Programming in

RPG

IV

Third Edition

Bryan Meyers & Judy Yaeger

A Division of
Penton Technology Media

221 E. 29th Street • Loveland, CO 80538 USA
(800) 650-1767 • (970) 663-4700 • www.iSeri

D0303154

Library of Congress Cataloging-in-Publication Data on file.

29th Street Press® is a division of
Penton Technology Media

© 2002 by Bryan Meyers and Judy Yaeger

This book was printed and bound in Canada.

ISBN 1-58304-094-3

2007 2006 2005 WL 2 1 10 9 8 7 6 5 4 3

To our families.
Thank you for your love and patience.

Acknowledgments

A new version of a new book is much like a new version of a programming language: It refines and enhances the previous versions, updating and reorganizing many of the original ideas and adding some new ones. Without the help of all the individuals involved in producing previous editions of *Programming in RPG IV*, this new edition would not have been possible. We want to extend our special thanks to those at 29th Street Press who encouraged us to do the earlier editions, especially Dave Bernard, Trish Faubion, Jan Hazen, and Tricia McConnell. We also thank Katie Tipton for her careful editing of the manuscript, Martha Nichols for her excellent production work, Matt Wiebe for the revamped cover design, and Wayne Madden for his leadership and enthusiasm.

Table of Contents at a Glance

Table of Contents

[*Italic type* indicates a sidebar.]

Preface

RPG IV, the version of the RPG language that participates in IBM's Integrated Language Environment (ILE), represents a dramatic step forward in RPG's evolution. RPG IV diverges from its predecessor, RPG III, in significant ways. However, to encourage adoption of the new ILE RPG/400 compiler and to prevent a nightmare for those programmers faced with maintaining older RPG programs, IBM made this latest release largely "backward-compatible" with older versions of RPG. Programs written before 1995 can easily be converted to RPG IV and subsequently modified, without the need for complete program rewrites. Although such backward compatibility is a practical solution for language developers, it means that the language must retain some components that, in fact, the new features make obsolete.

Writing a textbook about a new version of a language, then, presents authors with a difficult decision: How much emphasis should be given to those features that, although still available in the language, really represent an outmoded approach to programming? Giving obsolete syntax equal importance with the language's more modern features might inappropriately encourage students to write outdated code; at the very least, equal coverage can unnecessarily complicate the learning process. On the other hand, ignoring those obsolete features completely would give students an incomplete understanding of the language and would ill prepare them for program maintenance tasks. With Version 5, the challenge becomes even more problematic than before. The free-format specification represents a much more dramatic departure from traditional columnar RPG than did previous releases.

This textbook tries to solve the dilemma by initially presenting students with the most suitable, modern techniques that RPG IV offers for solving typical programming problems. As RPG IV matures and its use becomes widespread, it's important that students be presented with the language in its most current form, using the style and techniques that will serve them for the long term. Thus, the bulk of the book features the appropriate methods and strategies that contemporary programmers use, relegating many of the older styles and operations to sidebars that clearly indicate them as legacy methods. Appendix G details the still older features of RPG that are becoming rare as RPG IV becomes an integral part of many companies' application infrastructure. When students tackle maintenance tasks on older RPG programs (maybe even RPG III or RPG II programs), they will be able to refer to the information in Appendix G for help.

As for the fixed-format vs. free-format quandary, this textbook presumes Version 5 as the baseline release for RPG IV (pre–Version 5 material is clearly labeled). Once the concept of the free-format specification is introduced, and the differences between it and the older Calculation Specifications outlined, the book uses free-format whenever possible. By continuing to use the terms Factor 1, Factor 2, and Result, however, the text's explanations and examples should still be clear to students who will not be using free-format. Students should be encouraged to work in free-format as the best long-term style for their own programs.

Programming in RPG IV, like its predecessor, *Programming in RPG/400*, tries to bridge the gap between academia and the business world by presenting all the facets of RPG IV needed by a professional programmer. The material is introduced incrementally, and the book is organized so that students quickly begin writing complete — although simple — programs. Each successive chapter introduces additional information about RPG IV syntax and fundamental programming methods, so that students become increasingly proficient at developing RPG IV programs — programs that grow in complexity as students progress through the book.

Each chapter includes a brief overview, which orients students to the material contained in the chapter, and a chapter summary, which reviews the chapter's major points. The end-of-chapter sections include discussion/review questions, exercises, and programming assignments designed to help students develop their analytical and problem-solving skills, as well as their proficiency with RPG IV syntax. These end-of-chapter sections remain basically unchanged from *Programming in RPG/400*, although they now require solutions in RPG IV, rather than RPG III.

The programming assignments at the end of each chapter are arranged roughly in order of difficulty, so that instructors can assign programs appropriate to their time schedules and their students' abilities. Although none of the program solutions are long by commercial standards, some of the necessary algorithms are quite difficult; the assignments require time and effort on the part of the students to develop correct solutions. Unfortunately, there is no "easy road" to becoming a good programmer, nor can students learn to deal with program complexity by merely reading or talking it about it. Programming, as much as any other activity we know, is truly a matter of "learning by doing." Those students interested in becoming IT professionals must recognize that they have chosen a rewarding — but demanding and challenging — profession, and they need to realize that they must be willing to work hard to succeed in this profession.

To give students experience developing application systems, rather than programming in a vacuum, most of the programming assignments relate to three fictitious companies and their application needs (described in Appendix F). By working on these assignments, students should gain a sense of how a company's data files are repeatedly used by numerous applications for different, related purposes.

For the most part, the structure of this edition of *Programming in RPG IV* remains the same as it was in the previous edition. Chapters 11 and 12 contain information that had been crowded into a single chapter previously. Chapter 11 now concentrates on advanced data definition techniques, while Chapter 12 emphasizes data manipulation, built-in functions, and error handling. The material on advanced interactive programming is now in Chapter 13. The material on maintaining older programs is now in Appendix G. Appendix A has been noticeably expanded to become a useful reference summary after the student completes the class. All other material has been fully updated and is current to Version 5 Release 2.

Although a complete introduction to using the iSeries is beyond the scope of this text, Appendix C introduces students to working on the system using Programming Development Manager (PDM). Appendix D acquaints students with Source Entry Utility (SEU). Appendix E provides some insights into program testing and debugging — often bewildering processes for beginning programmers.

Depending on the length of the school term and the pace of the course, some instructors may choose to present this material over two terms. An instructor manual is available to those instructors adopting this text for classroom use. The manual provides answers to the review questions and solutions to the exercises. The manual also includes a CD with the data files needed for the programming assignments, the source code for the solutions to the programming assignments, and copies of the output produced by the solutions.

Chapter 1

Introduction to Programming and RPG

 Chapter Overview

This chapter introduces you to RPG as a programming language and describes how the language has evolved. It also explains general programming and computer-related concepts that you need to know as you begin learning to program in RPG IV

Programming

Computer programming involves writing instructions for a computer that tell it how to process, or manipulate, data. In many programming languages, these instructions depict a step-by-step procedure needed to produce a specific result or product, such as a sales report. These kinds of languages are called **procedural languages**. Procedural languages require you to explicitly state each processing step or instruction for the computer. Moreover, you must accurately describe the order or sequence in which the computer is to execute these steps for the program to produce correct results.

The computer is a binary device. Designed with electronic components that can depict only two states — on and off, or flow of current and no flow — computers internally store and manipulate instructions (and data) as patterns of **bits**, or **binary digits**. Programmers originally were forced to write computer instructions as strings of 1s and 0s, using machine language. Humans, however, do not function as well at this low representation level. Fortunately, advances in computer science soon led to the development of **high-level languages (HLLs)**.

Programs written in HLLs require translation into the bit patterns of machine language before a computer can actually execute their instructions. The computer itself can accomplish this translation using a special program called a **compiler**. A compiler translates a program written in an HLL into machine language that the computer can understand.

History of RPG

IBM introduced the **Report Program Generator (RPG)** programming language in the early 1960s. RPG filled a niche for providing quick solutions to a common business task: generating reports needed within the business. By designing RPG to be relatively easy to learn and use, IBM set the stage for today's **fourth-generation languages (4GLs)**.

Unlike the procedural languages in use at the time, RPG did not require the programmer to detail each processing step. Instead, the language included a fixed-logic cycle that automatically executed the normal cycle of read-calculate-write found in most report programs. In RPG, the programmer's job was to describe accurately to the computer the files, record layouts, calculations, and output desired for a specific program; the RPG compiler supplied the needed missing steps to provide a standard machine-language program for the computer to execute. RPG required that these descriptive specifications appear in a specific sequence within a program and that entries within a program line appear in fixed locations, or columns, within each line.

Another unique characteristic of RPG was its use of a special class of built-in variables called **indicators**. These variables, many of which simply had numbers for names, were predefined to the computer and could have only one of two values: '1' or '0' (corresponding to "on" or "off"). The indicators could be set on or off in one part of the program; their status would then be referenced in another part of the program to determine what processing was to occur.

RPG II

By the late 1960s, RPG had gained popularity, especially in small and midsized data-processing departments. Programmers were stretching the language beyond its original intended use, using RPG for complex computations and complicated file updating as well as for report generation.

Accordingly, IBM introduced an enhanced version of the language, RPG II, when it released its System/3 computer. Other computer vendors observed the popularity of RPG and developed RPG II compilers for their minicomputers, but for the most part, RPG remained a language associated with IBM installations.

RPG III

During the 1970s, several trends in data processing became apparent. First, as computers became less expensive and more powerful, and as operating systems became more sophisticated, interest in interactive programs began to mushroom. In **interactive applications**, a user interacts directly with the computer through a terminal or workstation to control the actions of a computer program as it is running. Previously, programs had involved only **batch processing**, in which the computer processes a "batch" of data (typically representing business transactions) without user intervention.

A second emerging trend was a growing interest in a database approach to data management. With a database approach, programmers define data independently of programs, in a central data dictionary. The files storing the data are rigorously designed and organized to minimize redundancy and to facilitate accessing data stored in separate files. Any program can use these database files without having to define the data within the program itself.

Finally, a third trend during that decade was an increasing concern with program design. This trend resulted in a methodology called **structured design**. As companies' libraries of developed programs continued to grow, the need to revise those programs to fit evolving business needs grew as well. It became apparent that computer professionals had paid too little attention to the initial design of programs. Poorly designed programs were causing inefficiencies in program maintenance. Experts attributed much of this inefficiency to "spaghetti code" — that is, to programs that included undisciplined, haphazard transfer of control from one part of a program to another.

Advocates of structured design recommended restricting indiscriminate flow of control within a program and using only those operations that kept tight controls on that flow. With this emphasis on structured design, concepts of modular programming and code reusability also began to emerge.

IBM addressed all these trends when it introduced the System/38 minicomputer in 1979. This computer's architecture was unique in that the design of the computer and its operating system featured a built-in database; the S/38 required data files to be predefined at a system level before a program could reference or use those files. This requirement alone forced IBM to release a new version of RPG to allow external file definition. IBM called this version RPG III.

At this time, IBM also made several other major changes to RPG. First, it added features that made it easier for programmers to develop interactive applications. Second, to address the issues of structured design, IBM included structured operations for looping and decision logic. Finally, to support modular code and reusability, IBM revamped the language to include the capability to perform calls to other programs and to pass data between programs.

RPG/400

In 1988, IBM announced its successor computer to the S/38: the Application System/400, or AS/400. With the new computer came a new version of RPG: RPG/400.

Despite its changed name, RPG/400 was really just a minor upgrade of RPG III, with a few new operations and enhancements. Following RPG/400's initial release, IBM periodically added additional features to the language, but these changes, too, were relatively minor.

RPG IV

Meanwhile, a growing number of critics accused RPG of being difficult to understand because of its short data names, abbreviated operation codes, and rigidly fixed format. The critics contended that the language was showing its age in its limited choice of data types (e.g., no direct support for date data types), its inability to handle multidimensional arrays, and its patchwork approach to data definition.

To address some of these criticisms, in 1994, concurrent with the release of Version 3 Release 1 of the AS/400's operating system (called OS/400), IBM introduced a version of RPG sufficiently unlike earlier versions that it warranted a change in name: RPG IV. In addition to trying to address the criticisms mentioned above, IBM included RPG as part of its newly introduced **Integrated Language Environment (ILE)**, a programming model that allows program modules to be first compiled and then bound together into executable programs. This change supported the growing interest in developing reusable units of code and improving system performance. Moreover, it let programmers develop a program using modules written in different languages and then bind these modules into a single program.

RPG IV relaxes many of the strict fixed-format requirements imposed by previous RPG versions, allowing free-format expressions and keyword notation in its specifications. Data naming limits have been extended, and many other artificial limits have been effectively removed from the language. In addition, RPG IV adds several new organizational concepts, including a central data-definition specification and procedure prototyping, which lets many program modules efficiently share information with each other. RPG IV borrows many of the best features of other programming languages, incorporating those features into its own new syntax.

In 2000, IBM rebranded several of its diverse computer lines, creating an all-inclusive *eServer* family; the AS/400 became the *eServer iSeries 400* (*iSeries* for short). Recent releases of RPG IV have focused on enabling the RPG IV architecture to coexist with Internet-based applications and objected-oriented languages, including Java. Modern e-business applications usually incorporate several hardware platforms (most notably, Intel-based computers, which IBM brands as *xSeries* in its eServer line) and software standards. As RPG IV evolves, its designers strive to maintain compatibility with these platforms and standards.

These changes have quieted, but not suppressed, RPG's critics. However, given the large base of existing RPG applications and IBM's present willingness to support RPG, it is likely that the language will continue to evolve and will remain the primary language for application development on the iSeries for many years to come.

If you compared RPG programs written 20 years ago with those written by RPG professionals today, you would be struck by their great design differences. These differences are not due solely to the use of operations unavailable in the past, although the new operations enabled the changes. The biggest change is that RPG, originally a language that emphasized specification instead of procedure, has been transformed by programming practices into a largely free-format procedural language. Today's programmers virtually ignore RPG's fixed-logic cycle — the feature that made the language unique in the 1960s. And most modern programmers use RPG's indicators only in those instances in which the language absolutely requires their use.

Learning the RPG Language

Most RPG texts start by instructing students in RPG II and introduce RPG III or RPG IV only after thoroughly indoctrinating the students in the fixed-logic cycle and the use of indicators. This book begins by teaching RPG as today's programmers use it. Only after you have mastered modern RPG will you become familiar with features of the language common in the past.

You may wonder why, if RPG programming has changed so much, you as a student need to bother learning features of the older versions of RPG. The reason is simple: For better or worse, most companies still use some programs that were written 10 or more years ago. Because your first job in the computer profession probably will involve maintenance programming, you no doubt will be working with some programs based on RPG III, or even RPG II. You will therefore need to understand the features of these language versions so that you can modify such programs when you encounter them. Appendix G of this text points out the important differences between RPG II, RPG III, and RPG IV that you will need to know to complete your understanding of this language.

The newest releases of the RPG IV compiler (starting with Version 5 Release 1) introduce free-format specifications for certain portions of a program. Free-format specifications bring with them many advantages, including enhanced readability, improved reliability, the ability to indent code, and a similarity to other languages you may already know. In this book, you'll generally find free-format illustrations, occasionally accompanied by fixed-format alternatives. Because free-format is a relatively new feature of RPG IV, however, it's likely that you will encounter many older, fixed-format RPG IV programs. While the free-format version is generally preferred, your organization's standards will dictate which alternative you use.

Now that you have an understanding of RPG's evolution, we can turn to some basic programming concepts that you need to know before you begin to learn RPG IV programming.

Note
Although this book refers to the iSeries hardware throughout, most RPG IV concepts also apply to older AS/400 hardware. Despite the hardware's name change, the operating system is still called OS/400.

Program Variables

Computer programs would be of little value if you needed a different program each time you wanted to change the values of the data to be processed. For example, assume you were developing a payroll program and one processing step was to multiply hours worked by pay rate. If you had to rewrite this step to explicitly state the number of hours worked and the hourly pay rate for each employee, you would be better off calculating wages by hand or with a calculator. The power and value of computer programming rests in the concept of variables.

A **program variable** represents a location in the memory of the computer that can store data. When a programming instruction involves the manipulation of a variable, the computer checks the value stored at that memory location and uses that value in the calculation. Thus, you can tell the computer to take the value stored in variable Hours, multiply that by the value stored in variable Rate, and store the answer in variable GrossPay. If Hours contained 35 and Rate 6, GrossPay would become 210. If Hours contained 40 and Rate 5, GrossPay would become 200. In a program, you might represent this process using variables names in this expression:

```
GrossPay = Hours * Rate
```

RPG generally uses the term **field** rather than variable. The language requires you to define all fields by naming them, assigning each field a fixed length that determines the amount of memory allocated for storing the field's values and declaring what type of data the field will contain. You will learn the methods RPG IV uses to define fields and the data types it allows in subsequent chapters of this book.

Data Files and the Data Hierarchy

In the business world, data processing typically centers on processing sets of data from files stored on disk or tape. Files containing data of temporary importance, generated during the course of the day's business, are **transaction files**. Once you have processed a transaction file, you typically have no further use for it. In contrast, most companies have sets of data that are of long-term importance to the company. These files, called **master files**, contain vital information about customers, products, accounts, and so on. Although you may update or change master files, companies regard master files as permanent files of data.

Files, Records, and Fields

All files, whether transaction or master, are organized into a data hierarchy of file-record-field. A **file** is a collection of data about a given kind of entity or object. For example, a business might have a customer master file that contains information about its customers.

A file, in turn, is broken down into **records** that contain data about one specific instance of the entity. Data about customer number 20 would be stored in a record within the customer file; data about customer number 321 would be stored in a separate record within that file.

Finally, each record contains several discrete pieces of data about each entity instance. For example, a customer record might contain the customer's account number, last name, first name, street address, city, state, zip code, phone number, date of last order, credit limit, and so on. Each of these items is a field. A field generally represents the smallest unit of data that we want to manipulate within a program. Figure 1.1 illustrates this data hierarchy.

Figure 1.1
Example of the Data Hierarchy

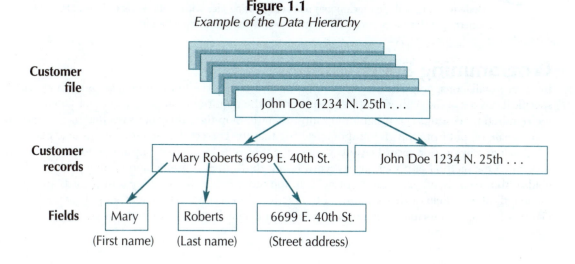

All records within a file usually contain the same fields of data. Because you define these fields to be fixed in length, if an alphanumeric value — for example, a person's last name — is shorter than the space allocated for it, blanks, or spaces, occupy the unused positions to the right of the value. If a numeric value is smaller than the space allocated for it, the system stores zeros in the unused positions. If quantity-on-hand, for example, is six positions long and has a value of 24, the value is stored in the file as 000024. Note that numeric values are stored as "pure" numbers, without dollar signs, commas, or decimal points.

A file occasionally may contain different record types, each with its own distinct format. In this case, each record usually contains a code field whose value signals which format the record represents. Figure 1.2 illustrates a data file with multiple record formats, with the format being determined by the Record code field.

Figure 1.2
Order File with Multiple Record Formats

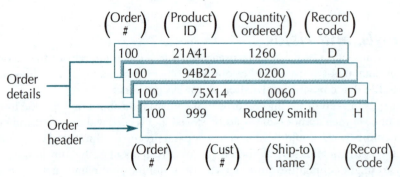

Note
Modern database design techniques discourage using files with multiple record formats, preferring instead to separate different record formats into separate files.

Programming Specifications
In many installations, programmers work from specifications given to them by systems analysts. These specifications detail the desired output of a program, the required input, and a general statement of the required processing. The programmer must then develop the instructions needed to generate the appropriate output from the given input, ensuring that the correct data manipulations take place.

Analysts may provide **record layouts** to describe the record formats of input files to be used by a program. One method of presenting a record layout shows the beginning and ending position of data fields within records; other methods list fields in the order in which they appear in records and give the length of each field or the positions of the fields within records. These methods, illustrated in Figure 1.3, include information about the number of decimal positions of numeric data.

Figure 1.3

Alternative Methods of Describing Record Layouts

Item number	Description	Quantity on hand (0 decimals)	Unit cost (2 decimals)	Vendor code	Reorder point (0 decimals)
1 5	6 25	26 34	35 39	40 42	43 51

Field	Length	Decimal positions
Item number	5	—
Description	20	—
Quantity on hand	9	0
Unit cost	5	2
Vendor code	3	—
Reorder point	9	0

Field	Positions	Decimal positions
Item number	1–5	—
Description	6–25	—
Quantity on hand	26–34	0
Unit cost	35–39	2
Vendor code	40–42	—
Reorder point	43–51	0

The Printer Spacing Chart

When the desired output includes a report, programmers may use a **printer spacing chart (PSC)** to provide the details of the desired report layout. The position of lines within the chart indicates the desired line spacing for the report. The printer spacing chart shows all constants (report headings or titles, column headings, and so on) that the report should include and where on the report they should appear. Printer spacing charts generally represent variable information using Xs, with each X representing one character of data.

We often want numeric data presented with special formats to facilitate comprehension. The printer spacing chart can depict the desired formatting, or **output editing**. Although there is no single accepted convention for indicating desired output editing, programmers generally recognize the notation presented in this chapter section (and used throughout this book). Commas, decimal points, and other insertion characters included within the Xs signal that these characters are to appear in the printed output. A zero within the Xs signals that zero suppression is desired.

Zero suppression means simply that leading, nonsignificant zeros are not printed. Thus, 000123 would be printed as ƀƀƀ123 (where ƀ = blank) if zero suppression were in effect. The location of the 0 within the Xs indicates the extent to which blanks, rather than leading zeros, are to be printed. X0XX signals "suppress up to and including the hundreds place but no farther." With this format, 0001 should be printed as ƀƀ01. A zero at the end of the format — for example, XXX0 — signals that zero suppression should continue to the rightmost digit; with this format, a value of 0000 should be printed as all blanks.

Currency symbols (typically, dollar signs) can appear two ways in output: as fixed or as floating symbols. A **fixed dollar sign** is positioned in a set column of the output, regardless of the number of significant digits in the number following the sign. A **floating dollar sign** is printed next to the leftmost significant digit of the number — its position varies, or "floats," depending on the value of the number with which it is associated. In a printer spacing chart, you can denote a fixed dollar sign by adding a single dollar sign to the immediate left of the Xs representing a numeric field. To signal a floating dollar sign, use two dollar signs, one at the far left of the Xs and the other in place of the zero-suppression character.

PSC notation	Meaning
$XXXX.XX	Fixed dollar sign, no zero suppression, no comma
$X,XX0.XX	Fixed dollar sign, zero suppress to units place, insert commas
X,XX.XX	Floating dollar sign, zero suppress to units place, insert commas
XX0	No dollar sign or decimal; complete zero suppression

Printer spacing charts also indicate how the analyst wants negative values to be printed. A single hyphen (–) at the left signals a fixed negative sign. Two hyphens, one to the left and one in place of a zero, indicate a floating negative sign. A single hyphen or the characters CR to the right of the Xs signal a fixed, trailing negative sign or credit notation.

PSC notation	Meaning
XXX	No sign to be displayed
–XX0	Fixed sign, complete zero suppression
–XX–.XX	Floating sign, zero suppress to units place
XX0.XX–	Zero suppress, trailing negative sign
XX0.XXCR	Zero suppress, indicate negative value with CR

Figure 1.4 shows a printer spacing chart that includes headings, lines of detailed information, departmental subtotals, and a grand total.

Figure 1.4
Sample Printer Spacing Chart

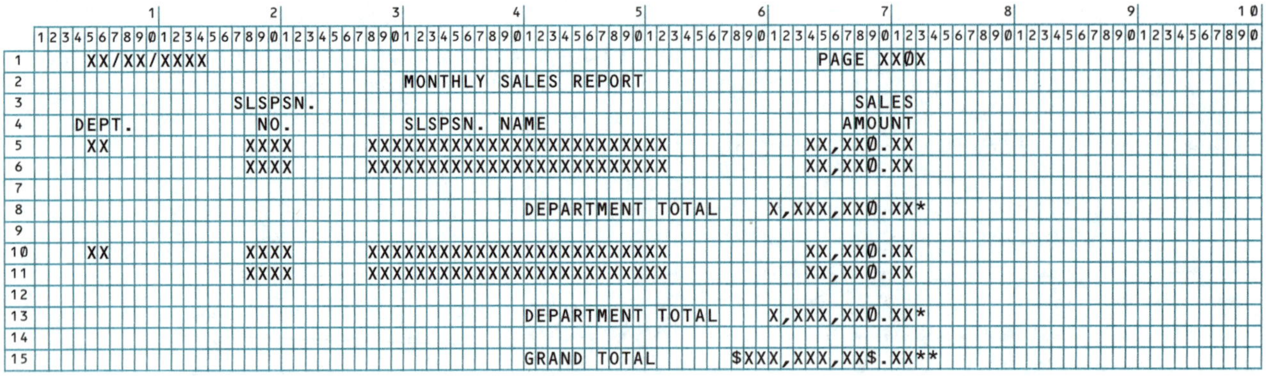

Note that the chart indicates that slashes should be inserted within the date and that asterisks are to appear to the right of totals.

The Program Development Cycle

The programmer's job is to develop a solution to a data-processing problem represented by the program specifications. The generally accepted method for achieving this solution is called the **program development cycle**. This cycle, which summarizes the sequence of activities required in programming, can be described as follows:

- Define the problem.
- Design the solution.
- Write the program.
- Enter the program.
- Test and debug the program.
- Document the program.
- Maintain the program.

The cycle starts with **problem definition**. It should be obvious that unless you understand the problem, as described in the programming specifications, you have little chance of coming up with a correct solution.

Once you understand the problem, you need to design a solution to the problem. **Program design** requires working out the solution, or **algorithm**, to the problem before expressing the solution in a given programming language. Formal design tools such as program flow charts, Warnier-Orr diagrams, or pseudocode can help clarify and illustrate program logic. Some programmers develop their own methods of sketching out a program solution.

Regardless of the method used, the importance of designing a solution *before* writing the program cannot be overemphasized. Developing a correct, well-structured design for a program represents the challenge of programming — this is the stage where most of your thinking should take place. Time spent at the design stage results in time saved fixing problems later in the cycle.

Writing the program is translating the design into a program using a particular programming language. This stage is often called coding. Beginning programmers may find this task difficult because they are unfamiliar with the rules of the language. Once you have mastered the syntax of a language, however, coding becomes almost a mechanical process that requires relatively little thought. The challenge of programming lies in design.

Entering the program consists of inputting the program statements into the computer. Years ago, program statements were punched onto cards; today, most program entry is done interactively on a terminal, using a system utility called an **editor**.

Testing the program is required to determine the existence of syntax or logic errors in your solution. **Syntax errors** are errors in your use of the rules of the language. The computer flags these errors, either as you enter the statements or later, when the computer tries to translate your statements into machine language. **Logic errors** are errors of design; it is up to the programmer to detect such errors through rigorous program testing by running the program with sets of test data and carefully checking the accuracy of the program's output. **Debugging** means discovering and correcting any errors. Testing should continue until you are convinced that the program is working correctly.

Documenting the program refers to providing material useful for understanding, using, or changing the program. Some documentation, such as system and program flow charts, user manuals, or operator instructions, may be **external** to the program. **Internal documentation** refers to comments included within the code itself. Such comments make the program more understandable to other programmers. Although documentation appears as one of the final stages in the program development cycle, documentation is best developed as you progress through the stages of the cycle. For example, it is easiest to provide comments within a program as you are actually entering the program, rather than waiting until the program is completely tested and running.

Program maintenance is making changes once the program is actually being used, or "in production." Estimates are that up to 70 percent of a programmer's time is spent modifying existing programs. The need for maintenance may arise from a "bug" discovered in the program or from changing user needs. Because maintenance is a way of life, any program you develop should be designed with ease of future maintenance in mind. This means, among other things, that your code's logic and organization should be clear, the variable names well chosen, and the internal comments appropriate and sufficient.

Program Entry and Testing

To complete the program entry and testing stages, you need to eliminate all program errors. As we've indicated, these errors fall into two general classes: syntax errors and logic errors. Syntax errors represent violations of the rules of the language itself; they are relatively easily detected and corrected. Logic errors are errors in your program that cause the program to produce incorrect results; these problems are detected by extensively testing the program with sets of test data and correcting any program statements that are causing incorrect processing.

As we mentioned above, you typically enter a program by interacting with the system's editor. Your program statements are called **source code**. The set of statements for one program module constitutes a **source member** (often called a **compile unit**) on the iSeries.

The iSeries editor will detect some syntax errors as you enter your program and will let you correct them immediately. Other syntax errors become apparent when you attempt to **compile** your program. Compiling means translating the source code into machine language, or **object code**. The iSeries has a program, called a compiler, that accomplishes this translation, provided you have not violated any rules of RPG IV in writing your program. If syntax errors prevent the translation from being completed, the compiler provides you with a list of the syntax errors it encountered. All such errors need to be fixed before you can progress to the next stage of testing. An OS/400 command, CRTRPGMOD (Create RPG Module), executes the RPG IV compiler.

If your program is free of syntax errors, the compiler creates a program module object. You must, in turn, **bind** the module (with other modules, if appropriate) to produce an executable program that can be run on the iSeries. The OS/400 command CRTPGM (Create Program) accomplishes this binding step. If your source code represents an entire program in one module, the OS/400 command CRTBNDRPG (Create Bound RPG Program) lets you combine compiling and binding into a single step.

Once you have successfully compiled and bound your program, you need to run it with test data to determine whether it is working correctly. Note that the computer executes the bound program object, or the translated version of your program. Errors discovered at this stage require you to back up, make changes to the program using the editor, and then recompile the program and bind it again before additional testing. Figure 1.5 illustrates this iterative process.

If you forget to recompile and rebind your program after making changes to the source code, the computer will run your old version of the program because you have not created a new object incorporating those changes.

Figure 1.5
Steps Required to Enter, Test, and Debug a Program

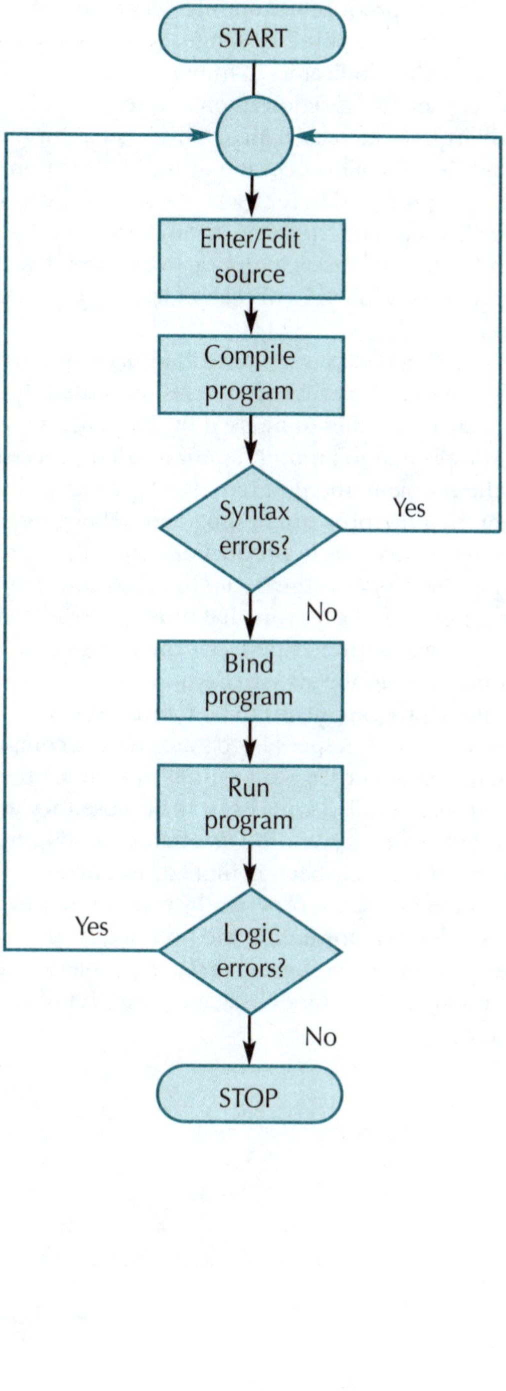

```
                    ( START )
                        |
                        v
                      (   )  <-----------------+
                        |                       |
                        v                       |
                  +------------+                |
                  | Enter/Edit |                |
                  |  source    |                |
                  +------------+                |
                        |                       |
                        v                       |
                  +------------+                |
                  |  Compile   |                |
                  |  program   |                |
                  +------------+                |
                        |                       |
                        v                       |
                    /  Syntax  \      Yes        |
                   <  errors?   >---------------+
                    \          /
                        | No
                        v
                  +------------+
                  |   Bind     |
                  |  program   |
                  +------------+
                        |
                        v
                  +------------+
                  |   Run      |
                  |  program   |
                  +------------+
                        |
          Yes           v
       +-------------/  Logic  \
       |            <  errors?   >
       |             \          /
       |                 | No
       |                 v
       |            ( STOP )
       |
       +--- (loops back to top circle)
```

Chapter Summary

Report Program Generator, or RPG, is a high-level programming language introduced by IBM in the early 1960s to provide an easy way to produce commonly needed business reports. Since introducing RPG, IBM has added enhancements to expand the language's functionality. Programmers originally used RPG's fixed-logic cycle and built-in indicators to minimize the need for explicit procedural instructions within their programs. As processing requirements have grown more complex and concerns about program understandability have increased, programmers have moved away from the fixed-logic cycle and now tend to explicitly include all processing instructions within their programs.

Variables enable programs to process different sets of data. RPG provides this flexibility through fixed-length fields that generally represent character or numeric data. Data is typically organized in a hierarchy of files, records, and fields. Relatively temporary data files that often need to be processed only once are called transaction files, while files of data of lasting importance to the company are called master files.

The process of developing a program is often described as the program development cycle. The cycle begins with problem definition. The problem often is presented through programming specifications, which include record layouts of files to be used by the program, printer spacing charts that describe the layout of desired reports, and an overview of needed processing.

In addition to defining the problem, the program development cycle includes designing the solution, writing the program, entering the program, testing and debugging, documenting, and — eventually — maintaining the program once it is in production. Too often, programmers short-cut the design stage and try to develop their logic as they write the program. This approach often leads to programs that are poorly designed or full of errors that must be corrected.

You enter an RPG IV program as source code using the iSeries editor. The program is stored as a source member within a source file on the system. Because computers actually execute machine-language instructions, your source program needs to be translated into an object program of machine language before the computer can run it. A special program called a compiler performs this translation.

As part of its translation, the compiler flags any entries in your source program that it cannot understand. These kinds of errors are called syntax errors because they are caused by your misuse of the rules of the language. Syntax errors prevent the creation of an object program.

Once your source code has successfully been compiled, you need to bind the resulting module into an executable program and then test the program by running it with input data. You must correct any logic errors in the program that are preventing the program from working correctly to produce the desired results. Each time you use the editor to correct a problem in your program, you must recompile the source member and bind the module again before running it to incorporate the changes into the executable program.

Key Terms

algorithm

batch processing

bind

bits (binary digits)

compile

compile unit

compiler

debugging

editor

external documentation

field

file

fixed dollar sign

floating dollar sign

fourth-generation languages (4GLs)

high-level languages (HLLs)

indicators

Integrated Language Environment (ILE)

interactive applications

internal documentation

logic errors

master files

object code

output editing

printer spacing chart (PSC)

problem definition

procedural languages

program design

program development cycle

program maintenance

program variable

record layouts

records

Report Program Generator (RPG)

source code

source member

structured design

syntax errors

transaction files

zero suppression

Discussion/Review Questions

1. What was the original purpose of RPG?

2. What is an indicator?

3. What trends emerged in the 1970s to influence the enhancements included in RPG III?

4. What criticisms influenced IBM's enhancements to RPG in RPG IV? What computer industry developments have contributed to the evolution of RPG IV?

5. Do you think that a programming language that requires revisions over time is poorly designed in the first place? Why or why not?

6. Give an example of a syntax error and a logic error in your native language (e.g., English).

7. Would it make sense to describe a person's complete address (street address, city, state, and zip code) as one field? Why or why not?

8. Would you define each letter in a person's last name as a separate field? Why or why not?

9. Keeping in mind the fact that all records within a file generally have the same, fixed number of fields, how do you think your school handles the problem of storing information about what courses you've taken?

10. Differentiate between source code and object code.

11. How many times do you need to compile a program?

12. Would you build a house without a blueprint? Is this a good analogy to writing a program without first designing it? Why or why not?

Exercises

1. Develop a list of data fields you think your school might store in its student master file. Then, design a record layout for this file that includes the length needed for each field, an indication of the data type (character or numeric), and the number of decimal positions of numeric fields.

2. For each printer spacing chart notation in the table below, show how the data value associated with the notation should appear when printed.

	PSC notation	Data value
a.	XXXXX	98100
b.	XXXXX	01254
c.	XX,XX0	31331
d.	XX,XX0	00010
e.	XX,XX0	01000
f.	XX,XX0	00000
g.	$XX,X0X	00872
h.	XX,XX	00298
i.	XX,XX	00000
j.	–XX,X–X	–07254
k.	–XX,X–X	00451
l.	XX,X0XDB	–00923
m.	XX,XX0–	–91486
n.	XX,XX0–	00000

Chapter 2

Getting Started

Chapter Overview

This chapter introduces you to RPG IV specifications. You'll learn how to write simple read/write programs using a procedural approach. You'll also learn how to include comments within your programs as documentation. Last, you'll see how RPG's techniques of output editing let you control the appearance of values on reports.

RPG IV Specifications

RPG IV programs consist of different kinds of lines, called specifications. Each type of specification has a particular purpose. You use **File Description Specifications**, for example, to identify the files your program uses, and you use **Calculation Specifications** to detail the arithmetic operations your program is to perform. Each kind of specification has a different identifier, or form type, which must appear in position 6 of each program line. A File Description Specification line of code, for example, must include an F in position 6.

Not every program requires the use of every kind of specification. However, all specifications that you use must appear in a specific order, or sequence, within your program, with all program lines that represent the same kind of specification grouped together. You will learn this order as we introduce the details of each specification type.

RPG IV specifications generally require fixed-position entries in at least part of the specification. **Fixed-position**, or **fixed-form**, means that the location of an entry within a program line is critical to the entry's interpretation by the RPG IV compiler. **Source Entry Utility (SEU)**, the iSeries editor you use to enter your program, can provide you with prompts to facilitate making your entries in the proper location. (Appendix D provides more information about SEU.)

The code samples in this book use two (or more) header lines to help you determine where to make your entries. The first header line indicates column position; the following line (or lines) contains "prompts" similar to those given within SEU.

Most specifications also support a **free-form** area of the specification, where you can code keywords and values with little or no regard for their specific location within the free-form portion of the specification.

Tip

As you begin to work with RPG specifications, don't be overwhelmed by what appear to be hundreds of entries with multiple options. Fortunately, many entries are optional, and you will use them only for complex processing or to achieve specific effects. This book introduces these entries gradually, initially showing you just those entries needed to write simple programs. As your mastery of the language grows, you will learn how to use additional specification entries required to develop more complex programs.

When you begin writing your first program, you will notice that an entry does not always take up all the positions allocated for it within a specification. When that happens, a good rule of thumb is that alphabetic entries start at the leftmost position of the allocated space, with unused positions to the right, while numeric entries are usually right adjusted, with unused positions to the left.

Program Specifications for a Sample Program

In this chapter, we cover the minimal entries needed to procedurally code a simple read/write program. To help you understand how to write such a program, we will walk through writing an RPG IV program to solve the following problem.

You have a file, SalesMast. Records in the file are laid out as follows:

Field	Positions	Decimal positions
Salesperson number	1–4	0
Salesperson name	5–34	—
Item sold	35–50	—
Date of sale	51–56	0
Sale price	57–63	2

You want to produce a report laid out as follows:

When you compare the desired output with the input record layout, you should note that all the output fields are present on the input records. No data transformation or generation needs to take place within the program. The required processing, then, consists of reading each record from the input file, writing that data to the report with appropriate headings, and formatting the variable data.

File Description Specifications

Our introductory RPG IV program begins with File Description Specifications (also known by the shorter name File Specifications, or sometimes F-specs). All File Specifications include an F in position 6. File Specifications describe the files your program uses and define how the files will be used within the program. Each file used by a program requires its own File Specification line. In our illustrative problem, file SalesMast contains the data we want to process.

The output of our program is a report. Although you usually think of a report as hard copy, rather than as a file per se, on the iSeries you produce a report through a printer file. We normally use a system-supplied printer file, QPRINT, as the destination file for our report lines. This file then resides as a spooled file in an output queue, where it will wait for you to release it to the printer. Your instructor will tell you which printer file to use in your programs and explain how to work with spooled files in the output queue. Appendix C of this text also contains helpful information about working with output on the iSeries.

You must code one File Specification for each file the program uses. Although you can describe the files in any order, it is customary to describe the input file first. The following header shows the layout of a File Specification. Note that in addition to column positions, the layout includes prompts to help you remember where to insert required entries.

```
*.. 1 ...+... 2 ...+... 3 ...+... 4 ...+... 5 ...+... 6 ...+... 7 ...+... 8
FFilename++IPEASFRLen+LKlen+AIDevice+.Keywords+++++++++++++++++++++++++++++++
```

Control Specifications

Although our sample program doesn't include them, **Control Specifications** (sometimes called Header Specifications) may be useful to control an RPG program's behavior. Control Specifications provide the following functions:

- default formats (e.g., date formats) for the program
- changes to normal processing modes (e.g., changing the internal method the program uses to evaluate expressions)
- special options to use when compiling the program
- language enhancements that affect the entire program

Control Specifications require an H in position 6. The remaining positions, 7–80, consist of reserved **keywords**, which have special values and meanings associated with them. The following header shows the layout of a Control Specification:

```
*.. 1 ...+... 2 ...+... 3 ...+... 4 ...+... 5 ...+... 6 ...+... 7 ...+... 8
HKeywords++++++++++++++++++++++++++++++++++++++++++++++++++++++++++++++++++++
```

In the following example, Control Specification keywords dictate the date and time formats to be used:

```
*.. 1 ...+... 2 ...+... 3 ...+... 4 ...+... 5 ...+... 6 ...+... 7 ...+... 8
HKeywords++++++++++++++++++++++++++++++++++++++++++++++++++++++++++++++++++++
H DATFMT(*USA) TIMFMT(*HMS)
```

A Control Specification can include more than one keyword, and a program can have multiple Control Specifications. Not all programs require Control Specifications, but if they are present, Control Specifications must appear as the first specifications in a program.

File Name (Positions 7–16)

First, in positions 7–16 (labeled Filename++ on the specification line), you enter the name of the file. In RPG IV, file names can be a maximum of 10 characters long. They must begin with an alphabetic character or the special character $, #, or @; the remaining characters may be alphabetic characters, numbers, or any of the four special characters _, #, $, and @. RPG IV lets you use both uppercase and lowercase alphabetic characters, but the language is not **case sensitive**. Thus, any lowercase letter you use within a file or variable name will be interpreted as its uppercase equivalent by the compiler. A file name cannot contain blanks embedded within the permissible characters.

Our practice problem input file is called SalesMast. The report file is QPRINT. Note that you code file names, like other alphabetic entries, beginning in the leftmost position allowed for that entry — in this case, position 7. Simply leave blank any unneeded positions to the right of the name.

File Type (Position 17)

Position 17 (labeled I on the specification line), specifies the type of file, or how the file will be used by the program. The two types we initially will work with are input (type I) and output (type O). An **input file** contains data to be read by the program; an **output file** is the destination for writing operations of the program. In our example, SalesMast is an input file, and QPRINT is an output file.

File Designation (Position 18; Input Files Only)

Every input file requires a file designation entry (position 18, labeled P). File designation refers to the way the program will access, or retrieve, the data in the file. In our example, we are going to retrieve data by explicitly reading records within our program rather than by using the built-in retrieval of RPG's fixed-logic cycle. In RPG terminology, that makes the file **full procedural**, so F is the appropriate entry for position 18.

File Format (Position 22)

The next required entry is file format. An F in position 22 (labeled F) stands for fixed format, which means that file records will be described within this program and that each record has the same, fixed length. Although it is preferable to describe files externally using OS/400's built-in database facilities, for simplicity's sake we will start with program-described files and progress to externally described files later (in Chapter 6). Because our files will be program described, an F is appropriate for both files of our sample program. All files, regardless of type, require an entry for file format.

Record Length (Positions 23–27)

You need to define the record length for each program-described file. Records of data files can be of almost any length; it is important that you code the correct value for this specification. Because SalesMast has a record length of 63, we enter 63 in positions 23–27. Note that record length is right adjusted within the positions allocated for this entry. This is typical of most RPG IV entries that require a numeric value.

Most printers support a line of 132 characters. As a result, records of printer files (which correspond to lines of report output) are 132 positions long. Accordingly, output file QPRINT is assigned a record length of 132 on its File Specification.

Device (Positions 36–42)

A final required entry is Device. Database files are stored on disk; accordingly, DISK is the appropriate device entry for the SalesMast file. The device associated with printer files is PRINTER. You enter these device names left-adjusted in positions 36–42 (labeled Device+).

No other File Specification entries are required to describe the files used by our sample program. The completed File Specifications for the program are shown below.

```
*.. 1 ...+... 2 ...+... 3 ...+... 4 ...+... 5 ...+... 6 ...+... 7 ...+... 8
FFilename++IPEASFRLen+LKlen+AIDevice+.Keywords+++++++++++++++++++++++++++++
FSalesMast IF   F   63        DISK
FQPRINT     O   F  132        PRINTER
```

Input Specifications

Input Specifications, identified by an I in position 6, come after the File Specifications in our introductory program. Input Specifications describe the records within program-described input files and define the fields within those records. Every program-described input file defined on the File Specifications must be represented by a set of Input Specification lines.

Input Specifications use two types of lines:

- lines representing record identification entries, which describe the input records at a general level
- lines representing field description entries, which describe the specific fields within the records

Each record identification line must precede the field entries for that record. The general layout for these two kinds of Input Specifications is shown below.

```
*.. 1 ...+... 2 ...+... 3 ...+... 4 ...+... 5 ...+... 6 ...+... 7 ...+... 8
IFilename++SqNORiPos1+NCCPos2+NCCPos3+NCC.................................
I......................Fmt+SPFrom+To+++DcField++++++++++L1M1FrP1MnZr......
```

Record Identification Entries

Record identification lines describe the input records at a general level. Each line takes the following form:

```
*.. 1 ...+... 2 ...+... 3 ...+... 4 ...+... 5 ...+... 6 ...+... 7 ...+... 8
IFilename++SqNORiPos1+NCCPos2+NCCPos3+NCC.................................
```

File Name (Positions 7–16)

In positions 7–16 (labeled Filename++ on the specification line), a record identification line must contain the name of the input file. This name must match the entry on the File Specification — in our case, SalesMast. The file name is a left-adjusted entry.

Sequence (Positions 17–18)

The next required record identification entry is Sequence, in positions 17–18 (labeled Sq). This entry signals whether the system should check the order of records in the file as the records are read during program execution. Sequence checking is relevant only when a file contains multiple record formats (that is, records with different field layouts). When sequence checking is not appropriate, code any two alphabetic characters in positions 17–18 to signal that sequence checking is not required. Many programmers use NS to signal "no sequence." Because the SalesMast file contains a single record format, we enter NS in positions 17–18.

The complete record identification specification is illustrated below.

```
*.. 1 ...+... 2 ...+... 3 ...+... 4 ...+... 5 ...+... 6 ...+... 7 ...+... 8
IFilename++SqNORiPos1+NCCPos2+NCCPos3+NCC.................................
ISalesMast NS
```

Note

Note that with the specification coded as shown, the compiler will issue a warning that a record identification indicator is missing from the line. Although record identification indicators are relevant in fixed-logic processing (discussed in Appendix G), they are not used in modern RPG programming. Simply ignore the compiler warning; it will not prevent your program from being compiled successfully.

Field Description Entries

Field description entries immediately follow the record identification entry. You define each field within the record by giving the field a valid name, specifying its length, and declaring its data type. Although you can define the fields of a record in any order, convention dictates that fields be described in order from the beginning of the record to the record's end.

Each field description entry takes the following form:

```
*.. 1 ...+... 2 ...+... 3 ...+... 4 ...+... 5 ...+... 6 ...+... 7 ...+... 8
I......................Fmt+SPFrom+To+++DcField++++++++L1M1FrP1MnZr......
```

Field Location (Positions 37–46)

You define a field's length by specifying the beginning position and ending position of the field within the input record. The beginning position is coded as the "from" location (positions 37–41 of the Input Specifications, labeled From+). The ending position is the "to" location (positions 42–46, labeled To+++). If the field is one byte long, the from and to entries will be identical because the field begins and ends in the same location of the record.

You enter the beginning and ending positions right-adjusted within the positions allocated for these entries. You do not need to enter leading, nonsignificant zeros.

Decimal Positions (Positions 47–48)

Numeric fields require a decimal position entry in positions 47–48 (labeled Dc), indicating the number of decimal positions to the right of the decimal point. In RPG IV, a field must be numeric to be used in arithmetic calculations or to be edited for output, so it is important not to overlook the decimal position entry. If a numeric field represents whole numbers, the appropriate entry for its decimal positions is 0 (zero). Numeric fields can contain a maximum of 30 positions to the right of the decimal point.

To define a field as a **character field**, simply leave the decimal position entry blank. (Chapter 3 provides a more complete discussion of RPG IV data types.)

Field Name (Positions 49–62)

The last required entry for a field description specification is a name for the field being described. This name, entered left-adjusted in positions 49–62 (labeled Field+++++++++), must adhere to the rules for valid field names in RPG IV. Within a record, a valid field name

- uses alphabetic letters, digits, or the special characters _, #, @, and $
- does not begin with a digit or an underscore
- does not include embedded blanks

In addition, a field name generally is 14 characters long or less. This is a practical limit, imposed by the fixed-format nature of the input specification.

The alphabetic characters can be upper case and/or lower case. RPG IV does not distinguish between letters on the basis of their case, but using a combination of upper- and lowercase characters makes your field names easier for others to understand.

Although not a requirement of RPG IV, it is also good programming practice to choose field names that reflect the data they represent by making full use of the 14-character name limit. For example, "LoanNumber" is far superior to "X" for the name of a field that will store loan numbers. Choosing good field names can prevent your accidental use of the wrong field as you write your program and can help clarify your program's processing to others who may have to modify the program.

The field description entries of the Input Specifications for our sample program are shown below.

```
*.. 1 ...+... 2 ...+... 3 ...+... 4 ...+... 5 ...+... 6 ...+... 7 ...+... 8
I......................Fmt+SPFrom+To+++DcField++++++++++L1M1FrP1MnZr......
I                          1     4 ØSlspNumber
I                          5    34  SlspName
I                         35    50  ItemNumber
I                         51    56 ØDateOfSale
I                         57    63 2Price
```

In these Input Specifications, we define fields SlspNumber (salesperson number), DateOfSale (date of sale), and Price (sale price) as numeric by including decimal position entries in positions 47–48.

Version 5 Release 2 Update

Numeric fields can now be up to 31 digits long with up to 31 decimal places.

Output Specifications

Although Calculation Specifications follow immediately after Input Specifications in RPG programs, we discuss **Output Specifications** next because their required entries parallel those required on Input Specifications in many ways. Every program-described output file named on the File Specifications needs a set of Output Specifications that provide details about the required output. All Output Specification lines require an O in position 6.

Output Specifications, like Input Specifications, include two kinds of lines: record identification lines, which deal with the output at the record level, and field description lines, which describe the content of a given output record. When the output is a report rather than a data file, "record" translates to "report line." Most reports include several different report-line formats; each needs definition on the Output Specifications.

To refresh your memory, our output file, QPRINT, is to contain a weekly sales report, formatted as shown in the printer spacing chart on page 16.

The desired report includes four different kinds of lines, or record formats. Three of the lines are headings, which should appear at the top of the report page, while the fourth is a **detail line** of variable information. The term "detail line" means that one line is to be printed for each record in an input file. The line contains detailed information about the data records being processed.

The following RPG IV code shows the complete Output Specifications to produce the report described above. You should refer to this code again as you read about the required Output Specification entries.

```
*.. 1 ...+... 2 ...+... 3 ...+... 4 ...+... 5 ...+... 6 ...+... 7 ...+... 8
OFilename++DF..N01N02N03Excnam++++B++A++Sb+Sa+...........................
O..............N01N02N03Field+++++++++YB.End++PConstant/editword/DTformat++
OQPRINT    E          Headings      2  2
O                                         8 'PAGE'
O                      PAGE            13
O                                        50 'WEEKLY SALES REPORT'
O                                        64 'DATE'
O                      *DATE      Y      75

O          E          Headings      1
O                                         7 'SLSPSN.'
O                                        48 'DATE OF'
O                                        77 'SALE'

O          E          Headings      2
O                                         3 'NO.'
O                                        21 'NAME'
O                                        46 'SALE'
O                                        61 'ITEM SOLD'
O                                        77 'PRICE'

O          E          Detail        1
O                      SlspNumber       4
O                      SlspName        37
O                      DateOfSale  Y   48
O                      ItemNumber      67
O                      Price       1   79
```

Record Identification Entries

Output Specifications require a record identification entry for each different line of the report. Each of these lines, representing a record format, must be followed with detailed information about what that record format (or report line) contains. Because our report has four different kinds of lines to describe, we have four record format descriptions in our Output Specifications.

The header that follows illustrates the layout for record identification entries. The following discussions refer to this layout.

```
*.. 1 ...+... 2 ...+... 3 ...+... 4 ...+... 5 ...+... 6 ...+... 7 ...+... 8
OFilename++DF..NØ1NØ2NØ3Excnam++++B++A++Sb+Sa+..............................
```

File Name (Positions 7–16)
The first record identification entry requires a file name entry in positions 7–16 (labeled Filename++). This file name serves to associate the record being described with the output file described on the File Specifications. Thus QPRINT, our output file, appears as the file name entered on the first record format line of the Output Specifications above. Although the Output Specifications include four record format descriptions, because each describes a format to be written to the same file (QPRINT), you do not have to repeat the file name entry on subsequent record format entry lines.

Type (Position 17)
Each record format description requires an entry in position 17 (labeled D) to indicate the type of line being described. In this context, "type" refers to the way RPG IV is to handle printing the line. Because we will be using procedural techniques to generate the report instead of relying on RPG's fixed-logic cycle, all the record format lines are Exception lines. As a consequence, we enter an E in position 17 of each record format line.

Exception Name (Positions 30–39)
In RPG IV, it is common practice to provide a name in positions 30–39 (labeled Excnam++++) for each exception line. Although not required, such names let you control printing without the use of indicators. By using exception names, you can easily reference lines to be printed from within your Calculation Specifications.

Moreover, you can assign the same name to lines that need to be printed as a group at the same time. Because our report has three lines that should be printed together at the top of the page, we have given each the name Headings. The fourth line, which will contain the variable information from our data file, is identified as Detail. Note that Headings and Detail are arbitrarily assigned names, not RPG-reserved terms. Exception-line names follow the same rules of naming as field names (up to 10 characters long), and they are left adjusted within the allocated area of the specification form.

Space and Skip Entries (Positions 40–51)
One more set of entries is needed to complete the record format line definitions. These entries describe the vertical alignment of a given line within a report page or relative to other report lines. Two kinds of entries control this vertical alignment: Space entries and Skip entries. Each variant offers "before" and "after" options.

For accurate placement of report lines, it is important to understand the differences between Space and Skip entries. Space entries specify vertical printer positioning relative to the current line. Space is analogous to the carriage return on a typewriter or the Enter key on a computer. Each Space is the equivalent of hitting the Return (or Enter) key. Space before (positions 40–42, labeled B++) is like hitting the Return key before you type a line, while Space after (positions 43–45, labeled A++) is like hitting Return after you type a line.

The same record format line can include both a Space-before and a Space-after entry. If both the Space-before and the Space-after entries are left blank within a record format description, the system defaults to Space 1 after printing — the equivalent of single-spacing. If you have either a Space-before or a Space-after entry explicitly coded and the other entry is blank, the blank entry defaults to 0.

In contrast to Space, Skip entries instruct the printer to "skip to" the designated line on a page. Skip entries specify an absolute vertical position on the page. Skip 3 before printing causes the printer to advance to the third line on a page before printing; Skip 20 after printing causes the printer to advance to the 20th line on the page after printing a line. If the printer is already past that position on a given page, a Skip entry causes the paper to advance to the designated position on the next page. Most often, you will have a Skip-before entry only for the first heading line of a report. Programmers most often use Skip entries to advance to the top of each new report page. Skip entries are also useful when you are printing information on a preprinted form, such as a check or an invoice.

You code any Skip-before entry in positions 46–48 (labeled Sb+), while Skip-after entries are made in positions 49–51 (labeled Sa+). If you do not code any Skip entries, the system assumes that you do not want any skipping to occur. The maximum value you can specify for any Space or Skip entry is 255.

Because we want the first heading of our report to be printed on the second line of a page, we code a Skip 2 before entry in positions 46–48 of the record format line describing that line. The Space 2 after entry (positions 43–45) for that same heading line will advance the printer head to the correct position for the second Headings line. The following header reproduces the record description entry for the first heading line to show how its entries correspond to the output record description labels.

```
*.. 1 ...+... 2 ...+... 3 ...+... 4 ...+... 5 ...+... 6 ...+... 7 ...+... 8
OFilename++DF..NØ1NØ2NØ3Excnam++++B++A++Sb+Sa+.............................
 OQPRINT    E            Headings      2  2
```

The second Headings line, with its Space 1 after entry, positions the printer head for the third Headings line, which in turn, with its Space 2 after entry, positions the printer head for the first Detail line of data to print. Because the report detail lines are to be printed single-spaced, exception line Detail contains a Space 1 after entry.

Field Description Entries

Each record format line of the Output Specifications is followed by field description entries that describe the contents of the line. Each field-level specification

- identifies an item to appear as part of the record format with which it is associated
- indicates where the item is to appear within the record format
- specifies any special output formatting for that item

Field-level items to be included within a record format may be entered in any order, although by convention programmers enter them in the order in which they actually are to appear in the output. The header below illustrates the layout for these field description entries.

```
*.. 1 ...+... 2 ...+... 3 ...+... 4 ...+... 5 ...+... 6 ...+... 7 ...+... 8
O.............NØ1NØ2NØ3Field++++++++YB.End++PConstant/editword/DTformat++
```

Field Name (Positions 30–43)

The name of each field whose value is to appear as part of the output record is coded in positions 30–43 (labeled Field++++++++). Any field appearing as part of the Output Specifications must have been defined earlier in the program.

In our sample program, most of the fields to be printed are part of the Detail record format. These are the same fields — SlspNumber, SlspName, DateOfSale, ItemNumber, and Price — that we defined as part of our input record. When we include these field names in the output, each time our program processes a successive record from the input file, each Detail line printed will contain the data values present in those fields of the input record.

In addition to the input fields, two RPG IV reserved words, which function as built-in, predefined fields, appear as part of the report headings. In the first Headings line on page 21, notice the field name PAGE. RPG supplies this field to automatically provide the correct page numbers for a report. PAGE, a four-byte numeric field, has an initial value of 1; this value is automatically incremented by 1 each time the report begins a new page.

The *DATE field, also appearing as part of the first Headings line, is another RPG IV reserved word. *DATE, an eight-byte numeric field, stores the current date, typically in *mmddyyyy* format. Any time your program needs to access the date on which the program is running, you can simply use *DATE as a field. RPG IV also stores a six-digit version of the date in reserved word UDATE. Reserved words *DAY, UDAY, *MONTH, UMONTH, *YEAR (four digits), and UYEAR (two digits) let you individually access the day, month, and year portions of the current date.

Constants (Positions 53–80)

In addition to fields, whose values change through the course of a program's execution, Output Specifications typically contain **constants**, or **literals** — characters that do not change and instead represent the actual values that are to appear on the report. You enter each constant, enclosed within apostrophes ('), in positions 53–80 (labeled Constant/editword/DTformat++) of the Output Specifications. The left apostrophe should appear in position 53; that is, you enter constants left-adjusted within positions 53–80. A constant cannot appear on the same Output Specification line as a field; each needs its own line.

In our sample program, the first heading is to contain the word PAGE as well as the page number. Accordingly, we code 'PAGE' as a constant within the first Heading line. Also, part of this first heading is the title, WEEKLY SALES REPORT. Although several words make up this constant, you enter the group of words as a single constant, enclosed in apostrophes; the spaces between the words form part of the constant.

The second and third report lines, or record formats, consist of column headings for the report. These, too, are handled as constants, with the appropriate values entered in positions 53–80. Notice, in the sample program, that the column heading lines are broken up into conveniently sized logical units and that each unit is then coded as a separate constant.

Note also that you can ignore blank, or unused, positions in output lines unless they appear within a string of characters that you want to handle as a single constant (e.g., 'DATE OF', or 'ITEM SOLD').

End Position in Output Record (Positions 47–51)

You denote where a field or constant appears within a line by coding its end position (the position of its rightmost character) within the line. Specify an end position by entering a numeric value that represents the actual position desired for the rightmost character of the field or constant. Such an entry should be right adjusted within positions 47–51 (labeled End++).

For example, because we want the E in constant 'PAGE' to appear in column 8 of the first heading line of our sample report, we code an 8 in position 51 of the specification entry for the constant 'PAGE'. The printer spacing chart indicates that the rightmost digit of the page number should appear in column 13 of the report line. Accordingly, 13 is the specified end position for field PAGE within its Output Specification line.

Our Output Specifications include an end position for each field or constant that is part of our report. If you omit an end position for a field or constant, that item is output immediately adjacent to the previous item, with no blanks separating the items.

You can also optionally specify the placement of a field or constant relative to the end position of the previously defined field. To use this alternative method, you put a plus sign (+) in position 47 and a right-adjusted numeric value in the remaining positions. The value tells how many blanks you want between the end of the previous field and the beginning position of the current field. The figure below illustrates how you would code the Detail line of our report using this relative notation.

The above code will end field SlspNumber in position 4 and put three blanks between the end of SlspNumber and the start of SlspName, three blanks between the end of SlspName and the start of DateOfSale, and so on.

Edit Codes (Position 44)

Three of the fields appearing in the output — *DATE, DateOfSale, and Price — have an entry in position 44, Edit codes (labeled Y). An **edit code** formats numeric values to make them more readable. The Y edit code associated with *DATE and DateOfSale inserts slashes within the printed date. Thus, if DateOfSale has a value of 122000, it will be printed as 12/20/00.

Edit code 1 causes commas and a decimal point to be inserted within the printed value of Price and signals that if Price is 0, the zero balance should appear on the report rather than being completely suppressed. RPG IV includes a large selection of editing alternatives to let you print or display values using a format most appropriate to your needs. A detailed discussion of these editing features appears at the end of this chapter.

Calculation Specifications

We have now defined the files to be used by our application, the format of the input records to be processed, and the desired output of the application. All we need to complete our program is to describe the processing steps required to obtain the input and write the report. We use Calculation Specifications to describe these processing steps.

Before coding Calculation Specifications, you need to develop the logic required to produce the desired output. In general, you would complete this stage of the program development cycle — designing the solution — before doing any program coding, but we delayed program design to introduce you to some of the RPG IV specifications and give you a taste of the language.

We can sketch out the required processing of our program using pseudocode. **Pseudocode** is simply stylized English that details the underlying logic needed for a program. Although no single standard exists for the format used with pseudocode, key control words generally appear in all capital letters, and indentation is used to show the scope of control of the logic structures. It is always a good idea to work out the design of your program before actually coding it in RPG IV (or in any other language). Pseudocode is language independent and lets you focus on what needs to be done rather than on the specific syntax requirements of a programming language.

Our program exemplifies a simple read/write program in which we want to read a record, write a line on the report, and repeat the process until no more records exist in the file (a condition called **end-of-file**). This kind of application is termed *batch processing* because once the program begins, a "batch" of data, accumulated in a file, directs its execution. Batch programs can be run unattended because they do not require control or instructions from a user.

The logic required by our read/write program is quite simple:

Correct algorithm
Write report headings
Read a record
WHILE there are more records
    Write a detail line
    Read the next record
ENDWHILE
END program

Note that WHILE indicates a repeated process, or loop. Within the loop, the processing requirements for a single record (in this case, simply writing a report line) are detailed and then the next record is read. Because we want to print report headings just once at the beginning of the report, rather than once for each record, that step is listed at the beginning of the pseudocode, outside the loop.

Output Continuation Lines

Although they are not appropriate for our current report, output continuation lines introduced in RPG IV let you code long constants as a single entry that spans more than one specification line. The layout for the continuation form of the Output Specification is as follows:

```
*.. 1 ...+... 2 ...+... 3 ...+... 4 ...+... 5 ...+... 6 ...+... 7 ...+... 8
O...............................................Constant/Editword-continues+
```

Assume, for example, that you're defining a report that is to be captioned "ACME EXPLOSIVES SALES REPORT" — a constant too long to fit on one specification line. You can code this caption as a single constant on two (or more) specification lines by using the continuation feature. Of course, you could also break the constant into two or more constants and then just code each constant on its own output line.

To use the continuation feature, you code the end position for the entire constant (e.g., 90) on the first line, together with some portion of the constant; then, signal that the constant is continued by terminating the entry on the first line with a hyphen (–) or a plus sign (+). A hyphen signals that the continuation resumes with the *first position* (i.e., position 53) of the continued constant on the next line, while a plus signals that the continuation resumes with the *first nonblank character* encountered in the continued constant on the next line.

The following code illustrates this output feature. Notice that you use an apostrophe only at the very beginning and the very end of the continued constant, rather than needing a set of apostrophes on each line.

```
*.. 1 ...+... 2 ...+... 3 ...+... 4 ...+... 5 ...+... 6 ...+... 7 ...+... 8
O...............N01N02N03Field+++++++++YB.End++PConstant/editword/DTformat++
O...............................................Constant/Editword-continues+
* The two examples below would produce the same output because of the use
* of the + and -.
O                                    90 'ACME EXPLOSIVES SALES +
O                                        REPORT'
O                                    90 'ACME EXPLOSIVES SALES -
O                                        REPORT'
```

You may wonder why the pseudocode contains two read statements. Why can't there be just a single read, as in the first step within the WHILE loop below?

Incorrect algorithm
Write report headings
WHILE there are more records
         Read the next record
         Write a detail line
ENDWHILE
END program

The preceding algorithm would work fine as long as each read operation retrieved a data record from the file. The problem is that eventually the system will try to read an input record and fail because there are no more records in the file to read. Once a program has reached end-of-file, it should not attempt to process any more input data. The incorrect algorithm above would inappropriately write a detail line after reaching end-of-file.

The correct algorithm places the read statement as the last step within the WHILE loop so that as soon as end-of-file is detected, no further writing will occur. However, if that were the only read, our algorithm would try to write the first detail line before reading any data. That's why the algorithm also requires an initial read (often called a **priming read**) just before the WHILE to "prime" the processing cycle.

After you have designed the program, it is a simple matter to express that logic in a programming language — once you have learned the language's syntax. The following free-format Calculation Specifications show the correct algorithm expressed in RPG IV. Notice the specifications' striking similarity to the pseudocode we sketched out earlier.

```
*.. 1 ...+... 2 ...+... 3 ...+... 4 ...+... 5 ...+... 6 ...+... 7 ...+... 8
 /FREE
   EXCEPT Headings;
   READ SalesMast;
   DOW NOT %EOF;
     EXCEPT Detail;
     READ SalesMast;
   ENDDO;
   EVAL *INLR = *ON;
   RETURN;
 /END-FREE
```

Calculation Specifications specify what processing needs to be done. Free-format Calculation Specifications are specified between /FREE and /END-FREE instructions; these instructions, called **compiler directives**, direct the RPG IV compiler to use free-format syntax rules for any instructions within the block. The /FREE and /END-FREE directives must be coded exactly as shown, beginning with a slash (/) character in position 7.

The instructions within the /FREE block usually begin with an operation that specifies an action to be taken (operations appear in all upper case in the example above). RPG IV supports a number of reserved words to identify valid operations. Many of these operations are followed by operand values, which RPG calls **factors**, to give the compiler the details necessary to perform an operation; other operation codes (DOW and EVAL in this example) are followed by expressions that the program will evaluate. Finally, each free-format Calculation Specification must end with a semicolon (;). Spacing usually is not important in a free-format Calculation Specification. You can code the specification in any position from 8 to 80; positions 6 and 7 must be blank. You can also indent certain operations to clarify the flow of the program.

If your version of RPG IV is earlier than Version 5, the compiler does not support free-format Calculation Specifications. In that case, the following equivalent fixed-format Calculation Specifications would be required instead.

```
*.. 1 ...+... 2 ...+... 3 ...+... 4 ...+... 5 ...+... 6 ...+... 7 ...+... 8
CLØN01Factor1+++++++Opcode(E)+Factor2+++++++Result++++++++Len++D+HiLoEq....
CLØN01Factor1+++++++Opcode(E)+Extended-factor2+++++++++++++++++++++++++++++
C                   EXCEPT    Headings
C                   READ      SalesMast
C                   DOW       NOT %EOF
C                   EXCEPT    Detail
C                   READ      SalesMast
C                   ENDDO
C                   EVAL      *INLR = *ON
C                   RETURN
```

Fixed-format Calculation Specifications do not require the /FREE and /END-FREE directives; instead, each line requires a C in position 6. Each Calculation Specification contains an operation, entered in positions 26–35 (labeled Opcode(E)+). Depending on the operation, specifications may also include a value in Factor 1 (positions 12–25), Factor 2 (positions 36–49), the Result field (positions 50–63), or the extended Factor 2 field (positions 36–80). Indicators associated with operations may also appear in positions 71–76, as discussed elsewhere in this chapter. Fixed-format Calculation Specifications do not require a semicolon delimiter at the end of the line.

RPG IV Operations

The Calculation Specifications are executed sequentially from beginning to end, unless the computer encounters an operation that redirects flow of control. Our program uses six operations: EXCEPT, READ, DOW, ENDDO, EVAL, and RETURN. Let's look at the specific operations used within the calculations of our program. The intent here is to provide you with sufficient information to understand our basic program and to write similar programs. Several of the operations described in the following section are discussed in more detail in subsequent chapters of this book.

EXCEPT (Calculation Time Output)

An EXCEPT operation directs the program to output an E line or lines from the Output Specifications. If no factor is coded with EXCEPT, the operation causes the system to output all unnamed E lines. In general, however, RPG programmers name their E lines and use the EXCEPT operation with an E-line name (in Factor 2 for fixed-format C-specs) to state explicitly which line or lines are to be involved in the output operation. In the sample program, the first EXCEPT operation specifies Headings as the name of the group of E lines to print. As a result, the three heading lines of our report will be printed. A second EXCEPT specifies Detail. When the program executes this line of code, our exception line named Detail will be printed. When using fixed-format, this operation never includes a value in Factor 1 or in the Result field.

READ (Read Sequentially)

READ is an input operation that instructs the computer to retrieve the next sequential record from the named input file — in this case, our SalesMast file. To use the READ operation with a file, you must have defined that file as input-capable on the File Specifications. When using fixed-format, Factor 2 specifies the file name.

DOW (Do While)

The DOW operation establishes a loop in RPG IV. An ENDDO operation signals the end of the loop. Note that this DOW and ENDDO correspond to the WHILE and ENDWHILE statements in our pseudocode. The DOW statement of our program reads, "Do while the end-of-file condition is not true." It is the direct equivalent of the pseudocode statement "While there are more records ..." because the end-of-file condition will come on only when our READ operation runs out of records.

The %EOF entry in this statement is an RPG IV **built-in function**, which returns a true ('1' or *ON) or false ('0' or *OFF) value to indicate whether the preceding file operation encountered end-of-file.

Indicators and Calculations

An **indicator** in RPG IV is a built-in character variable with only two possible values: '0' (*OFF) and '1' (*ON). Indicators signal whether or not certain events have occurred during processing and can be used, in turn, to control subsequent processing. RPG IV provides 99 numbered indicators (01, 02, 03, ..., 98, 99) for you to use in your programs.

In fixed-format syntax, many RPG IV operations can turn on an indicator or indicators depending on what happens during an operation's execution. These indicators are called resulting indicators because their status depends on the result of a calculation. You code these indicators in positions 71–76 (labeled HiLoEq) of the fixed-format Calculation Specifications. As its label implies, this area is actually divided into three two-position areas (positions 71–72, 73–74, and 75–76) for indicator specifications. Some RPG IV operations (particularly before Version 4 Release 2) require coding an indicator in one of these three areas to signal the results or effect of the operation when the program is running; other operations optionally let you associate indicators with their execution.

In turn, you can use these indicators as fields with operations that control subsequent processing. To reference an indicator as a field, you simply add *IN as a prefix to the indicator name. Thus, *IN90 is indicator 90 treated as a field. If the indicator has been turned on, its value will be '1' (also expressed as *ON); otherwise, its value is '0' (or *OFF).

Before OS/400 Version 4 Release 2, RPG IV did not support the %EOF built-in function used in our basic program; many of the programs you will work with will have been written before V4R2. In these versions of the language, the READ operation required you to code a resulting indicator to signal end-of-file. The calculations would have been coded as follows:

```
*.. 1 ...+... 2 ...+... 3 ...+... 4 ...+... 5 ...+... 6 ...+... 7 ...+... 8
CLØN01Factor1+++++++Opcode(E)+Factor2+++++++Result++++++++Len++D+HiLoEq....
CLØN01Factor1+++++++Opcode(E)+Extended-factor2++++++++++++++++++++++++++++
C                   EXCEPT    Headings
C                   READ      SalesMast                                90
C                   DOW       NOT *IN90
C                   EXCEPT    Detail
C                   READ      SalesMast                                90
C                   ENDDO
C                   EVAL      *INLR = *ON
C                   RETURN
```

Notice that each READ statement has a two-digit number entered in positions 75–76, the "Equal" indicator position, toward the right side of the specification. This number — in our case, 90 — designates which indicator we want to turn on when a READ operation encounters end-of-file (runs out of records). The subsequent DOW operation then refers to *IN90 instead of %EOF. You can use any one of RPG's indicators for this purpose, but most programmers used indicators in the 90s for end-of-file signals.

Modern RPG IV programs avoid the use of resulting indicators, opting instead for more descriptive built-in functions to query the outcome of an operation. Free-format Calculation Specifications do not support resulting indicators.

Built-in functions (sometimes called BIFs) perform specific operations and then return a value to the expression in which they are coded.

ENDDO (End Do Group)

This operation serves to mark the end of the scope of a DO operation. All the program statements between the DO operation and its associated ENDDO are repeated as long as the DO operation is in effect.

EVAL (Evaluate Expression)

EVAL is an operation used to assign a value to a variable. In the sample program, by evaluating the expression

```
*INLR = *ON
```

we are assigning the value *ON to a special indicator variable called Last Record. *INLR (commonly referred to simply as LR) performs a special function within RPG IV. If LR is on when the program ends, it signals the computer to close the files and free the memory associated with the program. If LR is not on, the program continues to tie up some of the system's resources even though the program is no longer running.

In most cases, specifying EVAL is optional in a free-format Calculation Specification; you can simply code the assignment expression without including the EVAL operation. EVAL is included in this example to provide easy comparison with the fixed-format code, where EVAL is required, but it could have been left out in the free-format C-spec.

RETURN (Return to Caller)

The RETURN operation returns control to the program that called it — either the computer's operating system or perhaps another program. Program execution stops when a RETURN is encountered. Although your program will end correctly without this instruction (provided you have turned on LR), including it is a good practice: RETURN clearly signals the endpoint of your program and lets the program become part of an application system of called programs. (Chapter 10 deals with called programs in detail.)

Internal Documentation

You might think that once you have a program written and running, you are finished with it forever and can move forward, developing new programs. Actually, about 70 percent of all programming is maintenance programming rather than new application development. Maintenance programming involves modifying existing programs to fix problems, address changing business needs, or satisfy user requests for modifications.

Because of the high probability that any program you write will be revised sometime in the future, either by yourself or by some other programmer in your company, it is your responsibility to make your program as understandable as possible to facilitate these future revisions. RPG programmers use several techniques to document their programs.

Program Overview

Most companies require overview documentation at the beginning of each program. This documentation states the function or purpose of the program, any special instructions or peculiarities of the program that those working with it should know, the program's author, and the date when the program was written. If the program is revised, entries detailing the revisions, including the author and the date of the revisions, usually are added to that initial documentation.

If a program uses several indicators, many programmers will provide an indicator "dictionary" as part of their initial set of comments to state the function or role of each indicator used within the program.

Comments

Another good way to help others understand what your program does is to include explanatory documentation internal to your program through the use of **comment lines**. In fixed-format RPG IV syntax, an asterisk (*) in position 7 of any line, regardless of the specification type, designates that line as a comment; you can enter any documentation, in any form that you like, within the remaining portion of the line.

When the RPG IV compiler encounters a commented line, it skips that line and does not try to translate it into machine code. Comments exist within the program at a source-code level only, for the benefit of programmers who may have to work with the program later. All the specification forms also include a comment area in positions 81–100 so that you can easily add a short comment to any line of code.

In addition to the asterisk in position 7, at Version 5 or later RPG IV also supports comments that begin with double slashes (//). In free-format specifications, these comments can make up an entire line (from position 8 to 80) or a portion of the line. Once the compiler encounters the // characters, it will ignore the rest of the line, treating the remainder as a comment. Using // to specify comments is not limited to free-format Calculation Specifications; you can use // comment lines anywhere in a program. In fixed-format specifications, the comments make up an entire line (from position 7 to 80); the line must begin with // characters. This book uses asterisk comments only for fixed-format examples, opting for // everywhere else.

You should include comments throughout your program as needed to help explain specific processing steps that are not obvious. In adding such comments, assume that anyone looking at your program has at least a basic proficiency with RPG IV; your documentation should help clarify your program to such a person. Documenting trivial, obvious aspects of your program is a waste of time. On the other hand, failing to document difficult-to-grasp processing can cost others valuable time. Inaccurate documentation is worse than no documentation at all because it supplies false clues that may mislead the person responsible for program modification.

Appropriately documenting a program is an important learned skill. If you are uncertain about what to document, ask yourself, "What would I want to know about this program if I were looking at it for the first time?"

Blank Lines

In addition to the use of comments, many programmers find that a program's structure is easier to understand when blank lines are used to break the code into logical units. To facilitate using blank lines within your code, RPG IV treats two types of lines as blank: First, any line that is completely blank between positions 6 and 80 can appear anywhere within your program. Second, if position 6 contains a valid specification type, and positions 7–80 are blank, the line is treated as a blank line; but the line must be located in that portion of the program appropriate for its designated specification type.

The Completed Program

Our completed sample RPG IV program is shown on the following pages (in both free-format and fixed-format versions). Note that the order of the program statements is File, Input, Calculations, and Output. RPG requires this order. Also note that you can use blank comment lines or lines of asterisks to visually break the program into logical units and that using lowercase lettering within internal documentation helps it stand out from program code.

Free-format (Version 5 or later)

```
*.. 1 ...+... 2 ...+... 3 ...+... 4 ...+... 5 ...+... 6 ...+... 7 ...+... 8
 // ***********************************************************************
 // This program produces a weekly sales report. The report data comes
 // directly from input file SalesMast.
 // Author:  J. Yaeger   Date Written:  12/10/1994.
 //                       Date Modified: 12/20/2001.
 // ***********************************************************************

FSalesMast IF   F   63        DISK
FQPRINT    O    F   132       PRINTER

ISalesMast NS
I                               1    4 0SlspNumber
I                               5   34  SlspName
I                              35   50  ItemNumber
I                              51   56 0DateOfSale
I                              57   63 2Price

  /FREE
     EXCEPT Headings;
     READ SalesMast;

     DOW NOT %EOF;
       EXCEPT Detail;
       READ SalesMast;
     ENDDO;

     EVAL *INLR = *ON;
     RETURN;
  /END-FREE

OQPRINT     E          Headings     2  2
O                                            8 'PAGE'
O                      PAGE                  13
O                                            50 'WEEKLY SALES REPORT'
O                                            64 'DATE'
O                      *DATE        Y        75

O           E          Headings     1
O                                            7 'SLSPSN.'
O                                            48 'DATE OF'
O                                            77 'SALE'

O           E          Headings     2
O                                            3 'NO.'
O                                            21 'NAME'
O                                            46 'SALE'
O                                            61 'ITEM SOLD'
O                                            77 'PRICE'

O           E          Detail       1
O                      SlspNumber            4
O                      SlspName              37
O                      DateOfSale   Y        48
O                      ItemNumber            67
O                      Price        1        79
```

Fixed-format (pre–Version 5)

```
*.. 1 ...+... 2 ...+... 3 ...+... 4 ...+... 5 ...+... 6 ...+... 7 ...+... 8
 *****************************************************************
 * This program produces a weekly sales report. The report data comes  *
 * directly from input file SalesMast.                                  *
 *    Author:  J. Yaeger   Date Written:  12/10/1994.                   *
 *                         Date Modified: 12/20/2001.                   *
 *****************************************************************

FSalesMast IF   F   63          DISK
FQPRINT    O    F   132         PRINTER

ISalesMast NS
I                                 1    4 ØSlspNumber
I                                 5   34  SlspName
I                                35   50  ItemNumber
I                                51   56 ØDateOfSale
I                                57   63 2Price

C                   EXCEPT    Headings
C                   READ      SalesMast

C                   DOW       NOT %EOF
C                   EXCEPT    Detail
C                   READ      SalesMast
C                   ENDDO

C                   EVAL      *INLR = *ON
C                   RETURN

OQPRINT    E         Headings      2  2
O                                           8 'PAGE'
O                     PAGE                  13
O                                          50 'WEEKLY SALES REPORT'
O                                          64 'DATE'
O                     *DATE         Y       75

O          E         Headings      1
O                                           7 'SLSPSN.'
O                                          48 'DATE OF'
O                                          77 'SALE'

O          E         Headings      2
O                                           3 'NO.'
O                                          21 'NAME'
O                                          46 'SALE'
O                                          61 'ITEM SOLD'
O                                          77 'PRICE'

O          E         Detail        1
O                     SlspNumber            4
O                     SlspName              37
O                     DateOfSale    Y       48
O                     ItemNumber            67
O                     Price         1       79
```

Now that you've seen how to write a complete RPG IV program, we can return to the concept of output editing to learn about RPG IV's editing features in greater detail.

Output Editing

Output editing refers to formatting output values by suppressing leading zeros and adding special characters — such as decimal points, commas, and dollar signs — to make the values easier for people looking at the output to comprehend. RPG IV allows numeric fields (but not character fields) to be edited as part of the Output Specifications. You often will use editing to obtain the output format requested in a printer spacing chart.

Editing is used in part because of the way numbers are stored in RPG. For example, if Amount, a field six bytes long with two decimal positions, is assigned the value 31.24, the iSeries stores that value as 003124. Although the computer keeps track of the decimal position, a decimal point is not actually stored as part of the numeric value. If you were to specify that Amount be printed without editing, the number would be printed as 003124; the nonsignificant zeros would appear, and there would be no indication of where the decimal point should be.

Edit Codes

To make it easier to specify the most commonly wanted kinds of editing, RPG IV includes several built-in edit codes you can use to indicate how you want a field's value to be printed. You associate an edit code with a field by entering the code in position 44 of the Output Specification containing that field. All commonly used edit codes automatically result in zero suppression — that is, printing blanks in place of nonsignificant leading zeros — because that is a standard desired format.

Editing Numbers

Some editing decisions vary with the application. Do you want numbers to be printed with commas inserted? How do you want to handle negative values — ignore them and omit any sign, print CR immediately after a negative value, print a floating minus sign (–) after the value, or print a floating

The Order of RPG IV Specifications

Not every program requires every type of RPG IV specification, but if a specification is included, it must be grouped with the other specifications of its type, in a specific order. Traditionally, an RPG IV program consists of the following specifications in this order:

- Control Specifications (H)
- File Description Specifications (F)
- Definition Specifications (D), described in Chapter 3
- Input Specifications (I)
- Calculation Specifications (C)
- Output Specifications (O)

In addition, modular programs written to use subprocedures (described in Chapter 10) will have one or more blocks of code to describe the subprocedure:

- Procedure boundary (P)
- Data definitions (D)
- Calculations (C)
- Procedure boundary (P)

These procedure blocks will appear at the end of the traditional specifications.

minus sign to the left of the value? And if a field has a value of zero, do you want to print zeros or leave that spot on the report blank? A set of 16 edit codes — 1 through 4, A through D, and J through Q — cover all combinations of these three options (commas, sign handling, and zero balances). The following table details the effects of the 16 codes.

	Option	Edit code			
Commas	Zero balances to print	No sign	CR	Right –	Floating –
Yes	Yes	1	A	J	N
Yes	No	2	B	K	O
No	Yes	3	C	L	P
No	No	4	D	M	Q

Thus, if you want commas, zero balances to print, and a floating negative sign, you would use edit code N; if you did not want commas or any sign but did want zero balances to print, you would use edit code 3.

To give you a clearer understanding of the effects of each of these edit codes, the two parts of the following table demonstrate how various values would appear when printed with each of the edit codes. Notice that if you use edit codes 1–4 with a field containing a negative value, the field will be printed like a positive number.

Value	Edit code							
	1	2	3	4	A	B	C	D
1234^56	1,234.56	1,234.56	1234.56	1234.56	1,234.56	1,234.56	1234.56	1234.56
1234^56–	1,234.56	1,234.56	1234.56	1234.56	1,234.56CR	1,234.56CR	1234.56CR	1234.56CR
0234^56–	234.56	234.56	234.56	234.56	234.56CR	234.56CR	234.56CR	234.56CR
0000^00	.00		.00		.00		.00	
000000^	0		0		0		0	

Value	Edit code							
	J	K	L	M	N	O	P	Q
1234^56	1,234.56	1,234.56	1234.56	1234.56	1,234.56	1,234.56	1234.56	1234.56
1234^56–	1,234.56–	1,234.56–	1234.56–	1234.56–	–1,234.56	–1,234.56	–1234.56	–1234.56
0234^56–	234.56–	234.56–	234.56–	234.56–	–234.56	–234.56	–234.56	–234.56
0000^00	.00		.00		.00		.00	
000000^	0		0		0		0	

RPG provides two additional useful edit codes: Y and Z. Edit code Y results in slashes being printed as part of a date. For example, if you run your program on December 11, 2002, field *DATE will contain 12112002. If edited with edit code Y, this date will be printed as 12/11/2002. Although edit code Y is normally used to edit dates, you can also use it with any field for which slash insertion is appropriate.

Edit code Z simply zero suppresses leading nonsignificant zeros. Z does *not* enable the printing of a decimal point or a negative sign, so if a field contained a value of –234.56, the Z edit code would cause the field to be printed as 23456. Z, if used at all, should be limited to **integer** (whole number) fields.

One additional edit code, X, was originally designed to convert positively signed values to unsigned values. Because the iSeries now performs this conversion automatically, this edit code has become obsolete. X is the only edit code that does not suppress leading zeros.

Currency Output Editing

You occasionally will want dollar signs (or another local currency symbol) to be printed as part of your report. As we mentioned in Chapter 1, you can position dollar signs in a fixed column of the report, or you can place them just to the left of the first significant digit of the values with which they are associated. This latter type of dollar sign is called a *floating dollar sign*:

Fixed dollar sign	Floating dollar sign
$ 12.34	$12.34
$ 6,342.11	$6,342.11
$ .00	$.00

In general, you want to use a dollar sign in addition to one of the editing codes. To specify a floating dollar sign, code '$' in the constant/edit word positions (columns 53–80) of the Output Specifications *on the same line* as the field and its edit code. To specify a fixed dollar sign, code '$' as a constant *on its own line* with its own end position.

You can use one additional feature along with edit codes. An asterisk coded in the constant/edit word position on the same line as the field and edit code specifies that insignificant leading zeros be replaced by asterisks, rather than simply being suppressed. This feature is sometimes called **check protection**, because its most common use is in printing checks, to prevent tampering with a check's face value. For example, a check worth $12.15 might include the amount written as $****12.15. The following examples illustrate the three currency output options.

```
*.. 1 ...+... 2 ...+... 3 ...+... 4 ...+... 5 ...+... 6 ...+... 7 ...+... 8
O..............N01N02N03Field+++++++++YB.End++PConstant/editword/DTformat++
O* The following line illustrates a floating dollar sign.
O                          Amount        1    65 '$'
O* The next two lines illustrate a fixed dollar sign.
O                                             56 '$'
O                          Amount        1    65
O* The following line illustrates asterisk fill.
O                          Amount        1    65 '*'
```

Edit Words

You would think that given the variety of edit codes built into RPG IV, you would be able to find a code to fit your every need. Unfortunately, that is not the case. Social Security and telephone numbers represent good examples of values that we are used to seeing in a format that an edit code cannot supply. RPG IV includes an alternative to edit codes, called **edit words**, that can help in this kind of situation.

You code an edit word in the constant/edit word portion of the Output Specifications on the same line as the field with which it is to be used. Edit words and edit codes are never used together for the same field, because they perform the same function. An edit word supplies a template into which a number is inserted. The template is enclosed with apostrophes. Within the template, a blank position indicates where a digit should appear, while a 0 indicates how far zero suppression should take place. With no zero in the edit word, the default is to zero suppress to the first significant digit.

You can use commas *or any other character* as insertion characters within the template. The insertion characters will be printed in the specified place, provided they are to the right of a significant digit. A dollar sign at the left of the edit word signals a fixed dollar sign; a dollar sign adjacent to a zero denotes a floating dollar sign. To indicate a blank as an insertion character, use an ampersand (&).

Examine the table below to see how edit words work.

This value	With this edit word	Is printed as
999999999	'ƀƀƀ-ƀƀ-ƀƀƀƀ'	999-99-9999
999999999	'ƀƀƀ&ƀƀ&ƀƀƀƀ'	999 99 9999
1234123412	'0(ƀƀƀ)ƀƀƀ-ƀƀƀƀ	(123)412-3412
00012^14	'ƀƀƀƀ$0.ƀƀ'	$12.14
00012^14	'$ƀƀƀƀ0.ƀƀ'	$ 12.14
05612^14	'$ƀƀ,ƀƀ0.ƀƀ'	$ 5,612.14

You can duplicate the effects of any edit code with an edit word. In general, RPG programmers use edit words only when there is no edit code that provides the format they want for their output.

Chapter Summary

RPG IV programs are written as fixed-format or free-format specifications. Different specification forms convey different kinds of information to the RPG IV compiler, which translates the program into machine language.

File Specifications contain descriptions of all files used within a program. Input Specifications provide detailed information about each program-described input file used by a program. There are two kinds of Input Specification lines: one that contains record identification entries, to generally describe a record format within a file, and one that contains field identification entries, to define the fields making up the record. Each field is described on a separate line.

Calculation Specifications center on operations, or processing steps, to be accomplished by the computer. Each Calculation Specification must include an RPG IV operation and may include additional entries, depending on the specific operation. The computer executes operations in the order they are given on the Calculation Specifications, unless the computer encounters an operation that specifically alters this flow of control. At Version 5 or later, RPG IV supports a free-format Calculation Specification, which sheds most of the positional requirements imposed by earlier versions.

Output Specifications provide details about each program-described output file. You use two kinds of Output Specification lines: a record identification line, to describe an output record format at a general level, and field description lines, to describe each field or constant that appears as part of a record format. You can use an optional third type of Output Specification to continue constants (or edit words) that are too long to fit on a single line. When the output is a report, you need a record identification line and corresponding field identification entries for each kind of line to appear on the report.

An important part of programming is documenting the program. Comment lines, signaled by an asterisk (*) in position 7 or by double slashes (//) in nearly any position of a specification line, can appear anywhere within a program. The RPG IV compiler ignores such comments. Positions 81–100 of all specification lines are also reserved for comments.

Within your code, you can insert completely blank lines and lines that are blank except for the specification type to visually break the code into sections.

It is customary to edit printed numeric values. RPG IV supplies ready-made edit codes for common editing requirements and lets you create special editing formats by using edit words.

Key Terms

built-in function

Calculation Specifications

case sensitive

character field

check protection

comment lines

compiler directive

constants/literals

Control Specifications

detail line

edit code

edit words

end-of-file

factor

File Description Specifications

fixed-position/fixed-form

free-form

full procedural

indicator

input file

Input Specifications

integer

keywords

numeric fields

output editing

output file

Output Specifications

priming read

pseudocode

Source Entry Utility (SEU)

Discussion/Review Questions

1. What is a fixed-form language? Can you give an example of a free-form language? Which form offers the most advantages?

2. Why do reports generated by RPG IV programs need to appear on File Specifications?

3. Why don't you need to enter a File Designation for output files?

4. Which of the following are invalid RPG IV variable names? Why?

```
X                    CUST#
ABC                  YR_END
@end                 avg.sales
_YTD_Sales           #3
YR END               CustNo
InvoiceNumber        $AMT
1STQTR               Day1
QTY-OH               Yearend
SALES                cusTnbR
```

5. What is an indicator? What specific methods of turning on indicators were introduced in this chapter? How can you use indicators to control processing? What alternative RPG IV feature can be used to reduce or eliminate indicators in a program?

6. Describe the difference between a Skip entry and a Space entry on the Output Specifications.

7. How could you obtain five blank lines between detail lines of a report?

8. What is the advantage of giving the same name to several exception lines of output?

9. What are some fields that are automatically provided by RPG IV for your use?

10. Why do you often need two read statements within a program?

11. What is the correct order of specifications within an RPG IV program?

12. What is the purpose of each kind of RPG IV specification introduced in this chapter?
13. What is LR? Why is it used?
14. What is maintenance programming? What programming techniques can you adopt to facilitate maintenance programming?
15. Why does RPG IV include both edit codes and edit words? What exceptions are there to the rule that an edit code and an edit word or constant should never appear together on the same Output Specification line?
16. What are the programming implications of the fact that RPG IV is not case sensitive?

Exercises

1. A program uses data from file Customers to generate a report that reflects all the data in the file. The record layout of file Customers follows:

Description	Positions	(Decimal positions)	Notes
Customer number	1–5	(0)	—
Customer name	6–25	—	—
Last order date	26–33	—	*mmddyyyy*
Balance owed	34–43	(2)	—

   Write the File Specifications for this program.
2. Given the above problem definition, write the Input Specifications.
3. Design a report for the application in Exercise 1, using the printer spacing chart notation of Chapter 1.
4. Develop Output Specifications based on your printer spacing chart from Exercise 3 and the File Specifications of Exercise 1.

Programming Assignments

All four of the following programming assignments center on a single company, CompuSell. CompuSell is a mail-order company specializing in computers and computer supplies. Appendix F provides a description of the company and the record layouts of its data files.

1. CompuSell would like you to write a program to produce a listing of all its customers. Use data file CSCSTP, the customer master file for CompuSell, as your input file. The listing should exactly match the format described in the following printer spacing chart.

2. CompuSell wants an inventory listing, formatted as shown in the following printer spacing chart. Write the program to produce this report, exactly matching the printer spacing chart specifications. The input file is CSINVP; its record layout is given in Appendix F.

```
          1         2         3         4         5         6         7         8         9         10
 1234567890123456789012345678901234567890123456789012345678901234567890123456789012345678901234567890
1     XX/XX/XX                            COMPUSELL INVENTORY LISTING                   PAGE XX0X
2
3 PROD.                          WEIGHT   QTY. ON      AVERAGE      CURRENT       SELLING
4 NUM.        DESCRIPTION        LBS. OZS.  HAND         COST         COST          PRICE
5
6 XXXXX   XXXXXXXXXXXXXXXXXXXXXXX  X0  XX    XX0X      X,XX0.XX     X,XX0.XX      $X,XX$.XX
7 XXXXX   XXXXXXXXXXXXXXXXXXXXXXX  X0  XX    XX0X      X,XX0.XX     X,XX0.XX      $X,XX$.XX
8
```

3. CompuSell wants to send out two separate mailings to each of its customers contained in file CSCSTP (see Appendix F for the record layout). Accordingly, the company asks you to write a label-printing program that will print two-across labels. Each of the labels reading across should represent the same customer. The printer will be loaded with continuous label stock when this program is run. Each label is five print lines long. The desired format for the labels is shown below. Note that the information in the parentheses is included to let you know what should appear on the label; it should not appear within your output.

```
          1         2         3         4         5         6         7         8         9         10
 1234567890123456789012345678901234567890123456789012345678901234567890123456789012345678901234567890
1    XXXXXXXXXX XXXXXXXXXXXXXXX        XXXXXXXXXX XXXXXXXXXXXXXXX      (FIRST, LAST NAME)
2    XXXXXXXXXXXXXXXXXXXXXXX           XXXXXXXXXXXXXXXXXXXXXXX         (STREET ADDRESS)
3    XXXXXXXXXXXXXXX  XX XXXXX-XXXX    XXXXXXXXXXXXXXX  XX XXXXX-XXXX  (CITY, STATE, ZIP)
4
5
6    XXXXXXXXXX XXXXXXXXXXXXXXX        XXXXXXXXXX XXXXXXXXXXXXXXX
7    XXXXXXXXXXXXXXXXXXXXXXX           XXXXXXXXXXXXXXXXXXXXXXX
8    XXXXXXXXXXXXXXX  XX XXXXX-XXXX    XXXXXXXXXXXXXXX  XX XXXXX-XXXX
9
```

4. CompuSell wants a telephone and address listing of all its suppliers. Write a program to produce this listing. Your input file, CSSUPP, is described in Appendix F.

```
          1         2         3         4         5         6         7         8         9         10
 1234567890123456789012345678901234567890123456789012345678901234567890123456789012345678901234567890
1     COMPUSELL SUPPLIER LIST AS OF XX/XX/XX                  PAGE XX0X
2
3  NAME/ADDRESS                   PHONE              CONTACT PERSON
4
5  XXXXXXXXXXXXXXXXXXXXXXXXXX     (XXX) XXX-XXXX    XXXXXXXXXXXXXXXXXXXXXXXXXXXXXXXXX
6  XXXXXXXXXXXXXXXXXXXXX
7  XXXXXXXXXXXXXX  XX XXXXX-XXXX
8
9
10 XXXXXXXXXXXXXXXXXXXXXXXXXX     (XXX) XXX-XXXX    XXXXXXXXXXXXXXXXXXXXXXXXXXXXXXXXX
11 XXXXXXXXXXXXXXXXXXXXX
12 XXXXXXXXXXXXXX  XX XXXXX-XXXX
13
14
15 XXXXXXXXXXXXXXXXXXXXXXXXXX     (XXX) XXX-XXXX    XXXXXXXXXXXXXXXXXXXXXXXXXXXXXXXXX
16 XXXXXXXXXXXXXXXXXXXXX
17 XXXXXXXXXXXXXX  XX XXXXX-XXXX
18
```

Chapter 3

Defining Data with Definition Specifications

 ## Chapter Overview

Now that you can write simple read/write programs in RPG IV, you will learn how to define work fields, data structures, and other data items your program might need to perform its tasks. RPG IV supports a rich set of data types; in this chapter, you'll discover which ones are appropriate for most business programming. You will also learn how to set the initial value for a data item and how to distinguish among program variables, literals, and constants.

Introducing Definition Specifications

RPG IV requires you to define all fields (or variables) used in your program by giving them valid names, specifying their lengths and data types, and, for numeric variables, designating the number of decimal positions they are to have.

At this point, you should have a good understanding of how to use RPG's Input Specifications to define fields that will receive values from records of a data file. The programs you have worked with so far simply wrote those field values to reports. Typically, however, program requirements include manipulating input data in other ways and storing the resulting values in preparation for output.

To enable this kind of processing, you need to identify to the computer the additional fields used to store such results. You perform such declarations in RPG IV by defining **standalone fields** (sometimes called work fields), so called because these fields are not part of a database record or any other kind of data structure.

You define standalone fields in Definition Specifications, identified by a D in position 6. If your program uses Definition Specifications, they must follow the File Specifications and precede any Input Specifications. The main purpose of Definition Specifications is to define data items your program may need in addition to file input and output fields; fields defined in Definition Specifications are not typically defined in data files. Because Definition Specifications concentrate data definition into a single group of consecutive statements near the beginning of your program, they facilitate later program maintenance.

To define a standalone field, code the name of the field anywhere in positions 7–21 (Name++++++++++) of the line, enter an S (for standalone) *left-adjusted* in positions 24–25 (Ds), enter the length of the field right-adjusted in positions 33–39 (To/Len+), and enter the number of decimal positions (for numeric fields) right-adjusted in positions 41–42 (Dc). A decimal position entry signals to the system that the field is numeric; the system generally interprets blanks in positions 41–42 to mean that the field is of character data type.

The following example defines two standalone fields: the numeric field TotalDue and the character field CtyStZip.

```
*.. 1 ...+... 2 ...+... 3 ...+... 4 ...+... 5 ...+... 6 ...+... 7 ...+... 8
DName++++++++++ETDsFrom+++To/Len+IDc.Keywords++++++++++++++++++++++++++++++++
 // Field TotalDue defined on a Definition Specification as a standalone
 // field seven positions long with two decimal positions
D TotalDue        S              7 2

 // Field CtyStZip defined as a character field 40 positions long
D CtyStZip        S             40
```

RPG IV allows numeric fields a maximum length of 30 (31 at V5R2) positions, up to 30 (31 at V5R2) of which may be decimal positions. Character fields can be up to 65,535 positions long. All numeric fields are signed and can store negative values without special specification. Recall, however, that negative values will be printed without a sign unless you use an appropriate edit code with the field on output.

Once you've defined a standalone field in a Definition Specification, you can assign it a value, use it with operations, or print it — just like an input field. Before you learn how to assign values to standalone fields, you need to understand three other kinds of data constructs: numeric literals, character literals, and figurative constants. You can use these constructs in Definition Specifications to assign initial values to a data item; you can also use literals and constants with operations in Calculation Specifications.

Numeric Literals

A **numeric literal** is a number per se; its value remains fixed throughout the program (unlike a field, whose value can change throughout the program). Numeric literals can be as long as 30 digits, including up to 30 decimal places. The literal may include a decimal point and/or a sign. If the numeric literal includes a sign, the sign must be the leftmost character of the literal. If the numeric literal does not include a sign, the computer assumes that the literal represents a positive number.

Other than a decimal point and a sign, the literal may include only the digits 0 through 9. You should never use commas, dollar signs, or percent signs in numeric literals. Numeric literals are not enclosed in apostrophes ('). Some examples of valid numeric literals follow:

−401230.12
0.0715
102
1
+3
−1
3.1416
.123456789

When entered in a Definition Specification or a Calculation Specification, numeric literals should be *left adjusted*; this is the one exception to the rule that numeric values are right adjusted when used as fixed-position entries.

Character Literals

Often, you will want to work with character data and fields as well as with numeric data. RPG IV lets you use character literals in Calculation Specifications when working with character-oriented operations. Like numeric literals, character literals maintain a constant value during the execution of the program. To indicate that a value is a character literal (and not a field name), simply enclose it within apostrophes. There is no restriction on what characters can make up the literal; any character that you can represent via the keyboard — including a blank — is acceptable. Character literals can be up to 1,024 bytes long. Some examples of character literals follow:

```
'John Doe'
'Abc   246   #18w'
'321444'
'45%'
```

Note

You cannot use a character literal — one enclosed within apostrophes — with an arithmetic operation even if all the characters of the literal are digits. Numeric literals do not use apostrophes.

Figurative Constants

RPG IV includes a special set of reserved words called figurative constants. **Figurative constants** are implied literals that can be used without a specified length. Figurative constants assume the length and decimal positions of the fields with which they are associated. Some of RPG's figurative constants are

- *BLANK (or *BLANKS)
- *HIVAL
- *LOVAL
- *ZERO (or *ZEROS)
- *ALL
- *OFF
- *ON
- *NULL

Assigning *BLANK or *BLANKS causes a character field to be filled with blanks.

Assigning *HIVAL fills a character field with X'FFFF...' (all bits on) and fills a numeric field with all 9s and a plus sign (+). Assigning *LOVAL fills a character field with X'0000...' (all bits off) and a numeric field with all 9s and a negative sign (–). Programmers often assign *HIVAL or *LOVAL to a field to ensure that the field's value will be greater than (for *HIVAL) or less than (for *LOVAL) any other value they may compare with that field.

RPG IV lets you assign *ZERO or *ZEROS to both numeric and character fields to fill the fields with 0s.

Assigning figurative constant *ALL immediately followed by one or more characters within apostrophes causes the string within the apostrophes to be cyclically repeated through the entire length of the result field.

Figurative constants *OFF and *ON represent character '0' and character '1', respectively. Although you can use *OFF and *ON with any character field of any length, programmers most often use *OFF and *ON to change the value of an RPG IV indicator or to compare an indicator's value. *ON is the equivalent of '1', while *OFF equates to '0'.

The constant *NULL represents a null value; *NULL is usually used to represent the absence of any value — not even blanks or zeros. RPG IV normally uses *NULL only in unusual situations, which we'll discuss later in the text.

Assigning Initial Values to Data

In addition to defining data items, such as standalone fields, in Definition Specifications, you can assign an **initial value** to those data items. If the data item is a field, its value can change during the execution of the program, but its initial value is the one the field contains when the program starts.

To inititalize (i.e., to assign an initial value to) a standalone field, you specify the value using the INZ keyword in the field's definition. The value is indicated using a literal or, in some cases, a figurative constant.

```
*.. 1 ...+... 2 ...+... 3 ...+... 4 ...+... 5 ...+... 6 ...+... 7 ...+... 8
DName++++++++++ETDsFrom+++To/Len+IDc.Keywords++++++++++++++++++++++++++++++++
 // Field MaxLimit defined as a numeric field seven positions long with two
 // decimal positions and an initial value
D MaxLimit        S              7  2 INZ(10500.00)
 // Field CompName defined as a character field 40 positions long, with an
 // initial value
D CompName        S             40    INZ('Kay Elmnop Enterprises')
 // Field HighLimit defined as a numeric field seven positions long with
 // two decimal positions and an initial value of 99999.99
D HighLimit       S              7  2 INZ(*HIVAL)
```

You should know that it is not always necessary to assign an initial value to a data item. RPG will automatically initialize data items to default values when the program starts unless you use the INZ keyword to initialize the field. The default values are typically blanks for character fields and zeros for numeric fields. If the default values are sufficient, you need not initialize the data item.

```
*.. 1 ...+... 2 ...+... 3 ...+... 4 ...+... 5 ...+... 6 ...+... 7 ...+... 8
DName++++++++++ETDsFrom+++To/Len+IDc.Keywords++++++++++++++++++++++++++++++++
 // The following definitions for TotalDue would result in identical
 // initial values.
D TotalDue        S              7  2 INZ(0)
D TotalDue        S              7  2 INZ(*ZEROS)
D TotalDue        S              7  2 INZ
D TotalDue        S              7  2

 // The following definitions for Title would result in identical
 // initial values.
D Title           S             25    INZ(' ')
D Title           S             25    INZ(*BLANKS)
D Title           S             25    INZ
D Title           S             25
```

Remember that keyword INZ assigns only the initial value for a field. In Chapter 4, we discuss how you can assign new values to a field once a program is running.

Data Types

So far, we've discussed only numeric and character data in general terms; these are the two basic classes of data used in most business processing. RPG IV actually supports several variations of numeric data, along with a few other classes of data that have special uses. You can specify any of these data types when you are describing a data item in Definition Specifications (or within a database file), using a code to signal the data type:

Data class	Data type	RPG code
Character	Character	A
Numeric	Zoned decimal	S
	Packed decimal	P
	Signed integer	I
	Unsigned integer	U
	Binary	B
	Floating point	F
Date	Date	D
	Time	T
	Timestamp	Z
Boolean	Indicator	N
DBCS	Graphic	G
	Unicode	C
Object	Object/class	O
Pointer	Pointer	*

To define a standalone field with a specific data type, you can simply include the code in column 40 of the Definition Specification. If the field is a character field, you need not code a data type in column 40; the system generally interprets blanks in positions 41–42 to mean that the field is of character data type.

```
*.. 1 ...+... 2 ...+... 3 ...+... 4 ...+... 5 ...+... 6 ...+... 7 ...+... 8
DName++++++++++ETDsFrom+++To/Len+IDc.Keywords+++++++++++++++++++++++++++++++
 // The following definitions are equivalent for a character field
D CtyStZip        S              40A
D CtyStZip        S              40
```

Zoned Decimal and Packed Decimal

Six data types deal with numbers; the differences among these data types are primarily in the way the iSeries stores the data. The two most common numeric types are **zoned decimal** and **packed decimal**. For a zoned decimal number, each digit of a numeric value requires a full byte of storage; the number's sign is stored within the rightmost digit. Packed decimal numbers, on the other hand, use a compressed storage format, wherein each digit and the sign require only one half-byte (four bits) of storage; in packed format, for example, a five-digit number would occupy three bytes of storage (five half-bytes for the digits and one half-byte for the sign). Although it's not required, packed decimal fields usually have an odd number of digits, to fully use every full byte allocated for them.

To define a specific numeric data type in a Definition Specification, include the appropriate code in column 40. For standalone fields, you usually need not code a data type. Simply enter the number of decimal positions right-adjusted in positions 41–42 (Dc); a decimal position entry signals to the system that the field is numeric. For a standalone field, RPG IV will define the field using the packed decimal format, which will usually be appropriate.

```
*.. 1 ...+... 2 ...+... 3 ...+... 4 ...+... 5 ...+... 6 ...+... 7 ...+... 8
DName++++++++++ETDsFrom+++To/Len+IDc.Keywords++++++++++++++++++++++++++++++++
 // The following definitions are equivalent for a packed decimal number
D TotalDue        S              7P 2
D TotalDue        S              7  2

 // To force zoned decimal representation, code the data type in column 40
D TotalDue        S              7S 2
```

Integers and binary numbers require even less memory than the decimal data types do. RPG can use these data types to store whole numbers. For example, unsigned integers can store values from 0 to 65,535 in just two bytes or store values from 0 to 4,294,967,295 in just four bytes; signed integers support half the range of unsigned integers in the same storage. Binary numbers, which are rarely used, use two bytes to store any whole number that is one to four digits long, or four bytes to store five- to nine-digit whole numbers.

```
*.. 1 ...+... 2 ...+... 3 ...+... 4 ...+... 5 ...+... 6 ...+... 7 ...+... 8
DName++++++++++ETDsFrom+++To/Len+IDc.Keywords++++++++++++++++++++++++++++++++
 // Field RecCount is an unsigned long (10-digit) integer
D RecCount        S             10U 0

 // Field UpDown is a signed short (5-digit) integer
D UpDown          S              5I 0
```

Date, Time, and Timestamp

Three data types deal with date- and time-related information: **date, time,** and **timestamp**. Dates and times are fairly self-explanatory. A timestamp is a combination of a date and a time. Each of these data types has specific requirements and capabilities, which we discuss later. RPG supports these data types in calendar-related operations, using certain operation codes and built-in functions, which we also discuss later.

To define standalone fields with the date/time data types, you specify a D (for dates), T (for times), or Z (for timestamps) in column 40. You do not specify a length or number of decimal positions; the system determines the length automatically.

```
*.. 1 ...+... 2 ...+... 3 ...+... 4 ...+... 5 ...+... 6 ...+... 7 ...+... 8
DName++++++++++ETDsFrom+++To/Len+IDc.Keywords++++++++++++++++++++++++++++++++
 // Field EnrollDate is a date field
D EnrollDate      S               D

 // Field StartTime is a time field
D StartTime       S               T

 // Field TransTime is a timestamp field
D TransTime       S               Z
```

Indicator Data Type

RPG IV also supports an **indicator data type**, which many other computer languages refer to as a **Boolean data type.** An indicator field is a single-byte field that can contain only two logical values: '1' or '0'. You can also refer to these values using the figurative constants *ON and *OFF, respectively. Indicator data is usually used within an RPG IV program to signal a true/false condition.

To code an indicator field, you type N for the data type in column 40. You do not need to code a length; the system will create a single-byte field.

```
*.. 1 ...+... 2 ...+... 3 ...+... 4 ...+... 5 ...+... 6 ...+... 7 ...+... 8
DName++++++++++ETDsFrom+++To/Len+IDc.Keywords++++++++++++++++++++++++++++++++
 // Field InpError is an indicator
D InpError        S               N   INZ(*OFF)
```

The remaining data types listed in the table on page 45 are seldom used in normal business processing. The DBCS (Double Byte Character Set) data types define and manipulate data in which two bytes represent a single graphic character or an extended-character-set character in multinational applications or Internet applications. Object definitions help RPG IV programs coexist with object-oriented languages, such as Java. Pointers let you dynamically access storage for data items and/or procedures associated with the pointers. We discuss many of these data types in more detail later in this text.

Defining Constants

You are already familiar with the concept of a constant (or literal). In addition to using Definition Specifications to define standalone fields, RPG IV lets you associate a data name with a constant so that you can reference the constant by its name throughout your program. A **named constant** differs from a standalone variable in two respects:

- Its value never changes during processing.
- It is defined with no specified length.

You define a named constant in the Definition Specifications by entering its name anywhere in positions 7–21 (Name+++++++++++); the name must follow the rules governing field names. The letter C, for constant, must appear in position 24 (Ds) of the specification. You enter the value of the constant in the Keywords area, positions 44–80. Enter numeric constant values with a decimal point or sign if appropriate, but never with commas. Enclose character constant values within apostrophes.

Note
You may occasionally see the value for a named constant coded within parentheses following the CONST keyword; this notation is valid but optional, and most programmers prefer simply to code the value without the CONST keyword.

In addition to numeric and character constants, you can define constants with other data values, such as dates and times. To express these values, you use **typed literals**. To code a typed literal, enclose the value within apostrophes, but precede it with a data-type code to indicate which data type the literal represents. To refer to a value of January 1, 2002, for example, you'd code D'2002-01-01' as the literal. Other common data-type codes for literals are T (for times), Z (for timestamps), and X (for hexadecimal literals). Here are more examples of typed literals:

Typed literal	Data type
D'2002-03-15'	Date
T'08.56.20'	Time
Z'2001-09-11-08.48.000000'	Timestamp
X'F0F0F0'	Hexadecimal

A named constant can be at most 1,024 bytes long; a numeric constant can contain up to 30 digits with up to 30 decimal positions. To enter a named constant too long to fit on a single line, continue the value into the Keywords area (positions 44–80) of one or more Definition Specification continuation lines. A hyphen (–) at the end of a line to be continued indicates that the constant continues in the first position of the Keywords area of the continuation line. A plus sign (+) signals that the constant resumes with the first nonblank character in the continuation line.

```
*.. 1 ...+... 2 ...+... 3 ...+... 4 ...+... 5 ...+... 6 ...+... 7 ...+... 8
DName++++++++++ETDsFrom+++To/L+++IDc.Keywords+++++++++++++++++++++++++++++++++
D...................................Keywords-continuation+++++++++++++++++
    // Examples of valid named constants
D FICA             C                   CONST(.0765)

D Pi               C                   3.142

D ExVicePres       C                   'John Adams'

D LongWord         C                   'ANTIDISESTABLISHMENTARIANISM'

D Example          C                   'This long constant has -
D                                       blanks where you would expect them-
D                                        to appear in a sentence.'

D PhoneEdtWd       C                   '(   )   -   '

D IndDay           C                   D'1776-07-04'
```

Once you've defined a named constant, you can use it in calculations appropriate to its type. The value of a named constant is fixed; you cannot change it during the course of program execution.

Named constants let you define constants in one place near the beginning of your program rather than coding them as literals throughout your calculations. This practice is a standard of good programming because it facilitates maintenance programming. If a value, such as FICA rate, needs to be changed, it is much easier and less error-prone to locate the named constant and change its value in that one place rather than have to search through an entire program looking for every calculation in which the literal value .0765 occurs.

Defining Data Structures

In addition to standalone fields and named constants, you can define **data structures** using Definition Specifications. Data structures are simply a means of organizing multiple fields within a single section of contiguous portions of memory. Data structures can give you flexibility in your handling of data by letting you subdivide fields into subfields and redefine fields with different data types or names. In this chapter, we introduce you to simple program-defined data structures; later in the text, we'll cover more complex data structures.

The data structure definition has two parts:

- the data structure definition itself (sometimes called the data structure header)
- the definition(s) for the subfield(s) within the data structure

DS, coded in positions 24–25 (Ds), signals the beginning of a data structure. You also may enter a name for the data structure in positions 7–21 (Name++++++++++); this name entry is optional, but it is required if you plan to reference the data structure as a whole elsewhere in your program.

Data structure names follow the same rules as field names. Although you can enter the length of the entire data structure in positions 33–39 (To/L+++) of the DS line, this entry is optional. If you omit it, the system derives the length of the structure as a whole from the lengths of the subfields.

Defining Data Structure Subfields

Subfields composing the data structure follow the DS header line. You define each subfield entry by giving it a name (in positions 7–21). The name can float (be indented) within its prescribed positions to make the hierarchical layout of the data structure easily visible.

Two methods exist for specifying the length of a subfield, which you can also conceptualize as the location of the subfield within the data structure as a whole. The first method, called *absolute notation*, involves using positions 26–32 (From+++) and positions 33–39 (To/L+++) to indicate the beginning and ending positions of the subfield within the data structure. The second method, *length notation*, entails leaving the From entry blank and entering the subfield's length in the To/L positions. The system will organize each subfield adjacent to the previously defined subfield within the data structure.

Most programmers prefer length notation because it is cleaner and more descriptive than absolute notation. The following code demonstrates these alternative methods.

```
*.. 1 ...+... 2 ...+... 3 ...+... 4 ...+... 5 ...+... 6 ...+... 7 ...+... 8
DName++++++++++ETDsFrom+++To/L+++IDc.Keywords+++++++++++++++++++++++++++++++
 // Defining subfields of a data structure using absolute notation
D OptName        DS
D   SubfieldA              1      3 0
D   SubfieldB              4      8 2

 // Defining the same structure using length notation
D OptName        DS
D   SubfieldA                     3 0
D   SubfieldB                     5 2
```

Regardless of the method you use, numeric subfields require a decimal position entry in positions 41–42 (Dc), as shown above. Code the data type of the subfield in position 40 (I). If the type is blank, the default is zoned decimal for numeric fields (fields with a decimal position entry) and character for fields with a blank decimal position entry.

Overlapping Subfields

The locations of subfields within a data structure can overlap, and the same position within a data structure can fall within the location of several subfields. When using absolute notation to define subfields, such overlapping is clearly indicated by the From and To position entries.

As an illustration of the concept of overlapping, or defining subfields within subfields, assume your program contains fields FirstName (15 bytes) and Phone (10 digits). The program needs to work with just the initial of the first name and with the area code, exchange, and local portions of the phone number as separate data items. Data structures let you easily access the data that way:

```
*.. 1 ...+... 2 ...+... 3 ...+... 4 ...+... 5 ...+... 6 ...+... 7 ...+... 8
DName++++++++++ETDsFrom+++To/L+++IDc.Keywords+++++++++++++++++++++++++++++++
 // Data structures to "split up" input fields into subfields
D                DS
D FirstName              1     15
D   Initial              1      1

D                DS
D Phone                  1     10 0
D   AreaCode             1      3 0
D   Exchange             4      6 0
D   LocalNbr             7     10 0
```

In the above code, Subfield Initial will contain the first letter of the value of FirstName, and the phone number of Phone will be broken into three pieces accessible through subfields AreaCode, Exchange, and LocalNbr.

If you want to use length notation to describe the above data definition, you need a way to indicate that Initial is supposed to be a part of FirstName rather than a subfield adjacent to it. RPG IV includes keyword OVERLAY to supplement length notation for this purpose. The format of the keyword is

```
OVERLAY(name{:pos})
```

OVERLAY indicates that the subfield overlays the storage of *name*, starting in the position within *name* indicated by *pos*. Note that {*:pos*} indicates that the position entry is optional; if you omit the entry, OVERLAY defaults to the first position of *name*. Recent releases of the RPG IV compiler also support the special value *NEXT with the OVERLAY keyword; specifying *NEXT instead of a position begins a subfield at the next available position of the overlaid field.

The following code reworks our example using length notation and OVERLAY.

```
DName+++++++++++ETDsFrom+++To/L+++IDc.Keywords++++++++++++++++++++++++++++++++
D                   DS
D FirstName                    15
D  Initial                      1      OVERLAY(FirstName)

 // Using OVERLAY with a position specified
D                   DS
D Phone                        10 0
D  AreaCode                     3 0    OVERLAY(Phone)
D  Exchange                     3 0    OVERLAY(Phone:4)
D  LocalNbr                     4 0    OVERLAY(Phone:7)

 // Using OVERLAY with *NEXT
D                   DS
D Phone                        10 0
D  AreaCode                     3 0    OVERLAY(Phone)
D  Exchange                     3 0    OVERLAY(Phone:*NEXT)
D  LocalNbr                     4 0    OVERLAY(Phone:*NEXT)
```

When you use keyword OVERLAY, the data name within the parentheses must be either a subfield already defined within the current data structure or the name of the current data structure itself, and the subfield being defined must be completely contained within the subfield or data structure it overlays.

Using Standalone Fields in a Program

In this chapter, we've discussed how to define data items to your program using Definition Specifications. To help you understand how you might use some of these definitions, we've added a few lines to the completed program from the preceding chapter. This modified program produces an enhanced sales report that counts the number of sales made (in standalone field Count) and the total sales prices of all the sales on the report (in standalone field TotPrice). The standalone fields are printed in the Totals exception output line.

Free-format (Version 5 or later)

```
*.. 1 ...+... 2 ...+... 3 ...+... 4 ...+... 5 ...+... 6 ...+... 7 ...+... 8
 // ****************************************************************
 // This program produces a weekly sales report, with total lines.
 // The report data comes directly from input file SalesMast.
 //      Author:  B. Meyers   Date Written:  12/20/1999.
 //                              Modified:  12/03/2001.
 // ****************************************************************

FSalesMast IF   F   63          DISK
FQPRINT     O   F  132          PRINTER
```

continued...

```
*.. 1 ...+... 2 ...+... 3 ...+... 4 ...+... 5 ...+... 6 ...+... 7 ...+... 8
D Count           S              5 0
D TotPrice        S              9 2

ISalesMast NS
I                                 1    4 0SlspNumber
I                                 5   34  SlspName
I                                35   50  ItemNumber
I                                51   56 0DateOfSale
I                                57   63 2Price

 /FREE
    EXCEPT Headings;
    READ SalesMast;

    DOW NOT %EOF;
      EXCEPT Detail;
      EVAL Count = Count + 1;
      EVAL TotPrice = TotPrice + Price;
      READ SalesMast;
    ENDDO;

    EXCEPT Totals;
    EVAL *INLR = *ON;
    RETURN;
 /END-FREE

OQPRINT     E        Headings     2  2
O                                         8 'PAGE'
O                    PAGE                13
O                                        50 'WEEKLY SALES REPORT'
O                                        64 'DATE'
O                    *DATE        Y      75
O           E        Headings     1
O                                         7 'SLSPSN.'
O                                        48 'DATE OF'
O                                        77 'SALE'
O           E        Headings     2
O                                         3 'NO.'
O                                        21 'NAME'
O                                        46 'SALE'
O                                        61 'ITEM SOLD'
O                                        77 'PRICE'
O           E        Detail       1
O                    SlspNumber          4
O                    SlspName           37
O                    DateOfSale   Y     48
O                    ItemNumber         67
O                    Price        1     79
O           E        Totals       1
O                    Count        Z      5
O                                       11 'SALES'
O                    TotPrice     1     79
O                                       85 'TOTAL'
```

Fixed-format (pre-Version 5)

```
*.. 1 ...+... 2 ...+... 3 ...+... 4 ...+... 5 ...+... 6 ...+... 7 ...+... 8
*****************************************************************
* This program produces a weekly sales report, with total lines.  *
* The report data comes directly from input file SalesMast.       *
*    Author:  B. Meyers   Date Written:  12/20/99.                 *
*****************************************************************
FSalesMast IF   F   63          DISK
FQPRINT     O   F  132          PRINTER

D Count            S              5 0
D TotPrice         S              9 2

ISalesMast NS
I                                     1    4 0SlspNumber
I                                     5   34  SlspName
I                                    35   50  ItemNumber
I                                    51   56 0DateOfSale
I                                    57   63 2Price

C                   EXCEPT    Headings
C                   READ      SalesMast
C                   DOW       NOT %EOF
C                   EXCEPT    Detail
C                   EVAL      Count = Count + 1
C                   EVAL      TotPrice = TotPrice + Price
C                   READ      SalesMast
C                   ENDDO

C                   EXCEPT    Totals
C                   EVAL      *INLR = *ON
C                   RETURN

OQPRINT    E        Headings      2 2
O                                        8 'PAGE'
O                   PAGE                13
O                                       50 'WEEKLY SALES REPORT'
O                                       64 'DATE'
O                   *DATE         Y     75
O          E        Headings      1
O                                        7 'SLSPSN.'
O                                       48 'DATE OF'
O                                       77 'SALE'
O          E        Headings      2
O                                        3 'NO.'
O                                       21 'NAME'
O                                       46 'SALE'
O                                       61 'ITEM SOLD'
O                                       77 'PRICE'
O          E        Detail        1
O                   SlspNumber           4
O                   SlspName            37
O                   DateOfSale    Y     48
O                   ItemNumber          67
O                   Price         1     79
O          E        Totals        1
O                   Count         Z      5
O                                       11 'SALES'
O                   TotPrice      1     79
O                                       85 'TOTAL'
```

Chapter Summary

RPG IV requires you to define all the fields your program will use, naming the fields and describing their data attributes (data type, length, and number of decimal positions, if any). Some fields are described within files, using Input Specifications, while Definition Specifications describe standalone fields that are not part of a database file.

Once you've defined a standalone field in a Definition Specification, you can assign it a value, use it with operations, or print it. You can use the INZ keyword with numeric literals, character literals, or figurative constants to assign initial values to a standalone field. Literals and constants do not change during the processing of an RPG IV program. You do not enclose numeric literals within apostrophes; apostrophes signal to the computer the presence of a character literal, which cannot participate in arithmetic operations.

Figurative constants are built-in literals with specified values. The length of a figurative constant automatically adjusts to match the length of the field with which the constant is used. Figurative constants include *BLANK, *BLANKS, *HIVAL, *LOVAL, *ZERO, *ZEROS, *ALL, *OFF, *ON, and *NULL.

RPG IV supports more than a dozen specific data types, which you can specify in Definition Specifications using a code in column 40. If you don't specify a code, RPG IV defaults to either character data or numeric data, depending on whether you specify a number of decimal positions. For standalone variables, numeric fields default to packed decimal; for data structures, numeric fields default to zoned decimal. The other most common numeric data types are signed and unsigned integers.

In addition to numeric and character data, other common data types include date-related data (date, time, and timestamp) and indicator data, which has a value of *ON or *OFF.

Definition Specifications let you define named constants as well as standalone fields. This feature lets you refer to a constant by name instead of having to code the constant as a literal. The value of a named constant never changes during processing. In addition to numeric and character constants, you can define constants with other data values, such as dates and times, using typed literals.

Data structures, also defined with Definition Specifications, organize multiple fields within a single section of contiguous portions of memory. Data structures let you subdivide fields into subfields and redefine fields with different data types or names. You can use either absolute notation or length notation to indicate the length and position of a subfield within a data structure. Most programmers prefer length notation, without a From position specified. The OVERLAY keyword lets you overlap fields within a data structure.

Key Terms

Boolean data type	named constant
character literals	numeric literal
data structures	packed decimal
date	standalone fields
Definition Specifications	time
figurative constants	timestamp
indicator data type	typed literals
initial value	zoned decimal

Discussion/Review Questions

1. What is the main purpose of Definition Specifications?
2. Why would you *not* use Definition Specifications to describe file input?
3. What is a named constant?
4. What are the advantages of using named constants in a program?
5. Compare and contrast literals, named constants, and figurative constants.
6. What is the main difference between a constant and a field?
7. When is it important to assign an initial value to a data item?
8. Which data types would be appropriate for storing money-related data? Why?
9. When would you use an indicator data type?
10. What kinds of capabilities can you gain by using data structures?
11. What is a figurative constant? What are possible uses for figurative constants? How does figurative constant *ALL work?

Exercises

1. Code the following standalone variables using Definition Specifications:
   - total sales, with 11 digits precision
   - product description, 30 bytes long
   - sales tax rate percent
   - transaction date

   Use field names, lengths, and data types appropriate to the variables' use.
2. Code the following values as named constants:
   - a commission rate of 2.5 percent
   - the company name "Acme Explosives Company"
   - the FICA cut-off income of $76,400
   - an edit word for editing Social Security numbers
   - the date January 1, 2000
3. Code a data structure for organizing information to be printed on a label. The subfields should include name, two address lines, city, state/province, postal code, and country. Field names and lengths should be appropriate to the fields' use.

Programming Assignment

1. Modify the CompuSell customer listing program from Chapter 2 (Programming Assignment 1) to include two total lines at the end of the report:
   - a count of the customer records listed
   - a total balance due

   The total balance due should appear in line below the balance due column in the rest of the report. Use standalone variables to store the count and the total.

Chapter 4

Assignment and Arithmetic Operations

 ## Chapter Overview

Now that you can write simple read/write programs in RPG IV, you're ready to learn how to perform arithmetic calculations in your programs. RPG was designed as a business language, and, as such, its mathematical capabilities don't extend much beyond the four basic arithmetic operations: addition, subtraction, multiplication, and division. You will learn how to express calculations using free-form expressions and appropriate operation codes. In addition, you will learn how to determine the correct size for fields that store the results of arithmetic operations and how to round calculations to avoid truncation.

Simple Numeric Assignment

RPG IV's primary **assignment operation** is EVAL (Evaluate Expression). Assigning a value to a field simply means giving the field a value. In previous chapters, we used the EVAL operation to assign the value *ON to an indicator. You can also use EVAL to assign values to numeric fields.

EVAL always works in conjunction with an assignment expression, which consists of a result (target) field, followed by the assignment operator (=), followed by an expression. An EVAL statement says, in effect, "Evaluate the expression to the right of the equal sign (=), and store its value in the result field to the left of the equal sign." When using the fixed-format version of the Calculation Specification, EVAL appears as the operation code in positions 26–35, and the extended Factor 2 area (positions 36–80) contains the assignment expression. The general format for an EVAL statement is shown below.

Free-format (Version 5 or later)
```
*.. 1 ...+... 2 ...+... 3 ...+... 4 ...+... 5 ...+... 6 ...+... 7 ...+... 8
 /FREE
    EVAL Result_field = expression;
 /END-FREE
```

Fixed-format (pre–Version 5)
```
*.. 1 ...+... 2 ...+... 3 ...+... 4 ...+... 5 ...+... 6 ...+... 7 ...+... 8
CLØNØ1Factor1+++++++Opcode(E)+Extended-factor2++++++++++++++++++++++++++++++++
C                   EVAL      Result_field = expression
```

The following examples demonstrate how to use EVAL for simple numeric assignment. In each case, the numeric field that appears to the left of the equal sign receives the value that appears to the right of the sign. The value to the right may be a numeric literal or a numeric field. You cannot define the result field within the EVAL statement; it must be defined elsewhere in the program (e.g., in a Definition Specification).

Free-format (Version 5 or later)

```
*.. 1 ...+... 2 ...+... 3 ...+... 4 ...+... 5 ...+... 6 ...+... 7 ...+... 8
 /FREE
    EVAL Counter = 0;            // Initialize a counter
    EVAL TaxRate = .045;         // Assign a value > 0
    EVAL AbslZero = -273.16;     // Assign a value < 0
    EVAL AmtOwed = BalDue;       // Assign a field value
 /END-FREE
```

Fixed-format (pre–Version 5)

```
*.. 1 ...+... 2 ...+... 3 ...+... 4 ...+... 5 ...+... 6 ...+... 7 ...+... 8
CL0N01Factor1++++++Opcode(E)+Extended-factor2++++++++++++++++++++++++++++++
 * Initialize a counter.
C                   EVAL      Counter = 0
 * Assign a value > 0.
C                   EVAL      TaxRate = .045
 * Assign a value < 0.
C                   EVAL      AbslZero = -273.16
 * Assign a field value.
C                   EVAL      AmtOwed  = BalDue
```

Note that even when you use the fixed-format syntax, the extended Factor 2 entry is *free-form*, which means that it can appear anywhere within positions 36–80, with as many (or as few) blanks between the entry's components as you want.

When you use the Version 5 free-format Calculation Specification, explicitly coding the EVAL operation is optional unless you need to use a special feature, such as rounding (discussed later). You can simply code the assignment expression, and the RPG IV compiler will make the assignment. The following free-format examples are equivalent to the ones shown above.

Free-format (Version 5 or later)

```
*.. 1 ...+... 2 ...+... 3 ...+... 4 ...+... 5 ...+... 6 ...+... 7 ...+... 8
 /FREE
    Counter = 0;              // Initialize a counter
    TaxRate = .045;           // Assign a value > 0
    AbslZero = -273.16;       // Assign a value < 0
    AmtOwed = BalDue;         // Assign a field value
 /END-FREE
```

For the remainder of this book, EVAL will not be explicitly coded in free-format examples unless it is required.

Arithmetic Operations

RPG IV does not include a wealth of mathematical operations. The four basic arithmetic operations — add, subtract, multiply, and divide — along with a few extras represent the range of RPG IV's mathematical offerings. Although the language has proven itself adequate to handle most of the mathematical processing required in the business environment, you probably wouldn't want to use RPG IV to calculate rocket trajectories.

The primary operation for arithmetic calculations in RPG IV is the EVAL operation. We will first look at this general-purpose operation and then consider several single-purpose operations you can use to handle special calculations that EVAL cannot perform in some earlier releases.

Using EVAL for Arithmetic

In a previous section, you saw how to use EVAL for simple numeric assignment. The EVAL operation also provides a flexible, powerful, relatively free-form method for assigning numeric fields the results of simple or complex arithmetic calculations in a single step.

The expression for evaluation can contain the arithmetic operators + (addition), − (subtraction), * (multiplication), / (division), and ** (**exponentiation**, or raising a value to a power), as well as parentheses, relational symbols (e.g., <, >), logical operators (e.g., AND, OR), and built-in functions (discussed later in the text).

A single expression can contain as many arithmetic operators, numeric literals, and numeric fields as needed to accomplish a desired calculation.

Free-format (Version 5 or later)

```
*.. 1 ...+... 2 ...+... 3 ...+... 4 ...+... 5 ...+... 6 ...+... 7 ...+... 8
 /FREE
    // Examples of calculations using the EVAL operation
    WithHold = FICA + StateTax + FedTax;
    NetPay = GrossPay − WithHold;
    GrssProfit = Cost * .6 * QtySold;
    AvgAmount = TotAmount / Counter;
    NumSquared = Number ** 2;
 /END-FREE
```

Fixed-format (pre–Version 5)

```
*.. 1 ...+... 2 ...+... 3 ...+... 4 ...+... 5 ...+... 6 ...+... 7 ...+... 8
CLØNØ1Factor1++++++Opcode(E)+Extended-factor2++++++++++++++++++++++++++++++
 * Examples of calculations using the EVAL operation
C                   EVAL      WithHold = FICA + StateTax + FedTax
C                   EVAL      NetPay = GrossPay − WithHold
C                   EVAL      GrssProfit = Cost * .6 * QtySold
C                   EVAL      AvgAmount = TotAmount / Counter
C                   EVAL      NumSquared = Number ** 2
```

All values used in the arithmetic expression to the right of the equal sign must, of course, be numeric fields or literals. One other restriction arises when you use division in an expression. Remember that division by zero is mathematically impossible. A runtime error occurs if, at the time of the division, the divisor (the part of an expression immediately to the right of the division sign) evaluates to zero.

When the arithmetic expression contains more than one operator, the computer uses the rules of precedence from mathematics to determine the order in which to perform the operations. Exponentiation has the highest precedence, followed by multiplication and division, and then addition and subtraction. When an expression contains operations of equal precedence, the system executes them in order from left to right. You can use parentheses to change the order in which the computer executes these operations; operations within parentheses are performed before any operations outside the parentheses.

Free-format (Version 5 or later)

```
*.. 1 ...+... 2 ...+... 3 ...+... 4 ...+... 5 ...+... 6 ...+... 7 ...+... 8
 /FREE
  // In this example, the multiplication will occur before the subtraction
    Answer = A * B − 1;

  // In this example, the parentheses cause the subtraction to take place
  // before the multiplication
    Answer = A * (B − 1);
 /END-FREE
```

Fixed-format (pre–Version 5)

```
*.. 1 ...+... 2 ...+... 3 ...+... 4 ...+... 5 ...+... 6 ...+... 7 ...+... 8
CLØNØ1Factor1+++++++Opcode(E)+Extended-factor2+++++++++++++++++++++++++++++++
 * In this example, the multiplication will occur before the subtraction
C                   EVAL      Answer = A * B - 1

 * In this example, the parentheses cause the subtraction to take place
 * before the multiplication
C                   EVAL      Answer = A * (B - 1)
```

The expression can include as many (or as few) blanks between fields, literals, and operations as you like to make the expression readable and easy to understand. If it is necessary, you can continue the expression to one or more lines. When using the free-format syntax, you can simply continue the expression anywhere on subsequent lines and then end it with a semicolon (;). When using the older fixed-format syntax, continuation lines must be blank between positions 7 and 35, with the expression continued in positions 36–80. The following code illustrates the use of a continuation line with the EVAL operation.

Free-format (Version 5 or later)

```
*.. 1 ...+... 2 ...+... 3 ...+... 4 ...+... 5 ...+... 6 ...+... 7 ...+... 8
/FREE
    Pay = HourlyRate * 40 +
          1.5 * HourlyRate * (HoursWorked - 40);
/END-FREE
```

Fixed-format (pre–Version 5)

```
*.. 1 ...+... 2 ...+... 3 ...+... 4 ...+... 5 ...+... 6 ...+... 7 ...+... 8
CLØNØ1Factor1+++++++Opcode(E)+Extended-factor2+++++++++++++++++++++++++++++++
C                   EVAL      Pay = HourlyRate * 40 +
C                                   1.5 * HourlyRate * (HoursWorked - 40)
```

Those of you who've studied algebra recognize the similarity between assignment expressions and algebraic equations. Don't be misled by this similarity, however. An algebraic equation asserts equality; an assignment expression instructs the computer to perform the calculation to the right of the equal sign and then assign the result to the field left of the equal sign. In algebra, the equation $x = x + 1$ is a logical impossibility; within an EVAL operation, $x = x + 1$ is a perfectly legitimate instruction that tells the computer to take the value of field x, add 1 to it, and store the result in field x.

In fact, this form of assignment expression is used frequently in RPG IV programming for counting and accumulating. For example, to count the number of customers in a file, you would increment a counter field (i.e., add 1 to it) each time you processed a customer record. Or, to accumulate employees' salaries, you would add each salary to a field representing the grand total of the salaries.

Free-format (Version 5 or later)

```
*.. 1 ...+... 2 ...+... 3 ...+... 4 ...+... 5 ...+... 6 ...+... 7 ...+... 8
/FREE
    Counter = Counter + 1;                         // Increment a counter
    GrandTotal = GrandTotal + EmpSalary;           // Accumulate a total
/END-FREE
```

Version 5 Release 2 Update

RPG IV now supports a series of arithmetic operators that you can use to simplify coding when the target of an operation is also the first operand in the operation. The += and -= operators increment or decrement an accumulator, respectively; moreover, the *=, /=, and **= operators simplify some multiplication, division, and exponentiation operations, respectively. Study the following examples:

```
*.. 1 ...+... 2 ...+... 3 ...+... 4 ...+... 5 ...+... 6 ...+... 7 ...+... 8
 /FREE
    Count += 1;                 // Same as: Count = Count + 1
    Inventory -= OrderQty;      // Same as: Inventory = Inventory - OrderQty
    NewPrc *= TaxPct;           // Same as: NewPrc = NewPrc * TaxPct
    Days /= 7;                  // Same as: Days = Days / 7
    Yards **= 2;                // Same as: Yards = Yards ** 2
 /END-FREE
```

Fixed-format (pre–Version 5)
```
*.. 1 ...+... 2 ...+... 3 ...+... 4 ...+... 5 ...+... 6 ...+... 7 ...+... 8
CLØN01Factor1+++++++Opcode(E)+Extended-factor2++++++++++++++++++++++++++++++
 * Increment a counter
C                   EVAL      Counter = Counter + 1
 * Accumulate a total
C                   EVAL      GrandTotal = GrandTotal + EmpSalary
```

You can also decrement a counter or decrease the value of an accumulator by using subtraction:

Free-format (Version 5 or later)
```
*.. 1 ...+... 2 ...+... 3 ...+... 4 ...+... 5 ...+... 6 ...+... 7 ...+... 8
 /FREE
    CountDown = CountDown - 1;
    Inventory = Inventory - OrderQty;
 /END-FREE
```

Fixed-format (pre–Version 5)
```
*.. 1 ...+... 2 ...+... 3 ...+... 4 ...+... 5 ...+... 6 ...+... 7 ...+... 8
CLØN01Factor1+++++++Opcode(E)+Extended-factor2++++++++++++++++++++++++++++++
C                   EVAL      CountDown = CountDown - 1
C                   EVAL      Inventory = Inventory   OrderQty
```

Numeric Truncation and Field Sizes

With all arithmetic operations, one of your jobs as a programmer is to determine appropriate length and decimal position entries for result fields. It is important to allow sufficient room; otherwise, if a calculation produces an answer too big to store in the result field, a runtime error or truncation will occur.

Truncation is the loss of digits from the right and/or left end of a result field. The iSeries stores the result of any arithmetic operation in the result field based on decimal position alignment. If the value to be stored is too large for the result field, truncation occurs. This digit loss may occur from the leftmost or rightmost digits of the answer (or both), depending on the operation used and the number of defined digit positions to the left and right of the decimal position in the result field. Digit loss from the left is called **high-order truncation**, while loss from the right is **low-order truncation**. The following table illustrates the concept of truncation.

| Calculated value | Result Field Definition | | Truncated result |
	Length	Decimal position	
413.29	4	1	413.2
413.29	4	2	13.29
413.29	4	0	0413
413.29	4	3	3.290

From these examples, you can see that truncation can occur for significant (leftmost) or insignificant (rightmost) digits, depending on the calculated value and the number of digit positions to the right and left of the decimal position in the result field. You should also notice that if the answer has fewer digits (left or right of the decimal position) than the result field, the system simply zero-fills the unneeded positions.

Truncation is important to understand because if it occurs during a program's execution, the program may simply continue to run without issuing a warning that digits have been lost, or the program may end abnormally (abend). Losing 1/1000 of a dollar may not be the end of the world (although on a large run, it could add up), but losing $10,000 would probably cause your company some distress. Furthermore, program abends reflect poorly on the programmer.

In RPG IV, all arithmetic operations automatically — and without warning — truncate extra decimal positions (low-order truncation) to fit the value in the result field. EVAL generates a runtime error that causes the program to end abnormally if high-order truncation is imminent.

How do you determine the size of a result field to ensure that truncation or abends do not inadvertently happen? EVAL keeps track of any intermediate results that occur during the evaluation of its expression, maintaining full precision internally (up to limits imposed by numeric data types) until the expression is completely evaluated and ready to be stored in the result field. However, you must analyze the expression — that is, consider the operations it performs and whether or not it occurs within a loop — to estimate the size needed for the final result. Fortunately, some guidelines exist for result field definition to help you ensure that your result fields are large enough to store the calculated answers. The following sections present some guidelines for determining field sizes of results occurring from two values and an operation. When in doubt, you can always manually perform some representative calculations that mirror what you want the computer to do to guide you in this matter.

Result Field Size for Addition

To avoid truncation when adding two values, you should define the result field with *one more* position *left of the decimal* than the larger of the addends' integer digit positions. Positions to the right of the decimal in the result field should equal the larger of the decimal positions of the addends. For example, if you're adding two fields, one defined as length 3 with two decimal positions (i.e., one to the left and two to the right of the decimal) and one defined as length 6 with three decimal positions (i.e., three to the left, three to the right of the decimal), your result field should be defined as length 7 with three decimal positions (four to the left, three to the right). To see why this rule eliminates the possibility of truncation, simply do the addition with the largest possible values the addends can contain — 9.99 and 999.999 — and you will understand its basis.

When you are using addition to count or accumulate, the value of the result keeps getting larger and larger each time the calculation is performed (for example, when accumulating individuals' calculated gross pay figures to generate a grand-total gross pay). In this case, to determine the necessary size of the result field, you need to have an approximate idea of how many times the calculation will be performed (i.e., how many employees you will process). Once you have this estimate, follow the rule for multiplication, given below.

Result Field Size for Subtraction

To eliminate the chance of truncation with subtraction, follow the rule given for addition. This advice may seem strange at first, until you realize that you must provide for the possibility of subtracting a negative number, which essentially turns the problem into one of addition.

Thus, to avoid high-order truncation when subtracting two values, define the result field to have one more digit position to the left of the decimal position than the larger of the high-order positions of the two values. And define the result field to have the same number of decimal positions as the larger of the number of decimal positions of the two values.

Result Field Size for Multiplication

When multiplying, to determine the needed number of digit positions in a result field, add the number of positions to the left of the decimal positions of the two multipliers and use the resulting value to determine the number of high-order digits in the result. The sum of the number of positions to the right of the decimal in the multipliers represents the number of positions your result field must have to the right of the decimal.

For example, if you were multiplying 999.99 by 99.99, your result field would require five places to the left of the decimal and four to the right to store the answer without truncation. In RPG IV, this would mean a field nine positions long, with four decimal positions.

Result Field Size for Division

When dividing by a value of 1 or greater, the maximum required positions to the left of the decimal in the result is the number of left-of-decimal positions in the dividend (the value *being* divided). To understand this point, recognize that dividing any value by 1 yields the original value; dividing by any value greater than 1 will yield a value smaller than the original value.

When dividing by values less than 1, computing the number of digit positions in the result becomes a more complicated process; the smaller the divisor, the more significant positions needed in the result field. If you are working with divisors less than 1, your safest approach is to hand-calculate with some representative values to get a sense of the size needed to store your answer.

Because few divisions work out evenly, there is no way to guarantee you will provide enough decimal positions to avoid low-order truncation. In general, you choose the number of decimal positions for the result field based on the degree of significance, or accuracy, that the calculation warrants. Because most business data processing deals with calculations involving dollars and cents, it usually makes sense to carry out intermediate calculations with the maximum needed or the maximum allowable number of decimal positions (whichever is smaller) and then reduce that to two decimal positions in the final calculation.

Rounding

When you store a value in a result field that has fewer decimal positions than the calculated answer, common business practice dictates that you should always round your answer rather than let the system truncate it. Rounding is sometimes called **half-adjusting** because of the technique computers use to accomplish this feat. The computer adds half the value of your rightmost desired decimal position to the digit immediately to the right of that decimal position before storing the answer in the result field. Because the value added is half the value of the least-significant digit position of your result, the term "half-adjust" came into being.

For example, assume the computer has calculated an answer of 3.14156 that you want to store, in rounded form, in a result field defined as length 4 with three decimal positions. The computer will add 0.0005 to the answer (i.e., 1/2 of 0.001, the lowest decimal position you are retaining in your result), yielding 3.14206. It then stores this value in the result field, truncated to three decimal positions, as 3.142. If you had defined the result as length 3 with two decimal positions, the computer would add 0.005 (1/2 of 0.01) to 3.14156, yielding 3.14656, and store that answer in the result as 3.14.

Fortunately, even if you don't completely understand how the computer rounds, the method RPG IV uses to specify that rounding should take place is simple: You just enter an H, for half-adjust, within parentheses immediately following the operation code of the calculation whose result you want rounded. This directive to round is called an **operation extender** in RPG IV. The following examples show the use of the (H) operation extender.

Free-format (Version 5 or later)

```
*.. 1 ...+... 2 ...+... 3 ...+... 4 ...+... 5 ...+... 6 ...+... 7 ...+... 8
  /FREE
    // Sample calculations specifying that the result should be rounded
      EVAL(H) Interest = Rate * LoanAmt;
      EVAL(H) AvgAmount = TotAmount / Counter;
      EVAL(H) Yards = SqYards **.5;
  /END-FREE
```

Fixed-format (pre–Version 5)

```
*.. 1 ...+... 2 ...+... 3 ...+... 4 ...+... 5 ...+... 6 ...+... 7 ...+... 8
CLØN01Factor1+++++++Opcode(E)+Extended-factor2+++++++++++++++++++++++++++++++
 * Sample calculations specifying that the result should be rounded
C                   EVAL(H)   Interest = Rate * LoanAmt
C                   EVAL(H)   AvgAmount = TotAmount / Counter
C                   EVAL(H)   Yards = SqYards **.5
```

Note that you must include the H in every calculation line where you want rounding to occur, even if those calculations use the same result field. The compiler will *not* warn you if you inadvertently omit an H entry. Note also that you must explicitly code the EVAL operation if you're going to use the (H) extender in the free-format syntax of the Calculation Specification.

Free-format (Version 5 or later)

```
*.. 1 ...+... 2 ...+... 3 ...+... 4 ...+... 5 ...+... 6 ...+... 7 ...+... 8
  /FREE
    // In the calcs below, rounding is specified in each calculation
    // that is to result in a rounded value for Interest
      EVAL(H) Interest = LoanAmt * StdRate;
      EVAL(H) Interest = AltAmt * PrimeRate;
  /END-FREE
```

Fixed-format (pre–Version 5)

```
*.. 1 ...+... 2 ...+... 3 ...+... 4 ...+... 5 ...+... 6 ...+... 7 ...+... 8
CLØN01Factor1+++++++Opcode(E)+Extended-factor2+++++++++++++++++++++++++++++++
 * In the calcs below, rounding is specified in each calculation that is to
 * result in a rounded value for Interest
C                   EVAL(H)   Interest = LoanAmt * StdRate
C                   EVAL(H)   Interest = AltAmt * PrimeRate
```

Although you most often need to round when multiplying or dividing, you can also specify rounding for addition and subtraction operations as well as for multiplication and division. Recognize that you do not always need to round when multiplying. For example, consider the following expression:

```
InvtyValue = QtyOnHand * UnitPrice
```

If QtyOnHand is an integer (whole number) and UnitPrice is stored as dollars and cents (e.g., length 4 with two decimal positions), the resulting answer will never have more than two decimal positions, so you do *not* need to round the answer to store it in InvtyValue, defined as length 6 with two decimal positions.

Caution
Sometimes, out of either uncertainty or laziness, students decide to play it safe by rounding all arithmetic operations, regardless of whether the rounding is needed. Avoid this practice. The RPG IV compiler will issue a warning message about unnecessary half-adjusting, and rounding when uncalled for reflects poorly on your programming skills and/or style.

Improving EVAL Precision

The EVAL operation automatically allocates memory for any intermediate values the operation may need to evaluate an expression. These intermediate numeric values are limited in size to 30 total digits, including digits to the right of the decimal. EVAL uses rules similar to those discussed above to avoid size overflow within these intermediate values. In some complex expressions, or with some large operands, EVAL may be forced to truncate decimal positions from an intermediate result in order to fit the intermediate field into 30 digits. This truncation may affect the precision of EVAL's results.

To ensure the best accuracy when using EVAL, you should instruct RPG that no intermediate value should have fewer decimal places than the end result. This instruction, called the **result decimal positions rule** for evaluating expressions, is *not* the rule RPG uses by default. There are two ways to invoke this rule:

- use the (R) operation code extender
- use the EXPROPTS Control Specification keyword

If you use the (R) extender, you'll need to include it with each EVAL operation in which you want the extender to apply. Note that you can combine several operation code extenders within the parentheses after the operation; in the following case, not only do we ensure EVAL precision, but we also round (half-adjust) the result.

Free-format (Version 5 or later)

```
*.. 1 ...+... 2 ...+... 3 ...+... 4 ...+... 5 ...+... 6 ...+... 7 ...+... 8
 /FREE
    EVAL(HR) Pay = HourlyRate * 40 + 1.5 * HourlyRate * (HoursWorked - 40);
 /END-FREE
```

Fixed-format (pre–Version 5)

```
*.. 1 ...+... 2 ...+... 3 ...+... 4 ...+... 5 ...+... 6 ...+... 7 ...+... 8
CLØN01Factor1+++++++Opcode(E)+Extended-factor2+++++++++++++++++++++++++++++
C                   EVAL(HR)  Pay = HourlyRate * 40 +
C                                   1.5 * HourlyRate * (HoursWorkd - 40)
```

Instead of remembering to code the (R) extender each time you need it, you should make the result decimal positions rule the default method within an RPG program by including the following Control Specification keyword at the beginning of each program:

```
*.. 1 ...+... 2 ...+... 3 ...+... 4 ...+... 5 ...+... 6 ...+... 7 ...+... 8
HKeywords+++++++++++++++++++++++++++++++++++++++++++++++++++++++++++++++++++
H EXPROPTS(*RESDECPOS)
```

Putting It All Together

You have learned how to perform arithmetic in RPG IV, and you understand the importance of correctly defining the size of result fields and appropriately rounding calculations. Now it's time to demonstrate the use of these concepts to give you a better flavor of RPG IV's approach to solving arithmetically oriented programming problems. The following example demonstrates how to use the arithmetic operations of RPG IV to solve a typical business problem.

A retail store wants you to write a routine to calculate selling prices for items it has received. The store uses a 60 percent markup for its goods. In addition to the required selling price, the store would like you to generate a projection of gross profit for each item and a grand-total projected gross profit for all items received. The gross-profit projections should assume that the store will sell all the items at the price calculated by your program.

An input file, NewItems, contains records with the following format:

Field	Positions	Decimal positions
Item description	1–30	—
Item cost	31–36	2
Quantity received	37–40	0

The following printer spacing chart depicts the desired report:

Pseudocode of a solution for this problem follows:

Print headings
Read a record
WHILE more records exist
         Calculate per-unit profit (cost * .6)
         Calculate selling price (cost + per-unit profit)
         Calculate total item gross profit (quantity * per-unit profit)
         Accumulate grand-total gross profit
         Write detail line
         Read a record
ENDWHILE
Print grand-total line
END program

Notice in the pseudocode that all calculations need to fall within the loop because each calculation needs to be performed for each data record. Printing headings is done just once before the loop, while printing the grand-total line is done just once, following the loop. The pseudocode also shows that the details of the required calculations have been worked out.

The File Specifications for this problem present no new challenges:

```
*.. 1 ...+... 2 ...+... 3 ...+... 4 ...+... 5 ...+... 6 ...+... 7 ...+... 8
FFilename++IPEASFRLen+LKLen+AIDevice+.Keywords+++++++++++++++++++++++++++++
FNewItems  IF   F   40        DISK
FQPRINT    O    F   132       PRINTER
```

On the Input Specifications, note that QtyRcvd must include a decimal positions entry of 0 because this field will be used in arithmetic operations:

```
*.. 1 ...+... 2 ...+... 3 ...+... 4 ...+... 5 ...+... 6 ...+... 7 ...+... 8
IFilename++SqNORiPos1+NCCPos2+NCCPos3+NCC............................
I.....................Fmt+SPFrom+To+++DcField++++++++L1M1FrP1MnZr......
I                          1   30  Descript
I                         31   36 2ItemCost
I                         37   40 0QtyRcvd
```

Looking at our pseudocode, we realize that we will need four fields that are not part of our input record: one representing unit profit for a given item, one for selling price, one for gross profit for that item, and one for grand-total gross profit of all items received. We define these fields as standalone fields on Definition Specifications (preceding the Input Specifications), as shown below:

```
*.. 1 ...+... 2 ...+... 3 ...+... 4 ...+... 5 ...+... 6 ...+... 7 ...+... 8
DName+++++++++++ETDsFrom+++To/L+++IDc.Keywords+++++++++++++++++++++++++++++++
D UnitProfit      S               6 2
D SellPrice       S               7 2
D GrssProfit      S              10 2
D TotProfit       S              14 2
```

The Calculation Specifications that follow show the algorithm to solve the problem.

Free-format (Version 5 or later)

```
*.. 1 ...+... 2 ...+... 3 ...+... 4 ...+... 5 ...+... 6 ...+... 7 ...+... 8
 /FREE
   EXCEPT Headings;
   READ NewItems;

   DOW NOT %EOF;
     EVAL(H) UnitProfit = ItemCost * .6;
     SellPrice = ItemCost + UnitProfit;
     GrssProfit = UnitProfit * QtyRcvd;
     TotProfit = GrssProfit + TotProfit;
     EXCEPT Detail;
     READ NewItems;
     ENDDO;

   EXCEPT TotalLine;
   *INLR = *ON;
   RETURN;
 /END-FREE
```

Fixed-format (pre–Version 5)

```
*.. 1 ...+... 2 ...+... 3 ...+... 4 ...+... 5 ...+... 6 ...+... 7 ...+... 8
CL0N01Factor1++++++Opcode(E)+Factor2++++++Result++++++++Len++D+HiLoEq....
CL0N01Factor1++++++Opcode(E)+Extended-factor2++++++++++++++++++++++++++++
C                   EXCEPT    Headings
C                   READ      NewItems

C                   DOW       NOT %EOF
C                   EVAL(H)   UnitProfit = ItemCost * .6
C                   EVAL      SellPrice  = ItemCost + UnitProfit
C                   EVAL      GrssProfit = UnitProfit * QtyRcvd
C                   EVAL      TotProfit  = GrssProfit + TotProfit
C                   EXCEPT    Detail
C                   READ      NewItems
C                   ENDDO

C                   EXCEPT    TotalLine
C                   EVAL      *INLR = *ON
C                   RETURN
```

Note that the expression used to obtain unit profit (UnitProfit) is rounded, while the one used to calculate gross profit (GrssProfit) is not. This difference is based on the relative number of decimal positions that the two multiplication operations generate, given the number of decimal positions in the multipliers.

Also note that to calculate grand-total gross profit (TotProfit), it is necessary in each pass through the loop to add the gross profit of the current item (GrssProfit) to the accumulator TotProfit.

All that remains to be completed are the Output Specifications for the program. In the following specification lines, we've omitted details of the coding for the heading lines because they present nothing new to consider. Note that the total line (TotalLine) appears in the output with a Space 1 before entry. This spacing is required to obtain one blank line between the last printed detail line and the total line. Notice also that the total line uses a continuation line to express the caption associated with the grand total. Last, note that a floating dollar sign is associated with field TotProfit, as requested in the printer spacing chart.

```
*.. 1 ...+... 2 ...+... 3 ...+... 4 ...+... 5 ...+... 6 ...+... 7 ...+... 8
OFilename++DF..N01N02N03Excnam++++B++A++Sb+Sa+..............................
O..............N01N02N03Field++++++++YB.End++PConstant/editword/DTformat++
OQPRINT    E              Headings         1
O                         . . .
O          E              Detail           1
O                         Descript            30
O                         ItemCost      1     41
O                         SellPrice     1     53
O                         QtyRcvd       1     62
O                         UnitProfit    1     74
O                         GrssProfit    1     92
O          E              TotalLine   1
O                                             70 'GRAND TOTAL GROSS PROFIT -
O                                                PROJECTED:'
O                         TotProfit     1     92 '$'
```

When we complete the Output Specifications for the heading lines, add some overview documentation, and put all the pieces of code together, we obtain the entire program:

Free-format (Version 5 or later)

```
*.. 1 ...+... 2 ...+... 3 ...+... 4 ...+... 5 ...+... 6 ...+... 7 ...+... 8
 // ****************************************************************
 // This program calculates selling prices for received items based on a
 // 60% markup over item cost. It also determines projected gross profit
 // for each item in the shipment and total gross profit for all the items
 //
 //      Author:  J. Yaeger
 //      Date Written:  Jan. 1995
 //      Date Modified: Dec. 2001
 //
 // ****************************************************************

FNewItems  IF   F   40        DISK
FQPRINT    O    F   132       PRINTER

 // Definition of all work fields used in program
D UnitProfit      S              6 2
D SellPrice       S              7 2
D GrssProfit      S             10 2
D TotProfit       S             14 2
 // Input file of received items defined within program
INewItems  NS
I                                1   30 Descript
```

continued...

continued...

```
I                                          31   36 2ItemCost
I                                          37   40 ØQtyRcvd

   // Calculations for program
 /FREE
    EXCEPT Headings;
    READ NewItems;

    DOW %NOT EOF;
      EVAL(H) UnitProfit = ItemCost * .6;
      SellPrice = ItemCost + UnitProfit;
      GrssProfit = UnitProfit *  QtyRcvd;
      TotProfit = GrssProfit + TotProfit;
      EXCEPT Detail;
      READ NewItems;
    ENDDO;

    EXCEPT TotalLine;
    *INLR = *ON;
    RETURN;
 /END-FREE

   // Output specifications
OQPRINT      E            Headings       1
O                         UDATE        Y   11
O                                          55 'GROSS PROFIT PROJECTION'
O                                          82 'PAGE'
O                         PAGE             87
O                         Headings     2 1
O                                          52 'SELLING'
O                                          74 'PER UNIT'
O                                          88 'TOTAL'
O                         Headings     2
O                                          10 'ITEM'
O                                          39 'COST'
O                                          51 'PRICE'
O                                          61 'QTY.'
O                                          73 'PROFIT'
O                                          92 'GROSS PROFIT'
O            E            Detail         1
O                         Descript         30
O                         ItemCost     1   41
O                         SellPrice    1   53
O                         QtyRcvd      1   62
O                         UnitProfit   1   74
O                         GrssProfit   1   92
O            E            TotalLine    1
O                                          70 'GRAND TOTAL GROSS PROFIT -
O                                             PROJECTED:'
O                         TotProfit    1   92 '$'
```

Note

By now, you should be familiar with the essential differences between the free-format and fixed-format versions of the Calculation Specifications. Free-format specifications became available with Version 5 of the ILE RPG/400 compiler. As RPG IV matures, free-format specifications will undoubtedly tend to be the preferred alternative to fixed-format C-specs. For the rest of this text, we'll show only free-format examples wherever practical. In addition, EVAL will not be explicitly coded unless it is necessary to do so.

Character Assignment

Now that you know how to use EVAL to assign values to numeric fields using free-form expressions, let's look at how to assign values to character fields. As you might guess, RPG IV's EVAL operation easily handles this task:

```
*.. 1 ...+... 2 ...+... 3 ...+... 4 ...+... 5 ...+... 6 ...+... 7 ...+... 8
/FREE
    EmailAdd = 'jdoe@rpgiv.com';
/END-FREE
```

Just as in numeric assignment operations, the value to be assigned (in this case, a character literal) appears to the right of the equal sign, and the receiving field appears to the left. If you need to continue a long literal to another line, use a continuation character (+ or –) to signal to the computer that the literal continues on the next line. When using the free-format syntax, end the entire expression (not each line) with a semicolon:

```
*.. 1 ...+... 2 ...+... 3 ...+... 4 ...+... 5 ...+... 6 ...+... 7 ...+... 8
/FREE
    ReportHead = 'Wexler University:  2000 +
                  Faculty Directory';
/END-FREE
```

Note

Remember that when you use the + continuation character with the fixed-format syntax, the continuation starts with the first nonblank character in the extended Factor 2 of the following line; a – directs the continuation to begin with whatever appears in column 36.

```
*.. 1 ...+... 2 ...+... 3 ...+... 4 ...+... 5 ...+... 6 ...+... 7 ...+... 8
CLØN01Factor1+++++++Opcode(E)+Extended-factor2+++++++++++++++++++++++++++++++
C                   EVAL      ReportHead = 'Wexler University:  2000 +
C                                          Faculty Directory'
```

The EVAL operation performs the assignment by transferring the literal character by character, starting with the leftmost character. If the result field that receives the literal is defined to be longer than the character literal, EVAL *right-pads* the field with blanks (i.e., it fills the unused positions at the right end of the field with blanks). If the result field is too small to store the literal, EVAL truncates the extra rightmost characters.

```
*.. 1 ...+... 2 ...+... 3 ...+... 4 ...+... 5 ...+... 6 ...+... 7 ...+... 8
/FREE
    // If the result field and the literal are the same length,
    // all characters are copied to the result field.
    Example = 'ABCDEFG';            // Field Example now contains 'ABCDEFG'

    // If the result field is longer than the literal by 5 positions, all
    // characters are copied to the left positions of the result field; the
    // rightmost 5 characters are blanks.
    Example2 = 'ABCDEFG';           // Example2 now contains 'ABCDEFG     '

    // If the result field is shorter than the literal by 3 positions, the
    // rightmost 3 characters of the literal are not copied to the result
    // field.
    Example3 = 'ABCDEFG';           // Field Example3 now contains 'ABCD'
/END-FREE
```

You can also use EVAL to assign the contents of one character field to another. The same rules apply regarding padding and truncation.

```
*.. 1 ...+... 2 ...+... 3 ...+... 4 ...+... 5 ...+... 6 ...+... 7 ...+... 8
 /FREE
    // Suppose PadCourse is 10 positions in length, CourseName contains
    // 'CS365', and Prefix is 2 positions in length
    PadCourse = CourseName;    // Field PadCourse now contains 'CS365      '
    Prefix = CourseName;       // Field Prefix contains 'CS'
 /END-FREE
```

Assigning Values with Figurative Constants

RPG IV lets you assign figurative constant *ZERO (or *ZEROS) both to numeric and to character fields to fill the fields with zeros. You can also assign *BLANK (or *BLANKS) to character fields to fill the fields with blanks. Assigning figurative constant *ALL immediately followed by one or more characters within apostrophes (') causes the string within the apostrophes to be cyclically repeated through the entire length of the result field.

```
*.. 1 ...+... 2 ...+... 3 ...+... 4 ...+... 5 ...+... 6 ...+... 7 ...+... 8
 /FREE
    // Examples of using figurative constants in assignment operations
    *IN50 = *ON;
    LastName = *BLANKS;
    ZeroField = *ZEROS;
    RecordKey = *HIVAL;
    CharField = *ALL'XYZ';
                      // If CharField has length 9, it contains 'XYZXYZXYZ'
    UnderLine = *ALL'-';
                      // If UnderLine has length 80, it contains 80 hyphens
 /END-FREE
```

Figurative constants *OFF and *ON represent character '0' and character '1', respectively. Although you can use *OFF and *ON with any character field of any length, programmers most often use these constants to change the value of an RPG IV indicator or to compare with an indicator's value. *ON is the equivalent of '1', while *OFF equates to '0'. We've used *ON previously in this text with EVAL to set on the LR indicator.

Data-Type Conversion

Occasionally, you may need to convert a value's data type from numeric to character, or vice versa, to use the value in operations that are valid only for a particular data type. For example, you might initially store a numeric value in a character field so you can check whether the value contains a particular digit (we discuss how to do this later in the text). After this check, you might transfer the value to a numeric field for use in arithmetic calculations or edited output.

You normally cannot use the EVAL operation to perform such data-type conversions; EVAL requires matching data types on either side of the assignment expression. You use another assignment operator, MOVE, to carry out data-type conversion.

The MOVE Operation

The MOVE operation uses the fixed form of the Calculation Specification; MOVE does not support the free-format syntax, even at Version 5. You do not use Factor 1 with MOVE. The value specified in Factor 2 is copied (or assigned) to the result field. The following examples show how to use MOVE to change data types.

```
*.. 1 ...+... 2 ...+... 3 ...+... 4 ...+... 5 ...+... 6 ...+... 7 ...+... 8
CLØN01Factor1+++++++Opcode(E)+Factor2++++++Result++++++++Len++D+HiLoEq....
 * Store a numeric value in character field Alpha (length 4)
C                   MOVE      1234        Alpha
 * Execute desired character operations on Alpha
                      . . .
 * Then move the value to a numeric field so that it can be used with
 * arithmetic operations or edited for output. Field Numeric has length 4,
 * with Ø decimal positions
C                   MOVE      Alpha       Numeric
```

Unlike EVAL, MOVE transfers characters from the sending field in Factor 2 to the receiving field in the result character by character from *right to left*. MOVE disregards the decimal positions of numeric fields, and it does not automatically pad a character field with blanks. (You would need to designate the operation extender (P) for this to occur.)

When you change data types with the MOVE operation, it is good programming practice to match the size of the result field with the size of the Factor 2 value to avoid errors in data transfer. Matching sizes with MOVE eliminates inadvertent changes to numeric values; it avoids the truncation of characters or the inclusion of carryover characters from the result field, which can occur if Factor 2 is shorter than the result. The following examples demonstrate how errors in data transfer can happen when using MOVE.

```
*.. 1 ...+... 2 ...+... 3 ...+... 4 ...+... 5 ...+... 6 ...+... 7 ...+... 8
CLØN01Factor1+++++++Opcode(E)+Factor2++++++Result++++++++Len++D+HiLoEq....
 * Alpha is a 4-position character field that contains Øs.
 * Numeric is a 5-position numeric field, with 1 decimal position,
 * previously initialized to Ø.
C                   MOVE      1.23        Alpha
C                   MOVE      Alpha       Numeric
 * Alpha now contains 'Ø123'; Numeric now contains ØØ12.3.

C                   MOVE      32767       Alpha
 * Alpha now contains '2767'.

C                   MOVE      59          Alpha
 * Alpha now contains '2759'.
```

The MOVEL (Move Left) Operation

Programmers sometimes use the MOVE operation to split off the rightmost portion of a data value that contains both alphabetic characters and digits to be treated as numeric data. To split off the leftmost portion, you can use another RPG IV assignment operation: MOVEL (Move Left). MOVEL performs identically to MOVE, except that data transfer proceeds from left to right. The following example shows how you can use MOVE and MOVEL to extract parts of a data value.

```
*.. 1 ...+... 2 ...+... 3 ...+... 4 ...+... 5 ...+... 6 ...+... 7 ...+... 8
CLØN01Factor1+++++++Opcode(E)+Factor2++++++Result++++++++Len++D+HiLoEq....
 * StateTax is a 6-byte character field that contains the value 'Ø725CA';
 * StateID is a 2-byte character field; TaxRate is a numeric field
 * of length 4, with 4 decimal positions.
C                   MOVE      StateTax    StateID
C                   MOVEL     StateTax    TaxRate
 * StateID now contains 'CA'; TaxRate contains .Ø725.
```

In Appendix G, we look further at how the MOVE and MOVEL operators were used in previous versions of RPG. You will also learn about other operators that were used before EVAL to carry out specific assignment operations.

Using Built-In Functions

RPG IV supports many **built-in functions (BIFs)** that you use in conjunction with free-form expressions. Some of the built-in functions mirror the roles of other "fixed-format" operation codes; others provide new functions that aren't available by any other means. Built-in functions always begin with a percent sign (%). You've already seen how to use the %EOF built-in function to return the end-of-file condition to a program. In addition to returning file-operation results, BIFs can simplify complex calculations, perform string operations, and perform data-type conversion.

%ABS (Absolute Value)

The %ABS (Absolute value) built-in function calculates the absolute value of a numeric expression (or a numeric field or literal). This BIF essentially removes the sign from an expression's result. You specify the expression within parentheses immediately following the %ABS notation in the extended Factor 2:

```
*.. 1 ...+... 2 ...+... 3 ...+... 4 ...+... 5 ...+... 6 ...+... 7 ...+... 8
 /FREE
     // In this example, TransTotal will be positive regardless of whether
     // the expression results in a positive or a negative number.
     TransTotal = %ABS(Debits - Credits);
 /END-FREE
```

%DIV (Divide)

The %DIV (Divide) built-in function performs integer division of two numbers (literals, fields, or expressions). The two numbers are passed as arguments, within parentheses and separated by a colon (:), immediately following the %DIV notation. The result of the division is always an integer (i.e., no decimal places). The division operator (/), on the other hand, performs precise division, including decimal places in the quotient if the result field is defined with decimal places.

```
*.. 1 ...+... 2 ...+... 3 ...+... 4 ...+... 5 ...+... 6 ...+... 7 ...+... 8
 /FREE
     // Convert total minutes to hours by dividing total minutes by 60.
     // Hours is be accurate to the number of decimal places defined for it.
     Hours = Minutes/60;

     // The %DIV BIF will return only the integer portion of Hours,
     // regardless of how many decimal places are defined for it.
     Hours = %DIV(Minutes:60);
 /END-FREE
```

%REM (Remainder)

The %REM (Remainder) built-in function returns the remainder (sometimes called the *modulus*) when dividing two numbers (literals, fields, or expressions). The two numbers are passed as two arguments immediately following the %REM notation. Although %REM is often used with the %DIV function, it is not necessary to actually perform the division operation in order to get the remainder.

```
*.. 1 ...+... 2 ...+... 3 ...+... 4 ...+... 5 ...+... 6 ...+... 7 ...+... 8
 /FREE
     // Convert total minutes to hours and minutes by dividing total minutes
     // by 60 to get hours and then returning the remainder as Minutes.
     Hours = %DIV(Minutes:60);
     Minutes = %REM(Minutes:60);
 /END-FREE
```

RPG IV supports many other built-in functions, and you'll learn about those functions throughout the text. Now, though, you know the key information about how to use built-in functions in your RPG IV program. BIFs always begin with a % sign. They are coded within free-form expressions. If you need to pass arguments to a BIF, pass them within parentheses immediately following the name of the BIF, and separate multiple arguments with colon separators:

%function(argument1:argument2:...)

Chapter Summary

RPG IV provides a limited number of arithmetic operators to use for computations. With the EVAL operation, you can express complex arithmetic calculations in a single, free-form expression that can continue over several lines, if necessary. Such expressions can include the arithmetic operators +, –, *, /, and **; parentheses; numeric fields; and numeric literals. You can use numeric fields and numeric literals in arithmetic calculations.

Calculations often involve creating new fields to store the results of the calculations. You must define these new fields by specifying their data type, length, and number of decimal positions (if numeric) within Definition Specifications. The size of result fields should be large enough to avoid high-order truncation and program abends. If the result of an arithmetic operation contains more decimal positions than you want to store, you should round the calculation.

You can also use EVAL to assign values to character fields. EVAL performs character data transfer from left to right and automatically right blank-pads the receiving field if it is longer than the sending field. If the receiving field is shorter than the sending field, EVAL truncates the rightmost extra characters. If you are coding your program using free-format specifications (beginning at Version 5), you may usually forego coding EVAL; simply code the assignment expression instead. To improve EVAL's precision in complex expressions and/or with large operands, you should always specify keyword EXPROPTS(*RESDECPOS) in the program's Control Specifications.

To change the data type of character or numeric data, use operation MOVE. MOVE transfers data from right to left, doesn't automatically blank-pad, and truncates extra leftmost characters. Good programmers match the sizes of fields and/or values in this kind of MOVE operation to avoid errors in data transfer.

You also can use MOVE and operation MOVEL to split off the rightmost and leftmost portions of a data value. MOVEL works like MOVE except that data transfer proceeds from left to right.

RPG IV supports many built-in functions to return file-operation results, simplify complex calculations, perform string operations, and perform data-type conversion. BIFs always begin with a % sign. They are coded within free-form expressions. To pass values to a built-in function, enclose the values within parentheses immediately following the name of the BIF; separate multiple values with colon (:) separators.

The following tables summarize the RPG IV operations and functions we've discussed in this chapter. These tables can help you recall the appropriate format for a Calculation Specification based on a particular operation.

Arithmetic and Assignment Operations

Data type	Operation	Factor 1	Extended Factor 2
Character/numeric	EVAL(HR)	—	RESULT-FIELD = EXPRESSION

continued...

continued...

Data type	Operation	Factor 1	Factor 2	Result
Character/numeric	MOVE(P)	—	FIELD/LITERAL	FIELD
Character/numeric	MOVEL(P)	—	FIELD/LITERAL	FIELD
Numeric	ADD(H)	field/literal	FIELD/LITERAL	FIELD
Numeric	SUB(H)	field/literal	FIELD/LITERAL	FIELD
Numeric	MULT(H)	field/literal	FIELD/LITERAL	FIELD
Numeric	DIV(H)	field/literal	FIELD/LITERAL	FIELD
Numeric	MVR	—	—	FIELD
Numeric	SQRT(H)	—	FIELD/LITERAL	FIELD

Notes: Uppercase entry = required; lowercase entry = optional.
Extended Factor 2 entries are free-form and may include built-in functions.
Operation extenders (optional):
    H = half-adjust (round) result
    P = pad result with blanks
    R = result decimal positions

Built-in Functions

Function	Return value
%ABS(*numeric-expression*)	Absolute value of *numeric-expression*
%DIV(*number1:number2*)	Integer portion of *number1* divided by *number2*
%REM(*number1:number2*)	Remainder of *number1* divided by *number2*

Introducing Specific Arithmetic Operators

The EVAL operation provides an efficient way for programmers to express complex calculations. Also, the free-form entry resembles the way we express calculations in algebra and the way other modern languages handle calculations. Moreover, using EVAL results in specifications that are easy to understand and maintain.

But RPG IV also supports a set of **specific** (or single-purpose) **arithmetic operations** that you may encounter in RPG programs. EVAL is usually preferred, but in some earlier releases of RPG IV, you may need to use one of the specific operations to perform a function that EVAL cannot perform in that release. In current releases of RPG IV, these specific arithmetic operators are considered obsolete.

Specific arithmetic operations, like many other RPG IV operations, require the standard form of the Calculation Specifications:

```
*.. 1 ...+... 2 ...+... 3 ...+... 4 ...+... 5 ...+... 6 ...+... 7 ...+... 8
CLØN01Factor1+++++++Opcode(E)+Factor2+++++++Result+++++++Len++D+HiLoEq....
```

The operations themselves are coded in positions 26–35 (Opcode(E)+). All require a Result field entry left-adjusted in positions 50–63, and most also include an entry left-adjusted in Factor 2 (positions 36–49) — or entries left-adjusted in both Factor 1 (positions 12–25) and Factor 2. The following paragraphs describe the exact format for each specific operation.

continued...

Introducing Specific Arithmetic Operators ... Continued

ADD and SUB (Subtract)

In its basic form, operation ADD adds the values of Factor 1 and Factor 2, storing the answer in the Result field. If Factor 1 and the Result field are the same field, you may omit Factor 1. The following code illustrates various forms and uses of ADD.

```
*.. 1 ...+... 2 ...+... 3 ...+... 4 ...+... 5 ...+... 6 ...+... 7 ...+... 8
CLØNØ1Factor1+++++++Opcode(E)+Factor2+++++++Result++++++++Len++D+HiLoEq....
 * Sample calculations using the ADD operation to add two numeric values.
 * The Result fields are defined within the specifications.
C     REGPAY        ADD       OVRPAY          TOTPAY
C     25            ADD       QTY             NEWQTY
C     RATE1         ADD(H)    .Ø45            RATE2
 * Calculations showing two equivalent ways of incrementing a counter.
C     COUNT         ADD       1               COUNT
C                   ADD       1               COUNT
 * Calculations showing two equivalent ways of accumulating net pay.
C     NETPAY        ADD       TOTNET          TOTNET
C                   ADD       NETPAY          TOTNET
```

The SUB (Subtract) operation subtracts Factor 2 from Factor 1, storing the answer in the Result field. Unlike with ADD, the order of the factors is significant. In algebra, the SUB operation would be expressed as

Result = Factor1 – Factor2

You can also decrement a counter or decrease the value of an accumulator by omitting Factor 1 on the SUB operation. This form of SUB says, in effect, "Subtract Factor 2 from the Result field, and store the answer in the Result field." The following code illustrates the SUB operation.

```
*.. 1 ...+... 2 ...+... 3 ...+... 4 ...+... 5 ...+... 6 ...+... 7 ...+... 8
CLØNØ1Factor1+++++++Opcode(E)+Factor2+++++++Result++++++++Len++D+HiLoEq....
C     GROSS         SUB       WTHHLD          NETPAY
C     65            SUB       AGE             WRKYRS
C                   SUB       1               COUNT
C                   SUB       AMT             RMDR
```

MULT (Multiply)

The MULT (Multiply) operation lets you multiply the contents of Factor 1 and Factor 2 and store the answer in the Result field. MULT also supports a second format, in which you omit Factor 1. With this format, the value of the Result field is multiplied by Factor 2, and the product is stored in the Result field. This form of MULT, used within a loop, was sometimes used to accomplish exponentiation because before RPG IV, there was no direct way to raise a number to a power. (EVAL supports the ** operator for this purpose.)

The following examples illustrate using MULT:

```
*.. 1 ...+... 2 ...+... 3 ...+... 4 ...+... 5 ...+... 6 ...+... 7 ...+... 8
CLØNØ1Factor1+++++++Opcode(E)+Factor2+++++++Result++++++++Len++D+HiLoEq....
C     SALES         MULT(H)   TAXRAT          SLSTAX
C     6Ø            MULT      HOURS           MINUTE
C     GROSS         MULT(H)   .Ø751           FICA
C                   MULT(H)   VALUE           EXPVAL
```

DIV (Divide) and MVR (Move Remainder)

The DIV (Divide) operation divides Factor 1 by Factor 2, storing the quotient in the Result field. DIV also supports the omission of Factor 1; in that case, the Result field is divided by Factor 2.

continued...

continued…

```
*.. 1 ...+... 2 ...+... 3 ...+... 4 ...+... 5 ...+... 6 ...+... 7 ...+... 8
CLØNØ1Factor1+++++++Opcode(E)+Factor2+++++++Result++++++++Len++D+HiLoEq....
C        TotMinutes     DIV(H)     60             Hours
C                       DIV(H)     2              Stocks
```

If you aren't sure what gets divided by what in the division format, mentally substitute a "divided by" sign (/) for the DIV operation to avoid reversing the factors. In algebra, this operation would be expressed as

Result = Factor1 / Factor2

Occasionally when dividing, you may want to capture the remainder of the division operation to use in a subsequent calculation or to print. Current releases of RPG IV support the %REM (Remainder) built-in function for this purpose. Previously, RPG IV provided the MVR (Move Remainder) operation, which you used in tandem with the specific division operation, DIV.

If a DIV operation is immediately followed by a MVR operation, the remainder from the division is stored in the Result field of the MVR specification. The following example demonstrates a use of this pair of operations:

```
*.. 1 ...+... 2 ...+... 3 ...+... 4 ...+... 5 ...+... 6 ...+... 7 ...+... 8
CLØNØ1Factor1+++++++Opcode(E)+Factor2+++++++Result++++++++Len++D+HiLoEq....
 * Convert total minutes to hours and minutes by dividing total minutes
 * by 60 to get hours and moving the remainder into a minutes field.
C        TotMinutes     DIV     60             Hours
C                       MVR                    Minutes
```

When you use the MVR operation, the definition you give the Result field should depend on the definitions of the values and Result field of the division operation whose remainder you want to capture. The system will carry out the division until the answer has the same number of decimal positions as the Result field; what's left at that point will be moved into the remainder field. To ensure you have your remainder field appropriately defined, hand-calculate some representative samples because there is no simple rule of thumb to guide you.

It is important to note that if you want to capture the remainder of a DIV operation with a subsequent MVR operation, you cannot round that division.

SQRT (Square Root)

Specific operation SQRT (Square Root) is used to calculate the square root of a numeric value. This operation does not use Factor 1. Factor 2 contains a numeric constant or numeric field whose square root you want to calculate, while the result must be a numeric field to store the answer. If the value of Factor 2 is 0, the result will be 0; if Factor 2 is a negative number, an error condition results because the square root of a negative value is an imaginary number.

```
*.. 1 ...+... 2 ...+... 3 ...+... 4 ...+... 5 ...+... 6 ...+... 7 ...+... 8
CLØNØ1Factor1+++++++Opcode(E)+Factor2+++++++Result++++++++Len++D+HiLoEq....
C                       SQRT     SqFeet         Feet
```

You may recall from algebra that you can express roots by using exponents. Raising a value to the one-half power is equivalent to finding the value's square root. You can use EVAL and the exponentiation (**) operator to perform this calculation:

```
*.. 1 ...+... 2 ...+... 3 ...+... 4 ...+... 5 ...+... 6 ...+... 7 ...+... 8
 /FREE
   EVAL(H) Feet = SqFeet ** .5;
 /END-FREE
```

If you use this technique to calculate roots, be sure to use the (H) operation extender to ensure accuracy. This is, perhaps, not as obvious a technique as using operation SQRT if someone else must read or maintain your code.

Key Terms

assignment operation

built-in functions (BIFs)

exponentiation

half-adjusting

high-order truncation

low-order truncation

operation extender

result decimal positions rule

specific arithmetic operations

truncation

Discussion/Review Questions

1. Why do you think RPG IV has relatively limited mathematical capabilities?

2. What is the difference between assigning a value to a field using the INZ keyword in Definition Specifications and assigning a value to a field in Calculation Specifications?

3. Why does it make sense that the result of a Calculation Specification or a free-form expression cannot be a literal?

4. What two mathematical impossibilities will result in a program error if your program tries to execute them?

5. Summarize the rules of thumb for determining how large to define result fields for arithmetic operations.

6. When should you round an arithmetic operation?

7. Discuss the differences among operations EVAL, MOVE, and MOVEL.

8. Name three uses for operation code extenders.

9. Why should you use EVAL rather than MOVE to assign values to numeric fields?

10. Would it be better to set EVAL precision rules to use the result decimal positions rule using a Control Specification keyword or an EVAL operation code extender? Why?

Exercises

1. Write the calculations to discount field OldPrice (six digits, two decimal positions) by 10 percent to yield NewPrice.

2. Write the calculations to convert a temperature in Fahrenheit to Centigrade, using the following formula:

$$C = 5(F - 32) / 9$$

Assume F and C are three positions each with zero decimal positions.

3. Write the calculations to convert a measurement taken in inches (field Inches, five positions with zero decimal positions) into the same measurement expressed as yards, feet, and inches.

4. Code the calculations needed to determine the cost of wall-to-wall carpeting for a room. Field RmLength (three positions, one decimal) contains the room's length in feet; field RmWidth (also three positions, one decimal) contains the room's width in feet; and field CostPerYard (four positions, two decimals) contains the cost per yard of the selected carpet.

5. Write the calculations to determine the Economic Order Quantity (EOQ), using the formula

$$EOQ = \text{square root of } (2DO/C)$$

where D (five positions, zero decimals) represents annual demand for product; O (five positions, two decimals) represents costs to place one order; and C (six positions, two decimals) represents carrying costs.

Programming Assignments

1. Wexler University wants a program that will produce a student grade report. Input file WUEXAMP (described in Appendix F) contains information about students in a class and five exam grades for each student.

   The program should calculate an average exam grade for each student. The school also wants to know the average exam grade for the class as a whole (i.e., the average of the averages). The desired report layout is shown below. Notice that just the initial of each student's first name is to be printed with the last name.

```
          1         2         3         4         5         6         7         8         9         1 0
 1234567890123456789012345678901234567890123456789012345678901234567890123456789012345678901234567890
 1    XX/XX/XX          WEXLER U. STUDENT GRADE REPORT          PAGE XXØX
 2
 3                                 EXAM  EXAM  EXAM  EXAM  EXAM   AVG.
 4 STUDENT NO.         NAME         1     2     3     4     5    GRADE
 5
 6 XXX-XX-XXXX    X. XXXXXXXXXXXXXXXX  XØX   XØX   XØX   XØX   XØX   XØX
 7 XXX-XX-XXXX    X. XXXXXXXXXXXXXXXX  XØX   XØX   XØX   XØX   XØX   XØX
 8 XXX-XX-XXXX    X. XXXXXXXXXXXXXXXX  XØX   XØX   XØX   XØX   XØX   XØX
 9
10                                              CLASS AVERAGE  XØX
```

2. CompuSell, the mail-order company, extends financing to some of its preferred customers. All financing is done for 12 months at a fixed rate of 14 percent. The company charges interest on the total amount financed, rather than on the unpaid balance remaining after each successive payment. Accordingly, the monthly payment is determined by calculating the interest due on the unpaid balance, adding the interest to the unpaid balance, and dividing that sum by 12.

   Write a program for CompuSell that will calculate monthly charges for each customer in the input file CSCFINP, described in Appendix F. The format of the desired report is shown below. Note that purchase date is to be printed using the format *dd-mm* and that the report requires a count of customers in the file.

```
          1         2         3         4         5         6         7         8         9         1 0
 1234567890123456789012345678901234567890123456789012345678901234567890123456789012345678901234567890
 1    XX/XX/XX                COMPUSELL FINANCE REPORT            PAGE XXØX
 2
 3    CUST.      PURCHASE    PURCHASE      DOWN        BALANCE      MONTHLY
 4    NUM.       AMOUNT      DATE         PAYMENT       OWED        PAYMENT
 5
 6    XXXXXX     X,XXØ.XX    ØX-XX      X,XXØ.XX     X,XXØ.XX     X,XXØ.XX
 7    XXXXXX     X,XXØ.XX    ØX-XX      X,XXØ.XX     X,XXØ.XX     X,XXØ.XX
 8
 9                          TOTALS     $XXX,XX$.XX  $XXX,XX$.XX  $XXX,XX$.XX
10
11    NUMBER OF CUSTOMERS PROCESSED XXØ
```

3. Wexler University wants a program to generate a payroll register for its hourly employees. Appendix F describes the input file for this program, WUHRLYP. The file contains information about regular and overtime hours worked and pay rate for hourly employees.

The school pays time and a half for overtime hours. Gross pay is the sum of regular and overtime pay. Net pay is gross pay less deductions for taxes and FICA. Eighteen percent federal tax is withheld, 5 percent state tax, and 7.51 percent for FICA.

The format of the desired payroll register is shown below. Note that just the initial of the first name is to be printed as part of each employee's name.

```
         1         2         3         4         5         6         7         8         9        10
1234567890123456789012345678901234567890123456789012345678901234567890123456789012345678901234567890
1     PAGE XX0X                                                                      XX/XX/XX
2
3                                   WEXLER U. PAYROLL REGISTER
4
5                                   GROSS        FEDERAL        STATE
6   SOC. SEC.        NAME            PAY          TAX            TAX          FICA          NET
7                                                                                          PAY
8   XXX-XX-XXXX  X. XXXXXXXXXXXXXX   X,XX0.XX     X,XX0.XX       XX0.XX       XX0.XX     X,XX0.XX
9   XXX-XX-XXXX  X. XXXXXXXXXXXXXX   X,XX0.XX     X,XX0.XX       XX0.XX       XX0.XX     X,XX0.XX
10
11              GRAND TOTALS        $XXX,XX$.XX   $XXX,XX$.XX   $XX,XX$.XX  $XX,XX$.XX  $XXX,XX$.XX
12
13
14
15
```

4. Ida Lapeer, Interior Decorator, wants a program that will estimate material costs for interior painting jobs based on data in file BIDS, described in Appendix F. Coverage per gallon represents the number of square feet of surface area that can be painted by one gallon. All room measurements were taken in terms of feet and inches (e.g., 14'10"). The percent figure given for windows and doors represents Ida's estimate of wall surface that will *not* need paint because of doors and windows. In calculating costs, include the cost of painting the ceiling as well as all four walls of the room.

Calculate final needed coverage to the nearest square foot and gallons needed to the nearest 1/100th of a gallon. Paint cost should be based on that figure. Ida has found that 5 percent of her paint costs represents a good estimate of other miscellaneous job costs, such as masking tape, brushes and rollers, and so on.

Your program should produce the report depicted in the following printer spacing chart.

```
         1         2         3         4         5         6         7         8         9        10
1234567890123456789012345678901234567890123456789012345678901234567890123456789012345678901234567890
1       XX/XX/XX              IDA LAPEER MATERIAL COST ESTIMATES
2
3   JOB      PAINT      COST      COVERAGE    SQ. FEET   GALLONS    ------ ESTIMATED COSTS ------
4   NO.      CODE       PER GAL.  PER GAL.    TO COVER   NEEDED     PAINT      MISC.      TOTAL
5
6   XXXX     XX-XXX     X0.XX     X0X         X,X0X      X0.XX     X,XX0.XX   XX0.XX    XX,XX0.XX
7   XXXX     XX-XXX     X0.XX     X0X         X,X0X      X0.XX     X,XX0.XX   XX0.XX    XX,XX0.XX
```

Chapter 5

Top-Down, Structured Program Design

 ## Chapter Overview

This chapter focuses on program design and introduces you to RPG IV operations that let you write well-designed programs using a top-down, structured approach. Loops, decision logic, and subroutines receive special attention. The chapter applies these design principles by teaching you how to code control-break problems.

Structured Design

You typically can solve programming problems in many different ways, each of which might produce correct output. Correct output, although an important goal, should not be the programmer's only goal. Producing code that is readable and easily changed is also important to programmers who are concerned with quality.

Changes in user requirements and processing errors discovered as programs are used dictate that programmers spend a lot of their time maintaining existing programs rather than developing new code. A well-designed, well-documented program facilitates such maintenance; a poorly designed program can be a maintenance nightmare.

Structured design is one development methodology that has become widely accepted over the past 20 years to facilitate quality program design. One important aspect of structured design is limiting control structures within your program to three basic logic structures:

- sequence
- selection (also called decision)
- iteration (also called repetition or looping)

Sequence lets you instruct the computer to execute operations serially. **Selection** lets you establish alternate paths of instructions within a program; which alternate path the program executes depends on the results of a test or condition within the program. And **iteration** permits instructions within the program to be repeated until a condition is met or is no longer met. Figure 5.1 illustrates these control structures in flowchart symbols so that you can understand easily how flow of control works with each structure.

Each of these control structures has a single entry point and a single exit point. Together, the structures can serve as basic building blocks to express the complex logic required to solve complicated programming problems while maintaining the tight control over program flow that facilitates program maintenance. Structured programming is sometimes called "GOTO-less programming" because this methodology discourages the indiscriminate use of GOTOs, the single operation most responsible for "spaghetti code."

Figure 5.1
Flowcharts Illustrating "Basic" Control Structures

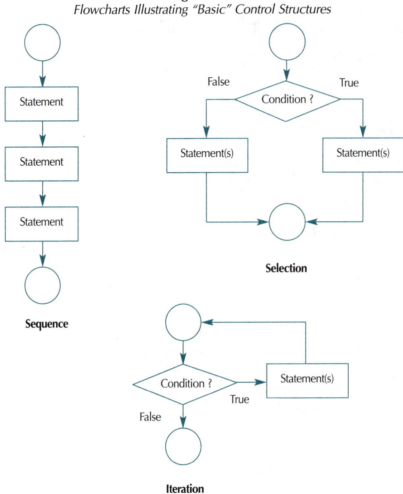

Sequential Flow of Control

Sequential control flow is inherent in RPG IV (and other programming languages) by default. The order in which you describe operations on the Calculation Specifications determines the order in which the computer executes them. The computer continues to execute the program statements in their order of occurrence unless it encounters an operation that explicitly transfers control to a different location within the program. To diverge from a sequential flow of control requires the use of explicit operations.

Relational Comparisons

RPG IV includes a variety of operations to let you express both decision and iteration logic. Both kinds of operations involve testing a condition to determine the appropriate course of action. This testing involves a **relational comparison** between two values.

To express the comparison, RPG IV supports six **relational symbols** that are used with many of the operations. The following table summarizes the symbols and their meanings.

Symbol	Meaning
>	Greater than
<	Less than
=	Equal to
<>	Not equal to
<=	Less than or equal to
>=	Greater than or equal to

The way the computer evaluates whether a comparison is true depends on the data type of the items being compared. If you are comparing two numeric items (whether fields or literals), the system compares them based on algebraic values. The length and number of decimal positions in the items being compared do not affect the outcome of the comparison. For example, 2.25 is equal to 00002.250000, while 00000002.12345 is smaller than 9. A positive value is always larger than a negative value. Only the algebraic values of the data items themselves determine the result of a relational comparison between numeric fields.

You can also perform relational tests between character values. This kind of comparison takes place somewhat differently from numeric comparisons. When you compare two character literals or fields, the system performs a character-by-character comparison, moving from left to right, until it finds an unmatched pair or finishes checking. When it encounters a character difference, the difference is interpreted in terms of the collating sequence of **EBCDIC**, the data-representation format used by IBM. (EBCDIC stands for "Extended Binary-Coded Decimal Interchange Code.") In EBCDIC, A is less than B, B less than C, and so on; lowercase letters are "smaller" than uppercase letters; letters are smaller than digits; and a blank is smaller than any other displayable character.

If you are comparing two character items of unequal sizes, the system blank-pads the smaller item to the right before making the character-by-character comparison. To understand character comparisons, consider the examples below. (In the examples, ƀ represents a blank within the data item.)

ART is less than BART
ARTHUR equals ARTHURƀƀƀƀ
ARTƀƀƀƀ is less than ARTHUR
AI is less than AL
123 is greater than ABC

RPG IV does not let you compare a numeric data item with a character data item. However, you can use indicators in relational comparisons, provided you preface the indicator with *IN. You can compare one indicator with another (in which case you're trying to determine whether their values are the same), or you can compare an indicator with the character literals '1' and '0' or the figurative constants *ON and *OFF, all of which represent the possible values an indicator may assume.

Selection Operations

Now that you understand how RPG IV makes relational comparisons, you can learn how to use the relational operators with those RPG IV operations that determine flow of program control. First we'll look at the options for sending control to alternate statements within a program: **decision** (or selection) **operations**.

IF (If)

RPG's primary decision operator is IF. The general format of the IF operation is

```
*.. 1 ...+... 2 ...+... 3 ...+... 4 ...+... 5 ...+... 6 ...+... 7 ...+... 8
 /FREE
    IF Conditional_expression;
       . . .
    ENDIF;
 /END-FREE
```

If the result of the conditional expression is true, all the calculations between the IF statement and its ENDIF are executed. If the relationship is not true, those statements are bypassed. (For fixed-format Calculation Specifications, IF uses the extended Factor 2; Factor 1 is always blank, and the extended Factor 2 contains the conditional expression to be tested.)

For example, if you wanted to count all senior citizens, you could write the following lines; the IF can be read, "If Age is greater than or equal to 65, then increment SeniorCnt by 1."

```
*.. 1 ...+... 2 ...+... 3 ...+... 4 ...+... 5 ...+... 6 ...+... 7 ...+... 8
 /FREE
    IF Age >= 65;
       SeniorCnt = SeniorCnt + 1;
    ENDIF;
 /END-FREE
```

You can also use the IF operation with an ELSE operator to set up an alternate path of instructions to be executed should the IF fail. For example, if you were asked to calculate pay and wanted to pay time and a half for any hours over 40, you could code the following:

```
*.. 1 ...+... 2 ...+... 3 ...+... 4 ...+... 5 ...+... 6 ...+... 7 ...+... 8
 /FREE
    IF Hours <= 40;
      EVAL(H) TotalPay = Hours * PayRate;
    ELSE;
      EVAL(H) TotalPay = 40 * PayRate + (Hours - 40) * PayRate * 1.5;
    ENDIF;
 /END-FREE
```

Sometimes, you want to execute a series of instructions based on multiple tests or conditions. RPG IV includes the binary operators AND and OR to allow such multiple conditions. When you use an AND to set up a compound condition, both relationships must be true for the IF to be evaluated as true. When you use an OR to connect two relational tests, the IF is evaluated to true if one or the other (or both) of the conditions is true:

```
*.. 1 ...+... 2 ...+... 3 ...+... 4 ...+... 5 ...+... 6 ...+... 7 ...+... 8
 /FREE
    IF Age >= 65 AND Status = 'R';
       // This block of code is executed only if Age >= 65 and Status = R.
       . . .
    ELSE;
       // If one or both conditions are not met, this code is executed.
       . . .
    ENDIF;
    IF Age >=65 OR Status = 'R';
       // This block is executed if one or both conditions are true.
       . . .
    ELSE;
       // This block is executed only if both conditions are false.
       . . .
    ENDIF;
 /END-FREE
```

You can combine ANDs and ORs to create more complex conditional tests. If a conditional expression requires more room than a single fixed-format specification offers, you can extend the expression to additional lines by using the extended Factor 2 continuation form of the Calculation Specifications. Note that ANDs are evaluated before ORs. However, you can use parentheses to change the order of evaluation; parentheses are always evaluated first.

To illustrate how ANDs and ORs are evaluated and to demonstrate the use of parentheses, consider the following scenario. A company wants to print a list of employees eligible for early retirement. Only salaried employees are eligible (code = 'S'); moreover, they must have worked more than 15 years for the company or be 55 (or more) years old. The following code shows an incorrect way and a correct way to express these conditions.

```
*.. 1 ...+... 2 ...+... 3 ...+... 4 ...+... 5 ...+... 6 ...+... 7 ...+... 8
/FREE
    // The IF below would select any employee who was salaried and had
    // worked more than 15 years; it also would incorrectly include any
    // employee at least 55 years old, whether or not (s)he was salaried.

    IF SalaryCode = 'S' AND YrsWorked > 15 OR Age >= 55;
      . . .
    ENDIF;

    // The parentheses in the IF below cause the correct selection of
    // employees who are salaried and who either have worked more than 15
    // years or are at least 55 years old.

    IF SalaryCode = 'S' AND (YrsWorked > 15 OR Age >= 55);
      . . .
    ENDIF;
/END-FREE
```

You can combine ANDs and ORs with other operations to form extremely complicated conditional tests. In these cases, order of precedence causes ANDs and ORs to be evaluated last, after any other operations, unless you use parentheses to change the order of precedence. The following code illustrates some complex IFs.

```
*.. 1 ...+... 2 ...+... 3 ...+... 4 ...+... 5 ...+... 6 ...+... 7 ...+... 8
/FREE
    // In the sample IF below, the order in which the operations would be
    // performed is as follows: first, multiplication (W*X); next, addition
    // (A + B); next, AND; and last, the two ORs, moving from left to right

    IF A + B > 85 AND X = 10 OR W*X <> G OR *IN90 = *ON;
      . . .
    ENDIF;

    // The sample IF below includes parentheses that change the order of
    // evaluation. Now, the multiplication (W*X) is done first; next, the
    // second OR is evaluated; next, the first OR; next, the addition;
    // and last, the AND

    IF A + B > 85 AND (X = 10 OR (W*X <> G OR *IN90 = *ON));
      . . .
    ENDIF;
/END-FREE
```

Caution
Although such IF logic is permitted in RPG IV, building conditions of such complexity leads to programs that are difficult to understand. You should avoid the practice if at all possible.

Nesting IFs

You can also nest IFs. That is, you can build IFs within IFs, with or without ELSEs. Each IF requires an ENDIF in the appropriate spot to indicate the end point of that IF's influence. The following example illustrates nested IF.

```
*.. 1 ...+... 2 ...+... 3 ...+... 4 ...+... 5 ...+... 6 ...+... 7 ...+... 8
/FREE
   // This code uses IF and EVAL to assign values to LifeExpect based on
   // age and sex.
   IF Age >= 65;
     IF Sex = 'F';
        LifeExpect = 84;
     ELSE;
        LifeExpect = 79;
     ENDIF;
   ELSE;
     IF Sex = 'F';
        LifeExpect = 81;
     ELSE;
        LifeExpect = 78;
     ENDIF;
   ENDIF;
/END-FREE
```

Sometimes, a program's logic requires that nesting take place only on the ELSE branches of the decision structure. The following example of assigning commission rates typifies this kind of construct, sometimes called **CASE logic**.

```
*.. 1 ...+... 2 ...+... 3 ...+... 4 ...+... 5 ...+... 6 ...+... 7 ...+... 8
/FREE
   // IF used to assign commission rates based on sales level
   IF Sales <= 5000;
     Rate = .005;
   ELSE;
     IF Sales <= 10000;
        Rate = .0075;
     ELSE;
        IF Sales <= 20000;
          Rate = .01;
        ELSE;
          Rate = .015;
        ENDIF;
     ENDIF;
   ENDIF;
/END-FREE
```

In this example, each IF statement requires its own corresponding ENDIF statement, resulting in a series of ENDIF statements to close individual nesting levels. As an alternative, the ELSEIF operation (available beginning with Version 5) combines ELSE and IF operations and requires only a single ENDIF at the end of the code block. The following example uses ELSEIF to simplify the nesting levels:

```
*.. 1 ...+... 2 ...+... 3 ...+... 4 ...+... 5 ...+... 6 ...+... 7 ...+... 8
/FREE
   // IF used to assign commission rates based on sales level
   IF Sales <= 5000;
     Rate = .005;
   ELSEIF Sales <= 10000;
     Rate = .0075;
   ELSEIF Sales <= 20000;
     Rate = .01;
   ELSE;
     Rate = .015;
   ENDIF;
/END-FREE
```

Notice in the examples presented so far in this chapter that the free-form syntax lets you indent code to make the logical groupings of conditions and the resulting actions more apparent.

IF and Page Overflow

Before we look at other RPG IV decision operations, one topic remains to be discussed in conjunction with decision logic: page overflow. In the reports we have written up to now, we have included page headings only on the first page. Because most business reports span multiple pages, we need a way to determine when it's time to advance to a new page and reprint heading lines.

RPG IV has built-in indicators called **overflow indicators**. The special indicators that may be used to signal overflow are OA, OB, OC, OD, OE, OF, OG, and OV. If you associate one of these indicators with the report file on the File Specifications, the indicator will automatically come on when the printer reaches the overflow line at the bottom of the page. To make that association, enter keyword OFLIND in the Keywords portion of the File Specification (positions 44–80), specifying the indicator you choose to use in parentheses after the keyword:

```
*.. 1 ...+... 2 ...+... 3 ...+... 4 ...+... 5 ...+... 6 ...+... 7 ...+... 8
FFilename++IPEASFRLen+LKLen+AIDevice+.Keywords++++++++++++++++++++++++++++++++
FQPRINT    O   F  132         PRINTER OFLIND(*INOF)
```

By referencing the status of the indicator in an IF statement just before printing a detail line, you can advance the page and print headings each time they are needed, as signaled by the overflow indicator; you will also need to turn off the indicator because it does not go off automatically:

```
*.. 1 ...+... 2 ...+... 3 ...+... 4 ...+... 5 ...+... 6 ...+... 7 ...+... 8
 /FREE
    // Demonstration of how to handle headings within a process loop
    IF *INOF;
      EXCEPT Headings;
      *INOF = *OFF;
    ENDIF;
    EXCEPT Detail;
 /END-FREE
```

Take special note of the IF statement in this example. Because *INOF is an indicator, which can have only the logical values *ON and *OFF, you can refer to it in a shortened logical expression. Coding IF *INOF is equivalent to coding IF *INOF = *ON. In either case, the tested condition will be true (*ON) if *INOF is *ON. Similarly, coding IF NOT *INOF would be equivalent to coding IF *INOF = *OFF.

SELECT (Conditionally Select Operations)

Although you can express even the most complex programming decisions with a series of IF, ELSE, and ELSEIF operations, nested IFs can be difficult to set up and hard for others to interpret. To overcome this problem, RPG IV use the SELECT (Conditionally Select Operations) operation to let you simplify the coding of CASE logic. The SELECT operation appears on a line alone to identify the start of a CASE construct. The SELECT is followed by one or more WHEN lines, each of which specifies a condition to be tested. Each WHEN is followed by one or more calculations to be performed when that condition is met. When the program is executed, it checks the WHEN conditions sequentially, starting with the first. As soon as it encounters a true condition, the computer executes the operation (or operations) following that WHEN statement and then sends control to the end of the SELECT construct, which is signaled by an ENDSL operation.

The following code uses SELECT to express the same logic for determining sales commission rates shown previously with nested IFs.

```
*.. 1 ...+... 2 ...+... 3 ...+... 4 ...+... 5 ...+... 6 ...+... 7 ...+... 8
 /FREE
     // Using SELECT/WHEN to assign a value to Rate based on level of sales
     SELECT;
       WHEN Sales <= 5000;
         Rate = .005;
       WHEN Sales <= 10000;
         Rate = .0075;
       WHEN Sales <= 20000;
         Rate = .01;
       OTHER;
         Rate = .015;
     ENDSL;
 /END-FREE
```

Notice in this example that the reserved word OTHER means "in all other cases." OTHER, if used, should be the final "catch-all" condition listed. When a SELECT includes an OTHER, the computer will always perform one of the sets of calculations. When a SELECT is composed only of WHEN conditions, none of the operations within the SELECT will be performed if none of the conditions are met.

Although not illustrated in the example above, just as in IF operations, multiple operations can follow each WHEN line — as many operations as are needed to accomplish the desired processing on that branch of the CASE structure. You also can couple the WHEN conditions with AND and OR to create compound selection criteria, which can continue on multiple specification lines if needed.

Operations for Iteration

The third logical construct of structured programming is iteration. Iteration lets your program repeat a series of instructions — a common necessity in programming. In batch processing, for example, you want to execute a series of instructions repeatedly, once for every record in a transaction file. You have already used one RPG IV operation that enables iteration, or looping: DOW.

DOW (Do While)

The DOW operation establishes a loop based on a conditional test expression (coded in the extended Factor 2 of the fixed-format Calculation Specifications). All the operations coded between this operator and its end statement (ENDDO) are repeated as long as the condition specified in the relational test remains true.

You have already used DOW to repeat processing until an end-of-file condition is turned on. You can use DOW for other kinds of repetition as well. Assume you want to add all the numbers between 1 and 100. With a counter field, Number, and an accumulator, Sum, you can use DOW to easily accomplish this summation, as shown in the following code.

```
*.. 1 ...+... 2 ...+... 3 ...+... 4 ...+... 5 ...+... 6 ...+... 7 ...+... 8
 /FREE
     // This routine adds all the numbers from 1 to 100.
     Number = 0;                        // Initialize Number to zero.
     Sum = 0;                           // Initialize Sum to zero.

     DOW Number < 100;                  // Loop while Number is less than 100.
       Number = Number + 1;             // Increment Number by 1.
       Sum = Sum + Number;              // Add Number to accumulator Sum.
     ENDDO;
 /END-FREE
```

The CAS*xx* (Conditionally Invoke Subroutine) Operation

In addition to IF and SELECT, existing RPG IV programs may include yet another selection operation, the CAS*xx* (Conditionally Invoke Subroutine) operation. The CAS*xx* structure is nearly identical to SELECT, with two important differences. First, instead of coding alternate sets of operations inline following each condition, you use the CAS*xx* operation to send control to subroutines elsewhere in the program. You name the subroutine to invoke in the Result field on the line that specifies the condition to be met to execute the subroutine. Control then returns to the Calculation Specification immediately following the ENDCS (End CAS*xx*) statement.

The second difference between SELECT and CAS*xx* concerns the layout of the CAS*xx* operation. Rather than using free-form conditional expressions, CAS*xx* uses a format reminiscent of older versions of RPG to express the conditional test. Instead of the relational symbols (<, >, and so on) that you've used so far in this chapter, CAS*xx* uses two-letter **relational codes** to indicate relationships:

Symbol	Meaning
GT	Greater than
LT	Less than
EQ	Equal to
NE	Not equal to
GE	Greater than or equal to
LE	Less than or equal to

Instead of using free-form expressions, CAS*xx* compares the values of Factor 1 and Factor 2, substituting one of these conditions for the *xx* in CAS*xx* (e.g., CASGT, CASLT). Consider the following example, which uses CAS*xx* to send program control to different subroutines based on the level of sales:

```
*.. 1 ...+... 2 ...+... 3 ...+... 4 ...+... 5 ...+... 6 ...+... 7 ...+... 8
CLØNØ1Factor1+++++++Opcode(E)+Factor2+++++++Result++++++++Len++D+HiLoEq....
 * Using CASxx to send control to different subroutines based on the level
 * of sales; commission rates might be assigned within the subroutines.
C        Sales        CASLE     5000           LowCommSR
C        Sales        CASLE     10000          MedCommSR
C        Sales        CASLE     20000          HighCommSR
C                     CAS                       VHighComSR
C                     ENDCS
```

The system compares the value in Factor 1 with that in Factor 2; if the relationship between the two values matches the relationship specified by the two-letter relational code appended to CAS (in the example, less than or equal to), the subroutine named in the result area is executed. As with SELECT, the first condition that is evaluated to true causes the operations associated with that condition (in this case, executing a subroutine) to be performed, and control then jumps to the end of the logic structure to bypass the remaining comparisons. ENDCS signals the end of the CAS*xx* operation.

CAS*xx* also lets you specify a subroutine to be performed if none of the tested conditions prove to be true. To include this option, simply use CAS without a relational code as the final operation within the structure.

The SELECT group is more flexible and readable than the CAS*xx* operation, and most RPG IV programmers prefer SELECT to CAS*xx*.

Like RPG IV's decision operations, the DOW operation lets you use AND and OR to form compound conditions to control the looping:

```
*.. 1 ...+... 2 ...+... 3 ...+... 4 ...+... 5 ...+... 6 ...+... 7 ...+... 8
 /FREE
      // Any processing specified within the loop would be repeated as long
      // as both indicators 90 and 99 remain off.

      DOW NOT *IN90 AND NOT *IN99;
         . . .
      ENDDO;
 /END-FREE
```

DOU (Do Until)

DOU (Do Until) is a structured iteration operation very similar to DOW. Like DOW, DOU includes a conditional test expression in the extended Factor 2. However, two major differences exist between a DOW and a DOU. First, a DOW operation repeats *while* the specified condition *remains* true, whereas a DOU operation repeats *until* the condition *becomes* true. Second, a DOW is a **leading decision loop**, which means the comparison is made before the instructions within the loop are executed for the first time. If the comparison is evaluated to false, the computer completely bypasses the instructions within the loop. A DOU, in contrast, is a **trailing decision loop**; because the comparison is made after the instructions within the loop have been executed, the instructions will always be executed at least once. In contrast, instructions within a loop controlled by a DOW may not be executed at all.

Figure 5.2 presents flowcharts of Do While and Do Until operations to illustrate their differences.

Figure 5.2
Do While vs. Do Until Loop

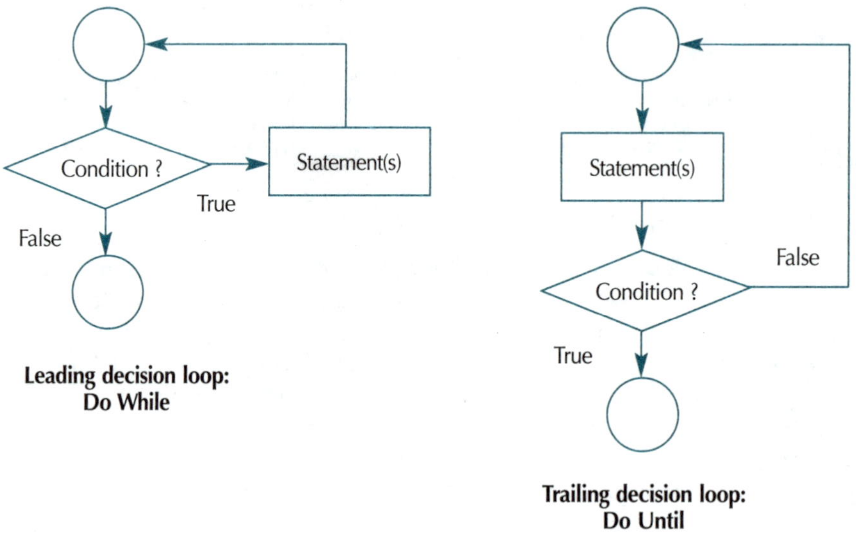

Leading decision loop:
Do While

Trailing decision loop:
Do Until

Do Whiles and Do Untils are often equally suited to setting up a looping structure. For instance, you could use a Do Until to solve the add-the-numbers problem; all you'd need to change is the operation and the relational test. The following code illustrates how to solve this problem using DOU.

```
*.. 1 ...+... 2 ...+... 3 ...+... 4 ...+... 5 ...+... 6 ...+... 7 ...+... 8
 /FREE
    // This routine uses DOU to add all the numbers from 1 to 100.
    Number = 0;                        // Initialize Number to zero.
    Sum = 0;                           // Initialize Sum to zero.

    DOU Number = 100;                  // Loop until Number equals 100.
      Number = Number + 1;             // Increment Number by 1.
      Sum = Sum + Number;              // Add Number to accumulator Sum.
    ENDDO;
 /END-FREE
```

FOR (For)

Often, as in the preceding example, you want a loop to be executed a specific number of times. To implement this kind of logic with Do Untils or Do Whiles, you need to define a field to serve as a counter. Each time through the loop, you increment the counter as part of your loop instructions and check the counter's value after each repetition to determine whether another iteration is needed.

RPG IV offers an operation designed specifically for count-controlled loops: FOR. As with DOW and DOU, an end operator, ENDFOR, signals the end of a FOR structure. Unlike those operations, the FOR operation automatically increments its counter to ensure that the repetition occurs the desired number of times.

The format of the FOR is a little more complicated than that of DOW or DOU because FOR provides more options and defaults. The general layout of a FOR loop is shown below.

```
*.. 1 ...+... 2 ...+... 3 ...+... 4 ...+... 5 ...+... 6 ...+... 7 ...+... 8
 /FREE
    FOR Counter = Start_value TO Limit_value BY Increment_value;
       . . .
    ENDFOR;
 /END-FREE
```

In general, a count-controlled operator in any language lets you specify four things:

- a field to serve as the counter
- the starting value of the counter
- the limiting value of the counter for looping to continue
- the amount to be added to the counter at the end of each repetition of the loop

Although RPG IV gives you the option to specify these four values, you also can omit any of them except the counter field.

The counter field must be defined as a numeric field with zero decimal positions. You can omit the initial value for the counter; if you do, the counter will begin with the same value it had before the program entered the FOR loop.

In the TO clause, specify a whole numeric field or literal as a limit value. If your limit value is a field rather than a literal, the value of the field determines the number of repetitions. You can also omit the TO clause with the limit value; if you do, the loop will continue indefinitely until the program processes a LEAVE operation.

In the BY clause, specify a whole numeric field or literal as the increment value. If your increment value is a field rather than a literal, the value of the field determines the increment value. You can also omit the BY clause with the increment value. If you do, RPG IV will assume an increment value of 1; that is, it will add 1 to the value of the counter at the start of each additional pass through the loop.

The following examples illustrate the FOR loop:

```
*.. 1 ...+... 2 ...+... 3 ...+... 4 ...+... 5 ...+... 6 ...+... 7 ...+... 8
/FREE
   FOR Idx = 1 TO 50;      // Processing in this loop would be done 50 times
      . . .
   ENDFOR;

   // The number of repetitions of this loop depends on the value of Iter
   FOR Idx = 1 TO Iter;
      . . .
   ENDFOR;

   // This loop will repeat until the program encounters a LEAVE operation
   FOR Idx = 1;
      . . .
      IF *INLR;
        LEAVE;
      ENDIF;
   ENDFOR;
/END-FREE
```

The following code shows the add-the-numbers problem implemented using FOR. Field Number is the counter field that the system automatically increments by 1 on each pass through the loop.

```
*.. 1 ...+... 2 ...+... 3 ...+... 4 ...+... 5 ...+... 6 ...+... 7 ...+... 8
/FREE
   // This routine will add all the numbers from 1 to 100 using a FOR.
   // Counter Number is automatically incremented on each pass through the
   // loop.

   Sum = 0;                              // Initialize accumulator to zero.

   FOR Number = 1 TO 100;
     Sum = Sum + Number;
   ENDFOR;
/END-FREE
```

FOR affords us great flexibility in changing the starting value and increment value. For example, we can easily change our sample solution to add all the even numbers from 1 to 100 if we set Number's starting value to 2 and the increment value to 2, as follows:

```
*.. 1 ...+... 2 ...+... 3 ...+... 4 ...+... 5 ...+... 6 ...+... 7 ...+... 8
/FREE
   // This routine will add all the even numbers from 2 to 100 using FOR.

   Sum = 0;                              // Initialize accumulator to zero.

   // Start Number at 2 and loop until it exceeds 100.
   FOR Number = 2 TO 100 BY 2;
     Sum = Sum + Number;
   ENDFOR;
/END-FREE
```

In the unlikely event that you need to decrement a counter instead of incrementing it, the FOR operation offers a variation that works in reverse, using a DOWNTO clause instead of TO:

```
*.. 1 ...+... 2 ...+... 3 ...+... 4 ...+... 5 ...+... 6 ...+... 7 ...+... 8
/FREE
    // This routine will add all the even numbers from 100 to 2 using FOR.

    Sum = 0;                              // Initialize accumulator to zero.

    // Start Number at 100; loop (decrementing by 2) until it goes below 2.
    FOR Number = 100 DOWNTO 2 BY 2;
      Sum = Sum + Number;
    ENDFOR;
/END-FREE
```

Loops and Early Exits

You sometimes may want to skip the remaining instructions within a loop to begin the next iteration or cycle. In other cases, you may want to exit the loop completely before the repetition is terminated by the relational comparison. Two RPG IV operations, ITER (Iterate) and LEAVE, give you these capabilities.

When the computer encounters an ITER within a loop, control skips past the remaining instructions in the loop and causes the next repetition to begin. LEAVE terminates the looping process completely and sends control to the statement immediately following the loop's END statement. You can use both of these statements with all the iterative operations (DOW, DOU, FOR, and DO).

Assume, for example, you are processing a file of customer records and printing a report line for those customers whose balance due exceeds zero. If amount due equals zero, you simply want to cycle around and read the next record from the file. The following code illustrates a solution that uses LEAVE and ITER.

```
*.. 1 ...+... 2 ...+... 3 ...+... 4 ...+... 5 ...+... 6 ...+... 7 ...+... 8
/FREE
    // This routine processes all records in CustFile and prints a detail
    // line for those customers whose AmountDue is not equal to 0.

    DOW NOT %EOF;
      READ CustFile;
      SELECT;
        WHEN %EOF;
          LEAVE;
        WHEN AmountDue = 0;
          ITER;
        OTHER;
          EXCEPT Detail;
      ENDSL;
    ENDDO;
/END-FREE
```

Top-Down Design

Up to now, this chapter has concentrated on structured design. A second design concept, top-down methodology, usually goes hand in hand with a structured approach. Top-down design means developing your program solution starting with a broad "outline" and then successively breaking the big pieces into smaller and smaller units. This technique is sometimes called hierarchical decomposition.

Hierarchical decomposition is the method your English teacher recommended for writing research papers: Work out an outline, starting with your main topics; then subdivide these into subtopics, and so on, until you have decomposed to a level of sufficient detail to allow you to write the paper (or in programming terms, the individual instructions of your program).

Top-down design lets you handle problems of great complexity by permitting you to initially ignore the detailed requirements of processing. Top-down design works in tandem with modular program development, which advocates that your program be structured into logical units, or modules. In top-down design, the first, or upper-level, design modules that you develop chiefly concern controlling flow to and from the lower-level modules you develop later.

Each module should be as independent of the others as possible, and the statements within a module should work together to perform a single function. Structural decomposition gives you a way to deal with complexity; when used with a modular approach, structural decomposition results in programs of functionally cohesive subroutines that are easier to maintain later.

The DO Operation

Current releases of RPG IV support the FOR operation as a free-form replacement for the older fixed-format DO operation. As the FOR operation finds its way into RPG IV programs, the DO operation will no doubt become obsolete. For now, expect to see either operation in existing RPG programs.

Like FOR, DO is a count-controlled loop instruction. As with FOR, an end operator, ENDDO, signals the end of a DO structure. Also as with FOR, the DO automatically increments its counter to ensure that the repetition occurs the desired number of times. The general layout of a DO loop is as follows:

```
*.. 1 ...+... 2 ...+... 3 ...+... 4 ...+... 5 ...+... 6 ...+... 7 ...+... 8
CL0N01Factor1+++++++Opcode(E)+Factor2+++++++Result+++++++Len++D+HiLoEq....
C     Start value  DO        Limit value   Counter
C                  . . .
C                  ENDDO     Increment value
```

Although DO gives you the option to specify these four values, you also can omit any of them. You can omit the counter's initial value and/or increment value; RPG IV assumes a default value of 1 for both. That is, it will start the counter at 1 and add 1 to it at the start of each additional pass through the loop, unless you specify differently.

You also can omit designating a field to serve as the counter. In this case, the system keeps track of the number of repetitions using an internal counter, but you are unable to directly reference the counter's value for calculations or printing.

You can also omit the limit of the counter; again, the default value is 1. To specify a different limit, enter a numeric integer field or literal in Factor 2. If your Factor 2 entry is a field rather than a literal, the value of the field determines the number of repetitions.

```
*.. 1 ...+... 2 ...+... 3 ...+... 4 ...+... 5 ...+... 6 ...+... 7 ...+... 8
CL0N01Factor1+++++++Opcode(E)+Factor2+++++++Result+++++++Len++D+HiLoEq....
 * Sample DO loop skeletons.
 * The processing within this loop would be done just once.
C                  DO
C                  . . .
C                  ENDDO
 * The processing within this loop would be done 50 times.
C                  DO        50
C                  . . .
C                  ENDDO
 * The number of repetitions of this loop depends on the value of Iter.
C                  DO        Iter
C                  . . .
C                  ENDDO
```

continued...

Defining Subroutines

One vehicle for top-down, modular program design in RPG IV is the **subroutine**. A subroutine is a block of code with an identifiable beginning and end. It is a set of operations coded elsewhere within the calculations and invoked as a unit by referencing the subroutine's name. After performing the subroutine, the program returns control to the statement immediately following the one that invoked the routine.

The first line of a subroutine contains the BEGSR (Begin a Subroutine) operation and the name of the subroutine (in Factor 1, if you're coding fixed-format specifications). The lines of code constituting the executable portion of the subroutine follow. The last line of a subroutine contains ENDSR as the operation code to signal the end of that subroutine.

continued...

If you need to know which iteration the computer is currently executing — for example, to print the value or to use it in a calculation — you need to designate a field to be used as the counter. You must define this field as a numeric field with zero decimal positions. To designate that the field is the counter used by the DO, enter it in the Result field position of the DO line.

The following code shows the add-the-numbers problem implemented using DO. Field Number is the counter field that the system automatically increments by 1 on each pass through the loop.

```
*.. 1 ...+... 2 ...+... 3 ...+... 4 ...+... 5 ...+... 6 ...+... 7 ...+... 8
CLØNØ1Factor1+++++++Opcode(E)+Extended-factor2+++++++++++++++++++++++++++++
CLØNØ1Factor1+++++++Opcode(E)+Factor2+++++++Result++++++++Len++D+HiLoEq....
 * This routine will add all the numbers from 1 to 100 using a DO operation.
 * Counter Number is automatically incremented on each pass through the loop.
 * Initialize accumulator Sum.
C                   EVAL      Sum = Ø
 * Loop until Number exceeds 100.
C                   DO        100           Number
C                   EVAL      Sum = Sum + Number
C                   ENDDO
```

If you want the counter to start at a value other than 1, you can enter an alternate starting value (as either a literal or a field) in Factor 1 of the DO statement. And if you want to use an increment amount other than 1, code this value (again, as a literal or a field) in Factor 2 of the ENDDO statement.

For example, we can easily change our sample solution to add all the even numbers from 1 to 100 if we set Number's starting value to 2 and the increment value to 2, as follows:

```
*.. 1 ...+... 2 ...+... 3 ...+... 4 ...+... 5 ...+... 6 ...+... 7 ...+... 8
CLØNØ1Factor1+++++++Opcode(E)+Extended-factor2+++++++++++++++++++++++++++++
CLØNØ1Factor1+++++++Opcode(E)+Factor2+++++++Result++++++++Len++D+HiLoEq....
 * This routine will add all the even numbers from 2 to 100 using DO.
 * Initialize accumulator to Ø.
C                   EVAL      Sum = Ø
 * Start Number at 2 and loop until it exceeds 100.
C     2             DO        100           Number
C                   EVAL      Sum = Sum + Number
C                   ENDDO     2
 * The 2 in the above ENDDO specifies the increment value for Number.
```

The following code shows the skeleton of a subroutine.

```
*.. 1 ...+... 2 ...+... 3 ...+... 4 ...+... 5 ...+... 6 ...+... 7 ...+... 8
 /FREE
    BEGSR CalcTax;
       . . .
    ENDSR;
 /END-FREE
```

Subroutines are coded as the last entries on the Calculation Specifications, following all other calculations. The order in which you list the subroutines does not matter, although many programmers prefer to specify them in alphabetical order for easy reference. A program can have an unlimited number of subroutines; each must have a unique name, based on the same rules that apply to RPG IV fields.

The EXSR (Execute Subroutine) Operation

To send control to a subroutine for execution, you use the EXSR (Execute Subroutine) operation. Specify the name of the subroutine to be performed (in Factor 2 for fixed format), as shown in the following example.

```
*.. 1 ...+... 2 ...+... 3 ...+... 4 ...+... 5 ...+... 6 ...+... 7 ...+... 8
 /FREE
    EXSR CalcTax;        // EXSR causes control to drop to subroutine CalcTax.

    // Control returns here when the subroutine finishes.
    .
    .
    .

    // Subroutines appear at the end of the Calculation Specifications.
    BEGSR CalcTax;
      EVAL(H) FICA =  Gross * .0751;
      EVAL(H) StateTax = Gross * .045;
      IF Gross > 5000;
        EVAL(H) FedTax = Gross * .31;
      ELSE;
        EVAL(H) FedTax = Gross * .25;
      ENDIF;
    ENDSR;
```

When the computer encounters an EXSR operation, control drops to the named subroutine. Upon completion of the subroutine, control returns to the operation immediately following the calculation that invoked the subroutine. The fact that control *returns* makes it possible to maintain tight control of program flow using EXSR.

Subroutines cannot contain other subroutines. They may execute other subroutines, but a subroutine should never execute itself. This latter coding technique, called **recursion**, is permitted in some programming languages but is treated as an error by the RPG IV compiler.

Control-Break Logic

To demonstrate how top-down, structured design can be used to help develop an easily maintained program, let's apply the techniques we have discussed to solve a common business programming problem: generating a report that includes subtotals.

Assume you have a file of sales records. Each record contains a salesperson's identification number, department, the amount of a given sale, and the date of the sale. A given salesperson may have many records in the file — depending on how successful a salesperson he or she is — and the data file is ordered by salesperson, so that all the records for a given salesperson are adjacent to one another in the file. You've been asked to write a program that will include the details of each sales transaction and a subtotal of each salesperson's sales. The printer spacing chart below shows the desired report format.

	1	2	3	4	5	6	7	8	9	10
1	XX/XX/XX	SALES REPORT	PAGE XXØX							
3	SLSPSN.		AMT.							
5	XXXX		X,XXØ.XX							
6	XXXX		X,XXØ.XX							
8	TOTAL		XX,XXØ.XX*							
10	XXXX		X,XXØ.XX							
11	XXXX		X,XXØ.XX							
12	XXXX		X,XXØ.XX							
14	TOTAL		XX,XXØ.XX*							
16	GRAND TOTAL		XXX,XXØ.XX**							

This kind of problem is often referred to as a **control-break problem**, because the solution involves checking the input records for a change, or "break," in the values of a control field. That occurrence signals the need for a subtotal and triggers special processing associated with printing the subtotal and preparing for the next control group.

Because the computer has only one record in memory at a time, to determine when a change in the control field's value has occurred, you need to define a standalone work field to hold the current value of the control field. Each time a record is read, its control-field value can then be compared with the work field; a comparison revealing that the two values are no longer equal signals that the first record of a new group has just been read. Before continuing with the detail processing of that record, it is necessary to "break" away from detail processing and complete any processing required by such a change. Typically, this processing entails printing a subtotal line, rolling over an accumulator, zeroing out the accumulator, and storing the new control-field value in the work field.

With that overview of control-break logic, let's develop the pseudocode for the calculations required by the program, using a top-down design strategy. Our design now also will include a provision for printing headings at the top of each page.

```
Do Initialization Routine
WHILE not end-of-file
    IF change in salesperson
        Do Slspbreak Routine
    ENDIF
    Do Detail Process Routine
    Read next record
ENDWHILE
Do Termination Routine
END program
```

The above pseudocode works out the "mainline" logic of the program. Notice that at several spots in the pseudocode, Do statements indicate that a number of processing steps need to be performed, but the details are not yet spelled out. This is the essence of top-down design.

Once you determine that the mainline logic is correct, you can develop the logic of the additional modules, or routines:

Initialization Routine
Read first record
Set up hold area
Print headings
END Initialization Routine

Slspbreak Routine
Print salesperson line
Add salesperson's total to grand total
Zero out salesperson's total
Move new value to hold area
END Slspbreak Routine

Detail Process Routine
IF page overflow
   Print headings
ENDIF
Print detail line
Accumulate sales in salesperson's total
END Detail Process Routine

Termination Routine
Do Slspbreak Routine
Print grand total
END Termination Routine

Notice that the processing in routine Slspbreak is representative of control-break logic in general. Also notice that Slspbreak is invoked from within the Termination routine. The break routine needs to be executed one last time to print the very last salesperson's subtotal line before printing the grand total.

The complete RPG IV program, including the calculations reflecting the logic expressed in the pseudocode, is shown in the following example.

```
*.. 1 ...+... 2 ...+... 3 ...+... 4 ...+... 5 ...+... 6 ...+... 7 ...+... 8
 // ************************************************************
 //    This program produces a Sales Report that lists subtotals  *
 //    for each salesperson.                                       *
 //    Author:  Yaeger      Date Written:  Dec. 1992               *
 //    Modified Jan 2002 to current RPG IV release. Meyers.        *
 // ************************************************************

FSalesFile IF   F   19          DISK
FQPRINT     O   F  132          PRINTER OFLIND(*INOF)

D HoldSlsp         S             4
D SlspTotal        S             6 2
D GrandTotal       S             8 2
```

continued...

continued...

```
*.. 1 ...+... 2 ...+... 3 ...+... 4 ...+... 5 ...+... 6 ...+... 7 ...+... 8

ISalesFile NS
I                              1    4  SalesPrsn
I                              5    7  Dept
I                              8   13 2SalesAmt
I                             14   19 ØSaleDate

 /FREE
  // *************************************************************
  //   Calculations required to produce the Sales Report.
  //   Mainline logic.
  // *************************************************************

     EXSR Initial;

     DOW NOT %EOF(SalesFile);
       IF HoldSlsp <> SalesPrsn;
         EXSR SlspBreak;
       ENDIF;

       EXSR DetailProc;
       READ SalesFile;
     ENDDO;

     EXSR Terminate;
     *INLR = *ON;
     RETURN;

  // *************************************************************
  //   Subroutine DetailProc ... executed for each input record.
  // *************************************************************
     BEGSR DetailProc;
       IF *INOF;          // If end-of-page, then print headings.
         EXCEPT Headings;
         *INOF = *OFF;
       ENDIF;
       EXCEPT DetailLine;
       SlspTotal = SlspTotal + SalesAmt;
     ENDSR;
  // *************************************************************
  //   Subroutine Initial ... to read first record, set up hold,
  //   and print first page headings.
  // *************************************************************
     BEGSR Initial;
       READ SalesFile;
       HoldSlsp = SalesPrsn;
       EXCEPT Headings;
     ENDSR;

  // *************************************************************
  //   Subroutine SlspBreak ... done when salesperson changes;
  //   print subtotal, roll over accumulator, zero out accumulator,
  //   and reset hold.
  // *************************************************************
     BEGSR SlspBreak;
       EXCEPT BreakLine;
       GrandTotal = GrandTotal + SlspTotal;
       SlspTotal = Ø;
       HoldSlsp = SalesPrsn;
     ENDSR;
```

continued...

continued...

```
*.. 1 ...+... 2 ...+... 3 ...+... 4 ...+... 5 ...+... 6 ...+... 7 ...+... 8
    // ***********************************************************
    //  Subroutine Terminate ... done at end-of-file; execute
    //  SlspBreak one last time and print grand-total line.
    // ***********************************************************
    BEGSR Terminate;
      EXSR SlspBreak;
      EXCEPT TotalLine;
    ENDSR;

  /END-FREE

    // ***********************************************************
OQPRINT     E           Headings       2 1
O                       UDATE          Y    17
O                                           33 'SALES REPORT'
O                                           40 'PAGE'
O                       PAGE                44
O           E           Headings       2
O                                           20 'SLSPSN.'
O                                           37 'AMT.'
O           E           DetailLine     1
O                       SalesPrsn           18
O                       SalesAmt       1    39
O           E           BreakLine      1 2
O                                           24 'TOTAL'
O                       SlspTotal      1    39
O                                           40 '*'
O           E           TotalLine
O                                           26 'GRAND TOTAL'
O                       GrandTotal     1    39
O                                           41 '**'
```

Multi-Level Control-Break Logic

Programmers often face coding solutions to multiple-level control-break problems, in which two or more different control fields of the input file are to be associated with subtotal lines. For example, our sample problem could have specified a need for department subtotals in addition to the salesperson subtotals. If the input file were ordered by department, and within department by salesperson, producing the desired report would take little additional programming effort because the logic of multiple-level control-break problems follows directly from that of a single-level problem.

To code a multiple-level control-break program, set up a standalone work field for each control field to hold the value of the group being processed. Code a separate break subroutine for each level; typically, the same processing steps take place in each kind of break (e.g., printing a subtotal line, rolling over an accumulator, zeroing out the accumulator, and moving the new control-field value into the work field), but using variables appropriate to that level.

Then, before the detail processing of each record, check each control field to see whether its value has changed, checking from major (biggest grouping) to minor (smallest grouping). If a break has occurred, execute the appropriate break subroutines, starting with the minor (smallest grouping) and finishing with the break routine that corresponds to the control field that triggered the break processing.

The following pseudocode illustrates the logic of a two-level control-break problem.

Mainline Logic for Two-Level Control Break
Do Initialization Routine
WHILE not end-of-file
   IF change in department
      Do Slspbreak Routine
      Do Deptbreak Routine
   ELSE
      IF change in salesperson
         Do Slspbreak Routine
      ENDIF
   ENDIF
   Do Detail Process Routine
   Read next record
ENDWHILE
Do Termination Routine
END program

Initialization Routine
Read first record
Set up hold areas for department and salesperson
Do headings
END Initialization Routine

Slspbreak Routine
Print salesperson line
Add salesperson's total to department's total
Zero out salesperson's total
Move new salesperson to salesperson hold area
END Slspbreak Routine

Deptbreak Routine
Print department line
Add department's total to grand total
Zero out department's total
Move new department to department hold area
END Deptbreak Routine

Detail Process Routine
IF page overflow
   Print headings
ENDIF
Print detail line
Add sales to salesperson's total
END Detail Process Routine

Termination Routine
Do Slspbreak Routine
Do Deptbreak Routine
Print grand total
END Termination Routine

Notice especially the order in which the pseudocode checks for changes in the control fields, the order in which it executes the break subroutines, and the parallels between the Slspbreak and Deptbreak routines. Once you understand the logic of a two-level break problem, you can write a program with any number of level breaks because the required processing steps can be exactly modeled on those required for a two-level control break.

Chapter Summary

The goal for this chapter has been to give you a basic understanding of structured design and how it is often used with a top-down, modular approach to program development. Structured program design means developing your program logic with flow of control tightly managed, by using structured operations. Top-down methodology requires you to approach designing your program hierarchically, working out its broad logic first — concentrating primarily on flow of control — and later attending to the detailed processing requirements. Both design concepts encourage a modular approach to programming, in which you design your program around subroutines of statements that form functionally cohesive units of code.

RPG IV provides structured operations IF and SELECT/WHEN (as well as CAS*xx*) to implement decision logic and structured operations DOW, DOU, FOR, and DO to implement looping logic. IF, SELECT/WHEN, DOW, DOU, FOR, and DO let you express the conditional test associated with the operation as a free-form logical expression.

All the structured operations mentioned above have a single entry point and a single exit point that help maintain tight flow of control within a program. The following tables can help you remember the formats for the operations presented in this chapter.

Decision and Iteration Operations

Factor 1	Operation	Extended Factor 2
—	IF	CONDITIONAL EXPRESSION
—	ELSE	—
—	ENDIF	—
—	SELECT	—
—	WHEN	CONDITIONAL EXPRESSION
—	OTHER	—
—	ENDSL	—
—	DOW	CONDITIONAL EXPRESSION
—	DOU	CONDITIONAL EXPRESSION
—	ENDDO	—
—	FOR	CONDITIONAL EXPRESSION
—	ENDFOR	—
—	ITER	—
—	LEAVE	—

Operation	Factor 1	Factor 2	Result
DO	field/literal	field/literal	field
ENDDO	—	field/literal	—
EXSR	—	SUBRNAME	—
BEGSR	SUBRNAME	—	—
ENDSR	—	—	—
CASxx	FIELD/LITERAL	FIELD/LITERAL	SUBRNAME
ENDCS	—	—	—

Notes: Uppercase entry = required; lowercase entry = optional.

Extended Factor 2 expressions are free-form.

xx = one of the relational codes (GT, LT, EQ, NE, GE, LE).

Key Terms

CASE logic

control-break problem

decision operations

EBCDIC

hierarchical decomposition

iteration

leading decision loop

overflow indicators

recursion

relational codes

relational comparison

relational symbols

selection

sequence

structured design

subroutine

top-down design

trailing decision loop

Discussion/Review Questions

1. Characterize structured design.

2. If RPG IV did not include a relational symbol or code to check for "not equal," what alternate way could you express the following logic in RPG IV? "If balance due <> 0, execute the calculation routine."

3. What does "tight" flow of control mean?

4. Describe how RPG IV compares numeric values.

5. Describe how RPG IV compares character values.

6. Now that RPG has a SELECT operation, can you always avoid writing nested IF statements? Explain your answer.

7. What's the difference between AND and OR?

8. How would you decide whether to use SELECT or CAS*xx*?

9. Why does RPG IV need looping operations other than FOR? Are both DOW and DOU essential from a logical standpoint?

10. Describe how ITER and LEAVE work. Would they be considered structured options? Explain.

11. Characterize a control-break problem.

12. In control-break processing, why is a "hold" or work field needed to store the value of the control field?

13. Can you think of an alternative way to handle page advance other than referencing an overflow indicator?

Exercises

1. Use IF to code the calculations needed to determine property tax based on a property's value, stored in Value (six positions, zero decimal positions). Use the information in the table below as the basis for your calculations:

Property value	Property tax
$0–$50,000	1% of value
$50,001–$75,000	$50 plus 2% of value
$75,001–$100,000	$70 plus 2.5% of value
over $100,000	$100 plus 3% of value

2. Solve the problem described in Exercise 1 using operation SELECT.

3. Write a routine to determine traffic fines based on the values of two input fields: MphOver (miles over speed limit) and NbrOffense (number of offenses). Fines are to be determined as follows:

MPH over limit	Fine
1–10	$25
11–20	$40
21–30	$70
over 30	$100

If the speeder is a first-time offender, there is no additional fine. However, second-time offenders are fined an additional $25 if they are no more than 20 miles over the limit and an additional $50 if they are more than 20 miles over the limit. Third-time offenders are fined an additional $50 if they are no more than 20 miles over the limit and an additional $100 if they are going more than 20 miles over the limit.

4. Use FOR to write the calculations needed to obtain the squares, cubes, and square roots of all numbers from 1 to 50.

5. A program to update a master file needs a routine that checks the update code stored in Code and sends control to one of three different subroutines (AddSR, ChangeSR, and DeleteSR), depending on whether the code is A, C, or D (Add, Change, or Delete records). Invalid codes should cause subroutine ErrorSR to be executed. Write this routine twice, each time using a different structured operator.

Programming Assignments

1. Wexler University wants a summary report of its student population that shows how many in-district, out-of-district, and international students there are at the freshman, sophomore, junior, and senior levels. The input file for this program is the school's student master file, WUSTDP. Appendix F provides the record layout for this file. The records in the file are ordered by Social Security number.

Note that district code is a code field where I = in-district, O = out-of-district, and F = international student status. The classification field differentiates G (graduate) from U (undergraduate) students. The school subdivides undergraduates based on earned credits: Students with fewer than 30 credits are freshmen; those with 30–59 credits are sophomores; those with 60–89 credits are juniors; and those with 90 or more credits are seniors.

The school wants the summary report to be formatted as shown in the following printer spacing chart.

```
      1         2         3         4         5         6         7         8         9         1 0
1234567890123456789012345678901234567890123456789012345678901234567890123456789012345678901234567890
 1   XX/XX/XX                              WEXLER U.                    PAGE XXØX
 2                         STUDENT POPULATION SUMMARY REPORT
 3
 4                         -----------------RESIDENCY----------------
 5   CLASSIFICATION    IN-DISTRICT    OUT-OF-DISTRICT    INTERNATIONAL    TOTAL
 6   --------------    -----------    ---------------    -------------    -----
 7       FRESHMEN         X,XØX           X,XØX             X,XØX        XX,XØX
 8       SOPHOMORES       X,XØX           X,XØX             X,XØX        XX,XØX
 9       JUNIORS          X,XØX           X,XØX             X,XØX        XX,XØX
10       SENIORS          X,XØX           X,XØX             X,XØX        XX,XØX
11
12       TOTAL           XX,XØX          XX,XØX            XX,XØX        XX,XØX
13
```

2. Wexler University needs a report to determine how equitable its faculty salaries are across sexes. Because salaries vary with academic rank and length of employment, the school wants average salaries broken down by rank, as well as by sex, and would also like average-length-of-employment figures. Appendix F describes the input file, WUINSTP. The desired report is shown below.

```
      1         2         3         4         5         6         7         8         9         1 0
1234567890123456789012345678901234567890123456789012345678901234567890123456789012345678901234567890
 1   WEXLER UNIVERSITY FACULTY SALARY REPORT   XX/XX/XX
 2
 3
 4                 AVERAGE SALARIES AND LENGTH OF EMPLOYMENT
 5                     MALE                          FEMALE
 6 RANK            SALARY      YEARS    N        SALARY      YEARS    N
 7 ----------      ------      -----    ---      ------      -----    ---
 8 INSTRUCTOR      XXX,XXØ.XX    ØX    (ØX)      XXX,XXØ.XX    ØX    (ØX)
 9 ASSISTANT       XXX,XXØ.XX    ØX    (ØX)      XXX,XXØ.XX    ØX    (ØX)
10 ASSOCIATE       XXX,XXØ.XX    ØX    (ØX)      XXX,XXØ.XX    ØX    (ØX)
11 PROFESSOR       XXX,XXØ.XX    ØX    (ØX)      XXX,XXØ.XX    ØX    (ØX)
12
13 ALL             XXX,XXØ.XX    ØX    (XØX)     XXX,XXØ.XX    ØX    (XØX)
14
15
16       NOTE: N==NUMBER IN EACH CATEGORY
17
```

3. The municipal water company needs a program that will calculate monthly water charges. The rates for city residents are

- $0.035 per unit for the first 500 units
- $0.030 per unit for the next 500 units
- $0.027 per unit for all units beyond 1,000

In addition, there is a service fee of $10.00 per month for all customers, regardless of usage. Water users who are not residents of the city pay 1.5 times the total bill.

An input file, MWC001P, described in Appendix F, contains customer information and old and new meter readings. Determine usage from the old and new meter readings. Note that the meters are like car odometers — when they reach their maximum value (9,999), the next unit's usage causes them to read 0000. You must take this feature into account in your calculations. You may assume that no one will ever use more than 9,999 units of water per month.

Output should appear as shown on the following printer spacing chart.

```
         1         2         3         4         5         6         7         8         9         10
1234567890123456789012345678901234567890123456789012345678901234567890123456789012345678901234567890
 1 XX/XX/XX                                               PAGE XXØX
 2                    GOTHAM CITY WATER BILLING REPORT
 3
 4 CUST.                      RES.   OLD    NEW              AMOUNT
 5  NUM.       NAME           CODE   METER  METER  USAGE     OWED
 6
 7 XXXXX   XXXXXXXXXXXXXXXXXXXXX  X   XXXX   XXXX   X,XØX    X,XXØ.XX
 8 XXXXX   XXXXXXXXXXXXXXXXXXXXX  X   XXXX   XXXX   X,XØX    X,XXØ.XX
 9
10
```

4. ACME manufacturing company wants you to write a payroll program. Each record in the input file, ACP001, described in Appendix F, represents one day's work for an employee. Records are accumulated for a week, so there will be several records per employee. Records in the file are ordered by Social Security number.

The company uses both an hourly rate and a piece rate to pay its employees. Everyone gets $5.50 per hour worked. In addition, if a person produces 0–500 units during the week, he or she receives 25 cents per unit; if he or she produces 501–1,000 units, he or she receives 30 cents per unit; if more than 1,000 units, 40 cents per unit. After using these figures to calculate gross pay, you must subtract a 4.6 percent state tax and a 15 percent federal tax from gross pay to obtain net pay.

Your program should generate the report illustrated in the following printer spacing chart.

```
         1         2         3         4         5         6         7         8         9         10
1234567890123456789012345678901234567890123456789012345678901234567890123456789012345678901234567890
 1   XX/XX/XX                          ACME PAYROLL REPORT                          PAGE XXØX
 2
 3                               HOURS              GROSS      STATE    FED.       NET
 4 SOC.  SEC.         NAME       WORKED    UNITS     PAY        TAX      TAX       PAY
 5
 6 XXX-XX-XXXX    XXXXXXXXXXXXXXXX   ØX     X,XØX   X,XXØ.XX   XØ.XX   XXØ.XX   X,XXØ.XX
 7 XXX-XX-XXXX    XXXXXXXXXXXXXXXX   ØX     X,XØX   X,XXØ.XX   XØ.XX   XXØ.XX   X,XXØ.XX
 8 XXX-XX-XXXX    XXXXXXXXXXXXXXXX   ØX     X,XØX   X,XXØ.XX   XØ.XX   XXØ.XX   X,XXØ.XX
 9
10          AVERAGE GROSS PAY:    $X,XXØ.XX
11          AVERAGE UNITS PER EMPLOYEE:   X,XØX
12          AVERAGE UNITS PER HOUR:   X,XØX
13
```

5. Wexler University's faculty members run a credit union. They want you to write a program to calculate monthly payments for loan applicants. The monthly payment is to be calculated using the formula shown below. Note that I represents monthly interest rate and N represents number of months for the loan. Also note that the N in the formula is an exponent, not a multiplier. The formula to be used in calculating payment amount is

$$\text{Payment} = \text{LoanAmt} * (I * (1 + I)^N) / ((1 + I)^N - 1)$$

Records in input file WULOANP, described in Appendix F, contain information about the loan amounts, interest rates, and length of loan. Generate a report formatted as follows:

```
           1         2         3         4         5         6         7         8         9        10
  12345678901234567890123456789012345678901234567890123456789012345678901234567890123456789012345678901234567890
 1 DATE XX/XX/XX         WEXLER U. FACULTY CREDIT UNION                      PAGE XXØX          .
 2                          NEW LOAN APPLICANTS REPORT
 3
 4 LOAN          CUSTOMER              LOAN        ANNUAL     NO. OF        MONTHLY
 5 NUM.            NAME               AMOUNT     INT. RATE    MONTHS        PAYMENT
 6
 7 XXXXX   XXXXXXXXXXXXXXXX        XX,XXØ.XX     XØ.XX%       XØX         XX,XXØ.XX
 8 XXXXX   XXXXXXXXXXXXXXXX        XX,XXØ.XX     XØ.XX%       XØX         XX,XXØ.XX
 9
10         GRAND TOTALS      X,XXX,XXØ.XX                             X,XXX,XXØ.XX
11
```

Chapter 6

Externally Described Files

 ## Chapter Overview
In this chapter, you will learn how the iSeries handles database files. The chapter explains the differences between physical and logical files and discusses field reference files. You will be introduced to the iSeries' data types and the storage implications of numeric and character data types. You will learn how to define database files at a system level and how to access these definitions from within RPG IV programs. You will also learn about externally described printer files.

The OS/400 Approach to Database Files

The iSeries is unique in the way it handles data. Unlike other systems, which require additional, costly software to provide them with database capabilities, the iSeries was designed with database applications in mind. Its operating system automatically treats all data files as part of a large relational database system. One consequence of this approach is that all data files need to be defined to the system independently of application programs. Even those applications that on the surface seem to be "creating" files are actually creating records and storing them in a file that must have been defined to OS/400 before program execution.

These files may be defined on the system at a record level (i.e., not broken down into individual fields) or at a field level. If you define a file only to the record level, any RPG IV program that uses that file must subdivide that record into the appropriate logical fields in the Input or Output Specifications. On the other hand, if you have externally defined the file at a field level — that is, created an **externally described file** — you do not need to code those field definitions within your application programs that use the file; the definitions will be brought into the program at compile time. Today, RPG IV programmers almost universally practice the use of externally defined files.

Defining data files externally to application programs has several advantages. First, if you design the files using database design principles, externally defined files can reduce the need for duplication of data across files. (This kind of duplication is called **redundancy**.) Because all programs using a given file use the same field definitions and names, externally defined files impose standardization among programmers and across applications.

External file description also increases programmer efficiency and reduces error because programmers don't need to duplicate the file definition effort each time they need to reference a file within a program. And last, if it is necessary to add a field to a file's records or to change a field's definition (e.g., expand zip code to nine digits), these changes need to be made in only one place (in the external file definition), rather than in every program that uses that file. This feature simplifies system maintenance.

Physical and Logical Files

OS/400 lets you define two kinds of database files: physical files and logical files. **Physical files** actually store data records. If you define a physical file at a field level and one of those fields is designated the key, you subsequently can access records stored in that file in either **key sequence** or **arrival sequence** (first-in, first-out). If you do not define a **key field**, access is limited to arrival sequence.

Logical files describe how data appears to be stored in the database. Logical files do not actually contain data records. Instead, they store access paths, or pointers, to records in physical files. Because you generally want these access paths to be based on values of key fields, logical files typically have one or more fields designated as a key. A logical file is always based on one or more physical files. Depending on which fields are specified and which are named as keys, the apparent record images and processing order of a logical file may vary greatly from those of the physical file (or files) underlying it. Logical files correspond to users' views of data, or **subschemas**, in database terminology.

To understand the relationship between physical and logical files, consider the example below, which shows records of an employee master physical file and two logical files based on the physical file. Employee number is the key field to the physical file. One of the logical files is keyed on a composite, or **concatenation**, of department and employee number, while the other has zip code as the key field.

The example shows the order in which the records would appear to an application program for each file if you stipulated sequential retrieval by key.

Physical file EMPMST (keyed on employee number)

Emp. no.	Last name	First name	Dept.	Salary	Street	City	State	Zip
111111111	Jones	Mary	MKT	54000	123 W. 45th	Decatur	MI	49065
222222222	Smith	Sam	ACT	61500	4422 N. Oak	Paw Paw	MI	49045
333333333	Adams	Arnold	MKT	34950	1120 W. Main	Kalamazoo	MI	49008
444444444	Houston	Wanda	MIS	29500	290 S. State	Kalamazoo	MI	49007
555555555	Jacobs	David	ACT	43275	9911 S. 88th	Mattawan	MI	49069
666666666	Salinger	Carol	MIS	38500	1300 Maple Lk.	Paw Paw	MI	49065
777777777	Riley	Thomas	MKT	24600	8824 E. Drake	Kalamazoo	MI	49008

Logical file EMPMSTL1 (keyed on department and employee number)

Emp. no.	Last name	First name	Dept.	Salary
222222222	Smith	Sam	ACT	61500
555555555	Jacobs	David	ACT	43275
444444444	Houston	Wanda	MIS	29500
666666666	Salinger	Carol	MIS	38500
111111111	Jones	Mary	MKT	54000
333333333	Adams	Arnold	MKT	34950
777777777	Riley	Thomas	MKT	24600

Logical file EMPMSTL2 (keyed on zip code)

Last name	First name	Street	City	State	Zip
Houston	Wanda	290 S. State	Kalamazoo	MI	49007
Adams	Arnold	1120 W. Main	Kalamazoo	MI	49008
Riley	Thomas	8824 E. Drake	Kalamazoo	MI	49008
Smith	Sam	4422 N. Oak	Paw Paw	MI	49045
Jones	Mary	123 W. 45th	Decatur	MI	49065
Salinger	Carol	1300 Maple Lk.	Paw Paw	MI	49065
Jacobs	David	9911 S. 88th	Mattawan	MI	49069

Although the actual data records are stored only in the physical file (remember that the logical files store only access paths to records), programs can use logical files just as though the logical files themselves contained the data.

You might use the first logical file to produce a salary report of employees, broken down by department, while the second logical file could be used to print mailing labels for employees, ordered by zip code. Note that logical file records do not need to include all the fields present in the physical records upon which they are based; what fields appear within a logical file depend on the logical file's definition.

Introduction to DDS

The procedure for creating database file definitions is similar to that of creating an RPG IV program. The first step is to use an editor, such as Source Entry Utility (SEU), to create a source member of definition statements. Most installations use a file named QDDSSRC to store members representing externally described files. The source type of a physical file member is PF; the type of a logical file member is LF. SEU automatically provides prompts appropriate to the member type you specify.

Data Description Specifications (DDS) are a fixed-format language that you can use to code the source definitions for physical and logical database files, as well as for display and printer files. The format for DDS definitions resembles RPG specifications — for a good reason: iSeries file definitions were closely modeled after RPG. All DDS lines include an A in position 6. As in RPG IV, an asterisk (*) in position 7 of a DDS source line signals a comment line. You can use comment lines throughout the file definition. Minimally, you should include a few comment lines at the beginning of each file definition to identify the nature of the file.

In addition to comment lines, DDS includes record format descriptions, which define a record type within the file; field definition lines, which describe fields within records; and perhaps key specifications, which designate which fields are to serve as keys to the file. The particular nature of these specifications depends on whether you are defining a physical file or a logical file.

DDS also extensively uses a variety of **keywords**, each with a special meaning. Some keywords, which apply to the file as a whole, are called **file-level keywords**; some apply to a specific record format within the file and are called **record-level keywords**; and some, which are associated only with a specific field, are called **field-level keywords**.

Although all externally defined files share those general features mentioned above, the details of a DDS definition depend on the type of file you are defining. Accordingly, let's first look at using DDS to define physical files.

Defining Physical Files

A physical file's source statements define the data contents the file will have. Physical files can contain only one record format. That means that every record within a physical file must have an identical record layout. Because of this requirement, a physical file's DDS can contain only one record type, or format. The record format is signaled by an R in position 17 (labeled T for Type), and you enter a name for the record format in positions 19–28 (Name++++++).

Following the record format specification, you must enter lines to define each field the record contains. Following the field definitions, you optionally can designate a key for the file. A K in position 17 denotes a key field. If you list a key field, its contents determine the sequence in which you can retrieve records from the file. The following example shows the DDS code for the employee master file EMPMST.

```
*.. 1 ...+... 2 ...+... 3 ...+... 4 ...+... 5 ...+... 6 ...+... 7 ...+... 8
A..........T.Name++++++RLen++TDpB......Functions++++++++++++++++++++++++++++
 * Employee master physical file EMPMST
A                                       UNIQUE
A          R EMPREC
A            EMPNO         9S 0          TEXT('Employee number')
A            LNAME         15A           TEXT('Last name')
A            FNAME         10A           TEXT('First name')
A            DEPT          3A            TEXT('Department')
A            SALARY        6P 0          TEXT('Annual salary')
A            STREET        15A           TEXT('Street address')
A            CITY          15A           TEXT('City')
A            STATE         2A            TEXT('State')
A            ZIP           5S 0          TEXT('Zip code')
A          K EMPNO
```

Let's look at the details of this definition. First, UNIQUE is a file-level keyword. (All file-level keywords appear at the beginning of the DDS, before the record format specification line.) UNIQUE stipulates that the file cannot contain records with duplicate key values. When you include this keyword, attempts to write a record to the file with a key value identical to a record already in the file will cause the system to generate an error message. Use of UNIQUE is optional; without its use, the system permits records with duplicate key values.

The record format line is next. Note the R in position 17 and the format name, EMPREC, left-justified in positions 19–28. DDS allows record format names (and field names, for that matter) up to 10 characters long. These names must begin with an alphabetic character (A–Z, @, $, or #). The remaining characters can be any of the alphabetic characters, any of the digits 0–9, or the underscore character (_). Unlike RPG IV, DDS source code cannot contain lowercase alphabetic characters, so all record format and field names in DDS source are entered as upper case.

You define the fields of a record on successive lines below the record format line. The field name begins in position 19. Next, you specify the length of the field, right-adjusted in positions 30–34 (Len++). As in RPG IV, any numeric field definition must include a decimal position entry (Dp, positions 36–37). You use position 35 to specify the data type, a concept we'll explore in detail in the next section.

Following the definition of all the fields to appear within the record, you can designate one or more fields as the record key by coding a K in position 17 and specifying the name of the key field in positions 19–28. In the example, EMPNO is named as the key field of the file. Notice that you must define the key field as part of the record prior to the K specification.

If you list more than one key line, you are specifying a composite or concatenated key. For a **composite key**, list the key fields in order from major to minor. Note that fields need not be adjacent to each other within the record to be key components.

The TEXT keyword entries are optional ways to provide documentation. In the example, TEXT is used with each field to explain what the field represents. You must enclose text comments with apostrophes (') and surround them with parentheses. Although text comments are not required, it makes good sense to include them, especially if your field names are somewhat cryptic. TEXT also can appear as a record-level keyword to document the record format.

Programmers new to DDS are sometimes confused by the fact that the name of the file is not included within the DDS (except, perhaps, within a comment line). The file name is determined by what you call the source member, which by default becomes the name of the compiled object, or database file.

Data Types and Data Storage

As we mentioned a few paragraphs ago, you must assign a **data type** to each field in a physical file. The data type assigned to a field determines how the field's values are stored, how much storage the field occupies, and what kinds of operations can be performed on the field when it is used within a program.

From previous chapters of this text, you are already familiar with two general types of data: character and numeric. To denote that a field is to contain **character** (or alphanumeric) data, you code an A for its type; if you leave the type entry blank and also leave the decimal position entry blank, the system assumes that the data type of the field is character.

Numeric fields (signaled by nonblank decimal position entries) are a little more complicated. DDS supports three commonly used data types:

- zoned decimal (type S)
- packed decimal (type P)
- binary (type B)

RPG IV does not differentiate among numeric data types in determining what kinds of operations you can perform on a field or what kinds of output editing are possible; however, the data type of a numeric field — zoned decimal, packed decimal, or binary — determines how that field is represented and stored within the database. If you leave the type entry blank for a numeric field, the system defaults to the packed decimal data type for the field.

An explanation of data representation must begin with EBCDIC. You know that computers manipulate data in binary form. You probably also know that any numeric value can be converted from its familiar decimal, or base 10, value to a corresponding value in binary, or base 2, notation. At first glance, then, data representation should be a simple matter of converting values from one base to another. The problem is that many characters and values that we want to represent to the computer are not numbers — letters of the alphabet, for example, or the characters $ and {.

IBM developed a coding scheme to allow any data character — numeric or non-numeric — to be represented to the computer. This coding scheme is called Extended Binary-Coded Decimal Interchange Code, or **EBCDIC**. EBCDIC assigns a unique eight-bit binary pattern to each representable character. Capital A, for example, is 11000001 in EBCDIC, while the digit 1 is represented as 11110001. The leftmost four bits are often called zone or **high-order bits**, while the rightmost four bits are digit or **low-order bits**. Because eight bits constitute a byte, it takes one byte of storage to store each character in EBCDIC. The iSeries stores all non-numeric, or character, data values this way.

Numbers can be handled slightly differently. The following table shows the EBCDIC codes for the digits 0 through 9.

Digit	EBCDIC
0	11110000
1	11110001
2	11110010
3	11110011
4	11110100
5	11110101
6	11110110
7	11110111
8	11111000
9	11111001

The first thing you should notice is that the zone bits of all digits are identical — 1111. This means that the zone portion is redundant for numeric data; that is, if the system knows the data is numeric, it knows that the zones of the data are all 1s. Two forms of numeric data storage take advantage of this redundancy.

The first form, **zoned** (or signed) **decimal**, takes a full byte to store each digit of a numeric value, except that the zone of the rightmost digit is used to store the sign of the data: 1111 represents a plus sign (+), while 1101 represents a negative sign (–). Zoned decimal representation, then, is almost identical to character representation, except that the sign is represented as part of the rightmost digit's byte.

The second form of numeric representation, **packed decimal**, takes greater advantage of the redundancy built into digit representation by simply not bothering to store the zones of numbers. Data in packed format takes just over half the amount of storage it would take to store the same number in zoned decimal format. In packed format, only the digit, or low-order, bits of a number are stored, with the sign of the number represented by an additional four bits. These sign bits always occupy the rightmost four bit positions of a packed decimal value.

Study the following table to understand the differences in data representation between these two formats. Notice the location of the signs (in bold type) in both representations and the elimination of the zone bits in the packed format.

Value to represent	Zoned decimal
+136	11110001 11110011 **1111**0110
–136	11110001 11110011 **1101**0110

	Packed decimal
+136	00010011 0110**1111**
–136	00010011 0110**1101**

The remaining form for representing numbers, **binary format**, dispenses completely with EBCDIC and stores a number as its direct binary equivalent. This format can result in the greatest savings in storage. A two-byte binary number can represent up to four digits, and a four-byte binary number can represent up to nine digits.

Many system programs use binary numbers (or integers, which are closely related to binary numbers), but most business programming can be accomplished using zoned or packed decimal format.

Although some programmers prefer to define numeric fields as zoned decimal (type S) because it's easier to print or view the raw data in the file when the data is stored in this format, the iSeries works most efficiently with numbers stored in packed decimal format.

The length of the entry you give a field in DDS represents the number of digit positions in the value to be represented, but the number of bytes of storage it will take to actually store the value may vary, given the data type. Packed fields take $(n + 1) / 2$ bytes of storage (rounded to the nearest whole byte), where n is the number of digit positions in the data value. The formula derives from the fact that in packed format, the sign and each digit require a half byte of storage; you need to round up to the nearest whole byte because data storage is allocated in byte-sized units. A number eight positions long would have a length of 5 if stored in packed format. (So would a number nine positions long. Because it takes the same amount of storage, many programming experts recommend that you always define packed numeric fields with an odd number of digit positions.) For zoned decimal format, storage length corresponds exactly to digit positions in the value to be stored. An eight-digit number would have a storage length of 4 if binary was the type specified for it.

DDS recognizes other data types besides A, S, P, and B; RPG IV recognizes still other data types as well. We will look at the additional RPG IV data types in Chapter 11. For now, we'll limit our scope to the character and numeric types presented above so that we can turn our attention to logical files.

Logical Files

Although you could, in theory, "get by" using only physical files to define your data, you are just scratching the surface of OS/400's database capabilities until you begin to use logical files.

As we discussed in the introduction of this chapter, logical files define access paths to data actually stored in physical files. You can use a logical file to restrict user views to a subset of fields contained in a physical file, to change the retrieval order of records from a file (by changing the designated key field), or to combine data stored in two or more separate physical files into one logical file. Although the data actually is stored in physical files, once you have defined logical files to the system you can reference these logical files in RPG IV programs as though the logical files themselves actually contained records. The advantage of using logical files is that they can provide alternate ways to look at data, including different orders of record access, without redundantly storing the actual data on the system.

Simple Logical Files

A logical file based on a single physical file is called a simple logical file. The method of defining simple logical files is similar to that of defining physical files. You first specify a record format, then follow that with a list of fields (optional), and follow that with one or more (optional) key fields. Because logical files provide views of physical files, you must include the keyword PFILE beginning in position 45 of the Functions area on the record format line, followed, in parentheses, by the name of the physical file upon which the logical record format is based.

The easiest way to code a simple logical file is to use the same record format name within the logical file as the record format name in the physical file on which the logical file is based. With this method, the system assumes the record layouts of the files are identical. As a result, you do not need to include fields within your logical record description. However, you can still designate one or more fields as a key, and this key does not have to match the key of the physical file.

The following example shows a logical file based on employee master file EMPMST:

```
*.. 1 ...+... 2 ...+... 3 ...+... 4 ...+... 5 ...+... 6 ...+... 7 ...+... 8
A..........T.Name++++++.Len++TDpB......Functions++++++++++++++++++++++++++++++
 * Logical file EMPMSTL3, keyed on last name
A          R EMPREC                   PFILE(EMPMST)
A          K LNAME
```

With this definition, all the fields defined within the physical file are included within the logical file. Because the logical file is keyed on last name, keyed sequential access of this logical file will retrieve the employee records in alphabetic order by last name. This kind of logical file definition is widely used to change the retrieval order of records in a file. Its effects are identical to that of physically sorting file records into a different order, but without the system overhead that a physical sort requires.

If you want to restrict the logical file so that it includes only some of the fields from the physical file, give the logical file a record format name different from that of the record format name in the physical file and then list just those fields to be included in the logical file. Again, you may designate one or more of these fields to serve as the key to the file. The logical file defined below would produce the logical view of employee data organized by department and employee number illustrated earlier in the chapter.

```
*.. 1 ...+... 2 ...+... 3 ...+... 4 ...+... 5 ...+... 6 ...+... 7 ...+... 8
A..........T.Name++++++.Len++TDpB......Functions++++++++++++++++++++++++++++++
 * Logical file EMPMSTL1, keyed on department and, within department,
 * on employee number. Only those fields listed are accessible
 * through the logical file.
A          R EMPRECL1                 PFILE(EMPMST)
A            EMPNO
A            LNAME
A            FNAME
A            DEPT
A            SALARY
A          K DEPT
A          K EMPNO
```

Notice that you do not need to specify length, type, and decimal positions for the fields in a logical file; these field attributes are already given in the physical file on which the logical file is based.

If you wanted to limit access to only name and address information in the employee master file and retrieve the records in zip-code order, you could define a logical file like the one that follows. Again, the data view resulting from this logical file was illustrated earlier.

```
*.. 1 ...+... 2 ...+... 3 ...+... 4 ...+... 5 ...+... 6 ...+... 7 ...+... 8
A..........T.Name++++++.Len++TDpB......Functions++++++++++++++++++++++++++++++
 * Logical file EMPMSTL2, keyed on zip code
A          R EMPRECL2                 PFILE(EMPMST)
A            LNAME
A            FNAME
A            STREET
A            CITY
A            STATE
A            ZIP
A          K ZIP
```

Record Selection/Omission

You can define logical files to exclude certain records contained in the physical file or to include only a subset of the records contained in the physical file by using Omit or Select specifications. You can use this feature only if the logical file contains a key specification. Your specifications base the record exclusion or inclusion on actual data values present in selected fields of the physical file records.

For example, assume you want to omit the MIS department from the salary report. You simply designate department as an omit field (O in position 17) and then in position 45 provide the basis for the omission. In this case, because you want to omit a specific department, simply use the field-level keyword VALUES, followed by the value or values you want to omit. If the field type is character, you must enclose each value with apostrophes:

```
*.. 1 ...+... 2 ...+... 3 ...+... 4 ...+... 5 ...+... 6 ...+... 7 ...+... 8
A..........T.Name++++++.Len++TDpB......Functions++++++++++++++++++++++++++++++
 * Logical file EMPMSTL4, keyed on department and, within department,
 * on employee number. MIS department employees are excluded from
 * the file.
A           R EMPRECL4                 PFILE(EMPMST)
A             EMPNO
A             LNAME
A             FNAME
A             DEPT
A             SALARY
A           K DEPT
A           K EMPNO
A           O DEPT                      VALUES('MIS')
```

If you wanted to include only the MIS and ACT departments, you could change the O in position 17 of the select/omit field to an S and specify MIS and ACT as values. In that case, the logical file would contain only employees of the MIS and ACT departments. Other departments would be excluded:

```
*.. 1 ...+... 2 ...+... 3 ...+... 4 ...+... 5 ...+... 6 ...+... 7 ...+... 8
A..........T.Name++++++.Len++TDpB......Functions++++++++++++++++++++++++++++++
 * Logical file EMPMSTL5, keyed on department and, within department,
 * on employee number. Only MIS and ACT departments are included
 * within the file.
A           R EMPRECL5                 PFILE(EMPMST)
A             EMPNO
A             LNAME
A             FNAME
A             DEPT
A             SALARY
A           K DEPT
A           K EMPNO
A           S DEPT                      VALUES('MIS' 'ACT')
```

Besides VALUES, two additional keywords let you specify the basis of record inclusion or exclusion: RANGE and COMP. Keyword RANGE, followed by parentheses containing two values, lets you specify the beginning value and the ending value of a range of values upon which the selection or omission is to be based. In the example that follows, only employees with zip codes 49400 through 50000 will be included in the logical file.

```
*.. 1 ...+... 2 ...+... 3 ...+... 4 ...+... 5 ...+... 6 ...+... 7 ...+... 8
A..........T.Name++++++.Len++TDpB......Functions++++++++++++++++++++++++++++++
 * Logical file EMPMSTL6, selecting specified records based on a
 * range of zip codes
A           R EMPRECL6                 PFILE(EMPMST)
A             LNAME
A             FNAME
A             STREET
A             CITY
A             STATE
A             ZIP
A           K ZIP
A           S ZIP                       RANGE(49400 50000)
```

With keyword COMP, you can specify a comparison between a field's value and a given value to serve as the basis of selection or omission. You specify the nature of the comparison by using one of eight relational operators:

- EQ (equal to)
- NE (not equal to)
- LT (less than)
- NL (not less than)
- GT (greater than)
- NG (not greater than)
- LE (less than or equal to)
- GE (greater than or equal to)

To use this feature, enter field-level keyword COMP; follow the keyword with parentheses containing first the relational operator and then a literal indicating the comparison value. In the following example, employees with zip codes below 49500 will be omitted from the logical file.

```
*.. 1 ...+... 2 ...+... 3 ...+... 4 ...+... 5 ...+... 6 ...+... 7 ...+... 8
A..........T.Name++++++.Len++TDpB......Functions++++++++++++++++++++++++++++++
 * Logical file EMPMSTL7, omitting those employees whose zip codes
 * are less than 49500
A          R EMPRECL7                    PFILE(EMPMST)
A            LNAME
A            FNAME
A            STREET
A            CITY
A            STATE
A            ZIP
A          K ZIP
A          O ZIP                          COMP(LT 49500)
```

You can designate multiple select and/or omit fields, set up alternate criteria using ORs (O in position 7), or list multiple criteria using ANDs (A in position 7) so that several specifications must hold true for record inclusion or exclusion to occur. (For additional details about these capabilities, see IBM's *iSeries DDS Reference*.)

Logical Files with Multiple Record Formats

In addition to defining simple logical files, you can define logical files based on two or more physical files. One way to do this is to define logical files with multiple record formats, where each format is based on a different physical file.

Consider the following scenario. You have a student master physical file that contains student number, name, major, date admitted, and so on. As students take courses, each course is recorded in a second physical file containing student number, course identification, semester taken, grade received, and so on. Here are partial definitions of these physical files:

```
*.. 1 ...+... 2 ...+... 3 ...+... 4 ...+... 5 ...+... 6 ...+... 7 ...+... 8
A..........T.Name++++++RLen++TDpB.....Functions++++++++++++++++++++++++++++++
 * physical file definition for student master file STUDMAST
A           R STUDREC
A             STUD_NO        9S Ø        TEXT('Student Number')
A             LNAME         20A          TEXT('Last Name')
A             FNAME         10A          TEXT('First Name')
A             MAJOR          6A          TEXT('Major')
A             ADM_DTE        6S Ø        TEXT('Date Admitted')
A           K STUD_NO
```

```
*.. 1 ...+... 2 ...+... 3 ...+... 4 ...+... 5 ...+... 6 ...+... 7 ...+... 8
A..........T.Name++++++RLen++TDpB.....Functions++++++++++++++++++++++++++++++
 * physical file definition of student courses taken, file STUDCRSE
A           R CRSEREC
A             STUD_NO        9S Ø        TEXT('Student Number')
A             CRSE_ID        6A          TEXT('Course Identifier')
A             SEMESTER       3A          TEXT('Semester Taken')
A             GRADE          2A          TEXT('Grade Received')
A           K STUD_NO
A           K CRSE_ID
```

Now, assume you want to produce a report that shows the name, number, and major for each student, followed immediately by a list of all the courses the student has taken and the grade received in each course. One way to handle this task would be to define a logical file based on the two physical files. The following code shows the logical file definition.

```
*.. 1 ...+... 2 ...+... 3 ...+... 4 ...+... 5 ...+... 6 ...+... 7 ...+... 8
A..........T.Name++++++.Len++TDpB.....Functions++++++++++++++++++++++++++++++
 * Logical file over STUDMAST and STUDCRSE physical files
A           R STUDREC              PFILE(STUDMAST)
A           K STUD_NO
 *
A           R CRSEREC              PFILE(STUDCRSE)
A           K STUD_NO
A           K SEMESTER
```

Notice that the logical file contains two record formats: one based on physical file STUDMAST and the other on physical file STUDCRSE. Both record formats use the student number as the major key; the second format, CRSEREC, also has semester as the minor portion of a concatenated key.

With this definition, sequentially reading the logical file will retrieve first a student record (the student with the lowest student number); then, one by one, each record from the course file for that student, arranged in semester order; then the next student's record, followed by the courses, in semester order, for that student; and so on. The logical file gives the appearance that the two physical files have been merged together, with records grouped by student and, within that grouping, arranged by semester. In reality, the data remains in the two separate physical files. The logical file interconnects them by building access paths to the records in both files.

Join Logical Files

You can define a second kind of logical file based on two or more physical files: a **join logical file**. In contrast to a logical file with multiple record formats, in which data from different physical files remains in separate records in the logical file, a join logical file combines fields from different physical files into a single record. To use this format, there must be a matching field across the physical files upon which the join can be based.

Take, for example, the case in which you want to generate invoice lines based on an inventory physical file whose records contain part number, description, unit cost, and selling price and an order physical file that contains order number, part number, and quantity ordered. You could set up a logical file to combine the description and price information from the inventory file with the order-number and quantity-ordered information from the order file by joining the two files on part number:

```
*.. 1 ...+... 2 ...+... 3 ...+... 4 ...+... 5 ...+... 6 ...+... 7 ...+... 8
A..........T.Name++++++RLen++TDpB......Functions+++++++++++++++++++++++++++++
 * Physical file of inventory, INVENT
A           R INVREC
A             PART_NO        6A          TEXT('Part Number')
A             DESCRPT       30A          TEXT('Part Description')
A             UNIT_COST      5P 2        TEXT('Unit Cost')
A             SELL_PRICE     5P 2        TEXT('Selling Price')
A             OH_QTY         5P 0        TEXT('On-hand Quantity')
A           K PART_NO

*.. 1 ...+... 2 ...+... 3 ...+... 4 ...+... 5 ...+... 6 ...+... 7 ...+... 8
A..........T.Name++++++RLen++TDpB......Functions+++++++++++++++++++++++++++++
 * Physical file of orders, ORDERS
A           R ORDREC
A             ORDER_NO       6A          TEXT('Order Number')
A             CUST_NO        5A          TEXT('Customer Number')
A             PART_NUM       6A          TEXT('Part Number')
A             QTY_ORD        3P 0        TEXT('Quantity Ordered')
A           K ORDER_NO
A           K PART_NUM

*.. 1 ...+... 2 ...+... 3 ...+... 4 ...+... 5 ...+... 6 ...+... 7 ...+... 8
A..........T.Name++++++.Len++TDpB......Functions+++++++++++++++++++++++++++++
 * Join logical file connecting files INVENT and ORDERS
A           R ORDLINE                    JFILE(ORDERS INVENT)
A           J                            JOIN(ORDERS INVENT)
A                                        JFLD(PART_NUM PART_NO)
A             ORDER_NO
A             CUST_NO
A             PART_NO
A             DESCRPT
A             SELL_PRICE
A             QTY_ORD
```

In the preceding logical file, keyword JFILE signals which physical files the logical file uses. The next two lines specify the nature of the join. Notice that the join specification requires a J in position 17 of the specification line. Keyword JOIN designates which files are used in this join. Because we expect every record from ORDERS to appear in the logical file, we list that file first. (It is likely that many of the parts represented in file INVENT are not part of anyone's current order and, accordingly, would not appear in the join logical file.)

Keyword JFLD indicates which fields' values are to be matched across the physical files named in the JOIN parameter. Following the join-level entries are the fields making up the logical record. Notice that some fields within the logical record come from INVENT, while others come from ORDERS. Records from these two files are "joined" together to create a single, logical record image. Any record (from either physical file) that does not have a corresponding record in the other file (based on a match of the part-number fields) will not appear in the join logical file.

Creating Database Files

The first step in actually creating a physical or logical file is to enter the DDS statements using an editor, such as SEU. As we mentioned, it is standard practice to use source file QDDSSRC to store database source members. Also recall that the source type is PF for physical file and LF for logical file.

Once you've entered your DDS code, you must compile it to create the file as an object on the system. If you are working from Programming Development Manager (PDM) or the Programmer's menu, follow the same procedure to compile a database object that you use to create a program module object. If you compile by directly entering a command at a command line rather than by working through menus, the appropriate commands are CRTPF (Create Physical File) and CRTLF (Create Logical File).

If the system encounters syntax errors while trying to create your file, you will receive a message indicating that the creation was not successful. Otherwise, the system will tell you that the job was completed normally and that the database object now exists. Once the file object exists, you can use it to store data. You can enter data into physical files by using a system utility called **Data File Utility (DFU)**, by writing values to the file through a program, or by copying records to the file from another file.

Caution
You must create a physical file before you can create logical files based on that physical file; failure to do so will result in error messages. If you want to change the definition of a physical file after you have created a logical file based on that definition, you must first delete the logical file object (although not the source) before the system will let you delete the physical file object and create a new one.

You should be aware of one additional caveat: If you want to change a physical file's definition after you have stored data in the file, *deleting the file deletes the data in the file as well*. You can avoid such data loss by copying the data temporarily to a different file or by using the CHGPF (Change Physical File) command; your instructor can provide you with this information, should you need it.

RPG IV Programming with Externally Defined Files

Now that you understand how to define and create files on the iSeries, you will find that it is simple to reference these external definitions within your programs. Basically, all you need to do is make a few minor changes to your File Specifications and eliminate your Input Specifications.

On the File Specifications in position 22, instead of an F for fixed format, code an E for externally defined. Next, omit a record-length entry — the system will supply that information automatically based on the external definition. Last, if the file is keyed and you want to access records based on keys, code a K in position 34. Omitting the K results in record retrieval based on arrival sequence (i.e., the order in which the records were originally written to the file). The following code illustrates a File Specification for an externally described file.

```
*.. 1 ...+... 2 ...+... 3 ...+... 4 ...+... 5 ...+... 6 ...+... 7 ...+... 8
FFilename++IPEASFRLen+LKlen+AIDevice+.Keywords+++++++++++++++++++++++++++++++
FEmpMaster IF   E        K DISK
```

EmpMaster is a physical file. If you wanted to use a logical file, you would enter the logical file name; the remaining entries would be identical to those shown for the physical file. At a program level, no distinction is made between physical and logical files.

If your input file is externally described, you do not need to code Input Specifications for the file. When you compile your program, the system will copy the file's definition into your source listing where the Input Specifications would normally appear. Obviously then, when you use external definition, the file must exist before your program can be compiled successfully.

Less obviously, if you change the definition of a physical or logical file after you have compiled a program that uses that file, you must recompile the program before the system will let the program be run. This feature, called **level checking**, prevents you from running a program based on an obsolete or inaccurate definition of a database file.

Calculation and Output Specifications can use any fields defined as part of the externally described input file just as though the fields were defined internally as part of the Input Specifications. You also can externally describe database files used as output; in that case, Output Specifications are unnecessary, and writing to the file can take place directly from your calculations. Chapter 7 explores this concept in detail. •

Additional Database File Concepts

The purpose of this chapter has been to give the beginning RPG IV programmer a basic understanding of externally defined files on the iSeries. OS/400 provides features for defining data far beyond what we have covered here. Variants on join logical files, for instance, can be much more complex than the simple examples we've illustrated. In addition to the keywords used in this chapter, the iSeries offers 30 or so other keywords used with data file definition. Some of these keywords let you establish data validity checks for interactive data entry; others let you specify how the field will be edited upon output to the screen.

Last, the iSeries lets you create a physical file that serves as a centralized **data dictionary** of fields used within an application system. Such a physical file is called a **field reference file**. You never actually use this kind of file for data storage; its sole purpose is to provide field definitions for use in subsequent physical file creation. Once you have created a field reference file, you can define the fields that make up your physical files simply by referring to the definitions contained in the field reference file.

Consider the examples of physical files that were part of the student records application system illustrated earlier in this chapter. Instead of defining each field within the physical database files, we could have first created a physical file containing the definitions of all the fields that the student record system will need to store. The following code illustrates this file — a field reference file.

```
*.. 1 ...+... 2 ...+... 3 ...+... 4 ...+... 5 ...+... 6 ...+... 7 ...+... 8
A..........T.Name++++++RLen++TDpB......Functions++++++++++++++++++++++++++++++
 * field reference file STUDREF for the student records system
A          R RECORD
A            STUD_NO        9S 0       TEXT('Student Number')
A            LNAME         20A         TEXT('Last Name')
A            FNAME         10A         TEXT('First Name')
A            MAJOR          6A         TEXT('Major')
A            ADM_DTE        6S 0       TEXT('Date Admitted')
A            CRSE_ID        6A         TEXT('Course Identifier')
A            SEMESTER       3A         TEXT('Semester Taken')
A            GRADE          2A         TEXT('Grade Received')
A            . . .
```

Once you have created the reference file, you can create physical database files whose field definitions are obtained from the reference file. To use this feature, simply include in your physical file the file-level keyword REF, with the name of the field reference file in parentheses. You can then define any field in this physical file whose definition already exists in the reference file simply by coding an R in position 29 (labeled R for Reference) and omitting the length, type, decimal entry, and relevant keyword information for that field. The two physical files that follow illustrate the use of the field reference file to supply field definitions.

```
*.. 1 ...+... 2 ...+... 3 ...+... 4 ...+... 5 ...+... 6 ...+... 7 ...+... 8
A..........T.Name++++++RLen++TDpB......Functions++++++++++++++++++++++++++++
 * physical file definition for student master file STUDMAST
A                                        REF(STUDREF)
A          R STUDREC
A            STUD_NO    R
A            LNAME      R
A            FNAME      R
A            MAJOR      R
A            ADM_DTE    R
A          K STUD_NO
```

```
*.. 1 ...+... 2 ...+... 3 ...+... 4 ...+... 5 ...+... 6 ...+... 7 ...+... 8
A..........T.Name++++++RLen++TDpB......Functions++++++++++++++++++++++++++++
 * physical file definition of student courses taken, file STUDCRSE
A                                        REF(STUDREF)
A          R CRSEREC
A            STUD_NO    R
A            CRSE_ID    R
A            SEMESTER   R
A            GRADE      R
A          K STUD_NO
A          K CRSE_ID
```

Field reference files can enforce a uniformity and consistency throughout an application system that facilitates program development and maintenance. Using such files, however, requires a thoughtful, structured approach to application system development because your data needs should be determined before any file creation or application development. The casual approach that many companies take toward developing new systems does not allow them to take advantage of field reference files.

Another related topic of concern to programmers is database design. A crucial step in application system development is determining the file structure for the system. What data fields will you need to store? What physical and logical files will you need? How do you determine what fields belong in what files? Whole books have been written on the subject of relational database design. Although this topic is beyond the scope of this book, realize that every professional programmer should have a solid understanding of relational database design.

As systems become complex and the number of files used in a system grows, it becomes increasingly important for an IS department to have file-naming conventions that provide some information about the function and type of each file. Although working with a maximum of 10-character file names imposes some restrictions on your ability to assign good file names, many installations use an agreed-upon mnemonic prefix to denote the system within which the file was designed to be used and use a short alphabetic mnemonic code — often related to the key of the file — to uniquely identify each file within the system. Some companies also use a suffix of P, L, or F to denote whether the file is a physical, logical, or field reference file and use a number to differentiate between similar files.

Externally Described Printer Files

In addition to allowing the external definition of database files, RPG IV lets you define reports externally. Although programmers use this feature less often than they use externally described database files, a significant number of programmers prefer to handle all their report programs by externally describing the reports.

Externally describing printer files offers two primary advantages. First, this method lets you change a report format without changing the source code of the program that produces the report — a wise approach to application maintenance. Second, if you externally define printer files, you can use an iSeries system utility, **Report Layout Utility (RLU)**, to help you design the layout of the report visually on the terminal; you don't need to use paper and printer spacing chart forms. RLU then generates the DDS required to describe the report so you don't have to do the "grunt work" of figuring out line position and spacing entries. (The details of using RLU fall outside the scope of this text; those persons interested in developing printer files using this method should consult the IBM manual *Report Layout Utility (RLU).*)

You use DDS to define printer files at the source level, the same as you do for database files. The source members of printer files, like those of database files, are generally stored in QDDSSRC; a printer file's type, however, is PRTF.

Once you have entered the source code using an editor, such as SEU or RLU, you compile the source to create a printer file object. Once the object exists, it can receive output from a program for printing. The DDS code for a printer file is analogous to that of a database file, except that its focus is the definition of record formats of information to be sent to a printer. Printer files, like logical files, can contain multiple record formats, each defining a different set of output lines. The DDS can also include keyword entries at the file level, the record level, and/or the field level to define the position and/or appearance of the output.

To illustrate how you would externally define a printer file, let's reconsider the sales report from Chapter 5. Recall that the desired report includes headings, individual sales figures, a sales total for each salesperson, and a grand total for all salespersons. The printer spacing chart for the report is reproduced below.

The RPG IV program in Chapter 5 defined five exception lines, grouped as Headings, DetailLine, BreakLine, and TotalLine, to generate this output. You would follow much the same procedure to externally describe this report in DDS.

The following code shows the DDS for the sales report. First, you must define one record format for each line or group of lines to be printed in a single output operation. Then, for each of those record formats, you need to specify what fields and/or literals are to be printed as part of that format, what line spacing each format should follow, where within a line the variable or constant data should appear, and what editing (if any) should be associated with the numeric fields.

```
*.. 1 ...+... 2 ...+... 3 ...+... 4 ...+... 5 ...+... 6 ...+... 7 ...+... 8
AAN01N02N03T.Name++++++RLen++TDpBLinPosFunctions+++++++++++++++++++++++++++++
 * Printer file SALESRPT, externally describing the sales report
A               R HEADINGS                    SKIPB(1)
A                                             10DATE EDTCDE(Y)
A                                             22'SALES REPORT'
A                                             37'PAGE'
A                                             42PAGNBR EDTCDE(3)
A                                               SPACEA(2)
A                                             14'SLSPSN.'
A                                             34'AMT.'
A                                               SPACEA(2)
 *
A               R DETAILLINE                    SPACEA(1)
A                 SALESPRSN     4              15
A                 SALESAMT      6 2            32EDTCDE(1)
 *
A               R BREAKLINE                     SPACEB(1) SPACEA(2)
A                                             20'TOTAL'
A                 SLSPTOTAL     6 2            31EDTCDE(1)
A                                             40'*'
 *
A               R TOTALLINE
A                                             16'GRAND TOTAL'
A                 GRANDTOTAL    8 2            30EDTCDE(1)
A                                             40'**'
```

You must begin each record format definition with an R in position 17, followed by the name of the format in positions 19–28. Next, for each record format, you need to define all the information that is to be printed as part of that format. Specify fields in positions 19–28, just as for database files. Constants are coded in positions 45–80 and must be enclosed in apostrophes.

To define each field within the DDS, provide its length in positions 30–34 and, for numeric fields, the number of decimal positions in positions 36–37; blanks in the decimal position columns signal a character field. Thus, in our example, SALESPRSN is defined as a four-byte character field, and SALESAMT is a six-byte numeric field with two decimal positions. Literals, such as 'SALES REPORT' and 'PAGE', are simply entered starting in position 45.

You also need to specify where within the report line each piece of information is to appear. Use positions 42–44 for this purpose. Note that in DDS, unlike in RPG IV, you must specify the field's or constant's beginning position (where it starts within the line), rather than its ending position. Thus, in our example, because SALES REPORT begins in column 22 of the first heading, you code 22 in positions 43–44 of the DDS line for that constant.

DDS handles the system date and the report page numbers a little bit differently than RPG IV does. RPG IV includes built-in variables UDATE and PAGE, which supply the system date and page number, respectively. In DDS, you access the same information through the keywords DATE and PAGNBR. As shown in the example, you enter these keywords on their own lines in DDS.

Edit Codes, Edit Words, and Line Positioning in DDS

The same edit codes and edit words available in RPG IV to change the appearance of numeric output are available within DDS. However, you indicate desired editing through the use of keywords EDTCDE or EDTWRD, followed by the appropriate edit code or word enclosed within parentheses. In our example, DATE will be printed with slashes as a result of the EDTCDE(Y) entry, while fields SALESAMT, SLSPTOTAL, and GRANDTOTAL will be printed with commas and zero balances because of keyword EDTCDE(1). EDTCDE(3) specifies that PAGNBR, a four-digit numeric value, should be zero suppressed and printed without commas.

The easiest way to specify line positioning on a page in DDS is to use four keywords:

- SPACEA
- SPACEB
- SKIPA
- SKIPB

The meaning of these keywords — space after or before and skip after or before — corresponds exactly to the meaning of these terms in RPG IV. You designate the number of lines to space (for SPACEA or SPACEB) or the line to skip to (for SKIPA and SKIPB) within parentheses after the keyword. You can use these keywords at the record level or at the field level. If you want line positioning to change within a record format, you use the appropriate keyword at a field level; if line positioning is to change for the record format as a whole, use the keyword at the record level.

In our example, because we want the headings to begin on the first line of each new page, we use the keyword entry SKIPB(1) at the record format level (that is, on the line containing the R entry or a line immediately following that entry and before any field or constant entry). But recall that record format HEADINGS contains information about two heading lines for our report, and we want to position the second line two lines below the first. In the DDS, the SPACEA(2) keyword entry immediately following the PAGNBR keyword entry produces the desired line spacing; immediately after the page number is printed, the paper is advanced two lines. Printing would then continue with the constant 'SLSPSN.' Note that multiple keywords can appear on the same code line, as shown by the record-level entry SPACEB(1) SPACEA(2) for record format BREAKLINE.

Other optional features of externally described printer files (e.g., changing fonts, printing bar codes, using indicators, defining fields by reference) are beyond the scope of this text. But with this introduction, you should be able to use DDS to externally describe most common types of printed output.

Externally Described Printer Files and RPG

How does external definition of printed output affect an RPG IV program? First, in the File Specification entry for the report file, include the actual name of the printer file, rather than the generic output file QPRINT. In addition, change the file format entry (position 22) to E — for externally described. Last, omit any entry for record length. You can associate an indicator field (or a numbered indicator, 01–99, but not OA–OF or OV) with this file to signal page overflow by using keyword OFLIND and your selected indicator enclosed within parentheses. The following example shows a File Specification for an externally described printer file.

```
*.. 1 ...+... 2 ...+... 3 ...+... 4 ...+... 5 ...+... 6 ...+... 7 ...+... 8
FFilename++IPEASFRLen+LKLen+AIDevice+.Keywords+++++++++++++++++++++++++++++
FSalesRept O    E              PRINTER OFLIND(EndOfPage)
```

The externally described printer file eliminates the need for Output Specifications in your program. How then do you direct the computer to print at the appropriate times as it executes the program? Instead of using the EXCEPT operation, which references lines defined on Output Specifications, you use the WRITE operation, specifying the name of the appropriate record format of your printer file in Factor 2. The following code illustrates the WRITE operation.

```
*.. 1 ...+... 2 ...+... 3 ...+... 4 ...+... 5 ...+... 6 ...+... 7 ...+... 8
CL0N01Factor1++++++Opcode(E)+Factor2++++++Result++++++++Len++D+HiLoEq....
 * Calculation showing output to an externally described printer file
C                    WRITE     Headings
```

Putting It All Together

Now that you have seen how database files and printer files can be externally described and you have a sense of how this approach to file definition affects RPG IV programs, we can rewrite our control-break program from Chapter 5 to take advantage of external definition. First, let's externally define the input file SALESFILE. The DDS for this file is shown in the following example. Because the file is keyed on SALESPRSN, data records later stored in the file will be kept ordered by salesperson number, a necessary condition for our control-break report.

```
*.. 1 ...+... 2 ...+... 3 ...+... 4 ...+... 5 ...+... 6 ...+... 7 ...+... 8
A..........T.Name++++++RLen++TDpB......Functions++++++++++++++++++++++++++++++
 * Definition of physical file SALESFILE
A          R SALESREC
A            SALESPRSN      4A            TEXT('Salesperson number')
A            DEPT           3A            TEXT('Department')
A            SALESAMT       6S2           TEXT('Sales amount')
A            SALEDATE       6S0           TEXT('Date of sale')
A          K SALESPRSN
```

We have already developed the DDS for the printer file SALESRPT.

Note

Remember that you must compile or create an object of each externally described file before it can be used. (Also remember that the physical file initially is empty; you would need to put actual data records into the file before it could meaningfully be used as input.)

With those files externally described, our RPG IV program becomes considerably shorter. In addition, we can now make changes to our report layout or to our data file definition without having to change the RPG IV program, except to recompile it.

```
*.. 1 ...+... 2 ...+... 3 ...+... 4 ...+... 5 ...+... 6 ...+... 7 ...+... 8
 // ****************************************************
 //   This program produces a Sales Report that lists subtotals  *
 //   for each salesperson.                                       *
 //   Author: Yaeger       Date Written:  Dec. 1992               *
 //   Modified Jan 2002 to current RPG IV release. Meyers.        *
 // ****************************************************

FSalesFile IF   E             DISK
FSalesRpt  O    E             PRINTER OFLIND(EndOfPage)

D HoldSlsp        S              4
D SlspTotal       S              6 2
D GrandTotal      S              8 2
D EndOfPage       S              N

ISalesFile NS
I                                     1    4  SalesPrsn
I                                     5    7  Dept
I                                     8   13 2SalesAmt
I                                    14   19 0SaleDate
```

continued…

continued...

```
*.. 1 ...+... 2 ...+... 3 ...+... 4 ...+... 5 ...+... 6 ...+... 7 ...+... 8
 /FREE
  // *************************************************************
  //    Calculations required to produce the Sales Report.
  //    Mainline logic.
  // *************************************************************

   EXSR Initial;

   DOW NOT %EOF(SalesFile);
     IF HoldSlsp <> SalesPrsn;
       EXSR SlspBreak;
     ENDIF;

     EXSR DetailProc;
     READ SalesFile;
   ENDDO;

   EXSR Terminate;
   *INLR = *ON;
   RETURN;

  // *************************************************************
  // Subroutine DetailProc ... executed for each input record.
  // *************************************************************
   BEGSR DetailProc;
     IF EndOfPage;          // If end-of-page, then print headings.
       WRITE Headings;
       EndOfPage = *OFF;
     ENDIF;
     WRITE DetailLine;
     SlspTotal = SlspTotal + SalesAmt;
   ENDSR;

  // *************************************************************
  // Subroutine Initial ... to read first record, set up hold,
  // and print first page headings.
  // *************************************************************
   BEGSR Initial;
     READ SalesFile;
     HoldSlsp = SalesPrsn;
     WRITE Headings;
   ENDSR;

  // *************************************************************
  // Subroutine SlspBreak ... done when salesperson changes;
  // print subtotal, roll over accumulator, zero out accumulator,
  // and reset hold.
  // *************************************************************
   BEGSR SlspBreak;
     WRITE BreakLine;
     GrandTotal = GrandTotal + SlspTotal;
     SlspTotal = 0;
     HoldSlsp = SalesPrsn;
   ENDSR;

  // *************************************************************
  // Subroutine Terminate ... done at end-of-file; execute
  // SlspBreak one last time and print grand-total line.
  // *************************************************************
   BEGSR Terminate;
     EXSR SlspBreak;
     WRITE TotalLine;
   ENDSR;

 /END-FREE
```

Chapter Summary

OS/400 defines data files independently of your programs. Such files, defined through DDS statements, exist as objects on the system and can be used by any program as externally described files. Physical files contain data records, while logical files provide access paths, or pointers, to the physical file records. A logical file is always associated with one or more physical files. Both physical and logical files can contain a key that lets you retrieve records based on the key's value. The key can consist of one or several data fields; in the latter case, the key is called a composite, or concatenation.

A physical file can contain only a single record format or type. Logical files can contain multiple record formats, based on records from two or more physical files. A logical file also can contain a single record format that actually combines data fields stored in different physical files; this kind of file is called a join logical file. You can also use logical files to specify records to be selected for inclusion or omitted from inclusion based on data values of the records in the physical file upon which the logical file is based.

You can use a special kind of physical file, a field reference file, to record field definitions. Physical database files then can reference this file rather than having the field definitions included directly within the physical files themselves.

OS/400 requires you to specify the type of data to be stored within fields. Two data classes the iSeries recognizes are character (or alphanumeric) and numeric. Furthermore, three distinct numeric data formats exist: zoned decimal, packed decimal, and binary. Zoned decimal is easiest to view but takes up the most room on disk. Packed decimal, the data format native to the iSeries, eliminates redundant high-order bits in storing digit values. Both zoned decimal and packed decimal formats use EBCDIC representation. Binary format stores the binary equivalent of a numeric value without first representing the number in EBCDIC.

Database design is an important part of application system design and development. A well-planned database can facilitate application development and maintenance; a poorly designed database can plague programmers for years. Once database files exist, using them within RPG IV programs is simple: Reference the file as externally described on the File Specifications. The system then will import the file's record definition to your program when you compile the program.

Some programmers use externally described printer files to define report formats. This practice offers several advantages: You can change report formats without modifying programs, you can use RLU to design the reports and generate the DDS, and you can eliminate Output Specifications from your programs.

Key Terms

arrival sequence
binary data type
character data type
composite key
concatenation
Data Description Specifications (DDS)
data dictionary
Data File Utility (DFU)
data type
EBCDIC
externally described file
field-level keywords
field reference file
file-level keywords
high-order bits

join logical file
key field
key sequence
keywords
level checking
logical files
low-order bits
packed decimal data type
physical files
record-level keywords
redundancy
Report Layout Utility (RLU)
subschemas
zoned decimal data type

Discussion/Review Questions

1. Explain the advantages of externally describing database files. Do externally described printer files share the same advantages?
2. Explain the difference between a logical file and a physical file.
3. What does concatenation mean? What is a concatenated key?
4. What are the advantages of logical files? Why not just create lots of physical files to store records in different orders or to present different combinations of data fields?
5. How does the system know whether you intend a keyword to be a file-level, record-level, or field-level keyword?
6. Why might you use UNIQUE as a keyword in a physical file?
7. Express the following values in zoned decimal and packed decimal format:
   +362
   −51024
8. How many bytes will it take to store the number 389,241,111 in zoned decimal? In packed decimal? In binary?
9. Provide several practical examples of using logical files.
10. Explain the differences among keywords COMP, RANGE, and VALUES.
11. If Select and Omit specifications were not available in logical file definitions, how could you produce a report that included only the employees of the ACT and MIS departments and excluded other employees?
12. What is a join logical file?
13. Explain the difference between arrival sequence and key sequence of sequential record retrieval.
14. Assume you wanted to write a program that used an externally described logical file that was based on a join of two physical files. What order would you use to create the four objects required to execute the program? Why?

15. Some programmers argue that standards in file and field naming and the use of features such as field reference files reduce their opportunities to be creative and should not be enforced. How would you respond to these people?

Exercises

1. A library wants a database file to store book title; author's last name, first name, and middle initial; catalog number; publisher; date published; number of pages; and number of copies owned. Code a physical file definition to store this data after determining what you believe to be the appropriate fields and the length and type for each field. Consider what the key field (if any) should be and whether use of keyword UNIQUE is appropriate.

2. The library wants to be able to access the catalog information described in Exercise 1 based on author's name. Among other things, staff members want to be able to print out listings by author so that all books by the same author appear together. Define a logical file that enables this kind of access.

3. The library also wants to store a description of each book. Because the books' descriptions vary greatly in length, from a few words to a long paragraph, the person designing the library's database has suggested storing the descriptions in a separate physical file, in which each record contains the catalog number, a description line number, and 40 characters of description. Define this physical file.

4. Define a multiple-record format logical file that combines the information in the physical files from Exercises 1 and 3 so that the initial book information will be followed sequentially by the lines of description, in order, for that book.

5. Define a field reference file for the library based on the data requirements of Exercises 1 and 3, and then rewrite the physical file definitions to take advantage of the field reference file.

Programming Assignments

Note
The following assignments all involve producing reports that either can be defined as part of your RPG IV program or can be described externally; your instructor will tell you which technique to use.

1. This assignment includes several parts.
   a. Create a physical file for Wexler University's student master file (file WUSTDP, in Appendix F). Key this file on student number, and specify that keys be unique.
   b. Enter records in the file, following your instructor's directions.
   c. Design a report for Wexler University that provides a listing of student information. Include student number, first and last name, credits earned, major, date admitted, and grade-point average in your report layout.
   d. Write a program to produce the report you designed in Part c, with your input file the externally described file you defined in Part a. The report should show students listed in order by Social Security number.
   e. Create a logical file over WUSTDP with last name and first name as a concatenated key.

f. Modify your program from Part d to use this logical file as the input file. The resulting report should list the students in alphabetic order by last name and, within last name, by first name.

2. This assignment includes several parts.
   a. Create a physical file for CompuSell's customer master file (file CSCSTP in Appendix F). Key the file on customer number, and specify that keys be unique.
   b. Enter records in the file, following your instructor's directions.
   c. Write a program using the file you created as input to produce the following report. All the customers should be listed, in order of customer number.

```
            1         2         3         4         5         6         7         8         9         10
   1234567890123456789012345678901234567890123456789012345678901234567890123456789012345678901234567890
 1      XX/XX/XX      COMPUSELL REPORT OF CUSTOMER BALANCES         PAGE XX0X
 2
 3         CUST. NO.      FIRST NAME      LAST NAME            BALANCE OWED
 4
 5         XXXXXX         XXXXXXXXXX      XXXXXXXXXXXXXXXX       -X,XX-.XX
 6         XXXXXX         XXXXXXXXXX      XXXXXXXXXXXXXXXX       -X,XX-.XX
 7         XXXXXX         XXXXXXXXXX      XXXXXXXXXXXXXXXX       -X,XX-.XX
 8
 9                                                  TOTAL      $XXX,XX$.XX
10
```

d. Create a logical file over the customer file keyed on last name and, within last name, by first name.

e. Change your program to use the file you created in Part d as the input file. The report should now list customers in name order.

f. Create another logical file over the customer file, this time keyed on balance due and selecting only those customers with a balance greater than zero.

g. Change your program to use the file you created in Part f as the input file. The report should now list customers in balance-owed order and include only those customers who owe the company money.

3. This assignment includes several parts.
   a. Create a physical file for Wexler University's student master file (file WUSTDP, in Appendix F). Key this file on student number, and specify that keys be unique.
   b. Create a physical file for Wexler University's department file (WUDPTP, in Appendix F), keyed on department code.
   c. Enter records in both files, following your instructor's directions.
   d. Create a multiple-record format logical file based on the department file and the student master file, with formats keyed on department code and on department of major and earned credits, respectively.

e. Use the logical file from Part d as an input file to produce the report shown below. Hint: You will have to use control-break logic. You may assume that the student major has been validated, so there will never be a student who does not belong within an existing department. However, there may be departments that do not currently have students enrolled in their programs. In that case, print the message shown in the printer spacing chart. Note that the date admitted should be printed in *mm/dd/yy* format.

```
     1         2         3         4         5         6         7         8         9        10
12345678901234567890123456789012345678901234567890123456789012345678901234567890123456789012345678901234567890
 1  XX/XX/XX              WEXLER U.  DEPARTMENTAL LISTING OF STUDENTS           PAGE XXØX
 2
 3
 4 DEPARTMENT                        STUDENTS
 5           SOC. SEC.    NAME: LAST        FIRST      CREDITS   GPA    DATE ADMIT.
 6
 7 XXXXXXXXXXXXXXXXXXXXX
 8           XXX-XX-XXXX  XXXXXXXXXXXXXXX XXXXXXXXXX    XØX     Ø.XX   XX/XX/XX
 9           XXX-XX-XXXX  XXXXXXXXXXXXXXX XXXXXXXXXX    XØX     Ø.XX   XX/XX/XX
10           XXX-XX-XXXX  XXXXXXXXXXXXXXX XXXXXXXXXX    XØX     Ø.XX   XX/XX/XX
11
12 XXXXXXXXXXXXXXXXXXXXX
13           (NO MAJORS AT THIS TIME)
14
15 XXXXXXXXXXXXXXXXXXXXX
16           XXX-XX-XXXX  XXXXXXXXXXXXXXX XXXXXXXXXX    XØX     Ø.XX   XX/XX/XX
17           XXX-XX-XXXX  XXXXXXXXXXXXXXX XXXXXXXXXX    XØX     Ø.XX   XX/XX/XX
18           XXX-XX-XXXX  XXXXXXXXXXXXXXX XXXXXXXXXX    XØX     Ø.XX   XX/XX/XX
19
```

4. Wexler University wants you to put together a University Catalog that lists all the courses of all departments. The format of the catalog is as follows:

```
     1         2         3         4         5         6         7         8         9        10
12345678901234567890123456789012345678901234567890123456789012345678901234567890123456789012345678901234567890
 1 XXØX
 2             WEXLER UNIVERSITY CATALOG
 3                      20XX
 4
 5 DEPARTMENT
 6 XXXXXXXXXXXXXXXXXXXXXX   CHAIR: XXXXXXXXXXXXXXXXXXXXXXXXXXX
 7     FOR INFORMATION CALL (XXX)XXX-XXXX OR VISIT ROOM XXXXXXXXXX
 8
 9
10 COURSES:
11     XXXXXX  XXXXXXXXXXXXXXXXXXXXXXXXXXXX      X CREDITS
12     XXXXXXXXXXXXXXXXXXXXXXXXXXXXXXXXXXXXXXXXXXXXXXXXX
13     XXXXXXXXXXXXXXXXXXXXXXXXXXXXXXXXXXXXXXXXXXXXXXXXXXXX
14     XXXXXXXXXXXXXXXXXXXXXXXXXXXXXXXXXXXXXXXXXXXXXXXXXX
15
16     XXXXXX  XXXXXXXXXXXXXXXXXXXXXXXXXXXX      X CREDITS
17     XXXXXXXXXXXXXXXXXXXXXXXXXXXXXXXXXXXXXXXXXXXXXXXXXXXX
18     XXXXXXXXXXXXXXXXXXXXXXXXXXXXXXXXXXXXXXXXXXXXXXXXXX
19     XXXXXXXXXXXXXXXXXXXXXXXXXXXXXXXXXXXXXXXXXXXXXXXXXXX
20     XXXXXXXXXXXXXXXXXXXXXXXXXXXXXXXXXXXXXXXXXXXXXXXXXX
21     XXXXXXXXXXXXXXXXXXXXXXXXXXXXXXXXXXXXXXXXXXXXXXXXXX
22
23     XXXXXX  XXXXXXXXXXXXXXXXXXXXXXXXXXXX      X CREDITS
24     XXXXXXXXXXXXXXXXXXXXXXXXXXXXXXXXXXXXXXXXXXXXXXXXXXXX
25     XXXXXXXXXXXXXXXXXXXXXXXXXXXXXXXXXXXXXXXXXXXXXXXXXXXXX
```

You will need to do the following to generate the catalog:

a. Create three physical files: one for the department file (WUDPTP), one for the course file (WUCRSP), and one for the course description file (WUCRSDSP). Appendix F describes the layouts of these files.

b. Put records in the files, following your instructor's directions.

c. Create a multiple-record format logical file over the three physical files.

d. Use the file to generate the catalog. You can assume that every course belongs to a department and that every department offers at least one course. However, some courses may not have a description.

Start each department on a new page. Use the system year in the catalog heading. Each course is identified by a course identification consisting of the department code and the course number; the course title follows the identification.

Chapter 7

File Access and Record Manipulation

Chapter Overview

This chapter introduces you to RPG IV's operations for reading, writing, and updating records. You will learn both sequential and random file-access techniques. The chapter also discusses file maintenance — adding, deleting, and changing records in a file — and record-locking considerations in update procedures.

Operations for Input Files

File access refers to how records can be retrieved, or read, from an input file. RPG IV offers several alternative operations for accessing data from full-procedural database files. Several of these operations are appropriate for sequential processing; you can use others for random access processing.

Sequential Access

In **sequential access**, records are retrieved in either key order, if the file is keyed and it is so noted in column 34 on the File Specifications, or in arrival, or first-in-first-out (FIFO), order for non-keyed files. Reading generally starts with the first record in the file, with each subsequent read operation retrieving the next record in the file until eventually you reach end-of-file. This kind of sequential access is especially suited for batch processing.

READ (Read a Record)

As you know, the READ (Read a Record) operation retrieves records sequentially. A file name in Factor 2 designates which file the READ accesses. You can code the %EOF built-in function to signal end-of-file when the READ finds no additional records in the file. (When you code the %EOF function, you can name a specific file in parentheses after the function; if you omit the file name, the %EOF function refers to the most recent file operation.) The following example demonstrates the use of READ and %EOF.

```
*.. 1 ...+... 2 ...+... 3 ...+... 4 ...+... 5 ...+... 6 ...+... 7 ...+... 8
 /FREE
    READ CustMast;
    IF %EOF(CustMast);
       // End-of-file processing goes here
    ENDIF;
 /END-FREE
```

For externally described files, Factor 2 can actually be a record format name rather than a file name. However, if the READ encounters a record format different from that named in Factor 2 — as could be the case when the input file is a logical file with multiple formats — the operation ends in error. You can optionally code an (E) operation code extender to detect such errors; you then use the %ERROR built-in function to handle them, as shown below, or you can use other error-handling techniques (discussed in Chapter 12). The (E) extender signals to RPG that you will be checking for the %ERROR built-in function. The %ERROR function is always turned on if the most recent operation code specified with an (E) extender resulted in an error.

```
*.. 1 ...+... 2 ...+... 3 ...+... 4 ...+... 5 ...+... 6 ...+... 7 ...+... 8
/FREE
   READ(E) CustRecord;
   IF %ERROR;
     EXSR ErrorSR;
   ENDIF;

   IF %EOF(CustMast);
     // End-of-file processing goes here
   ENDIF;
/END-FREE
```

Caution

If your program does not include some way to handle this kind of error, the program will terminate before reaching its normal ending point after issuing an error message. (This kind of abnormal ending is often called an *abend*.) Accordingly, unless you have a specific reason for reading a record format rather than the file, and unless you explicitly want to include an error handler, you are better off using a file name as Factor 2.

RPG IV includes additional operations that provide variations on sequential record access. Some of these operations control where in the file sequential reading will next occur; others determine the nature of the reading itself.

SETLL (Set Lower Limit)

The SETLL (Set Lower Limit) operation provides flexibility related to where sequential reading occurs within a file. SETLL lets you begin sequential processing at a record other than the first one in the file. It also can be used to reposition the file once end-of-file has been reached. The general format of a SETLL operation is

```
*.. 1 ...+... 2 ...+... 3 ...+... 4 ...+... 5 ...+... 6 ...+... 7 ...+... 8
/FREE
   SETLL Factor1 Factor2;                    // General format of SETLL
/END-FREE
```

SETLL positions a file at the first record whose key is greater than or equal to the value specified in Factor 1. Factor 1 can be a literal, field name, figurative constant, or KLIST name (we describe KLISTs later in this chapter). Factor 2 can be a file name or record format name (if the file is externally described).

You can use the %FOUND built-in function with SETLL; %FOUND is turned on if there is a record in the file that has a key equal to or greater than the value in Factor 1. The %EQUAL built-in function is turned on if a record is found whose key exactly matches the value of Factor 1.

To detect a system error that might occur upon execution of the SETLL operation, you can include the (E) extender and the %ERROR function when you use SETLL:

```
*.. 1 ...+... 2 ...+... 3 ...+... 4 ...+... 5 ...+... 6 ...+... 7 ...+... 8
/FREE
    SETLL(E) CustIn CustMast;
    SELECT;
      WHEN %ERROR(CustMast);
        EXSR SystemErr;
      WHEN %EQUAL(CustMast);
        EXSR ExactMatch;
      WHEN %FOUND(CustMast);
        EXSR GTMatch;
      OTHER;
        EXSR ValueTooHi;
    ENDSL;
/END-FREE
```

The SETLL operation does not actually retrieve a record; it simply positions the file to determine which record the next sequential read will access. An unsuccessful SETLL causes the file to be positioned at end-of-file.

SETLL has two common uses in RPG IV programming. The first is to reposition the file to the beginning during processing by using figurative constant *LOVAL as Factor 1. The next sequential read operation then retrieves the first record in the file:

```
*.. 1 ...+... 2 ...+... 3 ...+... 4 ...+... 5 ...+... 6 ...+... 7 ...+... 8
/FREE
  // Using SETLL to position pointer to first record in file
  // for subsequent read
    SETLL *LOVAL CustMast;
    READ CustMast;
/END-FREE
```

The second common use of SETLL is to position the file to the first record of a group of records with identical key values in preparation for processing that group of records. (We discuss details of this use when we cover the READE operation.)

You also can use SETLL to determine whether a record exists in a file without actually reading the record. If you simply need to check for the presence of a record with a given key without accessing the data contained in the record, using SETLL is more efficient than doing a READ operation:

```
*.. 1 ...+... 2 ...+... 3 ...+... 4 ...+... 5 ...+... 6 ...+... 7 ...+... 8
/FREE
  // Using SETLL to determine whether a record exists in a file
    SETLL CustIn CustMast;
    IF %EQUAL(CustMast);
      EXSR CustFound;
    ELSE;
      EXSR NoCustomer;
    ENDIF;
/END-FREE
```

SETGT (Set Greater Than)

The SETGT (Set Greater Than) operation works similarly to SETLL. The primary difference is that this operation positions the file to a record whose key value is greater than the value of Factor 1, rather than greater than or equal to the value of Factor 1. The SETGT operation takes the following general format.

```
*.. 1 ...+... 2 ...+... 3 ...+... 4 ...+... 5 ...+... 6 ...+... 7 ...+... 8
 /FREE
    SETGT Factor1 Factor2;
 /END-FREE
```

As with the SETLL operation, Factor 1 can be a field, literal, figurative constant, or KLIST; Factor 2 can be a file name or a record format name. You can use the %FOUND function, which is turned on if the positioning is successful, or code NOT %FOUND to detect unsuccessful positioning (in which case the file would be positioned at end-of-file). The %ERROR function is turned on if an error occurs during the operation, if you remember to use the (E) extender. The %EQUAL function does not apply to SETGT.

```
*.. 1 ...+... 2 ...+... 3 ...+... 4 ...+... 5 ...+... 6 ...+... 7 ...+... 8
 /FREE
    SETGT(E) CustIn CustMast;              // Demonstrating the use of SETGT
    SELECT;
      WHEN %ERROR;
        EXSR SystemErr;
      WHEN %FOUND(CustMast);
        EXSR GTMatch;
      OTHER;
        EXSR ValueTooHi;
    ENDSL;
 /END-FREE
```

To understand the value of the SETGT operation, assume you have a logical file over your orders file, keyed on order date in *yyyymmdd* format and you want to generate a report of orders from the last six months of 1999. If you use the SETGT operation with June 30 as the Factor 1 value, the system will position the file to the first record of July, regardless of what date that happens to be. The following code illustrates this example.

```
*.. 1 ...+... 2 ...+... 3 ...+... 4 ...+... 5 ...+... 6 ...+... 7 ...+... 8
 /FREE
 // Orders file keyed on date;
 // code uses SETGT to process all orders placed after June 30, 1999.
    SETGT 19990630 Orders;
    READ Orders;
    DOW NOT %EOF(Orders);
      . . .
      READ Orders;
    ENDDO;
 /END-FREE
```

SETGT is also used with figurative constant *HIVAL to position a file to end-of-file in preparation for a READP operation (which we discuss in a moment). Remember that a SETGT, like a SETLL, merely positions the file; it does not actually retrieve a record from the database.

READE (Read Equal Key)

The READE (Read Equal Key) operation sequentially reads the next record in a full-procedural file if the key of that record matches the value in Factor 1. If the record's key does not match, or if the file is at end-of-file, the %EOF function is turned on. You can also use the (E) extender and the %ERROR function to signal the occurrence of an error during the operation.

Factor 1 can be a field, literal, figurative constant, or KLIST name. Factor 2 can be a file name or a record format name.

Programmers use the READE operation within a loop to identically process sets of records with duplicate keys in a file. Programmers often precede the first READE with a SETLL operation to position the file initially, in preparation for processing those records with keys identical to the value specified by the SETLL.

Assume, for example, that you want to list all orders received on a specific date and that the order file is keyed on date. Further assume that field InDate stores the date whose orders are to be printed. The following processing would be appropriate.

```
*.. 1 ...+... 2 ...+... 3 ...+... 4 ...+... 5 ...+... 6 ...+... 7 ...+... 8
 /FREE
   // Code to list all orders placed on InDate
     SETLL InDate Orders;
     IF %EQUAL;
       READE InDate Orders;
       DOW NOT %EOF(Orders);
         EXCEPT OrderLine;
         READE InDate Orders;
       ENDDO;
     ELSE;
       EXCEPT NoOrders;
     ENDIF;
 /END-FREE
```

This code uses the value of InDate to position the Orders file to a key value that matches that of InDate. If a match exists, the %EQUAL function is turned on, and the program does an initial READE of the file and then sets up a loop with a DOW operation; within the loop, the program uses EXCEPT to write an order line and then reads the next equal record. The loop is continued as long as the READE is successful. If the initial SETLL fails (signaled by %EQUAL being off), flow bypasses the loop, drops down to the ELSE, and writes a "no orders" line using EXCEPT.

READP (Read Prior Record) and READPE (Read Prior Equal)

The READP (Read Prior Record) and READPE (Read Prior Equal) operations are sequential reading operations that have their parallels in READ and READE, respectively. The only difference between READP and READ, and between READPE and READE, is directionality; the Prior operations move "backwards" through the file. Like READE, READPE requires a Factor 1 entry; both Prior operations require a Factor 2 entry, which can be a file name or a record format name.

Like READ and READE, both READP and READPE support the %EOF function. This function is turned on at beginning-of-file (not end-of-file) for READP or when the key of the prior sequential record does not match the Factor 1 value for READPE. With both operations, you have the option to use the (E) extender with the %ERROR function.

Before using READP or READPE with a blank Factor 1, you must first position the file with some input operation. Programmers often use a SETGT operation for this initial positioning before beginning the reverse transversal through the file.

The concept of "backwards" sequential access is relatively easy to grasp; it is harder to visualize why such processing might be desired. To get a sense of when these operations might be appropriate, let's consider an example.

Imagine the following scenario. As part of an order-processing application, a program is to assign order numbers sequentially. Each day the program is run, the number assigned to the first order number is to be one larger than the number of the last order processed the previous day. Assume also that the order file is keyed on order number. The following code will determine the appropriate starting value for the day's orders.

```
*.. 1 ...+... 2 ...+... 3 ...+... 4 ...+... 5 ...+... 6 ...+... 7 ...+... 8
/FREE
  // Code using SETGT and READP to determine the next order number to use.
  // Orders file is keyed on field Order#.
    SETGT *HIVAL Orders;
    READP Orders;
    IF NOT %EOF(Orders);
      Order# = Order# + 1;
    ELSE;
      EXSR Error;
    ENDIF;
/END-FREE
```

In this code, SETGT positions the file at end-of-file. The READP operation retrieves the last record in the file (e.g., the record with the highest order number). Adding 1 to Order#, then, gives you the value for the first new order of the day. If %EOF is turned on, it indicates that you are at beginning-of-file, which means no records exist in the order file; in this case, an error routine should be performed.

In general, you might use the Prior read operations any time you want to process files in descending key order because ordinarily OS/400 organizes keyed files in sequence by ascending key value.

Random Access

All the operations we've discussed so far in this chapter deal with retrieving database records sequentially. Often, however, you want to be able to read a specific record, determined by its key value, without having to read through the file sequentially to reach that record. This kind of access is called **random access**. Random access lets you "reach into" a file and extract just the record you want. RPG IV supports random access of full-procedural database files through the CHAIN operation.

CHAIN (Random Retrieval from a File)

The CHAIN (Random Retrieval from a File) operation requires a Factor 1 entry. The literal or data-item name of Factor 1 contains the key value of the record to be randomly read. Factor 2, also required, contains the name of the file (or record format) from which the record is to be randomly retrieved. The %FOUND function is turned on if the random read is successful — that is, if a record in the file matches the specified key value of Factor 1. You can optionally include the (E) extender and the %ERROR function.

```
*.. 1 ...+... 2 ...+... 3 ...+... 4 ...+... 5 ...+... 6 ...+... 7 ...+... 8
/FREE
    CHAIN CustNbr CustMaster;
    IF %FOUND(CustMaster);
      EXSR CustFound;
    ELSE;
      EXSR NoCust;
    ENDIF;
/END-FREE
```

In the example shown above, CustNbr contains the key value of the CustMaster record you want to read. If the CHAIN finds a record, the program executes subroutine CustFound; if the record is not found, the program executes subroutine NoCust. If the file contains records with duplicate keys, such that more than one record would qualify as a match, the system retrieves the first record that matches.

If the CHAIN is successful (signaled by the %FOUND function), the system positions the file to the record immediately following the retrieved record. Accordingly, issuing a READ or READE to the file following a successful CHAIN results in sequentially accessing the file starting with the record immediately following the CHAINed record. Because of this feature, you can use the CHAIN operation to position the file in a manner similar to SETLL. The primary difference between these two approaches is that a successful CHAIN actually reads a record, whereas a successful SETLL merely repositions the file without retrieving a record.

If a CHAIN operation is unsuccessful, you cannot follow it with a sequential read operation without first successfully repositioning the file with another CHAIN, SETLL, or SETGT operation.

Referencing Composite Keys

As we discussed in Chapter 6, both physical and logical files can have keys based on more than one field. This kind of key is called a **composite key** or a **concatenated key**. The existence of composite keys raises a puzzling question: What can you use as a Factor 1 search argument for CHAIN, SETLL, READE, and so on when the records in the file you are trying to access are keyed on more than one field value? In other words, how can you indicate a corresponding composite value in a single data-item entry? RPG IV solves this problem with the KLIST operation.

KLIST (Define a Composite Key) and KFLD (Define Parts of a Key)

The KLIST (Define a Composite Key) operation lets you define a field for accessing records based on a composite key. Factor 1 specifies the name you want to give the KLIST. No entries other than Factor 1 are used with KLIST.

At least one KFLD (Define Parts of a Key) operation must immediately follow a KLIST operation. Each KFLD entry declares a field that is to participate in the concatenation; the field is entered as the Result field of the operation. The order in which the KFLDs are listed determines the order in which they are concatenated to form the KLIST.

The free-format specification does not support the KLIST and KFLD operations. You must code them in traditional Calculation Specifications. Most programmers consider it good style to define KLIST entries among the first lines of the Calculation Specifications, near other declarations in the Definition Specifications and the Input Specifications.

To understand how to form and use KLISTs, consider the following example. Assume you have a database file of student grades, StudGrades, which contains one record per student per course taken. The records contain four fields — StudNbr, CrseNbr, Grade, and Semester — and the file has a composite key based on StudNbr, Semester, and CrseNbr. You are writing a program that requires you to randomly access the StudGrades file to retrieve a grade that a given student received in a given class. The student, semester, and course you want to find are stored in fields Student, Smster, and Course, respectively.

```
*.. 1 ...+... 2 ...+... 3 ...+... 4 ...+... 5 ...+... 6 ...+... 7 ...+... 8
CLØN01Factor1+++++++Opcode(E)+Factor2+++++++Result+++++++Len++D+HiLoEq....
C     StdSemCrs     KLIST
C                   KFLD                      Student
C                   KFLD                      Smster
C                   KFLD                      Course
 . . .
 /FREE
   CHAIN StdSemCrs StudGrades;
 /END-FREE
```

In the code shown above, StdSemCrs is the KLIST name that stores the combined values of student number (Student), semester (Smster), and course (Course). That KLIST is then used to chain to the StudGrades file.

The KFLDs can have, but do not need to have, the same names as those of the file records' composite key. However, each KFLD field must agree in length, type, and number of decimal positions with the field it corresponds to in the file's composite key. Each KFLD is associated with a composite key field based on the ordinal positions of the corresponding fields. That is, the first KFLD field is matched to the first (or high-order) field of the composite key, and so on.

KLIST and KFLD are declarative operations, providing definitions rather than executable operations. You can use the same KLIST name to access different database files — provided it is appropriate to do so. You can also use one KLIST multiple times to access the same file within a program. A KLIST name can serve as the Factor 1 value in CHAIN, READE, READPE, SETLL, SETGT, and DELETE operations.

Partial Key Lists

KLIST offers an additional feature that makes processing groups of logically associated records relatively simple. Let's use the previous example, but this time, instead of wanting information about a grade for one course for one student, assume you want to be able to access all the records in StudGrades for a particular student for a given semester, perhaps to print out his or her grades earned that semester. The following code accomplishes the desired processing.

```
*.. 1 ...+... 2 ...+... 3 ...+... 4 ...+... 5 ...+... 6 ...+... 7 ...+... 8
CLØNØ1Factor1++++++Opcode(E)+Factor2++++++Result++++++++Len++D+HiLoEq....
  // Define a partial KLIST.
C      StudSmster    KLIST
C                    KFLD                      Student
C                    KFLD                      Smster

 /FREE
  // Use KLIST to access correct student and semester.
    CHAIN StudSmster StudGrades;
    IF %FOUND(StudGrades);
      // Loop through records for that student/semester.
      DOW NOT %EOF(StudGrades);
        EXSR PrintGrade;
        // READE sets %EOF when no more records are found
        // for that student/semester.
        READE StudSmster StudGrades;
      ENDDO;
    ELSE;
      EXSR NoGrades;
    ENDIF;
 /END-FREE
```

This code first defines KLIST StudSmster with only the student number and semester as the KFLDs of the list. StudSmster, then, is a *partial KLIST*, because the file it will be used with is keyed on a composite of student number, semester, and course number.

Using StudSmster, the program chains to the StudGrades file to read the first course for the given student in the given semester. If the CHAIN finds a record, the program sets up a loop that continues until %EOF comes on for StudGrades. Within the loop, the program executes subroutine PrintGrade to print grades and then executes a READE to bring in the next course for the student being processed. If the original CHAIN fails, control drops to the ELSE and the program executes subroutine NoGrades to indicate that the student/semester was not in the file.

Note that we could have achieved the same effects by issuing a SETLL to position the file and then, provided the operation was successful, using a READE to read the first record of the set. A successful CHAIN reads a record and positions the file to the desired location in one operation.

RPG IV lets you access a database file based on a partial key list provided the portion you want to use is the major, or high-order, key field (or fields). That is, given StudGrades keyed on StudNbr + Semester + CrseNbr, we can access the records with a partial key of student, or of student and semester, but not with a partial key of course or semester. Thus, we can get a list of all courses for a given student but not a list of all students who have taken a given course; the database file would need to be keyed differently, perhaps using a logical file, to allow this kind of access.

Version 5 Release 2 Update

Programmers can now avoid using the KLIST (Define a Composite Key) and KFLD (Define Parts of a Key) operations to specify key lists. The CHAIN (Random Retrieval from a File), SETLL (Set Lower Limit), READE (Read Equal Key), and READPE (Read Prior Equal) operations now support coding a list of fields or expressions instead of a single field or a KLIST name, as the following example illustrates.

```
*.. 1 ...+... 2 ...+... 3 ...+... 4 ...+... 5 ...+... 6 ...+... 7 ...+... 8
 /FREE
    CHAIN (Student:Smster) StudGrades;
 /END-FREE
```

As an alternative, you can specify a data structure containing the key fields and then refer to the data structure using the %KDS (Key Data Structure) function. The following code defines a data structure called StudSmstr and then uses it as a key to CHAIN to the StudGrades file.

```
*.. 1 ...+... 2 ...+... 3 ...+... 4 ...+... 5 ...+... 6 ...+... 7 ...+... 8
DName++++++++++ETDsFrom+++To/Len+IDc.Keywords+++++++++++++++++++++++++++++
D StudSmstr       DS
D   Student                       9 0
D   Smster                        1 0
D   Course                        5

 /FREE
    CHAIN %KDS(StudSmstr) StudGrades;
 /END-FREE
```

If you want to specify a partial key, you can code a second argument to the %KDS function to tell it how many key fields to use (only Student and Smster in the following example):

```
*.. 1 ...+... 2 ...+... 3 ...+... 4 ...+... 5 ...+... 6 ...+... 7 ...+... 8
 /FREE
    CHAIN %KDS(StudSmstr:2) StudGrades;
 /END-FREE
```

In connection with this support, V5R2 also enhances the EXTNAME keyword, to let you define an externally described data structure that will automatically extract just the key fields from a record format, eliminating the necessity to key the subfields explicitly. The following code would create a data structure identical to the program-described data structure:

```
*.. 1 ...+... 2 ...+... 3 ...+... 4 ...+... 5 ...+... 6 ...+... 7 ...+... 8
DName++++++++++ETDsFrom+++To/Len+IDc.Keywords+++++++++++++++++++++++++++++
D StudSmstr    E DS                  EXTNAME(StudGrades:*KEY)
```

Operations for Output Files

The operations we've looked at so far are appropriate for input files. A few input/output (I/O) operations deal with output — that is, writing records to database files. Until now, the output of your programs has been reports, but you can also designate a database file as program output. The File Specification entries in this case require the file name in positions 7–16; the type, O for output, in position 17; an E in position 22 (assuming the file is externally described); a K in position 34 (if the file is accessed via a key); and DISK, the device specification, in positions 36–42:

```
*.. 1 ...+... 2 ...+... 3 ...+... 4 ...+... 5 ...+... 6 ...+... 7 ...+... 8
FFilename++IPEASFRlen+LKlen+AIDevice+.Keywords+++++++++++++++++++++++++++++++
   // File specification for a program that writes records to a new file
FCustMast  O   E          K DISK
```

You may need to make one additional entry in the File Specification, depending on whether your program is performing an initial file load — that is, putting records into the file for the first time — or adding records to a file that already contains records. If you are adding records to an output file that already contains records, you must signal that fact by entering an A in position 20 of the File Specification:

```
*.. 1 ...+... 2 ...+... 3 ...+... 4 ...+... 5 ...+... 6 ...+... 7 ...+... 8
FFilename++IPEASFRlen+LKlen+AIDevice+.Keywords+++++++++++++++++++++++++++++++
   // File specification for a program that adds records
   // to those already in a file
FCustMast  O A E          K DISK
```

Once you've defined a database file as output, two RPG IV operations let you output records to the file: EXCEPT and WRITE.

EXCEPT (Calculation Time Output)

You have already used the EXCEPT (Calculation Time Output) operation to write to printer files; you can also use EXCEPT to write records to a database file. The form of the EXCEPT statement used to write to database files is no different than the form used for printer files.

The EXCEPT operation optionally can designate a named E line on the output. When the program reaches the EXCEPT operation, it writes the named E lines (if the EXCEPT includes a line name in Factor 2) or all unnamed E lines (if the EXCEPT operation appears alone on the Calculation Specification) from the Output Specifications.

In the Output Specifications, you need to enter the record format name of the externally described file, rather than the file name itself, in positions 7–16. Then either list all the fields composing the record or simply specify *ALL. Omitting a field or fields from the list causes either zeros or blanks (depending on the data type) to be written to the record for that field. Rather than listing all the fields, you can simply code *ALL, which has the same effect as including all the field names.

```
*.. 1 ...+... 2 ...+... 3 ...+... 4 ...+... 5 ...+... 6 ...+... 7 ...+... 8
OFilename++DF..N01N02N03Excnam++++B++A++Sb+Sa+............................
 /FREE
    EXCEPT Record;              // Writing to a database file with EXCEPT
 /END-FREE
                                // Exception lines for an initial file load
OCustRecordE        Record
O                   *ALL
```

The code shown above demonstrates how you could write records to a customer file for an initial file load. If you wanted to add records to records already in a file, you would need to include an ADD entry in positions 18–20 of the Output Specification E line, as shown below, in addition to entering an A in position 20 of the File Specification.

```
*.. 1 ...+... 2 ...+... 3 ...+... 4 ...+... 5 ...+... 6 ...+... 7 ...+... 8
OFilename++DF..NØ1NØ2NØ3Excnam++++B++A++Sb+Sa+.............................
                       // Exception line for adding records to an existing file
OCustRecordEADD        Record
O                      *ALL
```

WRITE (Write a Record to a File)

Today's RPG IV programmers generally output database records more directly in their calculations by using the WRITE operation. The WRITE operation must designate a record format name rather than a file name.

```
*.. 1 ...+... 2 ...+... 3 ...+... 4 ...+... 5 ...+... 6 ...+... 7 ...+... 8
 /FREE
    WRITE CustRecord;        // Writing a record to database file CustMaster
 /END-FREE
```

If the writing is adding records to a file that already contains records, the A in position 20 of the File Specification for that file is required.

With a WRITE operation, the current program values for all the fields making up the record definition are written to the file. You can include the (E) extender and the %ERROR function with this operation to signal an error.

Update Files and I/O Operations

A common data-processing task is file maintenance. File maintenance, or updating, involves adding or deleting records from database files, or changing the information in database records, to keep the information current and correct. Records that do not exist cannot be changed or deleted; if a file has unique keys, a second record with the same key should not be added to the file. Accordingly, file maintenance routines typically require first determining whether the record exists in the file (through a CHAIN or SETLL) and then determining what update option is valid, given the record's found status.

RPG IV includes an update file type, signaled by U in position 17 of the File Specifications, which lets you read, change, and then rewrite records to the file, as well as add and delete entire records. You can use any database file as an update file simply by coding it as such in the File Specifications. If the maintenance procedure involves adding new records, you must signal that fact in the File Specifications by entering an A (for Add) in position 20.

An update file supports both input and output operations. If you define a file as an update full-procedural file, you can use all the input operations we've discussed so far — CHAIN, READ, READE, READP, READPE, SETLL, and SETGT — to access records in the file. You also can use KLIST for externally described update files. If you defined the file for add capability (the A on the File Specifications), you can use the WRITE operation to add new records to the file. Two additional I/O operations can be used only for update files: DELETE and UPDATE.

DELETE (Delete Record)

The DELETE (Delete Record) operation deletes a single record from the file specified in Factor 2. Factor 2 can be a file name or, if the file is externally described, a record format name. The use of Factor 1 is optional. If you leave Factor 1 blank, the system deletes the record most recently read. If you use Factor 1 to specify which record is to be deleted, you can enter a field name, a literal, or a KLIST name. If duplicate records based on the Factor 1 value exist in the file, the system deletes only the first record.

If you code an entry in Factor 1, you should use the NOT %FOUND function to detect instances wherein the record to be deleted is not found in the file. DELETE also supports the optional (E) extender with the %ERROR function.

```
*.. 1 ...+... 2 ...+... 3 ...+... 4 ...+... 5 ...+... 6 ...+... 7 ...+... 8
/FREE
    // This code deletes the record of customer 100 if the record exists
    // in the file.
    CustNbr = '100';
    CHAIN CustNbr CustMaster;
    IF %FOUND(CustMaster);
      DELETE CustMaster;
    ENDIF;

    // The lines below produce the same result as the code above.
    CustNbr = '100';
    DELETE(E) CustNbr CustMaster;
    IF %ERROR(CustMaster);
      // Error processing goes here
    ENDIF;
/END-FREE
```

Note
Note that if you use DELETE without Factor 1 and without first retrieving a record from the file, you will get a system error message.

The DELETE operation logically deletes records from a file rather than physically removing them. Although as a result of DELETE a record is no longer accessible to programs or queries, the record actually remains on disk until the file containing the deleted record is reorganized.

UPDATE (Modify Existing Record)

The UPDATE (Modify Existing Record) operation modifies the record most recently read. You can use this operation only with files defined for update. This operation does not use Factor 1; if the file is externally described, Factor 2 must contain a record format name, not a file name. Moreover, your program must have successfully completed a READ, READE, READP, READPE, or CHAIN operation to retrieve that record format before it executes an UPDATE.

UPDATE causes the current program values of all the record's fields to be rewritten to the file. The typical procedure involving UPDATE is to retrieve a record, change one or more of its fields' values, and then use UPDATE to rewrite the record with its new values. You cannot issue multiple UPDATEs for a single read operation; each UPDATE must be preceded by a record retrieval.

```
*.. 1 ...+... 2 ...+... 3 ...+... 4 ...+... 5 ...+... 6 ...+... 7 ...+... 8
/FREE
    // Retrieve the customer record, add the current invoice amount to the
    // customer's balance due, and rewrite the record to the file.
    // If the customer is not in the file, perform an error routine.
    CHAIN CustNbr CustMaster;
    IF %FOUND(CustMaster);
      BalanceDue = BalanceDue + InvoiceAmt;
      UPDATE CustRecord;
    ELSE;
      EXSR NoCustomer;
    ENDIF;
/END-FREE
```

Updating Through EXCEPT

The UPDATE operation rewrites all of a database record's fields to a file. In the previous example, the current value of BalanceDue and every other field in CustRecord is incorporated into the record by the UPDATE. If your program logic has resulted in changes in field values that you do not want to be updated, you can use the EXCEPT operation to designate which fields are to be rewritten:

```
*.. 1 ...+... 2 ...+... 3 ...+... 4 ...+... 5 ...+... 6 ...+... 7 ...+... 8
OFilename++DF..NØ1NØ2NØ3Excnam++++B++A++Sb+Sa+.........................

/FREE
   // Retrieve the customer record, add the current invoice amount to the
   // customer's balance due, and rewrite via EXCEPT.
   // If the customer is not in the file, perform an error routine.
   CHAIN CustNbr CustMaster;
   IF %FOUND(CustMaster);
     BalanceDue = BalanceDue + InvoiceAmt;
     EXCEPT CustRewrit;
   ELSE;
     EXSR NoCustomer;
   ENDIF;
/END-FREE

   // Only the balance due field is updated to the file; other fields of the
   // customer record will retain whatever values they originally had when
   // the record was read, regardless of how their values have been changed
   // within the program.

OCustRecordE           CustRewrit
O                      BalanceDue
```

File and Record Locking

Any multiuser system needs to address the problems related to simultaneous use of the same database file. Otherwise, it is possible that if two users access the same record for update, make changes in the record, and then rewrite it to the file, one of the user's changes might get lost — a condition sometimes called **phantom updates**. Two approaches you can use to deal with this type of problem are **file locking** and **record locking**.

The easiest kind of locking is to limit access to a file to one user at a time — a condition known as file locking. Although OS/400 permits you to lock files at a system level by issuing CL commands,

Version 5 Release 2 Update

RPG IV's UPDATE (Modify Existing Record) operation now lets you update only selected fields in externally described files; previously you could do this only by using the EXCEPT operation and Output Specifications. The %FIELDS built-in function lets you list those fields that you want to update; all others will not be updated. For example, the following code would change only the BalanceDue and CreditFlag fields in the CustRecord record. The other fields would retain whatever values they originally had when the record was read, regardless of how their values had been changed within the program.

```
*.. 1 ...+... 2 ...+... 3 ...+... 4 ...+... 5 ...+... 6 ...+... 7 ...+... 8
/FREE
     UPDATE CustRecord %FIELDS(BalanceDue:CreditFlag);
/END-FREE
```

most of the time you want to allow multiple users access to the same files at the same time. RPG IV includes built-in, automatic locking features at a record level.

If your program designates a file as an update file, RPG IV *automatically* places a lock on a record when it is read within your program. Updating that record or reading another record releases the record from its locked state. While the record is locked, other application programs can access the record if they have defined the file as an input file but not if they, too, have defined the file as an update file. This solution eliminates the problem of lost updates.

However, record locking can cause waiting and access problems for users if programmers don't structure their code to avoid locks except when absolutely necessary. The nightmare scenario you should keep in mind when designing update programs is that of the user who keys in a request to update a record, pulls up the screen of data preparatory to making changes in the record, and then realizes it's lunch time and disappears for an hour. Meanwhile, the record lock prevents all other users from accessing the record.

One solution to this problem lies with operation extender (N), which you can use with READ, READE, READP, READPE, and CHAIN to specify that the input operation to an update file be done without locking the record. You can use this feature to avoid unnecessary locking. Another, less common, solution is the UNLOCK (Unlock a Data Area or Release a Record) operation. If you've read a record with a lock and want to release the lock, you can use this operation along with a file name in Factor 2 to release all locks to that file.

```
*.. 1 ...+... 2 ...+... 3 ...+... 4 ...+... 5 ...+... 6 ...+... 7 ...+... 8
/FREE
   // Random read of an update file automatically locks the record.
   CHAIN CustNbr CustMaster;

   // Random read of an update file with operation extender (N)
   // keeps the record unlocked.
   CHAIN(N) CustNbr CustMaster;

   // Release all current record locks for CustMaster.
   UNLOCK CustMaster;
/END-FREE
```

If you start releasing record locks in update procedures, however, be aware that you can easily code yourself right back into the phantom-update problem that caused systems to incorporate record locking in the first place. If you aren't including some provision that checks to make sure another user has not updated a record between the time you first accessed the record and the time you are about to rewrite the record with the values from your program, leave all record locking in place.

Beyond record-locking considerations, generally accepted programming practice dictates that a program should not keep a file open any longer than it needs to access the required data from the file. RPG IV automatically opens your files at the beginning of processing and then closes them all at the end of processing. If your program needs access to a file for only a portion of its total running time, you should take control of the file opening and closing rather than letting RPG IV manage those tasks for you. RPG IV includes two operations to give you this capability, OPEN and CLOSE:

```
*.. 1 ...+... 2 ...+... 3 ...+... 4 ...+... 5 ...+... 6 ...+... 7 ...+... 8
/FREE
   OPEN CustMaster;                    // Explicitly opening file CustMaster.

   CLOSE CustMaster;                   // Explicitly closing file CustMaster.
/END-FREE
```

You can close a file that RPG IV opened automatically. If you want to control the file opening with the OPEN operation, you must make an additional entry within the File Specification for the file you want to open. Keyword USROPN (User Open), coded in the Keywords area of the specification line, prevents the file from being implicitly opened by RPG IV and signals that the opening of the file will be explicitly coded within the program:

```
*.. 1 ...+... 2 ...+... 3 ...+... 4 ...+... 5 ...+... 6 ...+... 7 ...+... 8
FFilename++IPEASFRlen+LKlen+AIDevice+.Keywords+++++++++++++++++++++++++++++++
   // File is an update file, with record addition possible.
   // File opening is user-controlled.
FCustMasterUF A E          K DISK      USROPN
```

Trying to open a file that's already open causes an error. However, you can open a given file more than once within a program, provided the file is closed before each successive open.

I/O Errors

All the operations discussed above support the optional use of the (E) operation code extender in conjunction with the %ERROR built-in function to detect errors of input or output, such as trying to read a record locked by another program or issuing a read to a record format not next in the file.

```
*.. 1 ...+... 2 ...+... 3 ...+... 4 ...+... 5 ...+... 6 ...+... 7 ...+... 8
/FREE
   UPDATE(E) CustRecord;
   IF %ERROR;
     EXSR IOError;
   ENDIF;
/END-FREE
```

Chapter 12 will show you additional ways to detect these and other kinds of errors. Errors not handled by a program cause the program to end abnormally (abend). Abends upset users and operators and often result in frantic phone calls to the programmer, usually at 3 a.m. Good, defensive programmers always design programs to minimize the possibility of errors and then trap for unexpected errors to ensure their reputations and minimize middle-of-the-night wake-up calls.

Putting It All Together

Now that you've learned about RPG IV's input and output operations, you might find some sample programs helpful to demonstrate how to apply these operations. Accordingly, read the scenarios that follow and study the program solutions to develop a sense of when to use the various I/O operations.

In the first scenario, a company has decided to give all its employees a five percent pay raise. Assume that an externally described master file of employees (EmpMaster) exists, that the record format within the database file is EmpRecord, and that the pay field is Pay. The file is keyed on employee ID. Externally described printer file ErrReport contains two record formats: ReadProb, to signal problems that occur when reading, and UpdateProb, to signal problems that occur when updating.

The following code shows a solution for this problem.

```
*.. 1 ...+... 2 ...+... 3 ...+... 4 ...+... 5 ...+... 6 ...+... 7 ...+... 8
   // ********************************************************************
   // This program gives each employee in the EmpMaster file a 5% raise.
   // Any I/O errors are recorded in ErrReport.
   //   Author: Yaeger. Feb. 1995.
   //   Modified: Meyers. Jan. 2002.
   // ********************************************************************

FEmpMaster UF   E            K DISK
FErrReport O    E              PRINTER OFLIND(EndOfPage)

D EndOfPage      S              N INZ(*ON)

 /FREE
    READ(E) EmpMaster;

    DOW NOT %EOF(EmpMaster);
      IF %ERROR;
        EXSR Overflow;
        WRITE ReadProb;
      ELSE;
        EXSR Process;
      ENDIF;
      READ(E) EmpMaster;
    ENDDO;

    *INLR = *ON;
    RETURN;

   // ********************************************************************
   //
   // Subroutine to write Heading lines
   //
     BEGSR Overflow;
       IF EndOfPage;
         WRITE ErrHeads;
         EndOfPage = *OFF;
       ENDIF;
     ENDSR;

   // ********************************************************************
   //
   //   Subroutine to process EmpMast records
   //
     BEGSR Process;
       EVAL(H) Pay = Pay * 1.05;
       UPDATE(E) EmpRecord;
       IF %ERROR;
         EXSR Overflow;
         WRITE UpdateProb;
       ENDIF;
     ENDSR;
 /END-FREE
```

In this solution, the file is declared as an update file, but because we are not asked to add new records to the file, the program does not specify that record addition should be enabled. Because all employees are to receive the raise, the calculations consist of a simple loop that sequentially reads through the file and then processes each record within a subroutine, Process. Subroutine Process calculates the new pay for each employee and updates the employee's record. IF logic detects I/O errors and writes such problems to a report.

Now let's complicate the problem a little. Instead of giving every employee a raise, the company wants to give only selected employees a five percent raise; a transaction file called RaiseTrans contains the IDs of these employees (in field EmpID).

The processing requirements of this problem vary from the first scenario because now we need to access only those employees in EmpMaster who appear in file RaiseTrans. Every record in RaiseTrans, however, must be processed. Accordingly, we want to sequentially process RaiseTrans and use the information on each record to randomly access an EmpMaster record to update. To provide for the possible error where RaiseTrans contains one or more employee IDs not found in the master file, assume that the error report file includes an additional error line, NoEmpProb.

```
*.. 1 ...+... 2 ...+... 3 ...+... 4 ...+... 5 ...+... 6 ...+... 7 ...+... 8
 // ********************************************************************
 // This program updates employees' pay by 5% based on employee IDs
 // contained in file RaiseTrans. Problems of incorrect IDs and I/O errors
 // are recorded in ErrReport.
 //   Author: Yaeger.  Feb. 1995.
 //   Modified: Meyers. Jan. 2002.
 // ********************************************************************

FRaiseTransIF   E             DISK
FEmpMaster UF   E           K DISK
FErrReport O    E             Printer OFLIND(EndOfPage)

D EndOfPage     S               N INZ(*ON)

 /FREE
    READ(E) RaiseTrans;
    DOW NOT %EOF(RaiseTrans);
      IF %ERROR;
        EXSR Overflow;
        WRITE ReadProb;
      ELSE;
        EXSR Process;
      ENDIF;
      READ(E) RaiseTrans;
    ENDDO;

    *INLR = *ON;
    RETURN;

 // ********************************************************************
 //
 // Subroutine to write Heading lines
 //
    BEGSR Overflow;
      IF EndOfPage;
        WRITE ErrHeads;
        EndOfPage = *OFF;
      ENDIF;
    ENDSR;

 // ********************************************************************
 //
 // Subroutine to process EmpMaster records
 //
    BEGSR Process;
      CHAIN(E) EmpID EmpMaster;
      SELECT;
```

continued…

continued...

```
      WHEN NOT %FOUND(EmpMaster);
        EXSR Overflow;
        WRITE NoEmpProb;
      WHEN %ERROR;
        EXSR Overflow;
        WRITE ReadProb;
      OTHER;
        EVAL(H) Pay = Pay * 1.05;
        UPDATE(E) EmpRecord;
        IF %ERROR;
          EXSR Overflow;
          WRITE UpdateProb;
        ENDIF;
    ENDSL;
  ENDSR;
/END-FREE
```

Now let's change the problem again, complicating it further. This time, the employers want to give raises to all the employees in certain departments; the DeptTrans file contains the names of the departments to receive the raise.

The best way to solve this problem is to define a logical file over the EmpMaster file, keyed on department, and then use the logical file for updating the employees. This approach lets you use SETLL to locate the appropriate departments within the file and then use READE to process all the employees within each department. The following program shows a solution using this approach. Note that we've omitted the error handling to let you focus more easily on the file accessing used in the program.

```
*.. 1 ...+... 2 ...+... 3 ...+... 4 ...+... 5 ...+... 6 ...+... 7 ...+... 8
 // *****************************************************************
 // This program updates employees' pay by 5% based on departments
 // contained in file DeptTrans. EmpMasterL is a logical file of
 // employees, keyed on department.
 //    Author: Yaeger.  Feb. 1995.
 //    Modified: Meyers. Jan. 2002.
 // *****************************************************************

FDeptTrans IF    E             DISK
FEmpMasterLUF    E           K DISK

 /FREE
    READ DeptTrans;
    DOW NOT %EOF(DeptTrans);                // Loop to process each department.
      SETLL Dept EmpMasterL;
      IF %EQUAL(EmpMasterL);
        READE Dept EmpMasterL;
        DOW NOT %EOF(EmpMasterL);           // Loop for all employees in a dept.
          EVAL(H) Pay = Pay * 1.05;
          UPDATE EmpRecordL;
          READE Dept EmpMasterL;
        ENDDO;
      ENDIF;
      READ DeptTrans;
    ENDDO;

    *INLR = *ON;
    RETURN;
 /END-FREE
```

As you begin to write programs that require you to access several files, try to decide how to handle access to each file. Ask yourself how many records in each file you will need to process. If you need to access all the records in the file or a subset (or subsets) of the records based on a common value of a field, then sequential access, using READ or READE (for subsets of sequential records), is appropriate. If you need to select only certain records from the file, random access, using CHAIN, would be best. And don't forget that OS/400's facility for defining keyed logical files lets you retrieve records based on any field. Often, defining logical files goes hand-in-hand with developing programs.

Chapter Summary

In this chapter, you learned many I/O operations appropriate to input, output, and update files. READ, READE, READP, and READPE are input operations used to access records sequentially from a full-procedural file whose type is declared as input or update. You can use the SETLL and SETGT operations to position the file before a sequential read operation. CHAIN randomly retrieves a record and also positions the file for subsequent sequential reading, if desired.

The KLIST and KFLD operations let you position a file or retrieve a record based on a composite key. By using a partial KLIST, you can initiate access to sets of records that share a common value on the first field (or fields) of a composite key.

You can use WRITE or EXCEPT to put records into an output file or an update file. Operations UPDATE and DELETE are specific to update files. You cannot UPDATE a record without having first read it; you can, however, DELETE a record without first retrieving it if you indicate the key of the record to delete in Factor 1 of the DELETE operation.

OS/400 includes built-in record locking to prevent the problem of phantom updates. Techniques, including use of the UNLOCK operation, exist to minimize record locking, but you should not use them if their implementation might cause lost updates to occur.

You have read about a large number of operations dealing with input and output. The following table summarizes these operations for you, to help you see more clearly the differences among the operations and to serve as a quick reference as you write your programs.

Input/Output Operations

File types	Operation	Factor 1	Factor 2	Result	Result functions
I, U	READ (en)	—	FILE/RFMT	dtastr	%error, %eof
I, U	READE (en)	FLCK*	FILE/RFMT	dtastr	%error, %eof
I, U	READP (en)	—	FILE/RFMT	dtastr	%error, %eof
I, U	READPE (en)	FLCK*	FILE/RFMT	dtastr	%error, %eof
I, U	SETLL (e)	FLCK	FILE/RFMT	—	%error, %found, %equal
I, U	SETGT (e)	FLCK	FILE/RFMT	—	%found, %error
I, U	CHAIN (en)	FLCK	FILE/RFMT	dtastr	%found, %error
O, U	WRITE (e)	—	RFMT	dtastr	%error
O, U	EXCEPT	—	ename	—	—
U	UPDATE (e)	—	RFMT	dtastr	%error
U	DELETE (e)	flck	FILE/RFMT	—	%found, %error
U	UNLOCK (e)	—	FILE	—	%error

continued...

continued...

File types	Operation	Factor 1	Factor 2	Result	Result functions
I, O, U	OPEN (e)	—	FILE	—	%error
I, O, U	CLOSE (e)	—	FILE	—	%error
I, U	KLIST	NAME	—	—	—
I, U	KFLD	—	—	FIELD	—

Key: Uppercase entry = required; lowercase entry = optional

* = entry required in free-format specification; optional in fixed-format Calculation Specifications

I = input; U = update; O = output

flck = may be a field, literal, constant, or KLIST

Operation extender (optional):   e = Capture error

n = Do not lock record

FILE/RFMT = may be a file name or a record format name (for externally described files)

RFMT = must be a record format name for externally described files

ename = exception line name on output

FILE = must be a file name

dtastr = data structure (used only with program-described files)

Key Terms

abend

composite key

concatenated key

file access

file locking

phantom updates

random access

record locking

sequential access

Discussion/Review Questions

1. Describe the difference between sequential and random record retrieval.
2. What does "position the file" mean?
3. What are the differences between the SETGT and SETLL operations?
4. Because READE and READPE imply reading records with matching keys, would you ever use them in programs accessing files with UNIQUE keys? Explain your answer.
5. When is it appropriate to use a READE as opposed to a READ operation?
6. When can you omit an A in position 20 of the File Specification of an output file? Why don't you need this A on printer files?
7. What does the term "file maintenance" mean? What kinds of files are likely to need maintenance?
8. Is any difference in results possible when you update a file using EXCEPT rather than UPDATE?
9. Because designating a file type as update gives you maximum flexibility in which I/O operations you can use with that file, why don't programmers designate all their files as update files, just in case? That is, why bother with input and output files?

10. What is the difference between a file lock and a record lock? Which technique do you think is easier for an operating system to implement? Why? Which technique is preferable from a user standpoint? Why?

11. What is defensive programming? What defensive-programming technique is described in this chapter? Name several other ways to be a defensive programmer.

Exercises

1. Assume you had a logical file of customers, CustLZip, keyed on zip code. Write the Calculation Specifications that would let you print an exception line, CustLine, for every customer whose zip code matched ZipIn. If no customers have that zip code, print exception line NoCust.

2. Your company sequentially assigns a unique customer number to each new customer. Assume customer file CustMaster is keyed on customer number, field CustNbr. Write the Calculation Specifications necessary to determine what number should be assigned to the next new customer.

3. You have a sales file, SalesFile, keyed on a composite key of store, department, and salesperson. (Duplicate keys are present because each record represents one sale.) Write the Calculation Specifications needed to total all the sales for a given department within a given store. Field Dept contains the desired department; field Store holds the store. The sales field that you want to accumulate is SalesAmt. Modify your code so that it totals all the sales of the store represented in Store.

4. Write the File Specifications and Calculation Specifications needed to let you randomly retrieve a customer in file CustMast based on the customer number in CustNbr, subtract Payment from BalanceDue, and rewrite the record. Execute subroutine NoCust if the customer is not found in the file.

5. You have a transaction file, CustTrans, of records to be added, deleted, or changed in the CustMaster master file. The Code field of the transaction record contains an A, D, or C, denoting whether the record is to be added, deleted, or changed, respectively, while the number of the customer to add, delete, or change is contained in transaction field CustNo. Write the File Specifications and Calculation Specifications that will let you appropriately process each record in the transaction file. Add is a valid option if the customer does not already exist in CustMaster; Change and Delete are valid only if the customer does exist in CustMaster. Execute subroutine AddRecord for valid adds, ChgRecord for valid changes, and DltRecord for valid deletions; for all invalid transactions, execute subroutine TransError. (Don't code the details of these subroutines; stop at the point of coding the EXSR statements.)

Programming Assignments

1. GTC Telephone Company wants a program to update its customer master file (GTCSTP) based on data contained in the payments transaction file (GTCPAYP). Data files are described in Appendix F. For each record in the payment file, randomly retrieve the appropriate customer, subtract the payment amount from the amount owed, change the date-of-last-payment field, and rewrite the customer record. Also prepare the audit report shown in the following printer spacing chart. Notice that if a customer in the payment file is not found in the customer file, an error notation should appear on the report.

```
          1         2         3         4         5         6         7         8         9        10
 1234567890123456789012345678901234567890123456789012345678901234567890123456789012345678901234567890
1  XX/XX/XX        GTC PAYMENTS PROCESSED   PAGE XX0X
2                       AUDIT REPORT
3
4    CUSTOMER        DATE RECEIVED      AMOUNT
5
6  (XXX)XXX-XXXX     XX/XX/XX      X,XX0.XX
7  (XXX)XXX-XXXX     XX/XX/XX      X,XX0.XX ERROR
8  (XXX)XXX-XXXX     XX/XX/XX      X,XX0.XX
9
10                    TOTAL     XXX,XX0.XX
11
12    X0X CUSTOMERS NOT IN MASTER FILE
13
```

2. CompuSell wants a program that will generate purchase orders for those items in the inventory file that need reordering — that is, items whose quantity on hand is less than or equal to their reorder point. For any inventory item that meets this criterion and has not already been reordered (i.e., the reorder code field is still blank), include that item on a purchase order and rewrite the record to the inventory file with an R in the reorder code field to signal that the item has been reordered.

Only one purchase order should be completed per supplier — that is, all items to be purchased from the same supplier should appear on the same purchase order. The format of the purchase order is shown below. Note that the item number is the supplier's product number, not CompuSell's. The unit cost is the current cost figure, and the quantity (QTY) is the reorder quantity in the inventory file.

```
          1         2         3         4         5         6         7         8         9        10
 1234567890123456789012345678901234567890123456789012345678901234567890123456789012345678901234567890
1     XX/XX/XX                 COMPUSELL
2                              5260 HAWORTH
3                       KALAMAZOO  MI  49008-0010
4
5  PURCHASE ORDER TO:
6
7  SUPPLIER: XXXXXXXXXXXXXXXXXXXXXXXXXX   CONTACT: XXXXXXXXXXXXXXXXXXXXXXXXXXXXXX
8            XXXXXXXXXXXXXXXXXXXX                  (XXX)XXX-XXXX
9            XXXXXXXXXXXXXXX   XX XXXXX-XXXX
10
11 ITEM NUMBER        DESCRIPTION              UNIT COST    QTY         EXTENSION
12   XXXXXXXX   XXXXXXXXXXXXXXXXXXXXXXXXXXX    X,XX0.XX   X,X0X    XX,XXX,XX0.XX
13   XXXXXXXX   XXXXXXXXXXXXXXXXXXXXXXXXXXX    X,XX0.XX   X,X0X    XX,XXX,XX0.XX
14   XXXXXXXX   XXXXXXXXXXXXXXXXXXXXXXXXXXX    X,XX0.XX   X,X0X    XX,XXX,XX0.XX
15
16                                       ORDER TOTAL     $XXX,XXX,XX0.XX
17
18
19
20        AUTHORIZED SIGNATURE
21
```

You will need to use data from CompuSell's inventory master file (CSINVP) and supplier file (CSSUPP), both described in Appendix F. You also will need to create a logical file so that the inventory records can be processed in supplier number order.

3. CompuSell wants you to write a program to process goods received from suppliers. As the company receives ordered goods from suppliers, the items are added to inventory, and a record of each received item is added to the goods received file, CSRCVP. The contents of this file are then run in batch to update the inventory file, CSINVP. Appendix F describes these files. Note that you will need to create a logical file to access the records in CSINVP by supplier product ID.

For each item in CSRCVP, the following changes must be made in the corresponding record of CSINVP: a) the quantity on hand must be changed to reflect the additional goods; b) the reorder code should be changed to spaces; and c) if the current charge from the supplier is not identical to the current and average costs stored in the inventory file, two changes must be made — first, the inventory file's current cost must be changed to reflect the new cost, and, second, the average cost must be recalculated and updated.

To calculate new average cost, multiply the old average cost by the old quantity on hand, add this value to the cost of the items that have just come in, and divide by the new total quantity on hand. Thus, if you had 10 units in stock with an average cost of $3 and received 20 more units at a cost of $4, the new average cost would be

$$(10 * 3 + 20 * 4) / 30 = \$3.67$$

In addition to updating the inventory file, your program should produce the following report to serve as an audit trail of the updating. Note that if there is an error in an item number in CSRCVP, so that a corresponding item does not exist in CSINVP, the report should note that fact by printing two special lines, as shown. The second line contains an image of the problem record from CSRCVP.

```
      1         2         3         4         5         6         7         8         9         10
 1234567890123456789012345678901234567890123456789012345678901234567890123456789012345678901234567890
 1  XX/XX/XX           COMPUSELL INVENTORY UPDATE REPORT                    PAGE XXØX
 2                        RECEIVED GOODS PROCESSED
 3
 4 SUPPLIER    ITEM     QTY     NEW QTY    OLD           NEW          OLD AVG.     NEW AVG.
 5   ID         NO     RCVD    ON HAND     COST          COST           COST         COST
 6
 7 XXXXXXXX   XXXXXX   XXØX     XXØX      X,XXØ.XX     X,XXØ.XX      X,XXØ.XX     X,XXØ.XX
 8 XXXXXXXX   XXXXXX   XXØX     XXØX      X,XXØ.XX     X,XXØ.XX      X,XXØ.XX     X,XXØ.XX
 9 XXXXXXXX   ITEM NOT FOUND IN INVENTORY FILE; RECHECK SUPPLIER ID
10        XXXXXXXXXXXXXXXXXXXXXX   RECORD NOT PROCESSED
11 XXXXXXXX   XXXXXX   XXØX     XXØX      X,XXØ.XX     X,XXØ.XX      X,XXØ.XX     X,XXØ.XX
12
13
14
15
16
17
```

4. Wexler University wants you to write a program that will generate a transcript, shown on the following page, of completed courses for each student in the transcript request file, WUTRANSP. The program will also require the use of the student master file (WUSTDP), the course file (WUCRSP), and the earned credits file (WUCRDP). Appendix F describes each of these files.

Note that the line showing graduation date and degree granted should be printed only if the student has, in fact, graduated, as signaled by nonblank values in those fields of the student's master record.

Courses should be listed in chronological order. Note that under SEMESTER, the school wants WIN to be printed for semester code 1, SUM for semester code 2, and FAL for semester code 3; the XX to the right of this code represents the year the course was taken.

```
         1         2         3         4         5         6         7         8         9        10
1234567890123456789012345678901234567890123456789012345678901234567890123456789012345678901234567890
 1              WEXLER UNIVERSITY OFFICIAL TRANSCRIPT
 2                    DATE ISSUED: XX/XX/XX
 3
 4 STUDENT:   XXXXXXXXXXXXXXX XXXXXXXXXX   DATE ADMITTED: XX/XX/XX
 5            XXX-XX-XXXX                  MAJOR: XXX
 6
 7       CREDITS EARNED: XØX              GRADE POINT AVERAGE: Ø.XX
 8       GRADUATED:  XX/XX/XX             DEGREE GRANTED: XXX
 9
10    COURSE        TITLE                 SEMESTER    CREDITS      GRADE
11    XXXXXX    XXXXXXXXXXXXXXXXXXXXXXXXX  XXX XX        X          XX
12    XXXXXX    XXXXXXXXXXXXXXXXXXXXXXXXX  XXX XX        X          XX
13    XXXXXX    XXXXXXXXXXXXXXXXXXXXXXXXX  XXX XX        X          XX
14
15
16
17
```

5. Wexler University wants you to write a program that will generate class lists to distribute to all instructors. The class lists should be formatted as follows:

```
         1         2         3         4         5         6         7         8         9        10
1234567890123456789012345678901234567890123456789012345678901234567890123456789012345678901234567890
 1              WEXLER U. CLASS LIST 20XX
 2
 3 INSTRUCTOR:  XXXXXXXXXXXXXXX DEPT: XXX
 4
 5    DEPT  COURSE    TITLE                      CREDITS     SECTION
 6    XXX   XXX    XXXXXXXXXXXXXXXXXXXXXXXXX         X       XXXXX
 7
 8          STUDENT             SOC. SEC.     DCODE    MAJOR
 9       XXXXXXXXXXXXXXX XXXXXXXXXX  XXX-XX-XXXX    X     XXX
10       XXXXXXXXXXXXXXX XXXXXXXXXX  XXX-XX-XXXX    X     XXX
11       XXXXXXXXXXXXXXX XXXXXXXXXX  XXX-XX-XXXX    X     XXX
12
13          SECTION ENROLLMENT: XØX STUDENTS
14
15
16    DEPT  COURSE    TITLE                      CREDITS     SECTION
17    XXX   XXX    XXXXXXXXXXXXXXXXXXXXXXXXX         X       XXXXX
18
19          STUDENT             SOC. SEC.     DCODE    MAJOR
20       XXXXXXXXXXXXXXX XXXXXXXXXX  XXX-XX-XXXX    X     XXX
21       XXXXXXXXXXXXXXX XXXXXXXXXX  XXX-XX-XXXX    X     XXX
22       XXXXXXXXXXXXXXX XXXXXXXXXX  XXX-XX-XXXX    X     XXX
23       XXXXXXXXXXXXXXX XXXXXXXXXX  XXX-XX-XXXX    X     XXX
24
25          SECTION ENROLLMENT: XØX STUDENTS
```

Because these lists are sent to the instructors, begin each instructor's list on a new page. You will need to access data from several files to obtain the output: the current enrollment file (WUENRLP), the student master file (WUSTDP), the current sections file (WUSCTP), the course file (WUCRSP), and the instructor file (WUINSTP). Appendix F describes these data files. Follow your instructor's directions for accessing these files of data. Hint: You will need to use logical files to solve this problem.

Chapter 8

Interactive Applications

 ## Chapter Overview

In this chapter, you will learn how to define display files and how to use them to develop interactive applications.

Batch and Interactive Programs

So far, the applications you have written were designed to run in batch. In **batch processing**, once a program begins to run, it continues to execute instructions without human intervention or control. Most batch applications in the business environment involve processing one or more transaction files sequentially; the programs end when the transaction files reach end-of-file.

Interactive applications, in contrast, are user driven. As the program runs, a user at a workstation interacts with the computer — selecting options from menus, entering data, responding to prompts, and so on. The sequence of instructions the program executes is determined in part by the user; the program continues until the user signals that he or she is ready to quit.

This dialogue between the user and the computer is mediated through what, on the iSeries, are called display files. **Display files** define the screens that the program presents as it runs. Display files allow values keyed by the user in response to the screen to be input as data to the program. Thus, display files serve as the mechanism that lets the user and program interact.

Display Files

You define display files externally to the program that uses them. The procedure for creating a display file is similar to the procedure followed to create a physical or logical file. You code display files using Data Description Specifications (DDS), enter the specifications using Source Entry Utility (SEU) to create a source member (with type DSPF), and then compile the source code to create an object. IBM also provides a utility called **Screen Design Aid (SDA)**, which automatically generates the DDS source code as you design and create display screens in an interactive environment.

Just like database and printer file definitions, display file definitions include entries at a file, record, and field level. File-level entries appear at the very beginning of the definition and apply to all the record formats within the file. Record-level entries are associated with a single record format (usually a single screen). Field-level entries are coded for specific fields or constants within a record format.

Each record format defines what is written to or read from the workstation in a single input/output (I/O) operation. On an output operation, the record may fill an entire screen with prompts and/or values; on an input operation, the record may read several values keyed from the workstation. Unless you make special provisions, only one screen is displayed at a time. When a different record format is written, the first screen is erased before the display of the second.

As an introduction to DDS coding for display files, consider the following situation. A school identifies each of its semester offerings through a section number. For each section, the school stores information about the course with which this section is associated, the days and time it meets, the assigned room, the section enrollment, and the instructor. This data is stored in file SECTIONS; its physical file definition is

```
*.. 1 ...+... 2 ...+... 3 ...+... 4 ...+... 5 ...+... 6 ...+... 7 ...+... 8
A..........T.Name++++++RLen++TDpB......Functions++++++++++++++++++++++++++++
 * Physical file SECTIONS definition
A           R SECREC
A             SECTNO        5               TEXT('Section number')
A             DAYS          3               TEXT('Days class meets')
A             BEGTIME       4    0          TEXT('Time class starts')
A             ROOM          4    0          TEXT('Classroom')
A             ENROLL        3    0          TEXT('Current enrollment')
A             INSTR        15               TEXT('Instructor')
A             COURSE        6               TEXT('Course identifier')
A           K SECTNO
```

The school wants a simple online inquiry program that will let a user enter a section number and then display information about that section. The application displays the following input, or entry, screen:

```
                          Section Inquiry

       Type value, then Enter.

          Section number . . _____












       F3=Exit
```

The DDS of the display file record format needed to produce the above screen is shown below.

```
*.. 1 ...+... 2 ...+... 3 ...+... 4 ...+... 5 ...+... 6 ...+... 7 ...+... 8
AAN01N02N03T.Name++++++RLen++TDpBLinPosFunctions++++++++++++++++++++++++++++++
A           R SECT1
A                                         CA03(03 'F3=Exit')
A                                       1 28'Section Inquiry'
A                                       3  2'Type value, then Enter.'
A                                       5  5'Section number . .'
A             SECTION       5A  I       5 24
A                                      23  2'F3=Exit'
```

Notice that each record format begins with an identifier, an R in position 17, followed by a name for that format — in this case, SECT1 — beginning in position 19 (Name++++++). Below the record format line appear all the fields and literals that are to make up the format. You must indicate the location of each literal and field on this screen by specifying the screen line on which the literal or field is to appear (in positions 39–41, Lin) as well as its starting column position within that line (in positions 42–44, Pos). You code the literals themselves, such as 'Section Inquiry', in the Functions area, positions 45–80 of the DDS line. You must enclose them in apostrophes (').

You enter field names left-adjusted in positions 19–28. Each field needs an assigned usage, which you code in position 38 (labeled B). Usage codes include I for input, O for output, or B for both input and output. SECTION, the only field in the sample definition, is an input field because its value is to be entered by the user and read by (input to) the program. Its usage code is therefore I.

You must further define each field by specifying its length in positions 30–34 (Len++), data type in position 35 (T), and — for numeric fields — number of decimal positions in positions 36–37 (Dp).

For display files, column 35 is actually more appropriately called "data type/keyboard shift" because it allows many more possible values than are permitted for field definitions of physical files. These additional values affect the **keyboard-shift attribute** of different workstations to limit what characters users can enter. Although a complete description of allowable values is beyond the scope of this text, the following table describes four commonly used values.

Keyboard-shift value	Description
A (Alphanumeric shift)	Used for character fields; puts keyboard in lower shift; lets user enter any character
X (Alphabetic only)	Used for character fields; lets user enter only A–Z, commas, periods, dashes, and spaces; sends lowercase letters as upper case
S (Signed numeric)	Used for numeric fields; lets user enter digits 0–9 but no signs; uses Field– key for entering negative values
Y (Numeric only)	Used for numeric fields; lets the user enter digits 0–9, plus or minus signs, periods, commas, and spaces

One very important distinction between keyboard-shift values S and Y is that Y lets you associate edit codes and edit words with the field, while S does not.

Because our sample application treats SECTION as a character field, a decimal position entry is not appropriate. The type is A, or character. Because A is the default type for character fields, we could have omitted the A. The default type for numeric fields is S unless you associate an edit code or word with the field; in that case, the system assumes a default type value of Y.

The line below the record-format definition, CA03(03 'F3=Exit'), establishes a connection between function key F3 and the 03 indicator. You haven't used indicators much previously in this text. The need for them is rapidly disappearing from RPG IV, but an indicator is still the primary means by which a DDS display file communicates conditions with an RPG program. When you code interactive applications, indicators communicate between the screen and the program that uses the screen. Control generally returns from the screen to the program when the user presses the Enter key or a function key that has been assigned a special meaning. In this screen, for instance, the user is prompted to press F3 to exit the program. But because you cannot reference the function key directly within an RPG IV program, an indicator must serve as a mediator.

The DDS line CA03(03 'F3=Exit') accomplishes three things. First, the CA03 portion establishes F3 as a valid command key in this application; only those function keys explicitly referenced within the DDS are valid, or enabled, during program execution. Second, the 03 within the parentheses associates indicator 03 with F3 so that when F3 is pressed, indicator 03 is turned on. Although you can associate any indicator (01–99) with any function key, it makes good programming sense to associate a function key with its corresponding numeric indicator to avoid confusion. Last, by referencing the function key as CA (Command Attention) rather than CF (Command Function), the code is saying to return control to the program without the input data values (if any) that the user has just entered. If the line were coded CF03(03 'F3=Exit'), control would return to the program with the input data.

The information within apostrophes — 'F3=Exit' — serves only as documentation. You could omit it (e.g., code only CA03(03)) without affecting how the screen functions. Good programming practice, however, suggests including such documentation.

We can now look at the design of the second screen the application needs. It's an information screen, or panel, used to display the requested information. The specific values shown give you a sense of what the screen might look like when the program is running.

```
              Section Information

     Section number . . . . . . 12435
     Course . . . . . . . . . . BIS350
     Instructor . . . . . . . . Johnson
     Room . . . . . . . . . . . 1120
     Meets on days  . . . . . . MWF
     Starting time  . . . . . . 10:30
     Enrollment . . . . . . . . 36









     Press Enter to continue.

     F3=Exit  F12=Cancel
```

This screen will require a second record format within the display file. The DDS for this record format is

```
*.. 1 ...+... 2 ...+... 3 ...+... 4 ...+... 5 ...+... 6 ...+... 7 ...+... 8
AAN01N02N03T.Name++++++RLen++TDpBLinPosFunctions+++++++++++++++++++++++++++++
A                                      REF(SECTIONS)
A          R SECT2
A                                      CA03(03 'F3=Exit')
A                                      CA12(12 'F12=Cancel')
A                                    1 10'Section Information'
A                                    3  2'Section number . . . . . .'
A            SECTNO    R      0      3 29
A                                    4  2'Course . . . . . . . . . .'
A            COURSE    R      0      4 29
A                                    5  2'Instructor . . . . . . . .'
A            INSTR     R      0      5 29
A                                    6  2'Room . . . . . . . . . . .'
A            ROOM      R      0      6 29
A                                    7  2'Meets on days  . . . . . .'
A            DAYS      R      0      7 29
A                                    8  2'Starting time  . . . . . .'
A            BEGTIME   R      0      8 29
A                                    9  2'Enrollment . . . . . . . .'
A            ENROLL    R      0      9 29
A                                   21  2'Press Enter to continue.'
A                                   23  2'F3=Exit'
A                                   23 11'F12=Cancel'
```

This code represents a "bare-bones" record format to describe the screen. Note that the fields represented are given an O, for Output, usage. That's because their values are going to be sent from the program to the screen. Instead of including length and decimal position entries, these field entries contain an R in position 29. This R (for Reference) signals that the fields are defined elsewhere and that their definitions can be obtained from that source. The source, in this case, is the file SECTIONS, as indicated by the first line of the DDS, which specifies keyword REF followed by the file name in parentheses. REF is a file-level keyword that should appear at the beginning of the DDS, before any record format definitions.

If you define a field through referencing, and if the referenced database field includes an edit code or edit word associated with it in the database file, that editing is automatically incorporated into the display file. (If the referenced field is unedited, or if the field is defined within the display file itself, you can add editing within the display file; we discuss how to do this later in this chapter.)

Notice that record format SECT2 enables function key F12 as well as F3. Generally accepted iSeries screen-design standards use F12, Cancel, to signal that the user wants to back up to the previous screen, while F3, Exit, means to exit the entire application.

Putting the two format definitions together completes the DDS for the display file, called SECTINQR. We've added one file-level keyword, INDARA, to the DDS. INDARA organizes all the indicators that the display file uses into relative positions in a 99-byte data structure — indicator 03 in position 3, indicator 12 in position 12, and so on. We'll use this data structure in the RPG IV program to avoid referring to numbered indicators; instead, we'll be able to assign them meaningful names.

```
*.. 1 ...+... 2 ...+... 3 ...+... 4 ...+... 5 ...+... 6 ...+... 7 ...+... 8
AAN01N02N03T.Name++++++RLen++TDpBLinPosFunctions++++++++++++++++++++++++++++++
 * Display file SECTINQR, containing two record formats
A                                     REF(SECTIONS)
A                                     INDARA
A           R SECT1
A                                     CA03(03 'F3=Exit')
A                                   1 28'Section Inquiry'
A                                   3  2'Type value, then Enter.'
A                                   5  5'Section number . .'
A           SECTION      5A  I  5 24
A                                  23  2'F3=Exit'
A           R SECT2
A                                     CA03(03 'F3=Exit')
A                                     CA12(12 'F12=Cancel')
A                                   1 10'Section Information'
A                                   3  2'Section number . . . . . .'
A           SECTNO       R      0  3 29
A                                   4  2'Course . . . . . . . . . .'
A           COURSE       R      0  4 29
A                                   5  2'Instructor . . . . . . . .'
A           INSTR        R      0  5 29
A                                   6  2'Room . . . . . . . . . . .'
A           ROOM         R      0  6 29
A                                   7  2'Meets on days  . . . . . .'
A           DAYS         R      0  7 29
A                                   8  2'Starting time  . . . . . .'
A           BEGTIME      R      0  8 29
A                                   9  2'Enrollment . . . . . . . .'
A           ENROLL       R      0  9 29
A                                  21  2'Press Enter to continue.'
A                                  23  2'F3=Exit'
A                                  23 11'F12=Cancel'
```

Before looking at some of the many additional features available for defining display files, let's develop the section inquiry program to see how display files are used in interactive programs. Recall that the user wants to enter a section number to request section information from the SECTIONS file. The program should display the retrieved information on the screen. The user can then enter another section number or signal that he or she is finished by pressing F3.

In writing the program, you must define display file SECTINQR, like any other kind of file, in the File Specifications. Display files are full-procedural, externally described files. However, because the concept of "key" is not applicable to this kind of file, you leave position 34 blank. What about type (position 17)? You have worked with input files (I), output files (O), and update files (U). Display files represent a new type: combined, or C. A **combined file** supports both input and output, but as independent operations. You cannot update a combined file.

Next, the device for display files is WORKSTN. Finally, we'll code the INDDS keyword, which instructs RPG to store the indicators passed to and from this display file in the data structure named FKeys; we'll discuss this data structure a little later. The following code shows the complete File Specifications for the section inquiry program.

```
*.. 1 ...+... 2 ...+... 3 ...+... 4 ...+... 5 ...+... 6 ...+... 7 ...+... 8
FFilename++IPEASFRLen+LKLen+AIDevice+.Keywords+++++++++++++++++++++++++++++++++++
FSections  IF   E           K DISK
FSectInqr  CF   E             WORKSTN INDDS(FKeys)
```

Because both files are externally described, the program will have no Input Specifications, nor Output Specifications for that matter. The only part of the program left to code is the Calculation Specifications. Before we jump into this coding, however, it pays first to think through the logic of a solution. Interactive programs are extremely prone to "spaghetti coding," primarily because the flow of control is less straightforward — depending on which function key a user presses, you may need to repeat, back up, or early-exit out of different routines.

The present program will need to loop until the user presses F3 in response to either screen 1 or screen 2. If the user presses F12 at screen 2 to back up, that effectively is the same in this program as hitting the Enter key because in both cases the user should next see screen 1 again.

A rough solution written in pseudocode would look like the following:

```
WHILE user wants to continue (no Exit)
    Display first screen
    Obtain user's response to the screen
    IF user wants to continue (no Exit)
        Random read section file to get section information
        IF record found
            Display second screen
            Obtain user's response
        ENDIF
    ENDIF
ENDWHILE
```

You can easily develop the RPG IV calculations from the pseudocode once you know how to send screens of data to the user and read user input.

Performing Screen I/O

The allowable operations for screen I/O are WRITE, READ, and EXFMT (Execute Format). All three operations require a record format name in Factor 2.

The WRITE operation displays a screen and returns control to the program without waiting for user input. A subsequent READ operation sends control to the currently displayed screen, waits for the end of user input (signaled by the user's pressing either the Enter key or any other enabled special key), and returns control to the program.

The EXFMT operation combines the features of WRITE and READ; it first writes a record to the screen and then waits for user input to that screen. When the user has finished inputting, the system reads the data back from the screen and returns control to the program. Because in most screen I/O you want to display some information and then wait for a user response, EXFMT is the operation you will use most frequently in your interactive programs.

The following code shows an RPG IV implementation of the pseudocode solution to the section inquiry problem.

```
*.. 1 ...+... 2 ...+... 3 ...+... 4 ...+... 5 ...+... 6 ...+... 7 ...+... 8
 /FREE
    DOW NOT *IN03;
      EXFMT Sect1;
      IF NOT *IN03;
        CHAIN Section Sections;
        IF %FOUND(Sections);
          EXFMT Sect2;
        ENDIF;
      ENDIF;
    ENDDO;

    *INLR = *ON;
    RETURN;
 /END-FREE
```

In this code, indicator 03, which is turned on when the user presses F3, controls the main program loop. Because the user can signal "Exit" at screen SECT1, the calculations need an IF following the return from the SECT1 screen to check for this possibility. Because the user may have keyed in a wrong section number, which would cause the CHAIN operation to fail, the program executes the information panel, SECT2, only if the chaining found a record.

Using an Indicator Data Structure

We can eliminate the somewhat obscure reference to *IN03 in the above code by including a definition for a special data structure called an **indicator data structure**. You'll recall that the INDARA keyword in the DDS for the display file instructed the system to organize all the display file's indicators into a 99-byte data area. In the RPG IV program, the File Specification for the display file included the INDDS keyword; this keyword moves the data area from DDS into the data structure named as the keyword value. Given these two requirements (the INDARA keyword in DDS and the INDDS keyword in the File Specification), we can then include a Definition Specification for the data structure that will contain the indicators. The code for this definition is shown here:

```
*.. 1 ...+... 2 ...+... 3 ...+... 4 ...+... 5 ...+... 6 ...+... 7 ...+... 8
DName++++++++++ETDsFrom+++To/L+++IDc.Keywords++++++++++++++++++++++++++++++++
   // Indicator data structure
D FKeys           DS                  99
D  Exit                        3      3N
D  Cancel                     12     12N
```

In this definition, position 3 in the data structure corresponds to *IN03, and position 12 corresponds to *IN12; these positions are assigned to indicator (data type N) fields named Exit and Cancel, respectively. Note that this definition uses From and To positions to specify exact positions of fields within the data structure, instead of field length. In defining this special data structure, this notation serves us well in describing which indicator we are naming and in letting us skip over unused portions of the indicator data structure. Once we've included this definition, we can refer to Exit instead of *IN03 in the RPG IV code, making the program more readable:

```
*.. 1 ...+... 2 ...+... 3 ...+... 4 ...+... 5 ...+... 6 ...+... 7 ...+... 8
 /FREE
    DOW NOT Exit;
      EXFMT Sect1;
      IF NOT Exit;
        CHAIN Section Sections;
        IF %FOUND(Sections);
          EXFMT Sect2;
        ENDIF;
      ENDIF;
    ENDDO;

    *INLR = *ON;
    RETURN;
 /END-FREE
```

Additional DDS Keywords

Although the DDS definition for the previous example would work, it represents a minimalist approach to screen design — it contains no "bells and whistles." More important, perhaps, as the DDS is presently coded, numeric fields would be displayed without editing, and information about a possible important program event — a section not found in the file — is not conveyed to the user. You can include these and other kinds of special effects by using keywords.

You have already been introduced to three keywords used with display files (CA*nn*, CF*nn*, and REF). DDS includes a long list of permissible keywords for display files to let you change a screen's appearance or the interaction between screen and user. This section discusses some of the major keywords. Refer to IBM's manual *OS/400 DDS Reference* for more detail.

Keywords are always coded in positions 45–80 (the Functions area) of the DDS line. Keywords apply at a file, record, or field level. Some keywords can be used with two levels, while others are appropriate to just one level. Where you code the keyword determines the level with which the keyword is associated.

File-Level Keywords

File-level keywords must always appear as the first lines in the DDS, before any record format information. If you have several file-level keywords, the order in which you code them does not matter. You have already encountered two file-level keywords: REF, used to indicate a database file that contains definitions of fields used in the screen, and INDARA, used to organize indicators into a 99-byte data structure.

Keyword MSGLOC (Message Location) specifies the position of the message line for error and other messages. The keyword's format is

```
MSGLOC(line-number)
```

Without this keyword, the message-line position defaults to the last screen line (line 24 on a standard 24 × 80 screen).

The CA*nn* (Command Attention) and CF*nn* (Command Function) keywords, which we've already discussed, enable the use of function keys and associate the keys with program indicators. You can use as many function keys as are appropriate to your application by including a CA*nn* or CF*nn* keyword for each one.

If you code these keywords at a file level, they apply to all the record formats within the file. Alternatively, you can associate them with individual record formats, as we did in the section inquiry example; in that case, the keys are valid only during input operations for the screen or screens with which they are associated.

A commonly used file-level keyword is PRINT. This keyword enables the Print key during the interactive application to let the user print the current screen. Without this keyword, the Print key is disabled. You can also use PRINT as a record-level keyword to enable the key for some screens but not others.

Keyword VLDCMDKEY (Valid Command Key) is a file- or record-level keyword used to turn on an indicator when the user presses any valid (enabled) command key. Note that command keys include any special key, such as the Roll up key, in addition to function keys. The format for this keyword is

```
VLDCMDKEY(indicator ['text'])
```

The indicator can be any numbered indicator (01–99); the text description is optional and serves only as documentation.

VLDCMDKEY is useful because it lets the program differentiate between control returned as a result of the Enter key and control returned by any other key. You often need to set up separate logic branches based on this distinction.

Record-Level Keywords

Record-level keywords appear on the line on which the record format is named and/or on lines immediately following that line, preceding any field or literal definition. These kinds of keywords apply only to the screen with which they are associated. They do not carry over to or influence other record formats defined within the file.

You can use keywords CA*nn*, CF*nn*, PRINT, and VLDCMDKEY as record-level keywords as well as file-level keywords. Keyword BLINK, on the other hand, is strictly a record-level keyword. BLINK causes the cursor to blink during the display of the record format with which it is associated.

OVERLAY is a record-level keyword that specifies that the record format be displayed without clearing the previous display. OVERLAY works only when the record formats involved do not overlap lines on the screen.

The following DDS demonstrates the use of record-level keywords.

```
*.. 1 ...+... 2 ...+... 3 ...+... 4 ...+... 5 ...+... 6 ...+... 7 ...+... 8
AAN01N02N03T.Name++++++RLen++TDpBLinPosFunctions++++++++++++++++++++++++++++++
 * Sample DDS showing record-level keywords
A           R SAMPLE                       PRINT
A                                          CA03(03 'F3=Exit')
A                                          CA12(12 'F12=Cancel')
A                                          VLDCMDKEY(30 'Any valid key')
A                                          OVERLAY
```

Field-Level Keywords

A field-level keyword applies only to the specific field with which it is associated. A field can have several keywords. The first keyword appears on the same line as the field definition or on the line immediately following the definition. You can code additional keywords on the same line (provided there is room) or on successive lines. All keywords for a field must be coded before the next field-definition line.

Two field-level keywords control the format of numeric output fields on the display: EDTCDE (Edit Code) and EDTWRD (Edit Word). Recall that only numerically defined fields can be edited and that the field-type specification in column 35 of the DDS must be Y or blank to use editing for a displayed field.

Display file edit codes and edit words match those used within RPG IV itself and have the same meaning as in RPG IV. EDTCDE's format is

```
EDTCDE(edit-code [*|$])
```

The parentheses should contain a valid edit code, such as 1, optionally followed by a single asterisk (*) to provide asterisk protection or a single dollar sign ($) to supply a floating dollar sign.

The format for EDTWRD is

```
EDTWRD('edit-word')
```

To review RPG IV edit words and edit codes, see Chapter 2.

The following DDS sample shows the use of keywords EDTWRD and EDTCDE. Note that because editing is a concept related to output, the use of EDTWRD and EDTCDE is appropriate for fields defined for output usage or fields used for both input and output, but not for fields defined to be used for input only.

```
*.. 1 ...+... 2 ...+... 3 ...+... 4 ...+... 5 ...+... 6 ...+... 7 ...+... 8
AANØ1NØ2NØ3T.Name++++++RLen++TDpBLinPosFunctions++++++++++++++++++++++++++++
 * Sample DDS showing the use of editing keywords
A           R SAMPLE
A             SOCSEC        9Y ØØ  4 1ØEDTWRD('   -  -    ')
A             NAME         2Ø   Ø  5 1Ø
A             BILLDATE      6Y ØØ  6 1ØEDTCDE(Y)
A             AMOUNTDUE     7Y 2Ø  7 1ØEDTCDE(1 $)
```

Another field-level keyword, DSPATR (Display Attribute), determines the appearance of fields on the screen. You can use DSPATR more than once for a given field, and you can include more than one attribute with the same keyword. The keyword is followed by parentheses containing the codes of the desired attributes. The following attributes can be assigned to all types of fields (input, output, or both):

Attribute	Meaning
BL	Blinking field
CS	Column separator (a vertical bar separating each position within a field)
HI	High intensity
ND	Non-display (keyed characters don't appear on screen)
PC	Position cursor (position cursor to the first character of this field)
RI	Reverse image
UL	Underline

The following code illustrates the use of **display attributes**.

```
*.. 1 ...+... 2 ...+... 3 ...+... 4 ...+... 5 ...+... 6 ...+... 7 ...+... 8
AAN01N02N03T.Name++++++RLen++TDpBLinPosFunctions+++++++++++++++++++++++++++
 * Sample DDS illustrating display attributes
A           R SAMPLE
A             SOCSEC        9Y 00  4 10DSPATR(ND)
A                                    DSPATR(UL)
A             NAME         20    0  5 10DSPATR(BL UL)
A             BILLDATE      6Y 00  6 10EDTCDE(Y)
A                                    DSPATR(RI)
A                                    DSPATR(PC HI BL)
```

 Caution

This sample is not intended to set a style standard to be followed. A screen with so many bells and whistles would be distracting to the user. In general, you should use such features sparingly and consistently to draw attention to specific fields on the screen or to problems with which the user must deal.

Another important set of field-level keywords concerns **data validation**. Every programmer should recognize the extreme importance of preventing invalid data from entering the system; corrupt data files can cause abnormal endings or incorrect processing. Although no way exists to completely ensure that values a user enters are correct, by validating data as tightly as possible, you can eliminate some kinds of errors.

The four major keywords used for validating user entry are

- VALUES
- RANGE
- COMP
- CHECK

Each of these keywords lets you place restrictions on what the user can enter. Violating these restrictions causes the system to display an appropriate error message on the message line and to display the field in reverse image to force the user to change the entered value.

Keyword VALUES lets you specify the exact valid values allowed for a field. The keyword format is

```
VALUES(value1 value2 . . .)
```

Up to 100 values can be entered. You must enclose character values within apostrophes.

Keyword RANGE lets you specify a range within which the user's entry must fall to be considered valid. The format for this keyword is

```
RANGE(low-value high-value)
```

If you use RANGE with character fields, the low and high values must each be enclosed in apostrophes. The valid range includes the low and high values, so the entered value must be greater than or equal to the low value and less than or equal to the high value to be considered valid.

Keyword COMP lets you specify a relational comparison to be made with the user's entered value to determine validity. This keyword's format is

```
COMP(relational-operator value)
```

The relational operator can be one of the following:

Operator	Meaning
EQ	Equal to
NE	Not equal to
GT	Greater than
NG	Not greater than
LT	Less than
NL	Not less than
GE	Greater than or equal to
LE	Less than or equal to

CHECK is a field-level keyword that you can use for validity checking. Its format is

```
CHECK(code [. . .])
```

That is, you can associate one or more validity-checking codes with a single CHECK entry. Some of these validity codes are ME (Mandatory Enter), MF (Mandatory Fill), and AB (Allow Blank).

For Mandatory Enter fields, the user must enter at least one character of data (the character could be a blank); the user cannot simply bypass the field. Mandatory Fill specifies that each position in the field have a character in it. (Again, a blank is considered a character.) Allow Blank provides the user with an override option for a field that fails a validity check. For example, if a field has a VALUES keyword associated with it and the user is uncertain which value is appropriate to the record he or she is entering, the user can simply enter blanks and the value will be accepted. The following DDS demonstrates the use of keywords for data validation.

```
*.. 1 ...+... 2 ...+... 3 ...+... 4 ...+... 5 ...+... 6 ...+... 7 ...+... 8
AAN01N02N03T.Name++++++RLen++TDpBLinPosFunctions++++++++++++++++++++++++++++
 * Sample DDS illustrating the use of keywords for data validation
A          R SAMPLE
A            DEPT          3   I  4 10VALUES('CIS' 'DPR' 'MGT')
A                                    CHECK(MF AB)
A            MONTH         2Y 0I  6 10RANGE(1 12)
A            REGHOURS      3Y 1I  7 10COMP(LE 40)
```

The CHECK keyword also supports parameter values concerned with functions other than validity checking. CHECK(LC), for example, lets the user enter lowercase (as well as uppercase) letters for character fields. Without this keyword, all user-entered alphabetic characters are returned to the program as upper case. You can use CHECK at a field, record, or file level, depending on how broadly you want to enable lowercase data entry.

One field-level keyword of major importance is ERRMSG (Error Message). When an error message is in effect for a field, the message is displayed on the message line of the screen, and the field with which the message is associated appears on the screen in reverse image. The format for the ERRMSG keyword is

```
ERRMSG('message text' [indicator])
```

If you specify an indicator, the indicator is turned off as part of the input operation that follows the display of the error message. Error messages are useful for conveying information about program-processing problems to the user's screen.

Last, two field-level keywords serve as built-in variables to display the date and/or time on the screen. TIME, entered as a keyword along with screen-line and column-position values, causes the system time to be displayed in *hhmmss* format (hours, minutes, and seconds). The time is displayed with the default edit word 'Ob:bb:bb' unless you specify an alternate display format. You can display the current date by using keyword DATE along with line and column entries. DATE appears as a six-position, unedited value unless you associate an edit code or word with it.

```
*.. 1 ...+... 2 ...+... 3 ...+... 4 ...+... 5 ...+... 6 ...+... 7 ...+... 8
AANØ1NØ2NØ3T.Name++++++RLen++TDpBLinPosFunctions++++++++++++++++++++++++++++
 * Sample DDS illustrating the use of DATE and TIME keywords
A           R SAMPLE
A                                        1  5TIME
A                                        1 6ØDATE EDTCDE(Y)
```

Conditioning Indicators

So far, we've discussed field-level keywords as though they are always in effect. However, if this were the case, many would be of little value. Why, for instance, would you want an error message to be displayed each time a field appears on the screen? In fact, you can condition most individual field-level keywords on one or more indicators. The status of these indicators when the screen is displayed determines whether the keywords are in effect. In fact, not only can you condition keywords, but you can also associate fields and literals with indicators to control whether the field or literal appears on the screen.

Moreover, you can use multiple indicators, in AND and/or in OR relationships, to condition screen events. You can include up to three indicators on a DDS line; these indicators are in an AND relationship with one another, such that all the indicators on the line need to be on for the event they are conditioning to occur. If you need to use more than three indicators to control an event, you can signal an AND by coding A in position 7 of the DDS line.

If you want an event to occur if one of several indicators is on (i.e., you want to express an OR relationship), code one indicator per line, with an O in position 7 of the second (and successive) lines. The keyword, field, or literal conditioned by these indicators should appear on the last line of the set.

```
*.. 1 ...+... 2 ...+... 3 ...+... 4 ...+... 5 ...+... 6 ...+... 7 ...+... 8
AANØ1NØ2NØ3T.Name++++++RLen++TDpBLinPosFunctions++++++++++++++++++++++++++++
 * Sample DDS showing the use of indicators
A           R SAMPLE
A 1Ø          FLDA        1Ø    O  4 15
A N1Ø         FLDB        12    O  4 3Ø
A             FLDC         5    O  6  5
A 2Ø 25                              DSPATR(HI)
A 3Ø
AO 4Ø                                DSPATR(UL)
A 1Ø                            15  5'Indicator 1Ø is on'
```

The above code causes FLDA to be displayed if indicator 10 is on, while FLDB is displayed only if indicator 10 is off (signaled by the N in position 8). FLDC will always appear, but it will be displayed in high intensity only if indicators 20 and 25 are both on; it will be underlined if either indicator 30 or indicator 40 is on. The literal 'Indicator 10 is on' will be displayed only if indicator 10 is, in fact, on.

Because you can turn indicators on or off as part of your program logic, they provide a way for program events to control screen display. For example, in our sample program, if the user-entered section number didn't exist in the SECTIONS file, it would be nice not only to return the user to the first screen but also to return with the erroneous section number displayed in reverse video, with the message "Section not found" shown at the bottom of the screen and with the cursor positioned on the field. We can easily cause this to happen by making a few changes in the first screen format. First we'll use the ERRMSG keyword to display a message when an unsuccessful chain occurs; we'll use indicator 90 to condition the ERRMSG keyword, showing it only if *IN90 is off.

```
*.. 1 ...+... 2 ...+... 3 ...+... 4 ...+... 5 ...+... 6 ...+... 7 ...+... 8
AAN01N02N03T.Name++++++RLen++TDpBLinPosFunctions++++++++++++++++++++++++++++++
A* Display file SECTINQR, containing two record formats
A                                      REF(SECTIONS)
A                                      PRINT
A                                      INDARA
A           R SECT1
A                                      BLINK
A                                      CA03(03 'F3=Exit')
A                                    1 28'Section Inquiry'
A                                    3  2'Type value, then Enter.'
A                                    5  5'Section number . .'
A           SECTION     5A  B        5 24
A N90                                  DSPATR(UL)
A N90                                  DSPATR(HI)
A  90                                  ERRMSG('Section not found' 90)
A                                   23  2'F3=Exit'
A           R SECT2
A                                      CA03(03 'F3=Exit')
A                                      CA12(12 'F12=Cancel')
A                                    1 10'Section Information'
A                                    3  2'Section number . . . . . .'
A           SECTNO      R         O  3 29
A                                    4  2'Course . . . . . . . . . .'
A           COURSE      R         O  4 29
A                                    5  2'Instructor . . . . . . . .'
A           INSTR       R         O  5 29
A                                    6  2'Room . . . . . . . . . . .'
A           ROOM        R         O  6 29EDTCDE(Z)
A                                    7  2'Meets on days . . . . . .'
A           DAYS        R         O  7 29
A                                    8  2'Starting time  . . . . . .'
A           BEGTIME     R         O  8 29EDTWRD(' 0:  ')
A                                    9  2'Enrollment . . . . . . . .'
A           ENROLL      R         O  9 29EDTCDE(3)
A                                   21  2'Press Enter to continue.'
A                                   23  2'F3=Exit'
A                                   23 11'F12=Cancel'
```

Note that one of the changes includes changing the usage of field SECTION to B (both) so the erroneous section number will be returned to the screen. If indicator 90 is off, SECTION is displayed as an underlined field in bold, or high intensity. If 90 is on, the error message is displayed and the field automatically appears in reverse image.

A few extra keywords give the display file more functionality: PRINT (to enable the Print key) and BLINK (to cause the cursor to blink).

The only additions to record format SECT2 were to add editing to fields ROOM, DAYS, and ENROLL to achieve the format shown in the sample screen given earlier in the chapter (page 160).

A few simple changes to the RPG IV program will enable it to display the error message if the CHAIN fails. First, we'll define position 90 in the indicator data structure FKeys, to give it a name:

```
*.. 1 ...+... 2 ...+... 3 ...+... 4 ...+... 5 ...+... 6 ...+... 7 ...+... 8
DName++++++++++ETDsFrom+++To/L+++IDc.Keywords+++++++++++++++++++++++++++++++
   // Indicator data structure
D FKeys           DS            99
D   Exit                 3      3N
D   Cancel              12     12N
D   SectNotFnd          90     90N
```

Then, we'll make a simple change to the logic to support the SectNotFnd field:

```
*.. 1 ...+... 2 ...+... 3 ...+... 4 ...+... 5 ...+... 6 ...+... 7 ...+... 8
 /FREE
    DOW NOT Exit;
      EXFMT Sect1;
      IF NOT Exit;
        CHAIN Section Sections;
        SectNotFnd = NOT %FOUND(Sections);
        IF %FOUND(Sections);
          EXFMT Sect2;
        ENDIF;
      ENDIF;
    ENDDO;
 /END-FREE
```

Because SectNotFnd is an indicator, with a value of *ON or *OFF, we can simply use an EVAL operation to move the result of the %FOUND function (also either *ON or *OFF) to SectNotFnd and, consequently, to *IN90.

Interactive File Maintenance

A common data-processing task is **file maintenance** — that is, adding, deleting, and changing records in a company's database files. Over the past decade, programmers have implemented an increasing amount of such updating through interactive, rather than batch, processing.

In a typical update program, the user specifies the key of a record and signals whether that record is to be added, changed, or deleted. Because businesses typically want key-field values to master records to be unique (e.g., they would not want the same customer number to be assigned to two customers), a user request to add a record with a key that matches the key of a record already in the file generally is handled as an error. Similarly, it is impossible to change or delete a record that does not exist in the file.

As a result, the first tasks of an update program are to accept the user's update-option request (add, delete, or change) and the key of the record to be maintained and to check the file for the existence of a record with that key before giving the user the chance to actually enter data values.

A critical concern of interactive updates is how to detect invalid data entries to prevent corrupting the business's database files. On the iSeries, you have three methods of safeguarding against invalid data:

- using validation keywords within the database definitions themselves, provided those fields are displayed for input and reference back to the database file
- including validation keywords within the display file
- validating field values within the program, after they are read from the screen

OS/400 handles some validation automatically for you. For example, the system will not let a user enter a non-numeric value for a numerically defined field. Or, if you have specified type X for a character field, the system will permit alphabetic entries only. The use of validation keywords also automatically limits what the user can enter without the need for further programming on your part.

For example, if you specify VALUES('A' 'C' 'D') for field CODE, attempts by the user to enter any value other than 'A', 'C', or 'D' will automatically cause an error message to appear on the bottom line of the screen and field CODE to be displayed in reverse video.

You should always validate your data as tightly as possible, given the nature of the data. For some fields (e.g., name), the best you can do is ensure that the user enters some value rather than skipping over the field; for other fields (e.g., sex code), you will be able to specify permissible values for the entered data. Never overlook validating data at any point where it enters the system.

To illustrate screen and program design for interactive updating, we will develop a program to update the university's SECTIONS file. To refresh your memory, the file definition is reproduced here:

```
*.. 1 ...+... 2 ...+... 3 ...+... 4 ...+... 5 ...+... 6 ...+... 7 ...+... 8
A..........T.Name++++++RLen++TDpB......Functions++++++++++++++++++++++++++++++
 * Physical file SECTIONS definition
A          R SECREC
A            SECTNO         5            TEXT('Section number')
A            DAYS           3            TEXT('Days class meets')
A            BEGTIME        4   0        TEXT('Time class starts')
A            ROOM           4   0        TEXT('Classroom')
A            ENROLL         3   0        TEXT('Current enrollment')
A            INSTR         15            TEXT('Instructor')
A            COURSE         6            TEXT('Course identifier')
A          K SECTNO
```

The first screen of the application is shown below. The user keys in a section number and an action code to specify whether he or she wants to add, change, or delete the section.

```
                        Section File Maintenance

        Type values, then Enter.

          Section number . . _____
          Action code  . . . _       A=Add
                                      C=Change
                                      D=Delete














        F3=Exit
```

If the user tries to enter an invalid action code, an error message is displayed. If the user enters a section with an action code inappropriate for that section — that is, tries to add a section already in the file or tries to change or delete a section not in the file — an appropriate error message appears on the screen.

If the user's entries are valid and appropriate, screen 2 is displayed, with blank fields if the user is in Add mode or with the field values from the selected record displayed if the mode is Change or Delete. A prompt appropriate to each mode appears at the bottom of the screen. Some data validation takes place as the user enters values. When the user presses Enter, the program performs the appropriate action and then returns the user to the first screen. If the user presses F12 at the second screen, no maintenance is done for that record, and the user is returned to the first screen. Pressing F3 at the second screen causes a program exit without maintenance of the last displayed data. The following screen illustrates the layout of screen 2.

```
                         Section File Maintenance        ADD

       Section number . . . . . . XXXXX
       Course . . . . . . . . . XXXXXX
       Instructor . . . . . . . . XXXXXXXXXXXXXX
       Room . . . . . . . . . . XXXX
       Meets on days  . . . . . XXX
       Starting time  . . . . . XX:XX
       Enrollment . . . . . . . XXX




       Press Enter to add

       F3=Exit  F12=Cancel
```

The DDS for the display file, SECTMAIN, is coded as follows:

```
*.. 1 ...+... 2 ...+... 3 ...+... 4 ...+... 5 ...+... 6 ...+... 7 ...+... 8
AAN01N02N03T.Name++++++RLen++TDpBLinPosFunctions++++++++++++++++++++++++++++
 * Display file SECTMAIN, used for interactively maintaining the
 * SECTIONS file
A                                 REF(SECTIONS)
A                                 PRINT
A                                 INDARA
A                                 CA03(03 'F3=Exit')
A                                 VLDCMDKEY(10)
A           R SCREEN1
A                                 1 28'Section File Maintenance'
A                                 3  2'Type values, then Enter.'
A                                 5  5'Section number . .'
A             SECTION      5   B  5 24
A  30
AO 31
AO 32
AO 91                             DSPATR(PC)
A  30                             ERRMSG('Record already exists' 30)
A  31                             ERRMSG('No record for change' 31)
A  32                             ERRMSG('No record for delete' 32)
A  91                             ERRMSG('I/O error' 91)
A                                 6  5'Action code . . .'
A             ACTION       1   I  6 24VALUES('A' 'C' 'D')
A                                 6 30'A=Add'
A                                 7 30'C=Change'
A                                 8 30'D=Delete'
A                                24  2'F3=Exit'
```

continued...

continued...

```
*.. 1 ...+... 2 ...+... 3 ...+... 4 ...+... 5 ...+... 6 ...+... 7 ...+... 8
A           R SCREEN2                     CA12(12 'F12=Cancel')
A                                       1 28'Section File Maintenance'
A             MODE        6   0 1 60DSPATR(HI)
A                                       3  2'Section number . . . . . .'
A             SECTNO    R     0 3 29
A                                       4  2'Course . . . . . . . . .'
A             COURSE    R   B 4 29
A   40                            DSPATR(PR)
A                                       5  2'Instructor . . . . . . . .'
A             INSTR     R   B 5 29
A   40                            DSPATR(PR)
A                                       6  2'Room . . . . . . . . . .'
A             ROOM      R   B 6 29EDTCDE(Z)
A   40                            DSPATR(PR)
A                                       7  2'Meets on days  . . . . . .'
A             DAYS      R   B 7 29VALUES('MWF' 'TTH')
A   40                            DSPATR(PR)
A                                       8  2'Starting time  . . . . . .'
A             BEGTIME   R   B 8 29EDTWRD(' 0:   ')
A   40                            DSPATR(PR)
A                                       9  2'Enrollment . . . . . . . .'
A             ENROLL    R   B 9 29EDTCDE(3)
A   40                            DSPATR(PR)
A                                      21  2'Press Enter to '
A             MODE2       6   0 21 17DSPATR(HI)
A                                      23  2'F3=Exit'
A                                      23 11'F12=Cancel'
```

This DDS contains one DSPATR entry you have not seen before: DSPATR(PR) protects input-capable fields (i.e., usage I or B) from input keying. Because you can condition display attributes with indicators, you can use this attribute to permit or prevent a user from keying a value into a field, depending on processing needs at that time. The maintenance program shown later in this chapter uses DSPATR(PR) to prevent the user from changing field values within a record when he or she has selected the delete option.

Notice in the above DDS for record format SCREEN2 that SECTNO is Output only to prevent the user from modifying that field. Also, record format SCREEN1 uses indicators to display error messages differentially, depending on processing outcomes within the program. Because SECTION should appear in reverse image with the cursor positioned to that field for any file error, DSPATR(PC) is conditioned by four indicators in an "OR" relation; if any one of the four indicators is on, the display attributes will be in effect. DSPATR(PR), or protected, is enabled for all SCREEN2 input-capable fields during deletion mode to prevent the user from changing these fields.

Before jumping into the RPG IV code required to implement this interactive application, let's work out the logic of what the application should do. This "think-before-acting" approach to programming typically leads to more structured code. And remember, when coding for interactive applications, it is hard to resist falling into the GOTO habit. The pseudocode that follows illustrates the logic needed for this maintenance program. Notice that the pseudocode breaks the program into separate modules based on the function the code performs.

Program Mainline
WHILE user wants to continue
   Display screen 1
   Read screen 1
   SELECT
      WHEN user signals exit
         Leave
      WHEN action is Add
         Do subroutine AddRecord
      WHEN action is Change
         Do subroutine ChngRecord
      WHEN action is Delete
         Do subroutine DeltRecord
   ENDSELECT
ENDWHILE
END program

Subroutine AddRecord
Chain to Section file
IF record found
   Set on error indicator (AddError)
ELSE
   Zero and blank all record fields except section number
   Display screen 2
   Read screen 2
   IF not valid command key
      Write record to file
   ENDIF
ENDIF
END Subroutine

Subroutine ChngRecord
Chain to Section file
IF record not found
   Set on error indicator (ChgError)
ELSE
   Display screen 2
   Read screen 2
   IF not valid command key
      Update record to file
   ENDIF
ENDIF
END Subroutine

Subroutine DeltRecord
Chain to Section file
IF record not found
    Set on error indicator (DltError)
ELSE
    Display screen 2
    Read screen 2
    IF not valid command key
        Delete record from file
    ENDIF
ENDIF
END Subroutine

Once you have the pseudocode worked out, coding the RPG IV is simple. In the following program, notice that indicators turned on within the program to control screen display may need to be turned off. Those indicators associated with error messages in the screen are set off automatically.

```
*.. 1 ...+... 2 ...+... 3 ...+... 4 ...+... 5 ...+... 6 ...+... 7 ...+... 8
  // ****************************************************************
  // This program interactively maintains file SECTIONS.         *
  //    Author: Judy Yaeger.   Date Written: 11-92.              *
  //    Revised Jan 2002 by Meyers.                              *
  //                                                             *
  // ****************************************************************

FSections  UF A E          K DISK
FSectMain  CF   E            WORKSTN INDDS(Indicators)

  // Indicator data structure
D Indicators      DS
D  Exit                   3      3N
D  CmdKeyPressed         10     10N
D  Cancel                12     12N
D  AddError              30     30N
D  ChgError              31     31N
D  DltError              32     32N
D  Protect               40     40N
D  IOError               91     91N

 /FREE
    DOW NOT Exit;
      DspAtrPr = *OFF;
      Cancel = *OFF;
      IF NOT IOError AND NOT AddError AND NOT ChgError AND NOT DltError;
        Section = *BLANKS;
      ENDIF;
      EXFMT Screen1;
      SELECT;
        WHEN Exit;
          LEAVE;
        WHEN Cancel;
          ITER;
        WHEN Action = 'A';
          EXSR AddRecord;
        WHEN Action = 'C';
          EXSR ChgRecord;
```

continued...

continued…

```
*.. 1 ...+... 2 ...+... 3 ...+... 4 ...+... 5 ...+... 6 ...+... 7 ...+... 8
      WHEN Action = 'D';
        EXSR DltRecord;
    ENDSL;
  ENDDO;

  *INLR = *ON;
  RETURN;

// ****************************************************************
//   Subroutine AddRecord: Processes an Add action request        *
// ****************************************************************
  BEGSR AddRecord;
    CHAIN Section Sections;
    AddErr = %FOUND(Sections);        //Set AddErr if record already exists
    IF NOT %FOUND(Sections);
      Mode = 'ADD';
      Mode2 = 'add';
      SectNo = Section;
      EXSR Initial;
      EXFMT Screen2;
      IF NOT CmdKeyPressed;
        WRITE(E) SecRec;
        IOError = %ERROR;
      ENDIF;
    ENDIF;
  ENDSR;

// ****************************************************************
//   Subroutine ChgRecord: Processes a Change request             *
// ****************************************************************
  BEGSR ChgRecord;
    CHAIN Section Sections;
    ChgError = %NOT FOUND(Sections);
    IF %FOUND(Sections);
      Mode = 'CHANGE';
      Mode2 = 'change';
      EXFMT Screen2;
      IF NOT CmdKeyPressed;
        UPDATE(E) SecRec;
        IOError = %ERROR;
      ENDIF;
    ENDIF;
  ENDSR;

// ****************************************************************
//   Subroutine DltRecord: Processes a Delete request             *
// ****************************************************************
  BEGSR DltRecord;
    CHAIN Section Sections;
    DltError = NOT %FOUND(Sections);
    IF %FOUND(Sections);
      Mode =  'DELETE';
      Mode2 = 'delete';
      Protect = *ON;
      EXFMT Screen2;
      IF NOT CmdKeyPressed;
        DELETE(E) SecRec;
```

continued…

continued...

```
*.. 1 ...+... 2 ...+... 3 ...+... 4 ...+... 5 ...+... 6 ...+... 7 ...+... 8
          IOError = %ERROR;
        ENDIF;
      ENDIF;
    ENDSR;

   // ********************************************************
   // Subroutine Initial: Initializes record fields to blanks *
   // and zeros preparatory to an Add.                        *
   // ********************************************************
    BEGSR Initial;
      Course = *BLANKS;
      Instr = *BLANKS;
      Room = *ZEROS;
      Days = *BLANKS;
      BegTime = *ZEROS;
      Enroll = *ZEROS;
    ENDSR;
```

Many RPG IV programmers feel that the fields used in the display file should not be the same as the database fields, and in some applications, depending on the program design, such separate definition in fact may be necessary to prevent losing values input by the user (or read from the database). To implement this approach, simply define the display file fields independently, giving them new names. Then, in your RPG IV program, add two subroutines — one that assigns the screen field values to the database fields and one that does the reverse (assigns the database fields to the screen fields). Before you add or update a record, execute the subroutine that assigns the screen fields to the database fields. Before you display the data-entry screen for a change or delete, execute the subroutine that assigns the database fields to the screen fields.

Screen Design and CUA

The screens illustrated in this chapter are based on a set of design standards called **Common User Access (CUA)**. IBM developed and promotes CUA as a way of standardizing user interfaces across platforms. All the iSeries screens follow these standards.

Screens can be classified into one of four panel types:

- menu
- list
- entry
- information

Under CUA, all panels have the same general layout: a panel title on the first screen line, an optional information area, an instruction area, a panel body area (where either the menu, list, data-entry fields, or informational output occurs), and, at the bottom of the screen, a command area, a list of function keys, and a message line. The following screen illustrates the layout for these types of panels.

```
Panel ID                        Panel Title

Optional information area (on menu, list, or info)
   and/or controlling fields for list panel

Instruction area (on menu, entry, or list)

Panel body area
   -    Menu choices on menu panel
   -    List area on list panel
   -    Entry prompts on entry panel
   -    Information prompts on information panel




Optional command area
Function key area
Message area
```

CUA provides specific guidelines for row and column placement of screen items, vertical alignment of screen columns, capitalization and punctuation, function key use, error-condition handling, and so on. Although you may think such standards stifle creativity, there are two excellent reasons for standardizing the user interface.

First, a standardized interface makes it easier for users to learn new applications because the interface is consistent with other applications. If F3 is always the Exit key across applications, for instance, and F12 always backs up to the previous screen, users don't have to learn new commands counter to those they've used in other applications.

A second major reason for adopting CUA (or other) standards is that such standards can improve programmer productivity. If you adopt a set of design standards, you can easily develop a set of generic DDS descriptions — one for each panel type — that you can then easily tailor to your specific applications.

Chapter Summary

Display files, defined in DDS, are the mechanism that lets a user and a program interact. Each record screen format of a display file defines a screen. The screen format may include literals to be displayed and fields for output, input, or both. Each data item is positioned on the screen based on line and column DDS entries.

DDS relies on keywords to achieve specific desired effects. You can associate some keywords with the entire file, others with a specific record format, and others yet with specific fields. Keywords enable function keys, determine the appearance and format of displayed items, control what the user can enter as input values, and associate error messages with fields.

You can condition most keywords, as well as fields and literals, by indicators. If the indicator is on at display time, the keyword is in effect (or the field or literal is displayed); if the indicator is off, the effect or data item with which the indicator is associated is suppressed. The indicators are turned on within a program to control screen display. On the display side, you can associate valid command keys with indicators to convey information back to the program. While DDS requires the use of numbered indicators to condition fields, RPG lets you map those indicators to an indicator data structure wherein you can name the indicators.

Today's businesses frequently use interactive applications to display database information or the results of processing data; more and more companies also use interactive applications for file maintenance. In the latter case, you should pay special attention to validating user's entries to maintain data file integrity.

IBM has developed a set of screen-design guidelines called Common User Access (CUA) that can standardize iSeries interactive applications. Such standards of screen design can make it easier for users to learn new applications and for programmers to develop new applications more efficiently.

Key Terms

batch processing
combined file
Common User Access (CUA)
data validation
display attributes
display files
file maintenance
indicator data structure
interactive applications
keyboard-shift attribute
Screen Design Aid (SDA)

Discussion/Review Questions

1. Contrast batch and interactive applications.
2. What are the permissible I/O operations that can be used with record formats of display files? What are the effects of each?
3. Describe how a combined file differs from an update file.
4. What lets the system determine whether you are using a keyword as a file-, record-, or field-level keyword?
5. What's the difference between referring to a function key as CA (Command Attention) and CF (Command Function)? How does each affect your program?
6. Explain the meaning of each of the following display attribute codes: BL, CS, ND, HI, UL, RI, PC.
7. Why might you want to know, in general, whether a user pressed an enabled function key or a special key (i.e., use the VLDCMDKEY keyword) when each valid key has its own indicator whose status can be checked within your program?
8. What are the relational codes used with COMP in DDS display files?
9. What's the difference between Mandatory Enter and Mandatory Fill?
10. What happens when an error message (ERRMSG) is in effect for a field? Describe the screen effects.
11. How can program events influence screen display, and how can screen input influence program flow of control?
12. Describe how a record's existence affects the validity of adding, deleting, or changing the record when maintaining a file with unique keys.

13. Discuss the pros and cons of adopting IBM's CUA standards in your screen design.

14. What impact do you think graphical user interfaces (GUIs), as typified by Microsoft's Windows environment and Internet browsers, will have on future iSeries interactive applications?

Exercises

1. Assume that your school has a student file containing name, sex, total credits accumulated, residency code, grade point average, major (or degree program), and student classification. Write the DDS for a record format that prompts the user to enter values for these fields, including as many validation keywords as are appropriate.

2. Write a DDS record format that would prompt the user to enter salesperson number, date of sale, and amount of sale. The cursor should blink, salesperson number should be underlined with column separators, date of sale should be displayed in high intensity, and amount of sale should be in reverse image and blinking.

3. Rewrite the DDS from Exercise 2 so that the salesperson number is underlined if indicators 10 and 12 are on and displayed with column separators if 10 or 12 is on. Date of sale should be displayed in high intensity only if indicator 10 is on. Amount of sale should be in reverse image and blinking if 10 and 12 are on or if 14 and 16 are on.

4. Write the pseudocode for a program to allow interactive processing of received goods. The program should let a user enter a product number (on Screen1), determine whether that product number exists in the file, and either display an error message (on Screen1) if the product number is incorrect or display a second screen (Screen2) that asks the user to enter the quantity of the product received. The amount entered should be added to the current quantity on hand and the product record then updated. Include provisions for exiting and canceling.

5. Write the RPG IV for the pseudocode of Exercise 4. Don't code the DDS. Make up whatever file and field names you need. Document whatever indicators you use.

Programming Assignments

1. CompuSell wants you to develop an interactive application that will let the company enter its product number for an item and display a screen of information about the supplier of that product. The screen should include all the information in the supplier file CSSUPP. You also must use inventory file CSINVP to obtain the correct supplier number for the item in question. Appendix F describes the data files; follow your instructor's directions for obtaining the files.

   Develop the DDS and the RPG IV program for this application. Design your application with two screens: one inquiry screen and one informational display. Write your program to loop so that following the display of the requested information, the program prompts the user for a new product number; continue until the user signals that he or she is finished. Follow your instructor's directions for testing this program.

2. CompuSell wants you to write an interactive file-maintenance program for its customer master file, CSCSTP (described in Appendix F). If the user wants to add a new customer, your program must determine the appropriate number to assign the customer (numbers are assigned sequentially) and provide the number automatically for the user; also automatically use the system date for the date of last order and assign balance due a value of zero. For a change

request, let the user change any field except the customer number. Do not let the user delete a record if the customer has a balance greater than zero. Follow your instructor's directions for testing this program.

3. Wexler University wants you to write an interactive file-maintenance program for its instructor file, WUINSTP (see Appendix F). Design screens as appropriate for the application. Let the users add, delete, or change instructor records. Do not let them change the Social Security number or add a record with a duplicate Social Security number. Include as much data validation as you can, given the nature of the data fields being entered. Follow your instructor's directions for testing this program.

4. CompuSell wants you to write an interactive application to enter customer orders. The application should begin by determining the appropriate starting order number, based on the last order number in orders file CSORDP. The main process loop should then begin by requesting the customer number; only orders for established customers (those in customer master file CSCSTP) can be processed. If the customer exists, the program should set up a loop to let the user enter ordered items until the order is complete.

   For each item, the user should enter the product number and the quantity desired. If the product is not in inventory file CSINVP, or if the quantity on hand is less than the quantity desired, inform the user through error messages that the item cannot be ordered; otherwise, update the quantity-on-hand field of the inventory file to reflect the new, lower quantity on hand and write a record to the order/products file (CSORDPRP) for that item.

   When the user has finished entering items for a customer, determine whether payment was included in the order, and if so, for how much. A record should be written to the CSORDP file, leaving the amount due zero. (The files CSORDP and CSORDPRP will be used by different programs to generate pick lists and invoices.) See Appendix F for the file descriptions.

5. Wexler University wants you to write a program that will provide an online registration system for its students. The registration system should work as follows:

   a. The student should be prompted to enter his or her Social Security number. If the student is not found in the student master file, the program should not let the student proceed.

   b. If the student is in the file, he or she should be allowed to register for courses until signaling that he or she is finished.

   c. For each desired course, the student will enter the section number. If the section number is invalid, the student should be informed. If the number is valid, the program should display the course identification, title, and credits on the screen, along with the time and days the section meets and an indication of whether the section is full or not full (current enrollment < cap).

   d. If the section is not full, and if the student indicates that this is, in fact, the course and section into which he or she wants to enroll, the program should confirm the enrollment to the student, update the current enrollment figure in the current section record by adding 1 to it, and add a record to the current enrollment file for this student in this section.

   When the student has finished enrolling, the program should return to the initial screen to let the next student enroll. This process should continue until the user presses F3 to exit the application completely.

   Your program will use files WUSTDP, WUSCTP, WUCRSP, and WUENRLP (Appendix F describes these files). Follow your instructor's directions for testing this program.

Chapter 9

Tables and Arrays

Chapter Overview

In this chapter, you will learn how to create, store, and access tables of data. You will also learn how to define and use arrays, which are data structures that can simplify repetitive processing of similar data.

Representing Tables of Data

In common usage, a **table** is a collection of data organized into columns and rows. Similar kinds of data are stored within a column, and the data elements within a row of the table are related, or "belong" together. Typically, the data elements in the first column of a table are organized sequentially in ascending order to facilitate finding an item. Once you find the item you want in column 1, you then read across the row to extract the data related to that item.

The following three-column table, for example, would let you look up a U.S. state code to extract the name and sales tax rate of the state associated with that state code. (Note that the full table would include 50 codes and their corresponding names and tax rates, not just the eight shown.)

State code	State name	Tax rate
AK	Alaska	.0000
AL	Alabama	.0400
AR	Arkansas	.0000
AZ	Arizona	.0500
CA	California	.0725
CO	Colorado	.0300
CT	Connecticut	.0600
DE	Delaware	.0000
. . .	. . .	. . .

RPG IV provides two data structures that you can use to represent such collections of data: tables and arrays. Originally, RPG included only tables; IBM added arrays to the language later to allow greater flexibility than tables could offer.

Although tables and arrays have several similarities, the capabilities of arrays go beyond those of tables. In fact, some RPG programmers no longer use tables; they prefer to use arrays for any solution that requires addressing multiple data values with a single field name. In this chapter, we'll look at basic tables first and then investigate the added power that arrays provide.

RPG IV Tables

RPG IV lets you define table data structures so that your program can extract data in a way analogous to the way you use tables. The major difference between an RPG IV table and tables as we are used to thinking about them is that one RPG IV table represents only a single column of data. In RPG IV terms, the state table shown above is actually three related tables.

Table Definition

Data elements within an RPG IV table need to have the same length, the same data type, and, if they contain numeric data, the same number of decimal positions. In the state table, the state codes are all two-byte-long character data; the state names, however, have different lengths. To use the names in an RPG IV table, you would have to determine the length of the longest state name (South Carolina and North Carolina both have 14 characters) and pad the names of the other states with trailing blanks to make them all 14 characters long.

Definition Specifications define tables. Recall that when your program uses Definition Specifications, these specifications must follow the File Specifications and precede the Input Specifications. The Definition Specification entries required to define a table vary depending on the complexity and layout of the data you are storing in table format and where the table data values are coming from. However, table definitions always require the use of one or more keywords, coded in positions 44–80 (the Keywords area) of the Definition Specification. Within this area, you can enter keywords separated by one or more spaces in any order, with several keywords on the same line.

You can use a Definition Specification continuation line to complete a list of required keywords if you need additional room. If you use a continuation line, simply enter it immediately following the initial Definition Specification, specifying the additional keywords in positions 44–80. Other than leaving positions 7–43 of the continuation line blank, you need to give no additional signal that the line completes the previous statement. The following headers show the layout of a Definition Specification and a Definition Specification continuation line:

```
*.. 1 ...+... 2 ...+... 3 ...+... 4 ...+... 5 ...+... 6 ...+... 7 ...+... 8
DName++++++++++ETDsFrom+++To/L+++IDc.Keywords+++++++++++++++++++++++++++++++
D.................................Keywords-continuation++++++++++++++++++
```

With that overview completed, let's now look at how to define various kinds of tables. Consider first how RPG IV would handle a very simple table — a table of 50 state codes. Once you understand the definitional requirements for this table, you can expand your understanding to more complex examples. The table of state codes appears below.

State code
AK
AL
AR
AZ
CA
CO
CT
DE
. . .

An RPG IV table name must begin with the characters TAB (in uppercase, lowercase, or mixed-case letters), followed by additional characters to specifically name the table. You can enter the table name anywhere in positions 7–21 (Name+++++++++++) of the Definition Specifications. An S coded left-adjusted in positions 24–25 (Ds) declares the table to be a standalone field. Unlike other standalone fields we have worked with, however, a table stores multiple values. To indicate how many values, or elements, the table contains, you must include keyword DIM (for Dimension) in positions 44–80, specifying the number of table elements within parentheses after the keyword.

You also must indicate the length of each table element right-adjusted in positions 33–39 (To/L++) of the specification line, along with the number of decimal positions within each element (for numeric table data) in positions 41–42 (Dc). If the table data is arranged in order, you should indicate this order by including keyword ASCEND (for ascending data) or DESCEND (for descending data), although this entry is optional for most tables.

The following Definition Specification associates the table name TabCode with our state codes and specifies that the table contains 50 elements of two-position-long character data in ascending order.

```
*.. 1 ...+... 2 ...+... 3 ...+... 4 ...+... 5 ...+... 6 ...+... 7 ...+... 8
DName++++++++++ETDsFrom+++To/L+++IDc.Keywords+++++++++++++++++++++++++++++++
D TabCode        S              2    DIM(50) ASCEND
```

This table definition allocates memory so that the entire table of data can remain in memory throughout a program's execution.

Additional entries are required to complete this definition. These entries depend on the source of the data values to be stored in the table and the layout of the original data. You can put data values into a table in two ways: You can either hard-code the data within your program (this kind of table is often called a compile-time table), or you can instruct the computer to obtain the data from a separate disk file each time the program runs (a pre-runtime, or pre-execution, table).

Compile-Time Tables

A **compile-time table** obtains its data from the program's source code; the data is bound to the table when you compile the program. The table data must be entered at the very end of the program, following the last program entries (most often the last Output Specification).

RPG IV uses what is called a ****CTDATA record** as a delimiter (or separator line) to explicitly identify the table whose data follows. To code this delimiter, place an asterisk (*) in positions 1 and 2 of a line following the last line of program code; in positions 3–8, enter CTDATA (for compile-time data); leave position 9 blank; and, starting in position 10, enter the name of the table whose data follows.

The actual table data follows this separator line. How you enter the data at this point is up to you. You could put one table entry per line, two per line, three per line, and so on. In our example, because each state code is two bytes long, we could code all 50 state codes in two lines of 25 states each if we wanted to do so. The only stipulations are

- that the values must begin in the first position of each line (unlike most RPG specifications, which begin in position 6 of each line)
- that they must be entered in the order in which you want them to appear in the table
- that multiple entries per line be entered contiguously (without spaces separating them)
- that you are consistent in the number of entries you put on each line

If the number of entries per line is not an even multiple of the number of total table entries, the odd number of entries goes on the last line. For example, assume that you decide to enter four state codes on one line. There would be 12 lines of four codes, with a final thirteenth line containing only two codes. The coding would look as shown on the following page:

```
    *.. 1 ...+... 2 ...+... 3 ...+... 4 ...+... 5 ...+... 6 ...+... 7 ...+... 8
**CTDATA TabCode
AKALARAZ
CACOCTDE
. . .
WVWY
```

Every compile-time table requires a keyword, CTDATA, included within its Definition Specification to signal that the table's compile-time data appears at the end of the program. In addition, you may need to use keyword PERRCD to indicate how the data values are entered. Each program line in your source member is a record in the source file. Accordingly, if you have entered four state codes per line, there are four table entries per record. If you had entered only one state code per line, there would be one table entry per record. Including the PERRCD keyword, with the number of table entries per record (or code line) indicated within parentheses after the keyword, lets the system correctly obtain the data to load within the table. If you omit keyword PERRCD for a compile-time table, the system assumes you have entered the data with one entry per record.

The following code shows the Definition Specification for the state-code table as a compile-time table with four entries per record.

```
*.. 1 ...+... 2 ...+... 3 ...+... 4 ...+... 5 ...+... 6 ...+... 7 ...+... 8
DName+++++++++++ETDsFrom+++To/L+++IDc.Keywords++++++++++++++++++++++++++++++++
     // Compile-time table of 50 state codes, entered in ascending sequence,
     // 4 per record
D TabCode         S             2    DIM(50) ASCEND CTDATA PERRCD(4)
```

Compile-time tables are useful for relatively small tables whose data is not likely to change over time. With large tables, it would be a waste of a programmer's time to enter the data as part of the program. Moreover, if the table data is **volatile** (i.e., frequently changing), a programmer would have to go back to the source program, change the table data at the end of the program, and recompile the program each time the data needed updating. You should avoid this practice, because each time you enter Source Entry Utility (SEU) to change your source code, you run the risk of inadvertently introducing errors into the program.

Pre-Runtime Tables

An alternate way to handle data values required by a table is to store the data in a database file that is loaded into the table each time the program is run. This kind of table is called a **pre-runtime** or **pre-execution table**, because RPG IV automatically retrieves all the table data from the file before the program's procedural processing begins.

The Definition Specification for a pre-runtime table varies slightly from that of a compile-time table. Instead of using keyword CTDATA, pre-runtime tables require you to include keyword FROMFILE, specifying the name of the file containing the table data within parentheses following the keyword. The value indicated with keyword PERRCD should indicate how many table entries are coded per record within the table file; if only one value appears per record, you can omit the PERRCD keyword.

```
*.. 1 ...+... 2 ...+... 3 ...+... 4 ...+... 5 ...+... 6 ...+... 7 ...+... 8
DName+++++++++++ETDsFrom+++To/L+++IDc.Keywords++++++++++++++++++++++++++++++++
     // Pre-runtime table of 50 state codes, entered one per record in
     // ascending order
D TabCode         S             2    DIM(50) FROMFILE(States) ASCEND
```

Because the data for a pre-runtime table is obtained from a file, you must include a definition of this file within the File Specifications of the program that uses the table. The File Specification for a file that contains table data differs somewhat from that of other files with which you have worked. The file type (position 17) is I (Input) because the program reads the data, but the file's designation (position 18) is T (Table); this entry directs the system to read all the data into a table automatically at the program's start. Because the table is defined internally within the program, rather than externally, you code an F (for fixed format) in position 22 and include the appropriate record length in positions 23–27.

```
*.. 1 ...+... 2 ...+... 3 ...+... 4 ...+... 5 ...+... 6 ...+... 7 ...+... 8
FFilename++IPEASFRLen+LKlen+AIDevice+.Keywords+++++++++++++++++++++++++++++
   // Input table file of state codes, with one code per record.
FStates    IT F   2        DISK
```

If you want to write the table back to a file at the end of program execution — perhaps because your program has changed some of the table values and you want to update the file to reflect these changed values — you need to include keyword TOFILE as part of the table's Definition Specification, specifying the name of the target file in parentheses after the keyword. If the FROMFILE is different from the TOFILE, you would need an additional File Specification defining the TOFILE as an output file. If the table data is to be written back to the same file from which it was initially read, the file type should be C (for combined):

```
*.. 1 ...+... 2 ...+... 3 ...+... 4 ...+... 5 ...+... 6 ...+... 7 ...+... 8
FFilename++IPEASFRLen+LKlen+AIDevice+.Keywords+++++++++++++++++++++++++++++
DName+++++++++++ETDsFrom+++To/L+++IDc.Keywords+++++++++++++++++++++++++++++
D.................................Keywords-continuation++++++++++++++++++
   // Table file of 50 state codes, with one code per record; records to be
   // rewritten at end of processing
FStates    CT F   2        DISK

   // Pre-runtime table of 50 state codes, entered one per record in
   // ascending order; table file to be rewritten at end of processing
D TabCode        S           2  DIM(50) FROMFILE(States) ASCEND
D                               TOFILE(States)
```

Table Lookups

Tables are used for one primary purpose: to look up data values using RPG's %TLOOKUP function. The %TLOOKUP function is coded using this format:

```
%TLOOKUPxx(search-arg:table)
```

Typically, you have a field — either a field from an input file or a result field from a calculation — that you want to find in the table; this value is the search argument ("search-arg" in the above format). Next, enter the name of the table. The *xx* lets you signal the type of match you want to find between the table value and the Factor 1 value. Most of the time, you want an equal match, so you would simply code %TLOOKUP, but other values are valid as well:

- %TLOOKUP — find equal match
- %TLOOKUPLT — find table value closest to but less than search-arg
- %TLOOKUPLE — find equal match or value closest to but less than search-arg
- %TLOOKUPGE — find equal match or value closest to but greater than search-arg
- %TLOOKUPGT — find table value closest to but greater than search-arg

When %TLOOKUP is successful, an internal pointer is positioned at the matching table value, and the function returns the value *ON. An unsuccessful lookup returns the value *OFF. You can use this status to control subsequent processing within the program. The %FOUND and %EQUAL functions are not affected. The following code illustrates a simple **table lookup**.

```
*.. 1 ...+... 2 ...+... 3 ...+... 4 ...+... 5 ...+... 6 ...+... 7 ...+... 8
 /FREE
  // Use input field CodeIn as the search argument of a lookup within
  // table TabCode. %TLOOKUP returns *ON if an equal match is found.

    IF %TLOOKUP(CodeIn:TabCode);
      EXSR CodeFound;
    ELSE;
      EXSR BadCode;
    ENDIF;

 /END-FREE
```

A table lookup involving a single table is of limited value. Its primary purpose would be to validate the value of an input field. The more common use of tables — to look up a value in one column of a table to extract a related value from a second column — requires some additional table definition in RPG IV and a slight modification of the %TLOOKUP function.

Two Related Tables

Recall that in RPG IV a table corresponds to one column of information. Assume you wanted to represent the information in the following example in table format within RPG IV.

State code	State name
AK	Alaska
AL	Alabama
AR	Arkansas
AZ	Arizona
CA	California
CO	Colorado
CT	Connecticut
DE	Delaware
. . .	. . .

To represent both the state codes and the state names within RPG IV requires defining two tables. The form of those definitions depends on how you have entered the data supplying the table values. When you are entering pairs of related table data, it is often convenient to enter the pairs together, as the following example shows.

```
   *.. 1 ...+... 2 ...+... 3 ...+... 4 ...+... 5 ...+... 6 ...+... 7 ...+... 8
**CTDATA TabCode
AKAlaska
ALAlabama
ARArkansas
AZArizona
CACalifornia
COColorado
CTConnecticut
DEDelaware
 . . .
```

This form of table-data entry is called **alternating format**. The state codes would be considered the primary table, alternating with the state names in the data. To reflect this data organization, the Definition Specification for the primary table remains identical to the way it would be defined if it were a standalone table. A second Definition Specification is required to define the table that is in alternating format. In this definition, you must include keyword ALT followed by the name of the primary table enclosed in parentheses. Keyword DIM is also a required entry for the alternating table. However, you cannot include the CTDATA, FROMFILE, TOFILE, or PERRCD keyword in the alternating table's definition; the alternating table "inherits" these keywords from the table with which it alternates.

```
*.. 1 ...+... 2 ...+... 3 ...+... 4 ...+... 5 ...+... 6 ...+... 7 ...+... 8
DName++++++++++ETDsFrom+++To/L+++IDc.Keywords+++++++++++++++++++++++++++++++
   // Two compile-time tables are defined in alternating format; each table
   // has 50 elements, 1 per record. TabCode is in ascending sequence.
D TabCode         S              2    DIM(50) CTDATA ASCEND PERRCD(1)
D TabName         S             14    DIM(50) ALT(TabCode)
```

In the tables defined above, the state names are stored in table TabName, and the length of each name is stated as 14 — the length of the longest name. Note that the number-of-entries-per-record specification in keyword PERRCD is 1 because only one pair of values is coded on each line. If the data had been laid out so that several pairs of data were entered on the same line, that keyword entry would need to be adjusted to accurately reflect the data layout.

Although the example above deals with compile-time tables in alternating-format, pre-runtime tables can be in alternating format, too. Simply make sure the data is entered in alternating format in the file records, and include the file definition in the File Specifications; then, in the Definition Specification of the primary table, include the FROMFILE and TOFILE (if needed) keywords rather than keyword CTDATA. The table in alternating format with the primary table would require only the DIM and ALT keywords:

```
*.. 1 ...+... 2 ...+... 3 ...+... 4 ...+... 5 ...+... 6 ...+... 7 ...+... 8
FFilename++IPEASFRlen+LKlen+AIDevice+.Keywords+++++++++++++++++++++++++++++++
DName++++++++++ETDsFrom+++To/L+++IDc.Keywords+++++++++++++++++++++++++++++++
   // Table file of state codes and state names in alternating format
FStates    IT  F  16         DISK

   // Two pre-runtime tables whose data is stored in alternating format
   // in file States
D TabCode         S              2    DIM(50) PERRCD(1) FROMFILE(States)
D                                     ASCEND
D TabName         S             14    DIM(50) ALT(TabCode)
```

You can then use the tables to look up a state code to extract a state name. To extract the name related to the state code, TabName must appear as the third argument in the %TLOOKUP function. A successful code lookup causes the internal pointer to be positioned in TabName at the name that corresponds to the matched code in TabCode. The result is that TabName contains the desired state name, and you can print or display TabName or use it in any other operation for which you need the appropriate state name.

If the lookup of TabCode is not successful, TabName will contain the state name from the last successful lookup. Good programming practice suggests you should always provide for the possibility of unsuccessful lookups within your code, as the following example demonstrates.

```
*.. 1 ...+... 2 ...+... 3 ...+... 4 ...+... 5 ...+... 6 ...+... 7 ...+... 8
 /FREE
  // Look up CodeIn in TabCode to extract TabName.

    IF %TLOOKUP(CodeIn:TabCode:TabName);
      EXSR PrintName;
    ELSE;
      EXSR BadCode;
    ENDIF;

 /END-FREE
```

Multiple Related Tables

RPG IV lets you define only one table in alternating format with a primary table. How, then, can you represent the following data so you can look up a state code to extract both the state name and the sales tax rate?

State code	State name	Tax rate
AK	Alaska	.0000
AL	Alabama	.0400
AR	Arkansas	.0000
AZ	Arizona	.0500
CA	California	.0725
CO	Colorado	.0300
CT	Connecticut	.0600
DE	Delaware	.0000
. . .	. . .	. . .

The most direct way to handle multicolumn table data is to first enter all the data from one column, then all the data from the next, and so on, entering each table's data separately. A **CTDATA record must appear between each set of data:

```
    *.. 1 ...+... 2 ...+... 3 ...+... 4 ...+... 5 ...+... 6 ...+... 7 ...+... 8
**CTDATA TabCode
AK
AL
AR
AZ
. . .
**CTDATA TabName
Alaska
Alabama
Arkansas
Arizona
. . .
**CTDATA TabRate
0000
0400
0000
0500
. . .
```

With this data layout, you define each table independently on the Definition Specifications, as shown in the following example. The calculations would then require two separate lookups, one to extract the appropriate state name and the other to extract the tax rate.

```
*.. 1 ...+... 2 ...+... 3 ...+... 4 ...+... 5 ...+... 6 ...+... 7 ...+... 8
DName++++++++++ETDsFrom+++To/L+++IDc.Keywords++++++++++++++++++++++++++++++
   // Three tables independently defined
D TabCode        S              2    DIM(50) PERRCD(1) CTDATA ASCEND
D TabName        S             14    DIM(50) PERRCD(1) CTDATA
D TabRate        S              4  4 DIM(50) PERRCD(1) CTDATA

 /FREE
  // Look up state name and tax rate based on code;
  // then use the tax rate to calculate tax due.

    IF %TLOOKUPCodeIn:TabCode:TabName)
      AND %TLOOKUP(CodeIn:TabCode:TabRate);
      EVAL(H) TaxDue = Amount * TabRate;
    ELSE;
      EXSR BadCode;
    ENDIF;
 /END-FREE
```

Although the sample coding above uses compile-time tables, the same techniques of entering multicolumn data and performing lookups apply to pre-runtime tables as well, where the data is stored in a table file.

Range Tables

One final kind of table needs to be considered: a **range table**. Consider the following table of shipping charges:

Package weight (lb)	Shipping charge ($)
0–1	2.50
2–5	4.25
6–10	7.50
11–20	9.00
21–40	12.00
41–70	16.00

You would use this table to look up a package weight to determine the shipping charges for the package. Unlike the previous tables, in this table the weight column entries represent a range of values rather than discrete values.

How should these values be represented, and how should the LOOKUP be performed? One solution is to represent this data as two tables, storing only the upper end of the range of weights in the table along with the charges, as follows:

```
*.. 1 ...+... 2 ...+... 3 ...+... 4 ...+... 5 ...+... 6 ...+... 7 ...+... 8
DName++++++++++ETDsFrom+++To/L+++IDc.Keywords+++++++++++++++++++++++++++++++
D TabWeight      S                2 0 DIM(6) ASCEND CTDATA PERRCD(1)
D TabCharge      S                4 2 DIM(6) ALT(TabWeight)

. . .

**CTDATA TabWeight
010250
050425
100750
200900
401200
701600
```

The above Definition Specifications define TabWeight as a table of six elements, with one entry per record and each entry a two-byte numeric value with no decimal positions; TabCharge is defined as a table in alternating format with TabWeight, with each TabCharge entry a four-byte numeric value with two decimal positions. Range tables require a sequence entry; the weights are in ascending sequence, so keyword ASCEND appears as part of TabWeight's definition.

You use the %TLOOKUP function to access range tables. Because you are no longer looking for an exact match between an input value and a table value, you use one of the alternative %TLOOKUP options (LT, LE, GE, or GT). Given the sample table's layout, the following example uses %TLOOKUPGE.

```
*.. 1 ...+... 2 ...+... 3 ...+... 4 ...+... 5 ...+... 6 ...+... 7 ...+... 8
 /FREE
   // A table lookup to find a weight in the table of weights to determine
   // the appropriate shipping charge for a package

     IF %TLOOKUPGE(WeightIn:TabWeight:TabCharge);
       TotCharge = PkgCharge + TabCharge;
     ELSE;
       EXSR CannotShip;
     ENDIF;

 /END-FREE
```

The lookup statement above translates to "Find the first table weight that is greater than or equal to the input weight, and extract the shipping charge that corresponds to that table weight." Because the maximum table weight is 70, failure of the lookup indicates an input weight over the 70-pound limit. In such cases, the program executes an error routine to indicate that the package cannot be shipped.

Changing Table Values

Tables are generally used for extracting values. It is possible, however, to change table values — intentionally or accidentally — during program execution. Anytime you specify a table name as the result of a mathematical or an assignment operation, the value of the entry where the table is currently positioned will be changed. Failing to understand this fact can sometimes lead to inadvertent program errors.

For example, consider the shipping-weight problem. Assume that in the application developed, you want to add and print either the appropriate shipping charge or, for packages weighing more than 70 pounds, to add and print 0 to indicate that the package can't be shipped. The following incorrect solution may tempt you:

```
*.. 1 ...+... 2 ...+... 3 ...+... 4 ...+... 5 ...+... 6 ...+... 7 ...+... 8
 /FREE
  // Incorrect solution may change some of the values in TabCharge to 0.

    IF NOT %TLOOKUPGE(WeightIn:TabWeight:TabCharge);
      TabCharge = 0;
    ENDIF;
    TotCharge = PkgCharge + TabCharge;

 /END-FREE
```

The result of the above code would be that each time a package weighing more than 70 pounds is processed, the TabCharge value of the most recently successful lookup would be set to 0. The next time a package of that lower weight was processed, its shipping charge would incorrectly be extracted as 0.

You can deliberately change table values, if you wish, by first executing a %TLOOKUP function to position the table correctly and then moving the new value into the table. If the table data came from a file and you want to store the table with its revised values back in the file at the end of processing, you can accomplish this task quite simply with a few changes to the File and Definition Specifications.

First, designate the table file as a combined file rather than an input file. Then, include the file name with keyword TOFILE (as well as with FROMFILE) on the Definition Specification. These two changes will cause the (changed) table values to be written back to the file upon program completion.

Arrays

An **array** is a data structure similar to a table, in that it contains multiple elements, all defined with a common name. As with a table, each element within an array must be the same data type, with the same length and (if the elements are numeric) number of decimal positions.

You define arrays in Definition Specifications; the required entries are the same as those required for tables. As with tables, you can load data into an array at compile time, with values entered at the end of the program (such an array is called a **compile-time array**), or at pre-runtime, with values obtained from a table file (a **pre-runtime array**). Array data may be obtained in alternating format, again, like tables.

Basically the only definition difference between compile-time arrays and tables and pre-runtime arrays and tables is that array names cannot begin with TAB. For reasons soon explained, programmers keep array names shorter than 14 characters — usually no more than six to eight characters long. Examine the following definitions, and you will see that, other than the names, array definitions are identical to table definitions.

```
*.. 1 ...+... 2 ...+... 3 ...+... 4 ...+... 5 ...+... 6 ...+... 7 ...+... 8
FFilename++IPEASFRlen+LKlen+AIDevice+.Keywords++++++++++++++++++++++++++++++
DName++++++++++ETDsFrom+++To/L+++IDc.Keywords++++++++++++++++++++++++++++++++
D.................................Keywords-continuation++++++++++++++++++
  // Table file ZipCodes contains alternating arrays Zip and City.
FZipCodes  IT   F   20          DISK

  // Definitions of arrays from file ZipCodes: Zip contains 500 numeric
  // elements, each 5 digits long with 0 decimals; City contains 500
  // character elements, each 15 bytes long.
D Zip            S              5  0 FROMFILE(ZipCodes) DIM(500) ASCEND
D                                    PERRCD(1)
D City           S             15    ALT(Zip) DIM(500)

  // Array Charge is a compile-time array, with three elements per record;
  // it contains 100 elements, each 6 digits long with 2 decimal positions.
D Charge         S              6  2 DIM(100) CTDATA PERRCD(3)
```

Runtime Arrays

One major difference between arrays and tables is that unlike tables, arrays can be loaded with values during the course of program execution. This kind of array is called a **runtime array**.

A runtime array is signaled on the Definition Specifications by the omission of both the CTDATA and FROMFILE keywords from the array definition; keyword PERRCD is also not used with runtime arrays:

```
*.. 1 ...+... 2 ...+... 3 ...+... 4 ...+... 5 ...+... 6 ...+... 7 ...+... 8
DName++++++++++ETDsFrom+++To/L+++IDc.Keywords+++++++++++++++++++++++++++++++++
  // The system recognizes the arrays defined below as runtime arrays.
D TaxAry          S              7 2 DIM(12)
D SlsAry          S             13 2 DIM(12)
D Names           S             20   DIM(200)
```

Data values for a runtime array can come from records read during program execution or from calculations performed within the program.

Runtime Arrays and Input Data

It is common for programmers to want to define some fields within an input record as an array to facilitate coding repetitive operations. Although you cannot directly define fields as array elements within an externally described file, a method of data redefinition does exist that lets you convert separately defined input fields into elements of a single runtime array. This method involves a data structure, a topic that we discussed briefly in Chapter 3 and will explore extensively in the next chapter.

Assume you have a file of sales records from all of a company's sales staff. Each record contains a salesperson's identification number and that person's total sales for each month during the past year — 12 sales figures in all. Each sales figure is 10 digits long, with two decimal positions. Because you plan to redefine the sales figures as an array, you have defined the sales as one large character field, as shown in the following DDS specifications.

```
*.. 1 ...+... 2 ...+... 3 ...+... 4 ...+... 5 ...+... 6 ...+... 7 ...+... 8
A..........T.Name++++++RLen++TDpB......Functions+++++++++++++++++++++++++++++
 * Externally described file SalesFile with 12 sales figures defined as
 * a single field
A          R SALESREC
A            SLSNBR        5A            TEXT('Salesperson Number')
A            SALES       120A            TEXT('Twelve Months Sales')
```

You are writing a program that uses file SalesFile as input, and you want to refer to the 12 sales figures within each record as elements of an array. To do this, you must include within the program's Definition Specifications a data structure definition that references the sales input field and redefines it as an array. The following specifications illustrate such a data structure.

```
*.. 1 ...+... 2 ...+... 3 ...+... 4 ...+... 5 ...+... 6 ...+... 7 ...+... 8
DName++++++++++ETDsFrom+++To/L+++IDc.Keywords+++++++++++++++++++++++++++++++++
D                 DS
D Sales                        120
D SalAry                        10 2 DIM(12) OVERLAY(Sales)
```

The DS entry in positions 24–25 of the first line declares that what follows is a data structure definition (unnamed, in this case). The second line says that the character field Sales (from file SalesFile) occupies the first 120 bytes of the data structure. The third line defines SalAry as an array of 12 zoned decimal elements, each with two decimal positions. SalAry represents an **overlay**, or a redefinition of the Sales field, breaking the Sales field down into 12 array elements, each 10 bytes long; as a result, SalAry also occupies bytes 1–120 of the data structure.

An alternate way to externally describe the sales file is to define each month's sales figure separately, as the following DDS shows.

```
*.. 1 ...+... 2 ...+... 3 ...+... 4 ...+... 5 ...+... 6 ...+... 7 ...+... 8
A..........T.Name+++++RLen++TDpB......Functions++++++++++++++++++++++++++++
 * Externally described file SalesFile
A           R SALESREC
A             SLSNBR         5A        TEXT('Salesperson Number')
A             JANSALES      10S 2      TEXT('January Sales')
A             FEBSALES      10S 2      TEXT('February Sales')
A             MARSALES      10S 2      TEXT('March Sales')
A             APRSALES      10S 2      TEXT('April Sales')
A             MAYSALES      10S 2      TEXT('May Sales')
A             JUNSALES      10S 2      TEXT('June Sales')
A             JULSALES      10S 2      TEXT('July Sales')
A             AUGSALES      10S 2      TEXT('August Sales')
A             SEPSALES      10S 2      TEXT('September Sales')
A             OCTSALES      10S 2      TEXT('October Sales')
A             NOVSALES      10S 2      TEXT('November Sales')
A             DECSALES      10S 2      TEXT('December Sales')
```

Given the above file definition, you must slightly change the data structure to manipulate the sales figures as array elements:

```
*.. 1 ...+... 2 ...+... 3 ...+... 4 ...+... 5 ...+... 6 ...+... 7 ...+... 8
DName+++++++++++ETDsFrom+++To/L+++IDc.Keywords++++++++++++++++++++++++++++++
D                 DS
D SalAry                      10S 2 DIM(12)
D JanSales              1     10S 2
D FebSales             11     20S 2
D MarSales             21     30S 2
D AprSales             31     40S 2
D MaySales             41     50S 2
D JunSales             51     60S 2
D JulSales             61     70S 2
D AugSales             71     80S 2
D SepSales             81     90S 2
D OctSales             91    100S 2
D NovSales            101    110S 2
D DecSales            111    120S 2
```

In the above data structure, each month's sales is defined as a successive 10-byte area within the data structure; array SalAry, occupying the same 120 bytes of memory, redefines the 12 sales figures as its 12 elements. A more thorough discussion of data structures occurs in the next chapter; for now, simply understand that you can use data structures to convert database fields to elements within an array.

With either method of defining the input file and its associated data structure, each time you read a record from SalesFile, the 12 sales figures from that record will be stored in array SalAry. When a new input record is read, the sales figures from that record replace the previous contents of the array. Thus, the contents of SalAry change as the program is running, and that's the reason why we call SalAry a runtime array.

In addition to loading runtime arrays through input operations, you can also assign values to arrays through calculations performed by your program. Before looking at this method of loading a runtime array, you must learn about array indexes.

Arrays and Indexing

Unlike table elements, you can directly reference and manipulate *individual* elements of an array using an **index**, or element number. To indicate an array element in RPG IV, you use the array name followed by a set of parentheses that contains the location number of the element within the array. Thus, SalAry(3) means the third element in the array SalAry. TaxAry(10) is the tenth element in the array TaxAry. When you use an array name without an index, the system infers that you want to reference or manipulate the entire array — that is, all its elements.

The index that you use to reference an element of an array does not have to be a numeric literal. Instead, you can use a field as an index, provided you have defined the field as numeric with zero decimal positions. If the index is a field, the current value of that field determines which element of the array is referenced. Thus, if Index has a value of 3, TaxAry(Index) is the third element of TaxAry. If Index's value is 10, TaxAry(Index) is the tenth element of the array.

Calculations with Arrays

You can use any of RPG IV's arithmetic or assignment operations with arrays or their elements. If you just reference individual elements in your calculations, the effects are the same as if you were using fields:

```
*.. 1 ...+... 2 ...+... 3 ...+... 4 ...+... 5 ...+... 6 ...+... 7 ...+... 8
/FREE
  // Sample calculations involving array elements

  // Add the values of two elements and store result in a third element.
    Ary(12) = Ary(6) + Ary(3);

  // Divide the third element of array Ary by 60 and store the remainder in
  // RemAry(3).
    Quotient = %DIV(Ary(3):60);
    RemAry(3) = %REM(Ary(3):60);
/END-FREE
```

You can also use entire arrays, rather than just individual elements of the arrays, in calculations. In this case, the Result field entry must always be an array name.

If all the factors involved in the operation are arrays, the operation is performed successively on corresponding elements of the arrays until the array with the fewest number of elements has been completely processed.

```
*.. 1 ...+... 2 ...+... 3 ...+... 4 ...+... 5 ...+... 6 ...+... 7 ...+... 8
/FREE
  // Multiply corresponding elements of AryA and AryB,
  // storing the products in AryC.
    EVAL(H) AryC = AryA * AryB;

  // Assign the values of AryB to AryA.
    AryA = AryB;

  // Take the square root of each element of AryA and store the result
  // in the corresponding element of AryB.
    AryB = %SQRT(AryA);
/END-FREE
```

When you combine non-array values and arrays in calculations, the operation works with corresponding elements of the arrays, along with the non-array values in each case, and continues until all the elements in the shortest array have been processed:

```
*.. 1 ...+... 2 ...+... 3 ...+... 4 ...+... 5 ...+... 6 ...+... 7 ...+... 8
 /FREE
   // Calculate gross pay for employees who work overtime; arrays Rate and
   // Hours contain employee values; array GPay stores results.
     GPay = 40 * Rate + ((Hours-40)*1.5*Rate);

   // Store 'ABCDE' in each element of array AryD
     AryD = 'ABCDE';
```

In addition to the standard operations already presented in this text, three operations apply only to arrays: %XFOOT, SORTA, and MOVEA.

%XFOOT (Sum the Elements of an Array)

The %XFOOT (Sum the Elements of an Array) function — called "crossfoot" — sums the elements of an array. The function's only argument is the name of the array whose elements are to be added together; use an assignment expression to name the field in which the answer is to be stored. If you half-adjust this operation, the rounding takes place just before the final answer is stored.

Crossfooting is a term used in accounting to sum across a row of figures to develop a total for that row. The %XFOOT function is very useful in such applications, provided the figures to be added are array elements:

```
*.. 1 ...+... 2 ...+... 3 ...+... 4 ...+... 5 ...+... 6 ...+... 7 ...+... 8
 /FREE
   // Sum the elements of array AryA and store the answer in field Total.
     EVAL(H) Total = %XFOOT(AryA);
 /END-FREE
```

SORTA (Sort an Array)

SORTA (Sort an Array) is a simple but useful operation that rearranges the values of the elements of an array into ascending or descending sequence. The order used depends on the sequence keyword — ASCEND or DESCEND — specified within the array's definition on the Definition Specifications. If the definition includes neither keyword, the SORTA operation sorts the values in ascending sequence, the default order. The specification for this operation includes just the operation and the name of the array to be sorted:

```
*.. 1 ...+... 2 ...+... 3 ...+... 4 ...+... 5 ...+... 6 ...+... 7 ...+... 8
 /FREE
   // AryA is array of 5 numeric elements, each 2 bytes long, no decimals.
   // Before SORTA, the array element values, in order, are 10 92 33 85 12.
     SORTA AryA;
   // Following SORTA, the array contains, in order, 10 12 33 85 92.
 /END-FREE
```

MOVEA (Move Array)

The MOVEA (Move Array) operation transfers values from Factor 2 to the Result field of the operation. At least one of these entries — Factor 2 or the result — must contain an array name. MOVEA is restricted to the fixed-format Calculation Specifications and is not allowed in free-format specifications. Programmers generally use MOVEA with character data, although it can be used with numeric values if the entries in Factor 2 and the Result field have the same numeric length (although not necessarily the same number of decimal positions).

```
*.. 1 ...+... 2 ...+... 3 ...+... 4 ...+... 5 ...+... 6 ...+... 7 ...+... 8
CLØN01Factor1++++++Opcode(E)+Factor2++++++Result++++++++Len++D+HiLoEq....
      // Sample showing the format of the MOVEA operation. Note that at least
      // one of the data items used in the operation must be an array.
C                   MOVEA     Factor2       Result
```

What makes MOVEA unusual is that the operation ignores the element boundaries of the array and moves the values, character by character, from the sending to the receiving field or array until either there is nothing left to send or there is no more room in the receiving field.

The easiest way to understand how a MOVEA operation works is to look at some examples. Assume you have two arrays: AryA, a four-element character array, with each element three characters long; and AryB, a character array of five elements, each two characters long. FieldA is a field five characters long.

The following examples illustrate the effects of different MOVEA operations using the arrays defined above. Notice especially that the data movement takes place from left to right and that portions of the receiving field or array not used in the operation retain their original values.

Example 1

This example uses MOVEA with two arrays containing elements of different lengths; the target array elements are shorter than those of the sending array.

```
*.. 1 ...+... 2 ...+... 3 ...+... 4 ...+... 5 ...+... 6 ...+... 7 ...+... 8
CLØN01Factor1++++++Opcode(E)+Factor2++++++Result++++++++Len++D+HiLoEq....
C                   MOVEA     AryA          AryB
```

	AryA	AryB
Before MOVEA:	abc def ghi jkl	mn op qr st uv
After MOVEA:	abc def ghi jkl	ab cd ef gh ij

Example 2

This example uses MOVEA with two arrays containing elements of different lengths; the target array elements are longer than those of the sending array.

```
*.. 1 ...+... 2 ...+... 3 ...+... 4 ...+... 5 ...+... 6 ...+... 7 ...+... 8
CLØN01Factor1++++++Opcode(E)+Factor2++++++Result++++++++Len++D+HiLoEq....
C                   MOVEA     AryB          AryA
```

	AryB	AryA
Before MOVEA:	mn op qr st uv	abc def ghi jkl
After MOVEA:	mn op qr st uv	mno pqr stu vkl

Example 3

This example uses MOVEA to send the value of a field to a target array.

```
*.. 1 ...+... 2 ...+... 3 ...+... 4 ...+... 5 ...+... 6 ...+... 7 ...+... 8
CLØN01Factor1++++++Opcode(E)+Factor2++++++Result++++++++Len++D+HiLoEq....
C                   MOVEA     FieldA        AryA
```

	FieldA	AryA
Before MOVEA:	ZYXWV	abc def ghi jkl
After MOVEA:	ZYXWV	ZYX WVf ghi jkl

Example 4

This example uses MOVEA to send an array to a target field.

```
*.. 1 ...+... 2 ...+... 3 ...+... 4 ...+... 5 ...+... 6 ...+... 7 ...+... 8
CLØN01Factor1+++++++Opcode(E)+Factor2++++++Result++++++++Len++D+HiLoEq....
C                   MOVEA     AryA          FieldA
```

	AryA	FieldA
Before MOVEA:	abc def ghi jkl	ZYXWV
After MOVEA:	abc def ghi jkl	abcde

Factor 2 and/or the Result field can specify an array element rather than an entire array. In that case, the data movement starts at that array element; elements preceding the specified element are not involved in the MOVEA operation. Data movement continues until there is nothing left to move or until the receiving array or field has no more room. The following examples illustrate this kind of data movement.

Example 5

This example uses MOVEA to send an array element to a target array.

```
*.. 1 ...+... 2 ...+... 3 ...+... 4 ...+... 5 ...+... 6 ...+... 7 ...+... 8
CLØN01Factor1+++++++Opcode(E)+Factor2++++++Result++++++++Len++D+HiLoEq....
C                   MOVEA     AryA(3)       AryB
```

	AryA	AryB
Before MOVEA:	abc def ghi jkl	mn op qr st uv
After MOVEA:	abc def ghi jkl	gh ij kl st uv

Example 6

This example uses MOVEA to send an array to a target array element.

```
*.. 1 ...+... 2 ...+... 3 ...+... 4 ...+... 5 ...+... 6 ...+... 7 ...+... 8
CLØN01Factor1+++++++Opcode(E)+Factor2++++++Result++++++++Len++D+HiLoEq....
C                   MOVEA     AryA          AryB(4)
```

	AryA	AryB
Before MOVEA:	abc def ghi jkl	mn op qr st uv
After MOVEA:	abc def ghi jkl	mn op qr ab cd

Example 7

This example uses MOVEA to send an array element to a target array element.

```
*.. 1 ...+... 2 ...+... 3 ...+... 4 ...+... 5 ...+... 6 ...+... 7 ...+... 8
CLØN01Factor1+++++++Opcode(E)+Factor2++++++Result++++++++Len++D+HiLoEq....
C                   MOVEA     AryA(3)       AryB(2)
```

	AryA	AryB
Before MOVEA:	abc def ghi jkl	mn op qr st uv
After MOVEA:	abc def ghi jkl	mn gh ij kl uv

As you've probably noticed, those positions within the Result field that did not have new values moved to them by MOVEA retained their old values. By using operation extender (P) with the MOVEA operation, you can specify that the unused, rightmost bytes of the target data item be blank-padded. The following example illustrates this feature.

Example 8
This example uses MOVEA to send an array element to an array element, with padding specified.

```
*.. 1 ...+... 2 ...+... 3 ...+... 4 ...+... 5 ...+... 6 ...+... 7 ...+... 8
CLØN01Factor1+++++++Opcode(E)+Factor2+++++++Result+++++++++Len++D+HiLoEq....
C                   MOVEA(P)  AryA(3)        AryB(2)
```

	AryA	AryB
Before MOVEA:	abc def ghi jkl	mn op qr st uv
After MOVEA:	abc def ghi jkl	mn gh ij kl ƀƀ

The MOVEA operation can be extremely useful for manipulating portions of data fields and combining bits and pieces from different data sources into a single data item.

Using Arrays

Now that you understand how to define arrays and how to use them in different calculations or special array operations, you are ready to see how arrays can simplify or expedite solutions to different kinds of programming problems. The ability to index an array with a field, rather than a literal, adds tremendous flexibility to your ability to manipulate arrays and makes arrays the preferred data structure to handle problems requiring identical processing of similar data items.

Recall, for example, the SalesFile file we described earlier, in which each record contained a salesperson's number and 12 monthly sales totals for that salesperson:

```
*.. 1 ...+... 2 ...+... 3 ...+... 4 ...+... 5 ...+... 6 ...+... 7 ...+... 8
A..........T.Name++++++RLen++TDpB......Functions++++++++++++++++++++++++++++
 * Externally described file SalesFile
A          R SALESREC
A            SLSNBR        5A          TEXT('Salesperson Number')
A            JANSALES     10S 2        TEXT('January Sales')
A            FEBSALES     10S 2        TEXT('February Sales')
A            MARSALES     10S 2        TEXT('March Sales')
A            APRSALES     10S 2        TEXT('April Sales')
A            MAYSALES     10S 2        TEXT('May Sales')
A            JUNSALES     10S 2        TEXT('June Sales')
A            JULSALES     10S 2        TEXT('July Sales')
A            AUGSALES     10S 2        TEXT('August Sales')
A            SEPSALES     10S 2        TEXT('September Sales')
A            OCTSALES     10S 2        TEXT('October Sales')
A            NOVSALES     10S 2        TEXT('November Sales')
A            DECSALES     10S 2        TEXT('December Sales')
```

Assume that this file is to be used in a program to help a company determine the end-of-year bonuses to be paid to the sales force. The bonuses are determined on a monthly basis by the salesperson's sales for that month; any time the monthly sales exceeds $50,000, the bonus for that month is one-half percent of the sales; otherwise, there is no bonus for that month. The company wants to calculate the total annual bonus for each salesperson but also print the individual monthly bonuses. The following printer spacing chart shows the desired report.

```
                1         2         3         4         5         6         7         8         9        10
       1234567890123456789012345678901234567890123456789012345678901234567890123456789012345678901234567890
 1      XX/XX/XX
 2                                                ANNUAL SALES BONUS REPORT
 3
 4     SLSPSN     JAN.      FEB.      MAR.      APR.      MAY       JUNE      JULY      AUG.
 5     XXXXX   XXX,XX0   XXX,XX0   XXX,XX0   XXX,XX0   XXX,XX0   XXX,XX0   XXX,XX0   XXX,XX0
 6     XXXXX   XXX,XX0   XXX,XX0   XXX,XX0   XXX,XX0   XXX,XX0   XXX,XX0   XXX,XX0   XXX,XX0
 7     XXXXX   XXX,XX0   XXX,XX0   XXX,XX0   XXX,XX0   XXX,XX0   XXX,XX0   XXX,XX0   XXX,XX0
 8     XXXXX   XXX,XX0   XXX,XX0   XXX,XX0   XXX,XX0   XXX,XX0   XXX,XX0   XXX,XX0   XXX,XX0
 9
10
```

```
                1         2         3         4         5         6         7         8         9        10
       1234567890123456789012345678901234567890123456789012345678901234567890123456789012345678901234567890
 1                            PAGE XX
 2
 3
 4     SEPT.     OCT.      NOV.      DEC.        TOTAL
 5     XXX,XX0   XXX,XX0   XXX,XX0   XXX,XX0   XX,XXX,XX0
 6     XXX,XX0   XXX,XX0   XXX,XX0   XXX,XX0   XX,XXX,XX0
 7     XXX,XX0   XXX,XX0   XXX,XX0   XXX,XX0   XX,XXX,XX0
 8     XXX,XX0   XXX,XX0   XXX,XX0   XXX,XX0   XX,XXX,XX0
 9
10                  GRAND TOTAL  $XX,XXX,XXX,XX$
11
12
```

To program a solution without using arrays would require writing a set of calculations that would be replicated 12 times, each time with a different set of fields representing each of the 12 months. With sales for different salespersons handled as elements of an array and with another array to store the salesperson's bonus for each of the 12 months, you can considerably shorten the calculations.

First, recall that we can define the 12 monthly sales figures as elements of an array by using a data structure. The Definition Specifications that follow illustrate the data structure as well as define an additional array, Bonus, and some standalone work fields that we require for our solution.

```
*.. 1 ...+... 2 ...+... 3 ...+... 4 ...+... 5 ...+... 6 ...+... 7 ...+... 8
DName+++++++++++ETDsFrom+++To/L+++IDc.Keywords+++++++++++++++++++++++++++++++++
     // Data structure for converting sales fields to array elements
D                 DS
D SlsAry                         10S 2 DIM(12)
D JanSales              1        10S 2
D FebSales             11        20S 2
D MarSales             21        30S 2
D AprSales             31        40S 2
D MaySales             41        50S 2
D JunSales             51        60S 2
D JulSales             61        70S 2
D AugSales             71        80S 2
D SepSales             81        90S 2
D OctSales             91       100S 2
D NovSales            101       110S 2
D DecSales            111       120S 2

     // Array for bonuses
D Bonus           S               6S 0 DIM(12)

     // Standalone work fields
D GrandTotal      S              11S 0
D TotBonus        S               8S 0
D I               S               2S 0
     // I is a loop counter and the index for the sales and bonus arrays.
```

Given the above array definitions, the calculations for solving our problem are relatively short:

```
*.. 1 ...+... 2 ...+... 3 ...+... 4 ...+... 5 ...+... 6 ...+... 7 ...+... 8
 /FREE
   // Specifications for calculating and printing bonuses for all
   // salespersons in SalesFile
     GrandTotal = 0;
     EXCEPT Headings;
     READ SalesFile;
     DOW NOT %EOF(SalesFile);
       FOR I = 1 TO 12; // FOR loop through 12 sales figures for salesperson
         IF SlsAry(I) > 50000;
           EVAL(H) Bonus(I) = SlsAry(I) * .005;
         ELSE;
           Bonus(I) = 0;
         ENDIF;
       ENDFOR;
       TotBonus = %XFOOT(Bonus);
       GrandTotal = GrandTotal + TotBonus;
       IF EndOfPage;
         EXCEPT Headings;
         EndOfPage = *OFF;
       ENDIF;
       EXCEPT Detail;
       READ SalesFile;
     ENDDO;
     EXCEPT TotalLine;
     *INLR = *ON;
     RETURN;
 /END-FREE
```

The beauty of handling data with arrays and variable indexes, as this example shows, is that if there were 1,200 sales figures for each salesperson, instead of 12, the calculations to determine bonuses and totals would be no longer; the only required changes would be to increase the number of iterations of the FOR loop from 12 to 1,200 and to increase the lengths of the work fields to avoid truncation.

In fact, in the current release of RPG IV, you could make a small change to the above code that would make it even more flexible. The following change to the FOR loop combines the FOR operation and the %ELEM (Get Number of Elements) built-in function to make the program easier to maintain. The %ELEM function returns the number of elements in an array or table (in this case, 12 elements), so that you need not hard-code that number in case it changes in the future.

```
*.. 1 ...+... 2 ...+... 3 ...+... 4 ...+... 5 ...+... 6 ...+... 7 ...+... 8
 /FREE
     FOR I = 1 TO %ELEM(SlsAry);
       IF SlsAry(I) > 50000;
         EVAL(H) Bonus(I) = SlsAry(I) * .005;
       ELSE;
         EVAL Bonus(I) = 0;
       ENDIF;
     ENDDO;
 /END-FREE
```

Array Lookups

We began this chapter with a discussion of tables and the %TLOOKUP function. You can use a related function, %LOOKUP, to access arrays. %LOOKUP works only with arrays (conversely, %TLOOKUP works only with tables). %LOOKUP returns the number of the array index that matches a search argument; if there is no match, %LOOKUP returns a zero. %LOOKUP does not affect the value of the %FOUND or %EQUAL function. Like %TLOOKUP, the %LOOKUP function has several variations:

- %LOOKUP — find equal match
- %LOOKUPLT — find array element closest to but less than search-arg
- %LOOKUPLE — find equal match or element closest to but less than search-arg
- %LOOKUPGE — find equal match or element closest to but greater than search-arg
- %LOOKUPGT — find array element closest to but greater than search-arg

If you simply want to know whether a value exists as an element in an array, but you don't need to access the element or know its location within the array, you can compare the %LOOKUP result with zero:

```
*.. 1 ...+... 2 ...+... 3 ...+... 4 ...+... 5 ...+... 6 ...+... 7 ...+... 8
/FREE
  // This LOOKUP simply indicates whether or not an array element exists
  // that matches Value.
   IF %LOOKUP(Value:Ary) > 0;
     EXSR ValueFound;
   ELSE;
     EXSR NotFound;
   ENDIF;
/END-FREE
```

If, on the other hand, you want to know not only whether a value exists in the array but also its location in the array, you need to use an index variable in an assignment expression. To start the lookup at the beginning of the array, specify 1 as a third argument to the %LOOKUP function; you can also specify another starting point, using a literal or a variable.

```
*.. 1 ...+... 2 ...+... 3 ...+... 4 ...+... 5 ...+... 6 ...+... 7 ...+... 8
/FREE
  // This %LOOKUP, if successful, assigns index I the value that points to
  // the array element whose value matches Value. If the lookup is
  // unsuccessful, I will be zero.

   I = %LOOKUP(Value:Ary:1);
   IF I > 0;
     EXSR ValueFound;
   ELSE;
     EXSR NotFound;
   ENDIF;
/END-FREE
```

If the index is greater than zero following the lookup, it means that the value was found in the array. Moreover, index I's value points to the location of the array element that has the same value as Value. Thus, if the third element of Ary had the same value as Value, the value of index I would be 3 after the %LOOKUP.

To understand how you can use arrays and the LOOKUP operation to extract data from a "table" (in the popular sense), let's reconsider the three-column table of state codes, state names, and sales tax rates we discussed earlier in the chapter. Let's assume that the three columns of data are entered successively at the end of our program, as shown below, but as compile-time arrays, rather than compile-time tables.

```
     *.. 1 ...+... 2 ...+... 3 ...+... 4 ...+... 5 ...+... 6 ...+... 7 ...+... 8
**CTDATA Code
AK
AL
AR
AZ
. . .
**CTDATA Name
Alaska
Alabama
Arkansas
Arizona
. . .
**CTDATA Rate
0000
0400
0000
0500
. . .
```

The Definition Specifications for these arrays would be identical to those used in the RPG IV table solution, except for the data names:

```
*.. 1 ...+... 2 ...+... 3 ...+... 4 ...+... 5 ...+... 6 ...+... 7 ...+... 8
DName+++++++++++ETDsFrom+++To/L+++IDc.Keywords++++++++++++++++++++++++++++++++
   // Three arrays independently defined
D Code            S               2    DIM(50) PERRCD(1) CTDATA ASCEND
D Name            S              14    DIM(50) PERRCD(1) CTDATA
D Rate            S               4  4 DIM(50) PERRCD(1) CTDATA
```

Using arrays, however, the calculations would require only a single %LOOKUP of the primary array to determine the appropriate value for the index; you could then use that index to point to the corresponding element in each additional "table" column.

```
*.. 1 ...+... 2 ...+... 3 ...+... 4 ...+... 5 ...+... 6 ...+... 7 ...+... 8
 /FREE
   // Lookup code based on CodeIn. If the lookup is successful, Name(I) will
   // refer to the correct state name and Rate(I) to the correct tax rate.
    I = %LOOKUPCodeIn:Code:1);
    IF I > 0;
      EVAL(H) TaxDue = Amount * Rate(I);
    ELSE;
      EXSR BadCode;
    ENDIF;
```

By default, %LOOKUP searches the entire array, beginning either at the first element or at the element you specify in the third, optional, argument. A fourth argument, also optional, lets you specify the number of elements you want to search if you don't want to search the entire array.

Output with Arrays

When you specify a table name as part of an Output Specification, the current instance of the table (the value to which the table is positioned) is printed. In contrast, when you specify an array name to be printed, all the elements appear, separated with two blanks, with the last element ending in the ending position specified for the array. Any editing associated with the array applies to each element. Depending on the printer spacing chart you are following, you may be able to use this shortcut; the alternative is to list each element of the array individually, with an index, and give each its own ending position.

If you need to print all the elements of an array but require more than two blanks separating the elements on the report, you can use an edit word that includes blanks (&) to increase the distance between the elements. In the following examples, array Ary stores seven numeric values (each of length six with two decimal positions), which will be printed so that the last element ends in position 76.

```
*.. 1 ...+... 2 ...+... 3 ...+... 4 ...+... 5 ...+... 6 ...+... 7 ...+... 8
O..............NØ1NØ2NØ3Field+++++++++YB.End++PConstant/editword/DTformat++
    // All the elements of Ary will be printed, separated with two spaces and
    // containing commas. The last element will end in position 76.
O                     Ary             1   76
    // Alternatively, each element could be listed individually.
O                     Ary(1)          1   16
O                     Ary(2)          1   26
O                     Ary(3)          1   36
O                     Ary(4)          1   46
O                     Ary(5)          1   56
O                     Ary(6)          1   66
O                     Ary(7)          1   76

    // If you need more than two blanks between elements, you can still use
    // the array name without an index by using an edit word. The code below
    // results in 3 blanks separating Ary's elements.
O                     Ary                 76 '&  ,   Ø.  '
```

Chapter Summary

You can use both tables and arrays to store sets of similar elements in RPG IV. You can load both tables and arrays at compile time, from data hard-coded at the end of the source program, or at pre-execution time, from data contained in a table file. You can also load arrays during runtime, from values contained in input records or as the result of calculations.

RPG IV tables are useful for performing lookups with the %TLOOKUP function. You can look up a value in one table to extract information from a parallel table, provided the second table is named as the third argument in the %TLOOKUP function. Using a table name in a calculation or printing operation causes the element to which the table is currently positioned to be used.

Arrays offer more flexibility and power than tables. You can explicitly reference an individual array element by using an index, or you can manipulate the array as a whole by using the array name without an index. You can use a numeric literal or field as an index to point to a specific array element. You can use four special RPG IV operations/functions with arrays: %LOOKUP, %XFOOT, SORTA, and MOVEA. You most often use arrays to simplify processing of identical kinds of data or to manipulate portions of data fields.

Specifying an array name and an end position on Output Specifications causes all the array elements to be printed, separated by two spaces, with the last element finishing in the designated end position.

The LOOKUP and XFOOT Operations

The %LOOKUP, %TLOOKUP, and %XFOOT functions require that OS/400 be at Version 5 or later. At releases earlier than Version 5, the LOOKUP and XFOOT operation codes perform the same functions; their use is restricted to the fixed-format Calculation Specification. The LOOKUP operation code works with either tables or arrays.

For a table lookup, the search argument goes in Factor 1; the name of the table goes in Factor 2. The LOOKUP operation requires a resulting indicator to serve as a signal for the type of match you want to find between the table value and the Factor 1 value. Most of the time, you want an equal match, so you put the indicator in the Eq position (75–76); you can also specify indicators in the Hi (71–72) or Lo (73–74) positions to indicate greater-than or less-than lookups, respectively.

When a table lookup is successful, the resulting indicator is turned on and an internal pointer is positioned at the matching table value. A successful lookup operation also turns on the %FOUND built-in function and, in the case of an equal match, the %EQUAL built-in function. LOOKUP requires a resulting indicator, even though we don't necessarily use that indicator subsequently; you can use either the indicator's status or the functions' status to control subsequent processing within the program. The following code illustrates a simple table lookup.

```
*.. 1 ...+... 2 ...+... 3 ...+... 4 ...+... 5 ...+... 6 ...+... 7 ...+... 8
CL0N01Factor1+++++++Opcode(E)+Factor2+++++++Result++++++++Len++D+HiLoEq....
CL0N01Factor1+++++++Opcode(E)+Extended-factor2++++++++++++++++++++++++++++++
 * Use input field CodeIn as the search argument of a lookup within
 * table TabCode. Indicator 50 comes on if an equal match is found.
C     CodeIn        LOOKUP    TabCode                            50

C                   IF        %FOUND
C                   EXSR      CodeFound
C                   ELSE
C                   EXSR      BadCode
C                   ENDIF
```

You can also use LOOKUP with two tables, specifying the alternate table in the Result field entry. In the following example, a successful code lookup causes the internal pointer to be positioned in TabName at the name that corresponds to the matched code in TabCode. As with %TLOOKUP, an unsuccessful table lookup will cause the tables to retain their values from the last successful lookup.

```
*.. 1 ...+... 2 ...+... 3 ...+... 4 ...+... 5 ...+... 6 ...+... 7 ...+... 8
CL0N01Factor1+++++++Opcode(E)+Factor2+++++++Result++++++++Len++D+HiLoEq....
CL0N01Factor1+++++++Opcode(E)+Extended-factor2++++++++++++++++++++++++++++++
 * Look up CodeIn in TabCode to extract TabName.
C     CodeIn        LOOKUP    TabCode       TabName              50

C                   IF        %FOUND
C                   EXSR      PrintName
C                   ELSE
C                   EXSR      BadCode
C                   ENDIF
```

continued…

continued...

You can also use LOOKUP to access arrays. There are two variants of the array LOOKUP: one that uses an index and one that doesn't. If you simply want to know whether a value exists as an element in an array, but you don't need to access the element or know its location within the array, you can use LOOKUP without an index, as follows:

```
*.. 1 ...+... 2 ...+... 3 ...+... 4 ...+... 5 ...+... 6 ...+... 7 ...+... 8
CLØNØ1Factor1+++++++Opcode(E)+Factor2+++++++Result+++++++Len++D+HiLoEq....
CLØNØ1Factor1+++++++Opcode(E)+Extended-factor2+++++++++++++++++++++++++++++
 * This LOOKUP simply indicates whether or not an array element exists
 * that matches Value.
C     Value           LOOKUP    Ary                                    5Ø
C                     IF        %FOUND
C                     EXSR      ValueFound
C                     ELSE
C                     EXSR      NotFound
C                     ENDIF
```

If, on the other hand, you want to know not only whether a value exists in the array but also its location in the array, you need to use an index. To start the lookup at the beginning of the array, you must initialize the index to 1 before the LOOKUP operation.

```
*.. 1 ...+... 2 ...+... 3 ...+... 4 ...+... 5 ...+... 6 ...+... 7 ...+... 8
CLØNØ1Factor1+++++++Opcode(E)+Extended-factor2+++++++++++++++++++++++++++++
CLØNØ1Factor1+++++++Opcode(E)+Factor2+++++++Result+++++++Len++D+HiLoEq....
 * This LOOKUP, if successful, assigns index I the value that points to the
 * array element whose value matches Value.
C                     EVAL      I = 1
C     Value           LOOKUP    Ary(I)                                 5Ø
C                     IF        %FOUND
C                     EXSR      ValueFound
C                     ELSE
C                     EXSR      NotFound
C                     ENDIF
```

If the %FOUND (or the %EQUAL) function is on following the lookup, it means that the value was found in the array. Moreover, index I's value points to the location of the array element that has the same value as Value. Thus, if the third element of Ary had the same value as Value, the value of index I would be 3 after the LOOKUP. If the LOOKUP operation is unsuccessful, the array index I is set to a value of 1; this result is different from that of an unsuccessful %LOOKUP function, which would return a 0.

The XFOOT (Sum the Elements of an Array) operation performs the same function as the %XFOOT function: it sums the elements of an array. This operation does not use Factor 1 of the standard Calculation Specification. Factor 2 contains the name of the array whose elements are to be added together, and the Result field contains the name of the field in which the answer is to be stored.

```
*.. 1 ...+... 2 ...+... 3 ...+... 4 ...+... 5 ...+... 6 ...+... 7 ...+... 8
CLØNØ1Factor1+++++++Opcode(E)+Factor2+++++++Result+++++++Len++D+HiLoEq....
 * Sum the elements of array AryA and store the answer in field Total.
C                     XFOOT(H)  AryA          Total
```

Indicators as Array Elements

One special, predefined array exists in RPG IV: array *IN. *IN is an array of 99 one-position character elements that represent the indicators 01–99. Thus, *IN(1) and *IN01 are both references to indicator 01. Note that the non-numbered indicators (e.g., *INLR, *INOF) are not represented within this array. The elements of *IN can contain only the character values '0' (*OFF) or '1' (*ON). Any operation valid for an array of character elements is valid to use with *IN. RPG IV programmers sometimes use this feature of indicators to turn off or on a consecutive block of indicators in a single calculation:

```
*.. 1 ...+... 2 ...+... 3 ...+... 4 ...+... 5 ...+... 6 ...+... 7 ...+... 8
CLØNØ1Factor1+++++++Opcode(E)+Factor2+++++++Result++++++++Len++D+HiLoEq....
 // The following calculation turns off indicators 31-35.
C                   MOVEA     '00000'        *IN(31)
```

In general, it's best to avoid using this feature of RPG IV. It's easy to make mistakes in its use, and it results in code that is less understandable than other methods of manipulating indicator values.

Key Terms

alternating format	pre-runtime array
array	pre-runtime (pre-execution) table
compile-time array	range table
compile-time table	runtime array
crossfooting	table
**CTDATA record	table lookup
index	volatile
overlay	

Discussion/Review Questions

1. If you wanted to describe the telephone book as a table in RPG IV, how many tables would you define?

2. If a program uses tables, what additional specification form is required and where should these specifications appear in your program?

3. What is the difference between the "number of entries per table" and "number of entries per record" entries on the Definition Specifications?

4. What factors would you use to determine whether to hard-code a table or store the table data in a disk file?

5. What are the two techniques that can be used to define tables of more than two columns? What are the advantages and disadvantages of each technique?

6. What is a "range" table? Give an example of one.

7. When would you need to use keyword FROMFILE as part of a table or array definition on the Definition Specifications?

8. What are RPG IV's requirements for naming tables and arrays? What practical considerations add additional constraints to array names?

9. What do the terms compile-time, pre-runtime, and runtime refer to when used to describe tables or arrays?

10. Give four ways that arrays can obtain data values.

11. What is the difference between using a table name and an array name (without an index) in a calculation (i.e., what data is being represented)?

12. How are the effects of standard arithmetic operations dependent upon whether array elements or arrays are entered as factors in the calculations?

13. What RPG IV operations are used only with arrays? What does each do?

14. Describe appropriate uses for tables and arrays. How would you decide which (if either) to use in a given application?

Exercises

1. You are writing an application to process orders. Records include the date ordered in *yymmdd* format, but you want to print the name of the month ordered rather than the number of the month.
    a. Show how you would hard-code data for a two-column table relating month number to month name.
    b. Code the Definition Specifications for these compile-time tables, matching the definitions to the way in which you've laid out your data.
    c. Write the calculations needed to look up OrdMonth(*order-month*) in one table to extract the appropriate month name.

2. Modify your work in Exercise 1 by using arrays, rather than tables. Don't require your program to do more work than needed. (Hint: Can you think of a way to obtain the correct month name without performing a lookup?)

3. An input file contains records of sales. Each record represents one week of sales, with seven sales figures, each 10 with two decimal positions, in positions 21–90 of the input record. Code the Definition, Input, and portion of the Calculation Specifications needed to generate a weekly sales total and also to separately accumulate sales for each day of the week as input to the file is processed.

4. Assume the IRS wants you to use the following table to determine how much salary to withhold for federal taxes:

| | Tax rate | |
If weekly salary is	Single	Married
0–$150	.18	.15
$151–$250	.25	.18
$251–$500	.28	.25
$501–$1,000	.31	.28
over $1,000	.33	.31

    a. Hard-code this information so it can be handled with RPG IV tables.
    b. Define the Definition Specifications to reflect your hard-coding.
    c. Write the calculations needed to assign the proper value to field Rate based on Salary (salary) and MrtStatus (marital status: S = single, M = married) of an employee's input record.
    d. Modify your code as would be needed if the table data were stored in a table file, rather than hard-coded.

Programming Assignments

1. Wexler University wants a program that will produce a student grade report and assign final grades. An input file, WUEXAMP (Appendix F), contains student records with five exam grades per student.

   The program will need to calculate an average exam grade for each student. The school also wants to know class averages for each exam and for the course as a whole. The program should also assign final grades based on the following criteria:

Average grade	Final grade
93–100	A
88–92	B+
83–87	B
75–82	C+
70–74	C
65–69	D+
60–64	D
< 60	F

   The desired report layout is shown below. Note that the students' first and last names are to be printed together, with one blank between the last character of the first name and the first character of the last name.

2. CompuSell wants you to write an interactive program that its shipping department can use to calculate shipping charges based on destination and weight of package.

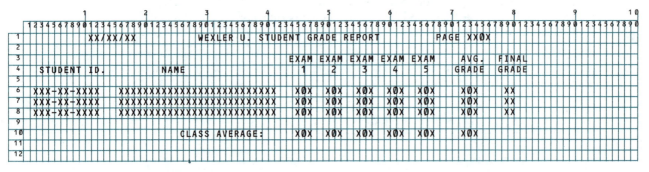

   Two files of table information related to shipping exist: the zip/zone table file (CSZPZNP) and the charges table file (CSCHGP). (Appendix F describes these files.)

   Your program should let a user enter the first three digits of the zip code of a package's destination and the pounds and ounces of the package weight and, based on the entered information, calculate the appropriate shipping charge and display the charge to the user.

   Note that any package with ounces greater than zero should get charged the rate appropriate for the next pound. That is, a package weighing seven pounds and three ounces should get charged at the eight-pound rate.

3. Wexler University wants you to write a program to score student tests. Each test is a 50-question, multiple-choice test. (Possible answers for each question are A, B, C, D, and E.) Student responses are scanned and stored in database file WUTSTP. Appendix F describes the format of these records; each record includes information about the course, the test, the student, and the student's test responses. The file is keyed on course ID, test number, and section number. An answer key to each test is prepared and stored in database file WUKEYP (Appendix F); this file is keyed on course ID and test number.

There will be several sets of tests, possibly from different sections and different courses, in file WUTSTP. The same key may be used to grade different sections' tests, provided the test number and course ID of the key record of file WUKEYP match those of the records to be graded.

You want to grade every record in WUTSTP; there may be keys in WUKEYP that don't match any of the current batches of tests, but there should not be any student test that does not have a corresponding key in WUKEYP.

Use arrays to do the scoring. Then use a compile-time table to assign letter grades. The table should reflect the following scale:

Score	Letter grade
<= 29	F
30–34	D
35–39	C
40–44	B
45–50	A

Prepare a report like the following. Start each new section and/or each new test on a new page with all headings. If a section takes more than one page, repeat all headings on successive pages. Note that an average grade for each section is required.

```
        1         2         3         4         5         6         7         8         9        10
 1234567890123456789012345678901234567890123456789012345678901234567890123456789012345678901234567890
 1                          WEXLER U. GRADE REPORT
 2
 3  COURSE ID:   XXXXXX    TEST:   XXXX                    DATE:   XX/XX/XX
 4
 5  SECTION:    XXXXXX    INSTRUCTOR:  XXXXXXXXXXXXXXXXX
 6
 7            STUDENT ID           TEST SCORE      LETTER GRADE
 8           XXX-XX-XXXX              0X               X
 9           XXX-XX-XXXX              0X               X
10           XXX-XX-XXXX              0X               X
11
12            SECTION AVERAGE        0X
13
```

4. GTC, a local telephone company, wants you to write a program to calculate costs of calls as part of a billing system. A calls transaction file, GTCLSP (described in Appendix F), is generated automatically as part of the company's switching system. Call data accumulates in this file during the course of the month. At the end of the month, the file is first used with this program and then used to print bills before being cleared for the next month's accumulation of call data. Note that the file includes a cost-of-call field, but the value for that field will be supplied by this program when it updates each record. When the record is read initially, this field contains zeros.

Cost of calls depends on two things: the area code and exchange of the number called, and the time of the call. Base daytime rates for all area codes and exchanges are contained in a rates file, GTCRATP (Appendix F). Each record contains the cost for the first minute and the per-minute charge for each additional minute for calls made to that area code/exchange. This file should be loaded into a table that can be used to look up the appropriate charges for each call in the calls file.

Time of call affects cost based on the following table. This table should be incorporated into a hard-coded table so it can be used for lookups during processing. The percents are discounts to the standard costs contained in the rate file.

Hours	Mon–Fri	Sat	Sun
8:00 A.M.–4:59 P.M.	0%	60%	60%
5:00 P.M.–10:59 P.M.	35%	60%	35%
11:00 P.M.–7:59 A.M.	60%	60%	60%

Notice that the time of call in the calls file is based on a 24-hour clock, such that 2:15 P.M. would be stored as 1415. To apply the discount, you need to know the day of the week. The following algorithm first converts a date to a sequential century-day and then from that figure derives a value (day-of-week) from 1 through 7 to represent the day of the week from Sunday through Saturday, respectively. Where the algorithm says INTEGER, truncate the value to a whole number (no rounding); where it says REMAINDER, use the %REM function (or the MVR operation, if %REM is not supported).

```
IF month > 2
    Add 1 to month
ELSE
    Add 13 to month
    Subtract 1 from year
ENDIF
century-day = INTEGER(years * 365.25) + INTEGER(month * 30.6) + days – 63
day-of-week = REMAINDER(century-day / 7) + 1
```

Your program is to determine the cost of each call in file GTCLSP, based on the area code and exchange of the called number and the time of the call; each call record should be updated with the cost calculated by your program.

Chapter 10

Modular Programming Concepts

 ## Chapter Overview

This chapter discusses modular programming and shows you how RPG IV programs can communicate with one another by passing data values as parameter arguments. You'll also learn how to code procedures, prototypes, and procedure interfaces to build your own functions. Finally, the chapter also introduces calling APIs from within an RPG IV program and sharing data among programs through data areas.

Modular Programming

As concern about program development and maintenance efficiencies has grown, programmers have become increasingly interested in developing small, standalone units of code (rather than writing monolithic programs thousands of lines long). This approach, which is often called **modular programming**, offers many advantages.

First, if you develop code in small, independent units, you often can reuse these units because it is common for several applications to share identical processing requirements for some parts of their logic. Furthermore, small programs are easier to test than large programs. In addition, code changes are less likely to cause unexpected — and unwanted — side effects when they're made within a small, standalone module rather than in a routine that is embedded within a gigantic program. Last, because you can separately develop and test such modules, a modular approach to programming makes it easier to divide an application development project among members of a programming team, each with responsibilities for developing different modules.

RPG IV provides the CALLP (Call a Prototyped Procedure or Program) operation to let you adopt this modular approach to program development. Before we discuss this operation in detail, you need to understand how the call affects flow of control. When program execution reaches a call statement, control passes to the called routine (which may itself be a program). The called routine executes until it reaches a RETURN statement; at this point, control returns to the calling program, at the statement immediately following the call.

Figure 10.1 illustrates this flow of control among calling and called programs.

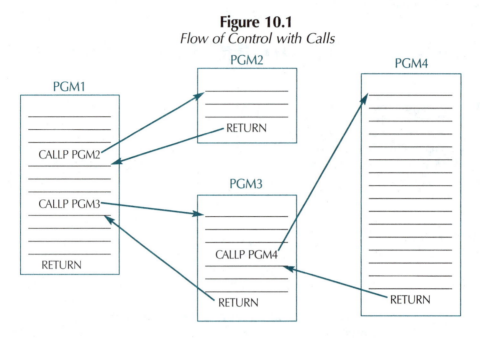

Figure 10.1
Flow of Control with Calls

As you can see, the flow of control with a call is like that of an EXSR operation, except that a call invokes an external program, module, or subprocedure rather than a subroutine internal to the program. A called program can in turn call other programs, but it should not recursively call its calling program.

Prototyping the Call Interface

A call would be of limited value if it did not permit the called and calling programs to share data. While an RPG IV program can normally access the value of any variable from anywhere within the program, this "global" feature of variables does not extend across program boundaries. That means if you want a called program to process some data and send the results of the processing back to the calling program, you need to make special provisions to let this sharing take place. The CALLP operation passes parameters to communicate values between caller and callee.

Before you can use CALLP to call a program, you must define the **call interface** to the RPG program. The basic program call interface includes the following information:

- the name of the program to call
- the number of parameters to pass, and their data attributes

To define this interface, you use a special structure called a **prototype**. The RPG IV compiler uses the prototype to call the program correctly and to ensure that the caller passes the correct parameters to the callee. A prototype must be in the Definition Specifications of the calling program; many programmers prefer to include prototypes at the beginning of the Definition Specifications. If the calling program calls more than one callee, it must include a prototype for each call interface.

To code a prototype, you define a structure similar to a data structure. The prototype definition has two parts:

- the prototype definition itself (the prototype header)
- the description(s) of parameter(s) to be shared between the caller and the callee

The following is an example of a prototype for a program call interface:

```
*.. 1 ...+... 2 ...+... 3 ...+... 4 ...+... 5 ...+... 6 ...+... 7 ...+... 8
DName+++++++++++ETDsFrom+++To/L+++IDc.Functions+++++++++++++++++++++++++++++
D UpdCust          PR                      EXTPGM('AR003')
D                                 5
D                                 7 0
```

PR, coded in positions 24–25 (Ds) signals the beginning of a prototyped call interface. You must name the prototype in positions 7–21 (Name+++++++++++). Code the external name of the program associated with this prototype, using the EXTPGM keyword; this name need not match the name of the prototype, although you may find it convenient to use a matching name. The program is the object that the caller will execute when you perform the call. The EXTPGM entry is usually a literal, but it could be a named constant or a field specifying the name of the program. In the example above, when you perform a call to the UpdCust prototype, program AR003 will actually be called.

If the call interface involves passing parameters, describe the parameters on subsequent lines, following the PR header. Indicate a parameter's length in positions 33–39 (To/L+++); for numeric fields, code a decimal positions entry in positions 41–42 (Dc). Code the parameter's data type in position 40 (I); if the type entry is blank, the default is packed decimal for numeric fields (fields with a decimal positions entry) and character for fields with blanks in positions 41–42. In the sample prototype above, there are two parameters: a five-character field and a seven-digit packed decimal field with zero decimals. Note that you need not name the parameters. You may find it convenient to document the parameter usage by naming the parameters (in positions 7–21), but the compiler will treat these names as comments.

CALLP (Call a Prototyped Procedure or Program)

The CALLP operation takes the form

```
CALLP(E) prototype(parm1: parm2: ... parmN)
```

CALLP passes control to the program object (*PGM) associated with the prototype named in Factor 2. You can also include the optional (E) operation code extender to indicate that the %ERROR function should be turned on if errors occur when the program attempts the call. List any parameters in parentheses immediately following the prototype name. If there are no parameters, Version 5 lets you code empty parentheses () instead; prior to Version 5, just omit the parentheses if there are no parameters.

```
*.. 1 ...+... 2 ...+... 3 ...+... 4 ...+... 5 ...+... 6 ...+... 7 ...+... 8
/FREE
   CALLP(E) UpdCust(Company:CustNbr);
   IF %ERROR;
     EXSR ERROR;
   ENDIF;
/END-FREE
```

The code in this example, when coupled with the prototype shown earlier, would call program AR003, named in the UpdCust prototype, passing fields Company (five characters) and CustNbr (seven digits) as parameters. Note that Company and CustNbr would be defined elsewhere in the program and that their definitions must match those in the prototype definition.

In the free-format specification, actually coding the CALLP operation is optional. You can let the compiler infer the CALLP operation, instead of explicitly coding it, as the following example illustrates:

```
*.. 1 ...+... 2 ...+... 3 ...+... 4 ...+... 5 ...+... 6 ...+... 7 ...+... 8
  /FREE
     UpdCust(Company:CustNbr);
  /END-FREE
```

Note, though, that you must explicitly code CALLP if you plan to use the (E) operation code extender.

The Procedure Interface

Recall the flow of control illustrated in Figure 10.1. In the calling program (e.g. PGM1), RPG IV uses the prototype definition to describe the list of parameters that it will pass on to the called program (e.g., PGM2). The called RPG IV program also uses a prototype definition to describe the corresponding list of parameters that it will receive from the caller. (Languages other than RPG IV may use mechanisms other than prototypes for this purpose.)

The prototypes in each program must match each other. That is, they must have the same number of parameters, and the corresponding parameters between the two programs must have the same data type and length. RPG IV passes parameter arguments by passing the address of the storage location represented by the field, so in fact these corresponding parameters reference the same storage location within the computer. The data names of the parameters used in the caller and callee need not be the same.

To access those storage locations passed by the calling program, the called program must include a **procedure interface** definition (in addition to a prototype). Like the prototype, the procedure interface describes the parameters that the callee will share with the caller. Unlike the prototype, however, the procedure interface defines variable names to hold the parameter values that the called program will receive, letting you refer to and manipulate those parameter values.

Tip
If there are no parameters involved in calling a program, the called program need not have a prototype or a procedure interface. You may still want to code each of them, however, for consistency among your programs and to promote future enhancements in the application. Regardless of any parameter-passing considerations, CALLP requires that the calling program always have a prototype.

The procedure interface is coded similarly to the prototype. Many programmers prefer to code the procedure interface immediately following any prototypes in the Definition Specifications. The procedure interface has two parts:

- the procedure interface itself (the header)
- the definition(s) for parameter(s) to be received by the callee

The following is an example of a prototype and a matching procedure interface:

```
*.. 1 ...+... 2 ...+... 3 ...+... 4 ...+... 5 ...+... 6 ...+... 7 ...+... 8
DName+++++++++++ETDsFrom+++To/L+++IDc.Functions++++++++++++++++++++++++++++
D Main            PR              EXTPGM('AR003')
D                               5
D                               7 0
D Main            PI
D   Company                     5
D   Customer                    7 0
```

PI, coded in positions 24–25 (Ds) signals the beginning of a prototyped call interface. You must name the prototype in positions 7–21 (Name+++++++++++). This name must match the name in the callee's prototype (but not necessarily the name for the caller's prototype).

Tip

Many programmers standardize on a common name, such as Main, for prototypes and procedure interfaces in called programs. This practice fortifies the role of the prototype and procedure interface to describe the "main procedure" in an RPG IV program.

If the call interface involves passing parameters, define the parameters on subsequent lines, following the PI header. Name the parameter variable in positions 7–21 (Name+++++++++++). Indicate its length in positions 33–39 (To/L+++); for numeric fields code a decimal positions entry in positions 41–42 (Dc). Code the parameter's data type in position 40 (I); if the type entry is blank, the default is packed decimal for numeric fields (fields with a decimal positions entry) and character for fields with blanks in positions 41–42. The data attributes and length of parameters in the procedure interface must match the corresponding parameter entries in the prototype. In the procedure interface above, there are two parameters: Company, a five-character field, and Customer, a seven-digit packed decimal field with zero decimals.

Changing Parameters, the RETURN Operation, and *INLR

Because RPG IV passes parameter arguments by passing the address of the storage location represented by the field — called **passing by reference** — rather than by passing the field's value — **passing by value** — changes in the parameter fields within the called program result in the same changes in the parameter fields of the calling program. In the following example, field Okay has a value of *OFF before the calling of another program. As part of its processing, the callee (next page) changes the value of the parameter Flag. When control is returned to the caller, Okay has a value of *ON because Okay and Flag reference the same storage location.

Caller

```
*.. 1 ...+... 2 ...+... 3 ...+... 4 ...+... 5 ...+... 6 ...+... 7 ...+... 8
DName++++++++++ETDsFrom+++To/L+++IDc.Functions++++++++++++++++++++++++++++

D NextPgm         PR                    EXTPGM('CALLEE')
D                                 N

D Okay            S                N    INZ(*OFF)

 /FREE
    CALLP NextPgm(Okay);                     // Okay = *OFF before call
                                             // Okay = *ON after call
 /END-FREE
```

Callee

```
*.. 1 ...+... 2 ...+... 3 ...+... 4 ...+... 5 ...+... 6 ...+... 7 ...+... 8
DName+++++++++++ETDsFrom+++To/L+++IDc.Functions+++++++++++++++++++++++++++++++

D Main            PR                    EXTPGM('CALLEE')
D                                 N

D Main            PI
D  Flag                           N

 /FREE
    Flag = *ON;                                 // Change value of Flag
    *INLR = *ON;
    RETURN;
 /END-FREE
```

The system returns control from the called program to the calling program when it encounters a RETURN statement in the called program. If the LR indicator is also on when the RETURN is executed, the system resources tied up by the called program are released; a subsequent call to the program causes it to start up again as though for the first time. On the other hand, if LR is not on within the called program upon return, the called program remains activated. As a result, a subsequent call to that program will find all the fields and indicators of the called program to have the values they had at the time of the previous RETURN. Moreover, any files used by the called program will still be open as a result of the previous call. The following examples illustrate this behavior.

```
*.. 1 ...+... 2 ...+... 3 ...+... 4 ...+... 5 ...+... 6 ...+... 7 ...+... 8
DName+++++++++++ETDsFrom+++To/L+++IDc.Functions+++++++++++++++++++++++++++++++
D SamplePgm        PR                    EXTPGM('SAMPLEPGM')
 . . .
 /FREE
  // Portion of a calling program that calls SAMPLEPGM within a loop
    DOW NOT %ERROR;
      CALLP(E) SamplePgm();
    ENDDO;
 /END-FREE

*.. 1 ...+... 2 ...+... 3 ...+... 4 ...+... 5 ...+... 6 ...+... 7 ...+... 8
 /FREE
  // Portion of called program SAMPLEPGM where RETURN is executed without
  // LR turned on; the program will remain active, and field Count will be
  // 1 greater each time the called program is entered from the calling
  // program.
    Count = Count + 1;
    RETURN;
 /END-FREE

*.. 1 ...+... 2 ...+... 3 ...+... 4 ...+... 5 ...+... 6 ...+... 7 ...+... 8
 /FREE
  // In this version of SAMPLEPGM, where LR is turned on before the RETURN,
  // the program is deactivated, and Count will be 0 each time SAMPLEPGM is
  // called.
    Count = Count + 1;
    *INLR = *ON;
    RETURN;
 /END-FREE
```

Whether or not you should turn on LR before returning from a called program, then, depends on whether you want the called program to start afresh each time the calling program evokes it or you want the called program to pick up where it left off on the previous call (within a given run). Failure to correctly handle the LR indicator can cause undesired effects in the called program.

Fitting the Pieces

Here is a summary of the requirements for having one RPG IV program call another RPG IV program. The calling program includes

- a prototype definition to describe the parameters to be passed
- the CALLP operation to execute the call

The called program includes

- a prototype definition to describe the parameters to be received
- a procedure interface to receive the parameters and define their variables
- the RETURN operation to return control to the calling program

In the following example "snippets," program AR001 calls AR003, passing it three parameters: CpyName (with a value of "CSELL"), CustNbr (10487), and Okay (*OFF). Study this example to understand the relationship between the caller and the callee as well as the relationship between the prototype and the procedure interface. (Program AR001 receives no parameters, but the example includes a prototype for the sake of consistency).

Program AR001
```
*.. 1 ...+... 2 ...+... 3 ...+... 4 ...+... 5 ...+... 6 ...+... 7 ...+... 8
DName++++++++++ETDsFrom+++To/L+++IDc.Functions++++++++++++++++++++++++++++++
D Main             PR                  EXTPGM('AR001')

D UpdCust          PR                  EXTPGM('AR003')
D                                 5
D                                 7 0
D                                 N

D CpyName          S                5
D CustNbr          S                7 0
D Okay             S                N    INZ(*OFF)

 /FREE
    CpyName = 'CSELL';
    CustNbr = 10487;

    UpdCust(CpyName:CustNbr:Okay);                    // Implied CALLP
    IF Okay;                  // If AR003 executed normally, Okay will be *ON
      EXSR Process;
    ENDIF;
 /END-FREE
```

Program AR003

```
*.. 1 ...+... 2 ...+... 3 ...+... 4 ...+... 5 ...+... 6 ...+... 7 ...+... 8
DName++++++++++ETDsFrom+++To/L+++IDc.Functions+++++++++++++++++++++++++++++++
D Main            PR                  EXTPGM('AR003')
D                                5
D                                7 0
D                                N

D Main            PI
D Company                        5
D Customer                       7 0
D Flag                           N

 /FREE
  // Company = 'CSELL' (Value received from first parameter)
  // Customer = 10487 (Value received from second parameter)
  // Flag = *OFF (Valued received from third parameter)

   Flag = *ON;                                      // Change value of Flag
   *INLR = *ON;
   RETURN;
 /END-FREE
```

Dynamic and Static Binding

Until RPG IV, CALL with **dynamic binding** was the only option for programmers who wanted to adopt a modular approach to their code. With this method, programmers compiled each program separately to create individual, executable *PGM objects. When you ran a program that used the CALL operation to invoke another program (*PGM object), the system then went "looking" for the called program and bound it to the calling program dynamically, during runtime.

The CALLP operation still uses dynamic binding to execute calls to an individual *PGM object. If an application is "call intensive" (that is, if one program calls another program hundreds, or even thousands, of times), this dynamic binding takes time and may degrade system performance — in some instances, severely — compared with performance if the programmer handled the code in the called programs as subroutines internal to the calling program.

When IBM introduced OS/400's Integrated Language Environment (ILE), it included the option of connecting RPG IV modules *before* runtime. This **static binding** alleviates some of the performance degradation found with dynamic binding.

Here is how static binding works. When you compile source code with the CL command CRTRPGMOD (Create RPG Module), the compiler creates a *MODULE object rather than an executable program (*PGM) object. To form the *PGM object, you must carry out a separate binding procedure, invoked through the CRTPGM (Create Program) command. If some *MODULEs are to call others, you can link them together during this binding step to form a single executable *PGM object. When the program runs, the binding has already been completed, so performance is not affected.

An alternate static binding command, the CRTSRVPGM (Create Service Program) command, binds *MODULE objects together to form a service program (*SRVPGM) object. Service programs are not executable objects but instead serve as containers for *MODULE code that programs can access. Service programs combine some of the performance advantages of basic static binding with the modularity and flexibility advantages of dynamic binding. A more complete discussion of service programs is beyond the scope of this text.

Using the CALL (Call a Program) Operation

While the CALLP operation is RPG IV's preferred method for having one program call another, you will likely maintain many programs that employ an older interface, using the CALL (Call a Program) operation. CALL is not as versatile as CALLP, and it does not support prototypes or procedure interfaces. CALL works only within the fixed-format Calculation Specifications.

The CALL operation passes control to the program object named in Factor 2. Factor 2 can contain a literal specifying the program to be executed (the called program), or it can contain a field, an array element, or a named constant that specifies the name of the program to be called. You can also include the optional (E) operation extender on the CALL to monitor for errors that might occur when the program attempts the call.

When you use a variable to represent the program name in a CALL operation, the program to be called is not fixed, or constant; it may change from one call to the next, depending on the value of the variable. Consider the following examples.

```
*.. 1 ...+... 2 ...+... 3 ...+... 4 ...+... 5 ...+... 6 ...+... 7 ...+... 8
CL0N01Factor1+++++++Opcode(E)+Factor2+++++++Result+++++++Len++D+HiLoEq....
 * A call to a program whose name is specified as a literal
C                   CALL(E)   'GL001R'
 * A call to a program whose name is the value of a variable
C                   CALL(E)   ProgName
```

Assume ProgName is a 10-position character field with the value 'GL001R'. In that case, the two CALL statements in these examples will have identical effects: the execution of program GL001R. However, with the second method, the value of ProgName could change during execution so that a repetition of that CALL statement could invoke a different program. Calling a program by supplying its name as a field value rather than as a literal causes more system overhead than coding the name as a literal. Accordingly, you should use a literal unless the program to be called actually may change within a run or between runs of the calling program.

Instead of a prototype, CALL uses the PARM (Identify Parameters) operation to indicate which field's values are to be shared between programs. PARMs are usually listed on subsequent lines following the CALL operation. A list of PARMs in the calling program must have a list of corresponding PARMs in the called program. Although the data names of the PARMs used in the calling and called programs do not need to be the same, corresponding PARMs in the two programs should have the same type and length.

Each PARM statement requires an entry in the Result field of the standard Calculation Specification. This entry can be a field, a data structure, or an array that is to serve as the parameter. It cannot be one of the reserved numbered indicators, a literal, a label, a constant, or a table name. If the field is a multiple-occurrence data structure, all occurrences of the data structure are passed as a single field.

You can list PARMs immediately following a call operation, or you can use the PLIST (Identify a Parameter List) operation, which can precede or follow the call operation. PLIST is merely a declarative operation that identifies a list of parameters to be shared between programs. PLIST requires an identifying entry in Factor 1; that entry should be either a PLIST name, if the PLIST is within a calling program, or *ENTRY, if the PLIST is within the called program. Reserved word *ENTRY signals that this PLIST (in the called program) contains the parameter arguments that the called program is to receive upon its invocation by the calling program. If a PLIST is used within a calling program, the name of the PLIST must appear as the Result field entry of the call associated with the list.

Look at the following examples to clarify the relationship between calling and called programs, PLISTs, and PARMs. In the following illustration, the calling program calls program Prog2, passing it PARMs FldA, FldB, and FldC. Because the PARMs appear immediately after a call operation, they do not require a PLIST header preceding them.

continued…

```
*.. 1 ...+... 2 ...+... 3 ...+... 4 ...+... 5 ...+... 6 ...+... 7 ...+... 8
CLØN01Factor1++++++Opcode(E)+Factor2++++++Result++++++++Len++D+HiLoEq....
 * This is a sample of a calling program. Notice how the PARMs follow the
 * CALL without a PLIST operation.
C                   CALL      'Prog2'
C                   PARM                    FldA
C                   PARM                    FldB
C                   PARM                    FldC
```

An alternate way to code the same logic is to include the PARMs within a PLIST and specify that PLIST within the call operation, as follows.

```
*.. 1 ...+... 2 ...+... 3 ...+... 4 ...+... 5 ...+... 6 ...+... 7 ...+... 8
CLØN01Factor1++++++Opcode(E)+Factor2++++++Result++++++++Len++D+HiLoEq....
 * This is a sample of a calling program. The PARMs appear in a PLIST,
 * which is referenced in the CALL operation. The effect is identical
 * to that of the preceding example.
C     PlistA        PLIST
C                   PARM                    FldA
C                   PARM                    FldB
C                   PARM                    FldC
 . . .
C                   CALL      'Prog2'       PlistA
```

Both examples accomplish the same effect — passing the addresses of FldA, FldB, and FldC to the called program, Prog2.

To access those storage locations passed by the calling program, the called program also must include PARMs. These PARMs occur within a PLIST labeled *ENTRY, as shown on the following page. A called program can contain only one *ENTRY PLIST, which serves a purpose similar to the procedure interface described elsewhere.

continued...

To call modules (*MODULE objects) that are to be statically bound, you can use the CALLP operation, just as you do for a dynamic program call. For statically bound modules, changes to the prototype definition dictate a **static procedure call.** The static procedure call is the method that RPG IV uses to call subprocedures, which we discuss next.

Tip

If you want to create an executable program from RPG IV source that does not require binding with other modules, you can complete the compiling and binding procedures in one step by using CL command CRTBNDRPG (Create Bound RPG Program).

Procedures and Subprocedures

Procedures are IBM's most recent RPG enhancement for developing modular, reusable code. In the past, RPG programs consisted of single-procedure programs with a single entry point. With the introduction of subprocedures, a program can now consist of a main procedure and, optionally, one or more **subprocedures**. Moreover, subprocedures can exist either within the same module as a main procedure (or program) or in standalone modules, where they can readily be bound to and accessed by several different programs.

continued...

```
*.. 1 ...+... 2 ...+... 3 ...+... 4 ...+... 5 ...+... 6 ...+... 7 ...+... 8
CLØNØ1Factor1+++++++Opcode(E)+Factor2++++++Result+++++++Len++D+HiLoEq....
 * This is the called program, Prog2. It includes an *ENTRY PLIST.
C     *ENTRY        PLIST
C                   PARM                    FldX
C                   PARM                    FldY
C                   PARM                    FldZ
```

Note that although the variable names in the corresponding PARMs of the calling and called programs may be different, they must agree in data type and length because they reference the same storage location. You must define the variables declared as PARMs within their respective programs on Definition Specifications.

Because RPG IV passes parameter arguments by reference, changes in the parameter fields within the called program result in the same changes in the parameter fields of the calling program. For example, assume in the above illustration that FldA had a value of 150 before the call to Prog2 and that, as part of its processing, Prog2 changes the value of FldX to 0. Upon return to the calling program, FldA will now have a value of 0 because that field and FldX of the called program reference the same storage location.

If this possible change in parameter field values could cause undesired effects, you can use Factor 2 with the PARM operation to eliminate this side effect. Simply enter the field whose value you want passed to the called program as Factor 2 and enter a different field as the Result field. When the call takes place, the system copies the value of the Factor 2 field into the Result field and passes the address of the Result field to the called program. Upon return from the called program, the Result field's value may be changed, but the Factor 2 field value remains undisturbed:

```
*.. 1 ...+... 2 ...+... 3 ...+... 4 ...+... 5 ...+... 6 ...+... 7 ...+... 8
CLØNØ1Factor1+++++++Opcode(E)+Factor2++++++Result+++++++Len++D+HiLoEq....
 * Example showing how to pass FldA's value to Prog1 without
 * the possibility of FldA's value being changed by Prog1
C                   CALL      'Prog1'
C                   PARM      FldA          FldX
```

A subprocedure is like a subroutine, but with two important differences. First, the subprocedure can be created independently of what we traditionally have called a program but now more accurately call a main procedure. The second important difference between a subprocedure and a subroutine lies in the scope of the variables used in the two kinds of routines. For a program containing subroutines, all data definition is global; that is, all variables are equally accessible by both the main procedure and the subroutines it calls. In contrast, subprocedures introduce the concept of **local variables** to RPG. Local variables are recognized only within the subprocedure in which they are defined. Data values are communicated from main procedures to subprocedures through passed parameters. A given subprocedure, like a built-in function, may return a value to the calling procedure outside the context of any parameter variable; this capability lets you incorporate user-defined functions into your programs. These differences make subprocedures much more similar to built-in functions than to traditional RPG subroutines.

Once a subprocedure has been created, you invoke it the same way you invoke a built-in function, if the subprocedure returns a value to the calling procedure. To invoke a subprocedure that does not return values, you use the CALLP operation.

Although the concept of subprocedures is relatively easy to understand, writing the code for subprocedures is somewhat more complex. The following example demonstrates how to use a subprocedure to convert a Fahrenheit temperature value into its Celsius equivalent.

```
*.. 1 ...+... 2 ...+... 3 ...+... 4 ...+... 5 ...+... 6 ...+... 7 ...+... 8
DName++++++++++ETDsFrom+++To/L+++IDc.Functions++++++++++++++++++++++++++++++++
PName++++++++++..T..................Functions++++++++++++++++++++++++++++++++
  // Module contains subprocedure only; no main procedure
H NOMAIN

  // Procedure prototype
D Celsius         PR              3 0
D                                 3 0

  // Begin subprocedure
P Celsius         B                        EXPORT

  // Procedure interface
D                 PI              3 0
D Fahrenheit                      3 0

  // Here is where variables local to the subprocedure are defined.
D Temperature     S               3 0

 /FREE
    EVAL(H) Temperature = (5/9) * (Fahrenheit - 32);
    RETURN Temperature;
 /END-FREE

  // End subprocedure
P Celsius         E
```

Note, first, the Control (Header) Specification. This specification, with its keyword NOMAIN, is required when a module contains no main procedure but only a subprocedure (or subprocedures).

Next in the code come Definition Specifications to define the procedure prototype. By now, you should be familiar with this structure. Notice the differences in the prototype header for this prototype compared with the prototypes we discussed earlier. In addition to naming the subprocedure (in this case, Celsius), the first line of the prototype identifies the length (positions 33–39), data type (position 40), and any decimal positions (positions 41–42) of the value that the subprocedure will return to the caller. This entry defines the subprocedure's **return value**.

Notice also that the prototype does not include the EXTPGM keyword; the EXTPGM keyword specifies a dynamic program call, so it is not appropriate for this static procedure call. (If the name of the prototype does not match the name of the procedure, you can use the EXTPROC keyword to name the procedure.)

The next Definition Specification (without any entry in positions 24–25) identifies the attributes of the parameter to be passed to the subprocedure by the caller. If there were additional parameters, you would code additional Definition Specifications.

This procedure prototype must appear in every module that calls this subprocedure, as well as in the subprocedure itself. These prototypes let the compiler compare the parameter definitions in the calling and the called procedures for inconsistencies that could cause difficult-to-locate bugs when the program is executed.

Following the procedure prototype is the **Procedure Boundary Specification**, a new type of specification that includes a P in position 6, the name of the subprocedure in positions 7–21 (Name+++++++++++), and a B in position 24 to indicate the beginning of the subprocedure itself. Including the keyword EXPORT on this specification lets the subprocedure be called by other modules within the program.

The next Definition Specification (with PI in positions 24–25) defines the **procedure interface** of the subprocedure. Like the prototype, the procedure interface includes the length and type of the subprocedure's return value. The following Definition Specification defines the variable (Fahrenheit) that is to receive the value of the parameter passed to the subprocedure. As with the prototype, had there been more parameters, we would have coded more Definition Specifications.

The final Definition Specification defines Temperature, a field that is local to subprocedure Celsius. In addition to standalone variables, you can code local data structures, arrays, tables, and named constants within a subprocedure.

The Calculation Specification converts the passed value to its Celsius equivalent. Note that the name of the variable containing the calculated value is included in the Factor 2 position of the RETURN operation to allow the subprocedure to return this value to the calling procedure. As an alternative to coding a variable in the RETURN statement's Factor 2 position, you can code an expression or a literal; the subprocedure will return the value of the expression or literal.

The subprocedure concludes with a second Procedure Specification, containing an E in position 24 to signal the end of the subprocedure.

This subprocedure can now be used like a built-in function in any procedure that needs to convert a Fahrenheit temperature to its Celsius equivalent. In the calling procedure, you could assign the value of the subprocedure to another variable or use it in a IF statement, as follows:

```
*.. 1 ...+... 2 ...+... 3 ...+... 4 ...+... 5 ...+... 6 ...+... 7 ...+... 8
DName++++++++++ETDsFrom+++To/L+++IDc.Functions+++++++++++++++++++++++++++++
   // Procedure prototype
D Celsius          PR             3 0
D                                 3 0

 /FREE
    ConvrtTemp = Celsius(TempIn);
    IF Celsius(TempIn) <= 0;
      Status = 'Freezing';
    ELSE;
      Status = 'Thawed';
    ENDIF;
 /END-FREE
```

Remember that the calling procedure must also include a prototype for the subprocedure.

You can also call subprocedures using the CALLP operation, using the form

```
CALLP prototype(parm1: parm2: ... parmN)
```

You should use this method for calling procedures only when the subprocedure does not return a value. Otherwise, invoke the subprocedure like a built-in function.

Before you can invoke a static procedure call, you must bind together those modules invoking the subprocedures with the modules containing the subprocedures they call into a single executable program with the CRTPGM command.

Tip

Don't be confused or overly concerned about the differences between a procedure and a subprocedure. The term "subprocedure" is simply used by RPG IV to distinguish a program's main procedure from other procedures in the program.

Using the CALLB (Call a Bound Module) Operation

While CALLP is the preferred operation code for invoking a *MODULE that has been statically bound with the calling program module, you may maintain programs that use an older operation code, CALLB (Call a Bound Module). CALLB is not as versatile as CALLP, does not support prototyping or return values, and is restricted to the fixed-format Calculation Specification.

The format of CALLB is identical to CALL. The Factor 2 specification must reference a *MODULE procedure that is contained within the same *PGM object as the calling program; CALLB cannot call a separately bound program (*PGM object type). Factor 2 must contain a literal, a named constant, or a procedure pointer — it cannot contain a field whose value is the procedure name. The following examples illustrate CALLB.

```
*.. 1 ...+... 2 ...+... 3 ...+... 4 ...+... 5 ...+... 6 ...+... 7 ...+... 8
DName++++++++++ETDsFrom+++To/L+++IDc.Keywords+++++++++++++++++++++++++++++++++
CLØNØ1Factor1+++++++Opcode(E)+Factor2+++++++Result++++++++Len++D+HiLoEq....
CLØNØ1Factor1+++++++Opcode(E)+Extended-factor2+++++++++++++++++++++++++++++++
D ProcName       C                 'ProcXYZ'
D PPtr           S                 PROCPTR

 * Examples of CALLB: one where the called procedure is specified as a
 * literal, one where a constant is used to specify the called procedure,
 * and one where a procedure pointer, PPtr, is used to indicate the called
 * procedure.
C                 CALLB      'ProcXYZ'
 . . .

C                 CALLB      ProcName
 . . .

C                 EVAL       PPtr = %PADDR('ProcXYZ')
C                 CALLB      PPtr
 . . .
```

Notice the use of %PADDR in the third example above. %PADDR (Get Procedure Address) is a built-in function similar to %ADDR (Get Address of Variable, discussed in Chapter 11), except that %PADDR returns the address of a procedure (*MODULE) entry point instead of the address of a variable's storage location. Calling a statically bound procedure using a procedure pointer is usually somewhat faster than using either a literal or a constant.

You can also use %PADDR to initialize a procedure pointer to the address of a procedure you will call later. You do this within the Definition Specification for the procedure pointer, as shown in the following example.

```
*.. 1 ...+... 2 ...+... 3 ...+... 4 ...+... 5 ...+... 6 ...+... 7 ...+... 8
DName++++++++++ETDsFrom+++To/L+++IDc.Keywords+++++++++++++++++++++++++++++++++
CLØNØ1Factor1+++++++Opcode(E)+Factor2+++++++Result++++++++Len++D+HiLoEq....
D PPtr           S             *   PROCPTR INZ(%PADDR('ProcXYZ'))

C                 CALLB(E)   PPtr
C                 IF         %ERROR
 . . .
C                 ENDIF
```

Note the data type * coded in position 40; this code indicates that the data item PPtr is a pointer, which points to an address in memory. (We'll discuss pointers more thoroughly in Chapter 11.) This practice facilitates program maintenance, because you can easily change the called procedure in one place in your program, without searching through Calculation Specifications for all the calls to that procedure.

Within a CALLB operation, you can include the optional (E) extender to turn on the %ERROR function if an error occurs when the program attempts the call, just as you can with operation CALL. Also, the status of LR (i.e., whether it is on or off) affects operation CALLB the same way it affects CALL.

Using Prototypes Effectively

Prototypes provide an effective way to define the data items to be passed between programs or procedures. Prototypes also offer a great deal of flexibility in the method the system will use to pass those parameters.

You'll recall from our earlier discussion that RPG IV, by default, passes parameter arguments by sharing the address of the storage location represented by the field (passing by reference). If the called program or procedure changes the value of the parameter field, the change will be recognized by the calling procedure or program. Prototypes offer you two other methods for passing parameters: passing by value and passing by read-only reference.

Passing Parameters by Value

When you include the VALUE keyword for a parameter within a prototype, you can pass the parameter's actual value instead of sharing the address of the parameter. The called procedure must allocate its own memory for the parameter instead of sharing the same memory address that the caller is using. If the called procedure changes the value of the parameter, the calling procedure will not recognize the change; its data is thus protected from being changed by the called procedure. Passing by value applies only to statically bound procedure calls.

```
*.. 1 ...+... 2 ...+... 3 ...+... 4 ...+... 5 ...+... 6 ...+... 7 ...+... 8
DName++++++++++ETDsFrom+++To/L+++IDc.Functions++++++++++++++++++++++++++++++
  // Procedure prototype passes all parameters by value
D Payment         PR             9 2
D                                9 2 VALUE
D                                5 5 VALUE
D                                5 0 VALUE
```

In the called procedure, the procedure interface definition must also specify the VALUE keyword to match the prototype.

You can mix passing methods if necessary. If you omit the VALUE keyword for a parameter, the parameter is passed by reference.

When you pass parameters by value, you can pass literals and expressions as well as variables. The following example passes three parameters to the Payment procedure.

```
*.. 1 ...+... 2 ...+... 3 ...+... 4 ...+... 5 ...+... 6 ...+... 7 ...+... 8
DName++++++++++ETDsFrom+++To/L+++IDc.Functions++++++++++++++++++++++++++++++
  // Declare procedure prototype.
D Payment         PR             9 2
D                                9 2 VALUE
D                                5 5 VALUE
D                                5 0 VALUE
  . . .
 /FREE
    Pmt = Payment(Principal + Interest:.075:Term);
 /END-FREE
```

Because the parameters are passed by value, the example can pass an expression (Principal + Interest) and a literal (.075), as well as the Term variable.

Tip

To improve the flexibility of your coding, and to protect the integrity of a procedure's data, always pass parameters by value, unless the calling procedure needs to access any changes made by the called procedure (in that case, pass by reference).

Passing Parameters by Read-Only Reference

On occasion, you may want to be able to pass expressions and literals to dynamically called programs in addition to procedures. Passing by value, however, applies only to procedures, not to programs. Prototypes offer the means to pass parameters to programs by read-only reference, a method that emulates passing by value. With this method, RPG IV can evaluate an expression or a literal and then make a copy of the value; the calling program will then pass a pointer to the memory occupied by the copy. The called program should not change the value of the parameter.

To specify read-only reference, you code the CONST keyword in the prototype:

```
*.. 1 ...+... 2 ...+... 3 ...+... 4 ...+... 5 ...+... 6 ...+... 7 ...+... 8
DName++++++++++ETDsFrom+++To/L+++IDc.Functions++++++++++++++++++++++++++++++
D UpdCust         PR                    EXTPGM('AR003')
D                                 5 0 CONST
D                                 7 0
 . . .
 /FREE
   // This is an example of calling a program using CALLP, passing a literal
   // and a variable.
     CALLP(E) UpdCust(5:CustNumber);
 /END-FREE
```

Both the VALUE and CONST keywords allow you some flexibility in passing parameters of slightly different data types than the prototype specifies. For example, you might pass a zoned decimal field when a prototype calls for a packed decimal field. As long as the field's value is appropriate for the data type, the prototype will manage this minor mismatch.

Using EXPORT and IMPORT

As we mentioned earlier, the CALLP operation uses parameters to share data. In addition, when using a static procedure call, you can define variables whose values are available across modules. You must define each variable in Definition Specifications within each relevant procedure. Then specify keyword EXPORT within the variable's definition in the module that will allocate storage. Finally, specify keyword IMPORT in the variable's definition in all remaining modules that reference it. Data items so defined should not be included as parameters. The procedure exporting the data item is responsible for any initialization of that variable.

```
*.. 1 ...+... 2 ...+... 3 ...+... 4 ...+... 5 ...+... 6 ...+... 7 ...+... 8
DName++++++++++ETDsFrom+++To/L+++IDc.Keywords+++++++++++++++++++++++++++++++
   // Example of a calling procedure EXPORTing a variable to the ProcA proc
D ProcA           PR

D FldA            S              9 2 EXPORT INZ(200)
 . . .
 /FREE
    CALLP ProcA;
 /END-FREE
```

```
*.. 1 ...+... 2 ...+... 3 ...+... 4 ...+... 5 ...+... 6 ...+... 7 ...+... 8
DName++++++++++ETDsFrom+++To/L+++IDc.Keywords+++++++++++++++++++++++++++++++
   // ProcA, which imports FldA's value from the calling procedure
D ProcA           PR

   // Superglobal field
D FldA            S              9 2 IMPORT

P ProcA           B
D                 PI
 . . .
P ProcA           E
```

You will usually find it more convenient and flexible to pass parameters between procedures rather than use EXPORT and IMPORT to define such intermodular "super-global" fields.

Using a Modular Approach

You'll find a wide variation in the extent to which different companies use RPG IV's calling features. Some companies incorporate calls within menu programs that present application choices to users; the menu programs then call the selected programs to perform the desired processing. Typically, this kind of program does not require passing data between the calling program and the programs it calls.

Another application of RPG IV's calling features is to access a routine that performs a specific task, without recoding the routine every time you need it. For example, in Chapter 11 we'll look at a routine to determine the day of the week for a given date in *ISO format. You could perform this day-of-the-week "calculation" within a called program or, better yet, as a subprocedure.

If you were to implement this function as a called program, the calling program would include two parameters: one to contain the given date and one to store the calculated day of the week. The called program would determine the day of the week of the value represented in the first parameter, store the result in the second parameter, and return control to the calling program.

If the function were a subprocedure, you'd pass to it a single parameter, the given date. The subprocedure would determine the day-of-week value for the passed date and then return that value to the calling procedure. With this implementation, the day-of-week procedure would be a user-defined function that you could reuse in many programs, coding it within an expression, just like a built-in function.

Another example of a routine that many programs or procedures might call is one that converts a numeric value representing dollars and cents (e.g., 123.43) to its representation in words (e.g., one hundred twenty-three dollars and 43 cents). The logic required for such a conversion is not trivial, and companies do not want to continually reinvent that particular wheel.

Calling an external routine offers an additional significant advantage over an EXSR operation: The called routine does not have to be an object created from RPG IV source. You can write a program in any high-level language (HLL) supported by the iSeries, or in OS/400's CL, compile it, and then call it from an RPG IV program.

Similarly, you can call an RPG IV program or procedure from a CL program or procedure or from one written in a different HLL supported by the iSeries. The RPG IV program's RETURN statement returns control to whatever program/procedure called it.

This flexibility lets you break down a problem into logical units, write each unit in the language best suited for developing the algorithm required by that unit, and then call the units to perform their processing as needed. Although this multilanguage approach to program development has not been not widely used in the iSeries world previously, its use is growing as cooperative processing and the use of graphical user interfaces (GUIs) demand more sophisticated capabilities than those RPG IV alone can offer. Moreover, the introduction of subprocedures has many programmers beginning to build "tool chests" of user-defined functions for reusability. As a result, modular programming is becoming more common in IT departments that use RPG IV.

APIs

You have learned how an RPG IV program can call another program (or procedure) written in RPG IV (or any other iSeries language) by using CALLP. You can also use CALLP to access application programming interfaces, or **APIs**. APIs are programs or commands built into the operating system that let you access lower-level machine functions or system data not otherwise available within an HLL program.

Many different APIs exist; each provides a different, specific capability. For example, API QUSLSPL (List Spooled Files) builds a list of spooled files from an output queue; a related API, QUSRSPLA (Retrieve Spooled File Attributes), retrieves this data into a program. You can use APIs to obtain information about a job, a database file, a library, or any other kind of object on the system. Almost all APIs have a required, specific set of parameters used to pass values from your program, return values to your program, or both. Many APIs also require a special kind of storage area, called a **user space**, to receive their output or to supply their input. User spaces are defined, permanent locations in storage; they are similar to data areas, which we describe in detail later in this chapter. How do user spaces originate? An API, QUSCRTUS (Create User Space), creates a user space for use by other APIs.

Although a complete discussion of APIs is beyond the scope of this text, we will take a closer look at two often-used APIs to give you a sense of how you might use APIs within your RPG IV programs. In general, you'll use a dynamic program call to execute an API, although you can use a static procedure call to execute a special group of APIs called "bindable" APIs.

The first API we'll consider is QUSCMDLN (Display Command Line Window). This API presents an OS/400 system command line as a pop-up window within your program. Say, for example, that you were writing an interactive application in which you wanted to give the user access to the system command line so he or she could check the status of a spooled file, send a message to another user, or whatever. In your display file, you would enable a function key (e.g., F21, mapped via an indicator data structure to field FKey21) to signal the user's request for a command line, and you would include a prompt at the bottom of the screen to inform the user of this feature (e.g., 'F21=Command Line'). Then, within your RPG IV program upon return from the display, you would check the status of the indicator associated with that function key. If the indicator's value indicated that the user had pressed the function key, your program would call API QUSCMDLN to pop up the command line on the current screen:

```
*.. 1 ...+... 2 ...+... 3 ...+... 4 ...+... 5 ...+... 6 ...+... 7 ...+... 8
DName++++++++++ETDsFrom+++To/L+++IDc.Keywords+++++++++++++++++++++++++++++++
    // Example showing a portion of an interactive program that lets the user
    // access a CL command line

D CmdLinAPI        PR                        EXTPGM('QUSCMDLN')

 /FREE
    EXFMT Screen1;
    IF FKey21;
      CALLP CmdLinAPI;
    ELSE;
      . . .
    ENDIF;
 /END-FREE
```

When the user finishes with the command line and exits from it, control returns to your program, which resumes processing from the point of the call.

Notice that QUSCMDLN, unlike most APIs, uses no parameters. The second API we'll look at, QCMDEXC (Execute Command), is more typical in its format.

What does QCMDEXC do? Occasionally within an RPG IV program, you would like to communicate directly with the operating system to issue a CL command. You might, for example, want to override one database file with another or send a message reporting on the program's progress to the user. API QCMDEXC lets you execute such a CL command from within an HLL program.

Any program can call QCMDEXC. QCMDEXC normally expects to receive arguments for two parameters: The first parameter should contain the command the system is to execute, and the second should contain the command's length. (The variable representing this length must be defined as a numeric field with 15 positions, five of which are decimal positions.)

The following example illustrates using an implied EVAL to command to set a parameter value and then using the implied CALLP to execute the command.

```
*.. 1 ...+... 2 ...+... 3 ...+... 4 ...+... 5 ...+... 6 ...+... 7 ...+... 8
DName++++++++++ETDsFrom+++To/L+++IDc.Keywords++++++++++++++++++++++++++++++++
   // Example showing the use of QCMDEXC to show the spooled files for the
   // current user.
D RunCmd          PR                    EXTPGM('QCMDEXC')
D                                3000    CONST OPTIONS(*VARSIZE)
D                                15   5  CONST

D Cmd                            3000    VARYING
D User                            10     INZ(*USER)
  . . .
  /FREE
     Cmd = 'WRKSPLF SELECT(' + User + ')';
     RunCmd(Cmd:%LEN(Cmd));
  /END-FREE
```

In this example, the prototype specifies passing by read-only reference (using the CONST keyword); this option allows embedding an expression as a parameter in the call (e.g., %LEN(Cmd)). Using a variable-length field, Cmd, simplifies the string expression used to construct the command, and specifying OPTIONS(*VARSIZE) in the prototype lets us pass less data than the prototype specifies.

You can see that APIs provide you with a variety of callable routines to access the resources of the iSeries in ways not possible with RPG IV alone. If you are interested in learning more details about APIs, see the IBM manual *AS/400 System API Reference*.

Data Areas

Parameters let calling and called programs/procedures share data. **Data areas** are OS/400 objects that represent storage locations used to share data between programs/procedures within a job or between jobs. However, one program does not have to call another to share the data if the data resides in a data area. You can use data areas to store information of limited size (up to 2,000 bytes), independent of database files or programs.

The system automatically creates a **local data area (LDA)** for each job in the system. Each LDA is 1,024 positions long, with type character; initially, blanks fill the LDA. When you submit a job with the CL SBMJOB (Submit Job) command, the value of your LDA is copied into the LDA of the submitted job so that the submitted job can access any data values stored in the LDA by your initial job. When a job ends, its LDA ceases to exist.

You also can create more permanent data areas with the CL command CRTDTAARA (Create Data Area). A data area created in this way remains an object on the system until it is explicitly removed; any program, regardless of its job, can access such a data area.

Programmers use data areas to store small quantities of data used frequently by several programs or by the same program each time it is run. For example, they might prefer storing within a data area the next order number or customer number to be assigned, to avoid having to retrieve that information from a database file of orders or customers. Programmers sometimes use a data area to store constant values used by several programs, such as tax rates or discounts, or to transfer the processing results of one program to another.

Using *DTAARA DEFINE, IN, and OUT

Usually, you'll define a data-area data structure to access data areas within your program. Older programs may access the contents of a data area through the *DTAARA DEFINE operation. This operation requires you to enter *DTAARA in Factor 1, and the Result field must contain a variable that is to receive the data area's contents. This variable can be a field, a data structure subfield, or a data structure (but not a data-area data structure — that is, no U in position 23). You must define this result variable within your program, and the definition must match that of the data area itself.

Factor 2 normally contains the external name of the data area whose contents you want to access. If you leave Factor 2 blank, the Result field must contain the external data-area name and also serve as the name you use to represent the data area within your program. If you want to use this operation with the LDA, code *LDA in Factor 2.

```
*.. 1 ...+... 2 ...+... 3 ...+... 4 ...+... 5 ...+... 6 ...+... 7 ...+... 8
DName++++++++++ETDsFrom+++To/L+++IDc.Keywords+++++++++++++++++++++++++++++++
CLØNØ1Factor1+++++++Opcode(E)+Factor2+++++++Result++++++++Len++D+HiLoEq....
 * Examples of using *DTAARA DEFINE to access data areas.
 * Data items used to receive the data areas' data are defined
 * on Definition Specifications below.

 * Standalone field InvNo        ·
D InvNo           S              8 0
 * Standalone field CheckNo
D CheckNo         S              6 0
 * Data structure Receipts
D Receipts        DS
D   Store1                      10 2
D   Store2                      10 2
D   Store3                      10 2

 * Data area Check associated with field CheckNo
C     *DTAARA        DEFINE    Check        CheckNo
 * Data area Receipts associated with data structure Receipts
C     *DTAARA        DEFINE                 Receipts
 * Local data area associated with InvNo
C     *DTAARA        DEFINE    *LDA         InvNo
```

Two important differences exist between accessing a data area with *DTAARA DEFINE and accessing it through a data-area data structure. First, the contents of the data area are not automatically retrieved into the result variable at the start of the program with *DTAARA DEFINE, as they are with a data-area data structure. Second, the Result field's contents are not automatically written back out to the data area at program termination. Instead, you must explicitly "read" and "write" the contents of the data area within your calculations. Specific operations (IN, OUT, and UNLOCK) let you control this explicit I/O of data areas. If you want to use these explicit operations with a data-area data structure, that structure must also appear as the Result field of a *DTAARA DEFINE statement, with the Factor 2 entry blank.

Operation IN (Retrieve a Data Area) "reads" the contents of the data area into your program. Factor 2 must contain the Result field of a *DTAARA DEFINE statement. By including the optional entry *LOCK as a Factor 1 entry, you can lock the data area from update by another program. If you leave Factor 1 blank and the data area has been retrieved previously, the locked status associated with the previous retrieval remains in effect. That is, if the data area was locked before this IN operation, it remains locked; if it was not locked, it remains unlocked. *LOCK cannot be used with the LDA.

continued…

continued...

```
*.. 1 ...+... 2 ...+... 3 ...+... 4 ...+... 5 ...+... 6 ...+... 7 ...+... 8
CLØNØ1Factor1+++++++Opcode(E)+Factor2+++++++Result++++++++Len++D+HiLoEq....
 * Examples showing *DTAARA DEFINE and subsequent use of IN:
 * Data area Check associated with field CheckNo
C     *DTAARA       DEFINE    Check           CheckNo
 * Data area Receipts associated with data structure Receipts
C     *DTAARA       DEFINE              Receipts
 * Local data area associated with InvNo
C     *DTAARA       DEFINE    *LDA            InvNo

 * Retrieves the contents of the LDA into InvNo
C                   IN        InvNo
 * Retrieves the contents of data area Check into CheckNo with lock
C     *LOCK         IN        CheckNo
 * Retrieves data area Receipts into data-area data structure Receipts
C                   IN        Receipts
```

Operation OUT (Write Out a Data Area) "writes" data back to (or updates) the data area referenced in Factor 2. Factor 2 must contain the result field of a *DTAARA DEFINE statement. Moreover, the operation cannot be used unless the data area has already been retrieved — either through the execution of an IN operation or through the implicit retrieval that results for data-area data structures.

If you include the optional entry *LOCK in Factor 1, a lock remains in effect for the data area following the OUT operation; if you leave Factor 1 blank, the data area is unlocked after it is updated. As with the IN operation, you cannot include a *LOCK entry for the LDA.

```
*.. 1 ...+... 2 ...+... 3 ...+... 4 ...+... 5 ...+... 6 ...+... 7 ...+... 8
CLØNØ1Factor1+++++++Opcode(E)+Factor2+++++++Result++++++++Len++D+HiLoEq....
 * Examples showing the use of OUT:
 * LDA is updated.
C                   OUT       InvNo
 * Receipts is updated, but the lock remains in effect.
C     *LOCK         OUT       Receipts
 * Data area Check is updated, and the lock is removed.
C                   OUT       CheckNo
```

Operation UNLOCK unlocks the data area referenced in Factor 2. This Factor 2 entry must be the result field of a *DTAARA DEFINE statement. Executing an UNLOCK operation on a data area already unlocked does not cause a system error. You cannot use the UNLOCK operation with the LDA.

```
*.. 1 ...+... 2 ...+... 3 ...+... 4 ...+... 5 ...+... 6 ...+... 7 ...+... 8
CLØNØ1Factor1+++++++Opcode(E)+Factor2+++++++Result++++++++Len++D+HiLoEq....
 * Examples showing the unlocking of data areas:
 * Unlocks data area Receipts
C                   UNLOCK    Receipts
 * Unlocks data area Check
C                   UNLOCK    CheckNo
```

For all three data-area operations — IN, OUT, and UNLOCK — if you enter *DTAARA as the Factor 2 entry, instead of a specific variable, all the data areas appearing as Result fields in *DTAARA DEFINE operations participate in the operation. All three operations also let you include the optional (E) extender to use the %ERROR function to signal that an error occurred during the operation.

Data-Area Data Structures

As a programmer, you should understand how to access data areas from within an RPG IV program. To make a data area accessible to an RPG IV program, define a data structure for the data area. A U in position 23 (T) of a data structure definition identifies it as a **data-area data structure**.

If you do not provide a name for a data-area data structure, the data structure automatically represents the LDA. If you want the data structure to contain data from a different data area, you must provide a name for the data structure; usually that name matches the external name of the data area in the system (otherwise, the DTAARA keyword provides the external name of the data area). The following code illustrates three data-area data structures.

```
*.. 1 ...+... 2 ...+... 3 ...+... 4 ...+... 5 ...+... 6 ...+... 7 ...+... 8
DName++++++++++ETDsFrom+++To/L+++IDc.Keywords++++++++++++++++++++++++++++++++
  // The data structure below represents the local data area (LDA).
D                 UDS
D InvNo                           8  0

  // The data structure below represents data area Receipts.
D Receipts        UDS
D   Store1                       10  2
D   Store2                       10  2
D   Store3                       10  2

  // The NextRes data structure represents the ResCounter data area.
D NextRes         UDS                   DTAARA(ResCounter)
D   NextResNbr                    7  0
```

The contents of any data area defined via a data structure, as in the examples above, are read into the program at program initialization. The data area is then locked to prevent other programs from accessing it. When the program ends, the system writes the contents of the data structure from the program back to the data area and removes the lock.

Chapter Summary

Programming experts advocate a modular approach to programming, in which you break complex processing down into separate programs or modules, each focused on accomplishing a single function. Other programs can then call these programs. If a routine is compiled and bound into a separate *PGM object, you use operation CALLP to invoke that program — a process called dynamic binding. The iSeries lets you write calling and called programs in any mix of languages available on the system, including CL.

In RPG IV, all variables are global within a program but local to the program. To share data between a calling and a called program, both programs use parameters to define the shared data. These parameters are described by a prototype definition and appear as arguments to a function call or CALLP operation. The procedure interface definition lets the called program accept parameter values and assign them to variables.

Support for subprocedures, the newest enhancement to modularity in RPG, lets you create stand-alone routines, or user-defined functions, that can be linked to other programs and used within them either through CALLP (if the subprocedure returns no value) or directly in code in the same way you use RPG's built-in functions (if the subprocedure returns a value). With subprocedures, separately compiled modules are connected to one another to form a single *PGM object — static binding. Static binding results in better system performance at runtime than does dynamic binding. Subprocedures also improve the modularity, maintainability, reliability, and reusability of commonly used code.

When you pass parameters by reference, the corresponding parameter variables in the calling and called programs/procedures share a common storage location. As a result, changes to a parameter's value in one of the programs affect the corresponding parameter's value in the other program. Using prototype definitions, you can also pass parameters by value or by read-only reference; these methods protect values in calling programs or procedures from being changed by called programs or procedures.

Breaking your programs into subprocedures lets a program contain local as well as globally defined variables. Values are passed to the subprocedure from the calling procedure, and the subprocedure itself can return a single value to the calling procedure.

IBM offers several built-in system programs, called APIs, which you can call from your RPG IV programs to accomplish various kinds of lower-level processing. API QUSCMDLN presents an OS/400 system command line for use within a program. API QCMDEXC lets you execute a CL command from within your program; you simply pass the command as a parameter to QCMDEXC, along with a second parameter that specifies the command's length.

The iSeries also provides data areas (special storage areas defined on the system) for sharing values between programs. The programs do not have to call one another to access the same data area. A temporary local data area (LDA) is automatically available for each job; you also can define permanent data areas that any program can subsequently access. You access the contents of a data area within an RPG IV program by defining a special data structure — a data-area data structure. Data contained in data-area data structures is automatically retrieved at the start of a program and written back to the data area at the end of the program.

Key Terms

APIs
call interface
data-area data structure
data areas
dynamic binding
local data area (LDA)
local variables
modular programming
passing by reference
passing by value

Procedure Boundary Specification
procedure interface
procedures
prototype
return value
static binding
static procedure call
subprocedures
user space

Discussion/Review Questions

1. What does "modular programming" mean?
2. What are the advantages of a modular approach to application development?
3. What effect does LR have on a called program?
4. Although static binding leads to improved system performance, when might you still want to use dynamic binding to call a program?
5. How do subprocedures improve the reusability and reliability of an application?
6. Describe the distinction between a parameter and a return value.
7. What is the purpose of the prototype definition?
8. What is the purpose of the procedure interface?
9. Explain the use of API QUSCMDLN and QCMDEXC.

10. What is an LDA?

11. Why might you use a data area rather than a database file to store values?

12. Describe how to access a data area through a data-area data structure.

Exercises

1. Write the RPG IV code to call ProgA, ProgB, or ProgC, depending on whether the value of field Option is 1, 2, or 3, respectively. No parameters are needed with any of the calls.

2. Write the portion of a calling program that passes a date of numeric data type in *yymmdd* format to a called program to convert the date to a date in month name, day, and four-digit year format (e.g., January 1, 1993).

3. Write the entire RPG IV program that would be called in Exercise 2 to convert the date to the desired format.

4. Assume a data area named CheckValue contains a six-position number representing the last check number used, a six-position date reflecting the most recent date on which the check-writing program was run, 10 positions containing the name of the last user running the check-writing program, and four positions reflecting the number of checks written during the last program run. Code a data-area data structure to enable access to this data area.

5. At a certain point in an RPG IV program, you need to delete a database file. The name of the file to be deleted is contained in field FileName, a 10-position character field. The CL command to delete a file is DLT (Delete File), used as follows:

```
DLTF FILE(*CURLIB/xxxxxxxxxx)
```

where *xxxxxxxxxx* represents a file name. Write the RPG IV code to incorporate the file name from field FileName in the proper location within the command and then call API QCMDEXC to carry out the command.

Programming Assignments

1. Develop an interactive menu application that presents the user with a choice for executing one of four programs you have written this semester. (Your instructor may tell you which applications to include; preferably, the programs will be part of the same application system and include at least one interactive application.) Your program should call the appropriate program based on the user's choice. Upon return from the called program, the user should again see the menu for another selection. This cycle should continue until the user signals Exit at the menu. Design your menu to be user-friendly and to include informational messages signaling the results of processing for noninteractive applications, so that the user knows the selected program has been executed. Also, let the user access a CL command line from the menu by pressing F21.

Note
At the instructor's discretion, Programming Assignments 2, 3, and 4 may be implemented with either dynamic program calls or static procedure calls.

2. As part of its billing procedure, GTC needs to convert military time to standard time in several programs. The company decides to perform this conversion through a called program. Write such a called program that will receive as a parameter argument the time in *hhmm* format, where the hours are based on a 24-hour clock (i.e., military time); convert that value to time expressed on a 12-hour clock, with "a.m." or "p.m." noted; and pass the converted value back to the calling program. For example, if the called program was passed 1530, it should convert that value to 3:30 p.m.

   To test your program, use GTC's calls transaction file, GTCLSP (described in Appendix F), as the input file to a calling program that passes the time-of-call value from each record to the called program and generates the following report to reflect the converted time returned by the called program:

```
        1         2         3         4         5         6         7         8         9         1 0
  1234567890123456789012345678901234567890123456789012345678901234567890123456789012345678901234567890
1 XX/XX/XX                   PAGE XX0X
2    GTC TIME CONVERSION TEST REPORT
3
4    MILITARY TIME   CONVERTED TIME
5
6         XXXX            0X:XX A.M.
7         XXXX            0X:XX P.M.
8         XXXX            0X:XX A.M.
```

3. GTC needs to convert time from military to standard time and determine the day of the week from a given date, both as part of its billing procedure. The programmers decide to implement each of these conversions as called programs. Write two called programs to accomplish these tasks. Programming Assignment 2, above, describes more details of the time conversion. For the called program that determines the day of the week, use the algorithm shown below, which compares a given date to a known Sunday (December 31, 1899). Hint: To convert a numeric date in *yymmdd* format to a date in *ISO format, use operation MOVE. Enter *YMD in Factor 1, the given date in Factor 2, and a *ISO date field in the Result field.

Algorithm to determine day of week from a date stored in yymmdd *numeric format:*
Initialize known date
Convert given date to date data type
Calculate number-of-days from known date to converted date
Calculate day-of-week (remainder from number-of-days / 7)
   IF day-of-week = 0
     name-of-day = "Sunday"
ELSE
   IF day-of-week = 1
     name-of-day = "Monday"
ELSE
   IF day-of-week = 2
     name-of-day = "Tuesday"
ELSE
. . .
ENDIF

Test your two called programs by generating the following report, using the date-of-call and time-of-call fields of GTC's calls transaction file (GTCLSP) for your test data. For the report's DAY column, print the appropriate name of the day (e.g., SUNDAY).

```
          1         2         3         4         5         6         7         8         9        10
 1234567890123456789012345678901234567890123456789012345678901234567890123456789012345678901234567890
1 XX/XX/XX                                      PAGE XXØX
2    GTC DATE AND TIME CONVERSION TEST REPORT
3
4 DATE            DAY        MILITARY TIME      CONVERTED TIME
5
6 XX/XX/XX     XXXXXXXXX      XXXX              ØX:XX A.M.
7 XX/XX/XX     XXXXXXXXX      XXXX              ØX:XX P.M.
8 XX/XX/XX     XXXXXXXXX      XXXX              ØX:XX A.M.
9
```

4. CompuSell wants you to write a label-printing program for its customers in file CSCSTP (Appendix F); the company wants your program to print two-across labels. Each of the labels reading across should represent the same customer. The printer will be loaded with continuous-label stock when this program is run. Each label is five print lines long. The desired format for the labels is shown below. Note that the information within parentheses is included to let you know what should appear on the label, but that information should not appear within your output.

```
          1         2         3         4         5         6         7         8         9        10
 1234567890123456789012345678901234567890123456789012345678901234567890123456789012345678901234567890
1     XXXXXXXXX XXXXXXXXXXXXXX          XXXXXXXXX XXXXXXXXXXXXXX     (FIRST, LAST NAME)
2     XXXXXXXXXXXXXXXXXXXXX             XXXXXXXXXXXXXXXXXXXXX        (STREET ADDRESS)
3     XXXXXXXXXXXXXX  XX XXXXX-XXXX     XXXXXXXXXXXXXX  XX XXXXX-XXXX (CITY, STATE, ZIP)
4
5
6     XXXXXXXXX XXXXXXXXXXXXXX          XXXXXXXXX XXXXXXXXXXXXXX
7     XXXXXXXXXXXXXXXXXXXXX             XXXXXXXXXXXXXXXXXXXXX
8     XXXXXXXXXXXXXX  XX XXXXX-XXXX     XXXXXXXXXXXXXX  XX XXXXX-XXXX
9
```

This assignment is a repeat of Chapter 2's Programming Assignment 3, except that now management has decided the labels will look nicer if the names, addresses, and city are printed in lower case (except for the first letter of each word). Rather than writing a conversion routine repeatedly for each of the fields, you decide to write the routine once as a called program so that it will be available for use in other programs as well.

Write a called program that converts a string of uppercase letters to a string in which the first character in the field and any other character immediately following a blank remain upper case but all other letters are converted to lower case. Include as parameters two character fields each 25 positions long. The program should process the value passed in the first parameter and store the converted string in the second parameter field before returning.

Once you have written the called program, in your label program successively call that program to convert first name, last name, street address, and city to the desired format for each customer before printing the label.

Chapter 11

Advanced Data Definition

Chapter Overview

This chapter gives you more detail about RPG IV data types and shows you how to perform "date arithmetic" using date operations and built-in functions. We also discuss pointers — how to define and use them. The chapter covers data structures in detail, showing you how to code, initialize, and use data structures. It also details some special data structures that RPG IV supplies to allow your program access to internal program information.

Data Types Revisited

You are already familiar with the use of Definition Specifications for defining standalone work fields, tables, arrays, data structures, and named constants. Definition Specifications consolidate the definitions of all data items used by your program in a single place within your source code for ease of understanding and program maintenance.

RPG IV, as you recall, requires you to define each data item used within your program by giving it a name, declaring its data type, and allocating a fixed amount of memory for storing that data item's value. In Chapter 3, you learned about some of the data types available in RPG IV. The following table, repeated from Chapter 3, shows all of RPG IV's data classes, the data types within those classes, and the code used to signal each data type within a definition.

Data class	Data type	RPG code
Character	Character	A
Numeric	Zoned decimal	S
	Packed decimal	P
	Signed integer	I
	Unsigned integer	U
	Binary	B
	Floating point	F
Date	Date	D
	Time	T
	Timestamp	Z
Boolean	Indicator	N
DBCS	Graphic	G
	Unicode	C
Object	Object/class	O
Pointer	Pointer	*

Data Types and Time

Three data types exist for dealing with time: **date, time,** and **timestamp**. Each data type has a default length and display format (*ISO), based on the International Standards Organization (ISO) standards. The default display format for type date (D) is a 10-byte-long field with format *yyyy-mm-dd*. Time (T) has a default length of 8 bytes, with format *hh.mm.ss*. The default display format for timestamp (Z) has a length of 26 bytes, with format *yyyy-mm-dd-hh.mm.ss.mmmmmm*.

The date and time (but not the timestamp) data types allow alternative display formats to the defaults. Date, for instance, supports eight different formats, and time supports five different formats. The following tables list the valid date and time formats.

DATFMT	Description	Representation	Example
*ISO	International Standards Org	yyyy-mm-dd	9999-12-31
*USA	IBM USA Standard	mm/dd/yyyy	12/31/9999
*EUR	IBM European Standard	dd.mm.yyyy	31.12.9999
*JIS	Japanese Industrial Standard	yyyy-mm-dd	9999-12-31
*YMD	Year/month/day	yy/mm/dd	99/12/31
*MDY	Month/day/year	mm/dd/yy	12/31/99
*DMY	Day/month/year	dd/mm/yy	31/12/99
*JUL	Julian	yy/ddd	99/365

TIMFMT	Description	Representation	Example
*ISO	International Standards Org	hh.mm.ss	23.59.59
*USA	IBM USA Standard	hh:mm xM	11:59 PM
*EUR	IBM European Standard	hh.mm.ss	23.59.59
*JIS	Japanese Industrial Standard	hh:mm:ss	23:59:59
*HMS	Hours/minutes/seconds	hh:mm:ss	23:59:59

To specify an alternative format for a date field, you use keyword DATFMT on the Definition Specification with the desired format code; for time fields, use keyword TIMFMT and the desired format code. You can also change the default display format of date and time fields for a program as a whole by specifying the DATFMT and/or TIMFMT keyword within the Control (Header) Specifications (or in a File Specification to indicate a default format for date/time fields within a program-described file).

Each display format includes a default separator character. For example, the separator character for the *ISO date format is the hyphen (–). Several of the formats let you change the separator character. For example, acceptable separator characters for the *DMY and *MDY date formats are the hyphen, the slash (/), the period (.), the comma (,), and the ampersand (&), which is displayed as a blank. Acceptable separator characters for the *HMS time format are the colon (:), the period, the comma, and the ampersand for blank. To change from the default separator, simply insert the separator character you want to use after the format code (e.g., *MDY– or *HMS,).

When defining data items with any of the date/time data types, you do not need to specify length because the system determines the length automatically. The following code illustrates how to define these kinds of fields (some using the default display formats and others specifying alternative formats).

```
*.. 1 ...+... 2 ...+... 3 ...+... 4 ...+... 5 ...+... 6 ...+... 7 ...+... 8
DName++++++++++ETDsFrom+++To/L+++IDc.Keywords++++++++++++++++++++++++++++++
    // Definitions of standalone fields with various date/time data types:

    // Define a date field in default format (*ISO): e.g., 1995-03-15.
D TodaysDate      S              D
    // Define a date field, *YMD format, default separator (/): 95/03/15.
D DueDateA        S              D    DATFMT(*YMD)
    // Define a date field, *YMD format, alternate separator (.): 95.03.15.
D DueDateB        S              D    DATFMT(*YMD.)

    // Define a time field in default format (*ISO):  e.g., 14.45.24.
D TimeA           S              T
    // Define a time field in *USA format: 2:45 PM.
D TimeB           S              T    TIMFMT(*USA)
    // Define a time field, *HMS format, blank separator: 14 45 24.
D TimeC           S              T    TIMFMT(*HMS&)

    //Define a timestamp field: e.g., 1995-03-15-06.15.37.000000.
D TimeStmp        S              Z
```

Caution

Be sure that you do not confuse the date, time, and timestamp data types with numeric fields that may be used to represent date-related data. Because the native date data types are a fairly recent development in the RPG world, many applications still use numeric fields to deal with date-related data. With these "legacy" date fields, it is up to the RPG program to provide any special processing required to validate or process those fields as if they were dates, times, or timestamps.

Date and Time Operations

You can use OS/400's native date-related data types in calculations involving times and/or dates. These operations use the following duration codes to indicate which portion of the date/time data you want to manipulate:

- *YEARS (or *Y)
- *MONTHS (or *M)
- *DAYS (or *D)
- *HOURS (or *H)
- *MINUTES (or *MN)
- *SECONDS (or *S)
- *MSECONDS (or *MS) (microseconds)

Date calculations also make use of the following built-in functions to convert a number to a duration:

- %YEARS
- %MONTHS
- %DAYS
- %HOURS
- %MINUTES
- %SECONDS
- %MSECONDS

In an assignment expression, these functions can appear on the right side of the expression. The left side of the expression must be a date, time, or timestamp variable, compatible with the function. The following examples illustrate the use of the duration functions in arithmetic expressions. Assume that fields BillDate, StartDate, and EndDate have been defined as type D (date) and that fields StartTime and EndTime have been defined as type T (time).

```
*.. 1 ...+... 2 ...+... 3 ...+... 4 ...+... 5 ...+... 6 ...+... 7 ...+... 8
/FREE

  // Add 30 days to BillDate to determine DueDate.
    DueDate = BillDate + %DAYS(30);

  // Add field Min, containing a number of minutes, to StartTime
  // to determine EndTime.
    EndTime = StartTime + %MINUTES(Min);

  // Add 5 years to DueDate.
    DueDate = DueDate + %YEARS(5);

  // Subtract 5 months from EndDate to get StartDate.
    StartDate = EndDate - %MONTHS(5);
    StartDate = EndDate + %MONTHS(-5);        // Equivalent to previous line

  // Subtract 30 days from DueDate to determine BillDate.
    BillDate = DueDate - %DAYS(30);

  // Subtract 5 years from DueDate.
    DueDate = DueDate - %YEARS(5);

/END-FREE
```

The %DIFF (Difference) Function

To calculate the duration between two date/time units, use the %DIFF (Difference) built-in function. Code data items of compatible types as the first two arguments; then, in the third argument, type the duration code that corresponds to the duration unit you want to determine. The result is a number, rounded down, with any remainder discarded. You can use the %DIFF function to find the duration between

- two dates
- two times
- two timestamps
- a date and the date portion of a timestamp
- a time and the time portion of a timestamp

For dates, the valid duration codes are *YEARS (*Y), *MONTHS (*M), and *DAYS (*D). For times, duration codes *HOURS (*H), *MINUTES (*MN), and *SECONDS (*S) are valid. Any of the duration codes are valid for two timestamps.

The following examples show the use of the %DIFF function.

```
*.. 1 ...+... 2 ...+... 3 ...+... 4 ...+... 5 ...+... 6 ...+... 7 ...+... 8
/FREE
  // Subtract a birth date from today to get age in years.
    Age = %DIFF(TodayDate:BirthDate:*YEARS);

  // Determine the number of days left to study for a test.
    CramTime = %DIFF(ExamDate:TodayDate:*DAYS);
/END-FREE
```

The %SUBDT (Extract from Date/Time/Timestamp) Function

The %SUBDT (Extract from Date/Time/Timestamp) function "substrings" a date; that is, %SUBDT extracts a portion of a date, time, or timestamp data item. The first argument is the date, time, or timestamp variable; it is followed by a compatible duration code that specifies the portion of the field you want to extract. The result is numeric. The %SUBDT function always treats the *DAYS code as the day of the month (even for *JUL format dates) and always returns a four-digit year when you specify the *YEARS code.

```
*.. 1 ...+... 2 ...+... 3 ...+... 4 ...+... 5 ...+... 6 ...+... 7 ...+... 8
 /FREE
   // Determine the birth year of a birth date
     BirthYear = %SUBDT(BirthDate:*YEARS);

   // Extract the month of a loan
     LoanMonth = %SUBDT(LoanDate:*MONTHS);
 /END-FREE
```

Using Dates and Times in Calculations

If you want to use any of the date data types with literals, you must use typed literals (i.e., literals preceded by a D for dates, T for times, or Z for timestamps). The following example demonstrates how you can use date/time literals in calculations.

```
*.. 1 ...+... 2 ...+... 3 ...+... 4 ...+... 5 ...+... 6 ...+... 7 ...+... 8
 /FREE
   // Calculate number of days from December 31, 1899
     DaysPassed = %DIFF(TodaysDate:D'1899-12-31':*DAYS);

   // Calculate times for late arrival or early leaving
     LateArrive = T'08:00:00' + %MINUTES(15);
     EarlyLeave = T'16:30:00' - %MINUTES(15);
 /END-FREE
```

If you've specified a DATFMT keyword in the Control Specifications of an RPG IV program, all date literals in that program must be in the same format that the DATFMT keyword specifies.

In addition to using expressions to assign values to date/time fields and to perform date/time arithmetic with the addition (+) and subtraction (−) operators, RPG IV supports operations MOVE, MOVEA, and MOVEL to move values between date/time data types and numeric or character fields. The rules for these movements depend on the kinds of data types involved in the move and can be somewhat complicated. Consult the *ILE RPG Reference* for details about how to use these operations.

RPG IV does not include an operation that determines the day of the week from a date field, but you can code a short routine that uses other RPG IV operations to perform this task. By comparing a given date with a known Sunday (e.g., December 31, 1899), you can determine the day of the week for any date. The following code produces a number between 0 and 6 (to represent the weekdays from Sunday to Saturday) and demonstrates some of the date/time data type concepts described in this chapter:

```
*.. 1 ...+... 2 ...+... 3 ...+... 4 ...+... 5 ...+... 6 ...+... 7 ...+... 8
DName+++++++++++ETDsFrom+++To/L+++IDc.Keywords+++++++++++++++++++++++++++++++
D ThisDate        S               D   INZ(*SYS)
D WorkField       S             5 0
D Weekday         S             1 0

 /FREE
   // Calculate number of days between ThisDate and 1899-12-31.
     WorkField = %DIFF(ThisDate: D'1899-12-31':*DAYS);
   // Calculate number of whole weeks in WorkField. Remainder is Weekday.
     WeekDay = %REM(WorkField:7);
 /END-FREE
```

Pointer Data Types

RPG IV includes two kinds of **pointer data types**: basing pointers and procedure pointers. Both kinds of pointers are used to access storage that is allocated dynamically throughout the program rather than once at the beginning of the program. Pointers (data type *, 16 bytes long) store addresses of memory locations rather than data values. A pointer tells you where to find something, not what is stored there. Basing pointers reference storage locations of variables, while procedure pointers reference storage locations of program modules.

Pointers can be standalone data items, subfields of a data structure, or elements of an array. You can also implicitly define a basing pointer by naming it as the pointer upon which an entity is "based." The following code shows some sample pointer definitions. You do not need to include a length entry as part of a pointer's definition. To indicate a procedure pointer, you must include the keyword PROCPTR as part of its definition.

Date-Specific Operations: ADDDUR, SUBDUR, and EXTRCT

At Version 5, you can use free-format expressions with date-related functions to perform date arithmetic. Before Version 5, RPG IV uses three specific operation codes for this purpose: ADDDUR (Add Duration), SUBDUR (Subtract Duration), and EXTRCT (Extract from Date/Time/Timestamp). These operation codes are not as flexible as the built-in functions, and they are restricted to the fixed-format Calculation Specifications. To help you maintain programs that may use these operations, they are detailed here.

The ADDDUR (Add Duration) operation lets you add a duration coded in Factor 2 to the date specified in Factor 1, storing the answer in the date, time, or timestamp field specified as the Result field. If Factor 1 is blank, the Factor 2 duration is simply added to the Result field. If Factor 1 is present, it may contain any data item representing one of the three date data types, but its type must match that of the Result field.

Factor 2 must contain an integer field (or literal), which represents the number to add, and one of the seven duration codes listed above, which indicates the kind of duration the number represents. You separate these two portions of Factor 2 with a colon. If the numeric portion of Factor 2 represents a negative value, the duration is subtracted rather than added.

The following examples illustrate the use of ADDDUR. Assume that fields BillDate, StartDate, and EndDate have been defined as type D (date) and fields StartTime and EndTime have been defined as type T (time).

```
*.. 1 ...+... 2 ...+... 3 ...+... 4 ...+... 5 ...+... 6 ...+... 7 ...+... 8
CLØNØ1Factor1++++++Opcode(E)+Factor2++++++Result++++++++Len++D+HiLoEq....
 * Add 3Ø days to BillDate to determine DueDate.
C     BillDate      ADDDUR    3Ø:*DAYS      DueDate

 * Add field Min, containing a number of minutes, to StartTime
 * to determine EndTime.
C     StartTime     ADDDUR    Min:*MN       EndTime

 * Add 5 years to DueDate.
C                   ADDDUR    5:*YEARS      DueDate

 * Subtract 5 months from EndDate to get StartDate.
C     EndDate       ADDDUR    -5:*MONTHS    StartDate
```

continued...

```
*.. 1 ...+... 2 ...+... 3 ...+... 4 ...+... 5 ...+... 6 ...+... 7 ...+... 8
DName++++++++++ETDsFrom+++To/L+++IDc.Keywords+++++++++++++++++++++++++++++++
  // Definitions of pointers in RPG IV
D Ptr1            S                *
D Ptr2            S                *    PROCPTR
D ArrayPtr        S                *    DIM(10)
D BField          S               8A    BASED(Ptr3)
```

In these definitions, Ptr1 is a basing pointer and Ptr2 is a procedure pointer (as indicated by keyword PROCPTR). ArrayPtr is an array of 10 pointers. Ptr1, Ptr2, and ArrayPtr are explicitly defined pointers; Ptr3 is an implicitly defined pointer because it is the pointer upon which the character field BField is "based."

---

continued...

Operation SUBDUR (Subtract Duration) has two uses: One is to subtract a date/time duration from a date/time value (similar to ADDDUR with a negative duration); the second is to calculate the duration between two date/time units (equivalent to Version 5's %DIFF function). To subtract a Factor 2 duration from a date/time data item in Factor 1 and store the answer in the Result field, you code the operation the same as you would ADDDUR. To calculate the duration between two date/time units, place data items of compatible types in both Factor 1 and Factor 2, and place an integer receiving field followed by a duration code that denotes the unit of time involved in the operation in the Result field. Again, a colon separates the two subfactors. The following examples show both uses of SUBDUR.

```
*.. 1 ...+... 2 ...+... 3 ...+... 4 ...+... 5 ...+... 6 ...+... 7 ...+... 8
CLØN01Factor1+++++++Opcode(E)+Factor2+++++++Result+++++++++Len++D+HiLoEq....
 * Subtract 30 days from DueDate to determine BillDate.
C     DueDate      SUBDUR   30:*DAYS      BillDate

 * Subtract 5 years from DueDate.
C                  SUBDUR   5:*Y          DueDate

 * Subtract a birth date from today to get age in years.
C     TodayDate    SUBDUR   BirthDate     Age:*YEARS

 * Determine the number of days left to study for a test.
C     ExamDate     SUBDUR   TodayDate     CramTime:*D
```

The third operation for manipulating dates and times, EXTRCT (Extract Date/Time/Timestamp), extracts a portion of a date, time, or timestamp data item and stores it in the Result field, which can be any numeric or character receiving field. The Factor 2 date/time data item must be coupled with a duration code to signal which portion of the date/time unit is to be extracted. Factor 1 is always blank for EXTRCT operations. At Version 5, the %SUBDT function performs this task.

```
*.. 1 ...+... 2 ...+... 3 ...+... 4 ...+... 5 ...+... 6 ...+... 7 ...+... 8
CLØN01Factor1+++++++Opcode(E)+Factor2+++++++Result+++++++++Len++D+HiLoEq....
 * Determine the birth year of a birth date.
C                  EXTRCT   BirthDate:*Y  BirthYear

 *Extract the month of a loan.
C                  EXTRCT   LoanDate:*M   LoanMonth
```

BField is an example of a based field, used to access the contents of the address (or storage location) to which a basing pointer "points." The following Definition Specifications illustrate definitions of basing pointers and their associated based fields.

```
*.. 1 ...+... 2 ...+... 3 ...+... 4 ...+... 5 ...+... 6 ...+... 7 ...+... 8
DName++++++++++ETDsFrom+++To/L+++IDc.Keywords+++++++++++++++++++++++++++++++
  // Definitions of pointers and based fields in RPG IV
D Ptr1            S               *
D FieldX          S               8  2 BASED(Ptr1)
D FieldY          S               6  2 BASED(Ptr2)
D Array1          S              10    DIM(20) BASED(Ptr3)
D Array2          S              20    DIM(10) BASED(Ptr4)
```

In this example, FieldX and FieldY are both based fields, while Array1 and Array2 are based arrays. You can use FieldX to access the contents of any numeric storage location to which Ptr1 points. FieldY accesses the contents of Ptr2's address. Array1 and Array2 access the contents of storage locations pointed to by Ptr3 and Ptr4, respectively.

Pointers acquire values in several ways. The default value of a pointer is *NULL, which means that the pointer does not point to any storage location. You can use EVAL to assign a pointer the value of another pointer. Moreover, you can use the %ADDR built-in function, which automatically returns the address of any field specified as its argument, to assign a value to a basing pointer.

Pointer concepts can be difficult to grasp for beginning programmers. To get a feeling for how based fields and basing pointers operate, study the following code.

```
*.. 1 ...+... 2 ...+... 3 ...+... 4 ...+... 5 ...+... 6 ...+... 7 ...+... 8
DName++++++++++ETDsFrom+++To/L+++IDc.Keywords+++++++++++++++++++++++++++++++
D Field1          S              15A    BASED(Ptr1)
D Field2          S              15A    BASED(Ptr2)
D NameA           S              15A    INZ('Moe')
D NameB           S              15A    INZ('Curley')

 /FREE
  // Calculations show how changing pointer values changes the values
  // of based fields.

  // Make Ptr1 "point to" the storage location allocated for NameA.
   Ptr1 = %ADDR(NameA);
  // Field1 automatically equals the contents stored at Ptr1's address
  // because it is based on Ptr1. That is, Field1 now equals 'Moe'.

   Field1 = 'Larry';
  // Field1 and NameA both are now 'Larry' because Field1 and NameA
  // represent the same storage location.

   Ptr2 = Ptr1;
  // Field2 is now 'Larry' also, because its pointer stores the same
  // address as Ptr1, which in turn stores the location of field NameA.

   Ptr2 = %ADDR(NameB);
  // Now Field2 equals 'Curley' because its pointer has changed.
 /END-FREE
```

Based variables have no storage assigned directly to them; instead, they dynamically access various storage locations depending on the value of their pointers. You can use a based entity within a program anywhere you can use a nonbased data item — provided its pointer has been assigned some address (i.e., it is not *NULL).

Pointers have proven very useful for languages such as C, but their use in RPG is not yet widespread because of the newness of this data type to the language.

LIKE (Field Definition)

RPG IV lets you define one field's length and type by referencing a second field that provides the definition; that is, it lets you say that one field is "like" another field. This practice can help simplify and standardize your work-field definitions, and, more important, it can make program maintenance more efficient and reliable.

The field being defined appears in positions 7–21 (Name++++++++++) of the Definition Specification. If it is a standalone field, code an S in position 24 (Ds). You include the field providing the definition as a parameter of keyword LIKE, coded in positions 44–80 (Keywords). The field that provides the definition can itself be defined internally or externally to the program. It can be a field, an array, or a table; if it is an array or a table, the attributes of one of the elements of the array or table provide the definition for the new field.

```
*.. 1 ...+... 2 ...+... 3 ...+... 4 ...+... 5 ...+... 6 ...+... 7 ...+... 8
DName++++++++++ETDsFrom+++To/L+++IDc.Keywords+++++++++++++++++++++++++++++++
D NewField        S                 LIKE(OldField)
```

The specification above defines field NewField by giving it the type, length, and decimal positions (if type is numeric) of field OldField. A variant of this basic format lets you lengthen or shorten the field being defined by entering a "signed" number (e.g., +4, –3), right-adjusted within positions 33–39 (To/L+++) to indicate that the field being defined should be larger or smaller than the defining field. The entered number signals the extent of the increase (+) or decrease (–) in field length. You cannot change the number of decimal positions of the field being defined.

Assume you are writing a payroll program and that Gross is an externally defined salary field. As part of your program, you need to define fields to store NetPay, FedTax, and StateTax as well as four accumulators for storing grand totals for each of these four fields. The following example shows how you could use LIKE to define the needed data items.

```
*.. 1 ...+... 2 ...+... 3 ...+... 4 ...+... 5 ...+... 6 ...+... 7 ...+... 8
DName++++++++++ETDsFrom+++To/L+++IDc.Keywords+++++++++++++++++++++++++++++++
D NetPay          S                 LIKE(Gross)
D FedTax          S           -2    LIKE(Gross)
D StateTax        S           -2    LIKE(Gross)
D TotalGross      S           +4    LIKE(Gross)
D TotalNet        S           +4    LIKE(NetPay)
D TotalFdTax      S           +4    LIKE(FedTax)
D TotalStTax      S           +4    LIKE(StateTax)
```

This example illustrates the value of defining fields with LIKE for easy program maintenance. Assume that the payroll program containing these definitions is put into production and that, after a few years, inflation causes salaries to become so high that the original definition for Gross is too small. Accordingly, you change the definition of Gross in the database file to make it large enough to hold new salary figures.

If you had defined the work fields in this program without using LIKE and instead had given each an absolute fixed length, you would need to carefully check the program's field definitions and manually modify any work field whose length needed to be increased. But because you used LIKE for those work fields, all you need to do is recompile the program; the work-field lengths will be adjusted automatically based on the new length of Gross.

You can also use LIKE to define display fields for interactive applications. Rather than directly referencing database fields within a display file, many programmers use work fields in their screen definitions to handle screen input and output; then, they transfer the data values between the work fields and the database fields within their RPG IV programs. By using LIKE to define an alternate field for each database field to be displayed, the programmer ensures that any future changes to the database-field definitions will not create maintenance problems for programs containing such display fields.

Data Structures

Data structures can give you flexibility in your handling of data by letting you subdivide fields into subfields, restructure records with different field layouts, change field data types, and add a second dimension to arrays. In Chapter 3, you were introduced to simple data structures as a means of organizing contiguous areas of memory; this section of the text will extend your understanding of how to define and use more complex data structures.

Data Structures and OVERLAY

You use Definition Specifications to define data structures. The subfields that make up the data structure follow the DS header line. Recall that you can use either absolute notation or length notation to indicate the length and position of subfields within the data structure:

```
*.. 1 ...+... 2 ...+... 3 ...+... 4 ...+... 5 ...+... 6 ...+... 7 ...+... 8
DName++++++++++ETDsFrom+++To/L+++IDc.Keywords+++++++++++++++++++++++++++++++
     // Defining subfields of a data structure using absolute notation
D OptName         DS
D   SubfieldA              1      3 0
D   SubfieldB              4      8 2

     // Defining the same structure using length notation
D OptName         DS
D   SubfieldA                     3 0
D   SubfieldB                     5 2
```

You'll remember that the OVERLAY keyword indicates that a subfield overlays the storage of another subfield — that is, the subfield is part of another subfield. When you use OVERLAY, the data name specified within the parentheses must be a subfield already defined within the current data structure, and the subfield being defined must be completely contained within the subfield it overlays.

```
*.. 1 ...+... 2 ...+... 3 ...+... 4 ...+... 5 ...+... 6 ...+... 7 ...+... 8
DName++++++++++ETDsFrom+++To/L+++IDc.Keywords+++++++++++++++++++++++++++++++
     // Data structures to "split up" input fields into subfields
D                 DS
D FirstName               15
D   Initial                1      OVERLAY(FirstName)
D                 DS
D Phone                   10 0
D   AreaCode               3 0 OVERLAY(Phone)
D   Exchange               3 0 OVERLAY(Phone:4)
D   LocalNbr               4 0 OVERLAY(Phone:7)
```

If the data item within parentheses is an array, OVERLAY applies to each element of the array; thus, the overlaid subfield itself becomes an array, without any explicit dimensioning:

```
*.. 1 ...+... 2 ...+... 3 ...+... 4 ...+... 5 ...+... 6 ...+... 7 ...+... 8
DName++++++++++ETDsFrom+++To/L+++IDc.Keywords+++++++++++++++++++++++++++++++
     // Given the definitions below, BigArray is an array of 300 elements,
     // each 10 characters long; because of the OVERLAY, SubArray is also
     // an array of 300 elements, each 2 characters long. Each element of
     // SubArray is identical to the first two bytes of the corresponding
     // elements in BigArray.
D                 DS
D BigArray                10    DIM(300)
D   SubArray               2    OVERLAY(BigArray)
```

Another use of a data structure is to group fields from non-adjacent locations on a data record. The following physical file definition contains fields WareHouse and PartNbr, but the fields are not adjacent to one another in the record.

```
*.. 1 ...+... 2 ...+... 3 ...+... 4 ...+... 5 ...+... 6 ...+... 7 ...+... 8
A..........T.Name++++++RLen++TDpB......Functions++++++++++++++++++++++++++++
A           R PARTREC
A             PARTNBR        5  0
A             DESCRPT       20
A             QTY            7  0
A             WAREHOUSE      3  0
A           K PARTNBR
```

By defining the following data structure, you can access WareHouse and PartNbr as a concatenation, or combined field, using the data structure name WarePart.

```
*.. 1 ...+... 2 ...+... 3 ...+... 4 ...+... 5 ...+... 6 ...+... 7 ...+... 8
DName++++++++++ETDsFrom+++To/L+++IDc.Keywords++++++++++++++++++++++++++++++++
D WarePart        DS
D   WareHouse              1     3  0
D   PartNbr                4     8  0
```

Consider another example. An externally described file contains student answers for a 100-problem, multiple-choice exam, and a second externally described file contains a key for the exam. You want to write a program to grade the exams, using array manipulation to compare each student's answers one at a time with the correct answer for that problem.

Because externally described files do not allow fields to be defined as arrays, the student answers have been defined as one large field, StdAns, and the answers on the key have been defined as one large field, KeyAns. You can use a data structure to convert these answer fields to arrays, in preparation for processing:

```
*.. 1 ...+... 2 ...+... 3 ...+... 4 ...+... 5 ...+... 6 ...+... 7 ...+... 8
DName++++++++++ETDsFrom+++To/L+++IDc.Keywords++++++++++++++++++++++++++++++++
  // Data structure redefining StdAns and KeyAns as arrays,
  // using mixed notation
D                 DS
D StdAns                 1   100
D StdAry                 1   100   DIM(100)
D KeyAns                     100
D KeyAry                      .1   OVERLAY(KeyAns) DIM(100)
```

Array StdAry provides a redefinition of field StdAns, using a technique we introduced in Chapter 9. Array KeyAry redefines KeyAns using keyword OVERLAY. Note that the data structure uses both absolute notation and length notation to define its subfields. When you use length notation for an array, the length entry refers to the length of each element of the array — 1 for KeyAry in this example.

Although you can also overlap field definitions or include the same positions in several fields within program-defined records in a way that looks identical to data structure subfield definitions, the results of these kinds of definitions are different than for data structures. When you define overlapping fields in a program-defined input record, the system establishes a separate storage location for each field so that changing the value of one field does not affect the value of any of the other fields. With data structures, in contrast, overlapping subfields reference the same memory locations.

```
*.. 1 ...+... 2 ...+... 3 ...+... 4 ...+... 5 ...+... 6 ...+... 7 ...+... 8
I......................Fmt+SPFrom+To+++DcField++++++++++L1M1FrP1MnZr......
IInRecord   NS
I                              1   15  FirstName
I                              1    1  Initial
```

Given the preceding input record definition, if FirstName were 'JACK' and our program assigned 'M' to Initial, FirstName would remain 'JACK'. In contrast, a data structure's overlapping subfields reference the same area of storage, so changing the value of one of the subfields also changes the value of any fields that overlap it. Thus, if the above were a data structure and FirstName were 'JACK', Initial would be 'J'; if we then assigned 'M' to Initial, FirstName would become 'MACK'.

Externally Described Data Structures

Up until now, we've discussed program-described data structures, explicitly coding each subfield within the data structure. You can also code **externally described data structures** in Definition Specifications. With this method, instead of coding each subfield for an externally described data structure, you define the subfields in the record format for a database file. Externally described data structures are useful when you want a data structure to mimic an existing record format or when you want to standardize a data structure, using the same data structure in many programs.

Two additions to the data structure definition make it an externally described data structure. Code an E in position 22 (E) of the data structure header to identify the data structure as being externally described. Then, name the external file that contains the format for the data structure using the EXTNAME keyword; if you omit EXTNAME, the name of the data structure must match the name of the external file. With externally described data structures, it usually is not necessary to code subfield definitions because the compiler will copy the subfields from the external file.

```
*.. 1 ...+... 2 ...+... 3 ...+... 4 ...+... 5 ...+... 6 ...+... 7 ...+... 8
DName+++++++++++ETDsFrom+++To/L+++IDc.Keywords+++++++++++++++++++++++++++++++
D EmployeeDS      E DS                  EXTNAME(EmpMaster)
```

LIKEDS (Data Structure Definition)

The LIKEDS keyword defines a data structure to be like another data structure. The subfields of the new data structure will be identical to the original data structure, without your having to explicitly code them. To refer to the subfields in the new data structure, you must *qualify* the subfield name, preceding it with the name of the data structure and a period (.).

```
*.. 1 ...+... 2 ...+... 3 ...+... 4 ...+... 5 ...+... 6 ...+... 7 ...+... 8
DName+++++++++++ETDsFrom+++To/L+++IDc.Keywords+++++++++++++++++++++++++++++++
D Contact         DS
D   Name                        35
D   Address                     35
D   City                        21
D   State                        2
D   ZipCode                     10

D Customer        DS                    LIKEDS(Contact)

D Vendor          DS                    LIKEDS(Contact)
```

In this example, data structures Customer and Vendor are both defined to be like the Contact data structure. They each have subfields Name, Address, City, State, and ZipCode, even though those subfields are not explicitly coded. To correctly identify the subfields, your program must qualify the subfield names with the data structure name. So, the program would refer to Customer.Name, Vendor.Name, Customer.Address, Vendor.Address, and so on.

Multiple-Occurrence Data Structures

You can define a "repeated" data structure by declaring it as a **multiple-occurrence data structure**. Keyword OCCURS signals this kind of data structure, and the numeric value you enter as the parameter of OCCURS determines how many times the structure is repeated in storage. (The maximum number of occurrences is 32,767). A multiple-occurrence data structure is similar to an array or a table because it enables the computer to store many values for a given field name. But because the entire data structure is repeated, you can build a much more complex collection of elements than you can with RPG IV arrays or tables.

Consider the problem of the state tax data we discussed in Chapter 9. We wanted to access the state name and the sales tax rate based on the state code, and we solved the problem two ways: once using tables and once using arrays. Each solution required us to define three separate tables or arrays. As the number of data items increases, however, implementing such access through tables or arrays becomes more and more awkward. If, for example, you wanted to access the state's capital, its lowest zip code, and its highest zip code in addition to the state name and the tax rate (based on the state code), you would need to define six separate tables or arrays. If you used tables, you also would need to perform five separate lookups to obtain the information.

Version 5 Release 2 Update

The new Version 5 Release 2 LIKEREC keyword performs a function similar to keyword LIKEDS. It defines a data structure to have the same subfields as a record format in an externally described file.

```
*.. 1 ...+... 2 ...+... 3 ...+... 4 ...+... 5 ...+... 6 ...+... 7 ...+... 8
FFilename++IPEASFRLen+LKlen+AIDevice+.Keywords+++++++++++++++++++++++++++++
DName++++++++++ETDsFrom+++To/L+++IDc.Keywords+++++++++++++++++++++++++++++++
FEmpMaster IF   E           K DISK

D Employee       DS                  LIKEREC(EmpRec)
```

You can specify an optional second parameter for the LIKEREC keyword to indicate which type of fields to use in the data structure:

- *ALL — The data structure will include all fields from the record format.
- *KEY — The data structure will include only key fields from the record format.
- *INPUT — The data structure will include only input fields from the record format.
- *OUTPUT — The data structure will include only output fields from the record format.

```
*.. 1 ...+... 2 ...+... 3 ...+... 4 ...+... 5 ...+... 6 ...+... 7 ...+... 8
FFilename++IPEASFRLen+LKlen+AIDevice+.Keywords+++++++++++++++++++++++++++++
DName++++++++++ETDsFrom+++To/L+++IDc.Keywords+++++++++++++++++++++++++++++++
FEmpMaster IF   E           K DISK

D EmployeeKey    DS                  LIKEREC(EmpRec:*KEY)
```

In the example above, only the key fields from the EmpRec format would be subfields in the EmployeeKey data structure. The LIKEREC keyword is useful for building key lists that will be used in conjunction with V5R2's %KDS (Key Data Structure) function.

A data structure handles this problem more simply:

```
*.. 1 ...+... 2 ...+... 3 ...+... 4 ...+... 5 ...+... 6 ...+... 7 ...+... 8
DName++++++++++ETDsFrom+++To/L+++IDc.Keywords+++++++++++++++++++++++++++++++
D DSState         DS                    OCCURS(50)
D   Code                        2
D   Name                       15
D   SalesTax                    4 4
D   Capital                    15
D   LowZip                      5 0
D   HiZip                       5 0
```

The data structure above occurs 50 times; each occurrence contains Code, Name, SalesTax, Capital, LowZip, and HiZip, which are the same names as the field names within file StatesFile. To load the data structure with the data from StatesFile, it is necessary to read each successive record from the file into a successive occurrence of the data structure. (This loading operation is illustrated in detail shortly.)

Multiple-occurrence data structures do not use subscripts or pointers directly to indicate which occurrence you want to work with. Instead, the %OCCUR (Set/Get Occurrence of a Data Structure) function establishes which occurrence of the data structure is to be used next within the program.

To set the current occurrence of a data structure, specify the %OCCUR function on the left side of an assignment expression. Name the data structure whose occurrence is being set as the only argument to the function:

```
*.. 1 ...+... 2 ...+... 3 ...+... 4 ...+... 5 ...+... 6 ...+... 7 ...+... 8
/FREE
  // Make the fifth occurrence of DSState active.
   %OCCUR(DSState) = 5;
  // Make the Nth occurrence of DSState active.
   %OCCUR(DSState) = N;
/END-FREE
```

If you want to determine which occurrence of a data structure is active, specify the %OCCUR function on the right side of the assignment expression. The result must be an integer numeric field that will be given the value of the current occurrence:

```
*.. 1 ...+... 2 ...+... 3 ...+... 4 ...+... 5 ...+... 6 ...+... 7 ...+... 8
/FREE
  // After the following line is executed, field S's value will indicate
  // which occurrence of DSState is currently active.
   S = %OCCUR(DSState);
/END-FREE
```

The following calculations illustrate how the state data could be obtained from a full-procedural input file to load the values into the multiple-occurrence data structure we defined earlier.

```
*.. 1 ...+... 2 ...+... 3 ...+... 4 ...+... 5 ...+... 6 ...+... 7 ...+... 8
/FREE
  // Loop 50 times to load DSState from StatesFile.
  // Exit early if the file contains fewer than 50 records.
   FOR I = 1 to 50;
     %OCCUR(DSState) = I;
     READ StatesFile;
     IF %EOF(StatesFile);
       LEAVE;
     ENDIF;
   ENDFOR;
/END-FREE
```

Once the data structure is loaded, the information is available for "lookups." To access the data structure information based on a match between an input state code (CodeIn) and the state codes in the data structure, you can code a loop to change the occurrence until a match is found; at that point, all the data structure fields contain values appropriate for CodeIn. The following calculations illustrate this technique:

```
*.. 1 ...+... 2 ...+... 3 ...+... 4 ...+... 5 ...+... 6 ...+... 7 ...+... 8
/FREE
  // Code to look up information when data is stored in a
  // multiple-occurrence data structure

  %OCCUR(DSState) = 1; // Set DSState to its first occurrence

  // Then loop, changing the occurrence, until either a match is found
  // or the last occurrence of the data structure has been examined.
  DOW CodeIn <> Code;
    I = %OCCUR(DSState);
    IF I < %ELEM(DSState);
      %OCCUR(DSState) = I + 1;
    ELSE
      EXSR BadCode;
      LEAVE;
    ENDIF;
  ENDDO;
/END-FREE
```

This code also uses the %ELEM (Get Number of Elements) built-in function, discussed later, to represent the total number of occurrences of the data structure, thus ensuring that the loop will not extend past the last occurrence.

Another use of a multiple-occurrence data structure is to provide capabilities equivalent to those of two-dimensional arrays. Unlike most other programming languages, RPG IV allows only one-dimensional arrays. Sometimes this limitation makes programming a solution to a problem more difficult than if the language included the capability to define arrays in two (or more) dimensions.

A simple analogy can help you understand the concept of a **two-dimensional array**. Most of you are familiar with spreadsheets. Each spreadsheet cell is addressed by a row position and a column position. The row represents one dimension; the column represents a second. Although most spreadsheets implement this addressing with an alphabetic "pointer" for the column and a numeric "pointer" for the row (e.g., cell B4), you can see how each cell is uniquely addressed by the combination of row and column values. Changing either the row address or the column address changes which cell (array element) you are referencing.

Although RPG IV does not directly support two-dimensional arrays, you can achieve the same effect by including an array within a multiple-occurrence data structure. The array subscripts would point to a value in one dimension (the "column"), while the occurrence of the data structure would point to the second dimension (the "row").

Consider the following problem. A company has an externally described file of sales transactions for the year; each record includes Amount (amount of sale), Date (date of sale in *yymmdd* format), and LocateIn (a numeric value, 1–50, designating the location at which the sale took place). The company wants a report that shows total monthly sales broken down by location.

One solution to this problem uses a multiple-occurrence data structure with 50 occurrences (each representing a location), where each occurrence contains an array of 12 elements (representing each month). The portion of the program that defines the data structure and shows the calculations to accumulate the sales is shown in the following code.

```
*.. 1 ...+... 2 ...+... 3 ...+... 4 ...+... 5 ...+... 6 ...+... 7 ...+... 8
DName++++++++++ETDsFrom+++To/L+++IDc.Keywords++++++++++++++++++++++++++++++++
    // A multiple-occurrence data structure with 50 occurrences;
    // each occurrence is an array.
D Location       DS                    OCCURS(50) INZ
D   Total                      10  2 DIM(12)

    // Data structure to access the month portion of input field Date.
D               DS
D Date                          6  0
D   Yr                          2  0 OVERLAY(Date)
D   Mon                         2  0 OVERLAY(Date:3)
D   Day                         2  0 OVERLAY(Date:5)

 /FREE
   // Calculations to process SalesFile to accumulate sales within the
   // appropriate accumulator of the data structure.
    READ SalesFile;
    DOW NOT %EOF(SalesFile);
   // Set the occurrence of the data structure based on Location's value.
      %OCCUR(Location) = LocateIn;
   // Check for an invalid month value.
      IF Mon < 1 OR Mon > 12;
        EXSR Error;
      ELSE;
        Total(Mon) = Total(Mon) + Amount;
      ENDIF;
      READ SalesFile;
    ENDDO;
 /END-FREE
```

At the end of the above routine, the year's sales have been accumulated within data structure Location, with each of the 50 occurrences of Location containing the 12 monthly sales totals for that location. You could then print the totals in a row/column format.

Initialization and Reinitialization of Variables

Data structures are considered character fields regardless of the data type of their subfields; as a result, they will contain blanks at the start of your program unless you explicitly initialize their subfields. In our sample code for accumulating sales, if we had not initialized all the elements within all the occurrences of Total to 0 (indicated by INZ in Location's header line), our program would have ended abnormally when we tried to add Amount to a Total element.

You initialize a data structure globally when you include keyword INZ in the Keywords area of the data structure header line. This use of INZ causes all subfields in the entire data structure to be automatically initialized to the default value appropriate for their data types (e.g., all numeric subfields are set to zero, all character fields to spaces, all pointers to *NULL).

As an alternative, you can initialize specific subfields of a data structure by including keyword INZ as part of their definitions. If you want to initialize the subfield to a value other than the default, you can include the desired value within parentheses following INZ. You can express this value as a literal or a named constant, but it must fit the data type of the subfield; moreover, it cannot be longer than the subfield or have more decimal positions than the subfield (if the type is numeric). If the value is too long to fit on one line, you can continue it over several lines in the same way you can continue values for named constants.

The use of keyword INZ is not limited to data structures; you can use it to initialize standalone fields and arrays as well. The rules for using INZ with data structure subfields also apply to these kinds of data items. Study the following code to gain a sense of how to use INZ.

```
*.. 1 ...+... 2 ...+... 3 ...+... 4 ...+... 5 ...+... 6 ...+... 7 ...+... 8
DName+++++++++++ETDsFrom+++To/L+++IDc.Keywords+++++++++++++++++++++++++++++++
     // The lines below define two named constants.
D NbrK            C                   14419
D CharK           C                   'ACCOUNTING'

     // The entire data structure below is globally initialized.
D Example1        DS                  INZ
D   CharSubFld                   30
D   NbrSubFld                     9 4

     // Specific subfield initialization is illustrated below.
     // Two subfields are initialized to named constants.
D Example2        DS
D   Nbr1                      1      4 0 INZ
D   Nbr2                      5      8 2 INZ(12.3)
D   Char1                     9     18   INZ
D   Char2                    19     28   INZ('ABCDEFG')
D   Char3                    29     69   INZ('This is an initial value +
D                                            for Char3.')
D   Nbr3                     70     74 0 INZ(NbrK)
D   Char4                    75     89   INZ(CharK)

     // Standalone fields can also be initialized using INZ.
D Example3        S             15   6 INZ
D Example4        S              5   1 INZ(1234.5)
D Example5        S             20     INZ(CharK)
D DateExmp        S               D   INZ(D'1995-03-15')
D PtrExmp         S               *   INZ

     // And even array elements can be assigned initial values.
D NbrAry          S              5   2 DIM(20) INZ(123.45)
D ChrAry          S             50     DIM(10) INZ(*ALL'-')
```

The OCCUR Operation

The %OCCUR function requires that your system be at Version 5 or later. Earlier releases of the RPG IV compiler use the OCCUR (Set/Get Occurrence of a Data Structure) operation for the same purpose. The OCCUR operation is restricted to the fixed-format Calculation Specification.

In an OCCUR operation, Factor 1 specifies which occurrence should be made active, and Factor 2 contains the name of the data structure whose occurrence is being set. Factor 1 can contain a literal, a numeric field, or a named constant. As an alternative, it can contain the name of a different multiple-occurrence data structure; in this case, the current occurrence of that data structure determines the occurrence of the data structure named in Factor 2. You can also optionally use the (E) operation extender with the %ERROR function; %ERROR is turned on if the specified occurrence is outside the range of the data structure.

```
*.. 1 ...+... 2 ...+... 3 ...+... 4 ...+... 5 ...+... 6 ...+... 7 ...+... 8
CL0N01Factor1+++++++Opcode(E)+Factor2+++++++Result++++++++Len++D+HiLoEq....
 * Make the fifth occurrence of DSState active.
C     5             OCCUR     DSState
 * Make the Nth occurrence of DSState active.
C     N             OCCUR     DSState
```

If you want to determine which occurrence of a data structure is active, you can leave Factor 1 blank and code an entry (which must be an integer numeric field) in the Result field position; the Result field will be given the value of the current occurrence:

```
*.. 1 ...+... 2 ...+... 3 ...+... 4 ...+... 5 ...+... 6 ...+... 7 ...+... 8
CL0N01Factor1++++++Opcode(E)+Factor2+++++++Result++++++++Len++D+HiLoEq....
 * After the following line is executed, field S's value will indicate
 * which occurrence of DSState is currently active.
C                   OCCUR     DSState       S
```

In the preceding sample code, keyword INZ initializes the entire Example1 data structure, such that any of its numeric subfields (e.g., NbrSubFld) are 0 and any character subfields (e.g., CharSubFld) are blank. All Example2 data structure subfields are initialized individually. Nbr1 is initialized to 0, and Char1 is initialized to blanks, because no alternate values are provided for those fields. Char2's initial value is 'ABCDEFG', and Char3's is 'This is an initial value for Char3.' Nbr3's value becomes 14419, and Char4's value becomes 'ACCOUNTING   ', because these subfields are initialized to named constants with those values. Note that in the standalone field definitions, DateExmp, a field of type date, is initialized to March 15, 1995; PtrExmp, a basing pointer, is initialized to *NULL. All the elements of array NbrAry are initialized to 123.45, while the figurative constant used to initialize array ChrAry fills each element with all hyphens.

Another way to handle initialization of data structure subfields, and of fields in general, is to explicitly assign them initial values within a subroutine that the program performs just once at the start of execution. RPG IV actually provides such a subroutine, named ***INZSR**. If you include a sub-routine with this name within your program, the subroutine is invoked automatically immediately after the program completes its other start-up tasks, such as opening the files and loading any arrays or tables. Although you can include other kinds of operations within *INZSR, good programming practice suggests that all operations within this subroutine focus on a single function — initializing variables.

```
*.. 1 ...+... 2 ...+... 3 ...+... 4 ...+... 5 ...+... 6 ...+... 7 ...+... 8
 /FREE
  // Sample code initializing variables using built-in subroutine *INZSR
    BEGSR *INZSR;
      RecordCnt = 0;
      Adds = 0;
      Changes = 0;
      Deletes = 0;
      ErrorCnt = 0;
    ENDSR;
 /END-FREE
```

Although RPG IV automatically initializes all numeric fields to 0, all character fields to blanks, all date, time, and timestamp fields to *LOVAL, and all pointers to *NULL at the start of a program, there are good reasons to explicitly initialize variables in an initialization subroutine or through the Definition Specifications. This practice makes the processing steps within your program more evident. Moreover, it relies less on the automatic features of RPG, in keeping with the movement toward complete procedural implementation of the language.

Version 5 Release 2 Update

Version 5 Release 2 lets you specify the DIM keyword on a data structure definition. By using DIM, you can now access a data structure occurrence using the same syntax you'd use for arrays, using an index instead of an occurrence. This support effectively renders multiple-occurrence data structures, the OCCUR operation, and the %OCCUR function obsolete. You can expect newer RPG IV programs to tend to drift away from using multiple-occurrence data structures in favor of the simpler, more flexible DIM data structure construction.

Version 5 Release 2 also lets you specify nested data structures, which can in turn be defined with the DIM keyword; this support effectively gives RPG IV access to multiple-dimension data structures.

You often need to reinitialize field values during processing. For instance, in control-break programs, you need to set subtotal accumulators back to 0. In interactive maintenance programs, you may want to clear data fields when you add new records. RPG IV provides two operations — CLEAR and RESET — to let you reinitialize variables.

CLEAR (Clear)

The CLEAR (Clear) operation changes the values of the data items with which it is used to their appropriate default values, based on data type (0 for numeric fields, blanks for character fields, *LOVAL for date, time, and timestamp fields, *NULL for pointers). You can CLEAR individual fields or whole structures (data structures, arrays, tables, record formats). A CLEAR operation requires an entry in the result area of the specification that tells which data item is to be cleared. If you specify an array, the system clears the entire array. If, however, you specify a multiple-occurrence data structure or a table for clearing, only the current occurrence or table element is cleared, unless you use keyword *ALL in Factor 2; in that case, all the occurrences or the entire table is cleared.

If the data item to be cleared is a database file record format, you can specify *NOKEY in Factor 1 to signal that all the record's fields except the record key are to be cleared. When you CLEAR a display record format, only fields that are output in that record format are affected. This means that if you clear a display file record format, only those fields with usage O (output) or B (both) are reinitialized.

```
*.. 1 ...+... 2 ...+... 3 ...+... 4 ...+... 5 ...+... 6 ...+... 7 ...+... 8
 /FREE

    CLEAR NbrFld;                 // Numeric field reinitialized to 0
    CLEAR CharFld;                // Character field reinitialized to blanks

  // The data structure subfields are set to the default values appropriate
  // for their individual data types.
    CLEAR DataStr;

  // All record fields except the key are set to the field's default values
    CLEAR *NOKEY Record;

  // All array elements are cleared.
    CLEAR Arry;

  // Only the current occurrence of the multiple-occurrence DS is cleared.
    CLEAR MultOcrDS;
  // All occurrences of the multiple-occurrence DS are cleared.
    CLEAR *ALL MultOcrDS;

 /END-FREE
```

RESET (Reset)

The RESET (Reset) operation is similar to CLEAR, except that instead of automatically reinitializing values to their appropriate default values based on data type, RESET restores the elements to whatever values they had at the end of the initialization step at the program's start. If you initialized data-structure subfields to specific values, turned on indicators, or assigned values to fields in *INZSR and these values subsequently changed during the program's execution, you can easily reassign those initial values with RESET.

The format of RESET is identical to that of CLEAR: The Result field entry can be a data structure, a record format, an array, a table, or a variable (field, subfield, or indicator). As with CLEAR, only the current occurrence of a data structure or the current element of a table is reset, unless keyword *ALL appears in Factor 2. If the result item is a display file record format, only those fields with usage O (output) or B (both) are reinitialized to their starting values.

```
*.. 1 ...+... 2 ...+... 3 ...+... 4 ...+... 5 ...+... 6 ...+... 7 ...+... 8
/FREE

  // All data structure subfields are reset to their originally initialized
  // values or to blanks, if no explicit INZ values were present.
   RESET DataStr;

  // All record fields except key are set to initialized values or to
  // default values, if not explicitly initialized to another value.
   RESET *NOKEY Record;

  // All array elements are reset to initialized value.
   RESET Arry;

  // Only the current occurrence of the multiple-occurrence DS is reset.
   RESET MultOcrDS;
  // All occurrences of the multiple-occurrence DS are reset.
   RESET *ALL MultOcrDS;

/END-FREE
```

File Information Data Structures

A file information data structure is a special data structure that you can define for each file used by your program. A **file information data structure** contains predefined subfields that can provide information to your program about the file and the outcomes of input and/or output operations to the file. Because much of this information details exception or error information, using a file information data structure can be helpful in debugging programs.

A file information data structure must be linked to the file with which it is associated by making an entry on that file's File Specification description. Use keyword INFDS, noting the name of the data structure serving as that file's file information data structure in parentheses after the keyword:

```
*.. 1 ...+... 2 ...+... 3 ...+... 4 ...+... 5 ...+... 6 ...+... 7 ...+... 8
FFilename++IPEASFRlen+LKlen+AIDevice+.Keywords++++++++++++++++++++++++++++++
  // File specification declaring data structure SampleDS
  // as the file information data structure file
FSample    UF   E           K DISK    INFDS(SampleDS)
```

The above code defines data structure SampleDS as the file information data structure for file Sample. Each such data structure is 528 positions long and is subdivided into predefined segments or subfields, each of which automatically will contain information about the file with which the data structure is associated. Your data structure needs only to include those subfields that contain data you want to reference within your program; you can ignore the others. To reference a particular subfield of information, you need to know its From and To positions within the data structure. You can look up these positions in the *ILE RPG Reference*.

As an alternative, IBM has provided keywords, which are more easily remembered, to represent the location of those subfields most often referenced. For these subfields, you can substitute the keyword for a subfield's actual location within the data structure. You must supply a name for the subfield, regardless of whether you reference its location through actual positions or through a keyword.

Although a complete discussion of file information data structures is beyond the scope of this text, the following paragraph describes some of the subfields and what they represent to give you a sense of the potential usefulness of file information data structures.

The subfield in positions 1–8 (keyword *FILE) contains the name of the file. Positions 16–21 (keyword *OPCODE) contain the name of the most recent operation processed on the file, such as READ. Positions 11–15 (keyword *STATUS) contain a five-digit numeric field (zero decimal positions) that contains the status code of the most recent input/output (I/O) operation.

Status codes are predefined values that signal specific I/O events. Status code 00000 reflects no error or exception. Status code 00002 indicates that a function key was used to end a display. Status code 00011 signals an end-of-file on a read. Status code 00012 signals a no-record-found condition on a chain operation. Any status code greater than 00099 is an error. Different error codes signal precisely what kind of error occurred. For example, 01211 indicates an attempt at I/O to a closed file, 01218 indicates a locked record, and status code 01021 indicates an attempt to write a record with a duplicate key to a file that is supposed to have unique keys.

Some of the subfields, such as the status code subfield, are useful for testing and debugging programs. Others may provide information your program needs as part of its normal processing. For example, if you are trying to develop an interactive application that is cursor sensitive, your program will need to be able to determine the cursor's location on the screen; positions 370–371 of the file information data structure contain (in binary representation) the row and column coordinates of the cursor upon return from a screen.

Other subfields of the file information data structure provide information about the position of the file "pointer," or current relative record number (positions 397–400); a count of the total number of records in the file (positions 156–159); or what function key was used to end a display (position 369).

The following example shows a sample file information data structure. Notice the use of keywords in place of location in three of the subfields. Rather than *FILE, you could access the file name by coding From 1 To 8.

```
*.. 1 ...+... 2 ...+... 3 ...+... 4 ...+... 5 ...+... 6 ...+... 7 ...+... 8
DName+++++++++++ETDsFrom+++To/L+++IDc.Keywords+++++++++++++++++++++++++++++++
    // Sample file information data structure
D SampleDS         DS
D   FileName            *FILE
D   FileStatus          *STATUS
D   OpCode              *OPCODE
D   RelRecNbr           397    400B 0
D   RecCnt              156    159B 0
```

In general, any time you write a program for which you need "behind-the-scenes" information about the files used by the program, remember file information data structures. Chances are you can obtain the data you need from a subfield within such a data structure.

Program Status Data Structures

Just as you can define file information data structures to provide information about data or events associated with the files used by your program, you can also define a **program status data structure** to provide information about the program itself and about exceptions or errors that occur during program execution.

Like a file information data structure, a program status data structure has predefined subfields that automatically acquire values during the course of your program's execution. Some of these subfields are useful in testing and debugging to determine what went wrong in the program; others provide information that might be needed to implement the logic of the program itself.

For example, a program status data structure can supply you with the name of the program, the job name and job number, the name of the user who called the program, and the specific number of any runtime exception or error that occurs while the program is running. A status code subfield also can provide information about program problems. To give you a sense of what kinds of errors the status code can report, the following table lists some possible values for the status code subfield:

Code	Meaning
00000	No error occurred
00101	Negative square root
00102	Divide by 0
00121	Array index not valid
00122	OCCUR outside range
00907	Decimal data error

An S in position 23 (T) of a data structure initial-definition line identifies a program status data structure. Any subfield of the data structure that you want to access must be defined within the data structure. The definition includes the location of the subfield, a decimal entry (if appropriate), and a name you assign to the subfield. IBM has provided keywords that can substitute for the location of the most commonly used subfields. A sample program status data structure is illustrated below. For more information about program status data structures, see the *ILE RPG Reference*.

```
*.. 1 ...+... 2 ...+... 3 ...+... 4 ...+... 5 ...+... 6 ...+... 7 ...+... 8
DName++++++++++ETDsFrom+++To/L+++IDc.Keywords+++++++++++++++++++++++++++++++
   // Sample program status data structure
D PSDS            SDS
D   PrgStatus       *STATUS         0
D   ErrType               40    42
D   ErrCode               43    46
D   JobName              244   253
D   JobNumber            264   269 0
D   UserName             354   363
```

Note

The %STATUS built-in function, discussed in Chapter 12, returns the file or program status information without requiring the use of a file information data structure or a program status data structure.

Note

You can initialize a character field (at least 10 character long) with the current user's name by specifying INZ(*USER) in its definition, without requiring the use of a program status data structure.

Chapter Summary

In addition to character and numeric types of fields, RPG IV offers other data types useful for specific purposes. Time, date, and timestamp data types let you declare that variables will hold date/time-related data. Once so declared, you can manipulate the data using special built-in functions to facilitate date computations. The basing pointer and procedure pointer data types let you dynamically access storage for the data items associated with the pointers.

You can define fields relative to other field definitions using keyword LIKE. A field defined in this way can exactly match its length to that of the field supplying the definition; as an alternative, you can specify a length longer (+ a number of positions) or shorter (– a number of positions) than the length of the second field.

You can define data structures that represent complex definitions of a given area of memory. A data structure is composed of subfields. These subfields can represent overlapping areas of storage or subdivisions of fields. Data structures can be program described or externally described. A multiple-occurrence data structure establishes repetitions of the data structure in memory to let you perform data manipulation more complex than what simple arrays or tables offer. Arrays can appear as subfields of multiple-occurrence data structures, a feature that provides the equivalent function of two-dimensional arrays in other languages.

You can easily initialize data structures or subfields of data structures in the data structure definition by using keyword INZ. RPG IV also provides subroutine *INZSR, which, if included within your program, is automatically executed at the program's startup. Programmers often use *INZSR to explicitly initialize fields and other data items. You can use operation CLEAR to initialize or reinitialize data items to the default values associated with their data types. RESET, on the other hand, reinitializes data items to whatever values they were given at the beginning of the program.

Two special data structures of predefined subfields exist in RPG IV to provide information about the status of files used by the program or about the processing of the program itself: the file information data structure and the program status data structure. You often access these data structures within RPG IV's *PSSR error subroutine to determine the cause of an execution error.

Key Terms

date data type	pointer data types
externally described data structures	program status data structure
file information data structure	time data type
*INZSR	timestamp data type
multiple-occurrence data structure	two-dimensional array

Discussion/Review Questions

1. What are the primary advantages offered by RPG IV's various date data types?
2. Compare and contrast RPG IV's basing pointers and array indexes.
3. What is the purpose of defining fields with keyword LIKE? Why might you use this RPG IV feature?
4. What is a multiple-occurrence data structure? Compare and contrast it with an RPG IV table.
5. Data structures use OCCUR; what parallel for OCCUR do you have when you are working with arrays? With tables?

6. What is variable initialization? What techniques are available in RPG IV to let you initialize fields and other data items?

7. Describe the difference between the CLEAR and RESET operations.

8. What built-in subroutines does RPG IV provide for your use? When is each executed?

9. Compare and contrast a file information data structure with a program status data structure.

10. How many file information data structures can you have within a program? How many program status data structures?

Exercises

1. A retail business's SALES file contains field DAYSALES, eight positions long with two decimal positions, that represents the store's sales from one day. Use LIKE to define fields that will hold the sales tax for a day's sales, a week's worth of sales, a week's sales tax, annual sales, and annual sales tax.

2. Data file WUTSTP contains student answers to 50-item, multiple-choice tests. The format of these records is as follows:

Field	Description	Positions
TEST	Test number	1–4
SECT	Section number	5–9
CRSE	Course ID	10–15
STID	Social Security number	16–24
ANS	Answers 1–50	25–74

Code a data structure that does the following:

- subdivides field CRSE into two three-position fields (the first represents the department offering the course, the second the course number)
- subdivides field STID into three-, two-, and four-position subfields
- defines field ANS as an array, with each answer a separate element of the array

3. To determine shipping charges, CompuSell uses a table file that contains shipping charges based on weight and zone. Each record contains a weight and six charges (one each for zones 2–7). There are 70 records in the file, sequentially reflecting weights 1–70. The record layout of file CSCHGP is

Field	Positions	(Decimal positions)
Weight (pounds)	1–2	(0)
Charge zone 2	3–6	(2)
Charge zone 3	7–10	(2)
Charge zone 4	11–14	(2)
Charge zone 5	15–18	(2)
Charge zone 6	19–22	(2)
Charge zone 7	23–26	(2)

Define a multiple-occurrence data structure that will hold the contents of this file and let you store all the table information at once in the data structure instead of in tables.

4. Write the code needed to determine whether or not a bill is more than 30 days past due. The due-date field, DateIn, and the system date, UDATE, are eight-byte numeric fields with zero decimal positions. (Hint: Define two date data-type fields, assign to them the values of DateIn and UDATE, and use one of the date operations to determine the difference between the two dates.)

Programming Assignments

1. Acme Explosive Company tracks its product sales by month. This sales information is stored in file PRDSLSP, described in Appendix F. There is only one record per product manufactured by the company. Each record includes sales totals for that product for each month of the previous year.

    The company wants you to write a program to produce a summary report of sales (below), highlighting the month with the lowest sales and the month with the highest sales for each product. The names of the months, rather than the month numbers, are to appear on the report. At the end of the report, the company wants the overall product sales for each month.

```
          1         2         3         4         5         6         7         8         9         10
 1234567890123456789012345678901234567890123456789012345678901234567890123456789012345678901234567890
 1 XX/XX/XX      ACME EXPLOSIVES ANNUAL SALES SUMMARY      PAGE XXØX
 2
 3 PRODUCT            BEST MONTH           WORST MONTH
 4 XXXXXX            XXX,XØX JANUARY      XXX,XØX SEPTEMBER
 5 XXXXXX            XXX,XØX MAY          XXX,XØX AUGUST
 6 XXXXXX            XXX,XØX JUNE         XXX,XØX DECEMBER
 7
 8 TOTAL MONTHLY SALES:
 9 JANUARY        $XX,XXX,X$X
10 FEBRUARY       $XX,XXX,X$X
11 MARCH          $XX,XXX,X$X
12 ...
13 DECEMBER       $XX,XXX,X$X
14
```

    To facilitate processing the sales figures, define the input record as a data structure containing an array. Define all work variables with LIKE. Handle the nomth names as a compile-time array.

2. Honest John's Used Cars employs 20 salespeople; each salesperson has a number assigned to him or her (numbers range from 1 to 20). During the course of a week, each sale a salesperson makes is recorded in a transaction file, HJSLSP (see Appendix F). Each record includes information about the salesperson number, the invoice number, and the amount of the sale. Each input record in the transaction file contains a record of a single sale. The file records are not sorted in any way. There may be several input records for a given salesperson, depending on how many successful sales he or she has had during the week.

    A salesperson file, HJSLPP, is also available, keyed on salesperson number and including the salesperson's name and weekly base pay (see Appendix F).

    Honest John wants you to determine the weekly pay due each salesperson. Pay is based on the weekly base pay plus a commission based on total weekly sales for each salesperson. If total sales is greater than $50,000, use a 3 percent commission rate; if it's between $25,000 and $50,000, use a 2 percent commission rate; if it's less than $25,000, use a 1 percent commission rate. It is possible that not every salesperson has had at least one sale this week; however, each should get paid at least his or her base pay.

Write a program to generate the report shown below, with the following restrictions on your program: 1) Do not define a logical file over HJSLSP; instead, use a multiple-occurrence data structure to accumulate sales for each salesperson. 2) Do not hard-code commission levels or rates in your calculations; instead, handle them as named constants. 3) Use LIKE to define any work variables needed within your program.

```
           1         2         3         4         5         6         7         8         9         10
  1234567890123456789012345678901234567890123456789012345678901234567890123456789012345678901234567890
 1      XX/XX/XX                    honest john's used cars
 2                          WEEKLY SALESPERSON PAY SCHEDULE
 3
 4   SLSP.                              BASE                          TOTAL
 5   NO.              NAME              PAY            COMMIS.        PAY
 6
 7     1    XXXXXXXXXXXXXXXXXXXXXXXXX   X,XX0.XX       X,XX0.XX       XX,XX0.XX
 8     2    XXXXXXXXXXXXXXXXXXXXXXXXX   X,XX0.XX       X,XX0.XX       XX,XX0.XX
 9     3    XXXXXXXXXXXXXXXXXXXXXXXXX   X,XX0.XX       X,XX0.XX       XX,XX0.XX
10                                       . . .
11
12                     TOTALS          $XXX,XX$.XX    $XXX,XX$.XX    $X,XXX,XX0.XX
13
```

3. Piper, a small commuter airline, runs three flights a day between two cities, seven days a week. Its plane holds 20 passengers. The airline wants an online reservation system that will do the following:

Let the user enter a day number (1–7, representing Monday–Sunday; see Note below), a flight number (1–3), and the number of requested seats. If that many seats are available, let the user enter the name and phone number of the customer making the reservation and reserve that many seats by adding a record to the reservation file. Confirm the reservation and then redisplay the original entry screen with no values showing. If that flight does not have enough vacant seats, display a message on the screen that tells how many seats are available and let the user change all or part of the reservation (i.e., redisplay with the old data).

Note

To simplify the problem, assume Piper does not take reservations more than a week in advance, nor on the day of the flight. Thus, if today is Tuesday, a reservation for day 2 would be interpreted to be for next Tuesday. Also assume that first thing each morning, a program is run that transfers all reservation records for that day's flight to another file, so you needn't worry about mixing up today's reservations with those for a week from now.

A physical file, PIPRESP (described in Appendix F), exists for use by your program. The file contains information about reservations for the flights for the week, including information about the person who made the reservation and the number of seats he or she reserved. This file should be updated as customers place reservations and should be used to determine availability of seats.

Tip

Load a multiple-occurrence data structure from the file at the beginning of the program before taking reservations. As you take reservations, make sure you update the data structure to keep it current and also write a record to the reservation file.

4. Wexler University wants you to write a program to prepare tuition bills for students based on their current enrollment. You will need to use four files: WUENRLP, WUSTDP, WUCRSP, and WUSCTP (see Appendix F). You may create whatever logical files you need to facilitate processing.

Each record in WUENRLP, which represents student current enrollment, should be processed in student order. For each section a student is enrolled in, you will need to determine the course identification and credits. Accumulate credits for the student. Then bill the student based on the total number of credits for which he or she is enrolled and on the student's residency and status, using the following per-credit-hour tuition figures:

	In-district ($)	Out-of-district ($)	International ($)
Lower division (< 61 credits)	77.50	155.25	200.50
Upper division (> 60 credits)	87.25	195.50	225.75
Graduate	111.50	250.50	276.00

In addition to tuition fees, the school levies the following fees:

- Enrollment fee — An enrollment fee will be charged to all students. Students enrolled in seven or more credit hours will be charged $194.00. Those enrolled in fewer than seven credit hours will be charged $72.50.
- Student activity fee — $8.00 is a student organization's assessment.
- MCC fee — Michigan Collegiality Congress fee of $0.50.

Define all fees and charges as named constants in your program because, as a student, you know these charges are bound to change soon. Use whatever other features discussed in this chapter (e.g., *INZSR) you feel will make your job easier.

Prepare a student tuition bill for each student, formatted as follows:

```
         1         2         3         4         5         6         7         8         9         1 0
1234567890123456789012345678901234567890123456789012345678901234567890123456789012345678901234567890
 1 WEXLER U. TUITION BILL     BILLING DATE: XX/XX/XX
 2
 3 TO:  XXXXXXXXXXXXXXX XXXXXXXXXX
 4      XXXXXXXXXXXXXXX
 5      XXXXXXXXXXXXXXX XX XXXXX-XXXX
 6
 7 ACCORDING TO OUR RECORDS, YOU HAVE ENROLLED IN THE
 8 FOLLOWING COURSES:
 9 COURSE      SECTION     DAYS    TIME       CREDITS
10 XXXXXX      XXXXXX      XXX     XØ:XX         X
11 XXXXXX      XXXXXX      XXX     XØ:XX         X
12 XXXXXX      XXXXXX      XXX     XØ:XX         X
13                        TOTAL CREDITS        XØ
14
15                        AMOUNT DUE
16          TUITION:          $X,XX$.XX
17          ENROLLMENT FEE:     XXØ.XX
18          ACTIVITY FEE:        XØ.XX
19          MCC FEE:              .XX
20
21          TOTAL DUE:        $X,XX$.XX
22
23 FAILURE TO PAY TOTAL WITHIN 21 DAYS OF BILLING
24 WILL RESULT IN YOUR BEING DROPPED FROM ALL
25 CLASSES.
```

5. Wexler University wants a report showing faculty earnings and number of years of employment. The data is contained in physical file WUINSTP (see Appendix F). The printer spacing chart of the desired report is shown below. Note that you are to list the faculty members in order of increasing salary within their respective departments. Also note that the names on the report represent a trimmed concatenation of last name, comma, and first name (e.g., "Doe, John"). The number of years employed should represent the number of whole years completed when considering date of hire and the current system date.

```
         1         2         3         4         5         6         7         8         9        10
1234567890123456789012345678901234567890123456789012345678901234567890123456789012345678901234567890
 1  XX/XX/XX                    WEXLER UNIVERSITY                    PAGE XXØX
 2                           FACULTY EARNINGS REPORT
 3
 4                                                              NO. YEARS
 5     DEPT.          NAME              RANK  SEX    SALARY      EMPLOYED
 6
 7     XXX    XXXXXXXXXXXXXXXXXXXXXXXXXX  X    X    XXX,XXØ.XX      ØX
 8            XXXXXXXXXXXXXXXXXXXXXXXXXX  X    X    XXX,XXØ.XX      ØX
 9
10     XXX    XXXXXXXXXXXXXXXXXXXXXXXXXX  X    X    XXX,XXØ.XX      ØX
11            XXXXXXXXXXXXXXXXXXXXXXXXXX  X    X    XXX,XXØ.XX      ØX
12            XXXXXXXXXXXXXXXXXXXXXXXXXX  X    X    XXX,XXØ.XX      ØX
13
```

6. GTC needs a listing of all customers who owe a balance and have not sent in a payment within the past 30 days. The company wants this listing to be in descending order by amount owed so it can concentrate on collecting from those customers who owe the most money first. The data upon which the report is to be based is stored in GTC's customer master file, GTCSTP (Appendix F). The desired listing format is shown below. The customer name should be a trimmed concatenation of first name followed by the last name (with a blank separator).

```
         1         2         3         4         5         6         7         8         9        10
1234567890123456789012345678901234567890123456789012345678901234567890123456789012345678901234567890
 1     XX/XX/XX              GTC OVERDUE PAYMENTS LISTING        PAGE XXØX
 2
 3      CUSTOMER                  PHONE            AMOUNT         DAYS SINCE
 4        NAME                   NUMBER             OWED         LAST PAYMENT
 5
 6    XXXXXXXXXXXXXXXXXXXXXXXXXX  (XXX) XXX-XXXX   X,XXØ.XX         XØX
 7    XXXXXXXXXXXXXXXXXXXXXXXXXX  (XXX) XXX-XXXX   X,XXØ.XX         XØX
 8    XXXXXXXXXXXXXXXXXXXXXXXXXX  (XXX) XXX-XXXX   X,XXØ.XX         XØX
 9    XXXXXXXXXXXXXXXXXXXXXXXXXX  (XXX) XXX-XXXX   X,XXØ.XX         XØX
10
11
```

Chapter 12

Advanced Functions and Error Handling

 ## Chapter Overview

This chapter covers a variety of RPG IV built-in functions and operations that let you inspect or manipulate individual positions or bytes within a field. In addition, the chapter shows you how to work with character strings, combining them and working with portions of them. You'll also learn how to work with bit patterns and when such manipulations are needed. Last, we'll discuss several error-handling techniques you can use to make your programs more reliable.

Although all the topics included in this chapter deal with data, they are basically independent, standalone concepts. You can incorporate any or all of these concepts within your programs to improve your programming style.

Field Inspection

RPG IV includes built-in functions and operations that let you inspect or manipulate individual bytes, or even bits of bytes, within data fields. These features provide options for processing data at a level that otherwise would be beyond our capabilities. Several RPG IV built-in functions and operations let you inspect the size and properties of data items or test individual positions, or bytes, within a character field.

%SIZE (Get Size in Bytes)

The **%SIZE** (Get Size in Bytes) built-in function returns the number of bytes, or length, of its argument. The function requires at least one parameter, which represents the data item whose size you want. You can use %SIZE to determine the size of a field, literal, named constant, data structure, subfield, array, or table. If the argument has only a single parameter and that parameter is the name of an array, table, or multiple-occurrence data structure, the returned value is the size of a single element or occurrence. If a second parameter, *ALL, follows the first, the returned value is the size of the entire table, array, or data structure.

The following examples demonstrate how to use %SIZE. Notice that the argument containing two parameters uses a colon (:) to separate them.

```
*.. 1 ...+... 2 ...+... 3 ...+... 4 ...+... 5 ...+... 6 ...+... 7 ...+... 8
 /FREE
  // Obtain the size of a field.
    SIZ = %SIZE(FieldA);
  // Obtain the size of one array element.
    SIZ = %SIZE(ArrayX);
  // Obtain the size of an entire table.
    SIZ = %SIZE(TableX:*ALL);
  // Obtain the size of a literal.
    SIZ = %SIZE('gurubesar');
 /END-FREE
```

When you use %SIZE to determine the length of a packed decimal value or a binary value, remember that it returns the number of bytes used to store the value, not the number of digits in the value. %SIZE always returns the declared byte size, regardless of the current value of the field. Consider the following examples:

```
*.. 1 ...+... 2 ...+... 3 ...+... 4 ...+... 5 ...+... 6 ...+... 7 ...+... 8
DName+++++++++++ETDsFrom+++To/L+++IDc.Keywords+++++++++++++++++++++++++++++
D Salary          S              5P 0
D BNumber         S              3B 0
D NumOfBytes      S              2  0

 /FREE
  // If Salary = 48600;
  // NumOfBytes = (number of digits + 1)/2 = (5 + 1)/2 = 3,
  // applying the formula from Chapter 6.
    NumOfBytes = %SIZE(Salary);

  // Suppose BNumber stores 750; NumOfBytes = 2, because 750 requires two
  // bytes to store its base 2 representation (1011101110).
    NumOfBytes = %SIZE(BNumber);
 /END-FREE
```

Programmers sometimes find the %SIZE function helpful when defining other data items, as shown in the next set of examples.

```
*.. 1 ...+... 2 ...+... 3 ...+... 4 ...+... 5 ...+... 6 ...+... 7 ...+... 8
DName+++++++++++ETDsFrom+++To/L+++IDc.Keywords+++++++++++++++++++++++++++++
  // Definition Specifications showing BIF %SIZE used to define data items
D FieldA          S             25

  // Number of elements of ArrayA based on the length of FieldA
D ArrayA          S              3    DIM(%SIZE(FieldA))

  // Initial value of Indx set to length of FieldA
D Indx            S              2  0 INZ(%SIZE(FieldA))

  // Constant MaxVal equals the entire length of ArrayA
D MaxVal          C                   CONST(%SIZE(ArrayA:*ALL))
```

%LEN (Get or Set Length)

The **%LEN** (Get or Set Length) function returns the number of digits or characters in an expression. %LEN is especially useful with character expressions, to determine the number of significant characters in the value of the expression. For numeric expressions, %LEN returns the precision of the expression, not necessarily the number of significant digits in the calculated value of the expression. For all other data types, %LEN returns the number of bytes, giving the same result as the %SIZE function. Here are some examples of the %LEN function:

```
*.. 1 ...+... 2 ...+... 3 ...+... 4 ...+... 5 ...+... 6 ...+... 7 ...+... 8
DName+++++++++++ETDsFrom+++To/L+++IDc.Keywords+++++++++++++++++++++++++++++
D Salary          S              9P 2 INZ(48600)
D Tenure          S              5P 0 INZ(1)
D FirstName       S             15    INZ('John')
D LastName        S             15    INZ('Doe')
D FullName        S             15    VARYING INZ('John Doe')

 /FREE
  // Length1 = 9, because Salary has 9 digits precision
    Length1 = %LEN(Salary);
  // Length2 = 14, the total precision (number of digits) of the expression
    Length2 = %LEN(Salary * Tenure);
```

continued...

continued...

```
  // Length3 and Size1 each will have a value of 15
    Length3 = %LEN(FirstName);
    Size1 = %SIZE(FirstName);
  // Length4 = 30
    Length4 = %LEN(FirstName + LastName);
  // Length5 = 4
    Length5 = %LEN(%TRIM(FirstName));
  // Length6 = 8
    Length6 = %LEN(%TRIM(FirstName) + ' ' + %TRIM(LastName));
  // Length7 = 8, Size7 = 15
    Length7 = %LEN(FullName);
    Size7 = %SIZE(FullName);
 /END-FREE
```

The fifth and sixth examples above also make use of the %TRIM built-in function, which trims the blanks from a string. We'll discuss %TRIM shortly. The last example shows %LEN used with a variable-length field (defined with VARYING). When used with variable-length fields, %LEN returns the *current length* of the field, which is dependent on the field's value; %SIZE returns the *declared length*, regardless of the field's value.

%DECPOS (Get Number of Decimal Positions)

The **%DECPOS** (Get Number of Decimal Positions) function returns the number of decimal positions in a numeric variable or expression. %DECPOS is sometimes used with the %LEN function to examine a data item or expression.

```
*.. 1 ...+... 2 ...+... 3 ...+... 4 ...+... 5 ...+... 6 ...+... 7 ...+... 8
DName++++++++++ETDsFrom+++To/L+++IDc.Keywords+++++++++++++++++++++++++++++++
D Salary          S              9P 2 INZ(48600)

 /FREE
    Length = %LEN(Salary);          // Length = 9
    Decimals = %DECPOS(Salary);     // Decimals = 2
 /END-FREE
```

%ELEM (Get Number of Elements)

Another size-related built-in function RPG IV supports is **%ELEM** (Get Number of Elements), which returns the number of elements in an array or a table or the number of occurrences in a multiple-occurrence data structure. Like %SIZE and %LEN, you can use %ELEM in calculations or when defining other fields. The latter use can result in code that is self-documented and easy to maintain, as the following example demonstrates.

```
*.. 1 ...+... 2 ...+... 3 ...+... 4 ...+... 5 ...+... 6 ...+... 7 ...+... 8
DName++++++++++ETDsFrom+++To/L+++IDc.Keywords+++++++++++++++++++++++++++++++
  // Example showing how to use BIF %ELEM within field definitions
D NumLocats       C                   CONST(100)
D NumMonths       C                   CONST(12)
D Location        S              4  0 DIM(NumLocats)
D MonthSales      DS                  OCCURS(NumMonths)
D   LocatTotal                   10  2 DIM(%ELEM(Location))
D Projection      DS                  OCCURS(%ELEM(MonthSales))
D   LocatProj                    10  2 DIM(%ELEM(LocatTotal))
```

In this example, array Location stores four-digit code numbers for 100 shop locations. MonthSales is a multiple-occurrence data structure that contains an array of monthly sales totals for each location. Projection is the same type of data structure, but it stores monthly sales projections for each location.

If the number of shop locations changes over time or the number of months per sales cycle changes, you need only update the named constants and recompile the program; the number of elements allocated for MonthSales and Projection will be adjusted automatically.

The following example shows how you might use %ELEM within Calculation Specifications.

```
*.. 1 ...+... 2 ...+... 3 ...+... 4 ...+... 5 ...+... 6 ...+... 7 ...+... 8
 /FREE
  // Assume field Indx was defined as a 4-digit integer value.
   FOR Indx = 1 to %ELEM(LocatTotal);
     . . .
   ENDDO;
```

In this example, we've matched the number of passes through the loop to the number of elements in LocatTotal. Should the number of locations change over time, you would not have to make any changes to these Calculation Specifications — the number of loop passes would automatically adjust to the updated number of elements of LocatTotal.

TESTN (Test Numeric)

You can use the TESTN (Test Numeric) operation to determine whether a character field contains all numeric characters, leading blanks followed by all numeric characters, or all blanks. The operation is useful for validating fields before you use them in mathematical operations or try to edit the fields, to prevent an abnormal program ending that would occur if the data were non-numeric. Because you can use TESTN only with character fields, you would need to move the field's value to a numeric field after validation or redefine the field as a numeric variable within a data structure before using it for arithmetic or editing.

TESTN works only with the fixed-format Calculation Specifications. The TESTN operation does not use Factors 1 and 2; the field to be tested occurs as the Result field. You must use at least one resulting indicator with this operation. Where you position that indicator depends on what you're trying to test for. You can, if you like, use indicators in all three resulting indicator positions.

An indicator specified in positions 71–72 (Hi) is turned on if all the characters within the field are numeric. An indicator in positions 73–74 (Lo) is turned on if the Result field contains numeric characters and one or more leading blanks. An indicator in positions 75–76 (Eq) is turned on if the Result field contains all blanks.

Because of the way RPG IV handles signed numbers, the rightmost character of the field may contain the EBCDIC representation of A–R and still be considered numeric because these are the same representations as signed (+ or –) digits 0–9.

Study the following examples to understand the use of indicators with this operation.

```
*.. 1 ...+... 2 ...+... 3 ...+... 4 ...+... 5 ...+... 6 ...+... 7 ...+... 8
CLØN01Factor1++++++Opcode(E)+Factor2++++++Result++++++++Len++D+HiLoEq....
 * TESTN with an indicator in the Hi position
C                   TESTN                   FieldA                10
```

Given the TESTN operation coded above, indicator 10, entered in the Hi resulting indicator position, would be off or on, depending on the value of FieldA:

FieldA	*IN10	Explanation
'123'	ON	Every character is numeric.
'1A3'	OFF	A is not numeric.
'12C'	ON	C is interpreted as positively signed 3.

If you included several indicators along with the TESTN operation, at most one would be turned on as a result of the check:

```
*.. 1 ...+... 2 ...+... 3 ...+... 4 ...+... 5 ...+... 6 ...+... 7 ...+... 8
CLØNØ1Factor1++++++Opcode(E)+Factor2++++++Result++++++++Len++D+HiLoEq....
 * TESTN with three resulting indicators specified
C                    TESTN               FieldA                    102030
```

The following table shows what the status of indicators 10, 20, and 30 would be following the TESTN above, given different values for FieldA.

FieldA	*IN10	*IN20	*IN30	Explanation
'123'	ON	OFF	OFF	All characters are digits.
' 23'	OFF	ON	OFF	Leading blank is present.
' 3'	OFF	ON	OFF	Both blanks are leading.
'1 3'	OFF	OFF	OFF	Blank is not leading.
' '	OFF	OFF	ON	All characters are blanks.
'A2C'	OFF	OFF	OFF	A is not a digit.

TEST (Test Date/Time/Timestamp)

The TEST (Test Date/Time/Timestamp) operation is similar to TESTN except that it checks the validity of date, time, or timestamp fields. You code the field to be tested as the Result field and leave Factor 1 and Factor 2 blank. The %ERROR function is turned on if the Result field contains an invalid date/time value. The following examples demonstrate this use of the TEST operation.

```
*.. 1 ...+... 2 ...+... 3 ...+... 4 ...+... 5 ...+... 6 ...+... 7 ...+... 8
 /FREE
  // Fields TodaysDate and StartTime are date (D) and time (T) data types.
   TEST(E) TodaysDate;
   TEST(E) StartTime;
 /END-FREE
```

To use TEST to check character and numeric fields for valid date/time data, you must include an operation extender (D for date, T for time, Z for timestamp) to identify which test you want to perform. Be sure to also include the (E) extender to support the %ERROR function. Factor 1 contains the date/time display format (e.g., *MDY, *USA) that you want to compare with your data. If Factor 1 is blank, RPG IV compares your data using the format specified in the Control Specification DATFMT keyword (or with the default *ISO format if there is no Control Specification keyword). Consider the following examples, in which UserDate and UserTime are numeric fields.

```
*.. 1 ...+... 2 ...+... 3 ...+... 4 ...+... 5 ...+... 6 ...+... 7 ...+... 8
 /FREE
   UserDate = 19950315;
   TEST(DE) UserDate;
 // Factor 1 is blank, so UserDate is checked to see whether it stores a
 // valid *ISO date; %ERROR is set off because the value is a valid date
 // for the default format.

   UserTime = 180000;
   TEST(TE) *HMS UserTime;
 // UserTime is a valid *HMS time value, so %ERROR is set off.
```

continued...

continued...

```
   UserDate = 12311995;
   TEST(DE) *EUR UserDate;
 // Now UserDate is tested to see whether it is a valid *EUR date value
 // (dd.mm.yyyy). Because it is not a valid date in this format,
 // %ERROR is set on.
/END-FREE
```

When testing the date/time validity of character fields, RPG IV also checks to see whether valid separator characters are included in the field. Assume UserDate is a 10-byte character field and UserTime is an eight-byte character field in the following examples.

```
*.. 1 ...+... 2 ...+... 3 ...+... 4 ...+... 5 ...+... 6 ...+... 7 ...+... 8
/FREE
   UserDate = '1995-03-15';
   TEST(DE) UserDate;
 // %ERROR is set off because UserDate is a valid *ISO date.

   UserTime = '18-00-00';
   TEST(TE) *HMS UserTime;
 // The hyphen (-) is not a valid separator for *HMS format,
 // so %ERROR is set on.

   UserTime2 = '180000';
   TEST(TE) *HMS0 UserTime2
 // The zero in Factor 1 (*HMS0) indicates that no separators should be
// present; %ERROR is set off.
/END-FREE
```

%SCAN (Scan String)

The **%SCAN** (Scan String) built-in function lets you look for a character or a string of characters within a character field. The direction of the scan is left to right. %SCAN takes the form

```
%SCAN(search-arg:string{:start})
```

%SCAN searches the string for the search argument, beginning with the specified start position (or beginning at position 1, if you don't specify a starting position). %SCAN is case sensitive; that is, 'A' is not the same as 'a'. If the string you are looking for includes blanks — whether leading, trailing, or embedded — the blanks are considered part of the pattern to find. Similarly, blanks within the searched field are not ignored. The function returns an integer value that represents the next position of the search argument in the source string; if the search argument is not found, the function returns a zero (the %FOUND function is not affected).

```
*.. 1 ...+... 2 ...+... 3 ...+... 4 ...+... 5 ...+... 6 ...+... 7 ...+... 8
/FREE
 // Search for FieldA within FieldB.
   Position = %SCAN(FieldA:FieldB);

 // Search for slash (/) character in FullName.
 // If FullName = 'DOE/JOHN' then Position = 4
   Position = %SCAN('/':FullName);

 // Look for FieldA in FieldB, beginning with the 3rd position of FieldB.
   Position = %SCAN(FieldA:FieldB:3);
/END-FREE
```

The %SCAN function is useful for inspecting text data. You could use it, for example, to scan addresses to locate all businesses or customers residing on the same street. Text-retrieval software uses operations like %SCAN to index text based on the presence of keywords within the text.

%CHECK (Check Characters)

The format of the **%CHECK** (Check Characters) function is similar to that of %SCAN. The first argument contains a character compare field, and the second contains a source or base string.

```
%CHECK(compare-str:string{:start})
```

Significant differences exist between %CHECK and %SCAN, however. %SCAN looks for the presence of the entire compare string within the base string and returns the location of its occurrence. %CHECK verifies that each character in the source string is among the valid characters in the compare string. If there is a mismatch, %CHECK returns the location of the mismatch; otherwise, if all the characters in the source string also appear in the compare string, %CHECK returns a zero.

%SCAN is used for locating substrings within a base string, while %CHECK is useful for verification of characters within the base string.

```
*.. 1 ...+... 2 ...+... 3 ...+... 4 ...+... 5 ...+... 6 ...+... 7 ...+... 8
 /FREE
    InvalidPos = %CHECK(LookFor:LookIn);
 /END-FREE
```

The compare string, represented in a character field, literal, named constant, data structure, array element, or table name, contains a list of valid characters. The base string contains the character field, literal, named constant, data structure, array element, or table name whose characters you want checked against those of the data item in the compare string. If %CHECK returns a nonzero number, that number is the first position in the string that contains a character not in the compare string.

The %CHECKR (Check Characters (Reversed)) function works exactly like %CHECK, except that it checks the base string from right to left rather than from left to right. You can use this operation to locate the rightmost invalid character in a string or to determine the length of a string of nonblank characters in a field.

```
*.. 1 ...+... 2 ...+... 3 ...+... 4 ...+... 5 ...+... 6 ...+... 7 ...+... 8
 /FREE
  // Assume Name contains 'Jones         '.
    Length = %CHECKR(' ':Name);
  // Length has a value of 5, the position of the rightmost nonblank
  // character of Name.
```

String Operation Codes

Some of the RPG IV programs you maintain might use a string operation code instead of the built-in function. The following operation codes are restricted to the fixed-format Calculation Specification.

The SCAN (Scan String) Operation

The SCAN (Scan String) operation, analogous to the %SCAN function, lets you look for a character or a string of characters within a character field. SCAN requires the search argument in Factor 1 and the base string in Factor 2. The %FOUND function is turned on if the SCAN is successful.

```
*.. 1 ...+... 2 ...+... 3 ...+... 4 ...+... 5 ...+... 6 ...+... 7 ...+... 8
CLØN01Factor1+++++++Opcode(E)+Factor2+++++++Result+++++++Len++D+HiLoEq....
 * Sample format of the SCAN operation. Look for FieldA's contents within
 * FieldB and turn on %FOUND if the string is found.
C     FieldA        SCAN      FieldB
C                   IF        %FOUND
 . . .
C                   ENDIF
```

Factor 1 contains the string you're looking for, sometimes called the compare string. This may be represented by a character field, array element, named constant, data structure name, literal, or table name. Moreover, you can specify that only a portion of the data item be used as the string to search for by following the data item with a colon (:) followed by an integer length, expressed as a literal, field, named constant, array element, or table name. The length determines how much of the Factor 1 entry the operation scans for.

For example, Factor 1 could be Code, in which case the entire value of the Code field would be the compare string, or it could be Code:3, in which case the first three characters of the Code field would be the compare string. If Factor 1 were Code:X, the value of X would determine how many characters of Code constituted the compare string.

Factor 2 contains the string to be scanned, sometimes called the base string. The base string can be a character field, array element, named constant, data structure name, literal, or table name. The base string can be followed by a colon, followed in turn by an integer literal, field, named constant, or array element that represents the starting location for the scan within the string. For example, if Factor 2 contains Name, the entire Name field will be scanned; if Factor 2 contains Name:4, the scan will begin at the fourth character in the Name field. The following examples illustrate using the various forms of Factor 1 and Factor 2.

```
*.. 1 ...+... 2 ...+... 3 ...+... 4 ...+... 5 ...+... 6 ...+... 7 ...+... 8
CLØN01Factor1+++++++Opcode(E)+Factor2+++++++Result+++++++Len++D+HiLoEq....
 * SCAN operations showing variant formats of Factor 1 and Factor 2

 * Search for FieldA within FieldB.
C     FieldA        SCAN      FieldB

 * Search string begins with the 4th character of FieldA; scan all of
 * FieldB.
C     FieldA:4      SCAN      FieldB

 * Look for all of FieldA in FieldB, beginning with the 3rd position
 * of FieldB.
C     FieldA        SCAN      FieldB:3

 * Look for a portion of FieldA within a portion of FieldB; the length of
 * FieldA's substring and the starting position within FieldB are based on
 * variables.
C     FieldA:X      SCAN      FieldB:Y
```

continued...

continued...

You can also include an optional Result field with SCAN. The result can be a field, array element, array name, or table name, but it must be defined as a numeric data type with no decimal positions (i.e., an integer). If a Result field is present and it is anything other than an array name, the SCAN operation will stop as soon as it locates an occurrence of the compare string within the base string, and a number representing the starting position of the compare string within the base string will be stored in the Result field. If the compare string is not found within the base string, the Result field will be set to 0.

To get a feeling for how SCAN works with a Result field, consider the following example.

```
*.. 1 ...+... 2 ...+... 3 ...+... 4 ...+... 5 ...+... 6 ...+... 7 ...+... 8
CLØNØ1Factor1++++++Opcode(E)+Factor2++++++Result++++++++Len++D+HiLoEq....
 * Sample SCAN with Result field, Found, a numeric integer field.
C       LookFor      SCAN      LookIn       Found
```

The following table shows the effects this SCAN operation would have on the contents of Found and %FOUND when LookFor = 'my' and LookIn takes on various values.

Field values		Results		
LookFor	**LookIn**	**Found**	**%FOUND**	**Explanation**
'my'	'Do it my way'	7	ON	Match of 'my' and 'my'.
'my'	'Amy knows best.'	2	ON	Match of 'my' and 'my'.
'my'	'It may harm you.'	0	OFF	'my' is not 'may' or 'm y'.
'my'	'My way is best.'	0	OFF	'my' is not 'My'.
'my'	'Amy knows my dad.'	2	ON	Stops at first 'my' match.

If the Result field is an array name, the SCAN does not stop when it finds the first match but instead continues to the end of the base field. The starting locations of each occurrence of the compare string within the base string are stored in successive elements of the array. If the array contains more elements than the number of compare-string occurrences within the base string, the unneeded array elements are set to 0.

```
*.. 1 ...+... 2 ...+... 3 ...+... 4 ...+... 5 ...+... 6 ...+... 7 ...+... 8
CLØNØ1Factor1++++++Opcode(E)+Factor2++++++Result++++++++Len++D+HiLoEq....
 * In the examples below, assume that FieldA's value is 'abcde',
 * while FieldB is 'mabcdeabczab'.
 * The comment below each example explains the results of the SCAN.

C       FieldA:3      SCAN      FieldB       FieldC
 * FieldC is 2 and %FOUND is on because compare value 'abc' is found
 * in FieldB at position 2.

C       FieldA:3      SCAN      FieldB:3     FieldC
 * FieldC is 7 and %FOUND is on because SCAN starts in position 3 of
 * FieldB.

C       FieldA:4      SCAN      FieldB:3     FieldC
 * FieldC is Ø and %FOUND is off because 'abcd' is not found
 * from position 3 to the end of FieldB.

C       FieldA:2      SCAN      FieldB       Arry
 * Arry is a 5-element array. Its values are 2, 7, 11, Ø, and Ø because
 * 'ab' was found in positions 2, 7, and 11 of FieldB. %FOUND is on.
```

When coding the SCAN operation, you optionally can include the (E) extender to monitor for the %ERROR function, which will be turned on if an error occurs during the operation.

continued...

String Operation Codes ... Continued

The CHECK (Check Characters) Operation

The CHECK (Check Characters) operation is similar to the %CHECK function. CHECK verifies that each character in Factor 2 is among the valid characters in Factor 1; if there is a mismatch, CHECK stores the location of the mismatch in the Result field.

```
*.. 1 ...+... 2 ...+... 3 ...+... 4 ...+... 5 ...+... 6 ...+... 7 ...+... 8
CLØNØ1Factor1+++++++Opcode(E)+Factor2+++++++Result++++++++Len++D+HiLoEq....
 * Example showing format of CHECK
C     LookFor         CHECK     LookIn          NotFound
```

The Factor 1 value of CHECK, represented in a character field, literal, named constant, data structure, array element, or table name, contains a list of valid characters. Factor 2 contains the character field, literal, named constant, data structure, array element, or table name whose characters you want checked against those of the data item in Factor 1. The Result field contains a numeric field, array element, data structure, table, or array name.

The CHECK operation proceeds from left to right as it checks the characters of the base string against those in the compare string. If the Result field is anything other than an array name, CHECK stores in it the position of the first character of the base string not found in the compare string. If all the base-string characters are present in the compare string, the Result field is set to 0. If the Result field is an array name, the CHECK operation does not stop at the first mismatch but continues to store the positions of unmatched base-string characters in successive elements of the named array. Unneeded array elements are set to 0.

As with the SCAN operation, you can use the colon notation with the base string to specify the position within the base string where the CHECK operation is to begin; the value represented by the field or literal following the colon determines the starting location for the CHECK.

If you don't need to know the position of invalid characters but simply want to know whether the base string contains one or more invalid characters, you can omit a Result field entry. The %FOUND function will be turned on if CHECK finds one or more incorrect characters in Factor 2.

```
*.. 1 ...+... 2 ...+... 3 ...+... 4 ...+... 5 ...+... 6 ...+... 7 ...+... 8
CLØNØ1Factor1+++++++Opcode(E)+Factor2+++++++Result++++++++Len++D+HiLoEq....
 * Examples illustrating the CHECK operation

 * Assume field Code contains 'X'.
C     'ABCDE'         CHECK     Code
C* %FOUND is turned on because X is not a character within Factor 1.

 * Assume Digits contains 'Ø123456789' and Amount contains '$125.50'.
```

continued...

Character Field Manipulation

RPG IV provides several features that enable string manipulation. These operations and functions let you change individual characters or strings of characters within a field.

+ (Concatenate Character Strings)

Using the + (Concatenate Character Strings) operator with EVAL is a convenient way to concatenate two (or more) strings to form a new string. You can combine string literals, named constants, and character fields in a free-form expression using one or more occurrences of +, coded in the extended Factor 2 region of the Calculation Specification. The following examples demonstrate how to use + to concatenate strings.

continued...

```
C     Digits          CHECK     Amount        Reslt
 * %FOUND is turned on and Reslt is 1 because the 1st-position character
 * of Amount, the $, is not contained within Digits.

 * Assume Digits contains '0123456789', Amount contains '$125.50',
 * and Arry is a 5-element numeric array.
C     Digits          CHECK     Amount        Arry
 * Arry(1) is 1 (position of $); Arry(2) is 5 (position of the decimal
 * point); the remaining array elements' values are 0. %FOUND is on.

 * Assume Digits contains '0123456789', Amount contains '$125.50',
 * and Arry is a 5-element numeric array.
C     Digits          CHECK     Amount:2      Arry
 * Arry(1) is 5 (position of the decimal point); all other elements are 0.
 * The position of the $ is not noted because the CHECK begins with
 * the 2nd position of Amount.
```

The CHECKR (Check Reverse) operation works exactly like CHECK, except that it checks the base string from right to left rather than from left to right. It is similar to the %CHECKR function.

```
*.. 1 ...+... 2 ...+... 3 ...+... 4 ...+... 5 ...+... 6 ...+... 7 ...+... 8
CL0N01Factor1++++++Opcode(E)+Factor2++++++Result++++++++Len++D+HiLoEq....
 * Examples of CHECKR

 * Assume field Code contains 'X'.
C     'ABCDE'         CHECKR    Code
C* %FOUND is turned on because X is not a character within Factor 1.

 * Assume Digits contains '0123456789' and Amount contains '$125.50'.
C     Digits          CHECKR    Amount        Reslt
 * %FOUND comes on, and Reslt is 5, because the 5th-position character
 * of Amount, the decimal point, is not contained within Digits.

 * Assume Digits contains '0123456789', Amount contains '$125.50',
 * and Arry is a 5-element numeric array.
C     Digits          CHECKR    Amount        Arry
 * Arry(1) is 5 (position of the decimal point); Arry(2) is 1 (position
 * of $); the remaining array elements' values are 0. %FOUND is on.

 * Assume Name contains 'Jones            '.
C     ' '             CHECKR    Name          Length
 * Length has a value of 5, the position of the rightmost nonblank
 * character of Name.
```

```
*.. 1 ...+... 2 ...+... 3 ...+... 4 ...+... 5 ...+... 6 ...+... 7 ...+... 8
/FREE
   Greeting = 'Hello ' + 'World';   // Greeting now contains 'Hello World'

   FullName = FirstName + ' ' + MidInitial + '. ' + LastName;
 // FullName contains the contents of field FirstName followed immediately
 // by a space, the contents of MidInitial, a period and another space,
 // and the contents of LastName.
/END-FREE
```

In the name example above, if FirstName contained the value 'Susan', MidInitial contained the value 'B', and LastName contained 'Anthony', FullName's value would be 'Susan B. Anthony'. However, if FirstName and LastName were both of length 10 and right-padded with blanks, FullName would retain the extra blanks: 'Susan   B. Anthony   '. To eliminate such unneeded blanks, RPG IV provides three built-in functions, which we'll discuss in the next section.

If the concatenated string is smaller than the result field to which it is assigned, EVAL right-pads the result field with blanks. If the concatenated string is too large to fit in the result field to which it is assigned, truncation occurs from the right end of the string.

```
*.. 1 ...+... 2 ...+... 3 ...+... 4 ...+... 5 ...+... 6 ...+... 7 ...+... 8
/FREE
  // The examples below are based on FName (5 positions), with a value of
  // 'John '; LName (12 positions), with a value of 'Jackson III ';
  // WholeName (25 positions); and ShortName (10 positions).

   WholeName = FName + LName;
  // WholeName contains 'John Jackson III          ', with blanks appearing
  // in its unused rightmost positions.

   ShortName = FName + LName
  // ShortName contains 'John Jacks'
  // because it can store only 10 characters.
/END-FREE
```

%TRIM, %TRIML, and %TRIMR (Trim Blanks)

Three built-in functions — **%TRIM** (Trim Blanks at Edges), **%TRIML** (Trim Leading Blanks), and **%TRIMR** (Trim Trailing Blanks) — remove leading and/or trailing blanks from their arguments. These functions each require a single argument, which must be a character data item. %TRIML removes leading, or leftmost, blanks from the argument; %TRIMR removes trailing, or rightmost, blanks; and %TRIM removes both leading and trailing blanks. The value returned by these functions is the trimmed result, a character string. You can use the trim functions with character variables, constants, or expressions. The following examples show how these trimming functions work.

Function	Returned value
%TRIML(' 1234 N. 25th St. ')	'1234 N. 25th St. '
%TRIMR(' 1234 N. 25th St. ')	' 1234 N. 25th St.'
%TRIM(' 1234 N. 25th St. ')	'1234 N. 25th St.'

```
*.. 1 ...+... 2 ...+... 3 ...+... 4 ...+... 5 ...+... 6 ...+... 7 ...+... 8
DName++++++++++ETDsFrom+++To/L+++IDc.Keywords+++++++++++++++++++++++++++++++
D FullName        S             30
D FirstName       S             15     INZ('John')
D LastName        S             15     INZ('Doe')

 /FREE
    LeftText = %TRIML(TextLine); // Left justification using %TRIML.

  // Concatenate first and last name, with one space in between.
    FullName = %TRIMR(FirstName) + ' ' + %TRIM(LastName);
  // FullName would have a value of 'John Doe'.

   Length5 = %LEN(%TRIM(FirstName));                         // Length5=4

   Length6 = %LEN(%TRIM(FirstName) + ' ' + %TRIM(LastName)); // Length6=8
 /END-FREE
```

Note in the preceding example that if FullName, FirstName, and LastName had been variable-length fields (defined with keyword VARYING), %TRIMming the blanks would have been unnecessary:

```
*.. 1 ...+... 2 ...+... 3 ...+... 4 ...+... 5 ...+... 6 ...+... 7 ...+... 8
DName++++++++++ETDsFrom+++To/L+++IDc.Keywords+++++++++++++++++++++++++++++++
D FullName        S              30      VARYING
D FirstName       S              15      INZ('John') VARYING
D LastName        S              15      INZ('Doe') VARYING

 /FREE
  // Concatenate first and last name, with one space in between.
   FullName = FirstName + ' ' + LastName;         // FullName = 'John Doe'

   Length5 = %LEN(FirstName);                               // Length5 = 4

   Length6 = %LEN(FirstName + ' ' + LastName);             // Length6 = 8
 /END-FREE
```

%SUBST (Get Substring)

Built-in function **%SUBST** (Get Substring) extracts a substring, or portion, of a character string. The argument parameters of %SUBST are, in order, the string from which the extraction is to occur, the position within that string where the substring is to start, and, optionally, the length of the substring. If you omit this third parameter, the substring will include all the bytes from the starting position to the final, rightmost byte of the string. Thus, the format of the substring function is

```
%SUBST(string:start{:length})
```

As shown above, you use colon separators between parameters. You can represent the starting position and the optional length using numeric variables, constants, or expressions that evaluate to integers greater than zero. If the length is too big given the starting position (i.e., the substring would extend beyond the end of the string), a runtime error will occur.

```
*.. 1 ...+... 2 ...+... 3 ...+... 4 ...+... 5 ...+... 6 ...+... 7 ...+... 8
 /FREE
  // Examples of accessing portions of character string
  // Phone (e.g., '9705551212') using %SUBST.
   AreaCode = %SUBST(Phone:1:3);
  // AreaCode contains the first three characters of Phone.
   Exchange = %SUBST(Phone:4:3);
  // Exchange contains the 4th, 5th, and 6th characters of Phone.
   Local = %SUBST(Phone:7);
  // Local contains all the characters of Phone from position 7 through
  // the end of the string.

  // Example demonstrating how to change Name from the form
  // 'Yaeger, Judy' to 'Judy Yaeger'.
   CommaPlace = %SCAN(',':Name);
   FirstName = %SUBST(Name:CommaPlace + 2);
   LastName = %SUBST(Name:1:CommaPlace - 1);
   NewName = %TRIM(FirstName) + ' ' + %TRIM(LastName);

  // The following code is equivalent.
   FirstName = %SUBST(Name:%SCAN(',':Name) + 2);
   LastName = %SUBST(Name:1:%SCAN(',':Name) - 1);
   NewName = %TRIM(FirstName) + ' ' + %TRIM(LastName);

  // The following code is also equivalent.
   NewName = %SUBST(Name:%SCAN(',':Name) + 2) + ' ' +
             %SUBST(Name:1:%SCAN(',':Name) - 1);
 /END-FREE
```

Like the other built-in functions we've discussed, %SUBST can be used to return a value needed within a calculation, as shown in the examples above. Unlike the other functions, you can also use %SUBST as the target (or result) of an EVAL assignment operation to change the value of a designated substring. For this use, the designated string must be a variable that can be assigned a value; a constant, for example, would be inappropriate. The following example illustrates this use of %SUBST.

```
*.. 1 ...+... 2 ...+... 3 ...+... 4 ...+... 5 ...+... 6 ...+... 7 ...+... 8
/FREE
  // In this example, '616' replaces the first three characters of Phone.
    %SUBST(Phone:1:3) = '616';
/END-FREE
```

%DEC (Convert to Packed Decimal Format)

The **%DEC** (Convert to Packed Decimal Format) function converts the result of an expression to a packed decimal format of the precision you specify. This function can be useful when you need to force the result of an expression into a specific data format or to avoid overflow. The numeric expression is coded as the first parameter within parentheses following %DEC. The next two parameters indicate the number of digits and the number of decimal positions in the result.

```
*.. 1 ...+... 2 ...+... 3 ...+... 4 ...+... 5 ...+... 6 ...+... 7 ...+... 8
/FREE
    Result = %DEC(Hours*Rate:7:2);

  // This formula calculates a monthly payment, converting it to a 13-digit
  // packed number with two decimal places.
    Payment = %DEC(Principal * (((Interest / 12) *
                  (1 + (Interest / 12)) ** Months) /
                  (((1 + (Interest / 12)) ** Months) - 1))
                  : 13 : 2);

  // This formula converts an expression to a packed number, with data
  // attributes matching Result.
    Result = %DEC(Hours*Rate:%LEN(Result):%DECPOS(Result));
/END-FREE
```

A related function, %DECH (Convert to Packed Decimal Format with Half Adjust), performs the same data conversion, but half-adjusts the result. In total, RPG IV supports the following built-in functions to convert expressions to specific numeric representations:

- %DEC, %DECH to convert to packed decimal format
- %INT, %INTH to convert to integer format
- %UNS, %UNSH to convert to unsigned integer format
- %FLOAT to convert to floating-point format

Here are some additional examples of the integer-related functions:

```
*.. 1 ...+... 2 ...+... 3 ...+... 4 ...+... 5 ...+... 6 ...+... 7 ...+... 8
/FREE
  // Find the area of a circle as a rounded whole number.
    Result = %INTH(3.14159 * Radius**2);

  // Truncate the decimal positions from a packed number,
  // to allow it to be used as an array element (no rounding).
    X = %UNS(HrsWorked);
/END-FREE
```

Version 5 Release 2 Update

Version 5 Release 2 now supports character expressions as arguments to the %DEC (Convert to Packed Decimal Format), %DECH (Convert to Packed Decimal Format with Half Adjust), **%INT** (Convert to Integer Format), %INTH (Convert to Integer Format with Half Adjust), %UNS (Convert to Unsigned Integer Format), %UNSH (Convert to Unsigned Integer Format with Half Adjust), and %FLOAT (Convert to Floating Point) functions. Before V5R2, the expressions had to be numeric. The new support affords your program an easy way to convert characters (with numeric values) to numbers. For example:

```
*.. 1 ...+... 2 ...+... 3 ...+... 4 ...+... 5 ...+... 6 ...+... 7 ...+... 8
 /FREE
    Char = '-123.56';
    Number = %DEC(Char:5:2);      // Number = -123.56
    Number = %UNSH(Char);         // Number = 124
 /END-FREE
```

Now that these functions support character expressions, they can be used to easily manipulate "legacy" date data, which is typically in a numeric format. Use the %DATE function to convert a number to a date; then use a combination of the %CHAR and %UNS functions to convert the date back to a character field, and finally to an integer:

```
*.. 1 ...+... 2 ...+... 3 ...+... 4 ...+... 5 ...+... 6 ...+... 7 ...+... 8
DName+++++++++++ETDsFrom+++To/L+++IDc.Keywords+++++++++++++++++++++++++++++++
D DueDate         S              8  0 INZ(20021231)
D WorkDate        S              D

 /FREE
    DueDate = 20021231;
    WorkDate = %DATE(DueDate:*ISO);            // WorkDate = D'2002-12-31'
    WorkDate = WorkDate + %DAYS(30);           // Add 30 days to WorkDate
    DueDate = %UNS(%CHAR(WorkDate:*ISO0));     // DueDate = 20030130
 /END-FREE
```

In this example, DueDate is a numeric field that stores a date value (typical of a legacy date field, perhaps in a database file). To perform date arithmetic on the numeric field, we first use the %DATE function to convert it to a native date field (WorkDate). After manipulating the date value in WorkDate, we use the %CHAR function, discussed in this chapter, to convert the date value to a character value and then use the %UNS function to convert that character value to an unsigned integer. The end result is a numeric value that we assign back to DueDate.

The following rules apply to character expressions used with these functions:

- The sign (+ or –) is optional, preceding or following the numeric data.
- The decimal point (. or ,) is optional.
- Blanks are allowed anywhere in the numeric data.
- Invalid numeric data will set %STATUS=00105.
- %DEC and %DECH require precision arguments (second and third arguments).
- Only %FLOAT allows floating-point data, with an optional exponent (E or e) preceding the numeric exponent.

%CHAR (Convert to Character Data)

The **%CHAR** (Convert to Character Data) function converts the result of an expression (usually numeric or date type) to a character value. If the expression is numeric, it is coded as the only argument, within parentheses following %CHAR. If the expression is a date, time, or timestamp, a second argument specifies the date format to use for the converted data. The converted date data will include separator characters unless you code a zero (0) following the format (e.g., *ISO0).

In addition to converting dates, the %CHAR function is especially useful when you need to include numeric data in a string expression. All the operands in a string expression must be in character format, so %CHAR is necessary to perform the conversion. A related function, %EDTCDE (Edit with an Edit Code), not only converts a number to a character field but also assigns an edit code (one of the same edit codes that Output Specifications and DDS support) to the number before converting it, optionally adding a currency symbol or asterisk leading fill (*****).

```
*.. 1 ...+... 2 ...+... 3 ...+... 4 ...+... 5 ...+... 6 ...+... 7 ...+... 8
DName++++++++++ETDsFrom+++To/L+++IDc.Keywords+++++++++++++++++++++++++++++++

D Message         S             80
D TodaysDate      S              D   INZ(*SYS)
D Points          S             10U 0 INZ(50273)
D Balance         S              9 2 INZ(-9876.54)

 /FREE
    Message = 'Today is ' + %CHAR(TodaysDate:*USA) + '.';
                   // Message: 'Today is 12/31/2002.'

    Message = 'Today is ' + %CHAR(TodaysDate:*MDY0) + '.';
                   // Message: 'Today is 123102.'

    Message = 'You have earned ' + %CHAR(Points) + ' Frequent Flier Miles.'
                   // Message: 'You have earned 50273 Frequent Flier Miles.'

    Message = 'Your account balance is ' + %EDTCDE(Balance:'A':'$');
                   // Message: 'Your account balance is $9,876.54CR'
 /END-FREE
```

%XLATE (Translate) Function

%XLATE (Translate) is a function that lets you translate, or convert, characters within a string to other characters. It take the form

```
%XLATE(from:to:string{:start})
```

The first two arguments serve as translation tables; the first one provides the characters that should be translated, and the second one specifies which characters they should be translated to. The third argument contains the source string to be converted. It can be a character field, array element, or table name. If you don't specify a starting location (fourth argument), the conversion starts at the first position of the source string. The function returns a translated version of the source string, which you can use in an assignment expression; you can, if you like, assign the result to the same field as the original source string.

The from string and the to string must have the same number of characters, with the characters ordered so that each character in the from string has a corresponding character in the to string. The from and to strings can be named constants, fields, literals, array elements, or table names. During execution of the %XLATE function, any character in the source string that is found in the from string is converted to the corresponding character in the to string. If a source string character does not appear in the from string, that character is unchanged in the return value.

If this sounds confusing, looking at some examples should help clarify how the %XLATE function works. The following examples convert uppercase letters to lowercase letters and vice versa; this kind of translation is the most frequent application of %XLATE. The from and to strings of alphabetic characters are defined through named constants UC and LC.

```
*.. 1 ...+... 2 ...+... 3 ...+... 4 ...+... 5 ...+... 6 ...+... 7 ...+... 8
DName++++++++++ETDsFrom+++To/L+++IDc.Keywords++++++++++++++++++++++++++++++++
  // Two named constants to serve as translation "tables"
D UC              C                   'ABCDEFGHIJKLMNOPQRSTUVWXYZ'
D LC              C                   'abcdefghijklmnopqrstuvwxyz'

 /FREE
  // LName (15 bytes) contains 'BYRNE-SMITH      '
  // Name (20 bytes) contains 'XXXXXXXXXXXXXXXXXXXX'
    Name = %XLATE(UC:LC:LName);        // Name now is 'byrne-smith         '
    Name = %XLATE(UC:LC:LName:2);      // Name now is 'Byrne-smith         '
    LName = %XLATE(UC:LC:LName:2);     // LName now is 'Byrne-smith    '

  // Assume that FieldA in the next example has a value of 'abc123ABC'.
    FieldA = %XLATE(LC:UC:FieldA);     // FieldA now is 'ABC123ABC'
 /END-FREE
```

Error Handling

Without explicit error handling within your program, any runtime error will cause the system to suspend the program and send a message to the interactive user or the system operator (when the program is running in batch). Assume you want to handle errors internally within your program rather than letting the errors cause a program **abend** (abnormal ending). You could use one of several alternative methods to handle errors.

One technique is to code the (E) error-handling extender with those operations that permit such an entry. If an error occurs during an operation that includes the (E), the %ERROR built-in function is turned on, and the program simply continues to the next sequential instruction. (Older RPG programs may use the Lo indicator, coded in positions 73–74, for the same purpose.)

```
*.. 1 ...+... 2 ...+... 3 ...+... 4 ...+... 5 ...+... 6 ...+... 7 ...+... 8
 /FREE
  // Using the (E) extender causes the program to simply continue if an
  // error occurs with any of the operations using the extender.
    READ(E) Sample;
    DOW NOT %EOF(Sample);
      CHAIN(E) Samp OtherFile;
      EXSR Calcs;
      READ(E) Sample;
    ENDDO;
 /END-FREE
```

Although this method prevents an abend of your program, it simply ignores the error — a potentially dangerous practice. A better method would be to include an error routine that the program executes immediately upon encountering an error. By checking the status of the %ERROR function after each operation that uses the (E) extender, your program could appropriately execute a special routine should any error occur.

```
*.. 1 ...+... 2 ...+... 3 ...+... 4 ...+... 5 ...+... 6 ...+... 7 ...+... 8
 /FREE
  // The %ERROR function is checked and subroutine Error executed
  // if an error occurs.
    READ(E) Sample;
    IF %ERROR;
      EXSR Error;
    ENDIF;
    DOW NOT %EOF(Sample);
      CHAIN(E) Samp OtherFile;
```

continued...

continued...

```
     IF %ERROR;
        EXSR Error;
     ENDIF;
     EXSR Calcs;
     READ(E) Sample;
     IF %ERROR;
        EXSR Error;
     ENDIF;
   ENDDO;
/END-FREE
```

The **%STATUS** (Return File or Program Status) built-in function provides the same information as the status code but without requiring a file information data structure. Usually, you'll use %STATUS in conjunction with the (E) extender and the %ERROR function, as the following example shows. You can code a file name with the %STATUS function; if you omit the file name, %STATUS will refer to the most recent change to the program or file status code.

```
*.. 1 ...+... 2 ...+... 3 ...+... 4 ...+... 5 ...+... 6 ...+... 7 ...+... 8
/FREE
  // Example of file error processing using %STATUS
    READ(E) SalesFile;
    SELECT;
      WHEN %ERROR AND %STATUS(SalesFile) = '01218';
        EXSR LockedRec;
      WHEN %ERROR;
        EXSR FileErr;
      WHEN %EOF(SalesFile);
        *INLR = *ON;
        RETURN;
      OTHER;
        EXSR Process;
    ENDSL;
/END-FREE
```

The XLATE Operation

Some programs that you maintain may use the older XLATE (Translate) operation instead of the %XLATE function. The XLATE operation is restricted to the fixed-format Calculation Specification. Factor 2 contains the source string to be converted, and the Result field specifies where the results of the translation should be placed. In Factor 2, you can use a colon and a value to designate the position where the translation is to begin (otherwise, the conversion starts at the first position of the Factor 2 string).

A Factor 1 entry supplies the from:to translation tables. The following code shows the format of an XLATE operation.

```
*.. 1 ...+... 2 ...+... 3 ...+... 4 ...+... 5 ...+... 6 ...+... 7 ...+... 8
CL0N01Factor1++++++Opcode(E)+Factor2+++++++Result++++++++Len++D+HiLoEq....
 * Sample format of XLATE operation
C     From:To       XLATE     Source        Changed
```

The Factor 2 source string and the Result field can be character fields, array elements, or table names. The Factor 1 from and to strings can be named constants, fields, literals, array elements, or table names. You can optionally use operation extender (P) to ensure that residual characters are not left in the Result field, should its length be larger than that of the source string.

Including all these checks, however, greatly increases the length of your program and still doesn't solve the problem of errors generated by operations (such as EVAL) that do not permit the use of the (E) extender.

Fortunately, two alternative methods of error trapping exist. The MONITOR and ON-ERROR operations let you check for errors that occur within a block of code in an RPG IV program. The ***PSSR** built-in subroutine lets you check for errors anywhere in the program that are not otherwise handled.

MONITOR and ON-ERROR Operations

The **MONITOR** (Begin a Monitor Group) and ENDMON (End a Monitor Group) operations form groups of code for which you will provide error-handling routines. If an error occurs while processing any line in a monitor group, control passes to the first ON-ERROR (On Error) operation within the monitor group.

Each ON-ERROR operation lists one or more errors for which it is responsible; these errors generally correspond to the %STATUS code from 00100 to 09999, or you can specify *FILE for file errors, *PROGRAM for program errors, or *ALL for any other errors. The code following an ON-ERROR operation is executed if the error that occurred matches the ON-ERROR statement. Only the first matching ON-ERROR statement is processed; if no matching ON-ERROR statements exist, none are processed. Once any ON-ERROR statements are processed, or if the monitor group is executed without error, control passes to the ENDMON statement that ends the group.

```
*.. 1 ...+... 2 ...+... 3 ...+... 4 ...+... 5 ...+... 6 ...+... 7 ...+... 8
 /FREE
  // Example of file error processing using MONITOR
    MONITOR;
      READ Sample;
      DOW NOT %EOF(Sample);
        CHAIN Samp OtherFile;
        EXSR Calcs;
        READ Sample;
      ENDDO;
    ON-ERROR 1218;
      EXSR LockedRec;
    ON-ERROR *FILE;
      EXSR FileErr;
    ON-ERROR *ALL;
      EXSR GenErr;
      *INLR = ON;
      RETURN;
    ENDMON;
 /END-FREE
```

A monitor group can appear anywhere in an RPG IV program, and you can nest monitor groups (innermost groups are considered first). Notice that the program no longer needs to use the (E) extender to monitor for errors. If any of the operations (READ, CHAIN, or EXSR) generates an error, the ON-ERROR groups automatically take control; in fact, if the Calcs subroutine generates an error, the ON-ERROR groups handle the error (unless Calcs also is coded with its own monitor blocks). It's a good idea to finish up the block with a "catch-all" ON-ERROR *ALL statement to handle generic errors.

The *PSSR Subroutine

If you include a subroutine named *PSSR within your program, that subroutine will automatically receive control when a program error occurs. To send control to this subroutine for file exceptions/errors as well, you must explicitly designate *PSSR as the error handler for the files. This assignment is quite straightforward; simply use keyword INFSR as part of the file definition and include *PSSR in parentheses after the keyword.

```
*.. 1 ...+... 2 ...+... 3 ...+... 4 ...+... 5 ...+... 6 ...+... 7 ...+... 8
FFilename++IPEASFRLen+LKLen+AIDevice+.Keywords+++++++++++++++++++++++++++++++
 // File definition with a file information data structure and
 // the *PSSR error handler defined for the file
FSample    UF   E          K DISK    INFDS(SampleDS) INFSR(*PSSR)
```

Keyword INFSR signals that its parameter is to serve as the error routine automatically invoked when a file exception/error occurs. Although any subroutine could be used for file error handling, most programmers prefer to combine program error handling and file error handling within a single subroutine, named *PSSR. With this method, any kind of error encountered while your program is running will cause control to be transferred to subroutine *PSSR. The *PSSR subroutine provides a "last defense" against errors — to handle those errors you haven't processed with the (E) extender, the %ERROR function, the %STATUS function, or MONITOR blocks.

Within *PSSR, you could check the status codes and other subfields of the file information and program status data structures to determine the best response to the error — perhaps ignoring the error and continuing, perhaps writing a line to an error report and continuing, or perhaps noting the error and bringing the program to a normal ending. The optimal design of *PSSR logic is beyond the scope of this text. As a programmer new to RPG IV, you should be aware of the need for error detection and understand the function and value of a *PSSR subroutine. As you gain more experience with the language, you will no doubt begin to incorporate such error handling within your programs.

Chapter Summary

RPG IV includes several operations and built-in functions to inspect fields and/or manipulate characters within fields. Function %SIZE lets you determine the length (or number of bytes) of a data item, %LEN returns the length of the value of an expression, and %ELEM returns the number of elements in an array or table or the number of occurrences in a multiple-occurrence data structure.

Operation TESTN determines whether the characters within a field are all numeric, all blanks, or leading blanks followed by numeric characters. You can use the TEST operation in two ways: to check date/time fields for valid date/time data or to test numeric and character fields for valid date/time data. When checking numeric/character fields, an operation extender (D, T, or Z) tells the computer which date/time test to perform.

%SCAN, %CHECK, and %CHECKR let you inspect the contents of character fields. %SCAN looks for the presence of a specified character or string of characters; %CHECK and %CHECKR detect the absence of specified characters. You store the position of the located character or string within the field for subsequent use.

The + concatenation operator, the %TRIM*x* and %SUBST built-in functions, and the %XLATE function let you change or manipulate characters within a field. You combine two fields' values into a third field by using + within an EVAL statement; you trim leading and/or trailing blanks from a field's contents with %TRIM, %TRIML, and %TRIMR. %SUBST extracts a substring from within a field, and %XLATE converts characters based on a translation table you provide.

The %DEC, %DECH, %INT, %INTH, %UNS, and %UNSH functions convert expression results to specific numeric data types. The %CHAR function coverts numeric and date expressions to character data.

Key Terms

abend	%SCAN function
%CHAR function	%SIZE function
%CHECK function	%STATUS function
%DEC function	%SUBST function
%INT function	%TRIM function
%LEN function	*PSSR
MONITOR operation	

Discussion/Review Questions

1. Discuss different options for trapping errors (or not trapping errors) within a program, giving the pros and cons of each method.

2. Discuss the role that the %SIZE, %LEN, %DECPOS, and %ELEM built-in functions play in improving the reliability and maintainability of an RPG application.

3. What is the primary advantage of using variable-length fields instead of fixed-length fields when you are performing string operations in an RPG program? Which approach is more readable? Which approach do you suspect performs faster?

4. Why might you want to convert one data type to another in an RPG program? For example, why might you want to convert a packed decimal number to a character field? Which built-in functions would you use to perform the conversion?

Exercises

1. Write the calculations that would be needed to load the data structure from Exercise 3 in Chapter 11 with the contents of file CSCHGP. Make up whatever data names you need, in addition to those of the data structure.

2. Write the calculations needed to locate the appropriate charge from the data structure of Exercises 3 and 4 in Chapter 11 based on an input weight (field WTIN) and zone (field ZIN). (That is, do the equivalent of a table lookup, using your data structure.)

3. Write the definitions and calculations to format a printed name and address from the following fixed-length fields:

SALUT (5 characters)
FIRSTNM (15 characters)
LASTNM (20 characters)
ADDRESS (35 characters)
CITY (21 characters)
STATPROV (2 characters)
MAILCODE (10 characters)
COUNTRY (35 characters)

The name and address should go into the following fields: LINE1, LINE2, LINE3, and LINE4 (35 characters each). For example:

LINE1 = 'Mr. John Doe'
LINE2 = '123 Main Street'
LINE3 = 'New York NY 10010'
LINE4 = 'USA'

4. Rewrite the definitions and calculations from Exercise 3 to use variable-length fields.

Programming Assignments

1. Wexler University wants an address and telephone listing for each of its students. The listing should include a formatted name and address as well as an edited phone number for each student. The specific report layout is left up to you, but each entry should generally look like this:

DOE John   555-555-5555
  123 Main Street
  New York NY 10010

The file WUSTDP (described in Appendix F) is the student master file, which contains the data you will need. Build a logical file over file WUSTDP, keyed on last name and first name. Use this file to list the records in alphabetic order.

2. GTC wants you to write a program that prepares customers' phone bills and updates two fields in the customer master file: current billing amount and balance owed. For the current billing amount, replace the field's previous contents with the amount due calculated for this month's charges. For the balance owed, add this month's charges to the previous amount.

Billing charges:
There is a set monthly charge for local service of $15.00 per month, regardless of calls made. In addition, there is an intrastate access charge of $4.39 per month, regardless of calls. A 3 percent federal excise tax applies to the total cost of calls only, but not to service charges. A 4 percent state sales tax applies to the cost of calls and the services charges.

You will need to use files GTCSTP (customer master) and GTCLSP (calls transaction) for this application; you can create whatever logical files you find helpful. Note that because of the monthly service charges, you will need to bill every customer, even if he or she has made no calls this month.

If you have written the program for Programming Assignment 2 in Chapter 10, call that program to convert the time from military time to standard time for printing; if you have not written that program, change the printer spacing chart to reflect military time (*hhmm* as stored in file GTCLSP).

Your bills should be formatted as shown below:

```
         1         2         3         4         5         6         7         8         9         10
1234567890123456789012345678901234567890123456789012345678901234567890123456789012345678901234567890
 1 GTC INC     PO BOX 123   LAWRENCE  MI   49067
 2
 3     BILL FOR:   X. XXXXXXXXXXXXXXX
 4                 XXXXXXXXXXXXXXXXXXXXX
 5                 XXXXXXXXXXXXXXX XX XXXXX
 6                 (XXX)XXX-XXXX
 7
 8 GTC CURRENT CHARGES
 9         LOCAL SERVICE                                    15.00
10         INTRASTATE ACCESS                                 4.39
11
12 DATE        CALLS MADE      MIN     TIME            COST
13 MMMDD       XXX-XXX-XXXX    XX0     HHMMA.M.        XX0.XX
14 MMMDD       XXX-XXX-XXXX    XX0     HHMMP.M.        XX0.XX
15 MMMDD       XXX-XXX-XXXX    XX0     HHMMP.M.        XX0.XX
16
17                                     CALLS TOTAL  X,XX0.XX
18
19     3% FEDERAL EXCISE TAX ON X,XX0.XX             XX0.XX
20     4% STATE TAX ON X,XX0.XX                      XX0.XX
21                                                 -----------------
22 CHARGES FOR THIS BILLING PERIOD                  X,XX0.XX
23 BALANCE PAST DUE                                 X,XX0.XX
24 AMOUNT DUE                                       X,XX0.XX
25
```

Chapter 13

Interactive Programs: Advanced Techniques

Chapter Overview

This chapter extends your ability to write interactive applications by introducing you to two new concepts: subfiles and online help.

Subfiles

In Chapter 8, you were introduced to interactive programs. You learned how to write inquiry and maintenance programs whose logic required the display of information one record at a time. Some kinds of applications require the use of **list panels**, in which data from many records is displayed on a screen for review, selection, or update. RPG IV has a special feature called subfiles to handle this kind of program requirement.

A **subfile** is a collection of records that is handled as a unit for screen input/output (I/O). Although subfile processing can get quite complicated, you can learn basic subfile processing techniques without great difficulty. As a prelude to discussing coding requirements for subfiles, consider the following problem description.

In Chapter 8, we worked with a file of course-section information and developed an interactive application to display detailed section information based on a section number entered by the user. The record layout of that file, SECTIONS, is repeated below.

```
*.. 1 ...+... 2 ...+... 3 ...+... 4 ...+... 5 ...+... 6 ...+... 7 ...+... 8
A..........T.Name++++++RLen++TDpB......Functions++++++++++++++++++++++++++++++
 * Physical file SECTIONS definition
A          R SECREC
A            SECTNO         5             TEXT('Section number')
A            DAYS           3             TEXT('Days class meets')
A            BEGTIME        4  0          TEXT('Time class starts')
A            ROOM           4  0          TEXT('Classroom')
A            ENROLL         3  0          TEXT('Current enrollment')
A            INSTR         15             TEXT('Instructor')
A            COURSE         6             TEXT('Course identifier')
A          K SECTNO
```

Now, assume that the same school wants an application in which the user can enter a course name to see a list of all the sections offered for that course. The desired screen layouts are shown below.

```
                          Course Inquiry

        Type value, then Enter.

            Course number . .  _____




        F3=Exit
```

```
                        XXXXXX Course Information

              Section    Instructor       Room  Days  Time   Enroll.
              XXXXX      XXXXXXXXXXXXXX    XXXX  XXX   XX:XX  XØX
              XXXXX      XXXXXXXXXXXXXX    XXXX  XXX   XX:XX  XØX
              XXXXX      XXXXXXXXXXXXXX    XXXX  XXX   XX:XX  XØX




        Press Enter to continue.

        F3=Exit  F12=Cancel
```

Notice that the second screen contains information from many section records rather than just one. This fact means that you will need to use subfiles to implement the solution.

Your first step, before beginning the screen definition, is to create a logical file over file SECTIONS to access the records in order by course and, within course, by section. The following DDS provides the definition for that logical file, SECTIONL:

```
*.. 1 ...+... 2 ...+... 3 ...+... 4 ...+... 5 ...+... 6 ...+... 7 ...+... 8
A..........T.Name++++++.Len++TDpB......Functions++++++++++++++++++++++++++++
 * Definition of SECTIONL, a logical file over physical file SECTIONS
A          R SECREC                    PFILE(SECTIONS)
A          K COURSE
A          K SECTNO
```

Now consider the display file, SECTINQ. The first screen definition is identical to the layout of the screen in Chapter 8; only the literals need to be changed. Note, though, that we've moved CA03 to make it a file-level keyword. The following DDS defines this screen.

```
*.. 1 ...+... 2 ...+... 3 ...+... 4 ...+... 5 ...+... 6 ...+... 7 ...+... 8
AAN01N02N03T.Name++++++RLen++TDpBLinPosFunctions+++++++++++++++++++++++++++++
A                                     INDARA
A                                     CA03(03 'F3=Exit')
A              R CRSEINQ
A                                     BLINK
A                              1 28'Course Inquiry'
A                              3  2'Type value, then Enter.'
A                              5  5'Course number . .'
A                COURSENO      6A  B  5 24
A N90                                 DSPATR(UL)
A N90                                 DSPATR(HI)
A  90                                 ERRMSG('Course not found' 90)
A                             23  2'F3=Exit'
```

The second screen will require subfile definition. Using a subfile to display multiple records on a screen requires two record formats: one to define a subfile record and one to control the subfile and its display.

Subfile Record Formats

The **subfile record format** describes the fields that are to appear on the screen. Because in this example the screen and database fields are the same, the database file containing the field definitions is noted with record-level keyword REF.

A new record-level keyword, SFL (Subfile), is also required; this keyword identifies the record format as a subfile. The remaining information in the subfile record format describes the fields to appear, their locations on the screen, and any editing or other special keywords desired. The line number associated with each field represents the line on which the first record of the subfile is to appear.

The following DDS illustrates the subfile record format of our application.

```
*.. 1 ...+... 2 ...+... 3 ...+... 4 ...+... 5 ...+... 6 ...+... 7 ...+... 8
AAN01N02N03T.Name++++++RLen++TDpBLinPosFunctions+++++++++++++++++++++++++++++
A                                     REF(SECTIONS)
A              R SFLSECT                SFL
A                SECTNO     R       O  4 14
A                INSTR      R       O  4 23
A                ROOM       R       O  4 41
A                DAYS       R       O  4 49
A                BEGTIME    R     Y O  4 57EDTWRD('0 :  ')
A                ENROLL     R     Y O  4 66EDTCDE(3)
```

Subfile Control Record Formats

The **subfile control record format** must immediately follow the subfile record format. This record format controls the display of the subfile records through the use of special record-level keywords. In addition, programmers often include the column headings for the subfile display as part of this record format.

The subfile control record format requires several record-level keywords. The required keywords and their functions are as follows:

- *SFLCTL (Subfile Control)*. Keyword SFLCTL identifies a record as the subfile control record for the subfile named within the parentheses after the keyword.

- *SFLDSP (Subfile Display)*. If keyword SFLDSP is active when an output operation is performed on the subfile control record, the subfile itself is also displayed. This keyword generally is conditioned by an indicator to control whether the subfile is displayed on a given output operation.

- *SFLPAG (Subfile Page)*. Keyword SFLPAG defines how many subfile records are to be displayed at one time on the screen. The number follows the keyword and is enclosed in parentheses. You typically determine this number by calculating the number of available screen lines, after taking into account all other lines to be displayed along with the subfile.

- *SFLSIZ (Subfile Size)*. The subfile size value, enclosed in parentheses immediately after the SFLSIZ keyword, should be either equal to or greater than the SFLPAG value. If the value is greater, you can make it large enough to accommodate the maximum number of records you would normally have in the subfile. (If you underestimate, however, the system will automatically extend the subfile to make room for the additional records.) A subfile cannot contain more than 9,999 records. If SFLSIZ is greater than SFLPAG, OS/400 automatically handles paging through the subfile when the user presses the page (or roll) keys and displays a plus sign (+) at the bottom of the screen to indicate there are subfile records not yet displayed.

Subfile control record-level keywords that are optional but usually used include the following:

- *SFLDSPCTL (Subfile Display Control)*. Keyword SFLDSPCTL enables the display of any output fields or constants described within the control record format. The keyword generally is conditioned with the same indicator used for the SFLDSP keyword.

- *SFLCLR (Subfile Clear)*. If keyword SFLCLR is active when an output operation is performed on the subfile control record, the subfile itself is cleared of records. An option indicator is required for this keyword, or the system would clear the subfile on every output operation to the control record. The indicator often is the reverse of the indicator used for keywords SFLDSP and SFLDSPCTL, so that you clear the subfile in one output operation and display the subfile and the control record information in a second output operation.

The following DDS illustrates a subfile control record format. Notice that when indicator 50 is on, the system will clear the subfile; when 50 is off, the system will display both the subfile record format and the subfile control record format. Also note that the control record format includes screen column headings for the subfile.

```
*.. 1 ...+... 2 ...+... 3 ...+... 4 ...+... 5 ...+... 6 ...+... 7 ...+... 8
AAN01N02N03T.Name++++++RLen++TDpBLinPosFunctions+++++++++++++++++++++++++++++
A* Subfile control record format for course inquiry application
A           R CTLSECT                    SFLCTL(SFLSECT)
A                                         SFLPAG(15)
A                                         SFLSIZ(80)
A  50                                     SFLCLR
A N50                                     SFLDSPCTL
A N50                                     SFLDSP
A             COURSENO      6A  O  1 28
A                                      1 35'Course Information'
A                                      3 12'Section'
A                                      3 24'Instructor'
A                                      3 41'Room'
A                                      3 49'Days'
A                                      3 57'Time'
A                                      3 64'Enroll.'
```

Loading the Subfile

As we indicated above, the relationship between subfile size and subfile page can vary. Programmers use several different approaches to defining this interrelationship and to loading data into the subfile. The method used depends in part on a program's anticipated processing requirements. We will develop our sample program using four different techniques to give you a sense of the variation and the rationale for each method.

Loading the Entire Subfile

The first approach to defining and loading a subfile involves defining the subfile size large enough to hold the maximum expected number of records and then loading all the appropriate data into the subfile before any record display. This method is the easiest to code but results in the slowest initial response time. Once display begins, however, paging through the subfile is fast. This method is least appropriate when there are a large number of records to be loaded and the user is unlikely to want to see most of them.

The following code shows the complete DDS for this application method. SFLSIZ is defined with a value of 80, and SFLPAG's value is 15.

```
*.. 1 ...+... 2 ...+... 3 ...+... 4 ...+... 5 ...+... 6 ...+... 7 ...+... 8
AAN01N02N03T.Name++++++RLen++TDpBLinPosFunctions++++++++++++++++++++++++++++
 * Display file SECTINQ, coded for loading the entire subfile at once
A                                       INDARA
A                                       CA03(03 'F3=Exit')
A                                       CA12(12 'F12=Cancel')
A                                       REF(SECTIONS)
 * Record format of initial inquiry screen
A           R CRSEINQ
A                                       BLINK
A                                     1 28'Course Inquiry'
A                                     3  2'Type value, then Enter.'
A                                     5  5'Course number . .'
A             COURSENO    6A  B  5 24
A N90                                   DSPATR(UL)
A N90                                   DSPATR(HI)
A  90                                   ERRMSG('Course not found' 90)
A                                    23  2'F3=Exit   F12=Cancel'
 * Record format for subfile
A           R SFLSECT                    SFL
A             SECTNO      R       0  4 14
A             INSTR       R       0  4 23
A             ROOM        R       0  4 41
A             DAYS        R       0  4 49
A             BEGTIME     R    Y  0  4 57EDTWRD('0 :  ')
A             ENROLL      R    Y  0  4 66EDTCDE(3)
 * Record format for subfile control
A           R CTLSECT                   SFLCTL(SFLSECT)
A                                       SFLPAG(15)
A                                       SFLSIZ(80)
A  50                                   SFLCLR
A N50                                   SFLDSPCTL
A N50                                   SFLDSP
A                                       OVERLAY
A             COURSENO    6A  O  1 28
A                                     1 35'Course Information'
A                                     3 12'Section'
A                                     3 24'Instructor'
A                                     3 41'Room'
A                                     3 49'Days'
A                                     3 57'Time'
A                                     3 64'Enroll.'
 * Footer record format
A           R FOOTER
A                                    21  2'Press Enter to continue.'
A                                    23  2'F3=Exit   F12=Cancel'
```

Notice the inclusion of a footer record definition, which contains prompts about active function keys. This record format is needed because the control record format cannot reference screen lines that would fall both above the subfile display (i.e., the column headings) and below the subfile (the function key prompts). The control record format includes the record-level keyword OVERLAY so that the footer record format will not be erased when the subfile is displayed.

With the display file definition complete, we can turn to the requirements for the program that will use it.

First, for all subfile applications, RPG IV requires you to identify a subfile within the File Specification of the display file with which you want to associate the subfile. In addition, as part of the display file's definition, you need to identify a field that your program will use to represent a subfile record's relative record number. **Relative record number** simply means the position of the record within the subfile (e.g., first subfile record, second subfile record). This field is needed because RPG IV writes records to a subfile (and retrieves records from a subfile) based on the value of the relative record number.

You associate the subfile and relative record number field with a workstation file by using keyword SFILE in the Keywords area of the File Specification (positions 44–80). The subfile record format name (e.g., SFLSECT), a colon (:), and the field to be used to store the relative record number (e.g., RRN) appear within parentheses following the keyword:

```
*.. 1 ...+... 2 ...+... 3 ...+... 4 ...+... 5 ...+... 6 ...+... 7 ...+... 8
FFilename++IPEASFRLen+LKLen+AIDevice+.Keywords+++++++++++++++++++++++++++++++
FSECTIONL  IF   E           K DISK
FSECTINQ   CF   E             WORKSTN SFILE(SFLSECT:RRN)
F                                     INDDS(Indicators)
```

Next, you need to design the calculations. In our application, once the user has entered the desired course, the program needs to use that value to access the appropriate records in logical file SECTIONL and write them to the subfile; loading the subfile continues until no additional appropriate records (i.e., no more sections for that course) exist. Then the subfile can be displayed by executing the subfile control record format. Because SLFPAG is less than SLFSIZ, the system will handle any user request to page up or page down. Upon return, the program should either end or request another course, depending on whether the user pressed F3 or Enter. The following pseudocode illustrates the logic needed for this application.

```
WHILE user wants to continue
   Display inquiry screen
   IF user doesn't want to exit
      Access start of appropriate sections
      IF section not found
         Turn on error indicator
      ELSE
         Clear subfile
         Load subfile
         Display subfile
      ENDIF
   ENDIF
ENDWHILE
```

The pseudocode for loading the subfile using this method of handling subfiles is as follows:

Read a matching section record
WHILE there are more appropriate section records
   Increment relative record number
   Write a record to the subfile
   Read a matching section record
ENDWHILE

The following code illustrates the RPG IV implementation of the design we've depicted in pseudocode.

```
*.. 1 ...+... 2 ...+... 3 ...+... 4 ...+... 5 ...+... 6 ...+... 7 ...+... 8
DName+++++++++++ETDsFrom+++To/L+++IDc.Keywords+++++++++++++++++++++++++++++++
CLØNØ1Factor1+++++++Opcode(E)+Factor2+++++++Result++++++++Len++D+HiLoEq....
  // Indicator data structure
D Indicators      DS
D  Exit                      3      3N
D  Cancel                   12     12N
D  SflClr                   50     50N
D  CrsNotFnd                90     90N
  // Partial key list to access SectionL file by course number
C     CourseKey      KLIST
C                    KFLD                    CourseNo

   . . .
 /FREE
  // Calculations for subfile application when entire subfile is loaded
  // before any display takes place
   DOW NOT Exit;                    // Process loop until user wants to exit
     EXFMT CrseInq;
     IF NOT Exit;
       SETLL CourseKey SectionL;
       IF NOT %EQUAL(SectionL);  // No matching section in file
         CrsNotFnd = *ON;          // Turn on error indicator
       ELSE;
         EXSR ClearSF;             // Otherwise, clear and then load subfile
         EXSR LoadSF;
         WRITE Footer;             // Write footer to screen
         EXFMT CtlSect;            // Show subfile via control record format
       ENDIF;
     ENDIF;
   ENDDO;

   *INLR = *ON;
   RETURN;

  // ********************************************************************
  //
  // Subroutine to clear the subfile and reset RRN to Ø
  //
   BEGSR ClearSF;
     SflClr = *ON;
     WRITE CtlSect;
     SflClr = *OFF;
     RRN = Ø;
   ENDSR;
```

continued…

continued...

```
// ********************************************************************
//
// Subroutine to load the subfile until no more section records
//
   BEGSR LoadSF;
     READE CourseKey SectionL;
     DOW NOT %EOF(SectionL);
       RRN = RRN + 1;
       WRITE SFLSect;
       READE CourseKey SectionL;
     ENDDO;
   ENDSR;
 /END-FREE
```

Note in these calculations that the subfile is loaded by writing records to the subfile record format based on the relative record number field, which is incremented before each successive write operation. The program displays the subfile by executing the subfile control record format. A WRITE operation to the control format clears the subfile (as long as the indicator for SFLCLR is on); the program also uses WRITE — rather than EXFMT — to display the Footer format because a user response to that display is not required. The KLIST lets you access the file using a partial key.

In this implementation of the subfile application, subfile size is greater than subfile page, and the size is large enough to handle the maximum number of records that the subfile normally would be expected to hold. The program stores all relevant database records in the subfile before any display. With this approach, OS/400 automatically enables the page keys and signals, through a plus sign in the lower-right screen corner, that more subfile records are available for viewing. From a programmer's viewpoint, this technique is the simplest to code. Unfortunately, this method can result in poor response time when the application is used.

The cause of the slow system response is that this technique requires the system to access all the records that meet the selection criterion and store them in the subfile before displaying the first page of the subfile. If the subfile size is small, performance will be satisfactory, but as the subfile size increases, response time will degrade noticeably. In that case, especially if the user typically does not scroll much throughout the subfile, it may make sense to build the subfile a page at a time as the user requests additional pages.

Loading the Subfile a Page at a Time
The other methods of subfile building load the subfile a page at a time. Three variations exist for this technique.

Variation 1: Subfile Size One Greater Than Page
This method of subfile handling relies on the fact that the system will automatically expand a subfile, regardless of its stated size, as your program adds more records to it. Because this additionally allocated room is not contiguous on disk, performance degrades as the number of pages in the subfile increases, but the technique works well when the number of records usually required within the subfile is small.

This method entails loading the subfile one page at a time based on the user's request for additional pages. Paging within the subfile records already loaded is handled automatically by the operating system. When the user attempts to scroll past the last page in the subfile, however, control returns to the program, which must load an additional page (if additional appropriate records exist).

To use this method, you must add three keywords to the subfile control record format. First, the PAGEDOWN keyword (or its equivalent, ROLLUP) must be associated with an indicator to let the system send control back to the program when a page-down request exceeds the current limits of the subfile. You must also add the SFLEND (Subfile End) keyword, conditioned by an indicator.

Keyword SFLEND, its associated indicator, and the Page down key work together to determine what happens when the user tries to scroll past the current limits of the subfile. If indicator SFLEND is off, the system displays a plus sign and returns control to the program to load the next page; if SFLEND is on, the plus sign is not displayed, and control is not returned to the program for additional loading. Thus, the program should turn on SFLEND when no additional records remain to be put into the subfile. The system will then prohibit user attempts to scroll past the last page of records in the subfile.

The third keyword needed is SFLRCDNBR (Subfile Record Number), coded within the subfile control record format opposite a hidden field. The value of the hidden field determines which page of the subfile is displayed when the subfile control format is written. Without this keyword and its associated field, when the program writes the control record after loading a new page into the subfile, it will by default display the first page of the subfile rather than the newly loaded page. Using parameter value CURSOR with keyword SFLRCDNBR causes the cursor to be positioned on that record upon display.

Note that you signify a hidden field by entering an H in position 38 (Usage) of the DDS specifications. Hidden fields do not include a screen-location specification because, although they are part of the screen, they are not displayed. Your program can write a value to a hidden field and read the field's value, but the user cannot see or change the value of the field.

The following DDS shows the changes this method requires in the subfile control record format. Note that because the initial inquiry screen, the portion of the control record format defining the column headings, and the footer record format are unchanged from our first example, this DDS does not repeat those lines.

```
*.. 1 ...+... 2 ...+... 3 ...+... 4 ...+... 5 ...+... 6 ...+... 7 ...+... 8
AAN01N02N03T.Name+++++RLen++TDpBLinPosFunctions++++++++++++++++++++++++++++++
 * Display file SECTINQ, coded for loading the subfile one page at a time,
 * with subfile size one greater than page
A                                       INDARA
A                                       CA03(03 'F3=Exit')
A                                       CA12(12 'F12=Cancel')
A                                       REF(SECTIONS)
              . . .
 * Record format for subfile
A           R SFLSECT                   SFL
A             SECTNO     R        0   4 14
A             INSTR      R        0   4 23
A             ROOM       R        0   4 41
A             DAYS       R        0   4 49
A             BEGTIME    R      Y 0   4 57EDTWRD('0 :  ')
A             ENROLL     R      Y 0   4 66EDTCDE(3)
 * Record format for subfile control
A           R CTLSECT                   SFLCTL(SFLSECT)
A                                       SFLPAG(15)
A                                       SFLSIZ(16)
A  50                                   SFLCLR
A N50                                   SFLDSPCTL
A N50                                   SFLDSP
A                                       OVERLAY
A                                       PAGEDOWN(21 'Page Down')
A  95                                   SFLEND
A             SFLRCD     4S 0H          SFLRCDNBR(CURSOR)
A             COURSENO   6A   0   1 28
A             . . .
```

The major logic changes in the RPG program center on loading the subfile a page at a time. Each time control returns to the program from the screen, if the page key triggered the return, the program must load the next page of the subfile and return control to the screen.

When there are no more records left to load, the program should turn on the SFLEND indicator to disable scrolling past the last subfile page. To determine whether additional pages can be built, the program needs to read one additional record after loading an entire subfile page before displaying the new page. The following code illustrates this technique. Note that the ClearSF subroutine is not included because it is identical to that of our first example.

```
*.. 1 ...+... 2 ...+... 3 ...+... 4 ...+... 5 ...+... 6 ...+... 7 ...+... 8
DName+++++++++++ETDsFrom+++To/L+++IDc.Keywords+++++++++++++++++++++++++++++++++
CLØNØ1Factor1+++++++Opcode(E)+Factor2+++++++Result+++++++Len++D+HiLoEq....
    // Indicator data structure
D Indicators      DS              99
D  Exit                    3      3N
D  Cancel                 12     12N
D  PagDwn                 21     21N
D  SflClr                 50     50N
D  CrsNotFnd              90     90N
D  SflEnd                 95     95N
    // Work field
D  Loop            S              10U 0
    // Partial key list to access SectionL file by course number
C     CourseKey    KLIST
C                  KFLD                   CourseNo


     . . .
   /FREE
    // Calculations for subfile application when subfile is built
    // one page at a time

      DOW NOT Exit;                    // Process loop until user wants to exit
        EXFMT CrseInq;
        IF NOT Exit;
          CHAIN CourseKey SectionL;
          IF NOT %FOUND(SectionL);    // No matching section in file
            CrsNotFnd = *ON;          // Turn on error indicator
          ELSE;                       // Clear and then load subfile
            EXSR ClearSF;
            EXSR LoadSF;
            SflEnd = *OFF;            // Initialize SFLEND indicator to off
            WRITE Footer;             // Write footer to screen
            EXFMT CtlSect;            // Show subfile via control record format
            DOW PagDwn;               // Load/display page when pag key pressed
              EXSR LoadSF;
              EXFMT CtlSect;
            ENDDO;
          ENDIF;
        ENDIF;
      ENDDO;

      *INLR = *ON;
      RETURN;
```

continued...

continued...

```
   // *********************************************************************
   //
   // Subroutine to clear the subfile and reset RRN to 0
   //
     BEGSR ClearSF;
       SflClr = *ON;
       WRITE CtlSect;
       SflClr = *OFF;
       RRN = 0;
     ENDSR;

   // *********************************************************************
   //
   // Subroutine to load one page of subfile or until no more records exist
   //
     BEGSR LoadSF;
       SflRcd = RRN + 1;

       FOR Loop = 1 TO 15;              // Loop 15 times to load the page
         RRN = RRN + 1;
         WRITE SFLSect;
         READE CourseKey SectionL;
         SflEnd = NOT %FOUND(SectionL);
         IF SflEnd;                     // Early exit if no more matching records
           LEAVE;
         ENDIF;
       ENDFOR;
     ENDSR;
 /END-FREE
```

Notice in this code that, in contrast to the code of the first method, subroutine LoadSF reads and writes only 15 records to the subfile — that is, one page. If no additional appropriate sections remain before the page is full, the looping ends. In the mainline, a loop of load-and-display continues until the user presses some key other than the Page down key.

Variation 2: Size Much Bigger Than Page

The second method of building subfiles a page at a time, setting size much bigger than page, is really just a variant of loading the entire subfile at once. However, like variation 1, this method builds the subfile just a page at a time instead of putting all the appropriate records in the subfile before any display.

This method is appropriate when you need to store a large number of records in a subfile, because the large specified size allocates adjacent disk space for faster access during subfile processing. Although each user request for an additional page still requires loading that page of the subfile, the system does not have to allocate additional disk space before each page load (unless the subfile begins to exceed the declared size). You should probably not use this method if the expected subfile size exceeds 100 records.

To use this technique, you need to make only slight changes to the display file; the program logic for this implementation is identical to that of variation 1. In the display file, you merely need to change the subfile size and move the PAGEDOWN keyword from the subfile control record format to the subfile record format. The following DDS illustrates these changes. Note that this code does not repeat the initial inquiry screen, the footer record, or the portion of the subfile control record that describes the screen column headings because these entries remain unchanged.

```
*.. 1 ...+... 2 ...+... 3 ...+... 4 ...+... 5 ...+... 6 ...+... 7 ...+... 8
AAN01N02N03T.Name++++++RLen++TDpBLinPosFunctions++++++++++++++++++++++++++++++
 * Display file SECTINQ, coded for loading the entire subfile one page
 * at a time, with subfile size much greater than page
A                                       INDARA
A                                       CA03(03 'F3=Exit')
A                                       CA12(12 'F12=Cancel')
A                                       REF(SECTIONS)
A               . . .
 * Record format for subfile
A            R SFLSECT                   SFL
A                                       PAGEDOWN(21 'Page Down')
A              SECTNO     R         0  4 14
A              INSTR      R         0  4 23
A              ROOM       R         0  4 41
A              DAYS       R         0  4 49
A              BEGTIME    R       Y 0  4 57EDTWRD('0 :  ')
A              ENROLL     R       Y 0  4 66EDTCDE(3)
 * Record format for subfile control
A            R CTLSECT                   SFLCTL(SFLSECT)
A                                       SFLPAG(15)
A                                       SFLSIZ(80)
A 50                                    SFLCLR
A N50                                   SFLDSPCTL
A N50                                   SFLDSP
A                                       OVERLAY
A 95                                    SFLEND
A              SFLRCD     4S 0H          SFLRCDNBR(CURSOR)
A              COURSENO   6A  0  1 28
A               . . .
```

Variation 3: Subfile Size Equals Page

Setting subfile size equal to page is most appropriate when the user is likely to want to scroll through a large number of records — for example, to do generic searches. Response time is medium and consistent regardless of the number of records viewed.

With this method, the subfile stores only one page of records. Scrolling forward requires replacing the existing page with the next page through loading; scrolling backward requires replacing the existing page with records already read. The program logic required by this technique is therefore more complicated than that of the other methods. Moreover, the method of backward scrolling used will depend on whether you are accessing records by unique keys, non-unique keys, partial keys, or relative record numbers. As an alternative to enabling PAGEUP (or ROLLDOWN), programmers often require users to restart the subfile at the beginning to review records already displayed. This is the method illustrated here.

The DDS for this implementation is similar to that used when subfile size is one greater than subfile page, except that subfile size equals subfile page and keyword SFLRCDNBR is not used. (Because the subfile is only one page long, positioning the subfile upon redisplay is not a problem with this technique.) Note that the control record format includes keywords PAGEDOWN and SFLEND, and function key F5 is enabled to signal restarting the course display. Also note that the illustration omits the initial inquiry screen and the screen column headings from the subfile control record format; these remain identical to those of the previous methods. The footer prompt line now indicates that F5 restarts the subfile.

```
*.. 1 ...+... 2 ...+... 3 ...+... 4 ...+... 5 ...+... 6 ...+... 7 ...+... 8
AAN01N02N03T.Name++++++RLen++TDpBLinPosFunctions+++++++++++++++++++++++++++++++
 * Display file SECTINQ, where subfile size equals subfile page
A                                       INDARA
A                                       CA03(03 'F3=Exit')
A                                       CA12(12 'F12=Cancel')
A                                       REF(SECTIONS)
            . . .
 * Record format for subfile
A            R SFLSECT                  SFL
A              SECTNO     R       O  4 14
A              INSTR      R       O  4 23
A              ROOM       R       O  4 41
A              DAYS       R       O  4 49
A              BEGTIME    R     Y O  4 57EDTWRD('0 :  ')
A              ENROLL     R     Y O  4 66EDTCDE(3)
 * Record format for subfile control
A            R CTLSECT                  SFLCTL(SFLSECT)
A                                       SFLPAG(15)
A                                       SFLSIZ(15)
A  50                                   SFLCLR
A N50                                   SFLDSPCTL
A N50                                   SFLDSP
A                                       OVERLAY
A                                       PAGEDOWN (21 'Page Down')
A  95                                   SFLEND
A                                       CA05(05 'Restart course')
A                                       VLDCMDKEY(06)
A              COURSENO   6A    O  1 28
            . . .
 * Footer record format
A            R FOOTER
A                                    21  2'Press Enter to continue.'
A                                    23  2'F3=Exit  F5=Restart Sections'
A                                    23 32'F12=Cancel'
```

Although the needed DDS changes are minimal, this method requires some major changes to the RPG IV program. First, before each loading of the subfile, the program must clear the subfile because the new records should completely replace those previously displayed. Second, the program must check the page key indicator and indicator 05 upon return from the screen to determine whether to put the next set of section records into the subfile or to chain to the first section record again and load the first set of records back into the subfile.

```
*.. 1 ...+... 2 ...+... 3 ...+... 4 ...+... 5 ...+... 6 ...+... 7 ...+... 8
DName++++++++++ETDsFrom+++To/L+++IDc.Keywords+++++++++++++++++++++++++++++++++++
CL0N01Factor1+++++++Opcode(E)+Factor2+++++++Result++++++++Len++D+HiLoEq....
  // Indicator data structure
D Indicators   DS             99
D   Exit                3       3N
D   Refresh             5       5N
D   Cancel             12      12N
D   PagDwn             21      21N
D   SflClr             50      50N
D   CrsNotFnd          90      90N
D   SflEnd             95      95N
  // Work field
D   Loop       S             10U 0
  // Partial key list to access SectionL file by course number
C     CourseKey    KLIST
C                  KFLD                 CourseNo
```

continued…

continued...

```
 . . .
 /FREE
  // Calculations for subfile application when subfile size equals page

    DOW NOT Exit;                          // Process loop until user exits
      EXFMT CrseInq;
      IF NOT Exit;
        CHAIN CourseKey SectionL;
        IF NOT %FOUND(SectionL);            // No match section in file
          CrsNotFnd = *ON;                  // Turn on error indicator
        ELSE;
          DOU NOT Refresh AND NOT PagDwn;   // Loop until no action
            IF Refresh;
              CHAIN CourseKey SectionL;
            ENDIF;
            EXSR ClearSF;                   // Clear and load subfile
            EXSR LoadSF;
            WRITE Footer;                   // Display footer and subfile
            EXFMT CtlSect;
          ENDDO;
        ENDIF;
      ENDIF;
ENDDO;

    *INLR = *ON;
    RETURN;

  // ********************************************************************
  //
  // Subroutine to clear the subfile and reset RRN to 0
  //
    BEGSR ClearSF;
      SflClr = *ON;
      WRITE CtlSect;
      EVAL SflClr = *OFF;
      RRN = 0;
    ENDSR;

  // ********************************************************************
  //
  // Subroutine to load one page of subfile or until no more records. First
  // record of page already read by CHAIN or previous READE.
    BEGSR LoadSF;
      FOR Loop = 1 TO 15;              // Loop 15 times to load the page
        RRN = RRN + 1;
        WRITE SFLSect;
        READE CourseKey SectionL;
        SflEnd = NOT %FOUND(SectionL);
        IF SflEnd;                      // Early exit if no more matching records
          LEAVE;
        ENDIF;
      ENDFOR;
    ENDSR;
 /END-FREE
```

Subfiles and Change

Assume you wanted to list sections of a course not just to inspect the data but also to make changes in the data — perhaps you need to assign different instructors to sections or reschedule some sections to different rooms. An RPG IV operation — READC (Read Next Changed Record), used only with subfiles — lets you develop such an application.

The READC operation requires a subfile name in Factor 2 and sets on the %EOF function to signal end-of-subfile. Generally used within a loop, the READC operation reads only those records from a subfile that were changed during a prior EXFMT operation; when no changed subfile records remain to be read, the indicator associated with the operation is turned on.

Because of the READC operation, a user can make as many changes as necessary to various records in the subfile in a single display; all these changes can then be processed when control is returned to the program.

You can use READC regardless of the technique used to load and display the subfile. For simplicity's sake, we'll modify the first version of our program, in which all the relevant records are loaded into the subfile at one time, to demonstrate how to use this operation.

We need to make a few changes in the display file. First, the subfile fields need to be different from the database fields. Without this change, rereading a database record preparatory to updating it would obliterate any changes to subfile field values. Also, the usage of most of the subfile fields needs to be B (both input and output) to let users change the fields' values; section number remains output only, to prevent changes to the key. Last, some of the screen captions and prompts require changes to better suit the new application. The following DDS reflects all these modifications.

```
*.. 1 ...+... 2 ...+... 3 ...+... 4 ...+... 5 ...+... 6 ...+... 7 ...+... 8
AAN01N02N03T.Name++++++RLen++TDpBLinPosFunctions+++++++++++++++++++++++++++++
 * Display file SECTUPDT, coded for loading the entire subfile at once
A                                       INDARA
A                                       CA03(03 'F3=Exit')
A                                       CA12(12 'F12=Cancel')
A                                       REF(SECTIONS)
 * Record format of initial inquiry screen
A          R CRSEINQ
A                                       BLINK
A                                     1 28'Course Section Update'
A                                     3  2'Type value, then Enter'
A                                     5  5'Course number . .'
A            COURSENO      6A   B    5 24
A N90                                    DSPATR(UL)
A N90                                    DSPATR(HI)
A  90                                    ERRMSG('Course not found' 90)
A                                    23  2'F3=Exit  F12=Cancel'
 * Record format for subfile
A          R SFLSECT              SFL
A            SECTNO     R       O  4 14
A            SINSTR        15   B  4 23
A            SROOM         4   0B  4 41
A            SDAYS         3    B  4 49
A            SBEGTIME      4Y  0B  4 57EDTWRD('0 :  ')
A            SENROLL       3Y  0B  4 66EDTCDE(3)

 * Record format for subfile control
A          R CTLSECT              SFLCTL(SFLSECT)
A                                 SFLPAG(15)
A                                 SFLSIZ(80)
A  50                             SFLCLR
```

continued...

continued…

```
A N50                              SFLDSPCTL
A N50                              SFLDSP
A                                  OVERLAY
A          COURSENO    6A  O  1 28
A                            1 35'Course Information'
A                            3 12'Section'
A                            3 24'Instructor'
A                            3 41'Room'
A                            3 49'Days'
A                            3 57'Time'
A                            3 64'Enroll.'
 * Footer record format
A          R FOOTER
A                           21  2'Change values as desired;-
A                              ' press Enter to continue.'
A                           23  2'F3=Exit  F12=Cancel'
```

The RPG program requires a few changes to enable the updating to take place. First, remember that the database file will be an update type so that records can be read and then rewritten to the file with any changes.

The program logic remains basically the same. The major difference occurs when control is returned to the program following the subfile display. At that point, provided the user did not press F3 or F12, the program needs to loop, using READC to read any changed subfile record and using that data to update the data file. The loop should continue until no more changed records exist.

Because specific database records need to be accessed by their complete key, the program needs a second KLIST, with both course and section as KFLDs. Finally, because the subfile and database fields are different, the program needs to move values back and forth between corresponding fields at appropriate times. The modified program is shown below.

```
*.. 1 ...+... 2 ...+... 3 ...+... 4 ...+... 5 ...+... 6 ...+... 7 ...+... 8
 // *************************************************************************
 // This interactive program displays sections of a course entered by the
 // user and lets the user update the section information.
 // Author:   Yaeger  Date Modified:  Mar. 1995.
 // Modified: Meyers  Date Modified:  Jan. 2002.
 *************************************************************************
FSectionL  UF   E    K    DISK
FSectUpdt  CF   E              WORKSTN SFILE(SFLSect:RRN)
F                                      INDDS(Indicators)

D Loop         S            10U 0
D RRN          S             2  0

   // Indicator data structure
D Indicators   DS                99
D  Exit                 3      3N
D  Cancel              12     12N
D  SflClr              50     50N
D  CrsNotFnd           90     90N
   // Partial key list to access SectionL file by course number
C     CourseKey     KLIST
C                   KFLD                      CourseNo
   // Full key list to access SectionL file
C     FullKey       KLIST
C                   KFLD                      CourseNo
C                   KFLD                      SectNo
```

continued…

continued...

```
/FREE
   DOW NOT Exit;                            // Process loop until user exits
     EXFMT CrseInq;
     IF NOT Exit;
       SETLL CourseKey SectionL;
       IF NOT %EQUAL(SectionL);             // No matching section in file
         CrsNotFnd = *ON;                   // Turn on error indicator
       ELSE;                                // Otherwise clear/load subfile
         EXSR ClearSF;                      // Clear/load subfile
         EXSR LoadSF;
         WRITE Footer;                      // Display footer/subfile
         EXFMT CtlSect;
         IF NOT Exit and NOT Cancel;        // Update database records
           EXSR UpdateSR;
         ENDIF;
       ENDIF;
     ENDIF;
   ENDDO;

   *INLR = *ON;
   RETURN;

   // ********************************************************************
   //
   // Subroutine to clear the subfile and reset RRN to 0
   //
   BEGSR ClearSF;
     SflClr = *ON;
     WRITE CtlSect;
     SflClr = *OFF;
     RRN = 0;
   ENDSR;

   // ********************************************************************
   //
   // Subroutine to load the subfile until no more section records exist
   //
   BEGSR LoadSF;
     READE CourseKey SectionL;
     DOW NOT %EOF(SectionL);
       RRN = RRN + 1;
       EXSR MoveDB;
       WRITE SFLSect;
       READE CourseKey SectionL;
     ENDDO;
   ENDSR;

   // ********************************************************************
   //
   // Subroutine to read changed records in the subfile and update the
   // database records
   //
   BEGSR UpdateSR;
     READC SFLSect;
     DOW NOT %EOF;
       CHAIN FullKey SectionL;
       IF %FOUND(SectionL);
         EXSR MoveSF;
         UPDATE SecRec;
```

continued...

continued...

```
        ENDIF;
        READC SFLSect;
      ENDDO;
   ENDSR;

   // *********************************************************************
   //
   // Subroutine to transfer values from database fields to subfile fields
   //
   BEGSR MoveDB;
     SDays = Days;
     SBegTime = BegTime;
     SRoom = Room;
     SEnroll = Enroll;
     SInstr = Instr;
   ENDSR;

   // *********************************************************************
   //
   // Subroutine to transfer values from subfile fields to database fields
   //
   BEGSR MoveSF;
     Days = SDays;
     BegTime = SBegTime;
     Room = SRoom;
     Enroll = Senroll;
     Instr = Sinstr;
   ENDSR;
 /END-FREE
```

Uses of Subfiles

You can use subfiles in a variety of ways. Subfiles can simply display data, when the user needs only to review information. You can use them for display with selection, so the user can select an entry to obtain more detailed information about the selected record; the user can then update the selected record if desired.

You can use subfiles for data entry of new records to database files, with or without validity checking. You can associate multiple subfiles with a given workstation file. You can display two subfiles simultaneously on the screen. You can transfer data between a program and a subfile by using CHAIN, UPDATE, and WRITE operations, as well as READC; such processing is always based on the relative record numbers of the subfile records. Last, you can display system messages through special message subfiles.

It should be obvious from the above discussion that subfile processing can become complex and that mastery of programming with subfiles, like any kind of programming, comes with practice and experience.

Online Help

Let's turn now to another important component of interactive programs: Well-designed interactive applications often let the user obtain additional information about what he or she is supposed to do. Because of space limitations, this kind of information, called help, normally does not appear on the standard display, but the user can invoke it by pressing the Help key.

The iSeries lets you build such help into your applications as part of your display file DDS. The actual help text may reside in records within a separate display file, through panel groups defined within OS/400's User Interface Manager (UIM), or as records within the display file used in the inter-active application. We will look at only this last technique; for information about the other methods, consult IBM's iSeries manual *OS/400 DDS Reference*.

To build online help into your display file, you first need to include the keyword HELP, at either the file or the record level, to enable the Help key. Once the Help key is enabled, pressing it will display help information associated either with the entire display or with a specific area of the display, depending on how you have implemented this feature.

Global Help

The simplest kind of help to code is help associated with the entire screen. For this kind of implementation, all you need in addition to keyword HELP is file-level keyword HLPRCD, coupled with the name of the record format containing the help text:

```
*.. 1 ...+... 2 ...+... 3 ...+... 4 ...+... 5 ...+... 6 ...+... 7 ...+... 8
AAN01N02N03T.Name++++++RLen++TDpBLinPosFunctions++++++++++++++++++++++++++++++
 * Sample DDS demonstrating global help
A                                       HELP
A                                       HLPRCD(RCD02)
A          R RCD01
            . . .
A          R RCD02
A                                   4  5'This is the record format'
A                                   5  5'containing the help text'
A                                   6  5'that will display when the'
A                                   7  5'user presses the Help key.'
```

Cursor-Sensitive Help

Rather than providing global help, you often want to be able to associate specific help text with specific portions of the screen. You can provide such cursor-sensitive help by including a new kind of format within the record specifications of your DDS — the **help specification format**. The help specification format associates a specific portion of the screen with a specific record of help text. You signal this kind of specification by entering an H in position 17 and the keyword HLPARA (Help Area) in positions 45–80. Help specifications are associated with standard record formats; the H line must appear after any record-level keywords but before any fields of the associated record.

The HLPARA keyword associated with the help specification defines a rectangular area on the screen; if the cursor is within this area when the user presses the Help key, the text of the record associated with the help specification is displayed. You define the rectangular area by specifying within parentheses four numeric values representing the line and column positions of the upper-left corner of the area and the line and column positions of the lower-right corner of the area. In addition to the HLPARA keyword and associated coordinates, the help specification includes keyword HLPRCD to designate which record should be displayed when the user requests help from within the designated screen area.

The following sample DDS illustrates how to provide cursor-sensitive help.

```
*.. 1 ...+... 2 ...+... 3 ...+... 4 ...+... 5 ...+... 6 ...+... 7 ...+... 8
AAN01N02N03T.Name++++++RLen++TdpBLinPosFunctions++++++++++++++++++++++++++++++
 * Sample DDS demonstrating cursor-sensitive help
A                                       INDARA
A                                       CA03(03 'F3=Exit')
A                                       HELP
A                                       HLPRCD(GENHLP)
```

continued...

continued...

```
*.. 1 ...+... 2 ...+... 3 ...+... 4 ...+... 5 ...+... 6 ...+... 7 ...+... 8
A           R INQREC
A           H                           HLPARA(2 10 4 40)
A                                       HLPRCD(REC1)
A           H                           HLPARA(5 15 20 70)
A                                       HLPRCD(REC2)
  . . .
A           R REC1
A                                  1  5'Help text 1'
A           R REC2
A                                  1  5'Help text 2'
A           R GENHLP
A                                  1  5'General help'
```

In this generic example, two different help areas are associated with record format INQREC. Each help area, in turn, evokes a different help record. If the user presses the Help key while viewing INQREC and the cursor is in the rectangular area defined by screen line 2, column 10 and line 4, column 40, then the contents of REC1 are displayed; if the cursor is within the area defined by line 5, column 15 and line 20, column 70, REC2's contents are displayed. If the cursor is outside both of these areas, record GENHLP is displayed.

To further demonstrate online help, the display file from the course-inquiry application is partially duplicated here with the addition of specific help (displayed if the user's cursor is on the screen line asking for course input) and general help instructions (displayed if the cursor is anywhere else on the screen).

```
*.. 1 ...+... 2 ...+... 3 ...+... 4 ...+... 5 ...+... 6 ...+... 7 ...+... 8
AAN01N02N03T.Name++++++RLen++TDpBLinPosFunctions++++++++++++++++++++++++++++++
A                                       INDARA
A                                       CA03(03 'F3=Exit')
A                                       CA12(12 'F12=Cancel')
A                                       HELP
A                                       HLPRCD(GENHLP)
A* Record format of initial inquiry screen
A           R CRSEINQ
A                                       BLINK
A           H                           HLPARA(5 5 5 24)
A                                       HLPRCD(CORHLP)
A                                  1 28'Course Section Update'
A                                  3  2'Type value, then Enter.'
A                                  5  5'Course number . .'
A             COURSENO     6A  B  5 24
A N90                                   DSPATR(UL)
A N90                                   DSPATR(HI)
A  90                                   ERRMSG('Course not found' 90)
A                                 23  2'F3=Exit   F12=Cancel'
A           R GENHLP
A                                  4  5'To get Help, position the'
A                                  4 30' cursor within the item f'
A                                  4 55'or which you want more   '
A                                  5  5'information and press Hel'
A                                  5 30'p.'
A           R CORHLP
A                                  5  5'Enter the 6-character ID '
A                                  5 30'of the course whose secti'
A                                  5 55'ons you want to see.     '
A                                  6  5'(For example, BIS264)'
```

You can have as many help specifications, each describing a different screen area, as you need. The area can be as big or as small as you want to make it. If the user presses the Help key outside all defined help areas, the file-level help record is displayed, if you have included one; otherwise, the system informs the user that no help is available. You cannot use help specifications within subfile record formats, but you can include them as part of subfile control record formats.

Chapter Summary

Subfiles let users work with more than one database record at a time in an interactive application. Records stored in a subfile are displayed in a single output operation to the workstation file; changes made to subfile records are returned to the program in a single input operation.

Defining subfiles within DDS requires two kinds of record formats: one that defines the fields within the subfile and describes the field locations within a screen line, and a second format, called a subfile control record format, that actually manages the displaying of the subfile information.

You use several required keywords with subfiles. Record-level keyword SFL identifies a record format as a subfile record, while record-level keyword SFLCTL identifies a format as a subfile control record format. Additional required keywords determine how many records appear on the screen at the same time, how much total storage the system allocates to the subfile, and when the subfile and its control record are displayed.

Several different techniques exist for loading and displaying subfiles. These methods differ in the relationship they establish between subfile page and subfile size and in when they write records to the subfile relative to when the subfile display begins. Regardless of the technique you use, all applications involving subfiles require additional entries on the File Specifications for the workstation files using the subfiles. You perform all input to and output from a subfile through relative record numbers. The READC operation lets your application program process just those subfile records that the user has changed.

The iSeries lets you associate online help with an entire screen or with specific areas of the screen that the user can access through the Help key.

Key Terms

help specification format
list panels
relative record number
subfile
subfile control record format
subfile record format

Discussion/Review Questions

1. What is a subfile?
2. What are the functions of a subfile record format and a subfile control record format in a display file?
3. Describe the meanings of the following display file keywords and which record format each is used with: SFL, SFLCTL, SFLPAG, SFLSIZ, SFLDSP, SFLCLR, SFLDSPCTL.
4. In subfile processing, how are column headings for the subfile and screen footings (i.e., information to be displayed below the subfile) generally handled?

5. What is a hidden field?

6. When do you need to use the keyword SFLRCDNBR?

7. Discuss the relative merits of different approaches to subfile definition and loading.

8. Discuss page-key control and action with the different approaches to subfile definition and loading.

9. How does the READC operation differ from the other read operations of RPG IV?

10. In using subfiles for updating, why do you need to use fields for the subfile that are different from the fields of the database file you are updating?

11. How do you establish cursor-sensitive help?

Exercises

1. Design the screens and write the DDS for an interactive application that lets a user enter a zip code to list the names of all the company's customers residing within that zip code. Create whatever fields you may need, and make subfile size much greater than page.

2. Write the RPG IV code for Exercise 1. Make up whatever file and field names you need, but be consistent with the definitions used in Exercise 1. Use the technique of loading the entire subfile prior to display.

3. Revise the DDS from Exercise 1 to make subfile size and page equal. Modify the RPG IV code from Exercise 2 to suit this change.

4. Write the pseudocode for an interactive application that displays a list of all a company's product numbers and their descriptions and lets the user place an X in front of those products for which he or she wants more information. The program should then display a screen of detailed product information — quantity on hand, cost, selling price, reorder point, and reorder quantity — for each product selected by the user.

5. Write the generic pseudocode needed to use subfiles for data entry (i.e., for adding large numbers of records to a file).

Programming Assignments

1. Write an interactive application for Wexler University that will let a user enter a department number to display all the instructors working within that department. Use a logical file built over file WUINSTP (described in Appendix F).

2. Write an interactive application for CompuSell that will let a user locate a customer based on a generic name search. That is, the user can enter one or more starting letters of the last name, and the program will display the customers by last name, starting with the first customer whose name meets the generic specification and ending when a customer's name no longer matches that specification.

   The subfile of customers displayed should include just the last name, first name, and identification of the customers, plus a selection field. If the user chooses (selects) one of the records, the program then should display all the detailed information about that customer (all the data fields of the customer master file). You will need to use file CSCSTP and a logical file keyed on last name built over this file (see Appendix F for a description of file CSCSTP). Include a generic help screen in your application.

3. Write an application for Wexler University that will let a user interactively add or change (but not delete) a course and/or its description in files WUCRSP and WUCRSDSP (see Appendix F). Do not let the user change the course identification or add a duplicate identification. All other fields of either file may be changed. Do not display the line numbers of the description on the screen.

4. GTC Telephone Company wants you to develop an interactive application to process payments from customers. The program should let a user enter a screen full of payments at one time by entering for each payer the payer's phone number and amount paid. This information should be used for two purposes: to update the amount-owed and data-of-last-payment fields in the customer master file (GTCSTP) and to write a record to the payments archive file (GTPAYP). Use the system date for date fields. See Appendix F for file layouts.

RPG IV Summary

This appendix summarizes RPG IV specifications, keywords, built-in functions, operation codes, and edit codes. The information is current for Version 5 Release 2 (V5R2) of the ILE RPG/400 compiler; earlier releases may not support some of the entries in this appendix. Entries new in V5R2 are indicated with a note ("V5R2 required"); those entries without a note can be assumed to work at V5R1.

Control Specification

```
*.. 1 ...+... 2 ...+... 3 ...+... 4 ...+... 5 ...+... 6 ...+... 7 ...+... 8
HKeywords++++++++++++++++++++++++++++++++++++++++++++++++++++++++++++++++++++
```

Specification Entries (SEU Format H)

Position(s)	Description
6	Form type = H
7–80	Keywords
81–100	Comments

Control Specification Keywords

ACTGRP	Activation group	ALTSEQ	Alternate collating sequence
ALWNULL	Allow null-capable fields	AUT	Authority
BNDDIR	Binding directories	CCSID	Default Coded Character Set
COPYNEST	Maximum /COPY nesting level		Identifier (CCSID)
COPYRIGHT	Copyright string	CURSYM	Currency symbol
CVTOPT	Convert options	DATEDIT	Y edit code character
DATFMT	Default date format	DEBUG	Debug option
DECEDIT	Decimal edit notation	DFTACTGRP	Default activation group
DFTNAME	Program/module name	ENBPFRCOL	Enable performance collection
EXPROPTS	Expression options	EXTBININT	Integer format for binary fields
FIXNBR	Fix decimal data	FLTDIV	Floating-point division
FORMSALIGN	Forms alignment	FTRANS	File translation
GENLVL	Generation level	INDENT	Source listing indenting
INTPREC	Integer precision	LANGID	Language identifier
NOMAIN	Module without main procedure	OPENOPT	Open printer file option
OPTIMIZE	Optimization level	OPTION	Compile options
PRFDTA	Profiling data	SRTSEQ	Sort sequence table
TEXT	Object text	TIMFMT	Default time format
TRUNCNBR	Move truncated value	USRPRF	User profile

File Specification

```
*.. 1 ...+... 2 ...+... 3 ...+... 4 ...+... 5 ...+... 6 ...+... 7 ...+... 8
FFilename++IPEASFRLen+LKLen+AIDevice+.Keywords++++++++++++++++++++++++++++++
```

Specification Entries (SEU Format F)

Position(s)	Description
6	Form type = F
7–16	File name
17	File type = I/O/U/C
18	File designation = b/P/S/R/T/F
19	End-of-file = b/E
20	File addition = b/A
21	Sequence = b/A/D
22	File format = F/E
23–27	Record length
28	Limits processing = b/L
29–33	Key field length
34	Record address type = b/A/P/K/G/D/T/Z/F
35	File organization = b/I/T
36–42	Device = PRINTER/DISK/WORKSTN/SPECIAL/SEQ
43	(Blank)
44–80	Keywords
81–100	Comments

File Specification Keywords

Keyword	Description	Keyword	Description
BLOCK	Record blocking	COMMIT	Commitment control
DATFMT	Date format	DEVID	Program device
EXTFILE	External file	EXTIND	External indicator
EXTMBR	External member	FORMLEN	Forms length
FORMOFL	Forms overflow line	IGNORE	Ignore record format
INCLUDE	Include record format	INDDS	Indicator data structure
INFDS	Feedback data structure	INFSR	File error subroutine
KEYLOC	Key field location	MAXDEV	Maximum number of devices
OFLIND	Printer file overflow indicator	PASS	Do not pass indicators
PGMNAME	Program for special device file	PLIST	Parameter list for special device file
PREFIX	Prefix characters	PRTCTL	Dynamic printer file
RAFDATA	Record address data file	RECNO	Process by relative record number
RENAME	Rename format	SAVEDS	Save data structure
SAVEIND	Save indicators	SFILE	Subfiles
SLN	Start line number	TIMFMT	Default time format
USROPN	User-controlled open		

Definition Specification

```
*.. 1 ...+... 2 ...+... 3 ...+... 4 ...+... 5 ...+... 6 ...+... 7 ...+... 8
DName+++++++++++ETDsFrom+++To/L+++IDc.Keywords+++++++++++++++++++++++++++++
```

Specification Entries (SEU Format D)

Position(s)	Description
6	Form type = D
7–21	Name
22	External description = Ƅ/E
23	Type of data structure = Ƅ/S/U
24–25	Definition type = Ƅ/C/DS/PI/PR/S
26–32	From position
33–39	To position/length
40	Data type = Ƅ/A/B/C/D/F/G/I/N/P/S/T/U/Z/*
41–42	Decimal positions
43	(Blank)
44–80	Keywords
81–100	Comments

Definition Specification Keywords

Keyword	Description	Keyword	Description
ALIGN	Align fields (data types I, F, U)	ALT	Alternating array
ALTSEQ	Alternate sequence	ASCEND	Ascending order
BASED	Based on pointer	CCSID	Character set ID
CLASS	Class object	CONST	Read-only parameter; constant value
CTDATA	Compile-time data	DATFMT	Date format
DESCEND	Descending order	DIM	Number of table/array elements
DTAARA	Data area name	EXPORT	Field can be exported
EXTFLD	Rename external field	EXTFMT	External format
EXTNAME	External file name	EXTPGM	External program name
EXTPROC	External procedure name	FROMFILE	Load pre-runtime array from file
IMPORT	Field can be imported	INZ	Initialize data
LIKE	Define like another field	LIKEDS	Define like another data structure
LIKEREC	Define like another record format (V5R2 required)	NOOPT	No optimization
		OCCURS	Number of occurrence
OPDESC	Operational descriptor	OPTIONS	Parameter-passing options
OVERLAY	Overlay data structure	PACKEVEN	Packed field has even number of digits
PERRCD	Number of elements per record	PREFIX	Prefix externally described fields
PROCPTR	Procedure pointer	QUALIFIED	Use qualified subfield names
STATIC	Static variable or method	TIMFMT	Time format
TOFILE	Write pre-runtime array to file	VALUE	Pass parameter by value
VARYING	Variable-length field		

Input Specification (Program-Described File)

```
*.. 1 ...+... 2 ...+... 3 ...+... 4 ...+... 5 ...+... 6 ...+... 7 ...+... 8
IFilename++SqNORiPos1+NCCPos2+NCCPos3+NCC.................................
I....................Fmt+SPFrom+To+++DcField++++++++L1M1FrPlMnZr......
```

Record Identification Entries (SEU Format I)

Position(s)	Description
6	Form type = I
7–16	File name
16–18	Logical relationship = AND/OR
17–18	Sequence
19	Number = ƀ/1/N
20	Option = ƀ/O
21–22	Record-identifying indicator
23–27	Position
28	Logical relationship = ƀ/N
29	Code part = C/Z/D
30	Character
31–35	Position
36	Logical relationship = ƀ/N
37	Code part = C/Z/D
38	Character
39–43	Position
44	Logical relationship = ƀ/N
45	Code part = C/Z/D
46	Character
47–80	(Blank)
81–100	Comments

Field Entries (SEU Format J)

Position(s)	Description
6	Form type = I
7–30	(Blank)
31–34	Data attributes
35	Date/time separator
36	Data format = ƀ/A/B/C/D/F/G/I/L/N/P/R/S/T/U/Z
37–41	From position
42–46	To position
47–48	Decimal positions
49–62	Field name

continued...

continued...

63–64	Control level indicator
65–66	Match field indicator
67–68	Field record relation indicator
69–74	Field indicators
75–80	(Blank)
81–100	Comments

Input Specification (Externally Described File)

```
*.. 1 ...+... 2 ...+... 3 ...+... 4 ...+... 5 ...+... 6 ...+... 7 ...+... 8
IRcdname+++....Ri.......................................................
I.............Ext-field+................Field++++++++L1M1..PlMnZr......
```

Record Identification Entries (SEU Format IX)

Position(s)	Description
6	Form type = I
7–16	Record name
17–20	(Blank)
21–22	Record-identifying indicators
23–80	(Blank)
81–100	Comments

Field Entries (SEU Format JX)

Position(s)	Description
6	Form type = I
7–20	(Blank)
21–30	External field name
31–48	(Blank)
49–62	RPG field name
63–64	Control level indicator
Position(s)	**Description**
65–66	Match field indicator
67–68	(Blank)
69–74	Field indicators
75–80	(Blank)
81–100	Comments

Calculation Specification

```
*.. 1 ...+... 2 ...+... 3 ...+... 4 ...+... 5 ...+... 6 ...+... 7 ...+... 8
CLØNØ1Factor1+++++++Opcode(E)+Factor2+++++++Result+++++++++Len++D+HiLoEq....
CLØNØ1Factor1+++++++Opcode(E)+Extended-factor2+++++++++++++++++++++++++++++
```

Traditional Format (SEU Format C)

Position(s)	Description
6	Form type = C
7–8	Control level indicator
9–11	Conditioning indicator
12–25	Factor 1
26–35	Operation code (and extender)
36–49	Factor 2
50–63	Result field
64–68	Result-field length
69–70	Result-field decimal positions
71–76	Resulting indicators
77–80	(Blank)
81–100	Comments

Extended Factor 2 Format (SEU Format CX)

Position(s)	Description
6	Form type = C
7–8	Control level indicator
9–11	Conditioning indicator
12–25	(Blank)
26–35	Operation code (and extender)
36–80	Extended Factor 2
81–100	Comments

Output Specification (Program-Described File)

```
*.. 1 ...+... 2 ...+... 3 ...+... 4 ...+... 5 ...+... 6 ...+... 7 ...+... 8
OFilename++DF..NØ1NØ2NØ3Excnam++++B++A++Sb+Sa+.............................
O..............NØ1NØ2NØ3Field++++++++++YB.End++PConstant/editword/DTformat++
```

Record Identification Entries (SEU Format OD)

Position(s)	Description
6	Form type = O
7–16	File name
16–18	Logical relationship = AND/OR
17	Type = H/D/T/E
18	Fetch overflow or release = b/F/R
18–20	Record addition = b/ADD/DEL
21–29	Output indicators
30–39	EXCEPT name
40–42	Space before
43–45	Space after
46–48	Skip before
49–51	Skip after
52–80	(Blank)
81–100	Comments

Field Entries (SEU Format P)

Position(s)	Description
6	Form type = O
7–20	(Blank)
21–29	Output indicators
30–43	Field name or *ALL
44	Edit code
45	Blank after = b/B
46	(Blank)
47–51	Ending output position
52	Data format = b/A/B/C/D/F/G/I/L/N/P/R/S/T/U/Z
53–80	Constant, edit word, data attribute, format name
81–100	Comments

Output Specification (Externally Described File)

```
*.. 1 ...+... 2 ...+... 3 ...+... 4 ...+... 5 ...+... 6 ...+... 7 ...+... 8
ORcdname+++D...NØ1NØ2NØ3Excnam++++..............................................
O.............NØ1NØ2NØ3Field+++++++++.B..........................................
```

Record Identification Entries (SEU Format O)

Position(s)	Description
6	Form type = O
7–16	Record name
16–18	Logical relationship = AND/OR
17	Type = H/D/T/E
18	Release = b/R
18–20	Record addition = b/ADD/DEL
21–29	Output indicators
30–39	EXCEPT name
40–80	(Blank)
81–100	Comments

Field Entries (SEU Format P)

Position(s)	Description
6	Form type = O
7–20	(Blank)
21–29	Output indicators
30–43	Field name or *ALL
44	(Blank)
45	Blank after = b/B
46–80	(Blank)
81–100	Comments

Procedure Specification

```
*.. 1 ...+... 2 ...+... 3 ...+... 4 ...+... 5 ...+... 6 ...+... 7 ...+... 8
PName++++++++++..B....................Keywords++++++++++++++++++++++++++++++++
```

Specification Entries (SEU Format PR)

Position(s)	Description
6	Form type = P
7–21	Procedure name
22–23	(Blank)
24	Begin, end = B/E
25–43	(Blank)
44–80	Keywords
81–100	Comments

Procedure Specification Keywords

EXPORT

Edit Codes

Common Edit Codes

Option		Edit code			
Commas	**Zero balances to print**	**No sign**	**CR**	**Right –**	**Floating –**
Yes	Yes	1	A	J	N
Yes	No	2	B	K	O
No	Yes	3	C	L	P
No	No	4	D	M	Q

Y = insert slashes (/) between month, day, and year; suppress leading zeros

Z = remove sign from a numeric field; suppress leading zeros

Operation Codes and Functions

This section lists RPG IV's operation codes and built-in functions using the following format:

%Function and Name

Function: %Function(required-entry:optional-entry)

Operation Code and Name

Free-form: Opcode(optional extenders) required-entry optional-entry

Factor 1		Factor 2	Result	HI	LO	EQ
Optional entry (not underlined)	Opcode (with optional extenders)	Required entry (underlined)		Req Ind	Opt Ind	

Note: In the examples above, the required and optional entries are underlined or not underlined, respectively, as examples of how the syntax descriptions will look.

Following each syntax example, you'll find a description of the operation code or function. If an operation code has a newer equivalent operation code or built-in function, the operation code will be labeled "Obsolete" and the new operation code or function will be noted.

%ABS Absolute value

Function: %ABS(numeric-expression)

Returns absolute value of expression, removing sign if negative.

ACQ Acquire a program device for a WORKSTN file

Free-form: ACQ(E) device-name workstn-file

Factor 1		Factor 2	Result	HI	LO	EQ
Device name	ACQ(E)	WORKSTN file			ER	

Attaches a device to a workstation file.

ADD Add two values together

Free-form: Not supported

Factor 1		Factor 2	Result	HI	LO	EQ
Addend 1	ADD(H)	Addend 2	Sum	+	–	Z

If there is a value in Factor 1, adds that value to the value in Factor 2. If there is not a value in Factor 1, adds the value in Factor 2 to the result. The sum is always placed in the Result field.

Note: *Obsolete.* Use + operator instead.

ADDDUR Add duration

Free-form: Not supported

Factor 1		Factor 2	Result	HI	LO	EQ
Date/Time 1	ADDDUR(E)	Duration:code	Date/Time 2		ER	

Adds a duration (e.g., a number of days) to a date, time, or timestamp.

Note: *Obsolete.* Use + operator with duration function (e.g., %DAYS, %MONTHS, %YEARS) instead.

%ADDR Get address pointer

Function: %ADDR(variable(index-expression))

Returns a basing pointer representing the storage address of the specified variable. On the left side of an assignment expression, assigns a storage address to a pointer.

%ALLOC Allocate storage

Function: %ALLOC(length)

Returns a pointer to uninitialized storage of the specified length.

ALLOC Allocate storage

Free-form: Not supported

Factor 1		Factor 2	Result	HI	LO	EQ
	ALLOC(E)	Length	Pointer		ER	

Allocates uninitialized storage of the specified length, setting a pointer to the new storage.

> **Note:** *Obsolete.* Use %ALLOC function instead.

AND*xx* And operation

Free-form: Not supported

Factor 1		Factor 2	Result	HI	LO	EQ
Compare value 1	AND*xx*	Compare value 2				

AND*xx* is an optional operation, used to specify a complex condition. When used, it must immediately follow a DOU*xx*, DOW*xx*, IF*xx*, OR*xx*, or WHEN*xx* operation. In the AND*xx* operation, the relationship *xx* can be

GT	Factor 1	>	Factor 2
LT	Factor 1	<	Factor 2
EQ	Factor 1	=	Factor 2
NE	Factor 1	<>	Factor 2
GE	Factor 1	>=	Factor 2
LE	Factor 1	<=	Factor 2

> **Note:** *Obsolete.* Use AND operator instead.

BEGSR Begin a subroutine

Free-form: BEGSR subroutine-name

Factor 1		Factor 2	Result	HI	LO	EQ
Subroutine name	BEGSR					

Identifies the beginning of a subroutine.

%BITAND Bitwise AND (V5R2 Required)

Function: %BITAND(expr1:expr2 {:exprn})

Returns bitwise ANDing of all arguments.

%BITNOT Bitwise NOT (V5R2 Required)

Function: %BITNOT(expr)

Returns bitwise inverse of bits in argument.

BITOFF Set bits off

Free-form: Not supported

Factor 1		Factor 2	Result	HI	LO	EQ
	BITOFF	Bit numbers	Character field			

Causes bits identified in Factor 2 to be set off (set to 0) in the Result field.

BITON Set bits on

Free-form: Not supported

Factor 1		Factor 2	Result	HI	LO	EQ
	BITON	Bit numbers	Character field			

Causes bits identified in Factor 2 to be set on (set to 1) in the Result field.

%BITOR Bitwise OR (V5R2 Required)

Function: %BITOR(expr1:expr2)

Returns bitwise ORing of arguments.

%BITXOR Bitwise Exclusive OR (V5R2 Required)

Function: %BITXOR(expr1:expr2)

Returns bitwise exclusive ORing of arguments.

CAB*xx* Compare and branch

Free-form: Not supported

Factor 1		Factor 2	Result	HI	LO	EQ
Compare value 1	CAB*xx*	Compare value 2	Label	HI	LO	EQ

Compares the two values specified by the *xx* portion of the operation and branches to the TAG or ENDSR operation. In the CAB.*xx* operation, the *xx* can be

GT	Factor 1	>	Factor 2
LT	Factor 1	<	Factor 2
EQ	Factor 1	=	Factor 2
NE	Factor 1	<>	Factor 2
GE	Factor 1	>=	Factor 2
LE	Factor 1	<=	Factor 2

Note: *Obsolete*. Use free-form expressions instead.

CALL Call a program

Free-form: Not supported

Factor 1		Factor 2	Result	HI	LO	EQ
	CALL(E)	Program name	Plist name		ER	LR

Passes control to the program specified in Factor 2.

Note: *Obsolete*. Use CALLP instead.

CALLB Call a bound procedure

Free-form: Not supported

Factor 1		Factor 2	Result	HI	LO	EQ
	CALLB(DE)	Procedure name or procedure pointer	Plist name		ER	LR

Passes control to the program specified in Factor 2.

Note: *Obsolete*. Use CALLP instead.

CALLP Call a prototyped procedure or program

Free-form: CALLP(EMR) name(parm1:parm2:...)

Factor 1		Extended Factor 2
	CALLP(EMR)	Name (Parm1:Parm2 ...)

Passes control to the procedure or program specified in the extended Factor 2 using any parameters specified in the extended Factor 2. You must include a prototype definition for the procedure or program to call.

CAS*xx* Conditionally invoke subroutine

Free-form: Not supported

Factor 1		Factor 2	Result	HI	LO	EQ
Compare value 1	CASxx	Compare value 2	Subroutine name	HI	LO	EQ

Conditionally invokes a subroutine. In the CAS*xx* operation, the *xx* relationship can be defined as

GT	Factor 1	>	Factor 2
LT	Factor 1	<	Factor 2
EQ	Factor 1	=	Factor 2
NE	Factor 1	<>	Factor 2
GE	Factor 1	>=	Factor 2
LE	Factor 1	<=	Factor 2
(Blank)	(No comparison made)		

Note: *Obsolete.* Use SELECT and WHEN instead.

CAT Concatenate two character strings

Free-form: Not supported

Factor 1		Factor 2	Result	HI	LO	EQ
Source string 1	CAT(P)	Source string 2: number of blanks	Target string			

Concatenates the character string specified in source string 2 to the end of the character string specified in source string 1. The concatenated string is placed in the target string in the Result field.

Note: *Obsolete.* Use free-form expressions instead.

CHAIN Random retrieval from a file based on key value or record number

Free-form: CHAIN(EN) search-argument file-format-name data-structure

Factor 1		Factor 2	Result	HI	LO	EQ
Search argument	CHAIN(EN)	File name or format name	Data structure	NR	ER	

Randomly retrieves a file based on key value or record number.

%CHAR Convert to character data

Function: %CHAR(<u>expression</u>:format)

Converts an expression (numeric, date, time, timestamp, graphic, or UCS-2 data) to character data.

%CHECK Check characters

Function: %CHECK(<u>compare-string:base-string</u>:start)

Verifies that each character in the base string is among the valid characters indicated in the compare string. Returns leftmost position of character in base string that is not in compare string.

CHECK Check characters

Free-form: Not supported

Factor 1		Factor 2	Result	HI	LO	EQ
<u>Compare string</u>	CHECK(E)	<u>Base string</u>:start	Left position(s)		ER	FD

Verifies that each character in the base string is among the valid characters indicated in the compare string.

> **Note:** *Obsolete.* Use %CHECK function instead.

%CHECKR Check characters (reversed)

Function: %CHECKR(<u>compare-string:base-string</u>:start)

Verifies that each character in the base string is among the valid characters indicated in the compare string. Checking begins with the rightmost character. Returns rightmost position of character in base string that is not in compare string.

CHECKR Check characters (reversed)

Free-form: Not supported

Factor 1		Factor 2	Result	HI	LO	EQ
<u>Compare string</u>	CHECKR(E)	<u>Base string</u>:start	Right position(s)		ER	FD

Verifies that each character in the source string is among the valid characters indicated in the compare string. Checking begins with the rightmost character.

> **Note:** *Obsolete.* Use %CHECKR function instead.

CLEAR Clear data structure, variable, or record format

Free-form: CLEAR *NOKEY *ALL structure-variable

Factor 1		Factor 2	Result	HI	LO	EQ
*NOKEY	CLEAR	*ALL	Structure or variable			

Clears a data structure, variable, or record format, setting it to its default value.

CLOSE Close files

Free-form: CLOSE(E) file-name

Factor 1		Factor 2	Result	HI	LO	EQ
	CLOSE(E)	File name			ER	

Closes one or more files or devices and disconnects them from the program.

COMMIT Commit group

Free-form: COMMIT(E) boundary

Factor 1		Factor 2	Result	HI	LO	EQ
Boundary	COMMIT(E)				ER	

Makes all the changes to files that have been specified in output operations since the previous COMMIT or ROLBK operation. Releases all the record locks for files under commitment control.

COMP Compare two values

Free-form: Not supported

Factor 1		Factor 2	Result	HI	LO	EQ
Compare value 1	COMP	Compare value 2		HI	LO	EQ

Compares two values, setting result indicators on or off depending upon the comparison.

Note: *Obsolete.* Use free-form expressions instead.

%DATE Convert to date

Function: %DATE(expression:format)

Converts expression (numeric, character, or timestamp data type), returning a date in *ISO format.

%DAYS   Number of days

Function: %DAYS(number)

Converts a number to a duration representing a number of days that can be added or subtracted to a date or timestamp.

DEALLOC   Free storage

Free-form: DEALLOC(EN) pointer

Factor 1		Factor 2	Result	HI	LO	EQ
	DEALLOC(EN)		Pointer		ER	

Frees storage previously allocated by ALLOC operation.

%DEC   Convert to packed decimal
%DECH   Convert to packed decimal with half-adjust

Function: %DEC(numeric-expression:precision:decimals)
        %DECH(numeric-expression:precision:decimals)

Converts a numeric expression to packed decimal format (optionally with half-adjusting) with the specified precision and number of decimal places. (**V5R2 enhancement:** Now supports character expressions.)

%DECPOS   Get number of decimal positions

Function: %DECPOS(numeric-expression)

Returns the number of decimal positions in the numeric expression or variable.

DEFINE   Field definition

Free-form: Not supported

Factor 1		Factor 2	Result	HI	LO	EQ
*LIKE	DEFINE	Referenced field	Defined field			
*DTAARA	DEFINE	External data area	Internal field			

Defines a field based on the attributes of another field (*LIKE), or defines a field as a data area (*DTAARA), depending on the entry in Factor 1.

Note: *Obsolete.* Use Definition Specifications (D-specs) with the LIKE or DTAARA keyword instead.

DELETE Delete record

Free-form: DELETE(E) search-argument <u>file-format-name</u>

Factor 1		Factor 2	Result	HI	LO	EQ
Search argument	DELETE(E)	<u>File name</u> or <u>Format name</u>		NR	ER	

Deletes a record from a database file. The file must be specified as an update file.

%DIFF Difference between two dates/times/timestamps

Function: %DIFF(<u>date1</u>:<u>date2</u>:<u>duration-code</u>)

Returns the difference (duration) between two date, time, or timestamp values.

%DIV Integer division

Function: %DIV(<u>dividend</u>:<u>divisor</u>)

Returns integer portion of quotient when dividing dividend by divisor.

DIV Divide operation

Free-form: Not supported

]Factor 1		Factor 2	Result	HI	LO	EQ
Dividend	DIV(H)	<u>Divisor</u>	<u>Quotient</u>	+	–	Z

If there is a value in Factor 1, divide that value by the value in Factor 2. If there is not a value in Factor 1, the result is divided by the value in Factor 2. The quotient is always placed in the Result field.

Note: *Obsolete.* Use / operator or %DIV function instead.

DO Begin a DO group

Free-form: Not supported

Factor 1		Factor 2	Result	HI	LO	EQ
Starting value	DO	Limit value	Index value			

Begins a DO group of operations and indicates the number of times the group is processed.

Note: *Obsolete.* Use FOR instead.

DOU Do until

Free-form: DOU(MR) <u>logical-expression</u>

Factor 1		Extended Factor 2
	DOU(MR)	<u>Logical expression</u>

Begins a group of operations you want to process at least one time, and usually more than once, until a logical expression is true.

DOU*xx* Do until *xx*

Free-form: Not supported

Factor 1		Factor 2	Result	HI	LO	EQ
<u>Compare value 1</u>	DOU*xx*	<u>Compare value 2</u>				

Begins a group of operations you want to process at least one time, and usually more than once, until a condition is satisfied. In the DOU*xx* operation, the *xx* can be

GT	Factor 1	>	Factor 2
LT	Factor 1	<	Factor 2
EQ	Factor 1	=	Factor 2
NE	Factor 1	<>	Factor 2
GE	Factor 1	>=	Factor 2
LE	Factor 1	<=	Factor 2

Note: *Obsolete.* Use DOU instead.

DOW Do while

Free-form: DOW(MR) <u>logical-expression</u>

Factor 1		Extended Factor 2
	DOW(MR)	<u>Logical expression</u>

Begins a group of operations you want to process while the logical expression is true.

DOW*xx* Do while *xx*

Free-form: Not supported

Factor 1		Factor 2	Result	HI	LO	EQ
<u>Compare value 1</u>	DOW*xx*	<u>Compare value 2</u>				

Begins a group of operations you want to process while the relationship *xx* exists. In the DOW*xx*, *xx* can be

GT   Factor 1   >   Factor 2
LT   Factor 1   <   Factor 2
EQ   Factor 1   =   Factor 2
NE   Factor 1   <>   Factor 2
GE   Factor 1   >=   Factor 2
LE   Factor 1   <=   Factor 2

Note: *Obsolete.* Use DOW instead.

DSPLY   Display function

Free-form: DSPLY(E) message message-queue response

Factor 1		Factor 2	Result	HI	LO	EQ
Message	DSPLY(E)	Message queue	Response		ER	

Lets the program communicate with a display workstation that requested the program.

DUMP   Program dump

Free-form: DUMP(A) identifier

Factor 1		Factor 2	Result	HI	LO	EQ
Identifier	DUMP(A)					

Provides a detailed listing of the values for all fields, files, indicators, data structures, arrays, and tables, to aid in debugging a program. The DUMP is performed if DEBUG(*YES) is specified in Control (Header) Specifications or if the (A) extender is coded.

%EDITC   Apply an edit code

Function: %EDITC(<u>numeric-expression</u>:<u>edit-code</u>:fill)

Returns a character result representing the edited number after applying an edit code to it.

%EDITFLT   Convert to floating point

Function: %EDITFLT(<u>numeric-expression</u>)

Converts a numeric expression to the external character display format for a floating-point number.

%EDITW Apply an edit word

Function: %EDITW(numeric-expression:edit-word)

Returns a character result representing the edited number after applying an edit word to it.

%ELEM Number of elements

Function: %ELEM(data-item)

Returns the number of elements in a table, array, or multiple-occurrence data structure.

ELSE

Free-form: ELSE

Factor 1		Factor 2	Result	HI	LO	EQ
	ELSE					

Used optionally with the IF and IF*xx* operations to indicate a block of code to process when the IF condition is not satisfied.

ELSEIF Else if

Free-form: ELSEIF(MR) logical-expression

Factor 1		Extended Factor 2
	ELSEIF(MR)	Logical expression

Lets a group of calculations be processed if a logical expression is true and if the logical expression for the previous IF/ELSEIF statement(s) in the IF block was false.

END*yy* End a structured group

Free-form: END*yy* increment-value

Factor 1		Factor 2	Result	HI	LO	EQ
	END*yy*	Increment value				

Used to end a structured group of code. Use one of the following values in place of *yy*:

(Blank)	Ends any structured group. Not supported by free-format syntax. *Obsolete.*
CS	Ends a CAS*xx* group. Not supported by free-format syntax.
DO	Ends a DO, DOU, DOW, DOU*xx*, or DOW*xx* group
FOR	Ends a FOR group
IF	Ends an IF or IF*xx* group
MON	Ends a MONITOR group
SL	Ends a SELECT group

ENDSR End of subroutine
Free-form: ENDSR return-point

Factor 1		Factor 2	Result	HI	LO	EQ
Label	ENDSR	Return point				

Marks the end of a subroutine.

%EOF End of file
Function: %EOF(file-name)

Returns the end-of-file (or beginning-of-file) condition — *ON or *OFF — after a read operation or a write to a subfile. %EOF applies to READ, READE, READP, READPE, READC, and WRITE (subfile only) operations and, with restrictions, to CHAIN, SETLL, SETGT, and OPEN operations.

%EQUAL Equal match
Function: %EQUAL(file-name)

Returns *ON if the most recent LOOKUP or SETLL operation found an exact match; otherwise, returns *OFF.

%ERROR Error
Function: %ERROR

Returns *ON if the most recent operation code with an (E) extender resulted in an error condition; otherwise, returns *OFF.

EVAL Evaluate expression
Free-form: EVAL(HMR) assignment-statement

Factor 1		Extended Factor 2
	EVAL(HMR)	Assignment statement

Assigns to a variable the result of an expression. With non-numeric (character, graphic, or UCS-2) expressions, the result will be left-adjusted, and padded or truncated on the right, if necessary.

EVALR Evaluate expression, right-adjust
Free-form: EVALR(MR) assignment-statement

Factor 1		Extended Factor 2
	EVALR(MR)	Assignment statement

Evaluates a non-numeric (character, graphic, or UCS-2) expression and assigns the result to a variable, right-adjusting the result, and padding or truncating on the left, if necessary.

EXCEPT Calculation time output
Free-form: EXCEPT name

Factor 1		Factor 2	Result	HI	LO	EQ
	EXCEPT	Name				

Writes one or more output records during calculations.

EXFMT Write then read format
Free-form: EXFMT(E) format-name

Factor 1		Factor 2	Result	HI	LO	EQ
	EXFMT(E)	Format name			ER	

The EXFMT operation is a combination of a WRITE followed by a READ to the same display record format.

EXSR Invoke subroutine
Free-form: EXSR subroutine-name

Factor 1		Factor 2	Result	HI	LO	EQ
	EXSR	Subroutine name				

Branches to a subroutine, then continues with the next Calculation Specification upon return from the subroutine.

EXTRCT Extract date/time/timestamp
Free-form: Not supported

Factor 1		Factor 2	Result	HI	LO	EQ
	EXTRCT(E)	Date/Time: duration code	Target		ER	

Returns a segment of a date, time, or timestamp field.

Note: *Obsolete.* Use %SUBDT function instead.

FEOD Force end of data

Free-form: FEOD(E) file-name

Factor 1		Factor 2	Result	HI	LO	EQ
	FEOD(E)	File name			ER	

Signals the logical end of data for a primary, secondary, or full procedural file.

%FLOAT Convert to floating point

Function: %FLOAT(numeric-expression)

Converts a numeric expression to floating-point format. (**V5R2 enhancement:** Now supports character expressions.)

FOR For

Free-form: FOR(MR) index = start BY increment TO|DOWNTO limit

Factor 1		Extended Factor 2
	FOR	Index = Start BY increment TO|DOWNTO limit

Begins a FOR group of operations and controls the number of times the group is processed.

FORCE Force a certain file to be read next cycle

Free-form: FORCE file-name

Factor 1		Factor 2	Result	HI	LO	EQ
	FORCE	File name				

Selects the file from which the next record will be read.

%FOUND Found

Function: %FOUND(file-name)

Returns *ON if the most recent relevant operation found a record or element; otherwise, returns *OFF. %FOUND applies to CHAIN, DELETE, SETLL, and SETGT file operations; CHECK, CHECKR, and SCAN string operations; and the LOOKUP search operation.

GOTO Go to label

Free-form: Not supported

Factor 1		Factor 2	Result	HI	LO	EQ
	GOTO	Label				

Branches to a specific location in a program, identified by a TAG operation.

%GRAPH Convert to graphic

Function: %GRAPH(expression:ccsid)

Converts a character, graphic, or UCS-2 expression to graphic format.

%HOURS Number of hours

Function: %HOURS(number)

Converts a number to a duration representing a number of hours that can be added to or subtracted from a time or timestamp.

IF If

Free-form: IF(MR) logical-expression

Factor 1		Extended Factor 2
	IF(MR)	Logical expression

Lets a group of calculations be processed if a logical expression is true.

IFxx If xx

Free-form: Not supported

Factor 1		Factor 2	Result	HI	LO	EQ
Compare value 1	IFxx	Compare value 2				

Lets a group of calculations be processed if a given relationship exists between factors. The xx in the IFxx operation can be

GT	Factor 1	>	Factor 2	
LT	Factor 1	<	Factor 2	
EQ	Factor 1	=	Factor 2	
NE	Factor 1	<>	Factor 2	
GE	Factor 1	>=	Factor 2	
LE	Factor 1	<=	Factor 2	

Note: *Obsolete.* Use IF instead.

IN Retrieve a data area

Free-form: IN(E) *LOCK <u>data-area-name</u>

Factor 1		Factor 2	Result	HI	LO	EQ
*LOCK	IN(E)	<u>Data area name</u>			ER	

Retrieves a data area and lets you specify whether or not the data area is to be locked from update by another program.

%INT Convert to integer format
%INTH Convert to integer format with half-adjust

Function: %INT(<u>numeric-expression</u>)
        %INTH(<u>numeric-expression</u>)

Converts a numeric expression to integer format (optionally with half-adjusting). (**V5R2 enhancement:** Now supports character expressions.)

ITER Iterate

Free-form: ITER

Factor 1		Factor 2	Result	HI	LO	EQ
	ITER					

Transfers control within a DO group to the ENDDO statement of the DO group.

%KDS Key Data Structure (V5R2 Required)

Function: %KDS(<u>ds-name</u>:number-of-fields)

Specifies data structure (and optional number of subfields) to use as the key list for CHAIN, DELETE, READE, READPE, SETLL, and SETGT operations.

KFLD Define parts of a key

Free-form: Not supported

Factor 1		Factor 2	Result	HI	LO	EQ
	KFLD		<u>Key field</u>			

Defines a field in a list of fields (KLIST) that make up the key to a file.

KLIST Define a composite key

Free-form: Not supported

Factor 1		Factor 2	Result	HI	LO	EQ
<u>Klist name</u>	KLIST					

Gives a name to a list of KFLDs. This list can be used as a search argument to retrieve records from files that have a composite key.

LEAVE Leave a DO group

Free-form: LEAVE

Factor 1		Factor 2	Result	HI	LO	EQ
	LEAVE					

Transfers control from within a DO group to the statement following the ENDDO operation.

LEAVESR Leave a subroutine

Free-form: LEAVESR

Factor 1		Factor 2	Result	HI	LO	EQ
	LEAVESR					

Transfers control to the ENDSR operation in a subroutine.

%LEN Get or set length

Function: %LEN(expression)

Returns the number of digits or characters in an expression, or sets the current length of a variable-length field.

%LOOKUP*xx* Look up element in an array

Function: %LOOKUP*xx*(search-argument:array:start:number-of-elements)

Searches an array for a specific element; returns the array index of the found element (or 0, if the search is unsuccessful). The *xx* in the %LOOKUP*xx* function can be

(Blank)	Find an exact match to search argument.
LT	Find element closest to but less than search argument.
LE	Find exact match, or element closest to but less than search argument.
GE	Find exact match, or element closest to but greater than search argument.
GT	Find element closest to but greater than search argument.

LOOKUP Look up element in an array or table

Free-form: Not supported

Factor 1		Factor 2	Result	HI	LO	EQ
Search argument	LOOKUP	Array name		HI	LO	EQ
Search argument	LOOKUP	Table name	Table name	HI	LO	EQ

Searches an array or table for a specific element.

Note: *Obsolete.* Use *%LOOKUPxx* or *%TLOOKUPxx* function instead.

MHHZO Move high to high zone

Free-form: Not supported

Factor 1		Factor 2	Result	HI	LO	EQ
	MHHZO	Source field	Target field			

Moves the zone portion of a character from the leftmost zone of the source field to the leftmost zone of the target field.

MHLZO Move high to low zone

Free-form: Not supported

Factor 1		Factor 2	Result	HI	LO	EQ
	MHLZO	Source field	Target field			

Moves the zone portion of a character from the leftmost zone of the source field to the rightmost zone of the target field.

%MINUTES Number of minutes

Function: %MINUTES(number)

Converts a number to a duration representing a number of minutes that can be added to or subtracted from a time or timestamp.

MLHZO Move low to high zone

Free-form: Not supported

Factor 1		Factor 2	Result	HI	LO	EQ
	MLHZO	Source field	Target field			

Moves the zone portion of a character from the rightmost zone of the source field to the leftmost zone of the target field.

MLLZO Move low to low zone

Free-form: Not supported

Factor 1		Factor 2	Result	HI	LO	EQ
	MLLZO	Source field	Target field			

Moves the zone portion of a character from the rightmost zone of the source field to the rightmost zone of the target field.

MONITOR Begin a monitor group

Free-form: MONITOR

Factor 1		Factor 2	Result	HI	LO	EQ
	MONITOR					

Begins a group of statements to be processed with specific conditional error handling, based on the status code. In addition to the statements to be processed, the monitor group will include one or more on-error blocks, which will be processed if specific exceptions occur within the monitor group.

%MONTHS Number of months

Function: %MONTHS(number)

Converts a number to a duration representing a number of months that can be added to or subtracted from a date or timestamp.

MOVE Move characters from source field to target field

Free-form: Not supported

Factor 1		Factor 2	Result	HI	LO	EQ
Date/Time format	MOVE(P)	Source field	Target field	+	–	ZB

Transfers characters from a source field to a target field. The move starts with rightmost character of the source field. If the source field is longer than the target field, the excess leftmost characters are not moved.

MOVEA Move array

Free-form: Not supported

Factor 1		Factor 2	Result	HI	LO	EQ
	MOVEA(P)	Source	Target	+	–	ZB

Transfers character, graphic, or numeric values from the source to the target; either the source or the target must be an array. The source and the target cannot specify the same array even if the array is indexed.

MOVEL Move left

Free-form: Not supported

Factor 1		Factor 2	Result	HI	LO	EQ
Date/Time format	MOVEL(P)	Source field	Target field	+	–	ZB

Transfers characters from the source to the target. The move begins with the leftmost character of the source field. If the source field is longer than the target field, the excess rightmost characters are not moved.

%MSECONDS Number of microseconds

Function: %MSECONDS(number)

Converts a number to a duration representing a number of microseconds that can be added or subtracted to a time or timestamp.

MULT Multiply

Free-form: Not supported

Factor 1		Factor 2	Result	HI	LO	EQ
Multiplicand	MULT(H)	Multiplier	Product	+	–	Z

Multiplies the value in the Factor 2 position by the value in Factor 1, if there is one. If there is not a value in Factor 1, the Factor 2 value is multiplied by the value in the Result field. The product is always placed in the Result field.

> **Note:** *Obsolete.* Use * operator instead.

MVR Move remainder

Free-form: Not supported

Factor 1		Factor 2	Result	HI	LO	EQ
	MVR		Remainder	+	–	Z

Moves the remainder of the immediately previous DIV operation to a separate field named in the Result field.

> **Note:** *Obsolete.* Use %REM function instead.

NEXT Specify next input for multiple-device file

Free-form: NEXT(E) program-device file-name

Factor 1		Factor 2	Result	HI	LO	EQ
Program device	NEXT(E)	File name			ER	

Forces the next input for a multiple-device file to come from a specific program device.

%NULLIND Get or set null indicator

Function: %NULLIND(field)

On the right side of an expression, returns the null indicator setting — *ON or *OFF — for a field; on the left side of an expression, sets the null indicator for a field.

%OCCUR Get or set occurrence of a data structure

Function: %OCCUR(data-structure)

On the right side of an expression, returns the current occurrence number of a multiple-occurrence data structure; on the left side of an expression, specifies which occurrence is to be used next.

OCCUR Get or set occurrence of a data structure

Free-form: Not supported

Factor 1		Factor 2	Result	HI	LO	EQ
Occurrence value 1	OCCUR(E)	Data structure	Occurrence value 2		ER	

Specifies which occurrence of a multiple-occurrence data structure is to be used next, or gets the current occurrence of a multiple-occurrence data structure.

Note: *Obsolete.* Use %OCCUR function instead.

ON-ERROR On error

Free-form: ON-ERROR exception-id1:exception-id2 ...

Factor 1		Extended Factor 2
	ON-ERROR	Exception-id1:exception-id2 ...

Specifies which error conditions are to be handled by an on-error block within a monitor group. After all the statements in the on-error block are processed, control passes to the statement following the monitor group's ENDMON statement.

%OPEN Return open file condition

Function: %OPEN(file-name)

Returns *ON if the specified file is open; otherwise, returns *OFF.

OPEN Open file for processing

Free-form: OPEN(E) file-name

Factor 1		Factor 2	Result	HI	LO	EQ
	OPEN(E)	File name			ER	

Explicitly opens the file named in Factor 2. The file named cannot be designated as a primary, secondary, or table file and must specify UC in positions 73–74 of the File Description Specifications.

ORxx Or condition xx

Free-form: Not supported

Factor 1		Factor 2	Result	HI	LO	EQ
Compare value 1	ORxx	Compare value 2				

Specified immediately following a DOUxx, DOWxx, IFxx, WHENxx, ANDxx, or ORxx statement, to further specify a condition. The xx in ORxx can be

GT	Factor 1	>	Factor 2
LT	Factor 1	<	Factor 2
EQ	Factor 1	=	Factor 2
NE	Factor 1	<>	Factor 2
GE	Factor 1	>=	Factor 2
LE	Factor 1	<=	Factor 2

Note: *Obsolete.* Use OR operator instead.

OTHER Otherwise select

Free-form: OTHER

Factor 1		Factor 2	Result	HI	LO	EQ
	OTHER					

Begins the sequence of operations to be processed if no WHENxx or WHEN condition is satisfied in a SELECT group. The sequence ends with the ENDSL or END operation.

OUT Write a data area

Free-form: OUT(E) *LOCK <u>data-area-name</u>

Factor 1		Factor 2	Result	HI	LO	EQ
*LOCK	OUT(E)	<u>Data area name</u>			ER	

Updates the data area named in Factor 2.

%PADDR Get procedure address

Function: %PADDR(<u>proc-name</u>)

Returns a procedure pointer representing the storage address of the specified procedure.

PARM Identify parameters

Free-form: Not supported

Factor 1		Factor 2	Result	HI	LO	EQ
Target field	PARM	Source field	<u>Parameter name</u>			

Names a field as part of a parameter list. This operation must immediately follow a PLIST, CALL, or CALLB operation.

 Note: *Obsolete.* Use prototype (PR) and procedure interface (PI) definitions instead.

%PARMS Number of parameters

Function: %PARMS

Returns the number of parameters passed to a procedure.

PLIST Identify a parameter list

Free-form: Not supported

Factor 1		Factor 2	Result	HI	LO	EQ
<u>Plist name</u>	PLIST					

Defines a unique symbolic name for a parameter list to be specified in a CALL or CALLB operation.

 Note: *Obsolete.* Use prototype (PR) and procedure interface (PI) definitions instead.

POST Put information into a file information data structure

Free-form: POST(E) program-device <u>file-name</u>

Factor 1		Factor 2	Result	HI	LO	EQ
Program device	POST(E)	File name	INFDS name		ER	

Puts information into an INFDS. The information is either the status of a specific program device or I/O feedback information associated with a file.

READ Read a record

Free-form: READ(EN) <u>file-format-name</u> data-structure

Factor 1		Factor 2	Result	HI	LO	EQ
	READ(EN)	<u>File name</u> or <u>record name</u>	Data structure		ER	EOF

Reads the record that is currently pointed to from a full-procedural file.

READC Read next changed record

Free-form: READC(E) <u>record-name</u>

Factor 1		Factor 2	Result	HI	LO	EQ
	READC(E)	<u>Record name</u>			ER	EOF

Reads next changed record in a subfile. Can be used only with an externally described WORKSTN file.

READE Read equal key

Free-form: READE(EN) search-argument <u>file-record-name</u> data-structure

Factor 1		Factor 2	Result	HI	LO	EQ
Search argument	READE(EN)	<u>File name</u> or <u>record name</u>	Data structure		ER	EOF

Retrieves the next sequential record from a full-procedural file if the key of the record matches the search argument.

READP Read prior record

Free-form: READP(EN) <u>file-record-name</u> data-structure

Factor 1		Factor 2	Result	HI	LO	EQ
	READP(EN)	<u>File name</u> or <u>record name</u>	Data structure		ER	BOF

Retrieves the prior record from a full procedural file.

READPE Read prior equal

Free-form: READPE(EN) search-argument <u>file-record-name</u> data-structure

Factor 1		Factor 2	Result	HI	LO	EQ
Search argument	READPE(N)	<u>File name</u> or <u>record name</u>	Data structure		ER	BOF

Retrieves the next prior sequential record from a full-procedural file if the key of the record matches the search argument.

%REALLOC Reallocate storage with new length

Function: %REALLOC(<u>pointer:length</u>)

Changes the length of the storage (previously allocated) pointed to by the pointer.

REALLOC Reallocate storage with new length

Free-form: Not supported

Factor 1		Factor 2	Result	HI	LO	EQ
	REALLOC(E)	<u>Length</u>	<u>Pointer</u>		ER	

Changes the length of the storage (previously allocated by ALLOC) pointed to by the Result field pointer.

Note: *Obsolete.* Use %REALLOC function instead.

REL Release program device

Free-form: REL(E) <u>program-device</u> <u>file-name</u>

Factor 1		Factor 2	Result	HI	LO	EQ
<u>Program device</u>	REL(E)	<u>File name</u>			ER	

Detaches the program device named in Factor 1 from a workstation file.

%REM Integer remainder

Function: %REM(dividend:divisor)

Returns integer remainder when dividing dividend by divisor.

%REPLACE Replace character string

Function: %REPLACE(replacement:source:start:length)

Returns character string that results from inserting a replacement string into a source string.

RESET Set variable to initial value

Free-form: RESET(E) *NOKEY *ALL structure-variable

Factor 1		Factor 2	Result	HI	LO	EQ
*NOKEY	RESET(E)	*ALL	Structure or variable		ER	

Resets a variable to the value it held after the *INIT phase of the program.

RETURN Return to caller

Free-form: RETURN(HMR) expression

Factor 1		Extended Factor 2	Result	HI	LO	EQ
	RETURN(HMR)	Expression				

Returns a program or procedure to its caller. If a value or expression is specified in the extended Factor 2, that value is returned to the calling procedure.

ROLBK Roll back

Free-form: ROLBK(E)

Factor 1		Factor 2	Result	HI	LO	EQ
	ROLBK(E)				ER	

Eliminates all changes made to files (under commitment control) that have been specified in output operations since the previous COMMIT or ROLBK operation.

%SCAN Scan character string

Function: %SCAN(search-argument:source:start)

Scans a character string for the specified substring; returns the leftmost position of the character string, or zero if the character string is not found.

SCAN Scan character string

Free-form: Not supported

Factor 1		Factor 2	Result	HI	LO	EQ
Search-arg: length	SCAN(E)	Source: start	Leftmost position		ER	FD

Scans a character string for the substring specified.

%SECONDS Number of seconds

Function: %SECONDS(number)

Converts a number to a duration representing a number of seconds that can be added to or subtracted from a time or timestamp.

SELECT Begin a select group

Free-form: SELECT

Factor 1		Factor 2	Result	HI	LO	EQ
	SELECT					

Conditionally processes one of several alternative sequences of operations. It includes a SELECT statement, zero or more WHEN*xx* or WHEN groups, an optional OTHER group, and an ENDSL or END statement.

SETGT Set greater than

Free-form: SETGT(E) search-argument file-name

Factor 1		Factor 2	Result	HI	LO	EQ
Search argument	SETGT(E)	File name		NR	ER	

Positions a file at the next record with a key or relative record number greater than the search argument.

SETLL Set lower limit

Free-form: SETLL(E) search-argument file-name

Factor 1		Factor 2	Result	HI	LO	EQ
Search argument	SETLL(E)	File name		NR	ER	EQ

Positions a file at the next record with a key or relative record number greater than or equal to the search argument.

SETOFF Set indicator off

Free-form: Not supported

Factor 1		Factor 2	Result	HI	LO	EQ
	SETOFF			OF	OF	OF

Sets off any indicators specified in columns 71–76.

   Note: *Obsolete.* Use free-form expression (*IN*xx* = *OFF) instead.

SETON Set indicator on

Free-form: Not supported

Factor 1		Factor 2	Result	HI	LO	EQ
	SETON			ON	ON	ON

Sets on any indicators specified in positions 71–76.

   Note: *Obsolete.* Use free-form expression (*IN*xx* = *ON) instead.

%SHTDN Shut down

Function: %SHTDN

Returns *ON if the system operator has requested a shutdown; otherwise, returns *OFF.

SHTDN Shut down

Free-form: Not supported

Factor 1		Factor 2	Result	HI	LO	EQ
	SHTDN			ON		

Lets the program determine whether or not the system is shutting down.

   Note: *Obsolete.* Use %SHTDN function instead.

%SIZE Size

Function: %SIZE(data-item:*ALL)

Returns the number of bytes occupied by a data item.

SORTA Sort array

Free-form: SORTA <u>array-name</u>

Factor 1		Factor 2	Result	HI	LO	EQ
	SORTA	<u>Array name</u>				

Sorts an array into the sequence specified by position 45 of the Definition Specifications.

%SQRT Square root

Function: %SQRT(<u>numeric-expression</u>)

Returns the square root of a numeric expression.

SQRT Square root

Free-form: Not supported

Factor 1		Factor 2	Result	HI	LO	EQ
	SQRT(H)	<u>Value</u>	<u>Root</u>			

Derives the square root of the field named in Factor 2.

>   **Note:** *Obsolete.* Use %SQRT function instead.

%STATUS File or program status

Function: %STATUS(file-name)

Returns the most recent value for the file or program status. %STATUS is usually used in conjunction with the %ERROR function to identify a specific error condition.

%STR Get or set null-terminated string

Function: %STR(<u>pointer</u>:length)

On the right side of an expression, gets the string indicated by a pointer up to (but not including) the first null (x'00') character. On the left side of an expression, creates a null-terminated string at the storage location indicated by a pointer.

SUB Subtract

Free-form: Not supported

Factor 1		Factor 2	Result	HI	LO	EQ
Minuend	SUB(H)	<u>Subtrahend</u>	<u>Difference</u>	+	–	Z

Subtracts one or two numeric items.

>   **Note:** *Obsolete.* Use – operator instead.

%SUBDT Subset of a date, time, or timestamp

Function: %SUBDT(date:duration-code)

Extracts a portion of a date, time, or timestamp; returns a number representing the extracted portion.

SUBDUR Subtract duration

Free-form: Not supported

Factor 1		Factor 2	Result	HI	LO	EQ
Date/Time 1	SUBDUR(E)	Duration: duration code	Date/Time 2		ER	
Date/Time 1	SUBDUR(E)	Date/Time 2	Duration: duration code		ER	

Subtracts a duration to establish a new date, time, or timestamp; or calculates a duration (difference).

> **Note:** *Obsolete*. Use – operator with duration function (e.g., %DAYS, %MONTHS, %YEARS), or use the %DIFF function instead.

%SUBST Get or set substring

Function: %SUBST(string:start:length)

On the right side of an expression, returns a substring from a string, starting at the given location for the specified length. On the left side of an expression, assigns a value to a substring within a field.

SUBST Substring

Free-form: Not supported

Factor 1		Factor 2	Result	HI	LO	EQ
Length to extract	SUBST(EP)	Base string: start	Target string		ER	

Calculates a substring from a string, starting at the given location for the specified length; assigns the substring to a target result.

> **Note:** *Obsolete*. Use %SUBST function instead.

TAG Tag

Free-form: Not supported

Factor 1		Factor 2	Result	HI	LO	EQ
Label	TAG					

Creates a label that identifies the destination of a GOTO or CAB*xx* operation.

TEST Test date/time/timestamp

Free-form: TEST(EDTZ) date-time-format tested-field

Factor 1		Factor 2	Result	HI	LO	EQ
	TEST(E)		Tested field		ER	
Date format	TEST(ED)		Tested field		ER	
Time format	TEST(ET)		Tested field		ER	
	TEST(EZ)		Tested field		ER	

Tests the validity of date, time, or timestamp fields before using them.

TESTB Test value of bit field

Free-form: Not supported

Factor 1		Factor 2	Result	HI	LO	EQ
	TESTB	Bit numbers	Character field	OF	ON	EQ

Compares the bits identified with the corresponding bits in the field named as the Result field.

TESTN Test numeric

Free-form: Not supported

Factor 1		Factor 2	Result	HI	LO	EQ
	TESTN		Character field	NU	BN	BL

Tests a character Result field for the presence of zoned decimal digits and blanks.

TESTZ Test zone
Free-form: Not supported

Factor 1		Factor 2	Result	HI	LO	EQ
	TESTZ		Character field	AI	JR	SZ

Tests the zone portion of the leftmost character in the Result field.

%THIS Class instance for native method
Function: %THIS

Returns an object value referring to the class instance on whose behalf a native method is being called.

%TIME Convert to time
Function: %TIME(expression:format)

Converts expression (numeric, character, or timestamp data type), returning a time in *ISO format.

TIME Time of day
Free-form: Not supported

Factor 1		Factor 2	Result	HI	LO	EQ
	TIME		Field			

Accesses the system time of day and, if specified, the system date at any time during program processing.

Note: *Obsolete.* Use %DATE, %TIME, or %TIMESTAMP function instead.

%TIMESTAMP Convert to timestamp
Function: %TIMESTAMP(expression:format)

Converts expression (numeric, character, or date data type), returning a timestamp.

%TLOOKUP*xx* Look up element in a table
Function: %TLOOKUP*xx*(search-argument:table:alternate-table)

Searches a table for a specific element; returns *ON if the lookup is successful, sets the current table element to the found element, and optionally sets the current table element of an alternate table to the same element (or returns *OFF, if the search is unsuccessful). The *xx* in the %TLOOKUP*xx* function can be

(Blank)	Find an exact match to search argument.
LT	Find element closest to but less than search argument.
LE	Find exact match, or element closest to but less than search argument.
GE	Find exact match, or element closest to but greater than search argument.
GT	Find element closest to but greater than search argument.

%TRIMx Trim blanks

Function: %TRIMx(string)

Returns a character, graphic, or UCS-2 string without leading and/or trailing blanks. The *x* in the %TRIMx function can be

(Blank)	Trim both leading and trailing blanks.
L	Trim left (leading) blanks only.
R	Trim right (trailing) blanks only.

%UCS2 Convert to UCS-2

Function: %UCS2(expression:ccsid)

Converts a character, graphic, or UCS-2 expression to UCS-2 format.

UNLOCK Unlock a data area or release a record

Free-form: UNLOCK(E) dtaara-record-file

Factor 1		Factor 2	Result	HI	LO	EQ
	UNLOCK(E)	Data area, record, or file name			ER	

Unlocks a data area or releases a record.

%UNS Convert to unsigned integer format
%UNSH Convert to unsigned integer format with half-adjust

Function: %UNS(numeric-expression)
%UNSH(numeric-expression)

Converts a numeric expression to unsigned integer format (optionally with half-adjusting). (**V5R2 enhancement:** Now supports character expressions.)

UPDATE Modify existing record

Free-form: UPDATE(E) file-format-name data-structure

Factor 1		Factor 2	Result	HI	LO	EQ
	UPDATE(E)	File name or record format	Data structure		ER	

Modifies the last record retrieved for processing from an update file.

WHEN When true then select

Free-form: WHEN(MR) <u>logical-expression</u>

Factor 1		Extended Factor 2
	WHEN(MR)	<u>Logical expression</u>

Performs the operations controlled by a WHEN operation in a SELECT group when the expression in Factor 2 is true.

WHEN*xx* When true then select

Free-form: Not supported

Factor 1		Factor 2	Result	HI	LO	EQ
<u>Compare value 1</u>	WHEN*xx*	<u>Compare value 2</u>				

Performs the operations controlled by a WHEN*xx* operation in a SELECT group when the relationship between Factor 1 and 2 is true. The *xx* relationship can be

GT   Factor 1   >   Factor 2
LT   Factor 1   <   Factor 2
EQ   Factor 1   =   Factor 2
NE   Factor 1   <> Factor 2
GE   Factor 1   >= Factor 2
LE   Factor 1   <= Factor 2

Note: *Obsolete.* Use WHEN instead.

WRITE Create new records

Free-form: WRITE(E) <u>file-format-name</u> data-structure

Factor 1		Factor 2	Result	HI	LO	EQ
	WRITE(E)	<u>File name</u> or <u>record format</u>	Data structure		ER	

Writes a new record to a file.

%XFOOT Sum array expression elements

Function: %XFOOT(<u>array-expression</u>)

Returns the sum of all the elements of an array expression.

XFOOT Sum the elements of an array

Free-form: Not supported

Factor 1		Factor 2	Result	HI	LO	EQ
	XFOOT(H)	Array name	Sum	+	–	Z

Adds the elements of an array together and places the sum into the field specified as the Result field.

> **Note:** *Obsolete.* Use the %XFOOT function instead.

%XLATE Translate

Function: %XLATE(from:to:string:start)

Translates characters in a string according to the From and To strings and returns the resulting string.

XLATE Translate

Free-form: Not supported

Factor 1		Factor 2	Result	HI	LO	EQ
From:To	XLATE(EP)	String:start	Target string		ER	

Translates characters in a source string according to the From and To strings and places them into a receiver (target) string.

> **Note:** *Obsolete.* Use %XLATE function insead.

%YEARS Number of years

Function: %YEARS(number)

Converts a number to a duration representing a number of years that can be added or subtracted to a date or timestamp.

Z-ADD Zero and add

Free-form: Not supported

Factor 1		Factor 2	Result	HI	LO	EQ
	Z-ADD(H)	Addend	Sum	+	–	Z

Adds the addend to a field of zeros and places the sum in the Result field.

> **Note:** *Obsolete.* Use free-form expression instead.

Z-SUB Zero and subtract

Free-form: Not supported

Factor 1		Factor 2	Result	HI	LO	EQ
	Z-SUB(H)	Subtrahend	Difference	+	–	Z

Subtracts the subtrahend from a field of zeros and places it in the Result field.

Note: *Obsolete*. Use free-form expression instead.

Appendix B

RPG IV Style Guide

Adapted with permission from "The Essential RPG IV Style Guide" by Bryan Meyers, NEWS/400, June 1998. Reprinted from RPG IV Jump Start: Your Guide to the New RPG, 4th ed., by Bryan Meyers, 29th Street Press, 2001.

Professional programmers appreciate the importance of standards in developing programs that are readable, understandable, and maintainable. The issue of programming style goes beyond any one language, but the introduction of the RPG IV syntax demands that we re-examine standards of RPG style. With that in mind, here are some simple rules of thumb you can use to ensure that bad code doesn't happen to good RPG software construction.

Comments

Good programming style can serve a documentary purpose in helping others understand the source code. If you practice good code-construction techniques, you'll find that "less is more" when it comes to commenting the source. Too many comments are as bad as too few.

    Use comments to clarify, not echo, your code. Comments that merely repeat the code add to a program's bulk, but not to its value. In general, you should use comments for just three purposes:

- to provide a brief program or procedure summary
- to give a title to a subroutine, procedure, or other section of code
- to explain a technique that isn't readily apparent by reading the source

    Always include a brief summary at the beginning of a program or procedure. This prologue should include the following information:

- a program or procedure title
- a brief description of the program's or procedure's purpose
- a chronology of changes that includes the date, programmer name, and purpose of each change
- a summary of indicator usage
- a description of the procedure interface (the return value and parameters)
- an example of how to call the procedure

    Use consistent "marker line" comments to divide major sections of code. For example, you should definitely section off with lines of dashes (–) or asterisks (*) the declarations, the main procedure, each subroutine, and any subprocedures. Identify each section for easy reference.

    Use blank lines to group related source lines and make them stand out. In general, you should use completely blank lines instead of blank comment lines to group lines of code, unless you're building a block of comments. Use only one blank line, though; multiple consecutive blank lines make your program hard to read.

    Avoid right-hand "end-line" comments in columns 81–100. Right-hand comments tend simply to echo the code, can be lost during program maintenance, and can easily become "out of synch" with the line they comment. If a source line is important enough to warrant a comment, it's important enough to warrant a comment on a separate line. Version 5's support for end-of-line comments (starting with //) relaxes this rule somewhat, but if the comment merely repeats the code, eliminate it entirely.

Declarations

With RPG IV, we finally have an area of the program source in which to declare all variables and constants associated with the program. The Definition Specifications organize all your declarations in one place.

RPG IV still supports the *LIKE DEFINE opcode, along with Z-ADD, Z-SUB, MOVEx, and CLEAR, to define program variables. But for ease of maintenance as well as program clarity, you'll want to dictate a standard that consolidates all data definition, including work fields, in Definition Specifications.

Declare all variables within Definition Specifications. Except for key lists and parameter lists, don't declare variables in Calculation Specifications — not even using *LIKE DEFINE. Define key lists and parameter lists in the first Calculation Specifications of the program, before any executable calculations. Use a prototype definition instead of an *ENTRY PLIST.

Whenever a literal has a specific meaning, declare it as a named constant in the Definition Specifications. This practice helps document your code and makes it easier to maintain. One obvious exception to this rule is the allowable use of 0 and 1 when they make perfect sense in the context of a statement. For example, if you're going to initialize an accumulator field or increment a counter, it's fine to use a hard-coded 0 or 1 in the source.

Indent data item names to improve readability and document data structures. Unlike many other RPG entries, the name of a defined item need not be left-justified in the Definition Specifications; take advantage of this feature to help document your code:

```
*.. 1 ...+... 2 ...+... 3 ...+... 4 ...+... 5 ...+... 6 ...+... 7 ...+... 8
DName++++++++++ETDsFrom+++To/L+++IDc.Functions++++++++++++++++++++++++++++++
D ErrMsgDSDS       DS
D   ErrPrefix                      3
D   ErrMsgID                       4
D   ErrMajor                       2    OVERLAY(ErrMsgID:1)
D   ErrMinor                       2    OVERLAY(ErrMsgID:3)
```

Use length notation instead of positional notation in data structure declarations. Definition Specifications let you code fields either with specific from and to positions or simply with the length of the field. To avoid confusion and to better document the field, use length notation consistently. For example, code

```
*.. 1 ...+... 2 ...+... 3 ...+... 4 ...+... 5 ...+... 6 ...+... 7 ...+... 8
DName++++++++++ETDsFrom+++To/L+++IDc.Functions++++++++++++++++++++++++++++++
D RtnCode          DS
D   PackedNbr                   15P 5
```

instead of

```
D RtnCode          DS
D   PackedNbr            1        8P 5
```

Use positional notation only when the actual position in a data structure is important. For example, when coding the program status data structure, the file information data structure, or the return data structure from an application programming interface (API), you'd use positional notation if your program ignores certain positions leading up to a field or between fields. Using positional notation is preferable to using unnecessary "filler" variables with length notation:

```
*.. 1 ...+... 2 ...+... 3 ...+... 4 ...+... 5 ...+... 6 ...+... 7 ...+... 8
DName++++++++++ETDsFrom+++To/L+++IDc.Functions++++++++++++++++++++++++++++++
D APIRtn           DS
D   PackedNbr          145      152P 5
```

In this example, to better document the variable, consider overlaying the positionally declared variable with another variable declared using length notation:

```
*.. 1 ...+... 2 ...+... 3 ...+... 4 ...+... 5 ...+... 6 ...+... 7 ...+... 8
DName+++++++++++ETDsFrom+++To/L+++IDc.Functions+++++++++++++++++++++++++++++
D APIRtn          DS
D  Pos145                   145    152
D  PackNbr                            15P 5 OVERLAY(Pos145)
```

When defining overlapping fields, use the OVERLAY keyword instead of positional notation. Keyword OVERLAY explicitly ties the declaration of a "child" variable to that of its "parent." Not only does OVERLAY document this relationship, but if the parent moves elsewhere within the program code, the child will follow.

If your program uses compile-time arrays, use the **CTDATA form to identify the compile-time data. This form effectively documents the identity of the compile-time data, tying the data at the end of the program to the array declaration in the Definition Specification. The **CTDATA syntax also helps you avoid errors by eliminating the need to code compile-time data in the same order in which you declare multiple arrays.

Naming Conventions

Perhaps the most important aspect of programming style deals with the names you give to data items (e.g., variables, named constants) and routines. Establish naming conventions that go beyond the traditional six characters, to fully identify variables and other identifiers. Those extra characters can make the difference between program "code" and a program "description."

When naming an item, be sure the name fully and accurately describes the item. The name should be unambiguous, easy to read, and obvious. Although you should exploit RPG IV's allowance for long names, don't make your names too long to be useful. Name lengths of 10 to 14 characters are usually sufficient, and longer names may not be practical in many specifications. When naming a data item, describe the item; when naming a subroutine or procedure, use a verb/object syntax (similar to a CL command) to describe the process. Maintain a dictionary of names, verbs, and objects, and use the dictionary to standardize your naming conventions.

When coding an RPG symbolic name, use mixed case to clarify the named item's meaning and use. RPG IV lets you type your source code in upper- and lowercase characters. Use this feature to clarify named data. For RPG-reserved words and operations, use all uppercase characters.

Avoid using special characters (e.g., @, #, $) when naming items. Although RPG IV allows an underscore (_) within a name, you can easily avoid using this "noise" character if you use mixed case intelligently.

Indicators

Historically, indicators have been an identifying characteristic of the RPG syntax, but with RPG IV they are fast becoming relics of an earlier era. Reducing a program's use of indicators may well be the single most important thing you can do to improve the program's readability.

Use indicators as sparingly as possible; go out of your way to eliminate them. At Version 5, RPG completely eliminates the need for conditioning indicators and resulting indicators and does not support them in any free-format specifications. In earlier releases, the only indicators present in a program should be resulting indicators for opcodes that absolutely require them (e.g., LOOKUP). Whenever possible, use built-in functions instead of indicators. Remember that you can indicate file exception conditions with error-handling functions (e.g., %EOF, %ERROR, %FOUND) and an (E) operation extender to avoid using indicators.

If you must use indicators, name them. As of Version 4 Release 2, RPG IV supports a Boolean data type (N) that serves the same purpose as an indicator. You can use the INDDS keyword with a display file specification to associate a data structure with the indicators for a display or printer file; you can then assign meaningful names to the indicators.

Use the EVAL opcode with *Inxx and *ON or *OFF to set the state of indicators. Do not use the SETON or SETOFF operation, and never use MOVEA to manipulate multiple indicators at once.

Use indicators only in close proximity to the point where your program sets their condition. For example, it's bad practice to set an indicator and then not test it until several pages later. If it's not possible to keep the related actions (setting and testing the indicator) together, move the indicator value to a meaningful variable instead.

Don't use conditioning indicators — ever. If a program must conditionally execute or avoid a block of source, explicitly code the condition with a structured comparison opcode, such as IF. If you're working with old System/36 code, get rid of the blocks of conditioning indicators in the source. The Version 5 free-format specification does not support conditioning indicators.

Include a description of any indicators you use. It's especially important to document indicators whose purpose isn't obvious by reading the program, such as indicators used to communicate with display or printer files or the U1–U8 external indicators, if you must use them.

Structured Programming Techniques

Give those who follow you a fighting chance to understand how your program works by implementing structured programming techniques at all times. The IF, DOU, DOW, FOR, and WHEN opcodes are positively elegant. Banish IFxx, DOUxx, DOWxx, and WHxx from your RPG IV code forever. By the way, you'd never use indicators to condition structured opcodes, would you? Good!

Don't use GOTO, CABxx, or COMP. Instead, substitute a structured alternative, such as nested IF statements, or status variables to skip code or to direct a program to a specific location. To compare two values, use the structured opcodes IF and ELSE. To perform loops, use DOU, DOW, and FOR. Never code your loops by comparing and branching with COMP (or even IF) and GOTO. Employ ITER to repeat a loop iteration, and use LEAVE to prematurely exit loops or LEAVESR to prematurely exit subroutines.

Don't use the obsolete IFxx, DOUxx, DOWxx, or WHxx opcodes. The newer forms of these opcodes — IF, DOU, DOW, and WHEN — support free-form expressions, making those alternatives more readable. In general, if an opcode offers a free-form alternative, use it. This rule applies to the DO opcode as well; the free-form FOR operation is usually a better choice, if you're at Version 4 Release 4 or later.

Perform multipath comparisons with SELECT/WHEN/OTHER/ENDSL. Deeply nested IFxx/ELSE/ENDIF code blocks are hard to read and result in an unwieldy accumulation of ENDIFs at the end of the group. Don't use the obsolete CASxx opcode; instead, use the more versatile SELECT/WHEN/OTHER/ENDSL construction.

Always qualify END opcodes. Use ENDIF, ENDDO, ENDFOR, ENDSL, or ENDCS as applicable. This practice can be a great help in deciphering complex blocks of source.

Avoid programming tricks and hidden code. Such maneuvers aren't so clever to someone who doesn't know the trick. If you think you must add comments to explain how a block of code works, consider rewriting the code to clarify its purpose. Use of the obscure "bit-twiddling" opcodes (BITON, BITOFF, MxxZO, TESTB, and TESTZ) may be a sign that your source needs updating.

Modular Programming Techniques

The RPG IV syntax, along with the iSeries Integrated Language Environment (ILE), encourages a modular approach to application programming. Modularity offers a way to organize an application, facilitate program maintenance, hide complex logic, and efficiently reuse code wherever it applies.

Use RPG IV's prototyping capabilities to define parameters and procedure interfaces. Prototypes (PR definitions) offer many advantages when you're passing data between modules and programs. For example, they avoid runtime errors by giving the compiler the ability to check the data type and number of parameters. Prototypes also let you code literals and expressions as parameters, declare parameter lists (even the *ENTRY PLIST) in the Definition Specifications, and pass parameters by value and by read-only reference, as well as by reference.

Store prototypes in /COPY members. For each module, code a /COPY member containing the procedure prototype for each exported procedure in that module. Then include a reference to that /COPY module in each module that refers to the procedures in the called module. This practice saves you from typing the prototypes each time you need them and reduces errors.

Include constant declarations for a module in the same /COPY member as the prototypes for that module. If you then reference the /COPY member in any module that refers to the called module, you've effectively "globalized" the declaration of those constants.

Use IMPORT and EXPORT only for global data items. The IMPORT and EXPORT keywords let you share data among the procedures in a program without explicitly passing the data as parameters — in other words, they provide a "hidden interface" between procedures. Limit use of these keywords to data items that are truly global in the program — usually values that are set once and then never changed.

Free the Factor 2

You can mix and match RPG III style, RPG IV fixed-format style, and RPG IV free-format style in your Calculation Specifications, but the result is inconsistent and difficult to read. Take full advantage of the more natural order and expanded space afforded by the free-format specification (or, previous to Version 5, the extended Factor 2). When you're coding loops and groups, you'll find that the code looks and feels better in free format.

Use free-form expressions (or EVAL) wherever possible. Instead of Z-ADD and Z-SUB, use assignment expressions. Use expressions for any arithmetic in your program. Instead of CAT and SUBST, use string expressions. Use expressions to set indicators (if you need them).

But don't completely abandon columnar alignment as a tool to aid readability in expressions. Especially when an expression must continue onto subsequent lines, align the expression to make it easier to understand.

Character String Manipulation

IBM has greatly enhanced RPG IV's ability to easily manipulate character strings. Many of the tricks that programmers had to use with earlier versions of RPG are now obsolete. Make your source "modern" by exploiting these new features.

Use a named constant to declare a string constant instead of storing it in an array or table. Declaring a string (such as a CL command string) as a named constant lets you refer to the string directly instead of forcing you to refer to it through its array name and index. Use a named constant to declare any value that you don't expect to change during program execution.

Avoid using arrays and data structures to manipulate character strings and text. Use the string manipulation opcodes and/or built-in functions instead.

Use EVAL's free-form assignment expressions whenever possible for string manipulation. When used with character strings, EVAL is usually equivalent to a MOVEL(P) opcode. When you don't want the result to be padded with blanks, use the %SUBST or %REPLACE function.

Use variable-length fields to simplify string handling. Use variable-length fields as CONST or VALUE parameters to every string-handling subprocedure, as well as for work fields. Not only does the code look better (eliminating the %TRIM function, for example), but it's also faster than using fixed-length fields. For example, code

```
*.. 1 ...+... 2 ...+... 3 ...+... 4 ...+... 5 ...+... 6 ...+... 7 ...+... 8
DName+++++++++++ETDsFrom+++To/L+++IDc.Functions++++++++++++++++++++++++++++
D QualName        S             33    VARYING
D Library         S             10    VARYING
D File            S             10    VARYING
D Member          S             10    VARYING

 /FREE
    QualName = Library + '/' + File + '(' + Member + ')';
 /END-FREE
```

instead of

```
D QualName        S             33
D Library         S             10
D File            S             10
D Member          S             10

 /FREE
    QualName = %TRIM(Library) + '/' + %TRIM(File)
               + '(' + %TRIM(Member) + ')';
 /END-FREE
```

Avoid Obsolescence

RPG is an old language. After more than 30 years, many of its original, obsolete features are still available. Don't use them.

Don't sequence program line numbers in columns 1–5. Chances are you'll never again drop that deck of punched cards, so the program sequence area is unnecessary. In RPG IV, the columns are commentary only. You can use them to identify changed lines in a program or structured indentation levels, but be aware that these columns may be subject to the same hazards as right-hand comments.

Avoid program-described files. Instead, use externally defined files whenever possible.

If an opcode offers a free-form syntax, use it instead of the fixed-form version. Opcodes to avoid include CABxx, CASxx, CAT, DO (at Version 4 Release 4), DOUxx, DOWxx, IFxx, and WHxx. At Version 5, avoid any opcode that the free-format specification doesn't support.

If a built-in function offers the same function as an opcode, use the function instead of the opcode. With some opcodes, you can substitute a built-in function for the opcode and use the function within an expression. As of Version 4 Release 1, the SCAN and SUBST opcodes have virtually equivalent built-in functions, %SCAN and %SUBST. In addition, you can usually substitute the concatenation operator (+) in combination with the %TRIMx functions in place of the CAT opcode. The free-form versions are preferable if they offer the same functionality as the opcodes.

Use the date operations to operate on dates. Get rid of the clever date and time routines that you (or your predecessors) have gathered and jealously guarded over the years. The RPG IV operation codes and built-in functions are more efficient, clear, and modern. Even if your database includes dates in "legacy" formats, you can use the date opcodes to manipulate them.

Shun obsolete opcodes. In addition to the opcodes mentioned earlier, some opcodes are no longer supported or have better alternatives:

- CALL, CALLB — The prototyped calls (CALLP or a function call) are just as efficient as CALL and CALLB and offer the advantages of prototyping and parameter passing by value. Neither CALL nor CALLB can accept a return value from a procedure.

- DEBUG — With OS/400's advanced debugging facilities, this opcode is no longer supported.

- DSPLY — You should use display file input/output (I/O) to display information or to acquire input.

- FREE — This opcode is no longer supported.

- PARM, PLIST — If you use prototyped calls, these opcodes are no longer necessary.

Miscellaneous Guidelines

Here's an assortment of other style guidelines that can help you improve your RPG IV code.

In all specifications that support keywords, observe a one-keyword-per-line limit. Instead of spreading multiple keywords and values across the entire specification, your program will be easier to read and let you more easily add or delete specifications if you limit each line to one keyword, or at least to closely related keywords (e.g., DATFMT and TIMFMT).

Begin all H-spec keywords in column 8, leaving column 7 blank. Separating the keyword from the required H in column 6 improves readability.

Relegate mysterious code to a well-documented, well-named procedure. Despite your best efforts, on extremely rare occasions you simply will not be able to make the meaning of a chunk of code clear without extensive comments. By separating such heavily documented, well-tested code into a procedure, you'll save future maintenance programmers the trouble of deciphering and dealing with the code unnecessarily.

Final Advice

Sometimes good style and efficient runtime performance don't mix. Wherever you face a conflict between the two, choose good style. Hard-to-read programs are hard to debug, hard to maintain, and hard to get right. Program correctness must always win out over speed. Keep in mind these admonitions from Brian Kernighan and P. J. Plauger's *The Elements of Programming Style*:

- Make it right before you make it faster.
- Keep it right when you make it faster.
- Make it clear before you make it faster.
- Don't sacrifice clarity for small gains in efficiency.

Appendix C

Developing Programs on the iSeries

As we described in Chapter 1, once you have written a program, you must enter it on the system, compile it, bind it, and then run the program. This appendix is designed to introduce you to those features of the iSeries that you need to know to complete these tasks.

OS/400 has a set of commands, called *Control Language (CL)*, that let you direct the computer's activities. The system also provides a series of menus that let you work on the iSeries without knowing CL. This appendix introduces you to the menus of Programming Development Manager, an iSeries facility that you can use to complete your assignments.

Before we look at the PDM menu, you need a basic understanding of OS/400 terminology. The iSeries uses *libraries* to organize stored information, called *objects*. A library is analogous to a PC directory (and is itself an object). The iSeries stores many kinds of objects — data files, job descriptions, commands, output queues, programs, and so on. The *type* associated with an object determines the kinds of actions you can perform on the object. All object types begin with an asterisk (*).

You will be working with three primary kinds of objects: *MODULE, *PGM, and *FILE. *MODULE objects result from successful program compilation and contain the machine-language version of your source code. An object with type *PGM is a bound program of executable code, based on one or more *MODULEs. When you call an object of type *PGM, you are telling the computer to carry out the instructions contained in that object.

Objects with type *FILE are files. Files are further differentiated by *attributes*, which categorize the nature of the file. The attribute PF-SRC indicates that a file is a source physical file that contains source code. Attribute PF-DTA indicates that an object is a physical database file; attribute LF indicates that an object is a logical database file.

The contents of all files, regardless of attribute, can be organized into *members*. A member is like a subdivision of a file. A file must exist before you can add members to it. Each program that you enter will be stored as a member within a source physical file; when you compile that member (or program), you will create a *MODULE object with the same name as the member.

Most companies use source file QRPGLESRC to store RPG IV source code. It is not unusual for installations to store their source code in libraries separate from their object (executable) code, although in the typical school environment, each student has a single library for storing all his or her own work. Your instructor will supply you with the name of the source file and the library name within which you will be working.

Programming Development Manager

Programming Development Manager (PDM) is the primary character-based means for accessing and manipulating libraries, objects, and members on the iSeries. This discussion focuses only on those features of PDM that you need to complete your assignments.

To access PDM from the iSeries Main menu, first select option 5, Programming; then, at the resulting Programming panel, select option 2, Programming Development Manager. You'll see the following PDM menu.

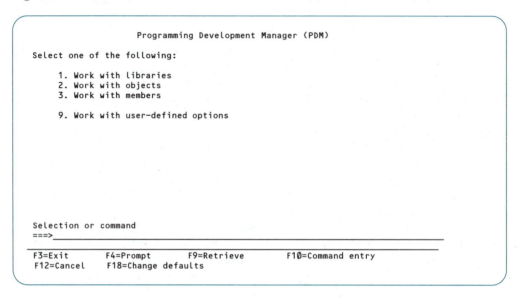

```
                    Programming Development Manager (PDM)

        Select one of the following:

              1. Work with libraries
              2. Work with objects
              3. Work with members

              9. Work with user-defined options




        Selection or command
        ===>_____
        _____
        F3=Exit      F4=Prompt      F9=Retrieve      F10=Command entry
        F12=Cancel   F18=Change defaults
```

Enter/Edit a Program

Select option 3, Work with members, from the PDM menu. You'll see the following display.

```
                    Specify Members to Work With

        Type choices, press Enter.

          File . . . . . . . . . .   QRPGLESRC_   Name, F4 for list

            Library . . . . . . . .     librname__ *LIBL, *CURLIB, name

          Member:
            Name . . . . . . . .     *ALL_____  *ALL, name, *generic*
            Type . . . . . . . .     *ALL_____  *ALL, type, *generic*, *BLANK






        F3=Exit    F4=Prompt    F5=Refresh    F12=Cancel
```

You may either enter the desired source file name or position your cursor on the File prompt and press F4 to see a list of the possible files. Once you've entered or selected the desired file name, the system will display all the members of that file:

```
                      Work with Members Using PDM                  xxxxxxxx

    File  . . . . . .   QRPGLESRC_
     Library . . . .    librrname__           Position to . . . . .   _____

    Type options, press Enter.
     2=Edit          3=Copy  4=Delete 5=Display      6=Print    7=Rename
     8=Display description  9=Save  13=Change text  14=Compile  15=Create module...

    Opt  Member      Type        Text
     __  ANZCRTDB___ RPGLE_____ _____
     __  ANZILECOPY_ RPGLE_____ /COPY member for prototypes, procedure interfaces_
     __  ANZILEPGM__ RPGLE_____ _____
     __  ANZILEPGM1_ RPGLE_____ _____
     __  ANZILEPGM2_ RPGLE_____ _____
     __  ANZILEPKG__ RPGLE_____ _____
     __  ANZSETUP___ RPGLE_____ _____
     __  CALCPMT____ RPGLE_____ Calculate monthly payment_____
                                                                        More...
    Parameters or command
    ===> _____
    F3=Exit          F4=Prompt           F5=Refresh          F6=Create
    F9=Retrieve      F10=Command entry   F23=More options    F24=More keys
```

From this screen you can select a source member to edit, print, or compile by keying a 2, 6, or 14, respectively, in the left column next to the member with which you want to work. Note that option 14 does not appear on the initial screen; pressing F23 (More options) reveals this and additional options for working with members. However, an option does not have to appear on the screen to be used — provided it is a valid option.

Edit/Enter a Member

To edit an existing member, enter a 2 to the left of the member name to bring that member into Source Entry Utility (SEU) and continue work on it. If you are creating a new member, press F6 (Create) to go to the Start SEU screen. You will need to enter the source file name, the member name, and the type.

Compile a Member and Create an Executable Program

Enter 14 to the left of the name of the member you want to compile and bind. If the *PGM object already exists, a Confirm Compile of Member screen (shown below) appears. To compile and bind your new version, you must respond Y (Yes) to the "Delete existing object" option.

```
                          Confirm Compile of Member

        The following object already exists for the compile operation:

           Object which exists . . . . . . . . :    ADDL
              Library . . . . . . . . . . . . . :      SRCLIB
           Object type . . . . . . . . . . . . :    *PGM

           Member to compile . . . . . . . . . :    ADDL
           File . . . . . . . . . . . . . . . . :    CMDSRC
              Library . . . . . . . . . . . . . :      ATEST

        Type choice, press Enter.
        Press F12=Cancel to return and not perform the compile operation.

           Delete existing object . . . . . . .     Y    Y=Yes, N=No




        F12=Cancel
```

Your program will not be ready to run until the system returns a message informing you that the processing was completed successfully. If the message reports that the processing ended abnormally, you must correct program errors and then reselect option 14.

Run a Program

Select option 2, Work with objects, from the PDM menu. The resulting screen will display a list of objects in your library:

```
                        Work with Objects Using PDM                 xxxxxxxx

        Library . . . .    librname__      Position to . . . . . . .
                                           Position to type  . . . . .

        Type options, press Enter.
          2=Change        3=Copy         4=Delete      5=Display      7=Rename
          8=Display description          9=Save       10=Restore     11=Move ...

        Opt   Object     Type      Attribute   Text
          __  CPYTOSAVF  *PGM      CLLE        Copy to save file
          __  DSPFDATE   *PGM      RPGLE
          __  DTAQCL     *PGM      RPGLE
          __  DTAQSR     *PGM      RPGLE
          __  ILEH01     *PGM      CLLE
          __  ILEN01     *PGM      CLLE
          __  MYPROGRAM  *PGM      CLP         Program to create a library and sourc
          __  NULLDATEST *PGM      RPGLE
                                                                        More...
        Parameters or command
        ===>_____
        F3=Exit          F4=Prompt        F5=Refresh         F6=Create
        F9=Retrieve      F10=Command entry  F23=More options   F24=More keys
```

Enter 16 next to the program object you want to run. Note that although 16 does not appear as an initial option, pressing F23 would reveal it (and other options, as well). As an alternative, you can enter **CALL** *program-name* on any command line.

Create a *Module Object

For most of your work in this course, PDM's option 14 will be the appropriate choice for you to compile and bind your program. However, if you'll be working with called programs (covered in Chapter 10), you may want to create a *MODULE object from your source code to bind together with other *MODULEs into a *PGM object. Option 15, Create module, is the proper choice in this case. Option 15 compiles the source code but does not bind it. To bind several modules together, use CL command CRTPGM (Create Program).

View or Print Output

Type **sp** in any option column on any of PDM's screens to obtain a list of your spooled files. (You can also key in **WRKSPLF** on any command line to execute the Work with Spooled Files CL command.) You will see the following screen, which includes a list of all spooled output.

```
                      Work with Printer Output
                                            System:   xxxxxxxx
 User . . . . . .    userid____   Name, *ALL, F4 for list

 Type options below, then press Enter.  To work with printers, press F22.
   2=Change   3=Hold   4=Delete   5=Display      6=Release   7=Message
   9=Work with printing status    10=Start printing   11=Restart printing


     Printer/
 Opt   Output      Status
     Not Assigned
 __    QPFRCOL     Not assigned to printer (use Opt 10)
 __    QSTRUPJD    Not assigned to printer (use Opt 10)
 __    QSYSSCD     Not assigned to printer (use Opt 10)
 __    QSERVER     Not assigned to printer (use Opt 10)
 __    QZLSSERVER  Not assigned to printer (use Opt 10)
 __    QDB2MULTI   Held (use Opt 6)
 __    QXOTJOB     Held (use Opt 6)
 __    QSYSWRKJOB  Held (use Opt 6)
 __    QFSIOPJOB   Held (use Opt 6)
                                                         Bottom
 F1=Help   F3=Exit   F5=Refresh    F11=Dates/pages/forms    F12=Cancel
 F14=Select other printer output    F20=Include system output   F24=More keys
```

You can see the dates, times, and number of pages of the output by pressing F11. The following screen shows the result of this action.

```
                        Work with Printer Output
                                                   System:   xxxxxxxx
     User . . . . . .   userid____   Name, *ALL, F4 for list

     Type options below, then press Enter.  To work with printers, press F22.
       2=Change    3=Hold    4=Delete    5=Display        6=Release    7=Message
       9=Work with printing status    10=Start printing   11=Restart printing

            Printer/
     Opt    Output      Date       Time       Pages   Copies   Form Type
            Not Assigned
       __   QPFRCOL     01/04/00   14:33:36      1       1      *STD
       __   QSTRUPJD    01/04/00   14:39:14     16       1      *STD
       __   QSYSSCD     01/04/00   14:40:22      1       1      *STD
       __   QSERVER     01/04/00   14:40:31      2       1      *STD
       __   QZLSSERVER  01/04/00   14:41:12      1       1      *STD
       __   QDB2MULTI   01/04/00   14:33:30      1       1      *STD
       __   QXOTJOB     01/04/00   14:33:38      1       1      *STD
       __   QSYSWRKJOB  01/04/00   14:33:44      1       1      *STD
       __   QFSIOPJOB   01/04/00   14:34:14      1       1      *STD
                                                                     Bottom
     F1=Help    F3=Exit    F5=Refresh    F11=Display statuses    F12=Cancel
     F14=Select other printer output    F20=Include system output    F24=More keys
```

To view a spooled file, enter option 5 next to the file name. To delete a spooled file, enter 4 and then press Enter at the resulting screen to confirm the deletion request. If you want to print a file, depending on how your system is set up, you may first have to assign the file to a printer by entering 10 next to the file name. At the resulting screen, shown below, enter PRT01 (or the name your instructor provides you).

```
                        Assign Output to a Printer

     Printer output  . . . . . . :   QPFRCOL

     This printer output is not assigned to a printer or the number of pages to be
        printed exceeds the limit specified.

        Printer . . . . . . . . .   _____   Name, F4 for list












     F1=Help    F3=Exit    F12=Cancel
```

You'll be returned to the Work with Printer Output screen, and the message "*Attempting to start" should appear next to the spooled file you chose to print. Pressing F5 (Refresh) will show you the progress the system is making in printing the file.

Display Messages

To display messages, type **DSPMSG** on the command line and press Enter, or type **dm** in any option column of your current screen.

WebSphere Development Studio for iSeries

Programming Development Manager and Source Entry Utility (discussed in Appendix D) are tools that IBM offers as part of its collection of application development tools called WebSphere Development Studio for iSeries. This comprehensive package includes the Application Development Toolset (ADTS) — a group of host-based utilities — and WebSphere Development Tools for iSeries (WDT) — a group of Microsoft Windows products that enhance the tools in the Application Development Toolset. At the time of this writing, at least 90 percent of the RPG IV programs written for the iSeries are developed using the older ADTS package. As the WDT product matures, you can expect its tools to gain favor and share; in this edition of this text, we discuss ADTS but encourage you to also explore WDT. Application Development Toolset includes the following tools (among others):

- Programming Development Manager (PDM) for organizing libraries, objects, and members
- Source Entry Utility (SEU) for editing source code
- Screen Design Aid (SDA) for designing screens

The utilities in WebSphere Development Tools perform many of the same functions as ADTS, but do so in a graphical Windows Environment, offloading the bulk of application development work from the host and onto Windows clients. Instead of PDM's "work with" screens, WDT uses Explorer-like windows to help you organize libraries, objects, and members. CODE/400, a part of WDT, provides a graphical editor with many more features than SEU. A DDS Design utility expands on the capabilities of SDA, and a robust interactive debugger rounds out the series of traditional tools.

WebSphere Development Studio also packages a full set of iSeries language compilers — including ILE RPG/400 (RPG IV), Control Language (CL), Cobol, and C — as well as a number of newer tools that fit into a modern interactive development environment. VisualAge for RPG is a development environment you can use to create RPG IV applications for Windows; these applications can use the iSeries database and interact with OS/400 from a client computer. VisualAge for Java is a development environment for developing Java language applications. WebSphere Studio is a suite of tools you can use to develop Internet Web applications in conjunction with the iSeries. These tools and more combine to make WebSphere Development Studio for iSeries a feature-filled application toolkit for the iSeries.

Appendix D

Source Entry Utility (SEU)

SEU Overview

Programmers generally enter RPG IV programs into the computer interactively using an editor called Source Entry Utility (SEU). An **editor** is like a limited word processor, in that it lets you easily enter, change, and delete text. Because the SEU editor has been designed specifically to facilitate entry of program source code, it includes some special features, such as line prompting and syntax checking, that a standard word processor would not provide. Another generally available editor for the iSeries is the CODE/400 editor, discussed briefly in Appendix C.

Source programs are stored as members of a source file. The file normally used to store RPG IV programs is QRPGLESRC; the member type is RPGLE. The name that you supply your program is the name that identifies that member.

You can reach SEU by selecting option 2, Edit, or option 5, Display, from Programming Development Manager's (PDM's) Work with Members Using PDM screen; or by directly entering the command STRSEU (Start SEU) on a command line. You can use SEU to create a new member or to edit, browse, or print an existing member.

When you enter SEU to create a new member, you see an Edit screen like the following one.

```
 Columns . . . :    6  76          Edit              librname/QRPGLESRC
 SEU==>                                                        membername
 FMT H    HKeywords+++++++++++++++++++++++++++++++++++++++++++++++++++++++++
          *************** Beginning of data ********************************
 ' ' ' ' ' ' '
 ' ' ' ' ' ' '
 ' ' ' ' ' ' '
 ' ' ' ' ' ' '
 ' ' ' ' ' ' '
 ' ' ' ' ' ' '
 ' ' ' ' ' ' '
 ' ' ' ' ' ' '
 ' ' ' ' ' ' '
 ' ' ' ' ' ' '
 ' ' ' ' ' ' '
 ' ' ' ' ' ' '
 ' ' ' ' ' ' '
 ' ' ' ' ' ' '
 ' ' ' ' ' ' '
          ****************** End of data **********************************

 F3=Exit    F4=Prompt    F5=Refresh    F9=Retrieve    F10=Cursor   F11=Toggle
 F16=Repeat find      F17=Repeat change        F24=More keys
 Member membername added to file librname/QRPGLESRC.                      +
```

The SEU command line appears at the top of the screen, the middle of the screen is used for code entry, and the bottom of the screen reminds you of enabled function keys and their uses and delivers system messages to you.

Press Enter to remove the blank lines between the Beginning of data and End of data lines. Once you've done so, you're ready to start entering your program.

As you enter the program, SEU tries to detect syntax errors in your code. When you enter a line containing such an error, the error is displayed in reverse video and the system provides a brief explanation of the error on the message line of the screen. When you have successfully corrected the error, the entry is displayed normally.

Tip

SEU, like other parts of OS/400, has lavish online help available. This help is cursor-position sensitive. When you find yourself in trouble or don't know what response is appropriate, try using the Help key.

Using Prompts

SEU can provide you with prompts to facilitate your code entry. For example, to obtain a line prompted appropriately for File Specifications, key **IPF** (Insert with Prompts for File Specifications) to the left on the Beginning of data line and press Enter. A prompt appropriate for File Specifications appears in the bottom part of the display, as shown in the following screen.

```
Columns . . . :    6  76          Edit              librname/QRPGLESRC
SEU==>  _____    membername
FMT H  HKeywords+++++++++++++++++++++++++++++++++++++++++++++++++++++++++++++
       *************** Beginning of data ********************************
'''''''
       ****************** End of data *********************************
Prompt type . . .   F       Sequence number . . .  '''''''

              File        File          End of       File
Filename      Type      Designation      File       Addition      Sequence

_____      _____      _____       _____     _____       _____
File        Record      Limits        Length of     Record
Format      Length     Processing     Key Field    Address Type
            _____      _____       _____      _____
   File
Organization      Device    Keywords
_____       _____    _____
Comment

_____


F3=Exit   F4=Prompt   F5=Refresh      F11=Previous record
F12=Cancel            F23=Select prompt   F24=More keys
```

Enter your first File Specification, using the Field exit key to move from entry to entry. When you have keyed the first line, press Enter. SEU assigns the line a sequence number and moves the line to the main portion of the screen; SEU also provides another prompted line for your next File Specification.

Each RPG IV specification form has one or more appropriate prompt formats available in SEU. The following table summarizes the prompt formats.

RPG IV Prompt Formats

Prompt format	Specification form
H	Control (H)
F	File (F)
FX	File (F) (External)
D	Definition (D)
DX	Definition (D) (Extended)

continued...

continued...

Prompt format	Specification form
I	Input (I) (Record Identification)
IX	Input (I) (Record Identification) (External)
J	Input (I) (Field Description)
JX	Input (I) (Field Description) (External)
C	Calculation (C)
CX	Calculation (C) (Extended Factor 2)
O	Output (O) (File Identification and Control)
OD	Output (O) (Output Disk)
P	Output (O) (Field Description)
PR	Procedure (P)
PX	Procedure (P) (Extended)
*	Comment (*)

To change the prompt format, press F23 and select the new format you want. Once selected, a prompt form will continue until you press F23 for a new prompt, press F12 to cancel the prompt and return to the Edit display, or press Enter without entering anything. This last method also returns your cursor to the Edit display.

In addition to formatted prompts, SEU can provide skeleton format lines based on the prompting codes shown in the preceding table. To obtain a format line appropriate for File Specifications, key **IFF** (Insert with Format for File Specifications) to the left on the Beginning of data line and press Enter. A formatted line appropriate for File Specifications appears just above the line you are entering:

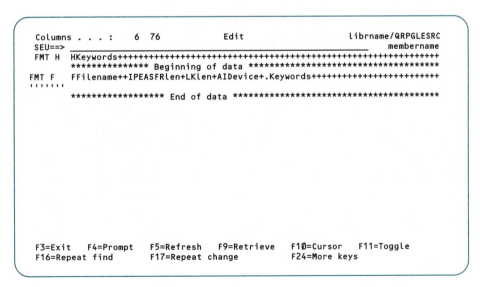

The format line works just like the prompting function to help with positioning code, but it will not become a permanent part of the source member.

Working Within the Edit Display

Sometimes it is more efficient to enter or edit code without the help of the prompts. The following list of features summarizes what you can do in Edit display mode and how to do it.

Position cursor

Use the arrow keys to move within a screen; use the roll keys to page up or down between screens.

Move to a specific line of code

Key the sequence number of the line to which you want to move over the sequence number of a line currently on the screen, and press Enter. The source will be repositioned to display the source code containing the desired line.

Insert within a line

The Insert key toggles insertion on and off.

Delete within a line

Use the Delete key to delete individual characters.

Note

The bold letter commands described below must be keyed over the sequence number of the line (or lines) involved in the operation.

Insert a line

Key an **I** on a line, and press Enter. A blank line will appear below the line you are on.

Insert a line with formatting

Key an **IF***f* (where *f* is one of the prompt formats discussed above) on a line, and press Enter. A blank line will appear below the line you are on, with a skeleton format line that shows fields based on the format code you entered.

Delete a line

Key a **D** on the line you want to delete, and press Enter.

Delete a block of lines

Key **DD** on the first line of the block, move the cursor to the last line of the block, again key **DD**, and press Enter.

Show a format line

Key an **F***f* (where *f* is one of the prompt formats discussed above) on a line, and press Enter. A skeleton format line will appear just above the line you are on, showing fields based on the format code you entered.

Move a line

Key **M** on the line to be moved, reposition the cursor to the desired location, key either **A** or **B**, and press Enter. The line will be moved either after (A) or before (B) the target line, depending on what you keyed.

Move a block of lines

Key **MM** on the first line of the block to be moved, position the cursor to the last line of the block, and key **MM**; then position the cursor to the target line, key **A** or **B**, and press Enter. The block will be moved either after (A) or before (B) the target line, depending on what you keyed.

Copy a line

Key **C** on the line to be copied, reposition the cursor to the desired location, key either **A** or **B**, and press Enter. The line will be copied either after (A) or before (B) the target line, depending on what you keyed.

Copy a block of lines
Key **CC** on the first line of the block to be copied, position the cursor to the last line of the block, and key **CC**; then position the cursor to the target line, key **A** or **B**, and press Enter. The block will be copied either after (A) or before (B) the target line, depending on what you keyed.

Repeat a line
Key **RP** and press Enter to repeat the line once immediately below the line on which you entered the RP.

Repeat a line n *times*
Key **RP***n*, where *n* is any number, and press Enter to repeat the line *n* number of times immediately below the line on which you entered the command.

Repeat a block of lines
Key **RPP** on the first line of the block to be copied, position the cursor to the last line of the block, key **RPP** again, and press Enter. The block will be repeated after the block you outlined.

Prompt an existing line
Key **P***f* on the line, where *f* is the prompt format you want, and press Enter.

Insert prompted lines
Key **IP***f*, where *f* is the prompt format you want, and press Enter. Doing so will return you to prompted mode.

Function Keys in SEU
Several function keys are active within SEU. The following list summarizes the keys you will use most often.

F3
You use F3 to go to the SEU Exit screen (described below).

F4
F4 places the line on which the cursor is located when the key is pressed into an appropriate prompt format.

F10
F10 toggles the cursor between the SEU command line and the Edit display.

F12
F12 cancels the current action; it is generally used to return to display editing from a prompted format.

F13 (Shift + F1)
F13 takes you to a screen that lets you change the SEU defaults for the current session; among other things, it lets you enable or disable lowercase alphabetic entry.

F15 (Shift + F3)
F15 splits the screen in two to let you browse a second member or a compile output while working in your source code; it also lets you copy code from one member into another.

F23 (Shift + F11)
F23 displays all possible prompt formats and lets you select the one you want to activate.

SEU's Command Line
To position the cursor on the SEU command line, press F10. Once there, you can enter an SEU command. Following are some possible commands:

SAVE
To save the member without exiting SEU

CANCEL
To leave SEU without saving and return to the previous menu

TOP or *T*
To move to the top of your source member

BOTTOM or *B*
To move to the bottom of your source member

FIND or *F*
To search for a string of characters in the source member. The string does not need to be enclosed in apostrophes unless it contains blanks, special values, apostrophes, or quotation marks.

CHANGE or *C*
To change a string of characters to some other string

Working with a Split Screen

Pressing F15 takes you to the screen shown below, which lets you divide the display into two halves, with the current member on the top and another member or spool file on the bottom.

```
                       Browse/Copy Options

   Type choices, press Enter.

      Selection . . . . . . . . . .   2            1=Member
                                                   2=Spool file
                                                   3=Output queue
      Copy all records  . . . . . .   N            Y=Yes, N=No
      Browse/copy member  . . . . .   membername   Name, F4 for list
        File . . . . . . . . . . .    QRPGLESRC_   Name, F4 for list
          Library . . . . . . . . .      librname__ Name, *CURLIB, *LIBL

      Browse/copy spool file  . . . .  spoolname_   Name, F4 for list
        Job . . . . . . . . . . . .       jobname____ Name
          User . . . . . . . . . . .       userid____ Name, F4 for list
          Job number  . . . . . . . .      *LAST_    Number, *LAST
        Spool number  . . . . . . .        *LAST     Number, *LAST, *ONLY

      Display output queue  . . . . .  QPRINT____   Name, *ALL
        Library . . . . . . . . . .    *LIBL_____  Name, *CURLIB, *LIBL

   F3=Exit       F4=Prompt       F5=Refresh        F12=Cancel
   F13=Change session defaults   F14=Find/Change options
```

If you select option 1, Member, on this screen, you should then enter the name of the member you want to display in the lower half of the screen. This option is useful for copying portions of code from one member to another or for checking field names in a database file while entering a program that uses that file. To copy lines from one member to the other in split-screen mode, use the same technique as when you are working within a single member; the arrow keys will take your cursor across the midscreen boundary. The roll keys affect the member in either the top or the bottom half of the screen, depending on where your cursor is positioned.

If you choose option 2, Spool file, the default values are such that the most recent compile listing of this member is brought into the lower half of the display, as shown on the following screen:

```
  Columns . . . :   6  76          Edit              librname/QRPGLESRC
  SEU==> _____         membername
  FMT *   *. 1 ...+... 2 ...+... 3 ...+... 4 ...+... 5 ...+... 6 ...+... 7 ...+.
          *************** Beginning of data ********************************
  0001.00 ****************************************************************
  0002.00 *
  0003.00 *    Module name - ANZILEPGM2 - Analyze ILE programs
  0004.00 *                          Build database
  0005.00 *
  0006.00 ****************************************************************

  Columns . . . :   1  71          Browse          Spool file  . . : spoolname
  SEU==> _____
          *************** Beginning of data ********************************
  0000.01 5769RG1 VxRxM0  xxxxxx RN        IBM ILE RPG          userid/member
  0000.02   Command . . . . . . . . . . . . :   CRTRPGMOD
  0000.03     Issued by . . . . . . . . . :      userid
  0000.04   Module . . . . . . . . . . . . :   modulename
  0000.05     Library . . . . . . . . . . :      librname
  0000.06   Text 'description' . . . . . . :   *SRCMBRTXT

   F3=Exit   F4=Prompt   F5=Refresh   F9=Retrieve   F11=Toggle   F12=Cancel
   F16=Repeat find       F17=Repeat change          F24=More keys
```

This feature is useful for correcting compile errors because it lets you scroll through the compile listing and make corrections in your source member based on the errors noted in the listing, without the need for a hard-copy version of the compile listing.

One particularly useful feature when displaying compiler listings in SEU is the FIND *ERR command. To use this command, position the cursor on the lower split window's SEU command line, and then enter

```
FIND *ERR
```

to locate errors that the compiler found.

Exiting SEU

When you press F3 to exit SEU, the Exit screen, shown below, appears, letting you accept preset default values or change them, as you desire.

```
                              Exit
  Type choices, press Enter.

    Change/create member . . . . . . .   N          Y=Yes, N=No
      Member . . . . . . . . . . . .     membername Name, F4 for list
      File . . . . . . . . . . . . .     filename__ Name, F4 for list
        Library . . . . . . . . . . .    librname__ Name
      Text . . . . . . . . . . . . .     _____

    Resequence member . . . . . . . .    Y          Y=Yes, N=No
      Start . . . . . . . . . . . .      0001.00    0000.01-9999.99
      Increment . . . . . . . . . .      01.00      00.01-99.99

    Print member . . . . . . . . . .     N          Y=Yes, N=No

    Return to editing . . . . . . . .    N          Y=Yes, N=No

    Go to member list . . . . . . . .    N          Y=Yes, N=No

   F3=Exit   F4=Prompt   F5=Refresh   F12=Cancel
```

By changing defaults, you can save the member with a name different from that with which you began the editing session, or you can cancel editing changes by specifying N for the Change/create member option. You also can get a printout of the member without having to compile it by changing the Print Member option to Y. Note that the Return to editing option's default value is N if you exited with no syntax errors in your source but Y if errors remained. You can exit with errors remaining if you change the Y default to N.

Appendix E

Program Testing and Debugging

A major part of a programmer's time is spent ensuring that the programs he or she has written are, in fact, accurately producing the desired results. This procedure involves carefully checking each program's correctness and fixing any errors this checking uncovers — a process often referred to as **debugging**. Program errors fall into one of two broad categories: syntax errors and logic errors.

Syntax Errors

Syntax errors are errors in your use of the programming language. Because the system points out these kinds of errors for you, they are simple to detect and easy to correct, once you have mastered the rules of the language in which you are programming.

On the iSeries, Source Entry Utility (SEU) detects some kinds of syntax errors as you enter program statements. For example, failing to make a required entry within a specification line, forgetting to right-adjust a numeric entry within its allocated columns, or including an invalid value in a column (e.g., an F instead of an I, O, U, or C for file type on the File Specifications) causes SEU to display the erroneous entry in reverse video, display an error message on the bottom of the screen, and lock the keyboard. You will need to press the Reset key before the system lets you proceed. Moreover, until you correct the error, the erroneous entry will remain in reverse video as a reminder of a problem.

Once you have completely entered your program and have eliminated all syntax errors detected by SEU, your next step is to compile and bind the program. Compiling and binding are processes that translate the statements in your source member into an object of machine-code instructions that the iSeries can then execute. In attempting to complete this translation process, the ILE RPG/400 compiler often detects additional syntax errors unnoticed by SEU.

If your program contains compile errors, the system sends you a message that your job ended abnormally. You can find the cause (or causes) of the difficulties by printing or displaying the *compile listing*, a report of the compilation generated by the compiler. A compile listing includes a listing of your program. The compiler numbers the program statements sequentially in increments of 100 and indicates the date on which each statement was entered (or modified).

Within the program listing, the compiler also indicates how it is interpreting any nesting of structured operators by inserting a B at the beginning of the structure, an E at the end of the structure, and an X for any ELSE it encounters within the structure. The compiler also prints a digit with each of these codes, representing the level of nesting the structure establishes. By cross-checking these digits, you can make sure that the computer has matched the beginnings and ends of the structures as you had intended. You can also instruct the compiler to indent the program listing so that you can more easily see your logic structures. Ask your instructor how to use this feature on your system.

The compiler also provides a cross-reference listing to help you diagnose problems. A cross-reference listing is a list of all fields and indicators used in your program; it logs every program statement within which each of the fields or indicators occurs. The statement defining the field is annotated with a D (for define), while any statement within which the field's or indicator's value is changed is annotated with an M (for modify). You can use this listing to quickly locate field and/or indicator use within your program listing.

If your program contains syntax errors, the compiler notes the errors by inserting an asterisk (*) and a numeric error code either under the line in error or within the cross-reference listing. At the end of the compile listing, a message summary lists these error codes and provides a message detailing the cause of the problem. Problems vary in severity. A message with a severity of 00 is an informational message noting a condition that will not prevent the program from being compiled; errors with severity of 10 or higher need to be corrected before the program can be compiled normally.

Once you have obtained a "clean compile" — that is, once the system has successfully translated your program into machine language and bound the program into a *PGM object — you can begin to check for logic errors that your program may contain.

Logic Errors

Logic errors are caused by faulty program design. You detect these kinds of errors by having the computer execute your program and then carefully checking the results of the execution. There are two broad classes of logic errors, sometimes called runtime errors and output errors.

Runtime Errors

Runtime errors are errors that prevent your program from reaching a normal end. Runtime errors are easy to detect: Either the program abruptly stops in the middle (an **abend**, or abnormal ending), or the program runs and runs and runs, until finally you or the operator intervenes. (The latter problem signals an infinite loop.) Although detecting the presence of a runtime error is not a problem, discovering the cause of the error can sometimes be difficult. Moreover, the kinds of logic problems that cause abends are different from those that cause infinite loops.

Diagnosing Abends

When your program ends abnormally, the system sends you an error message to inform you of the cause of the problem and where the problem occurred within your program. Sometimes these error messages are not completely clear. By putting your cursor on the message and pressing the Help key, you can obtain additional information about the problem. Typical causes of such runtime problems include trying to divide by zero, attempting to carry out a numeric operation on a field that contains non-numeric data, trying to reference an array element beyond the defined limits (or size) of the array, attempting to read past end-of-file, and trying to update a record before you have read a record.

Once you have located the problem statement and determined the nature of the problem, you often have to trace through your program logic to determine how your program allowed that problem to occur. For example, if the program statement

```
EVAL      C = A/B
```

causes an abnormal ending because of an attempt to divide by zero, you need to determine why field B has a value of 0 at the time the system is attempting the division operation. Is B an input field? If so, have you forgotten to read a record before the division? If B is a work field, have you neglected to assign it a nonzero value before the division? Or have you inadvertently assigned 0 to B at the wrong time in your program?

If you cannot locate the cause of the problem, you may find it useful to run the program in debug mode, a topic discussed later in this appendix.

Diagnosing Infinite Loops

If you have to cancel your job to prevent it from running forever, you know that you have an infinite loop within your program. An infinite loop is a faulty logic structure that causes the computer to repeat the same set of instructions over and over again. The following code shows two obvious infinite loops.

```
*.. 1 ...+... 2 ...+... 3 ...+... 4 ...+... 5 ...+... 6 ...+... 7 ...+... 8
CLØNØ1Factor1+++++++Opcode(E)+Extended-factor2+++++++++++++++++++++++++++++++
CLØNØ1Factor1+++++++Opcode(E)+Factor2+++++++Result++++++++Len++D+HiLoEq....
 * Two examples of infinite loops
C                   EVAL      *IN9Ø = *OFF
C                   DOW       *IN9Ø = *OFF
C                   EVAL      Count = Count + 1
C                   ENDDO
 . . .
C     Loop          TAG
C                   ADD       1             Count
C                   GOTO      Loop
```

In these examples, the causes of the infinite loops are simple to detect. In the case of the DOW, no statement exists within the loop to change the value of *IN90 to *ON — the condition needed to end the loop. In the second example, the GOTO unconditionally (that is, always) transfers control back to the TAG statement.

In general, the cause of an infinite loop within a real program is less obvious than it is in these examples. The first thing to realize in trying to diagnose your problem is that you can narrow your focus to the iterative operations in your program: DO, DOU, DOW, and FOR. The second thing to realize is that somehow the condition that specifies when the looping should stop is not occurring. For example, forgetting to include a READ operation within a DOW loop that continues until end-of-file is reached will result in an infinite loop. Forgetting to increment a counter in a count-controlled loop based on an operation other than DO will likewise prevent the loop from ending.

A common cause of infinite loops that you can easily overlook when modifying older, converted programs is a counter defined too small. Study the following example to see whether you can detect the cause of the infinite loop that would result if the program were run.

```
*.. 1 ...+... 2 ...+... 3 ...+... 4 ...+... 5 ...+... 6 ...+... 7 ...+... 8
DName++++++++++ETDsFrom+++To/Len+IDc.Keywords+++++++++++++++++++++++++++++++++
CLØNØ1Factor1++++++Opcode(E)+Factor2+++++++Result++++++++Len++D+HiLoEq....
 * A less obvious example of an infinite loop
D Count           S              2 Ø INZ(Ø)

C     Count         DOUEQ     1ØØ
 . . .
C                   ADD       1             Count
C                   ENDDO
```

This example results in an infinite loop because Count never attains the value 100. Count is defined as two positions (with zero decimals), so the largest value it can store is 99. Adding 1 to 99 causes the resulting value, 100, to be truncated to 00. You can easily avoid such a potential problem by using the modern features of RPG IV. The EVAL operation does not allow high-order truncation; it issues a runtime error to alert you to the problem.

Output Errors

The most insidious kinds of logic errors are not those that cause abnormal program endings or infinite loops, but those that simply result in incorrect output. Some of these errors are very obvious — neglecting to print heading lines on reports, for instance, or omitting an output entry that causes an entire column of information to be missing from a report. Other output errors are less easily detected and require careful checking by hand to discover. You are unlikely to notice errors in complex calculations, for example, if you simply scan the output visually.

Detecting Output Errors

Carefully checking output generated by the computer against the results of your hand calculations is called **desk checking**. How much desk checking is required depends on the complexity of the logic that the program expresses. In general, you should check out enough sets of data to test each logic branch within your program at least once. If, for example, you have written a payroll program that processes workers with overtime hours differently from workers without overtime, you should desk check the output for at least one worker with overtime hours and one without. The more conditional the logic within your program, the more desk checking required to ensure that your program is processing each case correctly.

Don't forget to check the accuracy of subtotals and grand totals. If you have many columns with totals, you generally do not have to hand-calculate the total for all columns. If you are doing all your accumulation in the same place within your program and the calculations are all set up in the same way, then if one column's total is correct, the rest should be correct as well — provided you are using the correct fields in the calculations and referencing the correct accumulators in your Output Specifications.

The final step in checking output is to rigorously compare the computer-generated output with design documents, such as printer spacing charts, to ensure that your output exactly matches the requested format. Are the column headings appropriately centered over the columns? Are the literals spelled correctly (e.g., "Quantity," not "Quanity")? Does the report's vertical alignment match that of the printer spacing chart? Did you edit the output correctly? The programmer's job is to give the designer exactly what he or she requested. Although concern with such formatting details may seem "picky," careful attention to detail is one facet of the preciseness expected of first-rate programmers.

Correcting Output Errors

Once you've discovered an output error, your next job is to discover the cause of the error so you can correct it. A good programmer never makes changes within a program without having a specific reason for doing so. You should locate the precise cause of a problem and fix it; do not, in other words, base your changes on hunches or trial and error.

To find the cause of an error, work backwards: Focus your attention initially on those calculations specifically involved in generating the incorrect output. If after carefully checking these program statements you still have not found a statement that is incorrect, broaden your search to those portions of the program that may be influencing the output more remotely.

It is impossible to be aware of every possible cause of erroneous output, but you should be alert to a number of common errors, many of which are described below, when you are working to debug a program.

Field Problems

Incorrectly defined variables cause truncation, a problem most likely to occur with fields used as accumulators or fields that are the result of complex calculations. Another common field-related problem is a failure to appropriately initialize or reinitialize fields. Forgetting to reset an indicator, counter, or flag variable during repetitive processing is a common cause of erroneous output.

Loops

Off-by-one errors, resulting in a count-controlled loop repeating one too few or one too many times, occur frequently in programs. This kind of error results when you establish the conditional test to end the looping process incorrectly. It often is related to an incorrect initialization of the counter field used to control the looping.

For example, both of the following pseudocode examples, designed to add all the numbers between 1 and 100, are erroneous. The first example would sum the numbers 1 through 101, while the second would add the values 1 through 99.

```
Initialize I to 0
Initialize Sum to 0
WHILE I is less than 101
    Add 1 to I
    Add I to Sum
ENDWHILE
```

```
Initialize I to 1
Initialize Sum to 0
WHILE I < 100
    Add I to Sum
    Add 1 to I
ENDWHILE
```

Another common loop problem is a failure to enter the loop. When you use a looping operator that tests the condition before executing the steps within the loop — when, for example, you want the system to read a file sequentially until it locates a desired code value within a record, process that record, and then resume reading until it finds the next record with that same code value — your program may fail to enter the loop. The following pseudocode will correctly find the first record containing the desired code but will continue to process the first record infinitely.

```
WHILE not end-of-file
    WHILE code <> desired value and not end-of-file
        Read a record
    ENDWHILE
    Process the record
ENDWHILE
```

Once the first appropriate record is located, the code field contains the desired value. As a result, the test of the inner loop will always be false and the inner loop will not be executed; no additional records will be read.

IF Logic

Programmers often incorrectly specify the relational comparison used within an IF that is testing for a range of values. For example, if specifications state that pay rate should be less than $45.00, the following pseudocode would be incorrect.

```
IF rate > 45
    Perform error routine
ENDIF
```

Sometimes output errors are caused by incorrectly nested IFs. Know how the system matches IFs, ELSEs, and ENDIFs, and check the notation of the compiler listing to make sure the system is interpreting your nested IFs the way you intended.

Another common IF problem is incorrectly used ANDs, ORs, or NOTs in compound IFs. NOTs, in particular, are prone to errors. For example, if you want to validate a code field that should have a value of S, H, or R, the following pseudocode would falsely signal valid values as errors.

```
IF code NOT = 'S' OR code NOT = 'H' OR code NOT = 'R'
    Perform error routine
ENDIF
```

Calculations

Sometimes steps in complex calculations are not executed in the correct order. Also, programmers occasionally overlook the possibility that a calculation can result in a negative value. This can be a difficult problem to locate because RPG IV prints or displays all values as absolute (unsigned) values unless field editing includes a provision for a negative sign (however, negative values are handled as negative values during calculation).

For example, when figuring income-tax withholding, you often need to subtract a dependent allowance from gross earnings before applying the withholding tax percentage. The relationship between gross earnings and the number of dependents may be such that this subtraction returns a negative value. If you did not anticipate this scenario, the tax will be added to gross earnings (subtracting a negative number), and the same negative tax liability will appear as a positive value on the payroll-register report unless the tax field is edited with a code specifying that negative signs should be printed.

Debug

On occasion, a visual examination of your program will not reveal the source of an output error. Rather than resorting to trial and error, you should use OS/400's debugging facility. A "debugger" lets you trace a program as it executes, stepping through the program one statement at a time or stopping it at "breakpoints" that you designate so you can examine the values of fields at particular points in execution. The Integrated Language Environment (ILE) source debugger lets you view your code as it is executed so that you can examine variable values while stepping through the code on the screen. This procedure can help you locate program errors that might otherwise elude you.

There are many options and methods for using the debugger; we describe the easiest and most commonly used method here. (For detailed information about the ILE source debugger, see *ILE RPG/400 Programmer's Guide*.) To begin using the source debugger, you need to compile your ILE programs with the DBGVIEW (Debug view) parameter set to *LIST or *SOURCE for the CRTRPGMOD (Create RPG Module) and CRTBNDRPG (Create Bound RPG Program) commands. Next, start a debug session with the STRDBG (Start Debug) command, naming the program (or programs) you want to debug, using the following syntax:

```
STRDBG PGM(program-name program-name ...)
```

A display like the following one will appear, showing the source for the entry module of the program you are debugging.

```
                        Display Module Source
Program:    PRTAUTUSR    Library:   BMEYERS       Module:    PRTAUTUSR
       1           *MODULE ENTRY AND MAIN PROCEDURE ENTRY
       2        1  ************************************************************
       3        2  * Object : RPG program DBGEXM
       4        3  * Author : Bryan Meyers, 5 January 2000
       5        4  ************************************************************
       6        5  *
       7        6 HALTSEQ(*EXT)
       8        7  *-----------------------------------------------------------
       9        8 FQPRINT    O    F  132          PRINTER FORMLEN( 66 ) FORMOFL(
      10        9 F                                       OFLIND( *IN63 )
      11       10  *
      12       11  *-----------------------------------------------------------
      13       12  *
      14       13  * Parms for the Create UserSpace (QUSCRTUS) API
      15       14  *
                                                                    More...
   Debug . . . _____

   F3=End program   F6=Add/Clear breakpoint    F10=Step    F11=Display variable
   F12=Resume       F17=Watch variable   F18=Work with watch   F24=More keys
```

Your program will remain in debug mode until you issue the command ENDDBG (End Debug).

Once in debug mode, you can specify *breakpoints* — statements within your program where you want execution to halt so you can examine the value of variables at particular points. Pressing F12 will resume operation. You can then run the program, which will execute until it reaches a breakpoint; then the debug display will reappear, positioned to the breakpoint. From the debug command line at the bottom of the screen, you can use several debug commands. The following table lists the most commonly used commands.

Most Commonly Used Debug Commands

Command	Usage	Examples
ATTR	Displays the attributes for a variable. The attributes are the type and size of the variable.	ATTR COMPNY
BREAK	Adds a breakpoint or a conditional breakpoint using the WHEN parameter.	BREAK 1000 BREAK 2000 WHEN COMPNY = '02'
CLEAR	Clears a breakpoint or all of the breakpoints.	CLEAR 2000 CLEAR PGM
EVAL	Displays or changes the value of a variable.	EVAL COMPNY EVAL COMPNY = '02'
FIND	Finds a line number of text in the source code.	FIND COMPNY
STEP	Causes the program to "step" through the code by executing the next statement.	STEP 1 STEP 5

Function keys can be used in place of debug commands in many cases. When a debug command or function returns information, the information is displayed on the message line at the bottom of the screen; if the information to be displayed exceeds a single line, a separate Evaluation Expression screen is displayed so you can view the entire variable information.

Breakpoints

When a breakpoint is reached, the program stops and lets you analyze the condition of the program at that line of code. On the debug screen, you specify breakpoints in either of two ways. You can place the display cursor on the sequence number for the line at which you want to set a breakpoint and then press F6, or you can type the **break** (or **br**) debug command on the Debug line at the bottom of the screen. For example, to set a breakpoint at line 85, you'd enter **break 85**. When the program executes, it would stop at statement 85, just before that statement's execution. Upon stopping, the system would again show you the debug display, indicating which breakpoint had been reached.

You could then examine the current value of a variable by positioning the cursor on the variable and pressing F11, or you could use the **eval** debug command to show the value of a variable. The **eval** command takes the following form:

```
eval variable
```

Another useful feature of debug is that you can actually change the value of a variable or variables to determine how your program executes when processing that value. To use this feature, wait until your program has reached the desired breakpoint and then issue the **eval** debug command using the form

```
eval variable = value
```

You can use this command with character or numeric fields; enclose character values in apostrophes (').

Conditional breakpoints are breakpoints defined to stop your program only when a specific condition is met. Conditional breakpoints are useful when you know your program needs to stop after a specific event. For example, if your program starts to print invalid information when the value of the company field, COMPNY, changes from '01' to '02', you can set your breakpoint to stop when that happens. To create a conditional breakpoint, you use the **break** debug command. To add a breakpoint to stop your program when the company field changes to '02', you'd enter the **break** command in the following format:

```
break 2000 when COMPNY = '02'
```

Conditional breakpoints can help you find the condition you want to evaluate quickly, without stopping the program several times in search of that condition.

To display all the breakpoints in your modules, use F13 to work with module breakpoints. All breakpoints are listed, with breakpoint conditions if applicable. The following screen shows a sample display of breakpoints.

```
                      Work with Module Breakpoints
                                                 System:   xxxxxxxx
    Program  . . . :   PRTAUTUSR            Library  . . . :   BMEYERS
      Module . . . :     PRTAUTUSR          Type . . . . . :   *PGM

    Type options, press Enter.
      1=Add   4=Clear

    Opt    Line      Condition
     _      ___      _____
     _       85
     _       99      ERRCODE > 0




                                                              Bottom
    Command
    ===>
    F3=Exit    F4=Prompt    F5=Refresh    F9=Retrieve    F12=Cancel
```

You can add new breakpoints using option 1, and you can remove existing breakpoints using option 4.

Step Mode

Another way to use debug is to trace the flow of statement execution, using a debugger feature called *stepping*, wherein the system executes all or part of your program one line at a time, stopping after each operation so you can examine the logic flow and program variables. To specify this single-stepping through your program, either press F10 or enter the **step** debug command.

Once you are finished with a debugging session, remember to issue the command ENDDBG to end the session; this command automatically removes all traces and breakpoints.

As a beginning programmer, you may feel frustrated at times by your inability to locate the cause of program errors. With practice, however, you'll find yourself beginning to recognize what kinds of logic errors cause certain output errors, and, as a result, you'll be able to correct your programs with increasing ease. The sign of an excellent programmer is the ability to detect such problems as they occur. But remember, even seasoned programmers make logic mistakes.

Appendix F

Data Files

This appendix contains definitions of the data files used in the Programming Assignments throughout this book. Most of the assignments focus on three companies to give you a sense of what it is like to develop an application system for a company. An application system is a series of programs that use the same set of data files to record and maintain data important to some facet of the company's business, process that data, permit online queries of the data, and produce needed reports. Depending on what programs your instructor assigns you, you will be working with several of the data files described below.

An overview of each company precedes the descriptions of the company's files to give you a context within which to understand each company's data and program needs. The key fields of each file, if any, are preceded by an asterisk (*).

Date fields are represented in these files using an eight-digit number in *ccyymmdd* format. Native date data types are not used.

Case 1: CompuSell

CompuSell is a small mail-order company specializing in computers and computer supplies. The company needs an integrated system of programs to handle its orders and inventory, as well as to generate needed reports for management. An analyst has already done the preliminary design work and determined the files needed as part of the system. The files, and their record layouts, are described below.

CSCFINP : Customer Finance File

This file contains information about customers who are financing purchases.

Record Layout of CSCFINP (Record Format FINREC)

Field	Description	Positions	(Decimal positions)	Notes
*CUSTNO	Customer number	1 – 6	(0)	—
PURAMT	Purchase amount	7 – 12	(2)	—
DWNPAY	Down payment	13 – 18	(2)	—
PDATE	Purchase date	19 – 26	(0)	*ccyymmdd*

CSCSTP : Customer Master File

This file stores basic information about CompuSell's customers. A unique customer number assigned to each new customer serves as that customer's identifier. In addition to storing name, address, and telephone information, this file tracks date of last order (for marketing purposes) and balance owed (for billing purposes). (Although most customers are cash customers, occasionally a customer will under- or overpay on an order.)

Record Layout of CSCSTP (Record Format CUSTREC)

Field	Description	Positions	(Decimal positions)	Notes
*CUSTNO	Customer number	1–6	(0)	—
CFNAME	First name	7–16	—	—
CLNAME	Last name	17–31	—	—
CSTRET	Street address	32–51	—	—
CCITY	City	52–66	—	—
CSTATE	State	67–68	—	—
CZIP	Zip+4	69–77	(0)	—
CPHONE	Phone	78–87	(0)	—
ORDDAT	Last order date	88–95	(0)	*ccyymmdd*
BALDUE	Balance due	96–101	(2 implied)	—

CSINVP: Inventory Master File

This file is used to maintain inventory records. When a company adds a new product to its line, the information is recorded in this file. Each item carried has a unique product number. As items are sold, they are subtracted from inventory; as stock comes in from suppliers, the stock is added to inventory. When quantity on hand drops to the reorder quantity, the item is reordered from the appropriate supplier. The reorder code field is used to prevent the same item from accidentally being reordered more than once. Supplier code is a supplier identification number assigned by CompuSell; supplier product ID is the supplier's identifier for that product. Current cost reflects the most recent cost paid for the item, and average cost is the average cost of the items in inventory. Selling price is what CompuSell currently charges for the item.

Record Layout of CSINVP (Record Format INVREC)

Field	Description	Positions	(Decimal positions)	Notes
*PRODNO	Product number	1–6	(0)	—
DESCRP	Description	7–31	—	—
SELLPR	Selling price	32–37	(2 implied)	—
SHIPWT	Shipping weight	38–41	—	1st 2 positions are pounds; last 2 are ounces
QTYOH	Quantity on hand	42–45	(0 implied)	—
RORPNT	Reorder point	46–49	(0 implied)	—
RORQTY	Reorder quantity	50–53	(0 implied)	—
RORCOD	Reorder code	54	—	Blank or R
SUPCOD	Supplier code	55–57	(0)	—
SUPPID	Supplier product ID	58–65	—	—
CURCST	Current cost	66–71	(2 implied)	—
AVGCST	Average cost	72–77	(2 implied)	—

CSORDP : Orders File

This file contains "header" information about each order placed with CompuSell. The detailed information about items ordered is stored in file CSORDPRP.

Record Layout of CSORDP (Record Format ORDRREC)

Field	Description	Positions	(Decimal positions)	Notes
*ORD#	Order number	1–5	(0)	—
ODATE	Date ordered	6–13	(0)	*ccyymmdd*
CUSTNO	Customer number	14–19	(0)	—
PAYMNT	Payment included	20–26	(2)	—
ORDTOT	Total cost of order	27–33	(2)	—

CSORDPRP : Order/Products File

This file, in conjunction with file CSORDP, contains information about customer orders.

Record Layout of CSORDPRP (Record Format ORDERREC)

Field	Description	Positions	(Decimal positions)
*ORD#	Order number	1–5	(0)
*PRODNO	Product number	6–11	(0)
QTYORD	Quantity ordered	12–15	(0)

CSRCVP : Goods Received File

The company uses a file of received goods. Each time goods are received from a supplier, the information is stored in this file until it can be processed in batch to update the inventory file.

Record Layout of CSRCVP (Record Format RCVREC)

Field	Description	Positions	(Decimal positions)
*SUPCOD	Supplier code	1–3	(0)
*SUPPID	Supplier product ID	4–11	—
QTYRCV	Quantity received	12–15	(0)
COST	Item cost	16–21	(2)

CSSUPP : Supplier File

This file stores information about the suppliers of CompuSell's products.

Record Layout of CSSUPP (Record Format SUPREC)

Field	Description	Positions	(Decimal positions)
*SUPCOD	Supplier code	1–3	—
SNAME	Supplier name	4–28	—
CONTAC	Contact person	29–58	—
SSTRET	Street address	59–78	—
SCITY	City	79–93	—
SSTAT	State	94–95	—
SZIP	Zip	96–104	(0)
SPHONE	Phone	105–114	(0)

CSZPZNP : Zip/Zone Table File

In addition to the above files, CompuSell will need two "table" files to help it determine what to charge its customers for shipping. The first table file, CSZPZNP, will be used to determine the correct shipping zone based on the first three digits of a customer's zip code. Zones range from 2 to 7, depending on zip code. CSZPZNP is a range table file, such that each zip-code record represents the highest of a range of zip codes.

Record Layout of CSZPZNP (Record Format ZIPREC)

Field	Description	Positions	(Decimal positions)
TZIP	Three zip digits	1–3	(0)
TZONE	Related shipping zone	4	(0)

CSCHGP : Charges Table File

This second table file contains shipping charges based on weight and zone. Each record contains a weight and six charges (one each for zones 2–7).

Record Layout of CSCHGP (Record Format CHGREC)

Field	Description	Positions	(Decimal positions)
TWGT	Weight in pounds	1–2	(0)
TCHG2	Charge zone 2	3–6	(2)
TCHG3	Charge zone 3	7–10	(2)
TCHG4	Charge zone 4	11–14	(2)
TCHG5	Charge zone 5	15–18	(2)
TCHG6	Charge zone 6	19–22	(2)
TCHG7	Charge zone 7	23–26	(2)

Case 2: Wexler University

Wexler University is a small midwestern university that wants a system for student records and registration. The system will store information about departments, instructors, courses, sections, students, and enrollment. The files required as part of the system are described below.

WUCRDP : Earned Credits File

This file contains a record for each course each student has completed.

Record Layout of WUCRDP (Record Format CRDTREC)

Field	Description	Positions	(Decimal positions)	Notes
*STUNO	Social Security number	1–9	(0)	—
DEPT	Course department	10–12	—	—
CRSNO	Course number	13–15	(0)	—
GRADE	Grade	16–17	—	—
SEMES	Semester taken	18–22	—	First 4 positions ccyy; 5th position is semester code, where 1 = winter; 2 = summer; 3 = fall

WUCRSDSP: Course Description File

Each course has a description of varying length; the description may include an overview of the course, prerequisites, and so on. One or more records in this file represent a description for a given course; the records for a given course are sequentially assigned a line number.

Record Layout of WUCRSDSP (Record Format CRSDREC)

Field	Description	Positions	(Decimal positions)
*DEPT	Course department	1–3	—
*CRSNO	Course number	4–6	(0)
*LINE	Description line number	7–8	(0)
CRSDSC	Description	9–58	—

WUCRSP: Course File

A record in this file represents each course the university offers. Each course is uniquely identified by a six-position identification of course department and course number (e.g., CIS264).

Record Layout of WUCRSP (Record Format CRSREC)

Field	Description	Positions	(Decimal positions)
*DEPT	Course department	1–3	—
*CRSNO	Course number	4–6	—
CRSTTL	Course title	7–31	—
CREDIT	Credits	32	(0)

WUDPTP: Department File

This file contains information about each department of Wexler University.

Record Layout of WUDPTP (Record Format DEPTREC)

Field	Description	Positions	(Decimal positions)
*DEPT	Department code	1–3	—
DNAME	Department name	4–23	—
CHAIR	Name of chair	24–48	—
DOFFIC	Department office	49–58	—
DPHONE	Department phone	59–68	(0)

WUENRLP: Current Enrollment File

A record is entered in this file for each student for each section in which he or she is enrolled. At the end of the semester, scanned grades are added to this file before preparing semester grade reports.

Record Layout of WUENRLP (Record Format ENRREC)

Field	Description	Positions	(Decimal positions)
SECT	Section number	1–5	(0)
STUNO	Social Security number	6–14	(0)
GRADE	Grade received	15–16	—

WUEXAMP: Student Exam File

This file contains information about students in a class and five exam grades for each student.

Record Layout of WUEXAMP (Record Format EXAMREC)

Field	Description	Positions	(Decimal positions)
*STUNO	Social Security number	1–9	(0)
SFNAME	First name	10–19	—
SLNAME	Last name	20–34	—
EXAM1	Exam 1 grade	35–37	(0)
EXAM2	Exam 2 grade	38–40	(0)
EXAM3	Exam 3 grade	41–43	(0)
EXAM4	Exam 4 grade	44–46	(0)
EXAM5	Exam 5 grade	47–49	(0)

WUHRLYP: Hourly Employees File

This file contains information about hourly employees at Wexler University.

Record Layout of WUHRLYP (Record Format EMPREC)

Field	Description	Positions	(Decimal positions)
EMPNO	Social Security number	1–9	(0)
LNAME	Last name	10–24	—
FNAME	First name	25–34	—
REGHRS	Regular hours	35–37	(1)
OTHRS	Overtime hours	38–40	(1)
RATE	Regular pay rate	41–44	(2)

WUINSTP: Instructor File

Each instructor at Wexler University has a record in this file.

Record Layout of WUINSTP (Record Format INSTREC)

Field	Description	Positions	(Decimal positions)	Notes
IFNAME	First name	1–10	—	—
ILNAME	Last name	11–25	—	—
*INSTNO	Social Security number	26–34	(0)	—
DEPT	Department	35–37	—	—
SALARY	Salary	38–45	(2)	—
RANK	Academic rank	46	—	1 = instructor; 2 = assistant professor; 3 = associate professor; 4 = full professor
SEX	Sex	47	—	M = male; F = female

continued...

continued...

Field	Description	Positions	(Decimal positions)	Notes
HIRDAT	Date of hire	48–55	(0)	*ccyymmdd*
MARSTS	Marital status	56	—	M = married; S = single; H = head of house
DEPEND	Number of dependents	57–58	(0)	—
TENURE	Tenured faculty	59	—	Y = yes; N = no
TITLE	Preferred title	60	—	1 = Dr.; 2 = Mr.; 3 = Mrs.; 4 = Ms.
STREET	Street address	61–80	—	—
CITY	City	81–95	—	—
STATE	State	96–97	—	—
ZIP	Zip	98–106	(0)	—

WUKEYP : File of Keys to Tests in WUTSTP

This file contains the keys (answers) to the tests contained in file WUTSTP, the student test file. There is one answer key (record) for each test. The file is keyed on course ID and test number; these values match those in the student test file.

Record Layout of WUKEYP (Record Format KEYREC)

Field	Description	Positions	(Decimal positions)
*TESTNO	Test number	1–4	(0)
*CRSID	Course ID	5–10	—
ILNAME	Instructor's last name	11–25	—
KEY	Correct answers 1–50	26–75	—

WULOANP : Faculty Credit Union Loan File

This file contains records for loan applications to the credit union.

Record Layout of WULOANP (Record Format LOANREC)

Field	Description	Positions	(Decimal positions)
*LOANNO	Loan number	1–5	(0)
CNAME	Customer name	6–20	—
LAMT	Loan amount	21–27	(2)
ANNRAT	Annual interest rate	28–31	(4)
YEARS	Years for loan	32–33	(0)

WUSCTP : Current Sections File

A record in this file represents every section of each course currently being offered. Each section has been assigned a unique number.

Record Layout of WUSCTP (Record Format SECREC)

Field	Description	Positions	(Decimal positions)	Notes
*SECT	Section number	1–5	(0)	—
DEPT	Course department	6–8	—	—
CRSNO	Course number	9–11	—	—
SECTIM	Meeting time	12–15	(0)	hhmm
SECDAY	Meeting days	16–18	—	—
ROOM	Meeting room	19–22	—	—
CAP	Maximum enrollment	23–25	(0)	—
CURENL	Current enrollment	26–28	(0)	—
ILNAME	Instructor's last name	29–43	—	—

WUSTDP : Student Master File

This file contains information about all Wexler University's students who are actively enrolled as well as those who have graduated within the past five years.

Record Layout of WUSTDP (Record Format STUDREC)

Field	Description	Positions	(Decimal positions)	Notes
*STUNO	Social Security number	1–9	(0)	—
SLNAME	Student last name	10–24	—	—
SFNAME	Student first name	25–34	—	—
SMNAME	Student middle name	35–44	—	—
STREET	Street address	45–64	—	—
CITY	City	65–79	—	—
STATE	State	80–81	—	—
ZIP	Zip	82–90	(0)	—
PHONE	Telephone	91–100	(0)	—
CRDTOT	Credits earned	101–103	(0)	—
DCODE	District code	104	—	I = in-district; O = out-of-district; F = international
ADMDAT	Date admitted	105–112	—	ccyymmdd
CLASS	Classification	113	—	U = undergraduate; G = graduate
GRDDAT	Date graduated	114–121	—	Blanks or ccyymmdd
SDEPT	Department of major	122–124	—	—
GPA	Grade point average	125–127	(2)	—
DEGREE	Degree granted	128–130	—	—

WUTRANSP : Transcript Request File

This file contains Social Security numbers for students requesting transcripts.

Record Layout of WUTRANSP (Record Format TRNSREC)

Field	Description	Positions	(Decimal positions)
*STUNO	Social Security number	1–9	(0)

WUTSTP : Student Test File

This file contains student answers to 50-question, multiple-choice tests. The file is keyed on course ID, test, and section number.

Record Layout of WUTSTP (Record Format TESTREC)

Field	Description	Positions	(Decimal positions)	Notes
*TESTNO	Test number	1–4	(0)	—
*SECTN	Section number	5–9	(0)	—
*CRSID	Course ID	10–15	—	—
STUID	Student ID	16–24	(0)	—
ANS	Answers 1–50	25–74	—	Values A, B, C, D, E

Case 3: GTC, Inc.

GTC is a small regional telephone company that needs an application system to maintain customer accounts, bill for calls, process payments, generate management reports, and so on. Four main files will be needed as part of the system. The files, and their record layouts, are described below.

GTCLSP : Calls Transaction File

The telephone switching system generates this file automatically. Records accumulate in the file during the month; once a month, the file is processed to determine monthly billing. The file is then cleared at the beginning of each new billing period.

Record Layout of GTCLSP (Record Format CALREC)

Field	Description	Positions	(Decimal positions)	Notes
CPHONE	Caller's number	1–10	(0)	—
CALLED	Called number	11–20	(0)	—
CALDAT	Date of call	21–28	(0)	*ccyymmdd*
CALLEN	Length of call	29–31	(0)	In minutes
CALTIM	Time of call	32–35	(0)	*hhmm* based on 24-hour clock
CALCST	Call cost	36–40	(2)	—

GTCSTP: Customer Master File

This file contains a record for each of GTC's customers.

Record Layout of GTCSTP (Record Format CUSREC)

Field	Description	Positions	(Decimal positions)	Notes
*CPHONE	Customer phone number	1–10	(0)	—
CLNAME	Last name	11–25	—	—
CFNAME	First name	26–35	—	—
CSTRET	Street address	36–55	—	—
CCITY	City	56–70	—	—
CSTAT	State	71–72	—	—
CZIP	Zip	73–77	(0)	—
CURBIL	Current billing amount	78–83	(2)	—
AMTOWE	Amount owed	84–89	(2)	—
PAYDAT	Date last payment	90–97	(0)	*ccyymmdd*

GTCPAYP: Payments Transaction File

This file is generated through optical character recognition (OCR) and manual entry techniques. Records are used once to update the customer account figures and generate a payment report and then archived.

Record Layout of GTPAYP (Record Format PAYREC)

Field	Description	Positions	(Decimal positions)	Notes
*CPHONE	Payer's phone number	1–10	(0)	—
AMTPD	Amount paid	11–16	(2)	—
DATRCV	Date payment received	17–24	(0)	*ccyymmdd*

GTCRATP: Rates Table File

This is a sequential file used as a table to determine cost of calls to a given area code and exchange.

Record Layout of GTCRATP (Record Format RATEREC)

Field	Description	Positions	(Decimal positions)
TAREA	Area code called	1–3	(0)
TEXCH	Exchange called	4–6	(0)
TCITY	City called	7–16	—
TSTATE	State called	17–18	—
CST1ST	Cost for first minute	19–20	(2)
CSTADL	Cost for each additional minute	21–22	(2)

Miscellaneous Files

The following files are not part of any of the above application systems. They represent "standalone" applications included as Programming Assignments to demonstrate certain programming concepts.

ACP001: Acme Work File

This file is used in Chapter 5, Programming Assignment 4.

Record Layout for ACP001 (Record Format ACMEREC)

Field	Description	Positions	(Decimal positions)	Notes
SOCSEC	Social Security number	1–9	(0)	—
NAME	Name	10–25	—	—
WKDATE	Date worked	26–31	(0)	*mmddyy*
*HOURS	Hours worked	32–33	(0)	—
QTY	Quantity produced	34–36	(0)	—

BIDS: Bids File

This file is used in Chapter 4, Programming Assignment 4.

Record Layout for BIDS (Record Format BIDREC)

Field	Description	Positions	(Decimal positions)
JOBNO	Job number	1–4	(0)
PCODE	Paint code	5–9	(0)
PCOST	Per gallon cost	10–13	(2)
COVRG	Coverage per gallon	14–16	(0)
LENFT	Room length, feet	17–18	(0)
LENIN	Room length, inches	19–20	(0)
WIDFT	Room width, feet	21–22	(0)
WIDIN	Room width, inches	23–24	(0)
HTFT	Room height, feet	25–26	(0)
HTIN	Room height, inches	27–28	(0)
PCT	Percent windows, doors	29–30	(2)

HJSLPP: Salesperson File

This file is used in Chapter 11, Programming Assignment 2.

Record Layout for HJSLPP (Record Format SLSPREC)

Field	Description	Positions	(Decimal positions)
*SLSMNO	Salesperson number	1–2	(0)
SNAME	Name	3–27	—
BASPAY	Weekly base pay	28–33	(2)

HJSLSP : Sales File

This file is used in Chapter 11, Programming Assignment 2.

Record Layout for HJSLSP (Record Format SLSREC)

Field	Description	Positions	(Decimal positions)
SLSMNO	Salesperson number	1–2	(0)
INVNO	Invoice number	3–7	(0)
AMT	Sale amount	8–14	(2)

MWC001P : Meter Reading File

This file is used in Chapter 5, Programming Assignment 3.

Record Layout for MWC001P (Record Format MWREC)

Field	Description	Positions	(Decimal positions)	Notes
CNAME	Customer name	1–20	—	—
CUSTNO	Customer number	21–25	(0)	—
OLDMTR	Old meter reading	26–29	(0)	—
NEWMTR	New meter reading	30–33	(0)	—
RCODE	Residency code	34	—	1 = city resident; 2 = non-city resident

PIPRESP : Airline Reservation File

This file is used in Chapter 11, Programming Assignment 3.

Record Layout for PIPRESP (Record Format PIPREC)

Field	Description	Positions	(Decimal positions)
*DY	Day of week	1	(0)
*FLIGHT	Flight number	2	(0)
RESERV	Seats reserved	3–4	(0)
FNAME	First name of reserver	5–14	—
LNAME	Last name of reserver	15–29	—
PHONE	Phone number of reserver	30–39	(0)

PRDSLSP : Sales Volume File

This file is used in Chapter 11, Programming Assignment 1. It contains a record for each of the company's products, showing the sales volume for each month.

Record Layout for PRDSLSP (Record Format PRDREC)

Field	Description	Positions	(Decimal positions)
PRODNO	Product number	1–6	(0)
SLS	12 monthly sales*	7–78	(0)

* Represents monthly total sales figures for that product, arranged sequentially from January to December; each sales figure is a six-digit integer.

Appendix G

Maintaining the Past

This appendix discusses the migration of older RPG programs to RPG IV. It also introduces you to features and operations used extensively in earlier versions of the language but now obsolete (although still supported) in RPG IV. The appendix also familiarizes you with RPG's fixed-logic cycle, as well as the use of conditioning, resulting, and level indicators.

Compatibility and Conversion

As RPG evolved, IBM's language developers tried to keep the language backward-compatible, so that old program source code could successfully be compiled and then executed with each new version of RPG. Typically, changes to RPG consisted of "add-ons" rather than replacements to older features, so that although the new version of the language might offer a better way to accomplish some programming task, the older method of accomplishing the task would still work. Thus, for example, RPG II programs could be compiled under RPG III with only slight, if any, modification to the source code.

RPG IV, however, introduced fundamental changes to the language. For example, source code lines were lengthened to 100 characters, while previous versions of the language used 80-column specifications. Moreover, RPG IV increased the permitted field-name length from six to 4,096 characters, allowed mixed-case entry and blank lines, changed the maximum length of operation names from five to six characters, shifted the location of some fixed-position entries, and changed some code requirements from fixed-position entries to more free-form keywords. All the specification types changed; some were eliminated, and a couple of new ones — the Definition Specification and the Procedure Boundary Specification — were introduced. As a result, the source code of programs written before RPG IV requires a "facelift" to be compatible with the RPG IV compiler.

To let RPG shops migrate code as effortlessly as possible to RPG IV, IBM supplies a CL command, CVTRPGSRC (Convert RPG Source), that converts pre–RPG IV source code to RPG IV syntax. This conversion utility automatically rearranges fixed-position entries to new locations, changes obsolete positional entries to appropriate keywords, creates Definition Specifications for tables and arrays to replace the eliminated Extension Specifications, substitutes new six-character operation codes for their obsolete five-character equivalents (e.g., LOOKUP for LOKUP, EXCEPT for EXCPT), and so on.

In general, companies using AS/400s traditionally stored RPG programs within source file QRPGSRC. As companies use command CVTRPGSRC to convert their old programs to RPG IV syntax, many choose to store the converted source code in the default source file QRPGLESRC. Depending on a company's approach to program migration, the business may have converted all its source code shortly after adopting RPG IV, or it may have taken a more leisurely approach, converting code on a member-by-member basis only as program maintenance needs required it.

But when you begin working as an RPG IV programmer (regardless of whether you need to convert source code to RPG IV or you are put to work on source code already converted), you need to understand the programming conventions and styles appropriate to earlier versions of the language to thoroughly understand the programs you encounter. CVTRPGSRC modifies only those syntactical variants that are no longer valid under RPG IV. In converted RPG IV source code, you can still find many coding styles and syntactical usage once necessary and/or appropriate for earlier versions of RPG. As a consequence, the code you maintain may not look much like the code you would write from scratch in RPG IV.

Holdovers from RPG III

First, don't be surprised to see variable names that are very short and written in all uppercase letters. Versions of RPG before RPG IV did not permit mixed-case entry, and they imposed a maximum length of six characters on field names. To give you a sense of what these earlier programs might look like once migrated to RPG IV, all the code in this appendix that illustrates pre–RPG IV techniques uses only uppercase characters and field names no longer than six characters. Program documentation, of course, does not extend beyond column 80.

Defining Work Fields

In RPG III, Definition Specifications did not exist. As a result, programs written during the RPG III era (and before it) defined each work field within the Calculation Specification in which that field appeared as a result. With this method, the length of the Result field is right adjusted in positions 64–68 (Len++). If the field is numeric — as it must be if it is the result of an arithmetic operation — the appropriate number of decimal positions is right adjusted in positions 69–70 (D+).

```
*.. 1 ...+... 2 ...+... 3 ...+... 4 ...+... 5 ...+... 6 ...+... 7 ...+... 8
CLØN01Factor1+++++++Opcode(E)+Factor2++++++Result++++++++Len++D+HiLoEq....
 * A division calculation that shows Result field definition
C       DAYS          DIV(H)    7             WEEKS             9 Ø
```

> **Note**
> All Calculation Specifications in pre-RPG IV versions of the language use the standard form rather than the extended Factor 2 form of the specification.

RPG III did let programmers define one variable "like" another, but in the absence of Definition Specifications this feature was implemented using a Calculation Specification. *LIKE was the Factor 1 value, DEFINE was the operation, the reference field was Factor 2, and the field being defined was the result. You could stipulate that the new field be longer or shorter than the defining field by including an entry in the length position: A plus sign (+) signaled that the new field should be longer than the defining field, while a minus sign (—) meant it should be shorter than the defining field. The value following the sign indicated the amount of increase or decrease. The following code illustrates this RPG III feature.

```
*.. 1 ...+... 2 ...+... 3 ...+... 4 ...+... 5 ...+... 6 ...+... 7 ...+... 8
CLØN01Factor1+++++++Opcode(E)+Factor2++++++Result++++++++Len++D+HiLoEq....
 * Older method of defining one field like another
C       *LIKE         DEFINE    OLDFLD        NEWFLD
C       *LIKE         DEFINE    SALES         SLSTOT            +  5
C       *LIKE         DEFINE    SLSTAX        SLSTOT            —  2
```

Performing Arithmetic and Numeric Assignment

The EVAL operation, with its free-form extended Factor 2 capabilities, was also not available before RPG IV. As a result, programmers used various fixed-form operations to express assignment and arithmetic logic. In Chapter 4, we briefly discussed the specific arithmetic operations ADD, SUB, MULT, and DIV. You can apply these operations to numeric fields or numeric literals, and the results of the operation must be stored in a numeric field designated as the Result field. Depending on the size of the answer relative to that of the Result field, these operations can result in high- or low-order truncation. You can specify rounding, or half-adjusting, for any of the operations by using the operation extender (H).

In its basic form, operation ADD adds the values of Factor 1 and Factor 2, storing the answer in the Result field. The SUB operation subtracts Factor 2 from Factor 1, storing its answer in the result. MULT multiplies the contents of Factor 1 and Factor 2, storing the product in the result; DIV divides Factor 1 by Factor 2, putting the quotient in the result. With RPG III, programmers could omit the Factor 1 entry if it repeated the result. The following code illustrates various forms and uses of ADD, SUB, MULT, and DIV.

```
*.. 1 ...+... 2 ...+... 3 ...+... 4 ...+... 5 ...+... 6 ...+... 7 ...+... 8
CLØNØ1Factor1+++++++Opcode(E)+Factor2+++++++Result++++++++Len++D+HiLoEq....
 * Sample calculations using the ADD operation to add two numeric values.
 * The result fields are defined within the specifications.
C        REGPAY        ADD       OVRPAY       TOTPAY        9 2
C        25            ADD       QTY          NEWQTY        7 0
C        RATE1         ADD(H)    .045         RATE2         4 2
 * Calculations showing two equivalent ways to increment a counter
C        COUNT         ADD       1            COUNT         3 0
C                      ADD       1            COUNT         3 0
 * Calculations showing two equivalent ways to accumulate net pay
C        NETPAY        ADD       TOTNET       TOTNET        9 2
C                      ADD       NETPAY       TOTNET        9 2
 * Examples of the use of the SUB operation
C        GROSS         SUB       WTHHLD       NETPAY        7 2
C        65            SUB       AGE          WRKYRS        2 0
C                      SUB       1            COUNT         5 0
C                      SUB       AMT          RMDR          5 2
 * Examples of the MULT operation
C        SALES         MULT(H)   TAXRAT       SLSTAX        5 2
C        60            MULT      HOURS        MINUTE        5 0
C        GROSS         MULT(H)   .0751        FICA          6 2
C                      MULT(H)   VALUE        EXPVAL       15 9
 * Examples of the DIV operation
C        TOTMINUTES    DIV(H)    60           HOURS         5 0
C                      DIV(H)    2            STOCKS        9 5
```

The advantage of RPG IV's EVAL over the individual arithmetic operators is obvious, especially when you need to execute a complex calculation. A calculation that might take dozens of specification lines using the fixed-form arithmetic operation codes can be accomplished with a single EVAL. The following example illustrates this contrast.

```
*.. 1 ...+... 2 ...+... 3 ...+... 4 ...+... 5 ...+... 6 ...+... 7 ...+... 8
CLØNØ1Factor1+++++++Opcode(E)+Extended-factor2+++++++++++++++++++++++++++++
CLØNØ1Factor1+++++++Opcode(E)+Factor2+++++++Result++++++++Len++D+HiLoEq....
 * The formula for converting a Fahrenheit temperature to Centigrade is
 *     C = 5(F - 32)/9. The following EVAL accomplishes this conversion.
C                      EVAL(H)   C = 5 * ( F - 32 ) / 9

 * Here's the same conversion using fixed-form arithmetic operations.
C        F             SUB       32           WRKFLD        4 0
C        WRKFLD        MULT      5            WRKFLD
C        WRKFLD        DIV(H)    9            C             4 0
```

Two additional operations — Z-ADD (Zero and Add) and Z-SUB (Zero and Subtract) — were commonly used to assign values to numeric variables before the introduction of EVAL. You can interpret Z-ADD, which requires a Factor 2 value and a Result field, as "Zero out the Result field and add Factor 2 to it." The effect of this operation was to assign the value of Factor 2 to the Result field. The most common use of this operation was to initialize or reinitialize a counter or accumulator to zero, but you could use Z-ADD to assign the value of any numeric literal or numeric field to the Result field.

Like Z-ADD, Z-SUB requires a Factor 2 entry and a Result field entry. The Z-SUB operator works similarly to Z-ADD, except that after zeroing out the Result field, it subtracts the value of Factor 2 from the Result field. Because this operation assigns the negative value of Factor 2 to the Result field, its effect is to reverse the sign of a field. The following examples illustrate the use of Z-ADD and Z-SUB.

```
*.. 1 ...+... 2 ...+... 3 ...+... 4 ...+... 5 ...+... 6 ...+... 7 ...+... 8
CLØNØ1Factor1+++++++Opcode(E)+Factor2++++++Result++++++++Len++D+HiLoEq....
 * Examples showing uses of Z-ADD and Z-SUB
 * Set COUNT to zero.
C                   Z-ADD     Ø              COUNT           3 Ø
 * Assign COUNT the same value as NBR.
C                   Z-ADD     NBR            COUNT
 * Set MAXMUM to 2Ø.
C                   Z-ADD     2Ø             MAXMUM          2 Ø
 * After the below calculation, MINMUM has a value of -2Ø.
C                   Z-SUB     2Ø             MINMUM          2 Ø
 * After the below calculation, X has a value of +15.
C                   Z-SUB     -15            X               3 Ø
 * In general, Z-SUB reverses signs.
C                   Z-SUB     POSVAL         NEGVAL          5 2
C                   Z-SUB     NEGVAL         POSVAL          5 2
```

Looping and Selecting

Another set of obsolete operators you may encounter in maintenance programming are DOW*xx*, DOU*xx*, IF*xx*, and WHEN*xx*. These fixed-form structured operators function identically to their modern counterparts DOW, DOU, IF, and WHEN. The major difference is that the older operations do not use free-form conditional expressions. Instead, each operation requires an entry in Factor 1, an entry in Factor 2, and a relational code (replacing the *xx* in the operation) to specify the way in which the two factor entries are to be compared. The following table lists these relational codes and their meanings.

Symbol	Code	Meaning
>	GT	Greater than
<	LT	Less than
=	EQ	Equal to
<>	NE	Not equal to
<=	LE	Less than or equal to
>=	GE	Greater than or equal to

Like their RPG IV counterparts, these RPG III structured operations require scope terminators to indicate their endpoints. Although the operation-specific terminators (e.g., ENDIF, ENDSL) were available in later versions of RPG III, initially only a generic END was used with these operations.

Because these older structured operations do not allow free-form expressions, to express a compound condition to check two (or more) relationships, you couple the comparisons with AND*xx* and/or OR*xx* operations to build complex conditional tests.

Carefully examine the following examples, which include converted RPG III code segments and their RPG IV equivalents, to understand how these RPG III structured operations work.

```
*.. 1 ...+... 2 ...+... 3 ...+... 4 ...+... 5 ...+... 6 ...+... 7 ...+... 8
CLØN01Factor1+++++++Opcode(E)+Factor2+++++++Result++++++++Len++D+HiLoEq....
CLØN01Factor1+++++++Opcode(E)+Extended-factor2+++++++++++++++++++++++++++++
 * Decision logic using IFxx
C         MILES        IFLE        50000
C         MONTHS       ANDLT       36
C                      EXSR        WRRNTY
C                      ELSE
C                      EXSR        YOUPAY
C                      END

 * Equivalent decision logic using IF
C                      IF          Mileage <= 50000 AND Months < 36
C                      EXSR        WarrantySR
C                      ELSE
C                      EXSR        YouPaySR
C                      ENDIF


 * Decision logic using SELECT and WHENxx
C                      SELECT
C         ADJGRS       WHENLE      8000
C                      Z-ADD       .00         RATE              2 2
C         ADJGRS       WHENLE      18000
C                      Z-ADD       .10         RATE
C         ADJGRS       WHENLE      35000
C                      Z-ADD       .21         RATE
C                      OTHER
C                      Z-ADD       .28         RATE
C                      END

 * Equivalent logic using SELECT and WHEN
C                      SELECT
C                      WHEN        AdjstGross <=8000
C                      EVAL        Rate = .00
C                      WHEN        AdjstGross <= 18000
C                      EVAL        Rate = .10
C                      WHEN        AdjstGross <= 35000
C                      EVAL        Rate = .21
C                      OTHER
C                      EVAL        Rate = .28
C                      ENDSL


 * Iteration implemented with DOWxx. Any processing specified within the
 * loop would be repeated as long as indicators 90 and 99 both remain off.
C         *IN90        DOWEQ       *OFF
C         *IN99        ANDEQ       *OFF
C                      . . .
C                      END

 * The same iteration logic implemented with DOW
C                      DOW         *IN90 = *OFF AND *IN99 = *OFF
C                      . . .
C                      ENDDO
```

continued…

continued…

```
*.. 1 ...+... 2 ...+... 3 ...+... 4 ...+... 5 ...+... 6 ...+... 7 ...+... 8
 * Iteration implemented with DOUxx. Any processing specified within the
 * loop would be repeated until either indicator 90 or 99 was turned on.
C     *IN90         DOUEQ      *ON
C     *IN99         OREQ       *ON
C                   . . .
C                   END

 * The same iteration logic implemented with DOU
C                   DOU        *IN90 = *ON OR *IN99 = *ON
C                   . . .
C                   ENDDO
```

In addition to the above structured operations, when maintaining older programs you may encounter two unstructured operations: CAB*xx* and GOTO. These operations are unstructured because neither has built-in constraints to limit how it directs flow of control.

The GOTO operation diverts control to a different location within a program. Factor 2 of the GOTO contains a label that identifies the location to which control should be transferred. The same label must appear as the Factor 1 entry of a TAG operation somewhere within the program. TAG, a non-executable operation, simply marks a program line as a label statement that identifies a location in the program. The same rules for forming RPG field names apply to RPG labels.

You can use GOTO to branch around a sequence of instructions if the TAG is below the GOTO or to set up a loop if the TAG is above the GOTO.

```
*.. 1 ...+... 2 ...+... 3 ...+... 4 ...+... 5 ...+... 6 ...+... 7 ...+... 8
CL0N01Factor1+++++++Opcode(E)+Factor2+++++++Result++++++++Len++D+HiLoEq....
 * This GOTO branches around instructions by sending control to SKIP.
C                   GOTO       SKIP
 . . .
C     SKIP          TAG
 . . .

C     LOOP          TAG
 . . .
 * This GOTO creates a loop by sending control back up to LOOP.
C                   GOTO       LOOP
```

The instructions above show the GOTO used to set up unconditional transfer of control. You will seldom, if ever, find unconditional transfer of control within a program — if you always want to bypass a set of instructions, why include them in the first place? And unconditional transfer to set up a loop results in an infinite loop that would cause a program to run forever. Accordingly, GOTOs are most often used with IF logic or conditioned by indicators (discussed later in this appendix) to transfer control based on some conditional test.

The CAB*xx* (Compare and Branch) operation is simply a GOTO in disguise. CAB*xx* combines a conditional test and the transfer of control in a single operation. CAB*xx* compares the value of Factor 1 with the value of Factor 2 based on the relational code included in the CAB*xx* operation; if the comparison is true, control is transferred to the TAG label designated in the Result field.

```
*.. 1 ...+... 2 ...+... 3 ...+... 4 ...+... 5 ...+... 6 ...+... 7 ...+... 8
CLØNØ1Factor1+++++++Opcode(E)+Factor2+++++++Result+++++++Len++D+HiLoEq....
 * This CABxx branches around instructions by sending control to SKIP
 * if A is greater than B.
C     A               CABGT     B              SKIP
 . . .
C     SKIP            TAG
 . . .

C     LOOP            TAG
 . . .
 * This CABxx creates a loop by sending control back up to LOOP
 * if indicator 4Ø is on.
C     *IN4Ø           CABEQ     *ON            LOOP
```

With both CAB*xx* and GOTO, transfer of control is unidirectional; flow simply continues on from the tag. Use of GOTO and CAB*xx* often makes programs harder to follow because these operators do not keep as tight a rein on flow of control as the structured operators do with their single-entry, single-exit points.

Manipulating Strings

In Chapter 12, you were introduced to RPG IV's techniques of string manipulation. You may still encounter two RPG III operations that no longer need to be used for handling strings: SUBST (Substring), which has been superseded by the built-in function %SUBST, and CAT (Concatenate), made obsolete by the concatenation (+) operator used within an EVAL operation.

SUBST (Substring)

The SUBST operation copies a portion of a character string into a different field. Factor 2, required for this operation, contains the base character string to be copied. The Result field serves as the receiving field for the SUBST operation. And Factor 1, also required, indicates the length of the string to be copied. The copying begins with the leftmost character of the base string unless the data item representing the base string is followed by a colon (:) and a start location.

An optional indicator in positions 73–74 (Lo) is turned on if the length specified in Factor 1 causes the substring to extend beyond the end of Factor 2. If the specified starting location is greater than the actual length of the base character string, the SUBST operation does not take place. If the substring is shorter than the Result field, the unused positions of the Result field will retain their previous contents unless you use operation extender (P) — pad — to blank-fill the unused portion of the Result field.

The following examples demonstrate the use of SUBST.

```
*.. 1 ...+... 2 ...+... 3 ...+... 4 ...+... 5 ...+... 6 ...+... 7 ...+... 8
CLØNØ1Factor1+++++++Opcode(E)+Factor2+++++++Result+++++++Len++D+HiLoEq....
 * All the examples below are based on FIELDA with value 'abcdefgh'
 * and field RESULT with value '12345' before the SUBST operation.

C     3               SUBST     FIELDA         RESULT                      9Ø
 * RESULT now contains 'abc45' because just the first 3 characters of
 * FIELDA are copied. Indicator 9Ø is off.

C     3               SUBST(P)  FIELDA         RESULT                      9Ø
 * RESULT is 'abc  ' because the operation specifies padding.
```

continued...

continued...

```
*.. 1 ...+... 2 ...+... 3 ...+... 4 ...+... 5 ...+... 6 ...+... 7 ...+... 8
C     4               SUBST(P)  FIELDA:3    RESULT               90
 * RESULT is 'cdef ' because 4 characters are copied, starting with the
 * third character of FIELDA. Indicator 90 is off.

C     3               SUBST     FIELDA:9    RESULT               90
 * The operation is not executed, because the starting position exceeds
 * the length of FIELDA.

C     6               SUBST     FIELDA:5    RESULT               90
 * Indicator 90 is turned on because the specified substring length, in
 * conjunction with the starting position, exceeds the length of FIELDA.
```

CAT (Concatenate)

RPG programmers used the CAT operation to combine the values of two strings to form a third string. The two character items to be combined are specified in Factor 1 and Factor 2; the Result field entry specifies where the results of the concatenation are to be placed.

You can optionally specify the number of blanks you want to appear between the nonblank characters of the concatenated fields by appending a colon to the Factor 2 item, followed by a data item that specifies the desired number of blanks. If you do not specify the number of desired blanks, all the trailing blanks (if they exist) within Factor 1 are included in the concatenation.

If the concatenation is too large to fit in the Result field, truncation occurs from the right of the string. No indicators are used with the CAT operation. As was the case with SUBST, CAT leaves residual characters in the unused leftmost positions of the Result field unless you indicate, through the use of operation extender (P), that you want to pad those unused positions with blanks.

To get a sense of how CAT works, examine the following examples.

```
*.. 1 ...+... 2 ...+... 3 ...+... 4 ...+... 5 ...+... 6 ...+... 7 ...+... 8
CL0N01Factor1+++++++Opcode(E)+Factor2++++++Result+++++++Len++D+HiLoEq....
CL0N01Factor1+++++++Opcode(E)+Extended-factor2+++++++++++++++++++++++++++
 * The examples below are all based on FNAME (10 positions) with a value of
 * 'John      ', LNAME (12 positions) with a value of 'Jackson     ', and
 *  WHLNAM (25 positions) with a value of 'abcdefghijklmnopqrstuvwxy'.

C     FNAME           CAT       LNAME       WHLNAM          25
 * WHLNAM contains 'John      Jackson      rstuvwxy' because nothing
 * about blanks or padding was specified.

C     FNAME           CAT       LNAME:1     WHLNAM
 * WHLNAM contains 'John Jackson       rstuvwxy' because 1 blank was
 * requested.

C     FNAME           CAT(P)    LNAME:1     WHLNAM
 * WHLNAM contains 'John Jackson             ' because 1 blank and
 * padding were requested.

C     FNAME           CAT(P)    LNAME:0     WHLNAM
 * WHLNAM contains 'JohnJackson              ' because 0 blanks
 * were requested.

 * SMLNAM, in the example below, is 10 bytes long.
C     FNAME           CAT(P)    LNAME:1     SMLNAM
 * SMLNAM contains 'John Jacks' because the field can store only 10
 * characters.
```

Delimiting Arrays and Tables

There is one additional RPG III feature that you may encounter when working with older programs that include compile-time arrays or tables: The required delimiter line between the end of the source code and the array or table data contains ****b̸** rather than ****CTDATA** and the array/table name. Because this older delimiter gives no indication of which array or table follows it, programs with multiple compile-time arrays or tables must define the arrays or tables in the same order as the data appears at the program's end.

Moving Data

Before we turn back the clock even further to consider RPG II, completing our discussion of RPG III requires us to take a second look at the MOVE, MOVEL, and MOVEA operations. Although these three operations have already appeared in this text in our discussion of RPG IV, in maintaining RPG III programs you will find that these operations were used much more extensively to accomplish a wider variety of processing needs than the earlier discussions in this text would lead you to believe.

   For example, before operation EVAL, programmers used MOVE and MOVEL for all character-assignment operations; they also used these two operations to split fields into smaller units or to rearrange subfields within fields. The following example typifies this use of MOVE and MOVEL. The RPG code below switches a "legacy" date (i.e., a date stored as a number or as a character string rather than as a date data-type value) stored in *yymmdd* format to *mmddyy* format.

```
*.. 1 ...+... 2 ...+... 3 ...+... 4 ...+... 5 ...+... 6 ...+... 7 ...+... 8
CLØN01Factor1+++++++Opcode(E)+Factor2+++++++Result++++++++Len++D+HiLoEq....
 * Assume YRMNDY is a date, 950329, in yymmdd format. Extract month
 * and day.
C                   MOVE      YRMNDY        MNDY              4
 * The above MOVE stores '0329' in field MNDY. Extract the year.
C                   MOVEL     YRMNDY        YR                2
 * The above MOVEL stores '95' in field YR. Store month and day.
C                   MOVEL(P)  MNDY          MNDYYR            6
 * The above MOVEL puts '0329  ' in field MNDYYR. Now move year.
C                   MOVE      YR            MNDYYR
 * MNDYYR now contains '032995'.
```

   Before the introduction of string operations and built-in functions in RPG IV, programmers used arrays and the MOVEA operation to inspect and manipulate characters within string fields. This approach involved using MOVEA to move field values into an array of one-character-long elements. By looping through the elements of the array, you could check each of the characters in the array while the array index served as a positional locator of the character. In this way, you could count, change, or rearrange characters within a string.

   To illustrate this concept, assume that a customer file contains records with the first-name field FNAME, 12 positions long, and the last-name field LNAME, 15 positions long. You want to use the file to generate letters to customers, but you want the letter salutation to read

```
Dear Judy Yaeger:
```

not

```
Dear Judy        Yaeger        :
```

The following code uses MOVEA and arrays to trim trailing blanks from the names and concatenate the desired string. ARY is a runtime array of 35 character elements, each one byte long. Read the comment lines carefully to understand how the program uses the array to build the salutation.

```
*.. 1 ...+... 2 ...+... 3 ...+... 4 ...+... 5 ...+... 6 ...+... 7 ...+... 8
CLØNØ1Factor1+++++++Opcode(E)+Factor2+++++++Result+++++++Len++D+HiLoEq....
 * Move "Dear" into the leftmost positions of ARY.
C                   MOVEA(P)  'Dear'          ARY
 * ARY now contains 'Dear                              '.
C
 * Now move FNAME into ARY, leaving a blank before the name.
C                   MOVEA     FNAME           ARY(6)
 * ARY now contains 'Dear Judy                         '.

 * Now loop to inspect the characters of ARY, moving backwards from the
 * last possible position for the last character of FNAME, until a
 * nonblank character is found.
C                   Z-ADD     17              I                 2 Ø
C     ARY(I)        DOWEQ     ' '
C                   SUB       1               I
C                   END
 * Given the example, I now has a value of 9.

 * Add 2 to I so it points to where LNAME should begin.
C                   Add       2               I
 * Move LNAME to array, beginning at that position.
C                   MOVEA     LNAME           ARY(I)
 * ARY now contains 'Dear Judy Yaeger                  '.

 * Now loop to move backwards from the end of the array, looking for
 * the last nonblank character.
C                   Z-ADD     35              I
C     ARY(I)        DOWEQ     ' '
C                   SUB       1               I
C                   END
 * Given the example, I now has a value of 16.

 * Add 1 to I for the colon position.
C                   ADD       1               I
C                   MOVEA     ':'             ARY(I)
 * ARY now contains 'Dear Judy Yaeger:                 '.
```

RPG II: An Initial Look

Because some RPG shops may be in a transitional stage between RPG III and RPG IV, you might find that some programmers still use the features discussed so far in this appendix. You will also frequently encounter these features in any maintenance programming you do. However, you may wonder, "Why bother with RPG II, a language version that IBM officially retired more than 15 years ago?" The primary reason why you should be familiar with RPG II is that you often will be asked to maintain programs that have been based in part, or perhaps entirely, on features from this version of the language. Some of the programs may be old, written before RPG III existed; others may be more recent but written by programmers who had not entirely embraced more modern styles of programming. If you don't understand how these RPG II features work, you will have little chance of success modifying programs that rely on them.

Note

Recognize that the inclusion of RPG II in this book is not an endorsement of these methods. However, you can implement all the features discussed in this section in RPG IV because of the backward-compatibility of the language. Also note that all RPG II examples that follow are showing code as it would look after CVTRPGSRC conversion because that would always be the first step in the maintenance of older programs.

To demonstrate the differences between RPG IV and RPG II, let's revisit the first program we wrote in Chapter 2 to see how it would be implemented in RPG II. The program is reproduced below as it appeared in the earlier chapter, except that an overflow indicator and check for page-advance has been added.

```
*.. 1 ...+... 2 ...+... 3 ...+... 4 ...+... 5 ...+... 6 ...+... 7 ...+... 8
****************************************************************
* This program produces a weekly sales report. The report data comes  *
* directly from input file SalesMast.                                 *
*     Author:  J. Yaeger   Date Written:  12/10/94.                    *
****************************************************************
FSalesMast IF   F   63        DISK
FQPRINT    O    F  132        PRINTER OFLIND(*INOF)

ISalesMast NS
I                              1    4 ØSlspNumber
I                              5   34  SlspName
I                             35   50  ItemNumber
I                             51   56 ØDateOfSale
I                             57   63 2Price

C                   EXCEPT    Headings
C                   READ      SalesMast

C                   DOW       NOT %EOF
C                   IF        *INOF = *ON
C                   EXCEPT    Headings
C                   EVAL      *INOF = *OFF
C                   ENDIF
C                   EXCEPT    Detail
C                   READ      SalesMast
C                   ENDDO

C                   EVAL      *INLR = *ON
C                   RETURN

OQprint    E              Headings      2  2
O                                            8 'PAGE'
O                         Page            13
O                                         50 'WEEKLY SALES REPORT'
O                                         64 'DATE'
O                         *DATE     Y     75
O          E              Headings      1
O                                          7 'SLSPSN.'
O                                         48 'DATE OF'
O                                         77 'SALE'
O          E              Headings      2
O                                          3 'NO.'
O                                         21 'NAME'
O                                         46 'SALE'
O                                         61 'ITEM SOLD'
O                                         77 'PRICE'
O          E              Detail        1
O                         SlspNumber       4
O                         SlspName        37
O                         DateOfSale Y    48
O                         ItemNumber      67
O                         Price      1    79
```

The program represents a simple read/write program. The calculations focus on setting up a loop to read records and write report lines. To express this logic in RPG II requires a few changes to our program.

First, RPG II programs rely on RPG's **fixed-logic cycle**. All versions of RPG (including RPG IV) have had a built-in read-process-write cycle that you could use to automate part of the processing requirements, but use of this cycle fell out of favor with the adoption of RPG III. This read-process-write cycle is repeated until all the desired records have been processed. To plug into the automated reading portion of the fixed-logic cycle, you need to designate the main input file as P (for Primary) rather than F (Full procedural). RPG automatically handles the reading of records from a primary file, so you do not (in fact, you cannot) explicitly issue an input instruction to that file. The File Specifications for our revised program appear below.

```
*.. 1 ...+... 2 ...+... 3 ...+... 4 ...+... 5 ...+... 6 ...+... 7 ...+... 8
FFilename++IPEASFRLen+LKLen+AIDevice+.Keywords+++++++++++++++++++++++++++++++
FSalesMast IP   F   63        DISK
FQPRINT     O   F  132        PRINTER OFLIND(*INOF)
```

We also need to make a minor addition to the Input Specifications of our program: adding a **record-identifying indicator** in positions 21–22 of the record identification line of the input file description. The indicator that we designate as the record-identifying indicator will be turned on each time RPG successfully reads a record from the file; the indicator is automatically turned off just before the next automatic attempt to read another record. If the system retrieves another record, the indicator is turned back on. On the other hand, if the system detects end-of-file, the record-identifying indicator remains off and indicator LR automatically is turned on instead.

You can use any one of RPG's numbered indicators (01–99) to serve as a record-identifying indicator. In our sample program, indicator 01 will serve this purpose. Note that you enter all indicators as two-digit numbers, even if the first digit is a zero:

```
*.. 1 ...+... 2 ...+... 3 ...+... 4 ...+... 5 ...+... 6 ...+... 7 ...+... 8
IFilename++SqNORiPos1+NCCPos2+NCCPos3+NCC................................
I..................Fmt+SPFrom+To+++DcField++++++++L1M1FrPlMnZr......
ISalesMast NS  01
I                            1    4 0SlspNumber
I                            5   34  SlspName
I                           35   50  ItemNumber
I                           51   56 0DateOfSale
I                           57   63 2Price
```

To automate the output portion of the cycle, so that writing is done automatically without explicit output operations, we need to change the record format type on the Output Specifications from E to the type appropriate for a given line:

- H for heading lines
- D for detail
- T for total

Also, we must remove the line names because names are permitted only for exception lines.

In addition to changing the line types and removing the line names, we now also will need to use indicators to condition whether a given line should be printed during the output portion of the fixed-logic cycle. Associating an indicator with an output line means that the indicator must be on for the line to be printed during the output phase of the current pass of the fixed-logic cycle. You enter indicators in positions 21–29 of the Output Specifications. Multiple indicators on a line are in an AND relationship, such that they all must be on for the line to be printed. To express an OR relationship between indicators, you code one indicator on a line, drop down a line and enter OR in positions 16–17, and enter the second indicator on this second line.

In the sample program, we want headings to be printed each time the overflow indicator OF is turned on. There is also a special indicator, 1P (First page), which is on for a very brief time at the beginning of the program. This indicator normally is used to produce headings on the first page, because the overflow indicator is not turned on until the first page is full. You condition heading lines, then, with 1P or OF. With the fixed-logic cycle, OF is turned off automatically after use; you do not need to explicitly turn it off within your calculations.

Because you want a detail line to be printed each time an input record is processed, we'll use indicator 01, the record-identifying indicator, to condition the detail line. The following code shows the modified Output Specifications.

```
*.. 1 ...+... 2 ...+... 3 ...+... 4 ...+... 5 ...+... 6 ...+... 7 ...+... 8
OFilename++DF..NØ1NØ2NØ3Excnam++++B++A++Sb+Sa+.............................
O..............NØ1NØ2NØ3Field+++++++++YB.End++PConstant/editword/DTformat++
OQPPRINT   H    1P                      2  2
O          OR   OF
O                                                8 'PAGE'
O                          PAGE                 13
O                                               50 'WEEKLY SALES REPORT'
O                                               64 'DATE'
O                          UDATE       Y        73
O          H    1P                      1
O          OR   OF
O                                                7 'SLSPSN.'
O                                               48 'DATE OF'
O                                               77 'SALE'
O          H    1P                      2
O          OR   OF
O                                                3 'NO.'
O                                               21 'NAME'
O                                               46 'SALE'
O                                               61 'ITEM SOLD'
O                                               77 'PRICE'
O          D    Ø1                      1
O                          SlspNumber           4
O                          SlspName            37
O                          DateOfSale  Y       48
O                          ItemNumber          67
O                          Price       1       79
```

What changes are required in the Calculation Specifications? Because this is a simple read/write program, there would be no calculations! In the RPG IV version of the program, the calculations consisted of setting up a processing loop, reading, and writing. All those steps are built into the fixed-logic cycle, so that none of them need to be explicit in the RPG II program. And when you use the fixed-logic cycle with a primary input file, indicator LR is turned on automatically at end-of-file; this signal serves to end the program automatically.

If our program had required arithmetic operations, decision processing, or repetitive processing for a given input record, these operations would appear in Calculation Specifications. In general, for a simple detailed report, the only Calculation Specifications needed are those that describe the processing required for each input record. Remember that the record retrieval, writing, and main process looping occurs automatically with the fixed-logic cycle.

The entire RPG II version of the sample program is shown below. (Notice that field names have been shortened and capitalized to conform to RPG's earlier standards.)

```
*.. 1 ...+... 2 ...+... 3 ...+... 4 ...+... 5 ...+... 6 ...+... 7 ...+... 8
F************************************************************************
F* This program produces a weekly sales report using RPG's fixed-logic  *
F* cycle.                                                                *
F*     Author:  J. Yaeger    Date Written:  12/10/94.                    *
F************************************************************************
FSALESMST  IP  F   63          DISK
FQPRINT    O   F  132          PRINTER OFLIND(*INOF)
I********************Input Specifications*******************************
ISALESMST  NS  01
I                                       1    4 0SLPNBR
I                                       5   34  SLPNAM
I                                      35   50  ITMNBR
I                                      51   56 0SLSDAT
I                                      57   63 2PRICE
O********************Output Specifications*****************************
OQPRINT    H    1P                     2  2
O          OR   OF
O                                              8 'PAGE'
O                           PAGE              13
O                                             50 'WEEKLY SALES REPORT'
O                                             64 'DATE'
O                           UDATE       Y     73
O          H    1P                     1
O          OR   OF
O                                              7 'SLSPSN.'
O                                             48 'DATE OF'
O                                             77 'SALE'
O          H    1P                     2
O          OR   OF
O                                              3 'NO.'
O                                             21 'NAME'
O                                             46 'SALE'
O                                             61 'ITEM SOLD'
O                                             77 'PRICE'
O          D    01                     1
O                           SLPNBR            4
O                           SLPNAM           37
O                           SLSDAT      Y    48
O                           ITMNBR           67
O                           PRICE       1    79
```

RPG's Fixed-Logic Cycle

As we mentioned above, RPG's fixed-logic cycle provides a built-in logical process of read-process-write that automatically overlays the descriptions you enter through your program specifications. The following pseudocode describes the steps of the logic cycle.

Pseudocode of RPG's fixed-logic cycle
Turn on 1P indicator
WHILE LR is off
   Print detail output (H and D lines)
   Turn off 1P, record-identifying, and level indicators
   Read record from primary file
   IF end-of-file
      Turn on LR and all level indicators

```
        ELSE
            Turn on record-identifying indicator
            IF change in control field
                Turn on level indicator(s)
            ENDIF
        ENDIF
        Perform total calculations
        Perform total output (T lines)
        IF LR is not on
            IF overflow indicator is on
                Print lines conditioned by overflow
            ENDIF
                Move data into input fields
            Perform detail calculations
        ENDIF
ENDWHILE
```

If you examine the above cycle carefully, you see that characterizing the fixed-logic cycle as read-calculate-write is a simplification. For one thing, at various points in the cycle different indicators automatically are turned on or turned off. For another, the calculations and writing each are actually broken down into two segments: total time and detail time, with total-time calculations and output preceding detail calculations and output. A more accurate characterization, then, would be read-calculate-write-calculate-write.

Total-time calculations are characterized by special indicators, called **level indicators**, coded in positions 7–8 of the Calculation Specifications. Calculations without an indicator in positions 7–8 are treated as detail calculations. On the Calculation Specifications, all detail calculations should be coded first, followed by total-time calculations, with subroutines appearing last within the calculations.

On the output, total-time output is represented by those lines designated as T lines, while H and D lines are considered detail output.

The Fixed-Logic Cycle and Control Breaks

The primary reason for breaking the fixed-logic cycle into two segments — total-time and detail-time — is to facilitate the automatic preparation of control-break reports. You'll recall from Chapter 5 that control-break reports require detecting a change in a control-field value and, when such a change is detected, executing special break processing: printing a subtotal line, rolling over accumulators, zeroing out accumulators, and resetting the hold field.

The following example reprints the control-break program developed procedurally in Chapter 5.

```
*.. 1 ...+... 2 ...+... 3 ...+... 4 ...+... 5 ...+... 6 ...+... 7 ...+... 8
*****************************************************************
* This program produces a Sales Report that lists subtotals  *
* for each salesperson.                                       *
*  Author:  Yaeger      Date Written:  Dec. 1992             *
*  Modified Dec 1999 to current RPG IV release. Meyers.      *
*****************************************************************

FSalesFile IF   F   19        DISK
FQPRINT    O    F   132       PRINTER OFLIND(*INOF)
```

continued...

continued...

```
*.. 1 ...+... 2 ...+... 3 ...+... 4 ...+... 5 ...+... 6 ...+... 7 ...+... 8
D HoldSlsp        S              4
D SlspTotal       S              6 2
D GrandTotal      S              8 2

ISalesFile NS
I                                     1    4  SalesPrsn
I                                     5    7  Dept
I                                     8   13 2SalesAmt
I                                    14   19 0SaleDate

     **********************************************************
     *  Calculations required to produce the Sales Report.
     *  Mainline logic
     **********************************************************
C                    EXSR      Initial

C                    DOW       NOT %EOF(SalesFile)
C                    IF        HoldSlsp <> SalesPrsn
C                    EXSR      SlspBreak
C                    ENDIF
C                    EXSR      DetailProc
C                    READ      SalesFile
C                    ENDDO

C                    EXSR      Terminate
C                    EVAL      *INLR = *ON
C                    RETURN

     **********************************************************
     * Subroutine to read first record, set up hold, and print
     * first page headings
     **********************************************************
C    Initial         BEGSR
C                    READ      SalesFile
C                    EVAL      HoldSlsp = SalesPrsn
C                    EXCEPT    Headings
C                    ENDSR

     **********************************************************
     * Subroutine done when salesperson changes; print subtotal,
     * rollover accumulator, zero out accumulator, and reset hold.
     **********************************************************
C    SlspBreak       BEGSR
C                    EXCEPT    BreakLine
C                    EVAL      GrandTotal = GrandTotal + SlspTotal
C                    EVAL      SlspTotal  = 0
C                    EVAL      HoldSlsp   = SalesPrsn
C                    ENDSR

     **********************************************************
     * Subroutine executed for each input record
     **********************************************************
C    DetailProc      BEGSR
C                    IF        *INOF = *ON
     * If end-of-page then print headings.
C                    EXCEPT    Headings
C                    EVAL      *INOF = *OFF
C                    ENDIF
C                    EXCEPT    DetailLine
C                    EVAL      SlspTotal = SlspTotal + SalesAmt
C                    ENDSR
```

continued...

continued...

```
*.. 1 ...+... 2 ...+... 3 ...+... 4 ...+... 5 ...+... 6 ...+... 7 ...+... 8
 ********************************************************
 * Subroutine done at end-of-file; execute SlspBreak one last
 * time and print grand total line.
 ********************************************************
C          Terminate     BEGSR
C                        EXSR      SlspBreak
C                        EXCEPT    TotalLine
C                        ENDSR


 ********************************************************
OQPrint      E            Headings      2  1
O                         UDATE         Y        17
O                                                33 'SALES REPORT'
O                                                40 'PAGE'
O                         PAGE                   44
O            E            Headings      2
O                                                20 'SLSPSN.'
O                                                37 'AMT.'
O            E            DetailLine    1
O                         SalesPrsn              18
O                         SalesAmt      1        39
O            E            BreakLine   1 2
O                                                24 'TOTAL'
O                         SlspTotal     1        39
O                                                40 '*'
O            E            TotalLine
O                                                26 'GRAND TOTAL'
O                         GrandTotal    1        39
O                                                41 '**'
```

Let's rework this program using the fixed-logic cycle. First, you need to know that RPG has special level indicators, L1–L9, that can be associated with control fields and that are turned on automatically when a change in the value of these fields is detected. Level indicators eliminate the need for explicit hold fields because RPG automatically detects changes in control-field values and turns on the appropriate level indicator (or indicators) when it detects a change.

You can use these level indicators to condition any calculations that would need to be done as part of break processing and also to condition printing of the appropriate subtotal line when a change in the control field occurs.

Again, you will recall that when you procedurally code a control-break problem, when a break occurs you need to complete the processing for the prior group before continuing with the detail processing of the record that triggered the break. It is for this reason that the fixed-logic cycle performs total calculations and output before detail calculations and output. It is also why, once end-of-file is detected, the cycle runs through total-time before ending. These final steps allow the wrap-up for the very last group in the report and the printing of grand totals, if the report requires them.

Because all total calculations are performed before total output, you cannot zero out a level's accumulator as part of total-time calculations; otherwise, the subtotals would always be printed as 0. RPG provides an alternate method of zeroing out these fields in the Output Specifications: You can code a B (for Blank after printing) in position 45 to have the field automatically set to zeros (if its type is numeric) or blanks (if its type is character) immediately after its value is printed.

The following code represents the sales report program written using the fixed-logic cycle and indicators. Fields SlspTotal and GrandTotal are defined on the Calculation Specifications rather than on Definition Specifications because the latter did not exist until RPG IV. Notice that the sales amount is rolled over into the grand-total accumulator as a total-time calculation conditioned by indicator L1. As a result, the program executes that calculation each time SalesPrsn changes. Also note that LR conditions the grand-total line, so that it is printed only once, just before the program ends.

```
*.. 1 ...+... 2 ...+... 3 ...+... 4 ...+... 5 ...+... 6 ...+... 7 ...+... 8
F*******************************************************************
F* This program produces a Sales Report that lists subtotals  *
F* for each salesperson.                                       *
F* Author: Yaeger      Date Written:  Mar. 1995                *
F*******************************************************************
FSalesFile IP   F   19        DISK
FQPRINT    O    F  132        PRINTER OFLIND(*INOF)
ISalesFile NS   01
I                            1    4  SalesPrsn       L1
I                            5    7  Dept
I                            8   13 2SalesAmt
I                           14   19 0SaleDate
C*******************************************************************
C*  Calculations required to produce the Sales Report
C*******************************************************************
C                 ADD    SalesAmt     SlspTotal        6 2
CL1               ADD    SlspTotal    GrandTotal       8 2
O*******************************************************************
OQPRINT   H    1P                      2  1
O         OR   OF
O                        UDATE       Y      17
O                                           33 'SALES REPORT'
O                                           40 'PAGE'
O                        PAGE               44
O         H    1P                      2
O         OR   OF
O                                           20 'SLSPSN.'
O                                           37 'AMT.'
O         D    01                      1
O                        SalesPrsn          18
O                        SalesAmt     1     39
O         T    L1                      1  2
O                                           24 'TOTAL'
O                        SlspTotal    1B    39
O                                           40 '*'
O         T    LR
O                                           26 'GRAND TOTAL'
O                        GrandTotal   1     39
O                                           41 '**'
```

If the sales file were sorted by department, and within department by salesperson, we could easily convert this program to a two-level control-break problem by associating indicator L2 with department and adding a department accumulator and a department total line (printed when L2 is on). Calculation modifications would be minimal. Instead of rolling SlspTotal into GrandTotal, we'd roll it into DeptTotal when L1 was on; when L2 came on, we'd roll DeptTotal into GrandTotal.

Note that a file does not have to be program described to use level indicators. If SalesFile were externally described, we could still use level indicators. All we would need to do is include just those input specifications necessary to make the association between the control field and L1.

Although RPG did not make use of externally described files until RPG III, as a maintenance programmer you may encounter any mix of techniques from different versions of the language.

The following examples show all the File and Input Specifications needed for our program if SalesFile were externally described. Notice that on the Input Specifications you use the record format name, not the file name, and positions 17–18 (Sq) are left blank. Also notice that From and To positions are omitted from the SalesPrsn field definition because that field is externally described.

```
*.. 1 ...+... 2 ...+... 3 ...+... 4 ...+... 5 ...+... 6 ...+... 7 ...+... 8
FFilename++IPEASFRLen+LKLen+AIDevice+.Keywords+++++++++++++++++++++++++++++++
IFilename++SqNORiPos1+NCCPos2+NCCPos3+NCC......................................
I......................Fmt+SPFrom+To+++DcField+++++++++L1M1FrPLMnZr......
 * Example showing SalesFile externally described
FSalesFile IP   E          K Disk
FQPRINT     O   E   132        Printer OFLIND(*INOF)

 * Example showing association of level indicator L1 with control
 * field SalesPrsn from externally described file SalesFile
ISalesRec       01
I                                   SalesPrsn      L1
```

At this point, you may be wondering why RPG II techniques, and especially the fixed-logic cycle, are no longer used much. After all, they appear to let you write code that is a lot shorter, and the code doesn't seem so difficult to understand. However, RPG II had many drawbacks. One of its major problems was its heavy reliance on indicators; as indicator use proliferates within a program, the code becomes increasingly difficult to understand. Indicators in RPG substituted for more sophisticated ways of controlling flow of execution within a program.

Decisions in RPG II

Originally, RPG had no operations to handle decision logic. Without the IF, IF*xx*, CAS*xx*, SELECT, and CAB*xx* operators, RPG II still needed some way to perform a relational test between two values and then execute alternate courses of action based on the outcome of that test. To provide that function, earlier versions of RPG relied on the COMP (Compare) operation and indicators.

Operation COMP compares the values of Factor 1 and Factor 2 and turns on an indicator in the Hi (positions 71–72), Lo (positions 73–74), or Eq (positions 75–76) column, depending on whether Factor 1 is greater than, less than, or equal to Factor 2, respectively. You can enter an indicator in just one or several of those locations and use one, two, or three different indicators, depending on the kind of comparison you are trying to make.

You would then use those indicators in calculations following the COMP to condition whether the operation was to be performed. The original 80-column RPG Calculation Specification let you code up to three **conditioning indicators** on a single line; RPG IV's 100-column Calculation Specification has room for only one indicator, in positions 9–11, but you can use multiple lines of code to condition a given calculation. Any calculation so conditioned is executed only if its associated indicators are on at that time.

Consider the following IF logic:

```
*.. 1 ...+... 2 ...+... 3 ...+... 4 ...+... 5 ...+... 6 ...+... 7 ...+... 8
CL0N01Factor1+++++++Opcode(E)+Extended-factor2++++++++++++++++++++++++++++++++
 * RPG IV example of decision logic
C                IF        Age >= 65
C                EVAL      SeniorCnt = SeniorCnt + 1
C                ENDIF
```

To express the same logic in RPG II syntax would require the following lines.

```
*.. 1 ...+... 2 ...+... 3 ...+... 4 ...+... 5 ...+... 6 ...+... 7 ...+... 8
CL0N01Factor1+++++++Opcode(E)+Factor2+++++++Result+++++++++Len++D+HiLoEq....
C* Example of decision logic using RPG II methods
C    AGE         COMP      65                              65 65
C   65SNRCNT     ADD       1             SNRCNT         3 0
```

Indicator 65 is turned on if AGE is greater than or equal to 65; indicator 65 conditions the addition operation. (Notice that, in keeping with RPG II limitations, field names are all capital letters and work fields are defined within the calculations that reference them.)

That doesn't look too bad, does it? But let's make the decision logic a little more complex. In the following example, the AN in positions 7–8 stands for "and" and means that the indicator in the preceding line, as well as the one in the current line, must be on for the calculation to be executed. Also note that if an N precedes an indicator, it means the indicator must be off for the calculation to be performed.

```
*.. 1 ...+... 2 ...+... 3 ...+... 4 ...+... 5 ...+... 6 ...+... 7 ...+... 8
CLØN01Factor1+++++++Opcode(E)+Factor2+++++++Result+++++++Len++D+HiLoEq....
C* Example showing compound decision logic using RPG II techniques
C        AGE          COMP      65                                      65  65
C        SEX          COMP      'F'                                         70
C   65
CAN 70                Z-ADD     84             LIFE              3 0
C   65
CANN70                Z-ADD     79             LIFE
C   N65
CAN 70                Z-ADD     81             LIFE
C   N65
CANN70                Z-ADD     70             LIFE
```

The following example shows the same decision logic expressed using RPG IV's IF operation to clarify the code.

```
*.. 1 ...+... 2 ...+... 3 ...+... 4 ...+... 5 ...+... 6 ...+... 7 ...+... 8
CLØN01Factor1+++++++Opcode(E)+Extended-factor2++++++++++++++++++++++++++++++
 * Example showing compound decision logic using RPG IV methods.
C               IF        Age >= 65 AND Sex = 'F'
C               EVAL         LifeExpect = 84
C               ELSE
C               IF        Age >= 65 AND Sex = 'M'
C               EVAL         LifeExpect = 79
C               ELSE
C               IF        Age < 65 AND Sex = 'F'
C               EVAL         LifeExpect = 81
C               ELSE
C               EVAL         LifeExpect = 78
C               ENDIF
C               ENDIF
C               ENDIF
```

While the above example is easier to understand than its RPG II counterpart, using the SELECT, WHEN, and OTHER operations makes the example even clearer:

```
*.. 1 ...+... 2 ...+... 3 ...+... 4 ...+... 5 ...+... 6 ...+... 7 ...+... 8
CLØN01Factor1+++++++Opcode(E)+Extended-factor2++++++++++++++++++++++++++++++
 * Example showing compound decision logic using RPG IV methods
C               SELECT
C               WHEN      Age >= 65 AND Sex = 'F'
C               EVAL         LifeExpect = 84
C               WHEN      Age >= 65 AND Sex = 'M'
C               EVAL         LifeExpect = 79
C               WHEN      Age < 65 AND Sex = 'F'
C               EVAL         LifeExpect = 81
C               OTHER
C               EVAL         LifeExpect = 78
C               ENDSL
```

You have seen that RPG indicator logic can become complex when you combine indicators in "and" relations and use an indicator's "off status" as a condition for a calculation (e.g., N75). You can also combine indicators in "or" relations, such that the calculation is performed if at least one of the indicators is on. The following code demonstrates this option.

```
*.. 1 ...+... 2 ...+... 3 ...+... 4 ...+... 5 ...+... 6 ...+... 7 ...+... 8
CLØN01Factor1+++++++Opcode(E)+Factor2+++++++Result++++++++Len++D+HiLoEq....
C* Example showing the use of OR and indicator conditioning; A and B
C* will be added if either indicator Ø5 or indicator 1Ø (or both) is on.
C     Ø5
COR 1ØA               ADD       B              C                  5 2
```

As the decision logic's complexity increases, the number of indicators needed to express that logic in RPG II increases, along with the difficulty of understanding the code. For example, can you figure out what the following code is trying to do?

```
*.. 1 ...+... 2 ...+... 3 ...+... 4 ...+... 5 ...+... 6 ...+... 7 ...+... 8
CLØN01Factor1+++++++Opcode(E)+Factor2+++++++Result++++++++Len++D+HiLoEq....
C                    Z-ADD     .15            RATE              2 2
C     SALARY         COMP      25000                               602030
C   60SALARY         COMP      40000                               603060
C   20SALARY         COMP      15000                               20  20
C   20               Z-ADD     .18            RATE
C   30               Z-ADD     .25            RATE
C   60               Z-ADD     .31            RATE
```

A conditioning indicator applies only to the line of code with which it is associated. If each of three calculations, for example, is to be executed only if indicator 10 is on, indicator 10 must appear with each calculation. RPG programmers sometimes tried to avoid this repetitive use of indicators on calculations by using the GOTO operation to branch around, or bypass, a group of calculations. The following example demonstrates how GOTO was sometimes used with decision logic in RPG II.

```
*.. 1 ...+... 2 ...+... 3 ...+... 4 ...+... 5 ...+... 6 ...+... 7 ...+... 8
CLØN01Factor1+++++++Opcode(E)+Factor2+++++++Result++++++++Len++D+HiLoEq....
C* Example showing use of GOTO with indicators
C     SALARY         COMP      15000                                  10
C   10               Z-ADD     .15            RATE              2 2
C   10               GOTO      EXTTAG
C     SALARY         COMP      25000                                  20
C   20               Z-ADD     .18            RATE
C   20               GOTO      EXTTAG
C     SALARY         COMP      40000                               603060
C   30               Z-ADD     .25            RATE
C   60               Z-ADD     .31            RATE
C     EXTTAG         TAG
```

The two preceding examples both express the same logic using RPG II techniques. You can see that using the structured operations and methods of RPG IV, as shown in the next example, results in code that is much easier to understand.

```
*.. 1 ...+... 2 ...+... 3 ...+... 4 ...+... 5 ...+... 6 ...+... 7 ...+... 8
CLØN01Factor1++++++Opcode(E)+Extended-factor2+++++++++++++++++++++++++++++
 * Example of RPG IV solution to previous example
C                   SELECT
C                   WHEN      Salary < 15000
C                   EVAL          Rate = .15
C                   WHEN      Salary < 25000
C                   EVAL          Rate = .18
C                   WHEN      Salary < 40000
C                   EVAL          Rate = .25
C                   OTHER
C                   EVAL          Rate = .31
C                   ENDSL
```

Resulting Indicators and Arithmetic

Another common use of indicators in RPG II was to include them as resulting indicators in conjunction with arithmetic operations. You can associate resulting indicators with any arithmetic or assignment operation; they are commonly used with ADD, SUB, MULT, and DIV.

Resulting indicators are turned on or off automatically when the operation with which they are associated is executed, depending on the value of the result of that operation. If the result is a positive value, an indicator in positions 71–72 is turned on; if the result is negative, an indicator in positions 73–74 is turned on; and if the result is zero, an indicator in positions 75–76 is turned on. Any resulting indicator in a position that does not reflect the sign of the result is turned off (or stays off). The following example demonstrates the use of resulting indicators.

```
*.. 1 ...+... 2 ...+... 3 ...+... 4 ...+... 5 ...+... 6 ...+... 7 ...+... 8
CLØN01Factor1++++++Opcode(E)+Factor2++++++Result+++++++Len++D+HiLoEq....
 * Examples showing how resulting indicators work:
 * Indicator 10 is turned on if C is 0.
C     A           MULT      B             C                        10

 * Indicator 10 is turned on if C is less than 0; otherwise, 20 is
 * turned on.
C     A           DIV       B             C                        201020

 * Indicator 10 is turned on if C is greater than 0, 20 if C is less than
 * 0, and 30 if C equals 0.
C     A           SUB       B             C                        102030
```

As you can see from these examples, you can use one or more of these indicator positions in a given calculation, repeating the same indicator (e.g., if you want it to signal that the result is greater than or equal to zero) or using a unique indicator in each position.

The main use of resulting indicators with arithmetic operations was to eliminate the need for a COMP operation in RPG II, in which the Result field would be compared with zero. In later versions of RPG, programmers sometimes used resulting indicators to eliminate the need for an IF*xx* operation involving the Result field's value:

```
*.. 1 ...+... 2 ...+... 3 ...+... 4 ...+... 5 ...+... 6 ...+... 7 ...+... 8
CLØN01Factor1++++++Opcode(E)+Factor2++++++Result+++++++Len++D+HiLoEq....
C* Examples showing three logically equivalent ways of specifying that if
C* taxable income is less than zero, reset taxable income to zero.
C* Method using resulting indicator
C     GROSS       SUB       DEPEND        TAXINC        7 2   20
C  20             Z-ADD     0             TAXINC
```

continued...

continued...

```
*.. 1 ...+... 2 ...+... 3 ...+... 4 ...+... 5 ...+... 6 ...+... 7 ...+... 8
C* Method using COMP
C      GROSS         SUB       DEPEND        TAXINC        7 2
C      TAXINC        COMP      0                                        20
C   20               Z-ADD     0             TAXINC

C* Method using IFxx
C      GROSS         SUB       DEPEND        TAXINC        7 2
C      TAXINC        IFLT      0
C                    Z-ADD     0             TAXINC
C                    ENDIF
```

Iteration and RPG II

Just as RPG II had no decision operations, it also had no operations to allow iteration. Without DO, DOW, DOU, DOW*xx*, and DOU*xx*, even with its built-in processing cycle RPG II still needed a way to create loops to perform repetitive processing for a single input record. In RPG II, programmers implemented loop logic using the COMP operation and indicators; the indicators conditioned a GOTO that sent control back to prior calculations to repeat processing steps.

The following example illustrates an RPG II technique of adding all the numbers from 1 to 100.

```
*.. 1 ...+... 2 ...+... 3 ...+... 4 ...+... 5 ...+... 6 ...+... 7 ...+... 8
CL0N01Factor1++++++Opcode(E)+Factor2++++++Result++++++++Len++D+HiLoEq....
C* Example showing RPG II techniques of adding the numbers from 1 to 100:
C* Initialize NUM and SUM to 0.
C                    Z-ADD     0             NUM           3 0
C                    Z-ADD     0             SUM           4 0
C* Loop while NUM is less than 100.
C      LOOP          TAG
C      NUM           ADD       1             NUM
C      SUM           ADD       NUM           SUM
C      NUM           COMP      100                                     50
C   50               GOTO      LOOP
```

Another pair of operations often used in RPG II was SETON and SETOFF. Because RPG II did not let you reference indicators directly as fields (e.g., *IN10), the only way to change the value of an indicator directly was to SETON or SETOFF the desired indicator (or indicators).

With these operations, Factor 1, Factor 2, and the Result field are always blank, but you can specify up to three indicators in positions 71–76 of the specification line.

```
*.. 1 ...+... 2 ...+... 3 ...+... 4 ...+... 5 ...+... 6 ...+... 7 ...+... 8
CL0N01Factor1++++++Opcode(E)+Factor2++++++Result++++++++Len++D+HiLoEq....
CL0N01Factor1++++++Opcode(E)+Extended-factor2++++++++++++++++++++++++++++
C* Turn on indicators 10, 20, and 30 using RPG II methods.
C                    SETON                                 102030

C* Equivalent results using RPG IV
C                    EVAL      *IN10 = *ON
C                    EVAL      *IN20 = *ON
C                    EVAL      *IN30 = *ON

C* Turn off indicators 10 and 20 using RPG II methods.
C                    SETOFF                                1020

C* Equivalent results using RPG IV
C                    EVAL      *IN10 = *OFF
C                    EVAL      *IN20 = *OFF
```

Improving on the Past

As you have seen, most of the features discussed in this appendix — features that at one time in RPG's history provided the only way to accomplish a given programming solution — have alternate, more modern counterparts to accomplish the same result in RPG IV. Specifically, you should avoid using conditioning indicators, arithmetic resulting indicators, COMP, and GOTOs — RPG's legacy from RPG II. Moreover, using EVAL and the new structured operators that let you write conditional tests as free-form expressions is preferable to using the older specific arithmetic operations, assignment operations, and fixed-format decision and iteration operations. Furthermore, data definition should always take place in Definition Specifications, rather than within Calculation Specifications.

Whether or not to completely abandon the fixed-logic cycle is an interesting issue. RPG's cycle still underlies every RPG program written, but, more and more, today's programmers are ignoring its automatic features in favor of taking complete procedural control over program logic. Figure G.1 contrasts program flow using the fixed-logic cycle with the procedural approach favored today. Rather than "riding" the basic process loop built into RPG, contemporary RPG programmers structure their own loops that are executed repeatedly during the first (and only) pass through RPG's cycle.

Figure G.1
The Fixed-Logic Cycle vs. Modern Process Logic

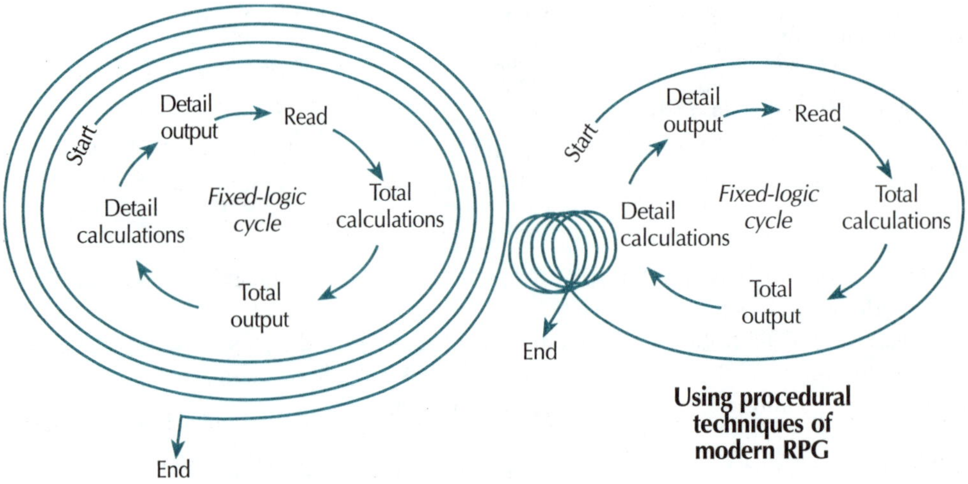

Using RPG fixed-logic cycle and RPG II techniques

The fixed-logic cycle truly is worthless for interactive applications because the cycle presupposes that you have a primary data file that you want to sequentially process from beginning to end-of-file. On the other hand, when all you require is a straightforward report of a data file's contents — with or without subtotals — using RPG's cycle may result in somewhat shorter programs, perhaps more quickly developed than if you coded full-procedural programs. Whether these shorter programs are as easy to maintain as procedural programs is open to debate.

Ultimately more important than whether or not you incorporate the fixed-logic cycle into your report programs — regardless of the method you use — is that you think before you code and that your work reflects a structured, modular approach to program design.

Glossary

Abend The condition in which a program prematurely terminates, or ends abnormally, after issuing an error message indicating the problem that prevented the program from reaching its normal ending point. (Chapters 7, 12; Appendix E)

Algorithm A step-by-step procedure for solving a problem. (Chapter 1)

Alphanumeric data Data treated as characters, rather than numbers, regardless of the actual make-up of the data; may be alphabetic, special characters, or digits. (Chapter 1)

Alternating format The form of data entry in tables or arrays in which pairs of related data are entered together. (Chapter 9)

APIs Application programming interfaces; programs or commands supplied as part of the operating system that let you access low-level system functions. You can call APIs from within RPG IV programs. (Chapter 10)

Array A data structure similar to a table in that it contains multiple elements defined with a common name; unlike tables, individual elements of arrays may be referenced by using an index. Also unlike tables, arrays can be loaded with values during the course of program execution; such arrays are called *runtime arrays*. (Chapter 9)

Arrival sequence The sequence in which database records are accessed in the order in which they were placed in the database file (first-in, first-out), rather than based on the value of a key field. (Chapter 6)

Assignment operation An operation that lets you assign a value to a variable. EVAL is RPG IV's primary assignment operator; other operations sometimes used for assignment include MOVE, MOVEL, Z-ADD, and Z-SUB. (Chapter 4; Appendix G)

Backward-compatible A characteristic of RPG that lets you compile and run previously written programs under a new version of the language without rewriting the programs. (Appendix G)

"Backwards" sequential access Accessing records in a database file in descending key order through the READP or READPE operations. (Chapter 7)

Base string The Factor 2 value of string operations (e.g., CHECK, SCAN, XLATE), which serves as the focus or target of the operation. (Chapter 12)

Based field A field that is not assigned static storage of its own; instead, its storage location is based on a pointer, whose value may change during program execution. (Chapter 11)

Basing pointer An RPG IV data type used to store addresses of storage locations of variables. (Chapter 11)

Batch processing Computer processing in which the computer processes a "batch" of data (typically representing business transactions) without user intervention, in contrast to applications that are interactively controlled by the user during execution. (Chapters 1, 8)

Binary A system of representing values based on powers of 2. For example, decimal value 8 is 1000 in binary. (Chapters 6, 11)

Binary data type Numeric data stored directly in base 2 representation rather than through EBCDIC encoding. (Chapter 6)

Bind A process that prepares a compiled object for execution by linking it with other modules (if needed) and creating a *PGM object. (Chapters 1, 10)

Bits (binary digits) Either 0 or 1. A group of eight adjacent binary digits represents one EBCDIC character and equals one byte. See also *decimal bits, zone bits*. (Chapters 1, 12)

Boolean data type Data containing only a logical true (*ON) or false (*OFF) indicator. (Chapter 3)

Built-in functions (BIFs)   Operation-like features of RPG IV that return a value based on the value of their argument. (Chapter 2, 4, 12)

Calculation Specifications   Lines in RPG IV programs that detail the procedural processing steps, including calculations, to be performed by the program. Each Calculation Specification line of code must include a C in position 6. (Chapter 2)

Call interface   The portion of an RPG program that enables a calling and a called program to share data by specifying the name of the program to call, the number of parameters to pass, and the data attributes of those parameters. (Chapter 10)

CASE logic   A logic construct that lets you specify multiple alternate branches of processing, in contrast to an IF structure, which allows only a single alternate branch. (Chapter 5)

Case sensitive   A condition in which uppercase alphabetic letters and their corresponding lowercase versions are treated as different characters. (Chapters 2, 12)

Character data type   A declaration that a field will contain alphanumeric data. (Chapter 6)

Character field   A field defined to represent alphanumeric characters. (Chapter 2)

%CHAR function   An RPG built-in function that converts an expression (numeric, date, time, timestamp, graphic, or UCS-2 data) to character data. (Chapter 12)

Character literals   Sequences of one or more keyboard characters that are enclosed within apostrophes (') and have fixed, non-numeric values; you can use character literals with character-oriented operations. (Chapter 3)

%CHECK function   An RPG built-in function that verifies whether each character in a source string is among the valid characters in a compare string. When a mismatch exists, %CHECK returns the location of the mismatch; otherwise, it returns a zero. (Chapter 12)

Check protection   A technique, most commonly used in printing checks, in which insignificant leading zeros in a number are replaced by asterisks (*) rather than simply suppressed, to prevent tampering with the check's face value. (Chapter 2)

Combined file   A file that supports both input and output, but as independent operations. Display files are combined files. (Chapter 8)

Comment lines   See *internal documentation*. (Chapters 1, 2)

Compare string   The Factor 1 value of a string operation (e.g., CHECK, CHECKR, SCAN) that contains the value to check for in the base string contained in Factor 2. (Chapter 12)

Compile   To translate the source code of a program into machine language, or object code. (Chapter 1)

Compile unit   On the iSeries, a set of source statements/instructions, representing a program module, that is compiled as a single unit. Also called a *source member*. (Chapter 1)

Compiler   A special computer program that translates a program written in a high-level programming language (HLL) into machine language that the computer can understand. (Chapter 1)

Compiler directives   Instructions, beginning with a slash (/) character in position 7, that direct the compiler to perform in some way. In the case of the /FREE and /END-FREE compiler directives, the compiler is instructed to use free-format syntax rules for any instructions within the block of code encompassed by the directives. (Chapter 2)

Compile-time array   An array whose values are hard coded at the end of the source program and whose values are bound to the array when the program is compiled. (Chapter 9)

Compile-time table   A table whose values are entered at the end of the source program and are bound to the table when the program is compiled. (Chapter 9)

Composite key   A key for a file or record format composed of more than one field. (Chapters 6, 7)

Concatenated key   Same as *composite key*. (Chapter 7)

Concatenation   A composite or combination of fields, as in a *composite* (or *concatenated*) *key*; also, an operation that joins two character strings in the order specified, forming a single string. (Chapters 6, 11, 12)

Conditioning indicators   Indicators in positions 9–11 of a Calculation Specification whose off/on status determines whether the calculation is performed. (Appendix G)

Constants   In an RPG IV program, those characters that do not change, representing the actual values that will be processed or printed out on a report; also called *literals*. (Chapter 2)

Continuation line   A line that lets you continue a line of code; you can use continuation lines with File, Definition, Calculation, and Output Specifications for completing keyword and free-form entries that are too long to fit on one line. (Chapters 2, 4, 9)

Control Specifications   Program lines that can be used to control aspects of an RPG program's behavior, including default formats, processing mode, compilation options, and language enhancements. (Chapter 2)

Control-break problem   A special type of batch-processing problem for files whose records are grouped by values of a control field and that require special processing based on a change in the control field's value; the special processing typically involves printing subtotals for each group of records. (Chapter 5)

Crossfooting   Summing across a row of figures to develop a total for the row; an accounting term. (Chapter 9)

Cross-reference listing   A list provided by the compiler that logs all fields and indicators used in a program; every program statement within which the fields or indicators occur appears in the listing. Useful for diagnosing problems when debugging programs. (Appendix E)

**CTDATA record   A line in a source member that appends the source code and serves as a delimiter (or separator line) to explicitly identify the table or array whose data follows; used with compile-time tables and arrays. (Chapter 9)

Common User Access (CUA)   A set of IBM design standards developed to promote standardized user interfaces across platforms. (Chapter 8)

Data areas   iSeries objects used to communicate data between programs within a job or between jobs. One program does not have to call another to access the same data if the data resides in a data area. (Chapter 10)

Data Description Specifications (DDS)   The name given to the RPG IV specification form in which database and display file definitions are developed. (Chapter 6)

Data dictionary   A central repository for storing definitions of data that is independent of programs and widely used in a database approach to data management. On the iSeries, a data dictionary can be developed through a special kind of physical file, called a *field reference file*. (Chapters 1, 6)

Data File Utility (DFU)   An iSeries program that facilitates entering data values into database files without the need for writing an HLL data-entry program. (Chapter 6)

Data structures   Single, contiguous portions of memory, which are then subdivided and referenced in different ways by a data structure's subfields. (Chapters 3, 9, 11)

Data type   A defined attribute of a data item that determines what kind of data the item can store and what kinds of operations it can be used with. (Chapters 6, 11)

Data validation Attempting to determine whether data is correct before accepting it as input. In RPG IV, the four major keywords used for validating user-entered data are CHECK, COMP, RANGE, and VALUES. (Chapter 8)

Data-area data structure A data structure defined specifically for a data area. See also *data area, data structure.* (Chapter 10)

Date data type An RPG IV data type (type D) used to store dates; its default display format is 10 bytes long, with format *yyyy-mm-dd.* (Chapter 3, 11, 12)

DBCS (Double-Byte Character Set) graphic data type An RPG IV data type in which two bytes represent a single character of a graphic character set. (Chapter 3, 11)

%DEC function An RPG built-in function that converts the result of an expression to a packed decimal format of the precision you specify. (Chapter 12)

Debugging Correcting any errors found in a computer program. (Chapter 1; Appendix E)

Decimal A system of representing values based on powers of 10. (Chapter 11)

Decimal bits The rightmost four bits of a byte, numbered 4, 5, 6, and 7; also called *low-order* or *digit bits.* See also *bits.* (Chapter 6, 11, 12)

Decision operations The options for sending control to alternate statements within a program. See also *selection.* (Chapter 5)

Definition Specifications Lines used in RPG IV programs to define data items used within a program; Definition Specifications require a D in position 6. (Chapters 3, 11)

Desk checking Checking output generated by the computer against the results of hand calculations. (Appendix E)

Detail line An output line based on data contained in a single record of an input file; the line prints detailed information about the data record being processed. (Chapter 2)

Digit bits The rightmost four bits of a byte; also called *low-order* or *decimal bits.* See also *bits.* (Chapter 6)

Display attributes Special characteristics that can be assigned to fields to affect their appearance on the screen; include such features as underlining, high intensity, and blinking. (Chapter 8)

Display files Files that define the screens that a program presents as it runs. Display files let values keyed by the user in response to the screen be input as data to the program; therefore, display files serve as the mechanism that lets the user and the program interact. (Chapter 8)

Dynamic binding Linking (or interconnecting) a calling program (*PGM) object with its called program (*PGM) object when the call is actually executed during runtime; the CALL operation is used with this kind of binding. (Chapter 10)

EBCDIC Extended Binary-Coded Decimal Interchange Code; the data-representation format used by IBM. EBCDIC assigns a unique eight-bit binary pattern to each representable character or digit. The leftmost four bits are called *zone* or *high-order bits;* the rightmost four bits are called *digit* or *low-order bits.* In this format, A is less than B, B is less than C, and so on. Lowercase letters are "smaller" than uppercase letters, letters are smaller than digits, and blank is smaller than any other displayable character. (Chapters 5, 6)

Edit code A letter or number that specifies how numeric values are to be formatted to make them more readable upon output; different edit codes evoke different formatting. (Chapter 2)

Edit words An alternative to edit codes for signaling the desired format for numeric output; an edit word supplies a template into which a numeric value is inserted and may include instructions for zero suppression and the insertion of special characters. Edit codes and edit words are never used together for the same field. (Chapter 2)

Editor   A computer program designed to let you enter, rearrange, change, and delete source-program statements (or other text) interactively. Source Entry Utility (SEU), the iSeries editor, also performs basic syntax checking as you enter program statements. (Chapter 1; Appendix D)

End-of-file   In sequential record access, the point when an attempt to read another record fails because no records remain unprocessed. (Chapter 2)

Exponentiation   The operation in which a value is raised to a power. (Chapter 4)

Extended Factor 2 format   A form of the Calculation Specifications in which there is no result entry; instead, positions 36–80 are used for a free-form expression. (Chapter 4)

Extension Specifications   An obsolete RPG specification type, formerly used to define tables and arrays. (Appendix G)

External documentation   Material added to (but not a direct part of) a program that is useful for understanding, using, or changing the program; external documentation can include such items as system and program flowcharts, user manuals, and operator instructions. (Chapter 1)

Externally described data structure   A data structure whose subfields are defined in the external record format for a database file rather than coded explicitly within the program source. (Chapter 11)

Externally described file   A file whose records are defined at a field level to the system when the file is created and whose external definition is used by a program referencing the file. (Chapter 6)

Factor   Operand value (either Factor 1 or Factor 2) that provides the compiler with the details necessary to perform an RPG operation. (Chapter 2)

Field   Generally represents the smallest unit of data to be manipulated within a program, such as a customer account number, last name, first name, street address, city, state, zip code, telephone number, and so on. See also *program variable*. (Chapter 1)

Field definition   The specification of variables to be used within a program by assigning each variable a name, length, and data type. (Chapter 2)

Field definition lines   Also called field description lines; lines in an RPG IV program that describe the content of a given input record for program-described files. (Chapter 2)

Field-level keywords   Keywords associated only with a specific field within a file in DDS specifications. (Chapter 6)

Field reference file   Another name for a centralized data dictionary of the fields in a physical file. See *data dictionary*. (Chapter 6)

Figurative constants   Implied literals that can be used without a specified length. Figurative constants assume the length and decimal positions of the fields with which they are associated. RPG IV's figurative constants are *BLANK (or *BLANKS), *ZERO (or *ZEROS), *HIVAL, *LOVAL, *OFF, *ON, *ALL, and *NULL. (Chapters 3, 11)

File   A named set of records stored or processed as a unit. In RPG IV, files are either physical files or logical files. See *physical file, logical file*. (Chapter 1)

File access   The means by which a file can be read, written to, or updated; methods include sequential and random access. See *sequential access, random access*. (Chapter 7)

File Description Specifications   Program lines that describe the files your program uses and how the files will be used within the program. File Description Specifications generally begin RPG IV programs, and they each include an F in position 6. Each file used by a program requires its own File Description Specification line. Also known as *File Specifications*. (Chapter 2)

File designation   Refers to the way the program will access, or retrieve, the data in an input, combined, or update file. (Chapter 2)

File information data structure A special data structure that can be defined for each file used by a program. File information data structures contain predefined subfields that provide information about the file following input/output (I/O) operations. (Chapter 11)

File locking Limiting access to a file to one user at a time. (Chapter 7)

File maintenance The process of adding, deleting, or changing records in a database files. (Chapter 8)

File Specifications A shortened synonym for *File Description Specifications.* (Chapter 2)

File-level keywords In DDS Specifications, keywords that apply to the file as a whole. (Chapter 6)

Fixed dollar sign In numeric data, a dollar sign ($) positioned in a set column of the output, regardless of the number of significant digits in the number following the sign. (Chapter 1)

Fixed format In File Specifications, an indication that a file's records will be described within the program and that each record of the file has the same, fixed length. (Chapter 2)

Fixed-form See *fixed-position.* (Chapter 2)

Fixed-logic cycle RPG's built-in read-process-write cycle that is repeated until all the desired records have been processed. (Appendix G)

Fixed-position Also called *fixed-form;* means that the location of an entry within a program line is critical to the entry's interpretation by the RPG IV compiler. (Chapter 2)

Floating dollar sign In numeric data, a dollar sign printed next to the leftmost significant digit of the number; the position of the dollar sign varies, or floats, depending on the value of the number with which it is associated. (Chapter 1)

Fourth-generation languages (4GLs) Languages designed to make programming easier by letting programmers specify the desired results to be accomplished instead of the detailed processing required to achieve the desired results; also called nonprocedural languages. (Chapter 1)

Free-form A characteristic of program syntax; implies that the meaning of the code does not depend on the location of the code within a line (i.e., the meaning is not positionally dependent). (Chapters 2, 4)

Full procedural The term used for a file whose records are explicitly read within the program, as opposed to using the built-in retrieval of RPG's fixed-logic cycle. Such files are identified by an F in position 16 of the entry for file designation on the File Specifications. (Chapter 2)

Graphical user interface (GUI) A visual computer interface that uses icons to represent actual objects; the user accesses and manipulates these icons using a pointing device, such as a mouse. The PC Windows environment typifies a GUI. (Chapter 8)

Half-adjusting The term often used to mean "rounding" a numeric answer on the computer. The computer adds half the value of the rightmost desired decimal position to the digit immediately to the right of that decimal position before storing the answer in the result field. Because the value added is half the value of the least-significant digit position of the result, the term "half-adjust" evolved. (Chapter 4)

Help specification format A format within the Data Description Specifications (DDS) that associates a specific portion of a screen with a specific record of help text. (Chapter 13)

Hexadecimal A system of representing values based on powers of 16. Digits 0–9 are used to represent 0–9 in hexadecimal; characters A–F are used to represent values 10–15, respectively. For example, hex B (usually represented as X'0B') is the equivalent of decimal 11. (Chapter 3)

Hierarchical decomposition See *top-down design.* (Chapter 5)

High-level languages (HLLs) Programming languages designed to make it easier for programmers to express instructions to computers; contrasted with low-level languages, such as machine language or assembly language. Programs written in an HLL need to be translated into machine language, a process called compiling, before the computer can actually execute the program. (Chapter 1)

High-order bits See *zone bits, EBCDIC.* (Chapter 6)

High-order truncation The loss of digits from the left end of a result field. (Chapter 4)

Index A value used to reference or indicate an individual element of an array. (Chapter 9)

Indicator data structure A special 99-byte data structure that maps the indicators used by a display file (01–99). (Chapter 8)

Indicator data type Logical (Boolean) data containing only a true (*ON) or false (*OFF) value. (Chapter 3)

Indicators Internal switches, or variables, with only two states or values — off or on (or '0' or '1') — used by a program to signal whether a particular event has occurred within the program and to control, or condition, subsequent processing within the program. (Chapters 1, 2; Appendix G)

Infinite loop A loop whose execution continues until you (or a system operator) intervene to terminate the job that contained the loop. (Appendix E)

Initial value The value stored in a field when a program starts. (Chapter 3)

Input file A file that contains data to be read by the program. (Chapter 2)

Input Specifications Specifications that describe the records within the program-described input files and define the fields within the records; identified by an I in position 6. (Chapter 2)

%INT function An RPG built-in function that converts a numeric expression to integer format. (Chapter 12)

Integer A type of data representing whole numbers. (Chapters 2, 3)

Integer numeric field A numeric field defined with zero decimal positions, such that it can store only whole numbers. (Chapter 2)

Integrated Language Environment (ILE) A term IBM introduced with Version 2 Release 3 of OS/400 to indicate a new approach to interconnecting high-level language (HLL) programs on the iSeries. The approach supports program development using modules written in different HLLs and statically bound into a single application. (Chapters 1, 10)

Interactive applications Applications in which a user interacts with the computer directly through a terminal or workstation to control the actions of a computer program as it is running. (Chapters 1, 8)

Internal documentation Comments included within the source code of a program to aid in understanding, using, or changing the program. In RPG IV, coding an asterisk (*) in position 7 or two slashes (//) anywhere on a line (positions 8–80 in free format specification; positions 7–80 in fixed format) designates that line to be a comment. (Chapters 1, 2)

*INZSR A subroutine that, when included in an RPG IV program, is automatically executed at the start of the program; usually used to initialize variables. (Chapter 11)

Iteration A control structure within a program that permits instructions within the program to be repeated until a condition is met or is no longer met; also called repetition or looping. (Chapter 5)

Join logical file A logical file that combines fields from different physical files into a single record. (Chapter 6)

Key field A field in a record whose contents are used to build access paths to records such that the records appear to be in sequence based on that field's values. (Chapter 6)

Key sequence   An access method in which database records are retrieved based on the key field defined for the records. (Chapter 6)

Key specifications   DDS specifications that declare which field (or fields) is to serve as the key to the file. (Chapter 6)

Keyboard-shift attribute   An entry associated with fields within display files that determines what kinds of data a user can input into a field or what kinds of data can be displayed. (Chapter 8)

Keywords   In RPG IV and DDS, reserved words with special meanings that are used, often with parameters, to complete definitions or to signal certain attributes. (Chapters 2, 6–12)

Leading decision loop   A program loop in which the test to determine whether the instructions within the loop are to be performed is made before the instructions within the loop are executed for the first time. (Chapter 5)

%LEN function   An RPG built-in function that returns the number of digits or characters in an expression. (Chapter 12)

Level checking   A feature of the iSeries that prevents running a program if changes have been made to the definition of a physical or logical file used by that program unless the program is first recompiled. This feature prevents executing a program using an obsolete or inaccurate definition of a database file. (Chapter 6)

Level indicators   Nine indicators, L1–L9, used to detect changes in control-field values in control-break processing when implementing the fixed-logic cycle. (Appendix G)

List panels   Term referring to the screen display of data from many records for review, selection, and update. (Chapter 13)

Literals   See *constants*. (Chapter 2)

Local data area (LDA)   A data area created for each job in the system. Each LDA is 1,024 positions long, with type character. See also *data area*. (Chapter 10)

Logic errors   Program errors caused by faulty program design that cause the program to end abnormally, loop infinitely, or process data incorrectly to produce incorrect output. (Chapter 1; Appendix E)

Logical files   Files that describe how data appears to be stored in the database. Logical files do not actually contain data records but rather access paths, or pointers, to records in physical files. Logical files must have one or more fields designated as a key, by which the access paths are identified. (Chapter 6)

Low-order bits   The four rightmost bits of a byte, also known as *decimal* or *digit bits*. See *high-order bits*, *EBCDIC*. (Chapter 6)

Low-order truncation   The loss of digits from the right end of a result field. (Chapter 4)

Master files   Sets of data, or files, of long-term or permanent importance; such files contain vital information for an organization's ongoing operations. (Chapter 1)

Mixed-case entry   A characteristic of programming languages that lets you enter alphabetic characters using either uppercase or lowercase letters. (Chapter 2, 4)

Modular programming   An approach to programming in which small, standalone units of code are developed (as opposed to monolithic programs thousands of lines long). (Chapter 10)

MONITOR operation   An RPG operation code that begins a group of statements to be processed with specific conditional error handling, based on the status code. In addition to the statements to be processed, the monitor group will include one or more on-error blocks, which will be processed if specific exceptions occur within the monitor group. (Chapter 12)

Multiple-occurrence data structure   Similar to a table or an array; enables multiple repetitions of the data structure in storage. (Chapter 11)

Named constant   In RPG IV, a constant value that has been given a name; the value can then be used throughout the program by referring to it by name rather than by entering the value itself. (Chapters 3, 11, 12)

Numeric data   Pertaining to non-alphabetic information (i.e., numbers); you can perform arithmetic calculations on numeric data. (Chapter 1)

Numeric fields   Fields that contain numeric values; numeric fields can be used in calculations and edited for output. (Chapters 2, 3, 4)

Numeric literal   A number per se whose value remains fixed throughout a program. A numeric literal can be up to 10 positions long and can include the digits 0–9 and a decimal point and/or a sign. (Chapter 3)

Object code   A program's code translated into executable machine language. (Chapter 1)

Operation extender   An extension to an RPG operation that enhances or modifies the effects of the operation. Enclosed within parentheses following the operation code, the extenders include (H) for rounding, (P) for blank padding, (D) for valid date testing, (T) for valid time testing, and (Z) for valid timestamp testing. (Chapters 4, 11, 12; Appendix G)

Output editing   Formatting numeric output values by suppressing leading zeros and adding special characters, such as decimal points, commas, and dollar signs, to make the values easier to comprehend for people looking at the output. (Chapters 1, 2)

Output errors   Logic errors that result in incorrect output when a program is run. (Appendix E)

Output file   The destination for writing operations of a computer program. (Chapter 2)

Output Specifications   Specifications used to define the desired format of output files when described within a program; identified by an O in position 6. (Chapter 2)

Overflow indicators   Special built-in indicators in RPG IV that signal end-of-page. Overflow indicators include OA, OB, OC, OD, OE, OF, OG, and OV. (Chapter 5)

Overlay   In a data structure, a redefinition of a field by an array; the array is defined to occupy the same bytes as the field. (Chapter 9)

Packed decimal data type   The numeric representation of data in EBCDIC format in which only the digit, or low-order, bits of a number are stored, with an additional four bits representing the sign of the number. The sign bits always occupy the rightmost four bit positions of a packed decimal value. (Chapters 3, 6)

Parameter   A value supplied to a command or program that is used either as input or to control the actions of the command or program. In ILE, an identifier that defines the types of arguments passed to a called procedure. (Chapter 10)

Passing by reference   RPG IV's method for passing a parameter argument between calling and called programs (or modules) by passing the address of the storage location represented by the field rather than the field's value; changing the parameter field within the called program results in the same change in the parameter field of the calling program. (Chapter 10)

Passing by value   A method for passing a parameter argument between calling and called programs (or modules) by passing a copy of the field's value rather than the address of the storage location represented by the field; changing the parameter field within the called program does not change the parameter field of the calling program. (Chapter 10)

Phantom updates   The condition that occurs if two users access the same record for update at the same time and, as a result of this concurrent access, the changes of one user are lost. Modern multiuser operating systems are designed to prevent phantom updates. (Chapter 7)

Physical files   Database files that actually store data records. (Chapter 6)

PLIST operation   An RPG IV declarative operation that identifies a list of parameters to be shared between programs. PLIST requires an identifying entry in Factor 1. (Chapter 10)

Pointer   A field whose value represents the address of a memory location. (Chapter 11)

Pointer data types   Data types of items used to access storage that is allocated dynamically throughout the program rather than once at the beginning of the program. See *basing pointer, procedure pointer.* (Chapter 11)

Pre-runtime array   An array whose values are obtained from a disk file at the start of a program's execution. (Chapter 9)

Pre-runtime (pre-execution) table   A table whose values are obtained from a disk file at the start of a program's execution. (Chapter 9)

Priming read   An initial read operation before the main process loop of a program, designed to provide the instructions within the loop with their first set of data to process. (Chapter 2)

Printer spacing chart (PSC)   A detailed representation of the desired report layout when desired output includes a report. The PSC shows all constants the report should include (e.g., report headings, column headings) and where on the report the constants should appear. Variable information is generally indicated by Xs, where each X represents one character of data. (Chapter 1)

Problem definition   The first step in the program development cycle; the process of identifying the problem in terms of the programming specifications. (Chapter 1)

Procedural languages   Programming languages that require explicit, step-by-step statements or instructions to the computer of the procedure required to produce a specific result or product (e.g., a sales report). (Chapter 1)

Procedure   IBM's most recent RPG enhancement for developing modular, reusable code. With the introduction of subprocedures and the CALLP operation, a program can now consist of a main procedure and (optionally) one or more subprocedures. (Chapter 10)

Procedure Boundary Specification   One of the lines in an RPG IV program that mark the beginning and ending boundaries of procedures. The line marking the beginning boundary includes the subprocedure name and a B in position 24; the line marking the ending boundary includes the subprocedure name and an E in position 24. Also referred to as Procedure Specifications. (Chapter 10)

Procedure interface   Program lines within a subprocedure that define the data type and size of the procedure's return value and the parameters the procedure will use. (Chapter 10)

Procedure pointer   An RPG IV data type used to store the address of an entry point of a program module. (Chapters 10, 11)

Procedure prototype   Program lines that identify a procedure (or subprocedure) in a program module; the prototype names the procedure and identifies the procedure's return value and the parameters to be passed to the procedure by the caller. (Chapter 10)

Program design   The second — and crucial — step in the program development cycle; this phase encompasses working out the solution (algorithm) to the problem using sound programming logic before expressing the solution in a given programming language. (Chapter 1)

Program development cycle   The sequence of activities required to develop a program, including defining the problem, designing the solution, writing the program, entering the program, testing and debugging the program, documenting the program, and maintaining the program. (Chapter 1)

Program maintenance   Making changes to a program once it is actually being used, or "in production." (Chapter 1)

Program module   An object of type *MODULE that is the result of a compile operation in RPG IV; a program module must be bound (either alone or with other modules) to produce an executable program. (Chapters 1, 10)

Program status data structure   A data structure that can provide information about the program itself and about exceptions or errors that occur during program execution. (Chapter 11)

Program variable   A program-defined construct that represents a location in the computer's memory; referencing a variable within a program causes the computer to access the memory location that corresponds to the variable and appropriately manipulate the data value stored at that location. In RPG, the term "field" is usually used instead of variable. Such fields, or variables, may represent alphanumeric (character) or numeric data. (Chapter 1)

Pseudocode   A tool of program design that uses stylized English to detail the underlying logic needed for a program. (Chapters 1, 2)

*PSSR   A subroutine which, when included in an RPG IV program, is executed automatically when a program runtime error occurs. (Chapter 12)

Random access   File access accomplished by just "reaching into" a file and extracting only the specific record you want (as opposed to retrieving database records sequentially). (Chapter 7)

Range table   A table in which the entries represent a range of values rather than discrete values. (Chapter 9).

Record   A set of one or more related data items grouped for processing. (Chapter 1)

Record layouts   Descriptions of the record formats of input files to be used by a program, including the beginning and ending positions of data fields within records, the order and length of the fields, and the number of decimal positions for numeric data. (Chapter 1)

Record locking   A mechanism for preventing two users from accessing the same database record for update at the same time. RPG IV automatically puts a lock on a record of an update file when the record is read. Updating the record or reading another record releases the record from the locked state. While the record is locked, other application programs can access the record if they have defined the file as an input file, but not if they have defined it as an update file. (Chapter 7)

Record-format descriptions   Those entries on Input and Output Specifications that describe one record type of a program-described input or output file. (Chapter 2)

Record-identifying indicator   An indicator associated with a record format of a primary input file that signals a record was successfully read; turned on and off automatically as part of the fixed-logic cycle. (Appendix G)

Record-level keywords   In DDS, the keywords that apply to a specific record format within a file. (Chapter 6)

Recursion   A programming technique in which subroutines execute or invoke themselves, either directly or indirectly through an intermediate subroutine; this technique is not permitted in RPG IV. (Chapter 5)

Redundancy   The duplication of data across files. (Chapter 6)

Relational codes In RPG IV programming, to make six two-letter codes used to make a relational comparison between two values. The codes are GT (greater than), LT (less than), EQ (equal to), NE (not equal to), LE (less than or equal to), and GE (greater than or equal to). (Chapter 5; Appendix G)

Relational comparison Testing a condition to determine the appropriate course of action within a program by making a comparison between two values using one of six criteria: greater than, less than, equal to, not equal to, less than or equal to, and greater than or equal to. (Chapter 5)

Relational symbols In RPG IV programming, six symbols used in making a relational comparison between two values. The six symbols are > (greater than), < (less than), = (equal to), <> (not equal to), <= (less than or equal to), and >= (greater than or equal to). (Chapter 5)

Relative record number A value that represents a record's ordinal position within a file or subfile. (Chapter 13)

Report Layout Utility (RLU) An iSeries utility to facilitate the design and definition of reports. (Chapter 6)

Report Program Generator (RPG) A high-level programming language introduced by IBM in the early 1960s. As originally designed, RPG included a fixed-logic cycle that eliminated the need for programmers to detail each processing step required for the computer to execute the program. Another unique characteristic of RPG was its use of a special class of built-in, predefined variables called *indicators*. (Chapter 1)

Result decimal positions rule An instruction, used in evaluating expressions, that tells the RPG compiler that no intermediate value should have fewer decimal places than the end result. (Chapter 4)

Resulting indicator An indicator coded in positions 71–76 of Calculation Specifications to signal whether the result of a computation is a positive value, zero, or a negative value. (Appendix G)

Runtime array Array that obtains or changes its values during the course of program execution, as a result of either input or calculations. (Chapter 9)

Runtime errors Errors that prevent your program from reaching a normal end; a runtime error can cause a program to abruptly stop in the middle of execution or cause it to run forever until you (or a system operator) intervene to terminate the job. (Appendix E)

%SCAN function An RPG built-in function that looks for a character or string of characters within a character field. (Chapter 12)

Screen Design Aid (SDA) An iSeries utility that automatically generates DDS source code as you design and create display screens in an interactive environment. (Chapter 8)

Selection The logic structure that lets you establish alternate paths of instructions within a program; which path the program executes depends on the results of a test or condition within the program. (Chapter 5)

Sequence The logic structure that lets you instruct the computer to execute operations serially. (Chapter 5)

Sequential access A method of retrieving or reading records serially, either in key order (if the file is keyed and so noted on the File Specifications) or in arrival or FIFO (first-in, first-out) order (for non-keyed files). (Chapter 7)

Simple logical file A logical file whose records are based on a single physical file. See *logical file*. (Chapter 6)

%SIZE function An RPG built-in function that returns the number of bytes occupied by a data item. (Chapter 12)

Source code   The statements/instructions of a program expressed in a high-level language. (Chapters 1, 8)

Source Entry Utility (SEU)   The iSeries editor you can use to enter your RPG IV program. (Chapters 2, 8; Appendix D)

Source member   On the iSeries, a subset of a file that contains a set of source statements/instructions representing a single program module. (Chapters 1, 8)

Spaghetti code   A program whose flow of control is difficult to follow; usually caused by undisciplined, haphazard transfer of control from one part of the program to another. (Chapters 1, 5, 8)

Specific arithmetic operations   Single-purpose, fixed-form operations to add, subtract, multiply, divide, or store remainders. Used by previous versions of RPG to perform all arithmetic calculations; their function largely has been replaced by the EVAL operation. (Chapter 4; Appendix G)

Standalone fields   Additional fields used to store the results of calculations; so called because these fields are not part of a database record or any other kind of data structure. (Chapter 3)

Static binding   Linking, or interconnecting, a calling module (*MODULE) object with its called module (*MODULE) object during the binding stage to form a single executable *PGM object; the CALLB operation is used with this kind of binding. (Chapter 10)

%STATUS function   An RPG built-in function that provides the status code of the most recent I/O operation. (Chapter 12)

Structured design   A program development methodology that advocates a systematic approach to program design and emphasizes limiting flow-of-control structures within a program to three basic logic structures: sequence, selection (also called decision), and iteration (also called repetition or looping). (Chapters 1, 5)

Subfile   A collection of record data from a database file that is handled as a unit for screen I/O. (Chapter 13)

Subfile control record format   The record format immediately following the subfile record format that controls the display of the subfile records through the use of special record-level keywords. Column headings for the subfile display also are often included as part of this record format. (Chapter 13)

Subfile record format   Describes the subfile fields that are to appear on the screen. (Chapter 13)

Subprocedures   Functional groupings of code that can be read independently of a main procedure and in which data definition is local. (Chapter 10)

Subroutine   A set of operations coded elsewhere within the calculations of a program and invoked as a unit by referencing the subroutine's name with an EXSR (Execute Subroutine) operation. (Chapter 5)

Subschemas   In database terminology, users' views of data. (Chapter 6)

%SUBST function   An RPG built-in function that extracts a substring, or portion, of a character string. (Chapter 12)

Syntax errors   Errors in programming caused by misuse of the rules of the programming language that prevent the creation of an object program for the computer to execute. (Chapter 1; Appendix E)

Table   Conceptually, a collection of data organized into columns and rows; similar kinds of data are stored within a column, and the data within a row of a table is "related," or belongs together. In RPG IV, one column of such a conceptual table. (Chapter 9)

Table lookup   An operation to locate a specified value in a table. In RPG IV, the common use of tables is to look up a value in one table to extract a related value from a second table. (Chapter 9)

Time data type   An RPG IV data type (type T) used to store time values; its default display format is eight bytes long, with the format *hh.mm.ss.* (Chapter 3, 11, 12)

Timestamp data type   An RPG IV data type (type Z) used to store combined date and time values; its default display format is 26 bytes long, with the format *yyyy-mm-dd-hh.mm.ss.mmmmmm.* (Chapters 3, 11, 12)

Top-down design   Program development that starts with a broad "outline" of the solution followed by successively breaking the big pieces into smaller and smaller units. Also sometimes called *hierarchical decomposition.* (Chapter 5)

Trailing decision loop   A program loop in which a test based on a comparison is made after the instructions within the loop have been executed; the outcome of the test determines whether the instructions within the loop are executed again. (Chapter 5)

Transaction files   Relatively temporary data files, usually generated during the course of a day's business, that often need to be processed only once. (Chapter 1)

%TRIM function   An RPG built-in function that returns a character, graphic, or UCS-2 string without leading or trailing blanks. (Chapter 12)

Truncation   The loss of digits from the right or the left end of a result field. (Chapter 4)

Two-dimensional array   An array that requires two indexes (or subscripts) to determine the identity of a given element of the array; one index points to the row and the second to the column location of the element. (Chapter 11)

Typed literals   Literal values enclosed within apostrophes and preceded by a data-type code to indicate what type of data the literal represents. (Chapters 3, 11)

User space   A defined, permanent location in storage that is created by an API and used by other APIs. (Chapter 10)

Volatile   In terms of programming, refers to data that is frequently changing. (Chapter 9)

Zero suppression   The elimination of leading, nonsignificant zeros when printing or displaying numeric data. (Chapter 1)

Zone bits   The leftmost four bits in IBM's EBCDIC coding scheme; bits 0, 1, 2, and 3. See also *bits, decimal bits, EBCDIC, high-order bits.* (Chapters 6)

Zoned decimal data type   The numeric representation of data in EBCDIC format in which a full byte is required to store each digit of a numeric value, except that the zone of the rightmost digit is used to store the sign of the data; 1111 represents a plus sign (+), and 1101 represents a minus sign (–). (Chapters 3, 6)

Index

Newest Books in the 29th Street Press® Library

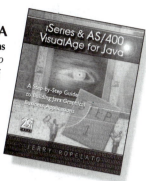

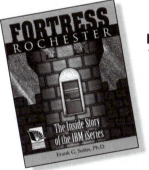

IMPLEMENTING AS/400 SECURITY, FOURTH EDITION
By Carol Woodbury and Wayne Madden

For years, AS/400 professionals have depended on earlier editions of *Implementing AS/400 Security* to learn and implement essential AS/400 security concepts. This latest edition not only brings together in one place the fundamental AS/400 security tools and experience-based recommendations you need but also includes specifics on the security enhancements available in OS/400 V4R5. In addition, you'll find expanded coverage of network, communications, and Internet security — including thwarting hacker activities — as well as updated chapters covering security system values, user profiles, object authorization, database security, output-queue and spooled-file security, auditing, contingency planning, and more. 454 pages.

ILE BY EXAMPLE
A Hands-on Guide to the AS/400's Integrated Language Environment
By Mike Cravitz

Learn the fundamentals of the AS/400's Integrated Language Environment (ILE) by following working examples that illustrate the ins and outs of this powerful programming model. Major topics include ILE program structure, bind by copy, ILE RPG subprocedures, service programs, activation groups, ILE condition handling and cancel handling, and more. A CD contains all sample programs discussed in the book, as well as a sample ILE condition handler to address record locks and ILE RPG software to synchronize system clocks using the Internet SNTP protocol. 165 pages.

SQL/400 DEVELOPER'S GUIDE
By Paul Conte and Mike Cravitz

SQL/400 Developer's Guide provides start-to-finish coverage of SQL/400, IBM's strategic language for the AS/400's integrated database. This textbook covers database and SQL fundamentals, SQL/400 Data Definition Language (DDL) and Data Manipulation Language (DML), and database modeling and design. Throughout the book, coding suggestions reinforce the topics covered and provide practical advice on how to produce robust, well-functioning code. Hands-on exercises reinforce comprehension of the concepts covered. 508 pages.

MASTERING THE AS/400, THIRD EDITION
A Practical, Hands-On Guide
By Jerry Fottral

The latest edition of this best-selling introduction to AS/400 concepts and facilities takes a utilitarian approach that stresses student participation. The book emphasizes mastery of system/user interface, member-object-library relationship, use of CL commands, basic database concepts, and program development utilities. The text prepares students to move directly into programming languages, database management, and system operations courses. Each lesson includes a lab that focuses on the essential topics presented in the lesson. 553 pages.

DOMINO R5 AND THE AS/400
By Justine Middleton, Wilfried Blankertz, Rosana Choruzy, Linda Defreyne, Dwight Egerton, Joanne Mindzora, Stephen Ryan, Juan van der Breggen, Felix Zalcmann, and Michelle Zolkos

Domino R5 and the AS/400 provides comprehensive installation and setup instructions for those installing Domino R5 "from scratch," upgrading from a previous version, or migrating from a platform other than the AS/400. In addition, you get detailed explanations of SMTP in Domino for AS/400, dial-up connectivity, directory synchronization, Advanced Services for Domino for AS/400, and Domino administration strategies, including backup strategies. 512 pages.

E-BUSINESS
Thriving in the Electronic Marketplace
By Nahid Jilovec

E-Business: Thriving in the Electronic Marketplace identifies key issues organizations face when they implement e-business projects and answers fundamental questions about entering and navigating the changing world of e-business. A concise guide to moving your business into the exciting world of collaborative e-business, the book introduces the four e-business models that drive today's economy and gives a clear summary of e-business technologies. It focuses on practical business-to-business applications. 172 pages.

INTRODUCTION TO AS/400 SYSTEM OPERATIONS, SECOND EDITION
By Heidi Rothenbuehler and Patrice Gapen

Here's the second edition of the textbook that covers what you need to know to become a successful AS/400 system operator or administrator. *Introduction to AS/400 System Operations, Second Edition* teaches you the basics of system operations so that you can manage printed reports, perform regularly scheduled procedures, and resolve end-user problems. New material covers the Integrated File System (IFS), AS/400 InfoSeeker, Operations Navigator, and much more. 182 pages.

CREATING CL COMMANDS BY EXAMPLE
By Lynn Nelson

Learn from an expert how to create CL commands that have the same functionality and power as the IBM commands you use every day. You'll see how to create commands with all the function found in IBM's commands, including parameter editing, function keys, F4 prompt for values, expanding lists of values, and conditional prompting. Whether you're in operations or programming, *Creating CL Commands by Example* can help you tap the tremendous power and flexibility of CL commands to automate tasks and enhance applications. 134 pages.

IMPLEMENTING WINDOWS NT ON THE AS/400
Installing, Configuring, and Troubleshooting
By Nick Harris, Phil Ainsworth, Steve Fullerton, and Antoine Sammut

Implementing Windows NT on the AS/400: Installing, Configuring, and Troubleshooting provides everything you need to know about using NT on your AS/400, including how to install NT Server 4.0 on the Integrated Netfinity Server, synchronize user profiles and passwords between the AS/400 and NT, administer NT disk storage and service packs from the AS/400, back up NT data from the AS/400, manage NT servers on remote AS/400s, and run Windows-based personal productivity applications on the AS/400. 393 pages.

DOMINO AND THE AS/400
Installation and Configuration
By Wilfried Blankertz, Rosana Choruzy, Joanne Mindzora, and Michelle Zolkos

Domino and the AS/400: Installation and Configuration gives you everything you need to implement Lotus Domino 4.6 on the AS/400, guiding you step by step through installation, configuration, customization, and administration. Here you get an introduction to Domino for AS/400 and full instructions for developing a backup and recovery plan for saving and restoring Domino data on the AS/400. 311 pages.

ESSENTIALS OF SUBFILE PROGRAMMING AND ADVANCED TOPICS IN RPG IV
By Phil Levinson

This textbook provides a solid background in AS/400 subfile programming in the newest version of the RPG language: RPG IV. Subfiles are the AS/400 tool that lets you display lists of data on the screen for user interaction. You learn to design and program subfiles via step-by-step instructions and real-world programming exercises that build from chapter to chapter. A section on the Integrated Language Environment (ILE), introduced concurrently with RPG IV, presents tools and techniques that support effective modular programming. An instructor's kit is available. 293 pages.

DDS KEYWORD REFERENCE
By James Coolbaugh

Reach for the *DDS Keyword Reference* when you need quick, at-your-fingertips information about DDS keywords for physical files, logical files, display files, printer files, and ICF files. In this no-nonsense volume, author Jim Coolbaugh gives you all the keywords you'll need, listed alphabetically in five sections. He explains each keyword, providing syntax rules and examples for coding the keyword. *DDS Keyword Reference* is a friendly and manageable alternative to IBM's bulky DDS reference manual. 212 pages.

SQL/400 BY EXAMPLE
By James Coolbaugh

Designed to help you make the most of SQL/400, *SQL/400 by Example* includes everything from SQL syntax and rules to the specifics of embedding SQL within an RPG program. For novice SQL users, this book features plenty of introductory-level text and examples, including all the features and terminology of SQL/400. For experienced AS/400 programmers, *SQL/400 by Example* offers a number of specific examples that will help you increase your understanding of SQL concepts and improve your programming skills. 204 pages.

OPNQRYF BY EXAMPLE
By Mike Dawson and Mike Manto

The OPNQRYF (Open Query File) command is the single most dynamic and versatile command on the AS/400. Drawing from real-life, real-job experiences, the authors explain the basics and the intricacies of OPNQRYF with lots of examples to make you productive quickly. An appendix provides the UPDQRYF (Update Query File) command — a powerful addition to AS/400 and System/38 file-update capabilities. CD included. 216 pages.

DDS PROGRAMMING FOR DISPLAY AND PRINTER FILES, SECOND EDITION
By James Coolbaugh

DDS Programming for Display and Printer Files, Second Edition helps you master DDS and — as a result — improve the quality of your display presentations and your printed jobs. The second edition offers a thorough, straightforward explanation of how to use DDS to program display files and printer files. It includes extensive DDS programming examples for CL and RPG that you can put to use immediately because a companion CD includes all the DDS, RPG, and CL source code presented in the book. 429 pages.

THE AS/400 EXPERT: READY-TO-RUN RPG/400 TECHNIQUES
By Julian Monypenny and Roger Pence

Ready-to-Run RPG/400 Techniques provides a variety of RPG templates, subroutines, and copy modules, sprinkled with fundamental advice, to help you write robust and effective RPG/400 programs. Highlights include string-handling routines, numeric editing routines, date routines, error-handling modules, and tips for using OS/400 APIs with RPG/400. The tested and ready-to-run code building blocks — provided on an accompanying CD — easily snap into existing RPG code and integrate well with new RPG/400 projects. 203 pages.

TCP/IP AND THE AS/400
By Michael Ryan

Transmission Control Protocol/Internet Protocol (TCP/IP) has become a major protocol in the AS/400 world because of TCP/IP's ubiquity and predominance in the networked world, as well as its being the protocol for the Internet, intranets, and extranets. *TCP/IP and the AS/400* provides background for AS/400 professionals to understand the capabilities of TCP/IP, its strengths and weaknesses, and how to configure and administer the TCP/IP protocol stack on the AS/400. It shows TCP/IP gurus on other types of systems how to configure and manage the AS/400 TCP/IP capabilities. 362 pages.

THE A TO Z OF EDI AND ITS ROLE IN E-COMMERCE, SECOND EDITION
By Nahid Jilovec

E-commerce expert Nahid Jilovec gives you the practical details of EDI implementation. Not only does this book show you how to cost justify EDI, but it also gives you job descriptions for EDI team members, detailed criteria and forms for evaluating EDI vendors, considerations for trading-partner agreements, an EDI glossary, and lists of EDI organizations and publications. The second edition includes new information about EDI and the Internet, system security, and auditing. 221 pages.

VISUALAGE FOR RPG BY EXAMPLE
By Bryan Meyers and Jef Sutherland

VisualAge for RPG (VARPG) is a rich, full-featured development environment that provides all the tools necessary to build Windows applications for the AS/400. *VisualAge for RPG by Example* brings the RPG language to the GUI world and lets you use your existing knowledge to develop Windows applications. Using a tutorial approach, *VisualAge for RPG by Example* lets you learn as you go and create simple yet functional programs from start to finish. The accompanying CD offers a scaled-down version of VARPG and complete source code for the sample project. 236 pages.
